pd for water
damage
10-02-15

D0164362

INTRODUCING
WORLD
RELIGIONS

INTRODUCING
WORLD
RELIGIONS

A CHRISTIAN ENGAGEMENT

CHARLES E. FARHADIAN

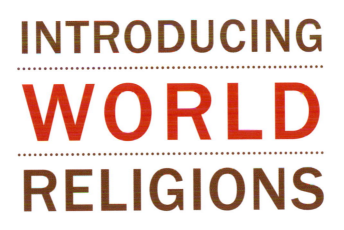

Baker Academic

a division of Baker Publishing Group
Grand Rapids, Michigan

Published by Baker Academic
a division of Baker Publishing Group
P.O. Box 6287, Grand Rapids, MI 49516-6287
www.bakeracademic.com

Printed in the United States of America

    Library of Congress Cataloging-in-Publication Data
Farhadian, Charles E., 1964–
    Introducing world religions: a Christian engage-
  ment / Charles E. Farhadian.
        pages cm
    Includes bibliographical references and index.
    ISBN 978-0-8010-3234-9 (cloth)
    1. Religions. 2. Christianity and other religions.
  I. Title
  BL80.3.F37 2015
  200—dc23   2014043637

15 16 17 18 19 20 21   7 6 5 4 3 2 1

To my family,
Katherine, Gabriel, Gideon,
Jeanette, Thea, Dorothy,
whose love and encouragement mean
the world to me

And to my students,
who make teaching such a joy

Contents

Illustrations

Acknowledgments

While it is impossible to thank all those who have shaped my thinking on the topics covered in the book, I want to share my gratitude for a few teachers and friends who have influenced my intellectual and personal formation: from Seattle Pacific University, Dan Berg and Miriam Adeney; from Yale University, Lamin Sanneh, David Kelsey, and Robert Johnson; from Boston University, Dana Robert, Robert Hefner, David Eckel, Livia Kohn, Charles Lindholm, and Chai-sik Chung; from the University of Edinburgh, Andrew Walls; from Calvin College, Joel Carpenter, John Witvliet, Rick Plantinga, Dan Harlow, and Dan Bays; from Papua, Benny Giay, Octo Mote, Noakh Nawipa, and Markus Kilungga; from The Mission Society, Darrell Whiteman; from Fuller Theological Seminary, Scott Sunquist; special friends and their families, Scott and Viji Cammauf, Chris and Michelle Hughes, Vijaysekhar and Jalene Jayaraman, Tim and Kim Notehelfer, Raul and Nora Ortiz, Mike and Chelsea Sheffey, and Matt and Karen Yonally. I thank the numerous religious communities and individuals who have opened their doors to me for research.

I am thankful to the administration at Westmont College, particularly the board of trustees, President Gayle Beebe, and Provost Mark Sargent, for providing me with professional development grants that afforded me time to write. Gratitude goes to Westmont colleagues Bruce Fisk, Maurice Lee, Tremper Longman, Chandra Mallampalli, William Nelson, Caryn Reeder, Helen Rhee, James Taylor, Curt Whiteman, and Telford Work for their support, collegiality, and humor. Appreciation goes to my students at Calvin College and Westmont College, whose enthusiasm to engage the religions of the world, sensitivity when visiting places of worship, and courage to wrestle with what it means to be a Christian in our world today, continues to enliven my teaching and writing. I am particularly grateful for Professor William Warner's generosity in providing me with office space during my sabbatical as visiting professor at the University of California, Santa Barbara, while he was chairman of the English Department at the same university. I greatly appreciate the opportunity to have served as the Underwood Distinguished Professor at Yonsei University in Seoul, Korea, in the fall of 2014, where I received warm hospitality from Dean Jeung Suk-Hwan, Professor Kwon Soo-Young, and other colleagues during the final phases of the preparation of this book. Special commendation goes to Steve Babuljak, whose photography continues to capture my attention. As my first photography teacher, Steve convinced me of the power of images to communicate persuasively. Thanks, Steve. I hope that I have convinced him of the potency of the written word. Particular thanks goes to Lewis Rambo for his enduring friendship and colleagueship over these past many years. Quick to provide a listening ear, engaging conversation, and warm spirit, Lewis has been mentor, friend, and collaborator on several writing projects.

My parents have been wonderful supporters of my work. My father, a second-generation Armenian, Edward Charles Farhadian, owned a small "Oriental" rug store in Berkeley, California—Imperial Rug Company—from which he had an endearing reputation among, in his words, "friends" rather than "customers." While we did not talk much about religion in his shop, mostly because he was a quiet man, I recall one day as a young boy when he mentioned that Muslims intentionally insert an incorrect knot into a rug, since they believe that only God is perfect. That statement intrigued me. To think, religion had something to do with rugs. And, as it turned out, in that little shop we were in fact hand repairing and selling prayer rugs, so the link between religion and rugs was far from artificial. My mother, Jeanette Farhadian, also a second-generation Armenian, is a remarkable model of Christian faith. Countless hours around the kitchen table, reflecting on questions she raised about everything from personality to religion to food to politics, have imbued me with a strong curiosity about a wide range of topics. I wish I could live several lives to explore the topics we discussed at the kitchen table. I am grateful for her kindness and her words of unfailing encouragement, wisdom, and prayer.

A word of appreciation should go to Baker Academic, and particularly James Kinney, whose editorial oversight, keen eye, and generous spirit made the completion of this project such an enjoyable experience. Thanks too, Brian Bolger, for your friendship and for your vision to acquire this project.

Finally, I want to extend my deepest appreciation to my family for the sacrifices they shouldered during my absence when traveling, researching, and writing. I am especially thankful to my wife, Katherine, for her support and encouragement throughout the writing of this book. Having traveled around much of the world together, we share meaningful memories from the forests of West Papua, cities of South Africa, to the villages of the Bavarian Alps. Thanks to my two sons, Gabriel and Gideon, who were brought into the adventure of this book through travels throughout Asia. I hope they have caught a vision for being world citizens and that their Christian faith will inspire them to "run the race" well, with a clarity of vision, strength of the Spirit, and confidence that they belong to Christ. Thank you, readers, for taking time to consider what is before you. I am responsible for any oversight or mistake.

Percentage majority religion by province, 2010

Percent of total population

▭	Christians
▭	Muslims
▭	Hindus
▭	Agnostics
▭	Buddhists
▭	Chinese folk-religionists
▭	Ethnoreligionists
▭	Sikhs
▭	Jews

10 40 60 75 85 90 95 100

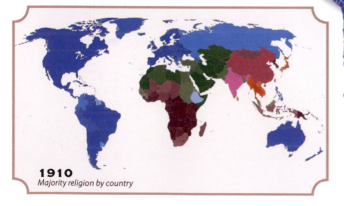

1910
Majority religion by country

Religions 1910–2010

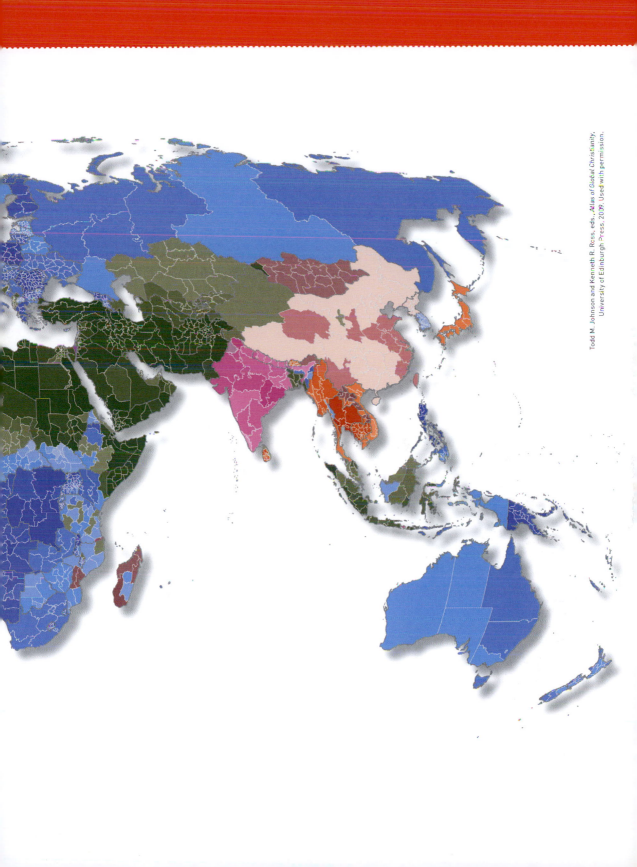

one

The Persistence of Religion

The Inescapable Context of Religion

We all live in contexts. We are contextual beings. No matter where we live, what we believe, or how we practice our faith, our contexts profoundly impact our formation as people. Yet it is far too easy to overlook the importance of our contexts. Contexts are universal, consisting of many shared elements. Our families serve as one of the most important and earliest contexts of our lives. We cannot understand religions without making sense of their broader psychological, social, cultural, historical, environmental, and religious contexts.

Religions have always been deeply influenced by their contexts, but just how have they been shaped by their local conditions? The kinds of human problems addressed by a religion are problems that emerge in part out of local contexts, and the human needs reflected in any given location are a mixture of universal needs and those unique to a particular people and region. Even the natural environment, climate, and weather patterns can impact religion and religious life. The bottom line is that there are many people around the world who live with gods in their midst.

Stephan Babuljak

Figure 1.1. We all live in contexts

David Haberlah

Charles E. Farhadian

Charles E. Farhadian

Figure 1.2. Families (Sudan, Papua, United States)

Defining Religion

This is a book about religion, but what is *religion*? In this book, I follow what has been called a phenomenological approach to understanding religion. Given the vast diversity of religious traditions in the world, it is nearly impossible to establish a concise and precise definition of religion broad enough to capture all phenomena in all religions, without inaccurately representing some aspect of a particular religious tradition. However, Winston King, who wrote the definition of religion for the *Encyclopedia of Religion*, offers eight characteristics of religion that are useful general categories, even if they do not provide a succinct definition of religion itself (see sidebar 1.1).

First, religions are marked by **traditionalism**.[1] King suggests that religions are inherently conservative and traditional because devotees continually find strength and guidance in the original creative action recorded by the religion. Whether it is the life and works of an individual founder or the words of foundational sacred scriptures, these original actions and words function

Stephan Babuljak

Figure 1.3. A Hindu-Balinese God keeps watch

as models of pristine purity, for faithful living, and of power. Believers often look back to the original scriptures or actions and words of the founder for guidance and direction in the contemporary world. These original actions and words are fully authoritative for the believing community. How do devotees make sense of changing social or cultural conditions? What are the sources

Eight Characteristics of Religion

According to Winston King, religions are characterized by the following:

1. *Traditionalism*: the importance of the original creative act or words of the founder
2. *Myth and symbol*: stories about origins carried in symbols (language, actions, objects)
3. *Ideas of salvation*: saving people from something, to something (a better reality)
4. *Sacred objects and places*: objects and places set apart from ordinary objects and places
5. *Sacred actions*: ritual actions that communicate with the divine or reality
6. *Sacred writings*: recorded words of the founder or early disciples
7. *Sacred community*: sense of belonging that provides structure and place of worship
8. *Sacred experience*: varieties of perceptions of transcendence or depth

King, "Religion," 12:284

Myth narrates a sacred history; it relates an event that took place in primordial Time, the fabled time of the "beginnings." In other words, myth tells how, through the deeds of Supernatural Beings, a reality came into existence, be it the whole of reality, the Cosmos, or only a fragment of reality—an island, a species of plant, a particular kind of human behavior, an institution. Myth, then, is always an account of a "creation"; it relates how something was produced, began to be. Myth tells only of that which really happened, which manifested itself completely.

Eliade, *Myth and Reality*, 5–6

Figure 1.4. Religious symbols. First row: Christian cross, Jewish Star of David, Taoist Yin Yang. Second row: Islamic star and crescent, Buddhist wheel of dharma, Shinto *torii*. Third Row: Sikh *khanda*, Baha'i star, Jain swastika.

of knowledge that they utilize to navigate their world? The sources for religious people lie in the religious traditions themselves. Indeed, Christian churches are often modeled on a "New Testament model" of the church. It would be strange for a church today to be modeled on a "medieval model" of church, since the paradigm of church was established in the New Testament. Reform movements seek to reform the religion in terms of its more holy past, for example, to "be the New Testament church."

Second, religions employ **myth** and **symbol**. Myths are stories about the origins of life. As such, myths serve an explanatory function—they explain all kinds of things, such as the creation of the universe, the emergence of human beings, and the origins of disease and death. Symbol is the language of myth, for myths are saturated with heavily symbolic meaning. Ordinary language simply cannot fully communicate a religion's truth, so symbolic language is necessary. Symbols can be linguistic or physical. Linguistic symbols consist of words, or discourse, that communicate more than their literal, surface meaning. Physical symbols point beyond themselves to communicate insights of the religion. To a Christian, a cross is not just two intersecting lines but rather conjures up the cost of salvation.

Third, religions promote concepts of **salvation**, **liberation**, and **release**. Winston King notes that all religions claim to save people from and to something. Religions presume that all kinds of problems need to be surmounted, and that a paradise, heaven, better existence, or even nonexistence awaits those who faithfully follow a particular religion. The promise of deliverance powerfully motivates people to adhere to the tradition and can be a source of courage in the face of tragedy or other personal or corporate trial. Additionally, each tradition offers the specific ways that one can be saved into paradise or at least out of the suffering of existence. Consequently, believers can spend much energy learning to live according to their religious tradition, with the hope of being delivered from the troubles of their present condition.

Wikimedia Commons

4

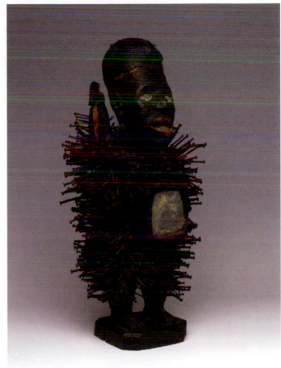

Figure 1.5. A nkisi nkondi (power figure) from Kongo Central Province in the Democratic Republic of the Congo. A nkisi nkondi serves as a container for potent ingredients used in magic and medicine. A ritual expert activates the figure by breathing into the cavity of the abdomen and immediately seals it off with a mirror. Nails and blades are driven into the figure, either to affirm an oath or to destroy an evil force.

Brooklyn Museum/Wikimedia Commons

Fourth, religions offer **sacred places** and **sacred objects**. The idea of the sacred denotes being set apart, a separation from and discontinuity with the surrounding world, from that which is ordinary, mundane, routine. Some areas and objects are considered special, set apart from ordinary areas and objects. Often physical actions accompany the entrance into the sacred place, for example, bowing, removing footwear, kneeling. The handling of sacred objects is not to be done casually but is usually accompanied by special words, chanting, or physical performance. Demarcating sacred places and objects are different types of boundaries that function to separate human beings from the sacred.

Boundaries of the sacred can be physical, ritual, and psychological. Crossing these boundaries requires some form of action on the part of the devotee. Physical boundaries, such as gates, doors, and curtains, require that one physically cross from the ordinary to the sacred space by passing through them. Ritual boundaries, such as bowing and kneeling or washing with water prior to entering the sacred place or encountering the sacred object, have a performative role in preparing an individual or community to communicate with the divine. And psychological boundaries entail recognition that since one is encountering the sacred, one must be prepared emotionally and psychologically, which is usually accompanied by the need to purify oneself, say, through confession or repentance, before facing the sacred.

> Allah made the Ka'ba [Qa'abah], the Sacred House, a means of support for men, as also the Sacred Months, the animals for offerings, and the garlands that mark them: that you may know that Allah has knowledge of what is in the heavens and on earth and that Allah is well-acquainted with all things.
>
> Qur'an 5:97[2]

Since sickness is the action of spirit, therapeutic action is sacramental. The sickness is only a symptom of the spiritual condition of the person, which is the underlying cause of the crisis, and it can only be cured by expiation—sacrifice—for the sin which has brought it about. This, then is a further characteristic of sin. It causes physical misfortune, usually sickness, which is identified with it, so that the healing of the sickness is felt to be also the wiping out of the sin.

Evans-Pritchard, *Nuer Religion*, 192

Fifth, religions employ **sacred actions (rituals)**. Human beings are ritual beings. So much of our lives is ritualistic, whether for sacred or communal ends, and we participate in ritual action in all sorts of ways. Ritual involves order and usually has a communicative function. Generally, rituals communicate something, either to a transcendent being or to other human beings. Rituals involve elements of order, routine, and a commonly accepted set of meanings, although specific rituals do not require universal acceptance. If you have traveled outside your own country or state, you quickly recognize that there are a host of ritual activities that need to be learned in order to avoid offending others. Ritual and culture are closely related. Moreover, ritual actions can be simple or complex, sacred or mundane. And they can involve stylized sayings or chanting, bowing, kneeling, or **sacrifices** (e.g., of animals, vegetables, money).

Ritual action pervades all communities, whether modern or traditional, urban or rural. We engage in simple ritual behaviors in our daily lives. When we enter an elevator, how do we act and move, and what do we say or not say? After entering an elevator, we immediately turn around—it would not seem quite normal to enter the elevator and remain facing the rear of the elevator when everyone else has turned around and faced the elevator doors. If the elevator is full, we may bump the person next to us. A social infraction has occurred, tearing the social fabric of that small space. A ritual needs to be performed—and we perform such mundane rituals daily. Typically, the offender of the social infraction will say something along the lines of, "Oh, excuse me, I'm sorry." And the response is: "That's okay" or "No problem." This simple, mundane ritual action mends the social fabric that was strained for a moment in that elevator space.

Figure 1.6. Hindu-Balinese village priest blessing students and workers for protection in Bali, Indonesia

Charles E. Farhadian

All people follow rituals, whether mundane and simple or extraordinary and complex. For some, it is difficult to think of Christianity as ritualistic, but we need to remember that Christianity and the Bible are full of ceremonies and rituals. Christians celebrate baptism, marriage, and the Lord's Supper (Eucharist, Mass) as rituals that help participants remember the past, be incorporated into the Christian community, and celebrate God's grace and the work of God's Holy Spirit. Since rituals usually refer to external actions, what is the relationship between the external nature of ritual life and the internal motivation of the participants? Would the ritual be valid without a proper internal response, such as humility, respect, or purity of heart? Likewise, would the ritual be valid if one has the correct internal motivation but fails to perform the ritual correctly? The New Testament states that priestly sacrifices cannot produce an inward purity, suggesting not that rituals are invalid but that Christ is what mediates a new relationship with God. According to Christianity, ritual life is not eliminated, but it is relativized under the light of Christ, who is incomparably superior:

> But when Christ came as a high priest of the good things that have come, then through the greater and perfect tent (not made with hands, that is, not of this creation) he entered once for all into the Holy Place, not with the blood of goats and calves, but with his own blood, thus obtaining eternal redemption. For if the blood of goats and bulls, with the sprinkling of the ashes of a heifer, sanctifies those who have been defiled so that their flesh is purified, how much more shall the blood of Christ, who through the eternal Spirit offered himself without blemish to God, purify your conscience from dead works to serve the living God! (Heb. 9:11–14)

Sacred ritual behavior is communicative action involving the divine. If an infringement has occurred, then a sacred ritual needs to be performed to restore the harmony between human beings and the divine. Some sacred actions can be simple, such as bowing before an image of a deity or ancestor, while others are incredibly complex, such as the yearlong horse sacrifice in early Hinduism. As we consider the world religions, we have to be aware of the role ritual plays in maintaining personal and corporate identity as well as harmony between human beings and the divine.

Sixth, religions utilize **sacred writings**. For literate societies, sacred writings are usually the words of holy people, such as the founder of the religious tradition, prophets, or saints. All the world religions that we will consider have sacred scriptures. Believers find guidance for their daily lives and wisdom about the human condition and the cosmos in their sacred writings. A religion's sacred writing can be contained in one book, such as the Bible, or in an immense corpus of materials, such as those found in Hinduism or Buddhism, written over a period of thousands of years. Sacred writings are not always in the vernacular language of the community, but such writings are often in language considered sacred, perhaps because the words are considered to be revealed from God. For instance, the Christian Bible, which was originally written primarily in Hebrew and Greek, has been translated into hundreds of languages throughout the world, without losing its sacred authority. Islam's sacred text, the Holy **Qur'an**, on the other hand, cannot be translated out of Arabic without losing its authority—upon translation the Holy Qur'an immediately becomes an "interpretation."

Figure 1.7. Three Hindu priests copying religious texts in the princely state of Jammu and Kashmir, India, in the 1890s

Other sacred writings are recorded in the vernacular, giving common people access to the stories, insights, and wisdom of the tradition. It is interesting to note, however, that sometimes particular segments of society are excluded from having access to the sacred writings or giving their interpretation of the texts. Whether sacred writings are recorded in a sacred language or in a vernacular language, the religious community needs interpreters who can provide greater insight and understanding of the sacred writings. Interpreters have received formal or informal education, usually involving work in language, history, and theologies, in order to illuminate the writings. Interpreters can be quite influential and powerful within the tradition, since they help to make sense of the religion under current conditions.

Seventh, religions include a **sacred community**. Winston King suggests that all religions have a communal sense and structure. Generally, there are common believers (e.g., Buddhists, Jews, Muslims), as well as the professional ritualists who lead the sacred rituals for the community. Believers worship in particular spaces, such as temples, mosques, or shrines, that can be simple structures or elaborate city-like sanctuary complexes. Worship can also be in the natural environment, such as around a tree or on the top of a

Are sacred communities all the same? One unique feature of the biblical church community was the makeup of its members, for it extended its hospitality to people regardless of their social, cultural, or economic status. The sacred community, called the church, looked beyond itself, as a sign and instrument of the kingdom of God.

> Hospitality, because it was such a fundamental human practice, always included family, friends, and influential contacts. The distinctive Christian contribution was the emphasis on including the poor and neediest, the ones who could not return the favor. This focus did not diminish the value of hospitality to family and friends; rather, it broadened the practice so that the close relations formed by table fellowship and conversation could be extended to the most vulnerable.[a]

Today, with Sunday being the most racially divided day of the week, the practice of Christian hospitality to all people remains a significant hurdle for many churches.

a. Pohl, *Making Room*, 6.

mountain. Many religions have a formal institutionalized subgroup within their communities that typically represents a greater degree of devotion to the religion, whose members seek an intensification of commitment for the purpose of getting closer to the divine or gaining deeper insight into and experience of the truths of the tradition. According to King, religion cannot be a lone affair—even the recluse hermit is living within the parameters of his or her tradition.

Finally, religions involve **sacred experience**. Beyond all the formalities of religion, such as scriptures and myths, are the actual experiences of the believers. What do people experience as religious people? Are their experiences similar across religions or distinct according to tradition? Religious people experience something—whether that be transcendence or a deep awareness. Sometimes it is easy to overlook the fact that studying religions entails taking people's religious experiences seriously. And those experiences, writes Winston King, occur within a declared religious context. There are innumerable religious experiences, and they vary from deep quiet in the presence of a holy God to intense joy because of a positively answered prayer. Experiences themselves can be like an electric shock or a peaceful calm.

In addition to considering religions as possessing the qualities suggested by King, we recognize that the scope of Christianity needs to include all branches of historic Christianity. **Orthodox**, **Catholic**, and **Protestant** (including

Figure 1.8. Sufi Whirling Dervish performing at a music festival in Purana Qila, New Delhi, India

Anabaptist) traditions are expressions of the Christian tradition. The term "Christianity" encompasses these three major branches of faith.

We need an ecumenical and charitable spirit even as we engage other Christian traditions, while not denying the differences within Christianity worldwide. The word "**ecumenical**" refers to the *whole household of God* and affirms common elements among the traditions. While particularities vary, these three branches of Christianity do indeed affirm that Jesus Christ is Lord and Savior, that his work of reconciliation has fundamentally altered all of life, and that the church and its members seek to be shaped by the biblical witness—the Bible.

Constructing Religion

The construct of "religion" as developed by Western academics remains a helpful, even if problematic, term. Definitions of religion are diverse, with some focusing on doctrine or emotional states or repetitive behaviors or reverence (for transcendent power) or ethics or a form of intuition. The etymology of the English word "religion" derives from the Latin *religio*, which has been interpreted as honor or reverence for the gods. As early as the ancient period, people traveling to new communities recognized that these groups worshiped gods with different names. When the ancient Greek historian Herodotus (484–425 BCE) encountered the Egyptian gods Amon and Horus, he tried to explain that they were equivalent to the Greek gods Zeus and Apollo. Herodotus was talking about religion—the reverence for gods.[3]

Although religion is not new, the way it is understood has changed immensely throughout history, with some of the most dramatic changes occurring in the modern period. **Friedrich Max Müller** (1823–1900), a German philosopher and Lutheran Christian who studied Sanskrit texts in England and became Oxford University's first professor of comparative theology (1868–75), was a well-known comparative philologist, particularly of Indo-European languages. During the Victorian era, when the theory of social Darwinism was highly influential, Müller sought to develop a "science of religion" that attempted to uphold the significance of religion in an era dominated by deism, the assertion that the God who created the world has remained indifferent to it.

In his *Introduction to the Science of Religion* (1873) and parts of his *Chips from a German Workshop* (1866), Müller attempted to convince a Western audience of the need to understand many religious traditions: "He who knows one, knows none."[4] In his famous "Westminster Lecture on Missions," Müller appealed to the study of comparative religions as a crucial part of Christian missionary preparation and even declared that for every Christian missionary he would rather send out ten more missionaries. Likewise, Müller advocated that the religions of Asia send missionaries to the West.[5] "Mission means that the encounter between the great human cultural types, that is the great powers of human ideas, becomes as deep and central and manysided as possible."[6] Ultimately, Müller was less interested in religious conversion than in exploring the origins of religion and myth.

Müller's case reminds us that the study of religions is influenced by the social, historical, cultural, and intellectual debates of the day. Müller, for instance, had to contend with **Charles Darwin**'s prominent evolutionary theory, which should remind us to consider the intellectual debates and insights that surround the theoretical perspectives on religion in any given period. While some may advocate eliminating the term "religion," perhaps because it is heavily laden with Western conceptual categories or because it fails to capture the essence of faith itself, it seems helpful to use the term, keeping in mind its history and limited ability to describe all things "religious."

Psychological Context

At first glance it seems strange to consider the psychological context of religion, but religions would be meaningless without people who believe and follow them. But what is the relationship between psychological processes and religion? And what about the relationship between psychology, religion, and culture? Does one aspect (psychology, religion, or culture) have greater impact than the other two? Or are they equally important to understanding religion? Have you ever wondered how your culture has impacted your emotion? There is an entire discipline called "psychological anthropology" that considers the interaction of psychological processes and culture. Some psychological anthropologists give ultimate weight to culture, suggesting that a person's emotions are determined by his or her culture. Others suggest that there is greater independence, with an individual's emotion being more determined by other factors, such as a combination of biology, chemistry, culture, and society.

Too often scholars of religion focus on the doctrine and practices of religion without considering the psychological context of the lived tradition. Our psychological, emotional, and personality makeup plays an important role in our religious life. All human beings have different personalities, even if we share salient characteristics; thus categories of "normal" and "abnormal" personalities to a great extent reflect the perspectives of our particular society, culture, and religion. A man who roams around a religious site, wearing few clothes, with matted hair and unkempt beard, relying on the food offerings of others, may be considered antisocial, psychotic, or to be suffering from some other "abnormal" psychological condition by Western standards. However, faithful Hindus may consider him a holy man whose asceticism reflects his high status as a purified soul.

Figure 1.9. Papua, Indonesia

Stephan Babuljak

> The mind is wavering and unsteady,
> Difficult to guard, hard to restrain.
> The wise one sets it straight,
> As a fletcher straightens the arrow's shaft.
>
> From the Buddhist text *Dhammapada* 3:33[7]

Psychological anthropologists who study the interaction between personality and culture note that culture influences the way we process our emotions. Likewise, our emotions and personality impact the way we engage religions. For instance, some religious people are more emotionally or physically demonstrative in worship, while others find meaning in worship that is quiet and still. Some process information, including their spiritual lives, cognitively more than emotionally.

The discussion of psychology and religion raises some interesting questions: Are certain psychological or emotional states required for religious belief? Do psychological or emotional states testify to the validity of the religious tradition itself? Likewise, does the lack of a particularly emotional response to a religion suggest that the tradition is invalid? Do believers—that is, those who follow religions—always need to come before the divine with great emotion? What is the relationship between "intention" and "right practice" in religious life? In other words, should we correlate emotional and psychological states with the universal truth of the religion, so that the more one is moved emotionally and psychologically, the more trustworthy the religion?

> Even with all the whistles and whistling,
> the calls of the birds,
> this, my mind, doesn't waver,
> for my delight is in
>   oneness.
>
> From the Buddhist text *Therigatha*, 1.49[8]

Furthermore, the way we make sense of our human struggles deeply impacts our psychological state with regard to religion. These struggles can be as small as a daily inconvenience or as large as genocide. How do religions provide psychological consolation in the midst of suffering and trauma? Countless individuals, communities, and nations have endured unthinkable tragedies, forcing them to consider the role of religion in maintaining one's identity, and to find the sources within one's religion to make sense of tragedy or deprivation. Likewise, how do religions provide the source for

Figure 1.10. Young victims of the Khmer Rouge genocide in Cambodia. Thousands of photos were taken at Security Prison 21 (S-21) prior to the prisoners being killed by the Khmer Rouge.

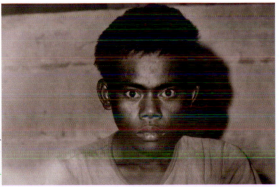

Stephan Babuljak

Stephan Babuljak

Figure 1.11. Female child standing in the Killing Fields outside Phnom Penh, Cambodia

happiness, contentment, and joy even in the midst of disappointments? Religions involve our human behaviors and emotions, so let us not forget the pervasive psychological context related to religions.

Social Context

Some revealing questions for modern people are, Where does the self find its home? How does religion help or hinder life in the modern world? How might religion provide continuity between the various social domains of life, even providing greater meaning and cohesiveness to one's identity, personality, ambitions, and goals? How much is religion a part of each social domain in the modern world, or is it absent outside religious institutions, like church or synagogue?

We live in communities that provide social networks that help to give us meaning and a sense of belonging. Much of our identity—who we believe we are—is given to us by our community, whether family, clan, state, or nation. Social structures change over time, influenced by such forces as modern technology, education, and increased migration to urban centers. Generally,

Wes Hargrove

Figure 1.12. Skyline of Amman, Jordan

14

social structures can be considered either traditional or modern. People today increasingly live in more globalized structures, whereby the events, products, and preferences of one location influence local life elsewhere in the world. Naturally, there are countless combinations of traditional and modern ways of living in society and structuring society.

> For the love of Christ urges us on, because we are convinced that one has died for all; therefore all have died. And he died for all, so that those who live might live no longer for themselves, but for him who died and was raised for them. From now on, therefore, we regard no one from a human point of view; even though we once knew Christ from a human point of view, we know him no longer in that way. So if anyone is in Christ, there is a new creation: everything old has passed away; see, everything has become new! All this is from God, who reconciled us to himself through Christ, and has given us the ministry of reconciliation; that is, in Christ God was reconciling the world to himself, not counting their trespasses against them, and entrusting the message of reconciliation to us.
>
> 2 Corinthians 5:14–19

For our purposes, it is enough to discuss briefly the differences between traditional and modern social structures because these two basic ways of organizing communities communicate something about religions. How are societies structured? Have you ever visited a society much different from your own? Who seems to be in control of those communities? Who makes the important decisions? How are important decisions made: by an individual or by group consensus? What kinds of media, messages, and ideas are promoted in the public squares in those societies? How do people relate differently than they do in your own community of origin? Does everybody have access to education, leadership positions, and religious life, or are some excluded? On what grounds are people excluded from different social domains or social positions?

Traditional societies are typically more closely knit, with fewer separate social domains than modern societies, which have greater distance between the separate social arenas. Traditional societies are characterized by multi-stranded relationships, where individuals are in several meaningful yet distinct, overlapping relationships. For instance, in a traditional society there may be several intersecting social roles played by members of the community; the person who cuts your hair can also be the religious leader as well as your teacher and your father. Social roles overlap much more in traditional societies than in modern societies. One would be less willing to speak untruths behind someone's back in a traditional society, since the entire community is watching!

Stephan Babuljak

Figure 1.13. Girls' school in Tamil Nadu, India

The multistranded nature of relationships points to the fact that there are fewer distinct social domains in a traditional world. In some traditional societies, the men clear the forest to establish the village garden, while women work daily in the gardens, harvest the yield, prepare the meals, and sell the crop yield at the local market. Thus her role is gardener, cook, and seller—and, probably, mother, wife, and more. What is more, because of the nature of overlapping social domains in the traditional world, it would not be unusual for a woman selling fruit from her family garden to give her daughter a haircut at the same time. Mom is simultaneously a seller and a barber. Since social domains are more likely to overlap in traditional societies, change in one area of social life may have a significant impact on other areas of life. Furthermore, social exchange, social hierarchy, and political power circulate within a more narrowly defined community rather than flowing outside the community to wider, national or global, spheres.

Authority roles in traditional societies are won either through heredity, such as the chiefdom patterns of leadership in Polynesia, or through competition or prowess, which is practiced in Melanesia (earning one's way to the top). Under traditional social conditions, the community functions fairly coherently and comprehensively. Yet change does occur in all societies. It is worthwhile to note that there are few truly isolated traditional communities that have absolutely no contact with people outside their own communities. Many people, even if they live in isolated regions, do in fact trade across vast frontiers, journeying on boat or foot to obtain items (and sometimes people) unavailable in their immediate locale.

Now the eleven disciples went to Galilee, to the mountain to which Jesus had directed them. When they saw him, they worshiped him; but some doubted. And Jesus came and said to them, "All authority in heaven and on earth has been given to me. Go therefore and make disciples of all nations, baptizing them in the name of the Father and of the Son and of the Holy Spirit, and teaching them to obey everything that I have commanded you. And remember, I am with you always, to the end of the age."

Matthew 28:16–20

The religious lives of traditional communities can remain fairly intact, but new ideas about the spirit world, the cosmos, and the natural world can be shared as traders and adventurers visit other communities and return with new knowledge. The social burdens for those living under traditional social conditions can be quite weighty. Change is not easy. And life options can be quite limited. If a woman is a seamstress, her daughter may be expected to follow in her mother's footsteps. If a man is a cattle herder, his son most likely will continue his father's work as an adult. The individual self is sustained and nurtured by the community because the self is oriented toward the social group for its identity. So one's identity is closely tied to the identity of the group, which can give an individual a deep sense of belonging.

Such close identification with the group can also cause one to feel confined by the limits of such a group and its expectations. Consequently, under traditional social conditions, the self is more **sociocentric**, for it is profoundly influenced by the group for its identity. Indeed the traditional world can be burdensome for an individual who desires to do things differently than the community does. The personal challenges confronting individuals moving from rural, traditional societies to urban, modern societies can be quite overwhelming, especially as individuals begin to make sense of a new world outside the contexts of their own villages, which had provided such meaning in the first place. If traditional societies are marked by relatively few distinct social domains and multistranded relationships, then modern societies tend to reflect some of the opposite social realities.

Modern societies are complicated but characterized in part by their multiple social domains and single-stranded connectedness. These are the kinds of societies that are the building blocks of urban centers throughout the world. And these social structures are not limited to urban centers, for they typify social structures prevalent in suburban contexts as well. Typical social domains include a wide range of institutions, such as schools, churches, businesses, gyms, houses, or apartments. For those living in a modern society, much of the day consists of moving from one social domain to another. We go to work. We exercise at gyms or in parks. We worship at churches. We study at school. We buy our groceries at a supermarket. We buy household items, technology, music, and books in all kinds of stores. These activities are punctuated by participation in other social domains, such as voluntary organizations like biking or running clubs. In significant ways, our entire lives are spent moving from one social domain to another.

All these social domains are separate, even when we fill up our cars at gas stations with attached fast-food restaurants. As we live in an area for some time, we may become familiar with some of the names and faces of the people we see routinely in these various locations, but we rarely see representatives of each social domain together in one location. In fact, it can be particularly surprising or even embarrassing to run into people in other domains than the one in which we are used to seeing them. Is it not somehow surprising to see your barber in line at the grocery store? Does it not catch your attention to see your pastor or priest standing in line at the post office? Those are small "ah-ha" moments! "Hey, great to see you!" In fact, if you have ever attempted to gather friends from the different domains of your life, say, for a birthday party, you know how hard it can be for each group to mingle with the others. It can be either humorous or disappointing. You assume they will all mesh well, because they are all your friends, but the contrary is usually the case. The different people typically do not relate well, if at all, and remain in their

Figure 1.14. Kolkata street, India: struggling in the midst of suffering

social enclaves, separated into groups of "school friends," "church friends," "family," and "workout buddies."

Under modern social conditions, replete with disparate social domains, it can be easy to remake one's self as we move from one domain to another. If we lack integrity, then our selves can be different in each social arena. And we can be left feeling quite alone and isolated. It is not surprising that one of the particular challenges of modern living is to maintain an integrated self through all life domains, rather than remaining in a state of existential crisis of self and identity.

Cultural Context

Everybody lives within a culture, but what is culture? Anthropologists provide a wide range of definitions of culture, depending on their theoretical perspective, but for our purposes let us consider culture to be "the sum total ways of living developed by a group of human beings and handed on from generation to generation."[9] It seems strange to me that "culture" is often understood as "how others live." We visit "cultures" when we travel but rarely think of our own values, foods, and clothes as part of "our" culture. Doing a quick internet search for "culture" pulls up images of people with bones through their noses or similar images of the "exotic other." But we all inhabit culture . . . and culture inhabits us! Culture refers to the beliefs, values, motives, attitudes, cosmologies, knowledge, practices, and meanings shared by a large group of people. Cultural patterns can be implicit or explicit. And symbols are often the carriers of culture, which means that learning about a culture entails learning something about the symbols of that culture.

Human cultures consist of material and nonmaterial items. Material culture refers generally to tangible, physical objects, produced by human activity, such as artwork, coins, utensils, weapons, handcrafts (e.g., clothing, textiles, jewelry), buildings (e.g., houses), food, tools, and technology. These material items are used by human beings and can communicate what is important about a particular culture, because they reflect something of the patterns of belief and practice of individuals and their communities. Nonmaterial culture consists of meanings, knowledge, beliefs, philosophies, and communication patterns (e.g., verbal and nonverbal communication). These include aspects of culture such as customs and traditions, institutions, gestures, and rules (e.g., government) that provide stability to the community. Globalization and the circulation of goods and commodities that travel across those channels of modern transportation and fiber optics also deeply impact the ways we relate to one another and create culture, while shaping our values and preferences.

Stephan Babujak

Figure 1.15. A tribe in Papua, Indonesia, encounters photo technology for the first time

Material and nonmaterial aspects of culture are constantly interacting. Some material items, such as flags, help create a shared identity for communities and nations. Ideas and values are not inherently present *in* the material object itself, but through common consent and belief, people give value to material culture. What are other examples of material culture that seem important in your culture? Why are they important? Who decides? Under what conditions do material cultural items lose their significance, and what helps sustain the value of a material item through time? How do "outsiders"—that is, those who did not originally value that item—begin to see worth in the material item? How do people resolve tension that emerges when two or more material items are present in the same space and appear to represent two significantly different values?

Religious symbols are typically items within the material culture of a community, but they are heavily laden with meaning, knowledge, and value that are passed down from generation to generation, giving communities a sense of continuity through time. We must look for religion not just behind the material culture but also within the material culture itself. Let us keep an eye on both material and nonmaterial cultural items, for both are deeply important to the religious life.

Cultures influence religions, and religions influence culture; culture and religion cannot be easily disentangled since they are so intimately connected. All foods, tastes, personalities,

Figure 1.16. Hindu-Balinese daily offerings at temple, and street merchant selling globalized goods in Bali, Indonesia

Charles E. Farhadian

priorities, relationships, and so on are shaped by the cultures in which we were raised. If you have ever traveled outside your own culture, you may have experienced a degree of culture shock, where you have felt disoriented, surprised, or anxious about encountering a different culture. Have you ever eaten monkey soup? I remember eating beetle grubs for the first time—I did not enjoy the flavor, but it was important to show my hosts in the jungles of New Guinea that I was thankful for their generous hospitality. Being world Christians requires that we become students of cultures so that we minimize the mistakes we are bound to make while traveling, living, or working in a culture different from our own. Most nations, in fact, consist of several cultures. Few places are completely culturally homogeneous. We carry our prejudices with us, seeing "the other" through our own cultural lenses. Studying world religions can help us see ourselves and others as equally "in-culturated."

Historical Context

The nature of creation has limited us to certain times and spaces. Our lives would be dramatically different had we lived one hundred or one thousand years ago. Even within our own time, we recognize that our lives would have been different had we been born into a different family or country, in a rural or urban setting, in poverty or affluence, or in a time of war or peace. Think about how much the world has changed just with the creation of computers and the internet! Commerce, dating, even book writing can all be done electronically. The historical moment of our lives is deeply momentous. The historical contexts of religions give us insight into the significant convictions and affirmations of each tradition, since religions often are contending against particular vices, sins, or falsehoods and offer new answers to universal questions.

Understanding the history of a religion gives us insight into the unique contribution that the religion made at the time of its birth as well as how it was sustained through time. No religion has emerged outside the confines of space and time. And we would do well to take seriously the historical moment of the emergence of the various religions as well as to ask ourselves how each religious tradition sustains itself over time. What seems to be significant for each tradition? What are its unique and more universally held affirmations? What unique answers did the religion offer at the time of its founding? Christian theology, for instance, emerged to a large extent because of Christian contact with other peoples and cultures. Throughout history the Christian missionary movement gave rise to the formalization of Christian theology, as Christians had to articulate themselves and their faith to those who had never heard the good news.

When communicating to Greeks, early Christians needed to speak Greek and use Greek philosophical concepts to make sense of Christian affirmations for Greek listeners. That is the story of Christian history, in which missionaries continually had to translate the message of the gospel into local idioms in order to communicate with the people they were meeting. At every turn, Christians needed to communicate Christian faith in terms that were meaningful to the recipients. As mission scholars **Lamin Sanneh** and **Andrew Walls** have suggested, Christianity is a movement of translation because the fundamental concepts of the faith find their final destination in local cultural idioms. Christianity has always been translated into local languages and concepts, and thus made meaningful to all people in their particular contexts. That process of translation continues today. We will revisit these themes in the chapter on Christianity.

> In the beginning was the Word, and the Word was with God, and the Word was God. He was in the beginning with God. All things came into being through him, and without him not one thing came into being. What has come into being in him was life, and the life was the light of all people. The light shines in the darkness, and the darkness did not overcome it. . . . And the Word became flesh and lived among us, and we have seen his glory, the glory as of a father's only son, full of grace and truth.
>
> John 1:1–5, 14

History recounts and interprets past events, furnishing readers with the story of the birth and demise of nations, economic systems, governmental regimes, and small- and large-scale societies. Economics, wars, periods of subjugation, developments in technologies, and the waxing and waning of nation-states are part of the larger story that historians try to describe. In a sense, everything (ideas, societies, the natural world, religions, and so on) has a history—each has some kind of beginning and a trajectory in time. Each religion has a unique history, although many show signs of connections with one another. The constellation of monotheistic religions (Judaism, Christianity, and Islam), which emerged roughly in the same area of the Middle East, shares several significant concepts.

Likewise, the traditions of Asia, such as Hinduism, Jainism, and Buddhism, share fundamentally important concepts, such as karma, reincarnation (**samsara**; Sanskrit, *samsāra*), and **dharma**, although these too are interpreted differently by each tradition. As we look at the different religions, we need to take the history of each tradition seriously, because often the religion is part of a larger constellation of religions (e.g., Judaism, Christianity, and Islam, or Hinduism, Jainism, and Buddhism) that was shaped by specific historical processes. As kings and emperors either embraced or denounced specific religions, those religions either advanced or declined, often in unpredictable ways.

Environmental Context

The natural world—including topography, flora, fauna, weather patterns, temperature, and sunlight—impacts religion in a variety of ways. First, for many the environment is considered to be animated by spiritual forces, so that material reality (e.g., trees, rocks, waterfalls) is more than what the eye alone can perceive. Recognizing that the natural world is filled with spiritual beings implicitly gives people a naturally spiritual orientation, since often the spirits are considered part of the community and must be appeased, feared, honored, and respected for the benefits they grant human beings. For many, the natural world is alive with significance. Second, even for those who do not recognize countless spirits in the natural world, many believe that creation, whether created by God or not, is imbued by natural laws that, when followed, promise long life and beneficial results, such as health, happiness, good crops, or a successful business.

Third, people "read" the natural world and its changes as somehow connected to God's activity and purpose. How does God speak? What nontextual means does God use to communicate? Natural catastrophes can be interpreted as signs from God, conveying judgment or blessing depending on which community is affected. Major environmental changes force people to inquire about God's purpose and design. Or maybe human beings have forgotten to live in line with the law of nature to such an extent that the very fabric of the universe tears or is at least stretched, and the natural world communicates a wake-up call for us to get our lives in order again—to align ourselves with the pattern of the universe. Fourth, the natural world provides items used for ritual sacrifices. Water, animals, fruits and vegetables, incense, and other substances offered in sacrifices tend to be locally produced. The environment itself yields the sacrificial elements, which are returned to God (or the gods) in ceremonial fashion.

> *There seems always and everywhere to be an awareness of the reality and possibility of a dedication, or even a sanctification of the life of man, on the basis of an individual or social striving, which is almost always and everywhere referred to an event which comes from beyond. As a result, the representation of the object and aim of the striving, or of the origin of the event, has always and everywhere been compressed into pictures of deities, with almost always and everywhere the picture of a supreme and only deity more or less clearly visible in the background.*
>
> K. Barth, *Church Dogmatics*, I/2:282

The memory of significant religious events, such as the birth or death of a prophet, or the location of divine-human interaction, is concretized and memorialized in specific natural spaces set apart for their sacredness. Religious memory is often tied to land. "This mountain is where God spoke to the prophet." "That valley is where God helped us win the battle."

Figure 1.17. Powerful memories of death and life. A Madonna of Sorrow at her son's grave (France, 1917)

When the entire nation had finished crossing over the Jordan, the LORD said to Joshua: "Select twelve men from the people, one from each tribe, and command them, 'Take twelve stones from here out of the middle of the Jordan, from the place where the priests' feet stood, carry them over with you, and lay them down in the place where you camp tonight.'" Then Joshua summoned the twelve men from the Israelites, whom he had appointed, one from each tribe. Joshua said to them, "Pass on before the ark of the LORD your God in the middle of the Jordan, and each of you take up a stone on his shoulder, one for each of the tribes of the Israelites, so that this may be a sign among you. When your children ask in time to come, 'What do those stones mean to you?' then you shall tell them that the waters of the Jordan were cut off in front of the ark of the covenant of the LORD. When it crossed over the Jordan, the waters of the Jordan were cut off. So these stones shall be to the Israelites a memorial forever."

Joshua 4:1–7

Memory of noteworthy religious events is frequently tied to the land, where people gather at pilgrimage centers, to remember God or the essentials of their religious tradition. In our contemporary world, the natural environment can also be the focus of hot debate, when indigenous people who have connected their religious worldview directly to the environment argue that the sacredness of land is desecrated when developers attempt to build on or destroy the natural world for economic gain. It is impossible to separate memory, religion, environment, and identity. For our purposes, however, it is enough to note that the natural world is a major element of the wider context of religion that should not be overlooked.

The Problem of Constructing Religion

Using the term "religion" does not bother most of us, especially when it is applied to other religious traditions. However, some Christians are turned off by the suggestion that the term be applied equally to Christianity—that Christianity itself is a "religion" as are the other traditions. Christians who are offended by using the term "religion" to describe their own tradition usually do so on the grounds that, so they say, "Christianity is not a religion, but a relationship."

The famous twentieth-century neoorthodox theologian **Karl Barth** (1886–1968) juxtaposed *religion* and *revelation*, arguing that any human attempt to know God, for instance, through religious rituals, practices, and beliefs, always fails because knowledge and communion with God can occur only if God takes the initiative to reveal himself. God has placed what in Pascal's words is a "God-shaped vacuum" in all human beings that can only be filled with God. Human beings are merely idol factories when they construct religions that attempt to bridge the gap between the human and the divine. *Revelation*, according to Barth, was God's unveiling of himself to humankind. Only through revelation can human beings know God. And God is known most fully through God's self-disclosure, Jesus Christ.

> Religion is "a set of symbolic forms and acts relating man to the ultimate conditions of his existence."
>
> Bellah and Tipton, *Robert Bellah Reader*, 28

For Barth, Christianity itself could be seen as a religion where humans attempt through ritual or otherwise to reach God rather than recognizing that God has stooped down to us. Christians who are uncomfortable using the term "religion" to refer to their own religious tradition reflect the same sorts of challenges implicit in most religious traditions. That is, many religionists differentiate between the superficial following of either their tradition or even other traditions and the deeper, essential aspects of their own religion. In Christianity's case, it may very well be offensive to suggest that Christianity is a religion to those who experience their faith as essentially a personal relationship with God through Jesus Christ. Whatever we may argue to be the "essentials of faith" of Christianity, the fact remains that

> Religions are confluences of organic-cultural flows that intensify joy and confront suffering by drawing on human and superhuman forces to make homes and cross boundaries.
>
> Tweed, *Crossing and Dwelling*, 54

> *If we say Jesus Christ, we also assert a human and therefore temporal presence. Every moment of the event of Jesus Christ is also a temporal moment, i.e., a present with a past behind it and a future in front of it, like the temporal moments in the sequence of which we exist ourselves. "The Word became flesh" also means "the Word became time.". . . [Revelation is] a temporal reality. So it is not a sort of ideal, yet in itself timeless content of all or some times. It does not remain transcendent over time, it does not merely meet it at a point, but it enters time; nay, it assumes time; nay, it creates time for itself.*
>
> K. Barth, *Church Dogmatics*, I/2:50

> *In the face of the cross of Christ it is monstrous to describe the uniqueness of God as an object of "natural knowledge."*
>
> K. Barth, *Church Dogmatics*, II/1:453

Christianity exhibits general characteristics similar to those of other religious traditions. And why cannot Christianity be both *religion* and *revelation*?

One of the major challenges for all believers is to recognize that there are insider and outsider perspectives on each tradition. As Christians, we know something of our tradition and may be rightly concerned if our tradition is misrepresented or misunderstood. Likewise, adherents of other religions may feel the same if their tradition is misrepresented. Naturally, an additional challenge for religions is that each tradition exhibits a degree of diversity, making essentialisms difficult to sustain. Anthropologists use the terms "**emic**" and "**etic**" to describe whether an interpretation of a given culture is from an insider's or an outsider's perspective, respectively. Emic descriptions are meaningful to insiders of the culture, religion, or society, whereas etic descriptions are meaningful to observers of that culture, religion, or society. Naturally, these terms can be applied to a wide range of topics, academic disciplines, and domains of knowledge. My point here is simply to suggest that even as Christians it is helpful to recognize that our perspectives on our own tradition and others' traditions will necessarily employ either an emic or an etic viewpoint. But which perspective is more valuable?

Emic perspectives may help us be sensitive to a person's lived experience and familiarity with a religion. When you want to learn about Islam, why not include conversations with Muslims in your research? If you want to learn about Buddhism, why not speak to Buddhists? Emic viewpoints typically represent an informant's insider perception, which is invaluable in understanding the subjective experience of religion. Etic, or outsider, perspectives are valuable partly because they are meaningful to a wider audience and employ terminology and conceptual schemes that are more universally useful to social scientists and scholars of religion. Although absolute objectivity is impossible to achieve, an etic perspective lends itself to comparative concepts and purposes. It seems best, however, to employ both emic and etic perspectives as much as possible, while recognizing the strengths and weaknesses of each.

Because religions are experienced by human beings and we are not uniform in the way we think, live, worship, feel, and love, there are often discrepancies between the doctrines, beliefs, and practices of a given faith tradition. Needless to say, although gathering as a body of Christ is a crucial part of a robust Christian faith, not all Christians go to church every Sunday. There are many disconnections between the religious ideals and the actual living out of the tradition. Religions are a messy business because they involve human beings. We also need to recognize Western and non-Western ways of thinking, to the best of our knowledge, since many aspects of religion cannot simply be pigeonholed into Western conceptual categories without denying or distorting the concepts we are trying to understand.

Simply put, there are significant so-called inconsistencies, intellectual discrepancies, and paradoxes in the various religious traditions of the world. And these inconsistencies and paradoxes provide natural tension and vitality within all religions. We can either try hard to tie up the loose ends of the tradition or simply allow the paradoxes to exist, recognizing them to be part of the tradition itself. The growing edge for many students will involve simply accepting the implicit inconsistencies of religion without forcing important concepts into neatly defined, hermetically sealed Western conceptual categories. Religions transcend Western categories of understanding. As such, studying world religions can help us grow intellectually as we make room for new insights and perspectives.

Theories of Religion

Beginning in the nineteenth century, several prominent intellectuals developed theories of religion that continue to influence our understanding of religion today.[10] It is worthwhile to note that the theoretical perspectives mentioned below are only representative viewpoints and should not be read as summarizing the entire theoretical perspective of a particular academic discipline. Needless to say, each discipline today consists of a mixture of scholars with a variety of perspectives on religion. The theorists below are presented here because their work represents some of the earliest significant theoretical insights of a given academic discipline or, as in the case of anthropologist **Clifford Geertz**, because of their overall impact on a wide range of disciplines. Each theorist is a major force in the field, so it is impossible to provide a complete summary of either their lives or their theories in any satisfactory way. While most of these theorists represent the first voices to seriously consider religion within each discipline, it is important to recognize that a Christian presence in these same disciplines has led to religion being seen in a different, and usually positive, light. Only a brief introduction to each theorist is provided to give you a sense of his general contribution to the discussion of the concept of religion. A footnote following each theoretical perspective provides suggestions for further reading.

A Psychological Theory of Religion

Sigmund Freud (1856–1939), the "father of psychoanalysis," has widely influenced the way many in the West understand human behavior. Many who reject Freud's theory of religion have nevertheless been impacted by particular aspects of his thought. Freud was born in Austria, the firstborn of his father's much younger second wife. Freud's own young life was characterized by divided emotions and contradictory feelings of both love and aggression. As a boy, Freud moved with his family to Vienna. He found it nearly impossible to develop any fondness for the predominately Roman Catholic city of Vienna, but he excelled brilliantly as a university student, working in Greek, Latin, Hebrew, French, English, Spanish, Italian, and German. In 1873 Freud entered the University of Vienna, where he studied anatomy and physiology; he graduated in 1881 as a doctor of medicine. Later Freud worked with mentally ill people, focusing primarily on neurotic, mostly wealthy, women. His vast corpus of writing addresses such topics as dreams, sexuality, neuroses, love, human development, civilizations, anxiety, and religion.

Freud's legacy includes his particular method of investigating and treating people, known as psychoanalysis, where he encouraged patients to say whatever came to mind in a stream of consciousness and **free association** so that repressed feelings could surface from the unconscious mind and be analyzed. Freud knew the stories of the Hebrew Bible, but he was, according to his biographer, "from beginning to end a natural atheist." Freud's *The Future of an Illusion* (1989 [1927]) outlined

Ferdinand Schmutzer/Wikimedia Commons

Figure 1.18. Sigmund Freud

his view of religion and God. Simply put, Freud argued that religion was a "wish fulfillment," "an illusion" that would disappear as people evolved into more rational beings, leaving behind the need and wish for religion itself. Freud's perspective arose from his view of the history of human societies and civilizations and the strength of the natural world. According to Freud, who was influenced profoundly by Charles Darwin's evolutionary theory, human life evolved out of the natural world, where nature continually threatened to destroy us through disease, predators, disasters, and physical decline.

For protection, human beings joined into clans, then tribes, then nations, and then civilizations. Motivating the human desire to gather into groups was the attempt to gain security from the constant threat of nature. Through developed civilizations we gained security, but this security required a great deal of personal and corporate restraint. We had to rein in our personal desires and instincts to maintain civilizational stability—how else could we survive in a civilization if all people acted on their desire to hurt or kill others? Yet even with these restraints, we discovered that civilization could not fully defend us from the threats of nature. Death and disease continued. So Freud suggested that we all are ultimately helpless—and death will win. Since civilization cannot protect us, and we desperately desire protection from the dangers of the night, we become like children again, when our fathers would protect us and provide childhood security. Since our most basic need for protection cannot be met by our families, nations, or civilizations, what are we to do?[11]

According to Freud, religious belief projects onto the external world a God (a heavenly Father) who dispels the terror of nature and gives us comfort in the darkness of death. Death loses its sting. Religion also facilitates living within societies and civilizations and thus has a social dimension—we are not just obeying the laws of humanity, but we also follow the laws of a righteous and just God. Since God is conceptualized as a person (i.e., Father), human beings can regain their sense of intimacy and protection that they cannot get from their earthly fathers. And religious education is in large measure responsible for the advancement of religion.

Religious beliefs are not truths revealed by God or about God but rather are ideas that we desperately want to be true. They are, in Freud's words, the "fulfillment of the oldest, strongest and most urgent wishes of mankind."[12] Freud was confident that science and its methods would expose the illusion

> *Think of the depressing contrast between the radiant intelligence of a healthy child and the feeble intellectual powers of the average adult. Can we be quite certain that it is not precisely religious education which bears a large share of the blame for this relative atrophy? I think it would be a very long time before a child who was not influenced began to trouble himself about God and things in another world.*
>
> Freud, *Future of an Illusion*, 60

of religion and be our future guide. Consequently, for Freud, religion was the result of a neurosis, which could only be overcome by the scientific method because only the "unbeliever can truly understand belief."[13]

Freud maintained that religion was only for the immature, and that as humanity grew, discarding its childish wishes, it would eliminate religion and replace it with reason and science. Religious resurgence, however, has been happening all over the world, even in the most scientifically oriented societies.

A Sociological Theory of Religion

Émile Durkheim (1858–1917) was born in France, the son of a rabbi. He was a gifted high school student and later became a professor at the University of Bordeaux, where he occupied the new chair in sociology. Durkheim is considered a founder of modern sociology. While not as antireligious as Freud, Durkheim was a secular Jew who was more concerned with analyzing social cohesion than the existence of God. Durkheim may have been less prone to pathologizing religion than Freud because as a young person Durkheim had been affected positively by a Roman Catholic schoolteacher.

Durkheim wrote extensively about the nature and function of religion, and his seminal work, *The Elementary Forms of the Religious Life* (1912), remains an indispensable part of an essential corpus of reading in the sociology of religion.

Society contains within *itself* the power to create religion. The society has all that is necessary to create the sensation of the divine in minds—because of the power of society over the individual. Like Freud, Durkheim presented his view of social development. According to Durkheim, individuals are born into social groups, such as families, clans, tribes, and nations. These social groups profoundly impact our self-understanding and our understanding of the wider world. Our languages, values, beliefs, and emotional responses are deeply affected by our social background. Furthermore, because social solidarity is so essential, all kinds of obligations keep individuals bound to the group, which, in the religious realm, teaches us morality and rituals of worship.

> *Religion would thus be the universal obsessional neurosis of humanity; like the obsessional neuroses of children, it arose out of the Oedipus Complex, out of the relation to the father. If this view is right, it is to be supposed that a turning-away from religion is bound to occur with the fatal inevitability of a process of growth, and that we find ourselves at this very juncture in the middle of that phase of development.*
>
> Freud, *Future of an Illusion*, 23

> *A society has all that is necessary to arouse the sensation of the divine in minds, merely by the power that it has over them; for to its members it is what a god is to his worshippers.*
>
> Durkheim, *Elementary Forms of the Religious Life*, 236–37

Henrik Hansson/Wikimedia Commons

Figure 1.19. Muslim girls enjoying friendships at the Istiqlal Mosque in Jakarta, Indonesia

Morality, which is the obligation of one to another and to the overall standards of the social group, is inseparable from religion. Society, morality, and religion are intimately connected—as the social structure changes, so too the morality and the religion. Rituals of worship are always communal, and religionists believe they are worshiping something "out there," beyond themselves, even if the focus of worship is a plant, a statue, or an icon that can control the natural world. Durkheim argued that worshipers of these powers believe that these powers can make them prosper in a host of different ways (e.g., send rain, health, long life).

However, Durkheim argued that something quite different was actually happening. During worship—that is, these awe-inspiring ceremonial occasions when the whole community gathers together for general rituals—worshipers seal their commitment to the clan or tribe. Worship enables individuals to merge themselves—to lose their individual selves into the group self, where worshipers solemnize their commitment to the social group (clan, tribe, nation), sinking their private selves into the great single self of the group. In the midst of such gatherings, people acquire sentiments and undertake actions that they would never think of embracing individually; they leave the realm of everyday routine (the

A religion is a unified system of beliefs and practices relative to sacred things, i.e., things set apart and forbidden— beliefs and practices which unite in one single moral community called a Church, all those who adhere to them.

Durkheim, *Elementary Forms of the Religious Life,* 47

Figure 1.20. Women at a traditional Nigerian coronation ceremony

profane) and enter the sphere of the sacred. Consequently, the origins of religion, according to Durkheim, are in ***collective experience***.

Durkheim employed terms such as "bubble up" and "effervescent" to describe the feelings of excitement that worshipers experience during group ceremonies. Out of these feelings, the notion of a god is projected out of the social group onto a heavenly canvas toward which prayers are addressed. Durkheim describes such moments as ritual times, full of energy, enthusiasm, joy, delight, and selfless commitment. Such ceremonial moments provide ontological security. From where does religion emerge? What are the origins of religion? For Durkheim religion is society writ large. It is from society that religion emerges and provides protection to individuals and communities.

In Durkheim's own words, "It is in the midst of these effervescent social environments and out of this effervescence itself that the religious idea seems to be born." Therefore, religion is "something eminently social. Religious representations are collective representations which express collective realities."[14] As individual selves merge with the collective self during ritual times of worship, the profane is left behind, and the sacred remains. Other terms employed by Durkheim to describe the power of society to create religion are "collective consciousness," "collective experience," and "collective representations," which illustrate his belief that religion and society are intimately connected and, in fact, that religion emerges from society itself—as a collectivity. For Durkheim, then, religion and society

> *Thus there is something eternal in religion that is destined to outlive the succession of particular symbols in which religious thought has clothed itself.*
>
> Durkheim, *Elementary Forms of Religious Life*, 427

Figure 1.21. Church in Tamil Nadu, India

are functionally related, with society determining religion.

An Economic Theory of Religion

One of the most influential thinkers of the nineteenth and twentieth centuries was **Karl Marx** (1818–83), who was born in the Rhineland region of Germany. Marx's vast legacy as the father of Communism remains a topic of robust discussion among economic theorists and ordinary people who continue to be impacted by his theory of economics, societies, and revolutionary change. Marx was born Jewish, and both his grandfathers were rabbis. He grew up in a comfortable and fairly prosperous middle-class home. It is interesting to note that, when Marx was a child, his father converted to Christianity. Marx studied law and philosophy at the University of Bonn and became a university teacher and journalist upon graduation. Some have compared Marx's influence on humankind to that of Jesus or Muhammad simply by the massive number of lives affected by his economic theory. Marx was known for being outspoken and confident, a scholar and a revolutionary, who was not content simply with reforming society. Marx wanted revolutionary social and economic change, and he is among a small number of people who have fundamentally changed the way people see the world and nonhuman relationships.

Unlike Freud and Durkheim, Marx's views of religion were recorded not in a single book but can be gleaned throughout his work as a partial subtheme that comes to the fore when Marx needs to address the subject. Marx had an all-embracing view of society, not a neatly packaged perspective on religion. Yet for some, Marx's work has been interpreted as a religion since it contains within it many of the characteristics associated

> *[Sacred things are] simply collective ideals that have fixed themselves on material objects. . . . They are only collective forces hypostasized, that is to say, moral forces; they are made up of the ideas and sentiments awakened in us by the spectacle of society, and not of sensations coming from the physical world.*
>
> Durkheim, "Dualism of Human Nature," 159

Wikimedia Commons

Figure 1.22. Karl Marx

with religion, such as sacred symbols, myths, rituals and ceremonies, sacred places and persons, and even missionaries. Marx's major works were **The Communist Manifesto** (1848), originally published as a political tract to introduce the Communist League's ideas and agenda, and **Das Kapital** (1867), a multi-volume work presenting Marx's history of economic thought and political economy.

The basis of irreligious criticism is this: man makes religion; religion does not make man. Religion is indeed man's self-consciousness and self-awareness so long as he has not found himself or has lost himself again. But man is not an abstract being, squatting outside the world. Man is the human world, the state, society.

Karl Marx, in Smelser,
*Karl Marx on Society and
Social Change,* 13

To appreciate Marx's insights we need to consider briefly the larger intellectual context of his day. Marx's thinking was opposed to another intellectual giant of his era, **Georg Wilhelm Friedrich Hegel** (1770–1831), a German philosopher who argued that material objects—that is, empirical reality—are secondary to "the absolute spirit," which is God. Hegel's views represented a philosophical school known as German idealism, which had been influenced by the work of **Immanuel Kant** (1724–1804) in the 1780s and 1790s. Hegel suggested that this "absolute spirit" animates material reality and events, much like an artist might express himself through beautiful works of art or an architect express herself through a building. Yet the material reality (e.g., art, building) never fully captures the ideal, suggesting that the material form is always inadequate. Hegel used the term "thesis" to refer to all material events in the world and argued that each time a thesis (event) occurs in the world, the spirit causes an opposite event (an "antithesis") that attempts to correct the specific material event.

Furthermore, the tension between material and mental/spiritual forces is resolved by a third force (event), the "synthesis," which Hegel suggested blended elements of both prior events (material and spiritual). Therefore, according to Hegel, a dialectical process emerges that explains the development of human societies. As a civilization (thesis) encounters another civilization (antithesis), a newer form of civilization emerges that is a blending of the two (thesis-antithesis) in a synthesis that explains the development of the entire world.

Marx rejected Hegel's idealism, believing that what was fundamentally real about the world was not spiritual or mental realities but material forces. However, Marx did not reject Hegel's notion of conflicting forces but instead introduced the idea that those forces were to be found within empirical (material) reality rather than in the dichotomy between material and spiritual, as Hegel had suggested.[15] *The Communist Manifesto* summarizes Marx's theory of class struggle, where one can hear the overtones of Hegelian dialectic.

I n 1971 Peruvian Catholic priest Gustavo Gutiérrez coined the term "liberation theology" to describe a theological perspective and practice that aimed to alleviate poverty caused by social injustice. Gutiérrez sought to identify the structures within society that oppressed people, arguing along with the Catholic Church at the time for the "preferential option for the poor." Some viewed Gutiérrez's book *A Theology of Liberation* (1971) as engaging in Marxist social analysis in its argument that Christians should participate in a class struggle to bridge the gulf between the rich and the poor. Gutiérrez contended that Christ liberates human beings from sin, the root of all injustice and oppression. According to Gutiérrez,

> Therefore, sin is not only an impediment to salvation in the afterlife. Insofar as it constitutes a break with God, sin is a historical reality, it is a breach of the communion of persons with each other, it is a turning in of individuals on themselves which manifests itself in a multifaceted withdrawal from others. And because sin is a personal and social intrahistorical reality, a part of the daily events of human life, it is also, and above all, an obstacle to life's reaching the fullness we call salvation.[a]

a. Gutiérrez, *Theology of Liberation*, 85.

Marx's belief is that economic realities determine the behavior of individuals and societies to such an extent that human history itself is a story of class struggle, a perpetual conflict between the rich and the poor, factory owners and workers. Marx's insights were based in large part on his observation of the unhappy lives of factory workers in England.

Marx's view of the history of humankind as a history of class struggle is exemplified in *The Communist Manifesto*:

> The history of all hitherto existing society is the history of class struggles. Freeman and slave, patrician and plebeian, lord and serf, guild-master and journeyman, in a word, oppressor and oppressed, stood in constant opposition to one another, carried on an uninterrupted, now hidden, now open fight, a fight that each time ended, either in a revolutionary re-constitution of society at large, or in the common ruin of the contending classes.[16]

The perpetual struggle, according to Marx, is between workers (proletariat), who are the salaried labor class, and capitalists (bourgeoisie), the employers of wage labor and thus the ones who exploit the proletariat for their surplus value. According to Marx, human beings are motivated by material concerns rather than by an idea of God. Their material concerns are their primary

Wikimedia Commons

Figure 1.23. *La Bourgeoisie*, 1894 (*The Bourgeoisie*)

motivation in life, and the overwhelming burdens of economic life make them subservient to an oppressive economic system benefiting the bourgeoisie.

What about religion? Like Freud, Marx argued that religion is pure illusion, and the primary target of his critique was Christianity. Religion functions as an ideology to maintain the status quo, keeping the oppressors in power. Marx's famous statement on religion and society emphasizes his view that religion is a drug, an opiate that camouflages economic, and therefore material, insecurity.

Religion enables people to enter an illusory world, where their immediate miseries and pains are eliminated. "I may have a horrible life here on earth, but life will be better once I enter heaven." Religion is "pure escapism"—and "fundamentally destructive"—because the energy the poor expend on religion could be spent on overturning society and its economic order through social and economic revolution.[17] According to Marx, there is no god—and religion works just like a drug that takes the sting out of our daily miserable condition; it prevents us from looking directly at the injustice of our own circumstances.

An Anthropological Theory of Religion

Clifford Geertz (1926–2006), considered by some to be the most influential American anthropologist and social scientist of all time, was born in San Francisco, California. After studying anthropology at Harvard University and doing field research on Java and Bali, Indonesia, and in Morocco, Geertz became the only anthropologist at the famous Institute for Advanced Study in Princeton, New Jersey. Geertz's work focused on ethnography of non-Western cultures. He is known for producing ethnographies of "thick description" that illuminate the contexts of human, cultural, and discursive interactions. "Thick description" describes the multilayered analysis he brought to bear on his investigations.

Take winking as an example: rather than simply noting that someone winked, Geertz attempted to present the structure of meaning behind the event of winking.

Religious suffering is at the same time the expression of real [economic] suffering and the protest against real suffering. Religion is the sigh of the oppressed creature, the sentiment of a heartless world, and the soul of soulless conditions. It is the opium of the people.

Marx, "Contribution to the Critique of Hegel's Philosophy of Right," 43–44 (emphasis in original)

Charles E. Farhadian

Figure 1.24. Traditional Balinese motifs in Bali, Indonesia

In Geertz's words, "a stratified hierarchy of meaningful structures in terms of which twitches, winks, fake-winks, parodies, rehearsals of parodies are produced, perceived, and interpreted, and without which they would not (not even for the zero-form twitches, which *as a cultural category*, are as much nonwinks as winks are nontwitches) in fact exist, no matter what anyone did or didn't do with his eyelids."[18] Moving past simple observation, for instance, Geertz's method involved unearthing the pattern of meanings within each culture and thus moving beyond simple "thin descriptions" (e.g., "that man winked") to "thick descriptions" that entailed substantial ethnographic data. One of his general contributions to anthropology and the social sciences was that he brought a humanistic perspective to bear on studying culture and peoples. Geertz's books include *The Interpretation of Cultures* (1973), *Islam Observed: Religious Development in Morocco and Indonesia* (1971), *Negara: The Theatre State in Nineteenth-Century Bali* (1981), and *The Religion of Java* (1960).

Geertz moved the discussion of religion away from its focus on the minds of people (e.g., Freud), social projection (e.g., Durkheim), and economic interests (e.g., Marx) and toward culture as a carrier of religion. Defining culture as "a pattern of meanings" carried in symbols, Geertz drew attention to the powerful role of culture, particularly symbols, in communicating religion. Religion is, according to Geertz, a cultural system. Unlike Marx, whose vision of religion is spread throughout his writing rather than presented in a single location, Geertz wrote specifically about religion and offered his own

Charles E. Farhadian

Figure 1.25. Spirit house in Thailand

comprehensive, "thick description" of religion. According to Geertz, religion is "(1) a system of symbols which acts to (2) establish powerful, pervasive, and long-lasting moods and motivations in men by (3) formulating conceptions of a general order or existence and (4) clothing these conceptions with such an aura of factuality that (5) the moods and motivations seem uniquely realistic."[19]

Think carefully about Geertz's definition of religion—namely, religion as a cultural system. It is striking to note the critical role that symbols play in religion, for they are the essential ingredients and carriers of religion. A religion is a system of symbols. Consequently, to understand a religion, one must illuminate the symbols of that religion and discuss how they function as an overall pattern that gives meaning to people's lives. Symbols are not passive communicative devices. Instead, they compel people to believe in the religion because symbols possess inherent force that shapes a person by "inducing in the worshipper a certain distinctive set of dispositions (tendencies, capacities, propensities, skills, habits, liabilities, proneness) which lend a chronic character to the flow of his activity and the quality of his experience."[20] Geertz believed that it was specifically in the arena of ritual that symbolic forms, as vehicles of meaning, induce in people the general conceptions of the order of existence— that is, religion.[21] According to Geertz, then, religion is a **worldview**—a set of beliefs that people have about what is real and that supports a set of moral values, emotions, and attitudes, guiding the way they live.

The Origins of Religions

What do you think of these theories of religion? How would you articulate their strengths and weaknesses? What is missing? What is new for you? Which aspects contribute to your understanding of religion in general? A major criticism of these theories, and a point difficult to overcome for anyone studying religions, is that they are often reductionistic. That is, each theory reduces the origin and existence of religion to a particular domain of life, whether to the mind (Freud), society (Durkheim), economics (Marx), or culture (Geertz). These robust theories raise important questions about origins. What are the origins of religion? Is religion simply a by-product of something else within the realm of human beings, such as mental, social, economic, or cultural processes? Is religion a product entirely dependent on other factors? Is religion a side effect of other processes or the initiator of processes and events? How independent is religion as a category? If religion is an independent variable, then how can it encounter the world of human beings? These challenging questions need to be answered explicitly by theorists of religion.

Because they wished to provide a nonreductionistic perspective, several theorists began reconceptualizing religion along wider parameters, attempting to avoid the notion that religion is a by-product of other processes. **Rudolf Otto** (1869–1937), a philosophical theologian and professor of systematic theology at the University of Marburg, Germany, wrote about the nonrational core of religion.

In *The Idea of the Holy* (1917), which has been translated into more than twenty languages, Otto focused attention on the numinous experience—that is, the experience of the "wholly other"—using the expression *mysterium tremendum fascinans*. As *mysterium*, the *numen* (Latin, "divinity," "wholly other") was revealed as mystery, as an objective value that can yet be subjectively known and encountered by human beings. As *tremendum*, the holy (*numen*) generates boundless wonder in the person who experiences it. As *fascinans*, the holy captivates, striking fear, awe, dread, as well as generating energy and vitality in individuals. Otto's ideas of the mysterious numinous, which is at once terrifying (*tremendum*) and fascinating (*fascinans*), influenced such diverse thinkers as the theologian Paul Tillich, the philosopher Hans-Georg Gadamer, and the medievalist and novelist C. S. Lewis. Otto's work stimulated a new approach to the phenomenological perspective with regard to religion, which was the central focus of the work of the great historian of religion **Mircea Eliade**.

Mircea Eliade (1907–86), who was born in Bucharest, Romania, spoke and wrote in several European languages (Romanian, English, French, German, Italian), as well as having a reading knowledge of Hebrew, Persian, and Sanskrit. Eliade was a Christian, and from an early age he was a natural multicultural thinker. He studied comparative religions and introduced a new method of understanding religions called the "**history of religions**" approach to religions. Even at a young age, Eliade was a prolific writer. By his eighteenth birthday, he had published his one hundredth article and was hired by a newspaper to write feature articles, book reviews, and opinion columns. In 1928 Eliade left Romania to study at the University of Calcutta, India, where he was attracted to the spiritual heritage of indigenous religions in India. He felt there a deep sense of spiritual life that was closely tied to the natural world, where simple peasants recognized the presence of the sacred in the mystery of life and death processes, including in the agricultural life

Tevaprapas Makklay/Wikimedia Commons

Figure 1.26. Preparing cow dung for fuel in Bihar, India

cycle. They viewed the world, and its continuous process, as "an unbroken cycle of life, death, and rebirth."[22] In 1931 Eliade returned to Romania, where he became a professor at the University of Bucharest (1933–39) and wrote critical pieces advocating Romanian nationalism, which led to his arrest and three-week imprisonment. In 1957 Eliade moved to the United States, where he taught at the University of Chicago and helped found a new method of studying religion, called the "Chicago School" or the "history of religions" approach, which in large part was a refinement of Rudolph Otto's earlier ideas of the holy.

Eliade's *The Sacred and the Profane: The Nature of Religion* (1957) presents his phenomenological perspective and thus became a foundational text for the history of religions approach to studying religion. Simply put, the "history of religions" approach was the attempt to discern elemental, timeless patterns of religious life. Eliade attempted to present a nonreductionistic understanding of religion, which preserved the independence of the sacred, rather than seeing it as a by-product of other human or cultural processes. He argued that religion must be studied on its own terms rather than as a dependent feature of other processes. When reading Eliade's work, it is important to keep in mind two of the primary axioms that shaped his method and perspective.

First, Eliade sought vigorously to present a nonreductionistic perspective on religion—that is, he insisted that religion itself should be seen as an independent variable. In Eliade's words, a religious phenomenon "will only be recognized as such if it is grasped at its own level, that is to say, if it is studied *as* something religious. To try to grasp the essence of such a phenomenon by means of physiology, psychology, sociology, economics, linguistics, art, or any other study is false; it misses the one unique and irreducible element in it—the element of the sacred."[23]

Essential to Eliade's perspective is the fundamental separation between the **sacred** and the **profane**. Rather than being normative, moral categories, the sacred and the profane are descriptions of realms. According to Eliade, the sacred is the sphere of the supernatural, the realm of the gods, heroes, ancestors, things extraordinary, memorable. The sacred is eternal, full of substance and reality. The sacred is Being, what is really Real, and is saturated with fullness. It is powerful, mysterious, and beautiful. The profane is the realm opposite to the sacred. That is, the profane is the realm of everyday business, ordinary things, and unimportant matters. The profane is described as fragile and full of shadows, vanishing, changeable, and chaotic, for it is the realm of human beings. Human beings encounter both sacred and profane realms all the time. Understanding religion, Eliade argued, begins with recognizing this fundamental separation between sacred and profane.[24]

Moses was keeping the flock of his father-in-law Jethro, the priest of Midian; he led his flock beyond the wilderness, and came to Horeb, the mountain of God. There the angel of the Lord appeared to him in a flame of fire out of a bush; he looked, and the bush was blazing, yet it was not consumed. Then Moses said, "I must turn aside and look at this great sight, and see why the bush is not burned up." When the Lord saw that he had turned aside to see, God called to him out of the bush, "Moses, Moses!" And he said, "Here I am." Then he said, "Come no closer! Remove the sandals from your feet, for the place on which you are standing is holy ground."

Exodus 3:1–5

Eliade's second axiom consists of his method of investigating the sacred and the profane.[25] How does one discover these realms? Eliade's method of understanding religion combined history and **phenomenology**. Through history Eliade attempted to look at religion through time, and his work is filled with examples of the sacred throughout history. Through his phenomenological perspective, Eliade attempted to uncover the manifestation of "Being." Phenomenology is the study of ways in which appearances manifest themselves, the investigation of things apprehended by consciousness and how human beings experience phenomena. Eliade's focus was more specifically on the appearance of the sacred—what he termed a "**hierophany**"—that breaks into the world and becomes an access point for human beings to get close to the sacred, that is, the realm of the gods, ancestors,

Being, and eternity. Hierophanies are the physical manifestations of the sacred and can be in the form of natural elements, symbols, rituals, and myths. Eliade's genius lay in his comparison through time of the appearance of the sacred (comparing hierophanies) to highlight the manifestation of something of a "wholly different order."[26] The history of religions consists of vast numbers of hierophanies, with the revelation of Jesus Christ being the utmost, highest expression of the sacred.

> *It could be said that the history of religions—from the most primitive to the most highly developed—is constituted by a great number of hierophanies, by manifestations of sacred realities. From the most elementary hierophany—e.g., manifestation of the sacred in some ordinary object, a stone or a tree—to the supreme hierophany (which, for a Christian, is the incarnation of God in Jesus Christ) there is no solution of continuity.*
>
> Eliade, *Sacred and the Profane*, 11

Because of the nature of the sacred—as the realm of the gods, permanence, and eternity—to be close to places and rituals and times that are animated by the sacred is to be close to the gods, which Eliade suggests is a natural yearning possessed by all human beings. *The Sacred and the Profane* is a monumental work tracing the separation of sacred and profane through major realms of reality, including space, time, nature, and human existence.[27] Eliade threw the interpretive net as wide as he could to include in his understanding of religion not only Christianity and other monotheistic religious traditions but also, more inclusively, both local religions and all other world religions. Some have accused Eliade of being a kind of academic Christian missionary because of the high view he had of Christianity. However, it is important to recognize that while Eliade clearly communicated significant unique features of Christianity, he also sought to demonstrate the universal features of religious experience throughout time. Like those of other theorists before him, Eliade's insights have drawn criticism. Among the typical criticisms are the imprecise ways in which he applied the terms "sacred" and "profane" and the ways in which he lifted his historical examples out of context to compare them, using his universal categories of religion, in a way that some scholars have suggested seems artificial.

For some Christians, perhaps Eliade has thrown the net too wide, and is too inclusive of other traditions, even though he so highly esteemed Christianity in the mix of other traditions. For others Eliade's phenomenological perspective provides profound insight that illuminates universal themes in all religious traditions. Is religion somehow neither an independent nor a dependent reality, but rather both at the same time? For instance, does religion somehow arise *out* of mental, social, cultural, personal, and economic processes, as well as being *infused* from an outside force—namely,

God? Let us keep in mind that the theoretical perspectives serve as helpful tools for more critically engaging our world and our own tradition as Christians. Everyone, either explicitly or implicitly, encounters the world through particular frameworks. As Christians, we try our best to engage the world in a manner consciously shaped by biblical affirmations, animated by the Holy Spirit. We do not want to see the world religions exclusively through any particular theoretical perspective. In fact, the most generous understanding of these religions will keep in mind the multivalent psychological, social, cultural, historical, and environmental contexts of the religions.

The Persistence of Indigenous Traditions

Many scholars of religion distinguish between so-called indigenous religions and world religions and organize their introductory textbooks on religion with indigenous religions in the beginning followed by the world religions. Indigenous religions are also referred to as popular, traditional, or folk religions, because they are the beliefs and practices found at a popular, indigenous level. They are "from below" in that they emerge from the context of local realities, rather than "from above" —that is, introduced by outsiders. The folk-urban typology was introduced by American social anthropologist **Robert Redfield** (1897–1958), who studied peasants in Mexico by contrasting folk society with modern urbanized society. Generally the term "**folk religion**" refers to religion occurring in local, small-scale communities. Referring to folk societies, Redfield wrote, "Such a society is small, isolated, nonliterate, and homogeneous, with a strong sense of group solidarity. The ways of living are conventionalized into that coherent system which we call 'a culture.' Behavior is traditional, spontaneous, uncritical, and personal. . . . The sacred prevails over the secular; the economy is one of status rather than of the market."[28]

My earlier discussions about traditional versus modern social structures, marked by single-stranded and multistranded connections, respectively, make a similar point. Although there are important connections between traditional and modern social systems, both world religions and indigenous religions are found in all kinds of groupings, from rural to urban communities. Naturally, indigenous and world religions are not equally present throughout all social groupings. What is important to recognize is that world religions and indigenous religions coexist in a blended and unpredictable fashion and influence each other, giving societies a rich environment of religious variety marked by local and universal features.

Broad Themes of Indigenous Religions

Indigenous religions affirm the existence of a world of spirits. In the past scholars tended to divide religions into two major camps, animists and world religionists, with strong evolutionary overtones. According to British anthropologist **Edward Burnett Tylor** (1832–1917), who was raised a Quaker and whose work was deeply influenced by the evolutionary theories of Charles Darwin (*Origin of Species*, 1859), all people in some early period believed in spirits. "Animism" (Latin, *anima*, "spirit" or "soul") is a term that describes belief in souls or spirits; more particularly, it is the belief that spirits dwell in objects, such as rocks, trees, mountains, and even people. Animists believe that the world is animated by spirits. Tylor's book *Primitive Culture* (1871) introduced the term "animism" and attempted to present an evolutionary view of religion, with animism being the first stage in the history of religions.

Later the Scottish anthropologist **James Frazer** (1854–1941), who read Tylor's *Primitive Culture* and suggested that in the evolutionary development of religion belief in magic preceded religion (magic, religion, science), argued that Africans worshiped fetishes, which were items believed to be endowed with special powers. Frazer and Tylor applied the logic of biological evolution to religions, even if they disagreed about its earliest stage (magic or animism). Tylor's views are compelling in part because they acknowledge the world of spirits present in material reality. By applying similar notions of biological evolution to religion, many scholars promoted the idea that religions were

Figure 1.27. Traditional welcome ceremony in Kheda district of Gujarat, India

also evolving, moving from "primitive" (e.g., traditional, folk, popular, indigenous) to **polytheism** (belief in many gods) to **monotheism** (belief in one God), eventually leading us to the demise of religion (or its great decline) altogether, to be replaced by science.

Evolutionary thinking in the realm of science and religion coalesced with the Enlightenment ideas of human progress to create an overly optimistic confidence among Westerners who believed all problems could be solved through science, if given enough time. That confidence waned as European colonizers at-

Figure 1.28. Traditional Dani village in the Baliem Valley of West Papua, Indonesia

tempted to "develop" their respective colonies in Africa, Asia, Latin America, and the Pacific, and problems of disease, social instability, environmental degradation, and cultural devastation burgeoned, leaving a problematic legacy inherited by our contemporary world. Within religious studies the term "animism" was used to describe the belief in spirits. What is important to keep in mind is that most religions, even world religions, affirm the existence of spirits. By recognizing the belief in spirits, we do not have to accept uncritically the evolutionary scheme introduced by Tylor and others.

Scholars suggest that the primary, though not exclusive, ways to seek guidance from the spirits are through practicing magic, presenting sacrifices, or offering praise. Some practices are aimed at getting close to the beneficent spirits and their power, while others focus on fending off maleficent spirits from the community. Many non-Western cultures are quite colorful because of the public nature of their religious practices. Anthropologist Clifford Geertz called the island of Bali, which is dominated by a Balinese form of Hinduism, a "theater state" because of the vast numbers of temples and ongoing participation of the community in the temple life, with the people making offerings of freshly cut flowers, fruits, and vegetables; caring for the temple grounds; and beautifying the statues of the gods.

The practices of indigenous religions are pragmatic, geared toward meeting practical needs and providing immediate guidance in the here and now. **Paul Hiebert**, **Daniel Shaw**, and **Tite Tiénou** suggest that there are "organic methods" and "mechanical methods" for obtaining guidance in the practice of the folk religions. Organic methods include practices such as making oaths and conditional curses, prophecies, necromancy,[29] dreams, visions, trances, and spirit possession. Mechanical methods of obtaining guidance include **divination** (the act of ascertaining information or foretelling an event), **astrology**, casting lots (**cleromancy**), ordeals, and omens.[30] Specific

Charles E. Farhadian

Figure 1.29. Karen traditional healer in northern Thailand

ritual practices can range from simple practices such as pouring drops of water on the earth or burning a leaf to ascertain the patterns of smoke, to complex practices such as elaborate ceremonies involving the entire community over a period of days or months.

Indigenous religions focus on the immediate, even daily, concerns of individuals and communities, rather than on the larger, more abstract questions of eternal salvation. Indigenous religions are more concerned with pressing matters, such as how to solve a problem that a person is faced with today. Questions that indigenous religions address concern the more existential issues of daily life rather than ultimate realities. Consequently, write Hiebert,

Christian Reflections

How do Christians obtain guidance? Some Christians engage in bibliomancy (using a book, the Bible, in divination—e.g., a person asks a question, then opens his or her Bible to a random page and points to a verse, believing that will be the answer to the question). Others pray alone or in a group. Some enter a natural environment and seek God. These practices seek to mediate the communication between the human and spirit worlds.

Shaw, and Tiénou, "they are interested more in issues of power and success than truth and logical consistency."[31] For instance, "How do I succeed in my work?" "How can I find love?" "How do I deal with fear of the dark?" "How do I get healed from this disease?" "How do we protect ourselves from that evil spirit?" "How do we find that lost pig?" "How do we determine the guilt or innocence of an individual or community?"

Because they focus on such quotidian matters, in significant ways indigenous traditions emerge "from below"—that is, they are deeply connected to the local context out of which they have emerged. Outside influences, such as a natural catastrophe or a foreign visitor with new ideas, may influence the questions and concerns of the local people, but the answers emerge out of the indigenous tradition itself, which is the primary source of knowledge.

Indigenous religions are also characterized by a degree of openness, informality, and pragmatism that sets them apart from the world religions. Although particular ritual practices may be quite formal, indigenous religions themselves lack the institutional and textual formality present within world religions. When delineating the main differences between the nature of indigenous religions and that of world religions, Hiebert, Shaw, and Tiénou suggest that world religions are marked by "large institutions, old leaders, normative religious texts, written commentaries, schools where young leaders are trained in the accepted beliefs, and large centers of worship and pilgrimage where people come for deep, authentic religious experiences."[32]

The absence of large institutions (e.g., seminaries, divinity schools) among the indigenous religions does not imply that knowledge of the religious tradition is stagnant or does not move from one generation to another. The ways that knowledge is received and employed in the indigenous traditions are less formalized—often knowledge of a tradition is communicated orally from one person to another or from one group to another group, following restrictions on gender, age, or class provided by the indigenous tradition. Ritual performances usually accompany the transference of knowledge, and rules of exclusion apply; for instance, in many regions men have greater access to religious knowledge, including myths of origin, than women in the same context.

By contrast, world religions offer standardized scriptures and interpretations, with clearly stated parameters rooted in **orthodoxy**—that is, what is considered inside the tradition. Practices or beliefs that fall outside the boundaries of orthodoxy are judged to be undesirable and can result in a variety of punishments for their adherents ranging from reprimands to death. Often, religions provide means of forgiveness so that those outside the parameters of orthodoxy can be reinstated into the community of believers.

In contrast, orthodoxy within the indigenous religions is less formalized, partly because of the absence of standardized scriptures and formal creeds.

Shinto

One of the most enduring religions that exhibits marks of both indigeneity and wide dispersion is **Shinto**, a Japanese religion focusing on the connection between the Japanese people and the spirits. Rather than being a universal creed for all people around the world, Shinto is the "**popular religion**" in Japan, a local religion writ large to encompass the entire nation. Shinto occupies a middle ground between indigenous religions, which are usually practiced by a relatively small group of people in a small locale, and a world religion, which covers larger geographic and historic scope. Furthermore, Shinto does not possess a tightly controlled system of thought and doctrine, unlike most of the world religions. There are three major traditions within Shinto, which will be introduced later in this chapter.

Generally, Shinto has helped to unify Japan and Japanese identity through its shared festivals and emphasis on harmony. Some have attributed Japanese economic and cultural strength to the way that Shinto has influenced productivity and creativity. The most popular forms of Shinto assert that spirits (*kami*) can possess a person, giving him or her incredible abilities to heal people of their immediate personal problems.

The term "Shinto" comes from a combination of *shen* (Chinese, "divine beings") and Tao (Chinese, "way"), and is usually translated "the way of the spirits," "the way of the gods," or "the way of the *kami*." It is common for followers of Shinto to blend ideas of Shinto with other religions in the region, particularly forms of Japanese Buddhism and Confucianism.

The meaning of *kami* in most cases is "purity," and its opposite is pollution (Japanese, *tsumi*). The major religious practice in Shinto is the engagement of *kami* through purification rituals that focus on mental, physical, and ritual purification. While *kami*, who are pure forces with great power and knowledge, reside

Wikimedia Commons

Figure 1.30. Izanami and Izanagi, the Shinto Celestial Parents who created the world (Kobayashi Eitaku, c. 1885)

48

in a heavenly realm, they can be cajoled to descend and reside in any number of material objects, even human beings.

Shinto consists of three major branches: **Shrine Shinto**, **State Shinto**, and **Sect Shinto**. While most Japanese consider themselves "nonreligious," the vast majority of those who are religious follow Shinto and some form of Buddhism. Shrine Shinto, by far the most popular form of Shinto, is practiced primarily at shrines, which can be as small as a shoebox or as large as hundreds of acres of spectacularly beautiful natural environment. A *torii* gate, a traditional Japanese gate commonly found at the entrance of a Shinto shrine, marks the separation between sacred and profane, mundane space. At shrines Shinto practitioners begin by seeking purification, and then they present offer-

Japan is the divine country. The heavenly ancestor it was who first laid its foundations, and the Sun Goddess left her descendants to reign over it forever and ever. This is true only of our country, and nothing similar may be found in foreign lands. That is why it is called the divine country.

"Kitabatake Chikafusa," in Tsunoda, deBary, and Keene, *Sources of Japanese Tradition,* 1:274

ings to the *kami* residing in the shrine and pray, thanking the *kami* for past bounty and petitioning the *kami* for a prosperous future.

State Shinto began in the late nineteenth century, during the **Meiji Restoration** (1868–1912), when all Shinto shrines throughout Japan were declared to be property of the central government of Japan. State Shinto was the Japanese

Wikimedia Commons

Figure 1.31. Iohi no Torii. Large *torii* gate at Toshogu, Nikko (Tochigi Prefecture, Japan, a UNESCO World Heritage Site)

state religion, a co-option of Shinto by the Japanese state as the ideological justification for modern Japanese nation building. State Shinto promoted the idea that the Japanese emperor was the incarnation of the Sun Goddess, **Okami Amaterasu**—a living *kami*—and justified Japanese militarism in World War II. State Shinto was disestablished in 1946 when **Emperor Hirohito** acknowledged that he was only a human being, thus losing his divine status, as part of the Allied reformation of Japan. In a New Year's statement referred to as his "Declaration of Humanity" or "Imperial Rescript on the Construction of New Japan," he stated, "The ties between us and our people have always stood upon mutual trust and affection. They do not depend upon mere legends and myths. They are not predicated on the false conception that the Emperor is divine, and that the Japanese people are superior to other races and fated to rule the world."[33]

Figure 1.32. The first meeting of General MacArthur and Emperor Hirohito at the end of World War II at the US Embassy (Tokyo, September 27, 1945)

Lt. Gaetano Faillace/Wikimedia Commons

With the dissolution of State Shinto after World War II, Sect Shinto grew more vigorously. Beginning in the nineteenth century, new religious movements developed in Japan, emerging in part as a result of the social unrest of the period. Shinto sects have provided another means to practice Shinto. Prior to World War II there were thirteen Shinto sects, while today there are many more. Shinto sects conduct religious activities focusing on nature (e.g., Mount Fuji) or people believed to be residences for *kami*. Many Shinto sects are faith-healing groups that focus on miraculous healings. Some of the more popular Shinto sects are **Tenrikyo**, **Konkokyo**, **Kurozumikyo**, and **Shinto Taikyo**. These new religious Shinto movements were based primarily on individual religious experiences of healing diseases or gaining spiritual insight.

A Religious World

Rather than being swept away by an all-encompassing scientific worldview or derailed by economic or cultural forces, religions appear to be doing quite well around the world. Religions are burgeoning globally, and their engagement with local realities provides one of the most compelling areas of study. The relationship between world religions and local contexts remains a fascinating one, as each world religion engages particular world regions in different, unpredictable, and uneven ways. According to a recent study of the Pew Forum on Religion and Public Life, over 80 percent of the world's people identify themselves with a religious group. The geographic distribution of religious groups also points to the importance of recognizing the historic spread of religions across the globe. Asia remains a significant location for the concentration of religions: for example, the Asia-Pacific region contains the vast majority of Hindus (99 percent), Buddhists (99 percent), and Muslims (62 percent), and most of the "religiously unaffiliated" (76 percent)—that is, those who do not identify themselves with any particular religion in surveys. Only about 20 percent of the world's Muslim population lives in the Middle East and North Africa, which means that understanding Islam requires us to broaden our focus to include all world regions. In terms of global religious distribution, Christians are the most evenly dispersed religious group worldwide, with roughly equal numbers of Christians living in Europe (26 percent), Latin America and the Caribbean (24 percent), and sub-Saharan Africa (24 percent).[34]

Religion is one of the most vital and significant elements of being human. Yet, given the immense diversity of social, cultural, environmental, and psychological contexts, no religion is experienced and practiced uniformly around the world. This is the messiness of religion, where local aspirations and cultures intermingle to shape religions. No pure world religion exists, apart from its local social, cultural, historical, and psychological contexts. The investigation of how local lifeways blend with a world religion is one of the

Religious Demography, 2010

Followers of Religion	Numbers Worldwide	Percentage of World Population
Christians	2.2 billion	32%
Muslims	1.6 billion	23%
Hindus	1 billion	15%
Buddhists	500 million	7%
Jews	14 million	0.2%

http://www.pewforum.org/2012/12/18/global-religious-landscape-exec/

most captivating areas in the study of religions today. Examples of the blending of world religions and local traditions are replete throughout the globe: Buddhists in Sri Lanka participating in ceremonies of possession, whereby spirits of local deities inhabit the bodies of the possessed; Muslims in Java incorporating local traditional Javanese sacrificial meals (**slamatan**) into their Islamic celebrations; Christian leaders in the Pacific Islands making offerings to powerful village spirits. On the ground, where we all live, popular religions blend with world religions and give people meaning and guidance for their lives, meeting both immediate longings (e.g., food, health, family) and more abstract concerns (e.g., salvation, peace with God). Many people are unconcerned about the logical contradictions between participation in a world religion and engagement in traditional religious practices.[35] We would be wise to resist the artificial separation of the religious world—what on the ground is a blended world of indigenous and formal religions that gives people meaning in their lives—into neatly sealed compartments.

Some Challenges to Studying World Religions

This book is directed to a broadly Christian audience, one that has interest in a sympathetic approach to learning about the major religious traditions of the world while being committed to Christian faith. When reading this book, Christian readers may face particular intellectual and religious challenges, especially if they have not yet seriously considered non-Christian religious traditions. Intellectually, some readers will be challenged to discard "black-and-white" thinking, as though truth lies only in one of two options. Some kinds of truth purported by the world religions are located somewhere in an area between the "black" and "white" absolutes with which some people have grown accustomed. Here I would suggest we distinguish between *truth*, indicating insights and common wisdom carried by cultures throughout the world, and *Truth*, indicating both common wisdom and the only means for salvation. Recognizing the *truth* found in other religions does not mean that Christians need to reject or minimize the *Truth* found in Christian faith alone.

Surely there is a mine for silver,
  and a place for gold to be refined.
Iron is taken out of the earth,
  and copper is smelted from ore. . . .
But where shall wisdom be found?
  And where is the place of understanding?

Job 28:1–2, 12

Of the many options for approaching world religions, there are two that are most basic. One of them is to pigeonhole, or force, what we learn into our inherited conceptual categories. This approach may make us feel more secure because it allows us, as learners, to control and categorize the knowledge we gain. The downside of this approach, however, is that while we may feel more secure about our neatly defined knowledge, we quite possibly have jettisoned the unique features of the religion itself. An alternative approach permits us to understand and appreciate world religions by recognizing that there are aspects of certain traditions (theologies, histories, etc.) that outside readers, such as ourselves, would be wise to let speak for themselves—to let them stand as they are. In this way, we have an opportunity to be challenged to (re)think Christian and non-Christian religious traditions. Such an approach does not preclude comparisons between Christianity and the other religious traditions; it does encourage sympathetic appreciation and intellectual responsibility to be faithful to understanding religions on their own terms. That said, there are particularly difficult hurdles that might both fascinate and challenge Christian readers.

First, many today practice religions and spiritualities that are self-constructed, more open, with permeable boundaries that allow for significant blending of elements from several traditions. It is more common today than ever for people to pull together aspects of various religions and spiritual orientations to create their own ad hoc smorgasbord religious tradition. Sociologists have used the analogy of the marketplace to interpret this practice

Charles E. Farhadian

Figure 1.33. A Hindu Brahmin priest blesses a new car at a Hindu temple in Malibu, California, USA

of pick-and-choose religious construction, as though one is a consumer of religious goods and services through which one seeks to meet one's needs. Such a religious life, whereby one builds one's own religion, means that individual *world religions* are engaged less comprehensively but instead on the basis of individual aspects of the religion that may be attractive to the religious practitioner (e.g., environmental concerns; meditation; views of the mind, body, or spirit). This sort of "smorgasbord" religion presents its own challenges to our understanding and raises questions about the role of an individual or community in constructing religious and spiritual orientation.

A second feature that may challenge Christian readers is making sense of the spiritual matrix of the world religions. Whereas monotheistic religions affirm the existence of God, other traditions recognize that the world is permeated with Gods as divine forces that can be cajoled or repelled, beneficent or malevolent. The house, the village, the town, the country, the nation, and the cosmos are all filled with Gods. The world is saturated with sacred, divine forces.

A third challenge is the philosophical affirmation of distinctly different views of reality (metaphysics). There are monistic views, which posit that all discrete entities, all existing things, can be explained in terms of a single reality. **Metaphysical monism** argues that all existing things are part of one substance or essence, rather than being a part of two distinct realities, as viewed from a dualistic perspective. That is, there is a fundamental unity of all things, substances, and essences. Some interpretations of Hinduism, Buddhism, Judaism, Christianity, and Islam affirm a religious monistic worldview. **Dualism** holds the view that there are two elements of existence, usually physical and spiritual. **Metaphysical dualism** has undergirded much of Christianity throughout its history. For example, a dualistic perspective is illustrated by the opposition between God and the devil or between good and evil.

A fourth challenge, which is related to the metaphysical assertions mentioned above, is the experience of **emptiness**, where the boundaries between cosmos, world, self, and sacred are removed in a final experience of oneness, often referred to as liberation or ultimate union with the divine. The Buddhist and Taoist traditions recognize the importance of "emptiness" and "**non-being**." Where is God in these perspectives? How can Christians reconcile the experience of emptiness and nonbeing with the affirmation of God's fullness, God's speech, and God's actions?

Who can hide in secret places so that I cannot see them? says the Lord. Do I not fill the heavens and earth? says the Lord.

Jeremiah 23:24

> Even though I walk through the darkest valley,
>   I fear no evil;
> for you are with me;
>   your rod and your staff
>   —they comfort me.
>
> Psalm 23:4

A fifth challenge concerns the relationship between history and myth. Many world religions believe that myth can carry truth. That is, the stories of Gods, demons, deities, and other powers bear truth, even if they refer to events that occurred prior to the creation of the world. Monotheistic religions are historically particular. For example, it is crucial for Christians to affirm the historicity of Jesus Christ and his life, death, and resurrection. While myth may be a part of the Judeo-Christian story, as communicated in the Bible, it consists of a story of real events, about God's dealings with people located in real time and space—that is, history. History contains the story of the people of Israel and God's self-disclosure in Jesus Christ. Asian religions, such as Hinduism, Buddhism, and Jainism, are less historically particular. Are there nonhistorical ways to convey truth that leads to salvation, or does salvation come only through a particular history?

Organization of Chapters

Now that your ears have been pricked a bit, you are ready to delve into an introduction of the major world religions with some Christian reflections. The organization of the chapters is straightforward: each has four major sections. The first section, "Contemporary Snapshot," provides a brief picture of the religion as it exists today. As you can well imagine, it is impossible to capture the entirety of a religion within a few sentences, so my goal here is simply to introduce each religion through an accessible story or incident. The second section, "Origins and Concepts," carries the lion's share of each chapter since it combines a summary history and introduction to major theological affirmations of a given religious tradition. Because this is an introduction to world religions, the presentation of a full-blown history is unfeasible, but this section does paint the historical data broadly enough so that you can easily comprehend the major historical moments of the religion. The third section, "Worship and Practice," explains the ways in which practitioners of a given religious tradition worship and seek salvation. The question to keep in mind here is "How does this religion claim to save or liberate its followers?" The fourth section, "Modern Movements," introduces some of the major individuals and institutions that have emerged in the modern period. Throughout each chapter I underscore some similarities and differences between certain topics and particular aspects within the Christian tradition. Because it is so important to know the essential terms within each religion, throughout each chapter new terms are clearly defined, with the hope that newcomers to these religions will be aided immensely and the mystery of these essential non-English terms will be minimized. Acquainting oneself with the crucial terms of each religion is tantamount to learning basic terms of anatomy as a foundation for learning physiology. This applies especially to the notion of "God," a term that will be capitalized when believers themselves would also do so.

Needless to say, an entire book could easily be dedicated to introducing a single tradition along with some Christian reflections. Given my ambitious goal to both introduce different religions and provide Christian reflections, neither may be accomplished entirely to everyone's satisfaction. Some readers will want more introduction and less reflection, while others will want less introduction and more reflection. Neither the introduction nor the reflection is complete, but my desire is to invite a conversation that can be continued through additional reading, such as the books mentioned in the footnotes, or through conversations with followers of different religions. My modus operandi in the world, and one that undergirds this book, begins by affirming the most obvious fact that all human beings, no matter what their religious traditions, are people first. Even the most intensely committed believer, one who may be directly opposed to

Figure 1.34. Small church in Chile

another's tradition, is first a human being. The humanization of human beings is far too easy to overlook, but the failure to acknowledge our common humanity can give rise to all sorts of horrendous problems that impede our Christian witness to our neighbors and the wider world. The church, which consists of the gathering of those who seek God, regardless of its size, is the witnessing body sent into the world as a sign and instrument of God's kingdom.

Finally, for the sake of clarity and to avoid repetitive topical discussions, the "Christian Reflections" provided in each chapter are limited to selected topics so that throughout the entire book as much thematic material as possible can be covered. It seems redundant, in other words, to discuss the Christian concept of God each time the topic of God, deities, or the divine appears in a chapter, especially since many of the religions address common themes, such as the concept of the divine, the human problem, the solution for the human problem, and the vision of salvation.

Key Terms

Anabaptist

astrology

Barth, Karl

Catholic

cleromancy

collective experience

Communist Manifesto, The

Darwin, Charles

Das Kapital

dharma

divination

dualism

Durkheim, Émile

ecumenical

Eliade, Mircea

emic

Emperor Hirohito

emptiness

etic

folk religion

Frazer, James

free association

Freud, Sigmund

Geertz, Clifford

Hegel, Georg Wilhelm Friedrich

Hiebert, Paul

hierophany

history of religions

kami

Kant, Immanuel

Konkokyo

Kurozumikyo

liberation

Marx, Karl

Meiji Restoration

metaphysical dualism

metaphysical monism

monotheism

Müller, Friedrich Max

myth

nonbeing

Okami Amaterasu

Orthodox

orthodoxy

Otto, Rudolf

phenomenology

polytheism

popular religion

profane

Protestant

Qur'an

Redfield, Robert

release

rituals

sacred

sacred actions (rituals)

Sacred and the Profane, The

sacred community

sacred experience

sacred objects

sacred places

sacred writings

sacrifices

salvation

samsara

Sanneh, Lamin

Sect Shinto	*slamatan*	*torii*
Shaw, Daniel	sociocentric	traditionalism
shen	State Shinto	*tsumi*
Shinto	symbol	Tylor, Edward Burnett
Shinto Taikyo	Tenrikyo	Walls, Andrew
Shrine Shinto	Tiénou, Tite	worldview

Further Reading

Beckford, James A. *Social Theory and Religion*. Cambridge, UK: Cambridge University Press, 2003.

Durkheim, Émile. *The Elementary Forms of the Religious Life*. Translated by Joseph Ward Swain. New York: The Free Press, 1965.

Eliade, Mircea. *The Sacred and the Profane*. Translated by Willard R. Trask. New York: Harcourt Brace Jovanovich, 1959.

Evans-Pritchard, E. E. *Nuer Religion*. New York: Oxford University Press, 1956.

Freud, Sigmund. *Future of an Illusion*. Translated by James Strachey. New York: W. W. Norton, 1989.

Geertz, Clifford. *The Interpretation of Cultures*. New York: Basic Books, 1973.

Kitagawa, Joseph M. *Religious Traditions of Asia: Religion, History, and Culture*. London: Routledge, 2002.

Küng, Hans. *Christianity and World Religions: Paths to Dialogue*. 2nd ed. Translated by Peter Heinegg. Maryknoll: Orbis, 1993.

Pals, Daniel L. *Eight Theories of Religion*. New York: Oxford University Press, 2006.

Sharpe, Eric J. *Comparative Religion: A History*. La Salle, IL: Open Court, 1986.

Stark, Rodney. *The Triumph of Christianity: How the Jesus Movement Became the World's Largest Religion*. New York: HarperCollins, 2011.

Tennent, Timothy. *Christianity at the Religious Roundtable*. Grand Rapids: Baker Academic, 2002.

Tweed, Thomas A. *Crossing and Dwelling: A Theory of Religion*. Cambridge, MA: Harvard University Press, 2006.

two

Hinduism

Contemporary Snapshot

Mahatma Gandhi was one of the most recognized names and influential persons in the twentieth century. His legacy was the liberation of India from British colonial rule. Gandhi's inspiration has motivated leaders around the world to engage in peaceful, nonviolent action to overcome political subjugation. People as diverse as Rosa Parks, Albert Einstein, Martin Luther King Jr., and Archbishop Oscar Romero were deeply influenced by Gandhi's notion of nonviolence. One of the greatest influences on Gandhi's life was the Hindu scripture the **Bhagavad Gita**, which Gandhi read for the first

Figure 2.1. Young woman in traditional dress in Mamallampuran, India

Figure 2.2. Mahatma Gandhi (right) and Jawaharlal Nehru (left) in India, 1942

time while living in England. Because of its emphasis on selfless action in the midst of the human struggle against evil, Gandhi frequently drew comfort for his own life and his struggle to free India from British colonial rule through meditating on the Bhagavad Gita.

> *When doubts haunt me, when disappointments stare me in the face, and I see not one ray of hope on the horizon, I turn to Bhagavad Gita and find a verse to comfort me; and I immediately begin to smile in the midst of overwhelming sorrow.*
>
> Mahatma Gandhi, quoted in Fischer, *Quotes from Gandhi*, 15

I bow to you,
I prostrate my body,
I beg you to be gracious,
Worshipful Lord—
as a father to a son,
a friend to a friend,
a love to a beloved,
O God, bear with me.

I am thrilled,
and yet my mind
trembles with fear
at seeing
what has not been seen before.
Show me, God, the form I know—
be gracious, Lord of Gods,
Shelter of the World.

Bhagavad Gita 11:44–45[1]

The Bhagavad Gita is one of the most cherished sacred texts in the Hindu tradition and one of the most popular world scriptures.

Christian Reflections

Many of the verses from the Bhagavad Gita could easily be mistaken for words from a Christian prayer, since there seems to be much in this book that can be affirmed by Christians, such as deference to God, worshipful hearts, and request for grace. I imagine that if these verses were read or prayed in church, many Christians would not recognize them as coming from the Hindu tradition.

These verses in the Bhagavad Gita extol the majesty of **Vishnu**, perhaps the most popular God of Hinduism. The massive appeal of the Bhagavad Gita is due to its profound reflection on the universal themes of suffering, love, duty, and sacrifice. Its words reflect the overwhelming intimacy between the God (Vishnu) and the believer (**Krishna**), where the believer eventually sees himself or herself as absorbed into God, a self-realization of the divine within the believer and the believer within the divine.

To Hindus living all over the world, the Bhagavad Gita is a source of reassurance and guidance for daily life. Theologically, as we will see later in the chapter, the Bhagavad Gita represents a new development within the Vedic tradition, which continues to be a source of encouragement and spiritual sustenance for Hindus today, while confronting prideful self-centeredness. Throughout South and Southeast Asia and other regions with large Hindu populations, the story of the Bhagavad Gita is memorialized in cartoons, television series, feature-length films, poetry, and fiction.

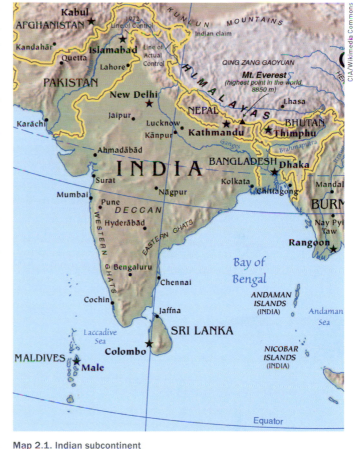

Map 2.1. Indian subcontinent

Origins and Concepts

What Is Hindu?

We begin our journey in South Asia, out of which have come some of the oldest and most enduring religious traditions of the world. South Asia gave birth to the traditions of Hinduism, Buddhism, Jainism, Sikhism, and a host of other lesser-known religious traditions. What we refer to as Hinduism began as a compilation of indigenous religions of South Asia (i.e., primarily the countries of India, Nepal, Bhutan, and Sri Lanka). Hinduism emerged as a combination of popular practices, organized cults, and specialized philosophies that emerged out of this South Asian context. Today there are well over 800 million adherents to Hinduism worldwide, making it the third largest religion in the world. The vast majority of Hindus, about 80 percent, live in India itself.

Additionally, Hinduism has one of the longest recorded histories of any world religion. The word "Hindu" comes from the word "Sindhu" (in Sanskrit, Hindi, and Persian), the Persian name of the Indus River, the longest river in Pakistan and one of the most significant rivers in the entire South Asian region. The etymology of the term "Hindu" can be traced to the Persians, who referred to the people living in the Indus River region as "the Sindhus." The Hindu tradition is also referred to as Sanatana Dharma (Sanskrit, *Sanātana Dharma*, "the teaching of truth").

What Is Hinduism?

Today most people think of Hinduism as a religion, but there is no separate word for "religion" in ancient South Asian languages. Despite this fact, the indigenous people of South Asia did have a plethora of rituals, Gods, and religious practices and beliefs that shaped their identities and made sense of their daily lives and struggles. An "ism" (e.g., as in Hindu*ism*, Buddh*ism*) communicates an institutionalized system of thought, a system of doctrines, and way of systematizing ideas in the fashion of Western abstraction. On the ground, where people have to make sense of their daily lives, there is little need to be so systematic. This tension between "Hinduism" and "Hindu" reflects the inherent tension between emic and etic perspectives, which, as we've seen, are the perspectives of a person from within and from outside the religion, respectively. Both of these perspectives are valuable in different ways. So what is a Hindu? And what is Hinduism? Some historians have argued that the term "Hindu" means anything indigenous to India, which may refer to religious life or not. A native to India would be Hindu, whether she is a follower of Christ or of Hindu dharma. It is important to recognize that the origin of the term "Hinduism" is strongly debated within South Asian scholarship.

The Influence of Orientalism on Western Perspectives

Orientalism refers to the study of Near Eastern and Asian societies, languages, and cultures by Westerners that attempts to construct identities, societies, and cultures in terms of Western consciousness and learning. Orientalism tends to be heavily biased and overgeneralizes "the other" (e.g., as anti-Western, primitive, backward, ignorant), often negatively depicting non-Western peoples as strange and exotic by Western norms. Some scholars argue that the term Hinduism results from the influential ideas of Orientalism, suggesting that Western colonizers fashioned the idea of "Hinduism" as a single world religion. On the other hand, some scholars of the nineteenth century contend that the term emerged after high-caste **Brahmins** collected their own sacred texts, systematizing and publishing their formal knowledge of the tradition.

Scholars continue to contest the origins of the term "Hinduism." But whether the term was imposed entirely by Western Orientalists or by Hindu

Charles E. Farhadian

Figure 2.3. Brahmin priest in India

intellectuals (i.e., Brahmins), or somehow emerged from a combination of these two forces among others, modern readers have inherited the term "Hinduism," and that is the term we will use here. The debate represents a larger academic discussion about the role of indigenous people in creating their own identities on their own terms. Was Edward Said correct in his view that Westerners' prejudicial perspective created the exotic "other" in the eighteenth and nineteenth centuries, and thus "Hinduism," or did Hinduism emerge from the discussions and efforts of Hindu intellectuals?

The German philologist Max Müller was an Orientalist who edited a massive fifty-volume set of Asian sacred writings known as the *Sacred Books of the East* (1879–1910), published by Oxford University Press, which also served as an initial step in encouraging knowledge about India and Indian religions for a Western audience. In spite of his biases, it became a valuable resource for Western scholars and students of religion.

Hinduism: A Blending of Local Religions

Hinduism, then, is a broad term that describes the indigenous religions of India, without a particular founder, without a single unified history, and without a prescribed, unified practice of worship. Some argue that all Hindus share the belief in the same sacred texts, but that notion is difficult to sustain because textual learning is not necessary for faithful Hindu living. However,

Origins are important. The history of the terms we use to describe religious traditions communicates something about the tradition itself. "Hindu-ism" may not be the best term to describe such a diverse religious tradition, especially since "Hindu" may very well refer to anything indigenous to the subcontinent. It is worthwhile to note that "Hindu" was a transliteration of the term "Sindhu," which underscores the artificial usage of this particular term. Likewise, the term "Christian" was used early on in a pejorative sense by Agrippa (Acts 26:28) and meant something along the lines of "followers of the anointed one," a group that recognized Jesus as Messiah. The prominent Roman historian Publius Cornelius Tacitus (c. 55–117), in his *Annals of Imperial Rome*, wrote that Christians were people who were despised for their evil deeds.[a] Followers of Christ in first-century Antioch were disdained and scorned, and the term "Christian" was applied to these early believers. While there is no such word as "Christ-ism," in some respects the meaning of that improbable term is how Christianity has come to be understood—as an institutionalized system of knowledge. Herein lies a perspective among some Christians that Christianity is not a religion (a system of knowledge) but rather a living relationship with God.

a. See Publius Cornelius Tacitus, *Annals of Imperial Rome*, 15.6.

Hinduism does have a historical and theological trajectory that makes it understandable. As we move into the material on South Asian traditions, I will use dates broadly, particularly when discussing the early material, since most South Asian religionists were unconcerned with specific dates.

Indus Valley Civilization (c. 3000–1000 BCE)

ARCHEOLOGICAL FINDINGS AT HARRAPA
AND MOHENJODARO

Let us begin with the earliest record of Hinduism, which is believed to be in the **Indus River Valley**, in today's Pakistan. The Indus Valley civilization (c. 3000–1000 BCE) was contemporaneous with the pharaohs of Egypt and other people groups in parts of modern Pakistan. While no decipherable written sources have survived, archaeologists in the late nineteenth century began excavating two of the largest cities in the Indus Valley, **Mohenjodaro** (250

Wikimedia Commons

Map 2.2. Indus Valley civilization

miles from the mouth of the Indus) and **Harappa** (another 400 miles further northwest). Archaeologists continue to discover and excavate other cities in the Indus River Valley that provide insight into the religion, culture, and traditions of the Indus Valley civilization, and thus the earliest sources of religious expressions in Indian religions.

Archaeological findings included well-structured cities, with a regular, rectangular layout and straight streets, some quite wide. Standardized brick sizes and large houses with baths covering an area of about thirty square feet were also discovered. The large public baths, with elaborate sewer systems, indicate a high sense of purity, since water functioned as an instrument of ritual purification. Also discovered were cult objects, such as a mother/earth Goddess image, probably associated with fertility and related to feminine power (Sanskrit, **Shakti**) that animates Goddesses, which typically function as reproduction-oriented deities. There were female figurines with large breasts and buttocks, and phallic symbols, probably indicating a high fertility cult of an agricultural society.

The sites of Harrapa and Mohenjodaro contained statues of animals, especially bulls, and a squatting God in a position of a *yogin*, a practitioner of **yoga** (Sanskrit, "union"; a discipline leading to union with the divine). Scholars have interpreted this sitting being as **Shiva**, one of the most popular deities later in Hinduism, in a lotus posture. The presence of animal figurines may indicate that the Indus Valley civilization fervently venerated animal life—perhaps suggesting that these societies were vegetarian in their dietary orientation. There were many kinds of domesticated animals, including cattle, camels, water buffalo, monkeys, goats, fowls (including chickens), dogs, pigs, horses, and, most likely, elephants. Tools were fairly simple, mostly of stone, with little copper and bronze. Families had seals, such as

Figure 2.4. Harappa figurines, c. 2500 BCE

emblems that were engravings of images, probably used for religious symbolism. Homes were constructed with bricks, and some were two stories high. The indigenous people were depicted as having dark skin color and short statures. They were speakers and writers of a Dravidian language, a language family that consists of 73 languages spoken by over 222 million people mainly in southern India and parts of Sri Lanka, Pakistan, Nepal, and Bangladesh.

Aryan Entry into the Indus Valley Civilization

Beginning around 1500 BCE, significant social, cultural, religious, and linguistic changes occurred among the inhabitants of the Indus Valley civilization that left indelible marks on Hinduism. Until that time the massive Himalayas, presenting a geographic barrier isolating the South Asian landmass, enabled the indigenous populations to develop largely on their own. The transformation of the indigenous Indus Valley civilization was due in large part to the immigration of the **Aryan** people, who were wandering all over the Eurasian landmass.

The Sanskrit term "Aryan" means "noble people," a term used as a self-description of the Indo-European people from North Asia, some of whom entered the Indus Valley region while others settled as far away as Iceland, leaving traces of their mythology from Iran to Iceland. Contrary to the physical makeup of the indigenous inhabitants, the Aryans were taller and had fairer skin. Aryans possessed techniques for working with bronze, rode horses and chariots, and were skilled as warriors, enabling them to conquer the indigenous populations of the Indus River civilization.

A few decades ago most scholars believed that the Aryans had conquered the indigenous populations through physical violence, forcing them further south into South Asia. More-recent scholarship challenges this "invasion" thesis, with the suggestion that the Aryans dominated the region more gradually. If the local inhabitants were sedentary agriculturalists, they had little chance of defending themselves against the Aryans. Whether the conflict between the indigenous people and the Aryans was public and swift or slow and steady, the results were the same: by around 1500 BCE, the Aryans had become the dominant people in the Indus Valley region. What the Aryans introduced to the region would permanently change the local people and their religion.

Vedic Religions (c. 1500–900 BCE)

Aryan Influences on Indus Valley Civilization

The **Vedas** (Sanskrit, "sacred knowledge") are the oldest sacred scriptures of Hinduism, and they introduce some of the most important notions of Hinduism, especially the liturgies, **mantras**, praises, and chants used by priests in religious rituals. Beginning in the Indus Valley region, then spreading into South Asia, the Vedic religion laid the foundation for further developments within Hinduism. Vedic religion itself contains some of the most ancient sacred scriptures in the world, with a new language and social structure that would leave their mark on Hinduism that endures even today.

SIDEBAR 2.1

Similarities in Sanskrit, Greek, Latin, and English

Sanskrit	dyaus-pater	deva	nama	bhrater	jna
Greek	Zeus-pater	theos	onoma	phrater	gno
Latin	Jupiter	deus	nomen	frater	cogno
English	Jupiter	deity	name	brother	know

The most important influences of the Aryans on local Indian life around 1500 BCE were the introduction of the Aryan religious language (Sanskrit), social structure, and religion (e.g., mythology). **Sanskrit** was used by Aryans for sacred oral and literary purposes. Like Greek, Latin, and English, Sanskrit is an Indo-European language.

Sanskrit was introduced by the Aryans, and it was used as a religious language for delivering praises to the early nature deities. Since its introduction into South Asia, Sanskrit has been the language of religious and philosophical discourse, setting it apart from the numerous local languages found throughout the region. It is interesting to note that the pervasiveness of Sanskrit would eventually extend to South Asia and Southeast Asia, where the modern lingua franca of those regions (e.g., Bahasa Indonesia) contain several Sanskrit words. Sanskrit communicated sacred lore and hymns composed over a period of five hundred years by religious priests of the Aryans, known as the Brahmins, who were masters of the sacred Sanskrit language and skilled in the intricacies of the early sacrificial rites.

The Aryans also introduced a new social structure that would significantly impact South Asian life until today. The *varna* (Sanskrit, "class" and "color") system is more popularly known today as the caste or class system of

SIDEBAR 2.2

The Four Classes of Hinduism

1. **Brahmins** (priests, scholarly community, e.g., doctors and teachers)
2. **Kshatriyas** (warriors, nobles, kings, politicians)
3. **Vaishyas** (producers, artisans, mercantile and business community)
4. **Shudras** (laborers, service-providing community)

The **Harijans** are those outside the caste system entirely, known as **Dalit** (downtrodden), scheduled classes, outcastes, non-castes, untouchables, polluted laborers, and members of the *avarna* (Sanskrit, "without class"). Mahatma Gandhi called this community the Harijans (Children of God), thus dignifying them, although he was a supporter of the *varna* system because he believed it was necessary for the distribution of labor within Indian society.

India, and reflects the belief that each Hindu is born into one of four social classes. The *varna* system included particular occupations, thus providing early South Asian societies with a stable social system where every member would have his or her own tasks. These classes were descriptive categories of Hindus in South Asia.

The Meanings of *Varna*

The *varna* (class) system informs people about religion and occupation. Many nineteenth-century Western researchers believed that *varna* referred to skin color, with light-skinned Brahmins at the top of the social hierarchy and dark-skinned Shudras (and Dalits) on the lowest rung. This assumption reflected the researchers' own race theories. It is true that each class was associated with a specific color, not for racist reasons but to follow the cosmological and religious qualities within Hinduism, particularly the "three qualities" (*triguna*) of Hinduism: Brahmins are associated with white (truthful), Kshatriyas with red (energetic), Vaishyas with yellow (a blending of qualities), and Shudras with black (inert, solid). Today, scholars understand *varna* to refer not literally to outdated notions of race (i.e., skin color), but rather to distinctive qualities of the larger South Asian population.

Notions of Purity and Occupation within the Class System

The *varna* system also was inherently religious, since notions of purity were a central concept of Hinduism generally. The Brahmins were closer to

Figure 2.5. Hindu devotees bathing in the Ganges River in Haridwar, India

68

liberation (Sanskrit, ***moksha***) and the Gods, and thus deemed purer than the other classes. Within the *varna* system, the higher the class, the greater the purity, making the Brahmins the highest, purest human beings and the Shudras the least pure within the system. Dalits were considered so impure and polluted that they were outside the *varna* system. Because Hindu rituals are concerned with purity, the *varna* system came to be reinforced by the practical application of the concepts of purity and impurity, with strong prohibitions against the contamination of high-caste Hindus by contact with those lower in the class system, especially by untouchables (Dalits, *avarna*, outcastes).

Furthermore, the four *varna* denote a specific range of occupations and levels of social and religious power and influence. *Varna* does not relate to material wealth and did not always reflect the material wealth of those within each class. For instance, the Brahmins are more powerful than the Kshatriyas, but the Kshatriyas have more social influence than the Shudras. According to the Hindu tradition, all people are born into this system. Within each class (e.g., Brahmin, Kshatriya) there are numerous castes (***jati***) consisting of various mixtures of classes that in part reflect the local occupational specialties in each region of South Asia.

Generally, marriage should be restricted to one's own group, although this constraint is loosening in modern times. *Jati* identifications are more important than class identifications. And the thousands of castes usually have strong prohibitions about interaction with one another.

Aryans instituted this stratified social structure, placing themselves in the first three classes of the *varna* and relegating the indigenous people to the Shudra and outcaste statuses. Known as the "twice-born," those who occupied the three highest castes (Brahmin, Kshatriya, and Vaishya) were privileged with the knowledge of Sanskrit, the religious texts, and the performance of the early Vedic rituals. During twice-born ceremonies, boys and girls "come of age," much like a Christian confirmation service or a

Figure 2.6. Faces of India

SIDEBAR 2.3

Understanding the Hindu Caste System

It is far too easy for outsiders to judge the Indian caste system as a form of social imprisonment. We should recognize that Western societies have similar social stratifications, for example, presidents, businesspersons, teachers, and laborers. Some of the most successful Christian missionaries from the West have worked within the class system rather than challenging it (e.g., Roberto de Nobili and Bartholomaeus Ziegenbalg). Modern India reflects great social complexity. After the introduction of modern (i.e., Western) education and railroads that enabled social movement across vast regions, Indian identity became an increasingly complicated matter, permitting circumstances where, for instance, highly educated Dalits could teach high-caste Hindus. Intermarriage between classes has also led to social change as individuals have aligned with different classes.

Jewish bar or bat mitzvah. The twice-born boys and girls memorize chants and ritual gestures for use in religious rituals.

The Importance of Sacrifice

When the Aryans arrived in the Indus Valley region, the priests, known as Brahmins, carried with them the memories of how to sustain good relations with the deities and thus maintain healthy crops, bodies, and human relationships. The origins of Hindu sacrifice are unclear, but early sacrifice may have been performed to bribe or to win favor from deities, or to venerate the deities by expressing fear or gratitude. Mircea Eliade suggests that early Hindu sacrifices were a reenacting and re-enlivening of a mythical past event. Sacrifices were first used to communicate with the Gods but were later understood to yield desired results immediately by the will of the deities. At the least, the early Hindu sacrifices were thought to somehow erase the misdeeds of the community.

The performance of sacrifice was central to the well-being of the community, the natural world, and the cosmos. Harmony between people, the natural world, and the deities depended on the correct performance of sacrifices. Since the Brahmins were the only ones who knew the sacred language, Sanskrit, and the sacred praises, they were the most powerful group within the community. Even kings and nobles would hire Brahmins to make sacrifices before going to war or to appease the nature deities during times of crisis. And the Vedic nature deities had no free will: if the sacrifice was performed correctly, then the nature deities would have to respond accordingly by bringing rain, or withholding rain, or whatever was requested by the priest and needed by the community.

How are religions carried through time and space? This is a question not only about the origins of religions but also about their maintenance and growth. Hinduism was significantly influenced by local Indus Valley culture and religion, yet its highest articulation remained in the hands of the dominating forces, the Aryans, and their priests, the Brahmins. Hinduism was sustained to a large extent by Brahmins, who maintained the sacred language and ritual actions that enabled the human community and cosmos to function harmoniously. How is Christianity carried through time and space? Who has the authority to interpret Christianity? How does it expand through societies and cultures? Early Hinduism provided a total lifeway, making sense of all people and their respective places within the larger social world of classes and castes. Does Christianity require a particular social structure? Yes and no. The Christian tradition does seem to affirm social structures that enable human flourishing and liberty, without making the distinction between classes: "There is no longer Jew or Greek, there is no longer slave or free, there is no longer male and female; for all of you are one in Christ Jesus" (Gal. 3:28). The New Testament also addresses slaves and free in order to inject new content of kinship through shared fellowship in Christ. This question of social structure appears frequently, even inherently, as part of the larger discussion about the relationship between Christianity and the political order, political theory, and democracy.

How did the Aryans justify the system of *varna*? In a word—sacrifice. Even the act of creation was the result of sacrifice. The earliest Hindu sacred scriptures, the Vedas, record the creation of the world and the sacrifice of the primordial man, **Purusha**, as the foundation of the four *varna*.

> The sacrificial victim, namely, Purusha, born at the very beginning, was sprinkled with sacred water upon the sacrificial grass. With him as oblation the gods performed the sacrifice, and also the Sadhyas and the *rishis*.
>
> From that wholly offered sacrificial oblation were born the verses and the sacred chants; from it were born the meters; the sacrificial formula was born from it.
>
> From it horses were born and also those animals who have double rows of teeth; cows were born from it, from it were born goats and sheep.
>
> When they divided Purusha, in how many different portions did they arrange him? What became of his mouth, what of his two arms? What were his two thighs and his two feet called?
>
> His mouth became the energy of the universe [i.e., Brahmins]; his two

arms were made into the Rájanya [Kshatriyas]; his two thighs the Vaishyas; from his two feet the Shudra were born.

The moon was born from the mind, from the eye the sun was born; from the mouth Indra and Agni, from the breath the wind was born.

From the navel was the atmosphere created, from the head the heaven issued forth; from the two feet was born the earth, and the quarters (the cardinal directions) from the ear. Thus did they fashion the worlds. . . .

With this sacrificial oblation did the gods offer the sacrifice. These were the first norm (dharma) of sacrifice. These greatnesses reached to the sky wherein live the ancient Sadhyas and gods.

Rig Veda 10.90[2]

Sacrifice of Purusha gave rise to creation and the four *varnas*. From Purusha's mouth came the Brahmins, from his two arms came the Kshatriyas, from his two thighs came the Vaishyas, and from his two feet the Shudras were born. As the Aryans dominated the indigenous population of the Indus Valley civilization, they added the Shudras and outcaste categories. The class system was an ideal that never worked exactly as prescribed by the *varna* system, even with the vast number of prescriptions for what people should and should not do. Many Brahmins, for instance, did work in business if there were no jobs as priests or teachers or in government service.

KINDS OF HINDU SCRIPTURES: *SHRUTI* AND *SHMRITI*

Vedic religion was carried in memory by the Aryans to the Indus Valley region. The oral tradition of the hymns of praise, chants, and mantras directed to the nature deities was transmitted orally from Brahmins to priests-in-training, written down later over a period of a few hundred years. That collection is called the Vedas. There are two main kinds of Hindu scripture, called **shruti** and **shmriti** literature. *Shruti* texts are considered "from the Gods," absolute truth, revealed by the Gods to human beings. Hindu orthodoxy is defined as acceptance of the authority of the *shruti* revelation. *Shmriti* texts are "remembered" by previous generations and transmitted from one generation to another, in an oral chain of transmission.

Abdel Sinoctou/Wikimedia Commons

Figure 2.7. *Sadhu* with cow in India. Hindus typically follow the Vedic injunction "mahimsyat sarva bhutani," which means "do not cause harm to any living entity."

As you might imagine, *shruti* literature maintains the highest level of authority within Hinduism, because it is believed to be the result of direct revelation. *Shmriti* material is still considered sacred scripture but has less authority than the revealed texts. Although there are discussions among Hindus about which texts should be considered *shruti* texts, all agree about the *shruti* nature of the Vedas.

Four Vedas

RIG VEDA

The Vedas are divided into four parts, with three main attachments at the end of each division. The four divisions of the Vedas are the **Rig Veda**, the **Yajur Veda**, the **Sama Veda**, and the **Atharva Veda**.[3] The Rig Veda is the oldest and most important Veda. It consists of about one thousand hymns recited during sacrifice that implore the blessings of the nature deities. The hymns are of varying lengths and are arranged by the family that recorded them and the deities they addressed. Specific Brahmin priests (called *hotri* priests) led the sacrifices outlined in the Rig Veda. Families had a hereditary monopoly, similar to a copyright, on the hymns. The hymns were written with careful literary craftsmanship in Sanskrit, giving us insight into the religious values and practices of the Vedic period. The hymns address mostly nature deities (e.g., sun, dawn, wind, rain).

The most prominent nature deities praised and cajoled in Vedic religion were **Varuna**, **Indra**, **Agni**, and **Soma**. Varuna is the God of cosmic order and the protector of truth. He is depicted carrying a thunderbolt. Varuna has power due to his knowledge, and he is a fierce administrator. Hymns addressed to Varuna are like plea bargains, asking for forgiveness since Varuna is all-seeing and all-knowing and presides over the orderliness of the cosmos. He guards the sacred pattern underlying the cosmic and social life (called *rita*, "sacred pattern of cosmos," "natural law," "order of things"). Varuna's role as the administrator of *rita* is extremely significant, since without *rita* the entire social and cosmic order could collapse into chaos.

> O Varuna, what was the terrible crime for which you wish to destroy your friend who praises you? Proclaim it to me so that I may hasten to prostrate myself before you and be free from sin, for you are hard to deceive and are ruled by yourself alone. . . .
>
> The mischief was not done by my own free will, Varuna; wine, anger, dice, or carelessness led me astray. The older shares in the mistake of the younger. Even sleep does not avert evil.
>
> As a slave serves a generous master, so would I serve the furious god and be free from sin.

> The noble god gave understanding to those who did not understand; being yet wiser, he speeds the clever man to wealth.
>
> O Varuna, you who are ruled by yourself alone, let this praise lodge in your very heart. Let it go well for us always with your blessings.
>
> Rig Veda 7.84.4, 6, 7, 8[4]

Figure 2.8. Selection from the Rig Veda, Sanskrit language

As moral judge, Varuna knows the secrets of the human heart. Varuna is the deity of the sky, the rain, and the law that sustains the universe and society.

Indra is another popular Vedic nature deity. Depicted as a warrior God and thus the God of the Kshatriyas, Indra is the mighty hero who subdued the evil dragon Vritra, which held back the waters of the world. Indra appears as a drunken clown in some later Hindu myths. In Vedic scripture Indra drinks soma, the intoxicating drink, and leads the rough warriors to win battles.

> Let me now sing the heroic deeds of Indra, the first that the thunderbolt-wielder performed. He killed the dragon and pierced an opening for the waters; he split open the bellies of mountains. . . .
>
> Wildly excited like a bull, he took the Soma for himself and drank the extract from the three bowls in the three-day Soma ceremony. Indra the Generous seized his thunderbolt to hurl it as a weapon; he killed the first-born of dragons. . . .
>
> With his great weapon, the thunderbolt, Indra killed the shoulderless Vṛtra, his greatest enemy. Like the trunk of a tree whose branches have been lopped off by an axe, the dragon lies flat upon the ground.
>
> Rig Veda 1.32.1, 3, 5[5]

Agni is the mouth of the Gods. His Sanskrit name means "fire" (Latin, *ignis*; English, "ignite"). As fire itself, Agni transmits offerings during sacrifice (e.g., meat, rice, milk) to the Gods. Sacrificially, Agni is extremely important because fire occupies the central place in the sacrificial rituals. Fire is vital to the performance of sacrifice because it consumes and transforms that which is offered, delivering what is sacrificed to the Gods. These are the very first verses of the Rig Veda:

> I pray to Agni, the household priest who is the god of the Sacrifice, the one who chants and invokes and brings most treasure. . . .

> Agni, the sacrificial ritual that you encompass on all sides—only that one goes to the gods.
>
> Agni, the priest with the sharp sight of a poet, the true and most brilliant, the god will come with the gods.
>
> Rig Veda 1.1.1, 4, 5[6]

Agni has three forms: fire, lightning, and the sun. Sacrifices made to Agni go immediately to the Gods, and he is considered the mediator between human beings and the Gods, as well as their protector and witness to their actions. Since the sacrificial fire is lit every day, Agni is eternally young.

Soma is the deity of sleep and is also an intoxicating plant prepared and drunk as a sacrifice. Soma gave people glimpses of the divine realm. As intoxicating juice, soma is used as part of the warriors' sacrifice before entering war.

> I have tasted the sweet drink of life, knowing that it inspires good thoughts and joyous expansiveness to the extreme, that all the gods and mortals seek it together, calling it honey. . . .
>
> We have drunk the Soma; we have become immortal; we have gone to the light; we have found the gods. What can hatred and the malice of a mortal do to us now, O immortal one? . . .
>
> The glorious drops that I have drunk set me free in wide space. You have bound me together in my limbs as thongs bind a chariot. Let me drops protect me from the foot that stumbles and keep lameness away from me.
>
> Rig Veda 8.48.1, 3, 5[7]

It is important to note that Agni and Soma are at once substances (fire and drink) as well as deities. The changing quality of Hindu deities points to the fact that many of them can morph into other Gods, change genders, and be a variety of kinds all at once. Alongside the male nature deities, several female nature deities are also the focus of sacrifice. Among them are Usha (dawn) and Vac (or Vak), the Goddess of sacred speech, the power of right words, and correct chants expressed during sacrifice.

Yajur Veda, Sama Veda, Atharva Veda

Beyond the Rig Veda, three other sacred writings make up the collection known as the Vedas: Yajur Veda, Sama Veda, and Atharva Veda. The Yajur Veda contains the same material as the Rig Veda, the only major difference being that the contents of the Yajur Veda are arranged according to sacrifice (*yajus* means sacrifice) and performed by Brahmin Adhvaryu priests. The Sama Veda also contains the same hymns and mantras as the Rig Veda and the Yajur Veda, but they are arranged by musical accompaniment, which is why the Sama Veda is also called the "singing Veda." Sama Veda hymns and mantras are performed by Brahmin Udgatri priests. The Atharva Veda is based on the Rig Veda but is a collection of curses, charms, spells, and incantations to be used for immediate concerns, such as against sickness, snakes, or demons, or to obtain love or success in business.

Here is an example of a mantra used against coughing from the Atharva Veda:

> As the soul with the soul's desires swiftly to a distance flies, thus do thou, O cough, fly forth along the soul's course of flight! As a well-sharpened arrow swiftly to a distance flies, thus do thou, O cough, fly forth along the expanse of the earth! As the rays of the sun swiftly to a distance fly, thus do thou, O cough, fly forth along the flood of the sea!
>
> Atharva Veda 6.105.1–3[8]

The Atharva Veda is the most unique of the four texts that make up the Vedas because of its contents, which are based on the Rig Veda but are more directly applicable to the daily challenges of life for ordinary people.

Additions to the Vedas

Each part of the Vedas (Rig, Yajur, Sama, Atharva) has three additional Vedic texts attached to it. These addendums provide commentary on the Vedas and reflect further philosophical and religious developments within early Hinduism. The first attachment consists of the **Brahmanas** (900–500 BCE), a collection of interpretations of ritual acts alluded to in the Vedas. Brahmanas show that even in the early days of Hinduism an attempt was being made to interpret the ancient truths according to the changing patterns of life. The Brahmanas contain detailed allegories that highlight the exact etymological meaning of Sanskrit words.

The second attachment is the **Aranyakas** ("Forest Books"), which attempt to understand the hidden truths of the Brahmanical rituals. The Aranyakas are the result of the insights produced by people who retreated

Wikimedia Commons

Figure 2.9. Shiva Nataraja, the Dancing Shiva. Shiva's leg is over a demon (*Apasmara*), who symbolizes ignorance and illusion. The dance represents the cosmic cycles of creation and destruction.

into the forest for meditation in an attempt to comprehend the hidden truths of the rituals. The Aranyakas detail the symbols of the rituals and thus represent a further development away from the literary application to a more philosophical and symbolic interpretation of rituals. With the development of the Brahmanas and the Aranyakas, we see greater religious and philosophical reflection on the meaning of the rituals that for centuries people had assumed would provide social and cosmic stability and well-being.

By approximately 500 BCE, a whole new range of ideas and practices became important. Built on the Vedas, including the Brahmanas and the Aranyakas, a new transition period was set in motion through the inclusion of the last addition to the Vedas, the **Upanishads**, which brought significant new interpretations to the older Brahmanical (Vedic) religion. The Upanishads are called the **Vedanta** ("end of the Vedas," "summation of the Vedas"), since they are the last of the addendums to the Vedas (following the Brahmanas and the Aranyakas) and also since they provide the most important summary statement of the truth contained in the entire Vedic tradition. The wisdom from the Upanishads is intended only for the spiritually mature.

The word "Upanishad" carries the meaning of "sitting down near a spiritual teacher to receive instruction" or "secret or sacred knowledge" or "discussions of ultimate wisdom." The etymology consists of *upa-* (near), *ni-* (down), and *shad* (to sit)—that is, to sit at the feet of the **guru** (teacher) to receive sacred knowledge. The Upanishads introduced and developed some of the major philosophical tenets of Hinduism that have maintained their significance throughout the centuries. It is important to recognize that at the time of the earliest recording of the Upanishads (1000–500 BCE), to the east of the Aryan area, the new religious movements of Buddhism, Jainism, and other religions provided a formidable challenge to Hindu ideas and practices. How would Hinduism define itself in the midst of these new religions? We will visit Buddhism and Jainism in later chapters of this book, but suffice it to say that these traditions, like any new religious tradition, would force Hindus to reexamine their beliefs and reinterpret their theology. Brahmins were in control in the Hindu areas and were sought by kings for their expertise in religious rituals. On the other hand, Brahmanical beliefs were being challenged by people seeking access to the secret knowledge of the Brahmin class. Through writings of the Upanishads, Brahmin ideas became more directly accessible, particularly the meaning of the sacrificial rites.

Upanishads—The Vedanta

The Upanishads consist of more than one hundred works, most of which are later and considered *shmriti* literature. However, the oldest thirteen belong to the ancient tradition and thus are *shruti* because they form part of the revealed corpus of the Vedas. Building on the insights provided by the Brahmanas and the Aranyakas, the Upanishads asked new questions about the sacrificial tradition. The most dramatic change was the move from focusing on ritual details to meditation and concentration. The move marked a turn inward—to seek the unchangeable reality that is identical with that which underlies the essence of humans and of the universe. The Upanishads pointed adherents to the inner and final meaning of all things, explaining the personal transformation that results from participation in the rituals. That is, the Upanishads moved away from a focus on ritual alone and the physical performance of the chant and toward seeking the essence of the ritual without going through it. The attempt to get underneath the ritual, to its essence, means looking underneath the material world to what is permanent and unchanging.

New Concepts Introduced in the Upanishads

BRAHMAN

Four major concepts that continue to be fundamental to Hindu life were first developed in the Upanishads. First, the Upanishads introduced the notion of Brahman, the essence of the universe. Brahman is the power that holds everything together, including the cosmos, human life, the natural environment, and sacrificial rituals. Brahman is portrayed in both nontheistic and theistic terms, known as the divinity without attributes (nontheism) and the divinity with attributes (theism). A God described as "nontheistic" means that the God is not known personally and directly, so the God is impersonal. According to Hindu scriptures, "this [universe] was Being (Sat) alone, one only without a second. Some say that in the beginning this was non-being (asat) alone, one only without a second; and from that non-being, being was born" (Chandogya Upanishad 6.2.1).[9] Yet Brahman is also seen in theistic terms. This

Christian Reflections

Who is God? What is God? These are important questions that help determine the general orientations of believers to God, to one another, and to the natural world. All Gods within Hinduism are emanations of the Absolute (**Brahman**), the divine essence, the powerhouse for all other Gods within the tradition. Indeed, Hindu theism is broad and includes both polytheistic and monotheistic perspectives. For example, it is said that there are 330 million Gods in Hinduism, yet Hindus also recognize that there is one God. This is a theological tension in Hindu theology that has been the basis for the immense diversity within Hinduism.

The Afterlife according to the Upanishads

In the Upanishads, the soul takes one of two paths after death, either the way of the fathers (the southern path that leads back to earth), or the way of the Gods (the northern path that leads to liberation). Taking the southern path, the soul passes into the smoke of the funeral pyre, from there into the night, then into the waxing half of the moon, then, in the six months when the sun is moving south, to the world of the fathers. From there it goes into space and then to the moon. After remaining there for as long as its merit allows, the soul returns again into space, wind, smoke, mist, cloud, rain, and then into a plant. When eaten by a man, the soul goes into his semen and then into a womb, and the cycle begins again. Those who follow the northern path go into the flames of the pyre, then into light, day, and the waxing half of the moon. The soul travels six months, when the sun is going north, then it enters the sun and the moon and then goes into lightning. From there the soul is led to Brahman.

means that Brahman is recognized as a personal being, with attributes that are recognizable. Therefore, Brahman is seen as both impersonal, without attributes, and personal, with attributes.

According to the Upanishads, Brahman is unknowable. But Brahman is the sacred power operative in the sacrifice and in the Brahmin class. Brahman is universal cosmic energy, described as being in the world like salt in water or like clay in statues. Brahman is the "thread of the thread." Brahman is the underlying power of the whole universe, the vital energy of the cosmos, omnipotent, omnipresent, and the source of all manifestations. Yet the Upanishads speak of the ineffability of Brahman as follows:

> not coarse, not fine, not short, not long, not glowing [like fire], not adhesive [like water], without shadow and without darkness, without air and without space, without stickiness, (intangible), odorless, tasteless, without eye, without ear, without voice, without wind, without energy, without breath, without mouth (without personal or family name, unaging, undying, without fear, immortal, stainless, not uncovered, not covered), without measure, without inside and without outside.
>
> Brihadaranyaka Upanishads 3.8.8[10]

Brahman cannot be described. Yet from Brahman springs the multiplicity of forms, including human beings. Although Brahman cannot be described, it can be worshiped in any number of forms and is equally present in any number and kind of beings. "Om" (or "aum") is chanted by the Brahmin priests because it is the sound that expresses Brahman.

SAMSARA

Second, the Upanishads introduce the South Asian concept of **samsara** (Sanskrit, "wandering"), translated as the transmigration of souls, the cycle of death and rebirth, or simply reincarnation. Liberation (Sanskrit, *moksha*) is release from samsara, conceived as either going beyond samsara or recognizing it to be an illusion (**maya**). Although the term "samsara" does not appear in the Vedas, thus suggesting it is non-Vedic in origin, the concept of the cycle of death and rebirth does appear in the Upanishads.

It is important to recognize that the portrayal of the paths of the soul's journey is rich, imaginative poetry. Samsara was scary, a heavy burden that filled people with fear that they had to go through death over and over again. Liberation (*moksha*) meant being free of the cycle of death and rebirth, so Hindu spirituality aimed for victory over the illusion of death—that is,

Christian Reflections

History is a fundamental feature of human identity, since it helps us understand our past and makes sense of our present experiences. The religions of the world present different notions of history. The two major distinctions are between linear and cyclical visions of nature. Between these two general perspectives there are other, more nuanced, perspectives. Religions that advocate linear histories believe that world and cosmos have a specific beginning and end, the details of which may not be known. Religions that advocate a cyclical view of history believe that major themes and forces of life will be repeated, usually indefinitely. Hinduism, along with other major Indian religious traditions, affirms both the cyclical and the linear nature of history and the religious life. From the Hindu viewpoint, at a cosmic level, creation and dissolution continue into perpetuity, but the world will be re-created. At the point where **dharma** is not followed, the world will be dissolved and re-created, with the same material of creation. Dissolution gives rise to new creation. On an individual level, the cycle is seen in the doctrine of samsara, the burden of reincarnation. That is, the cyclical notion of history is intimately connected to individual existence and the way of salvation. Existence itself becomes a necessary burden that must be overcome. Freedom from existence is ultimate freedom—liberation. According to many Christian thinkers, history is perceived in a linear fashion, which begins with creation and culminates in the consummation of time. For many Christians, like Hindus, life on earth can be a burden, but the Christian approach does not see existence itself as the same sort of burden to be overcome as Hindus typically view it under the doctrine of samsara.

over the illusory nature of samsara. This illusion is referred to as maya. And one must see through maya in order to be liberated. More specifically, the desire is to be released from existence, since the merging of soul with matter (spirit and body) binds people to existence. If one is not liberated, then that soul is punished in hell.

ATMAN

Third, the notion of the real self, called **atman**, first appears in the Upanishads. Atman originally meant "extended self," referring to one's body, social status, family, and image one had of oneself. Then atman was interpreted on a more sophisticated inner level as the core of one's inner being—the divine moment within. Atman is free from evil, old age, death, grief,

Figure 2.10. *Sadhu* in Haridwar, India. As *sannyasi* (renunciate), *sadhus* leave behind all material attachments in order to seek liberation.

hunger, and thirst. Ultimately, atman is beyond the senses and intellect. Through the practice of meditation one attempts to enter a state of consciousness that allows one to get a glimpse of atman—the true self.

Here is the deep message of the Upanishads, and it is, according to Hindu tradition, only for the spiritually elite: liberation comes through the realization of Brahman within. In the Upanishadic tradition, the believer seeks to discover the inner connections among all things, for all things are bound together not only by likeness of activity but in actuality—in *being*. The great insight of the Upanishads is that all reality is one—all is one; atman = Brahman—"I am Brahman" (*Aham Brahman asmi*). The great pronouncement of the Upanishads is *Tat twam asi* (Thou art that), meaning that the atman (thou) is the same as Brahman (that), which is the basis for all life.[11] This is the deepest insight of Hinduism and gives believers knowledge of the interconnectedness of all things, particularly the identification of the individual atman (self, soul) with the divine (Brahman).

KARMA

Finally, the concept of **karma** first appears in the Upanishads. Karma (Sanskrit, "action") refers to all actions and the consequences of actions. Karma (action) determines one's current and future lives. It is as though every action is a seed, and a person's individual life is the fruit or result of his or her actions. Where the seed falls, fruition occurs and brings forth the seed inside. All present life is the fruit of one's former life. What kinds of actions are there? Simply put, there are physical actions and mental actions. Physical actions include anything one does with one's body, while mental actions involve activities of the mind and the emotions. All karma directly impacts one's present or future life.

> Now as a man or woman is like this or like that, as he or she acts and behaves, so will he or she be. A man or woman of good deeds becomes good, a man or woman of bad deeds becomes bad. He or she becomes pure by pure acts, impure by impure acts.
>
> Brihadaranyaka Upanishad 4.4.5[12]

> Those of noble conduct soon attain good birth, as a Brahman, warrior, or merchant, but those of wicked conduct reach an evil birth, dog, hot, or social outcast.
>
> Chandogya Upanishad 5.10.7[13]

So, for instance, anger (bad seed) will produce bad consequences in one's life. Love (good seed) will produce good consequences. The Upanishads convey three kinds of karma: (1) bad karma, (2) good karma, and (3) neutral karma. Bad karma, produced by negative emotions and actions such as those stemming from egoism, fear, and anger, can accumulate into karmic clusters that can result in a more miserable life for the person. Good karma, produced by good emotions, yields clusters of friendliness, wisdom, and blessing. Only actions that are helpful to others produce good karma. Neutral karma is a more advanced vision of karma—that is, accepting everything as it is, not distinguishing between good and bad. Karmic law states that people suffer the consequences of their actions, in their present and future lives. Lesser

---

SIDEBAR 2.5

330 Million Is One

Indian lore contains a well-known tale about a Hindu man who spent his entire life as a kind of theistic census taker. He went from village to village, house to house, occupation to occupation, caste to caste, inquiring at every location about which deities were worshipped at that place by those people. After traveling throughout India and recording the names of all the deities who were worshipped, tradition states that he chronicled the list in a great book. The number is traditionally held to have been 330 million. When the weary traveler finally returned to his home village, exhausted and in his ninety-third year, he was asked to count how many Gods were in his book. He spent seven years counting the Gods, and at the end of the book he wrote the grand total—one. He declared in his dying breath that there is "one God worshipped in India."

Tennent, *Christianity at the Religious Roundtable*, 38

Hindus themselves disagree on the ontological status of the many Gods of Hindu tradition. Is the ultimate deity of Hinduism the same as the Christian God? The classic Christian theological affirmation is that God is at once transcendent and immanent, a combination of mystery and knowability. That is, on the one hand, God is fully other, so holy that anything unholy cannot be in fellowship with him. Yet on the other hand, God has descended into our time and space in Jesus Christ—breaking into human history—taking on the flesh of human beings in order to conquer sin and make a way for human beings to know God and have fellowship with him. Similarly, the Hindu notion of **avatar** ("divine descent," "incarnation"; the descent of Brahman into the world in a tangible form) means that God descends into human form. Since the sixth century, the term "avatar" has been used primarily to describe the incarnation of Lord Vishnu, who descended into *mythical time*, rather than into human flesh.

karma finds its rewards immediately on earth. Hindus have various theories about karma. *Moksha* (liberation) is beyond good and evil, so doing good (producing good karma) does not necessarily bring *moksha,* but it can help one be reincarnated into a better life.

Belief in karma is responsible for the strong emphasis on charity in the Hindu tradition, as well as in many other South Asian religions. One must do good deeds and be compassionate in order to accumulate good karma. This includes a strong respect for all life, such as a tendency toward vegetarianism. Doing good and not harming others will cause one to be born into a better existence. Consequently, an individual is responsible for whatever situation she or he is born into.

Late Vedic Period

LIFE STAGES

The Vedic period introduced three life stages (***ashrama***) through which all the faithful traveled. Additional detail comes from the *Laws of Manu* (c. 200 BCE–200 CE), which tells of the duties expected in the caste system and the different *ashrama*. The first *ashram* is the Brahmacharya (celibate student), the stage of the student, when a boy beginning around the age of seven lives in the house of his teacher (guru). The guru gives the student a mantra that will become his slogan for life and teaches the student the Vedas and ritual sacrifices. The student stage often lasts around ten to fifteen years. Girls also go through a similar stage, but they learn household duties from their mothers rather than living with a guru.

The second *ashram* is Grahastha, the stage of the married householder, which entails being married, having children, overseeing a household, and working to provide for one's family, especially for future generations. It is also important for the householder to keep the sacred fire going and pay daily homage to the deities in the house. Householders can range from between eighteen to fifty years of age.

The third *ashram* is known as Vanaprastha, the stage of retirement, when one stays in one place and studies the Vedas and meditates. It is the grandparent stage, when individuals are no longer responsible for making money or for overseeing the household. Ideally, at this stage the grandparents teach younger generations about the family and the heart of the traditions.

The fourth *ashram*, the stage of the **sannyasi**, is introduced in the Upanishads, and with it comes a new path of spiritual life. It is burdensome to be born over and over again. The search for Brahman causes people to leave society, often naked, wandering around homeless, relying on others for food donations, and living in forests as hermits and ascetics. These are the *sannyasis*, the wandering mendicants, ascetics, or renunciants. The term "*sannyasi*" comes from the Sanskrit *sam* (together), *ni* (down), and *asyati* (he throws), thus one who "throws down" or "puts aside."

Two Religious Paths (Vedic and Upanishadic)

During the Upanishadic period (900–400 BCE), two options for the spiritual life were available. These spiritual orientations represented a fundamental split in early Indian society but were not contradictory in nature. That is, followers of one path did not claim that followers of the other path were heretical. Upanishadic logic suggested that if karma bound one to samsara (to existence itself), then the one way to gain liberation was not to act at all. The stage of the *sannyasi* was an optional stage that theoretically could be taken up at any point in one's life but more popularly was taken after the stage of retirement. Becoming a houseless wanderer meant giving up all connection to family and possessions, taking a new name, becoming homeless, and relying on the goodwill of others. The point is not to act, and so not create karma.

How does one know *how* to act in any given situation? One acts according to one's dharma (duty, law, virtuousness, justice, way of the cosmos; "the right way of living"), which is similar to the earlier Vedic notion of *rita*, the universal law or cosmic order. To improve one's current and future life, one must follow one's dharma. **Varnashrama-dharma** more fully expresses the relative and dynamic nature of dharma, for *varnashrama-dharma* consists of duties (dharma) in accord with class (*varna*), caste, and stage of life (*ashrama*).

The Vedic and the Upanishadic Paths

Ordinary Path (Vedic)	Extraordinary Path (Upanishadic)
Good actions (karma)	No action (renunciation, *sannyasi*)
Good rebirth (samsara)	No rebirth (*moksha*)
Impermanent result	Permanent result
Individual and caste identity	Loss of individual and caste identity
Individual responsibility	No individual responsibility
Varnashrama-dharma (better rebirth)	*Moksha*

Each *varna* and *ashrama* has its own dharma—so much so that even if one can perform the dharma of another's class, it would be better to perform one's own dharma. *Adharma*, literally "mis-dharma" (nonrighteousness, misdeeds), guarantees a worse condition for the doer of such actions. The aims of dharma differ according to one's station and stage in life. A Brahmin had different standards of study and liberation from others. Furthermore, a Brahmin had different duties (dharma) at each stage in his or her life.

> Better to do one's own duty imperfectly than to do another man's well.
>
> Bhagavad Gita 18:47

In the era of Vedic speculation, when the Upanishads were recorded and Hinduism was challenged by the non-Brahmanical religions of Buddhism and Jainism, Hindu spirituality was split between two possible religious orientations, the ordinary (Vedic) and the extraordinary (Upanishadic) paths. Each spiritual path was a valid expression of the Hindu tradition, both guaranteeing a certain spiritual attainment. On the one hand, the Vedic path consisted of performing good karma and following one's dharma, with the assurance that one's next life would be an improvement on one's current condition. On the other hand, the Upanishadic path emphasized performing no actions at all, thus going beyond samsara altogether, which would give rise to liberation.

Followers of the Vedic path remain within their families and societies and maintain the hope that faithful dharmic living will give them better lives, even if they are not liberated completely. Conversely, the followers of the Upanishadic path seek to recognize the identity between their atman and divine Brahman (*tat twam asi*), accumulating no karmic weight, and thus being liberated from their existence. The *sannyasi* is a "no-person" who has obliterated the "I" that acts and has consequently gone beyond the Gods and the "ordinary" way of karma. In the period of Vedic speculation (c. 1000–500 BCE) the Vedic and the Upanishadic religionists coexisted in Indian society.

Burgeoning of the Hindu Tradition (c. 500 BCE–300 CE)

THE EMERGENCE OF THEISM

The Upanishadic insights contributed immensely to the development of Vedic religion, connecting the inner state of human beings to the divine. While Brahman was conceived of as nontheistic, the Upanishads moved the tradition beyond a mere mechanistic view of the centrally important sacrificial rituals toward a more internalized vision of the divine, which democratized it, making the "secret knowledge" of the ritual life more accessible to people. What is crucial at this point in the history of the Hindu tradition is that this period introduces another way of salvation, one that differs from the Vedic and Upanishadic notions.

The growth of theism is an integral part of the Hindu tradition. This theistic movement, while not fully developed at this point in the history of Hinduism, when people were devoted to a particular God with specific characteristics, may have its roots in the worship of the ancient Vedic nature deities, or it may reflect the influence from the non-Aryan religions of India. Whatever the case, it is probable that some form of deity worship in which religionists were devoted to a particular God for aid and protection was widespread among ordinary people. Although people recognized that several Gods existed, and many were worshiped, the two Gods of particular importance that emerge are Vishnu and Shiva. From this period onward, these two dominate the religious scene of Hinduism.

Christian Reflections

How many ways can one be saved? Christianity claims that "salvation comes from the Lord" to those who believe. In the Christian tradition salvation is initiated by God as a gift, rather than being something earned through hard work or ritual performance. The scandal of the cross means that salvation is a free gift, based on God's love for human beings: for example, "God proves his love for us in that while we still were sinners Christ died for us" (Rom. 5:8). Yet the biblical writers also noted the importance of "works"—that is, actions and deeds done by Christians, as part of Christian faith: for example, "Those who say, 'I love God,' and hate their brothers or sisters, are liars" (1 John 4:20), and "faith apart from works is barren [dead]" (James 2:20). The Christian story says that since human beings are so fundamentally and inherently scarred by sin (i.e., impure), there is no way apart from God's help that human beings can be saved. Yet it is worthwhile to note that Christianity, like Hinduism, promotes a balance between faith and deeds.

THE GREAT EPIC POEMS: THE RAMAYANA AND THE MAHABHARATA

During the Epic period (roughly 500–200 BCE) the two great *shmriti* texts, the Hindu Epic poems the **Ramayana** and the **Mahabharata**, were composed. Here we find less interest in Vedic ritual per se, but a growing attraction to the Gods Vishnu and Shiva. Having ten avatars, Vishnu is perhaps the most popular God in Hinduism today. According to the tradition, Vishnu descends as an avatar when people no longer follow dharma. The purpose of his descent is to save dharma from vanishing.

Vishnu appears as Matsya (fish), Kurma (tortoise), Varaha (bear), Narasimha (half man/half lion), Vamana (dwarf), Parashurama (Rama-with-the-axe), Rama (Ramachandra, king of Ayodhya), Krishna (young cowherd boy; young prince; chariot driver), Buddha (Enlightened One), Kalki ("Eternity"; "Time"). A believer knows the divine through particular avatars. The Ramayana and the Mahabharata are among the most loved texts in Southeast Asia, with wide impact on the religious traditions in that region. They are presented in a variety of ways, including cartoon strips, television series, life dramas, books, and songs.

The Ramayana (Story of Rama) was completed by 200 BCE. It tells of the exiled Prince Rama, an avatar of Vishnu, and his beloved wife, Sita. Sita is kidnapped by the demon Ravana. Much of the Ramayana recounts the adventures of Prince Rama and the monkey God, Hanuman, as they search for and eventually save Sita. The Ramayana teaches Hindus two significant lessons. First, Rama and Sita are model spouses to Hindus. They demonstrate a commitment to each other. Rama's commitment is seen in his persistence to find Sita. Sita's commitment is demonstrated by her chastity, her refusal to give up on being reunited with Rama. Second, Sita's commitment to Rama exemplifies an ideal of religious dedication. Since Rama is a God, the

Figure 2.11. Vishnu's incarnation as Krishna

Figure 2.12. Vishnu's incarnation as Rama

incarnation of Vishnu, Sita's dedication to Rama is the same as a devotee's dedication to a God. They are faithful to each other.

The Mahabharata ("Great [story of the] Bharatas") (c. 400 BCE–400 CE) is an epic poem that tells the incredible story of an early Indian dynasty. The Mahabharata is about four times as long as the Bible, with about one hundred thousand verses, and is a repository of Indian myths and legends. The epic story is about a feud between two sides of the Bharata family. The Mahabharata discusses the inner workings of the human heart, the conflicting visions of the kingdom, and the immensely interesting activities of the Gods in the divine realm as well as in their relationship with human beings. The Mahabharata recounts the conflict between the Pandavas and the Kauravas, two sides of a family that ruled in northern India, near today's New Delhi.

Around 1500–1200 BCE the kingdom passed to a king, Dhritarashtra, whose blindness kept him from ruling the kingdom; therefore his younger brother ruled in his place. Because of a curse, Dhritarashtra's younger brother had to leave the country, returning the kingship back to Dhritarashtra after all. Following the rules of succession, the eldest son of the brother, who was the rightful king due to Dhritarashtra's blindness, was designated the heir apparent. Upon the death of Dhritarashtra, the eldest son and his four brothers, called the Kauravas, were ready to take over the country. However, Dhritarashtra had also adopted five sons from his brother, called the Pandavas, and while they were not directly his own children, Dhritarashtra loved them as his own. Members of the Pandavas also claimed to be the heir apparent, so the impending conflict between the Pandavas and the Kauravas reaches a climax in the section of the Mahabharata called the Bhagavad Gita.

The Bhagavad Gita

The most popular section of the Mahabharata is the Bhagavad Gita, which records the climax of the conflict between the two sides of the dynasty, the Pandavas and the Kauravas, and offers new insights into the nature of the Gods and the spiritual path. As a sacred text, the Bhagavad Gita provides comfort and guidance for Hindus today. Many Hindus form groups to study the Bhagavad Gita devotionally, to glean insights from its immensely beautiful words.

The Bhagavad Gita (Dialogue/Song of the Supreme Exalted One) tells of the dialogue between Arjuna, a Pandava of the Kshatriya (warrior) class, and his chariot driver, Krishna (an avatar of Lord Vishnu). The dialogue takes place before the battle between two massive opposing forces, the Kauravas and the Pandavas, as Arjuna is supposed to follow his dharma and lead his brothers and their armies into battle. Krishna drives Arjuna to the center of the battlefield to start the battle, and Arjuna is alone. As he looks at his enemies, he realizes they are his own brothers, the ones with whom he was raised, and whom he loves. Yet Arjuna has to act—to fight—that is his dharma.

Unless he follows his dharma, Arjuna will be reborn into a more miserable condition. When Arjuna enters the battlefield, the Bhagavad Gita introduces a dramatic moral crisis: Does a person do his duty (dharma) even if it causes harm to the people he loves? Or does he act out of pity and fear of causing harm? When Arjuna stands on the battlefield and sees his opponents arrayed against him, he is filled with grief and pity, and he attempts to renounce his responsibility for action, trying to escape his dharma by following the *sannyasi* route. What will Arjuna do? His duty to fight will cause much suffering, and Arjuna questions his duty (Bhagavad Gita 1.42–2.1). Krishna provides counsel, giving Arjuna insight into how one can act and also be fully liberated—even in the midst of action. Krishna's teaching can be summarized in three disciplines (yogas).

Lessons from the Bhagavad Gita

First, Krishna teaches Arjuna the discipline of knowledge (*jnana* yoga)—that is, the knowledge that the soul (atman) is not killed when the body is killed. Arjuna is told to be detached, to let things go. Since the body is not the self, that which is killed is not the person. This is knowledge of the nature of the eternal soul. Second, Krishna teaches Arjuna about the discipline of action (karma yoga), developing the concept of dharma in a way that transcends the split between the ordinary and the extraordinary norms.

Duty impels Arjuna to act in the world of material nature, even while he remains detached from it. If Arjuna fulfills his responsibilities as a warrior (Kshatriya) without being attached to the results of his actions, he can be liberated in the midst of action itself. The notion that liberation can occur *in the midst of action* is a new insight in the Hindu tradition, for before the Epic period it was believed that action (karma) results in the bondage of reincarnation. Krishna points out the hypocrisy of many within the ascetic tradition, of those who attempt "not to act":

A man cannot escape the force
of action by abstaining from actions;
he does not attain success
just by renunciation.

No one exists for even an instant
without performing action;
however unwilling, every being is forced
to act by the qualities of nature.

> When his senses are controlled
> but he keeps recalling
> sense objects with his mind,
> he is a self-deluded hypocrite.
>
> When he controls his senses
> with his mind and engages in the discipline
> of action with his faculties of action,
> detachment sets him apart.
>
> Perform necessary action;
> it is more powerful than inaction;
> without action you even fail
> to sustain your own body.
>
> Bhagavad Gita 3:4–8

Krishna counsels Arjuna to be detached, calm, and liberated in the midst of action (karma), detached not from action itself but from the *fruits of action*. The third discipline Krishna teaches is called the discipline of devotion (bhakti yoga). **Bhakti** (Sanskrit, "loving [warm] devotion") refers to the action of loving, worshiping, and revering, and is one of the paths to liberation. If one remains detached from the fruits of one's actions, then where should those fruits be directed?

In the teaching of bhakti yoga, Krishna reveals himself (theophany), explaining in more detail and with more-striking imagery his own divine nature and the relationship that he envisions between living beings, such as Arjuna, and himself. Until this point, Arjuna does not recognize Krishna as anything other than his chariot driver. But when Krishna reveals his true identity, Arjuna recognizes him as a God—indeed, as Vishnu himself—in the beautiful language of Hindu sacred literature, that which describes the purifying capacity of the divine.

> Nothing is higher than I am;
> Arjuna, all that exists
> is woven on me,
> like a web of pearls on a thread.
>
> Bhagavad Gita 7:7

> I am the self abiding in the heart of all creatures.
> I am Vishnu striking among the sun gods.
>
> Bhagavad Gita 10:20, 21

> As roiling
> river waters

> stream headlong
> toward the sea,
> so do these human
> heroes enter
> into your blazing
> mouths.
>
> As moths
> in the frenzy
> of destruction
> fly into a blazing flame,
> worlds
> in the frenzy
> of destruction
> enter your mouths.
>
> You lick at the worlds
> around you,
> devouring them
> with flaming mouths;
> and your terrible fires
> scorch the entire universe,
> filling it, Vishnu,
> with violent rays.
>
> Bhagavad Gita 11:28–30

Arjuna is called to offer the fruit of his actions to the God, for he is lovingly devoted to him. Krishna humbles Arjuna with the powerful vision of Vishnu's divine splendor—and Arjuna surrenders to the deity, even seeing himself in the deity. All beings are in the divine, and the divine is in all beings.

Bhakti yoga is elevated above other kinds of yoga.

> Of all the men of discipline [yoga],
> the faithful man devoted to me,
> with his inner self deep in mine,
> I deem most disciplined.
>
> Bhagavad Gita 6:47

In the Bhagavad Gita the ordinary way and the extraordinary way to salvation come together. In the teaching about the nature of the divine, Krishna takes the combined issues of detachment and commitment to a deeper level and connects them to a speculative tradition that gave us the **monism** of the nontheistic Upanishads and the theistic vision pronounced in the Epic period.

Arjuna is being told that his deepest nature is not simply his own immortal soul but the divine—that which surrounds him, controlling the entire cosmic process, and also dwells within him as his innermost self (atman). There are many commentaries on the Bhagavad Gita, but how one interprets the indwelling nature of the divine depends on whether one believes that divine reality is ultimately personal and different from creation and empirical reality (theism) or is ultimately one (monism), such as the vision presented in Upanishadic monism.

The revolutionary lesson offered by the Bhagavad Gita is that one can in fact be liberated in the midst of action, as long as one offers the fruit of one's action to a God, with loving devotion. This idea would free Hindus to engage their current lives as students, householders, and retirees, without the burden of having to renounce everything to be liberated from <u>samsara</u>.

Christian Reflections

How is one saved? What makes the promise of salvation efficacious? Does greater insight alone provide salvation? Do greater efforts directed toward the divine or the human community necessarily procure liberation from our human predicament? Perhaps more importantly, who actually does the *work* of salvation? According to the Roman Catholic and Protestant perspectives, the fall encompassed all of creation and left a permanent mark on humanity, which Christians call "sin." Reconciliation and harmony begin with God's initiative to conquer sin.

As the self-disclosure of God, Jesus Christ pays the price for the sin that objectively marks humankind and the natural world. Since the human problem of sin is so severe and pervasive, there is nothing humanly possible that we can do to earn our salvation. Christians recognize that human beings need a savior, but no human being is "good enough" to be such a savior. How can a being marked by sin overcome sin? Christians recognize that the God-man, Jesus Christ, is fully human and fully divine: "And you who were once estranged and hostile in mind, doing evil deeds, he has now reconciled in his fleshly body through death, so as to present you holy and blameless and irreproachable before him—provided that you continue securely established and steadfast in the faith, without shifting from the hope promised by the gospel that you heard, which has been proclaimed to every creature under heaven" (Col. 1:21–23). Martin Luther's description of Christians as *simul justus et peccator* (simultaneously justified and sinner) illuminates the dual status of a follower of Christ. What parallels do you see between the new insights highlighted in the Bhagavad Gita and biblical notions of salvation and the role of human agency in effecting salvation?

Worship and Practice

How are people liberated within Hinduism? The Hindu tradition has no mandated adherence to a particular sacred text, no requirement to worship in a temple, nor even universal belief in a God or Gods. Despite its openness to incorporating or recognizing new Gods (e.g., Jesus) into its pantheon of deities, the Hindu tradition affirms the importance of worshiping individual Gods (e.g., Kali, Shiva), which helps to guide worshipers' devotion. For our purposes, let us consider two of the major practices of worship—meditation and faith in a God. These prominent ways of attempting to achieve liberation (*moksha*) exist today in India and have been present in significant ways throughout the tradition's history.

Alongside these two are the various ways of liberation exhibited by the renunciants (*sannyasi*), who have given up karma (action) in an attempt to rise above the Gods and the system of caste and individual responsibility. The renunciant option is underscored in the Upanishads, also referred to

Figure 2.13. Temple entrance in Haridwar, India

as the Vedanta. Generally there are no conflicts between these different styles of religious practice and orientation. The Gods are not jealous of one another, and neither are the practitioners of various religious customs.

Meditation: Patañjali's Yogasutras

Sometime during the classical period of Hinduism (c. 300–650 CE), the **Yogasutras** were composed for the purpose of organizing the search for Brahman, the highest reality, into several states. The path outlined by the Yogasutras begins with the practitioners following moral rules and bodily exercises, and culminating in union with Brahman. Yoga (Sanskrit, "discipline") is combined with sutras (Sanskrit, "thread," "manuals," "chapters," "literature," "collection of discourses"), offering the first outline of the process of meditation that would be inherited by other South Asian religionists and in part form the foundation of contemporary meditation practiced worldwide.

Many scholars debate the authorship of the text, but Patañjali's name is connected with the collection more than that of any other individual figure. The eight-stage process, where each stage is referred to as a "limb," begins with external behaviors and bodily postures and moves progressively inward in an attempt to unite with the infinite. It is important to note that not all practitioners are able to reach the final level of the Yogasutra meditation. And the practice is not engaged in frivolously but rather requires discipline that begins with how one orders one's daily life. Most will not attain the final stage, but devotees report that the process itself liberates one into new awareness of the divine, the nature of the self, and the world. It is possible that the author of the Yogasutras composed, or compiled, the sutras in response to the Eightfold Path of Buddhism.

Faith in a God: The Puranas and the Growth of Bhakti (c. 400–1000 CE)

Following the Epic period and the composition of the Yogasutras, Indian mythology and bhakti flourished, giving rise to full-blown theism. Theism here means simply divinity with attributes. Theism is contrasted with nontheism, where the divine remains unknowable, without attributes. The **Puranas** (Sanskrit, *purānas*, "ancient") are a set of eighteen sacred books that reflect popular theistic traditions.[14] They present Gods that are knowable, with histories, genealogies, and personalities.

Each of these *shmriti* texts focuses on a specific deity, for the first time presenting the mythology of the Gods and Goddesses, and containing stories, legends, and hymns about the creation of the universe, the incarnations of Brahman, and the instructions of various deities and spiritual legacies of ancient sages. Although each deity is depicted as the Supreme Being responsible for creating and ordering the world, there is no competition among them, since they are all fully gods and are of Brahman. The Puranas cover five topics: (1) the creation of the world, (2) the dissolution of the world, (3) the ages of the world, (4) genealogies of the Gods and Goddesses, and (5) stories of the descendants of the genealogies. The eighteen major Puranas are divided into three groups in honor of Vishnu, **Brahma**, and Shiva.

TRIMURTI

Together the three Gods are referred to as **Trimurti** (Sanskrit, *trimūrti*, "three forms," "three images"). In comparison to the intellectual nature of the Bhagavad Gita, the Puranas tend to be more emotional and tactile in their presentation of the Gods. The Puranas highlight Brahma, Vishnu, and

Charles E. Farhadian

Figure 2.14. Shiva temple at Mahabalipuram in Tamil Nadu, India

Shiva, using bhakti poetry written in the vernacular rather than in Sanskrit, and emphasize the tactile union with the divine, the direct experience of the gods, and the inner feelings of the devotee.

Brahma: The Creator

Brahma is the first of the Gods, the creator of the world, who precedes the universe and takes care that all created things are the way they should be. The Puranas, written in rich, poetic, imaginative language, record that Brahma was born from a golden egg floating on primal waters. He is depicted with four heads, four faces, and four hands, which sprang up when he created a female from his own pure essence and fell in love with her. He needed four heads so that he could follow her around with his eyes. Another purpose of his four heads was to create the four Vedas; out of each head emerged a Veda. He is red in color, dressed in white, and rides a goose.

Brahma is referred to as the Lord of Creatures, Great Patriarch, Self-Existent, Chief Sacrificer, and "Born of the Golden Egg." Brahma is a challenging concept because some Hindu traditions believe that he really originates from Vishnu. The Puranas also state that Brahma is a creation of Brahman. Today few temples in India honor Brahma, as he is the least worshiped of the Trimurti, perhaps because he is considered a creator similar to a deistic notion of God. The myths of the Trimurti function as poetic devices to communicate the grandeur and power of these beings.

Was Brahma really born from a golden egg floating on primal waters? Imaginative language is employed throughout Hindu scriptures. Similarly, such figurative language is a powerful way that biblical writers conveyed notions about God and Jesus. For example, referring to God, the Bible states, "Can a woman forget her nursing child, or show no compassion for the child of her womb? Even these she may forget, yet I will not forget you" (Isa. 49:15).

The writer of Deuteronomy states,

> He sustained him in a desert land,
> in a howling wilderness waste;
> he shielded him, cared for him,
> guarded him as the apple of his eye.
> As an eagle stirs up its nest,
> and hovers over its young;
> as it spreads its wings, takes them up,
> and bears them aloft on its pinions,
> the LORD alone guided him;
> no foreign god was with him. (32:10–12)

Likewise, "Jerusalem, Jerusalem, the city that kills the prophets and stones those who are sent to it! How often have I desired to gather your children together as a hen gathers her brood under her wings, and you were not willing" (Matt. 23:37). Other biblical verses use poetic language to express the holiness and grandeur of Jesus: for example, "His head and

Vishnu: The Sustainer

Vishnu is by far the most popular God within Hinduism. Within the Trimurti, Vishnu is considered the sustainer and preserver of creation. Those who consider Vishnu the highest God are called Vaishnava and frequently mark their foreheads with a large "V." Vishnu is associated with the doctrine of avatars (incarnations), which appear to preserve order (dharma) whenever unrighteousness (*adharma*) threatens the world. The idea of the successive avatars of Vishnu enables Vishnu to absorb different religious traditions, such as Buddhism, into Hinduism. According to the universalism of Hinduism, all people are Hindus. For instance, some Hindus believe that the Buddha himself was an incarnation of Vishnu, which may reflect the attempt of early Hinduism to supersede Buddhism at a time when Buddhism was gaining popularity and thus challenging Hinduism. At any rate, Vishnu's avatars are

his hair were white as white wool, white as snow; his eyes were like a flame of fire. . . . In his right hand he held seven stars, and from his mouth came a sharp, two-edged sword, and his face was like the sun shining with full force" (Rev. 1:14, 16).

Paradise Lost, the epic poem written by the seventeenth-century English poet John Milton, renders creation as a brooding dove impregnating the egg of Chaos and incubating it until it hatches: "And chiefly Thou O Spirit, that dost prefer / Before all Temples th' upright heart and pure, / Instruct me, for Thou know'st; Thou from the first / Wast present, and with mighty wings outspread / Dove-like sat'st brooding on the vast Abyss / And mad'st it pregnant" (book I, 17–22).

There is an immense challenge when speaking about God. How do we use human language to preserve the knowability and mystery of God? Christians affirm that God is knowable, made known in Jesus Christ and Scripture, but God is also transcendent, "wholly other." Therefore our best language cannot exhaustively capture the notion of God. The challenge of religious language is to communicate in a way that preserves the knowability and mystery in our language about God. Religious language utilizes both metaphors and analogies to communicate about God. For example, while God is not literally a rock, God is the rock (of our salvation). Likewise, Jesus is not exactly a vine, but he says about himself, "I am the vine, you are the branches" (John 15:5), teaching us a lesson about abiding in him. All religions have a similar challenge regarding the use of religious language—that is, using ordinary, mundane language to convey truths about God.

not limited to the ten incarnations noted in the Puranas. Vaishnavas believe that all deities came from Vishnu, including the creator God, Brahma. The different avatars of Vishnu appear to meet the needs of the specific eras.

Shiva: The Destroyer

Shiva is the third member of the Trimurti, the God of destruction, and he is considered as the supreme God by the Shaivas, who may be identified by three horizontal lines on their foreheads. Shiva is a God of paradoxes—simultaneously a renunciant and a householder, a celibate yogi (practitioner of yoga) and a husband. The Dancing Shiva, called Nataraja, is one of Shiva's

V&A Museum/Wikimedia Commons

Figure 2.15. Trimurti showing Brahma, Shiva, Vishnu, and their consorts (c. 1700)

Figure 2.16. Statue of Shiva in Delhi, India

popular depictions. To devotees of Shiva, Nataraja is the God of creation and destruction. Shiva is depicted in a host of different ways, but he is usually wrapped in a necklace of live cobras and has matted hair from which falls the sacred Ganges River.

THE GODDESS AS SUPREME BEING

Brahman manifests itself in both male and female forms. Although some female deities are revered in the Vedas, prior to the Puranas there is little evidence for worship of the supreme deity as a Goddess. Early Goddesses typically defeat demons intent on disturbing the process of creation and destroying dharma. Other than the Trimurti, there are several Goddesses whose powers contribute to the potency of the Gods with whom they are paired. And the God's power is exemplified by the fact that he has a consort, a Goddess, attached to him. Her power is called Shakti—the creative female power manifested as Goddess—that is able to bring things into appearance. Shakti power is understood as either the Supreme Being conceived as female or a consort (Goddess) of one of the major Hindu Gods.

Devi is the active power (Shakti) that manifests as the universe. She is the mother of everything but is not a maternal

Christian Reflections

According to the Bible, Jesus is the Light of the world, the Lamb of God, the Messiah, and the Son of God. These titles are different names that refer to Jesus Christ; the names do not represent various entities. Similarly, the different names of the Hindu Gods do not necessarily imply distinct beings.

Shiva is not mentioned by name in the Vedas, although he was later identified with the Vedic deity Rudra. In the Upanishads, Shiva is described as the supreme God equal to Brahman as the source of the universe. Shiva is often depicted in artwork as an ascetic dressed in tiger's skin, with white complexion and thickly matted hair coiled like a snake. He has a third eye on his forehead and wanders as an ascetic carrying a human skull in one hand and a begging bowl in the other. His third eye developed after his wife playfully approached him from behind and held her hands over his eyes, throwing the entire world instantaneously into darkness. The third eye developed immediately and saved the universe from darkness.

Shiva is worshiped widely in the form of a lingam (phallus) with his wife, the Goddess Sati, as a yoni (female organs, represented by a conch shell), together representing the close connection between destruction and creation. Worship of Shiva can involve magical practices, self-immolation, and ecstatic trances.

figure; rather, she is the embodiment of creative and destructive power. Although all Goddesses are theoretically subsumed within Devi, the individual entities receive bhakti as adherents focus on different manifestations as they face different challenges within their lives. Consequently, some suggest that all Goddesses have their origin in the same general category of Goddess, called **Deva** (Sanskrit, "shining sky," "celestial power"), a particular "manifestation (*not* personification) of a natural power, generally beneficent, especially if propitiated through offerings."[15] Most of the Goddesses are consorts of either Vishnu or Shiva. Uma, who is first mentioned in the Upanishads, is a mediator between Brahma and the other Gods and is Shiva's consort. Later Uma is identified with many Goddesses, including **Parvati** and **Durga**.

Parvati (Sanskrit, *Pārvatī*, "daughter of the mountain") is the daughter of the mountain Himalaya. Parvati and Shiva's famous progeny was **Ganesha** (Lord of the hosts), who is known as the elephant-headed God of wisdom and good fortune. Ganesha is the remover of obstacles and is invoked as one of the most popular Gods. Tradition credits Ganesha with writing the Mahabharata by dictation from Vyasa.

Figure 2.17. Statue of Lakshmi and Narayana from the eleventh century (National Museum, India)

Durga is fearsome, a slayer of demons who threatened the destruction of dharma. Depicted with ten arms, carrying a variety of weapons, and riding a lion or a tiger, Durga is accompanied by eight female demons who assist her in the destruction of forces that threaten dharma. Durga is portrayed as beautiful and warlike, and Hindu legend credits her with slaying several demons. Durga is an aspect of another fierce Goddess, **Kali** (Sanskrit, *Kālī*, "she who is black"), a ferocious Goddess with a terrifying appearance, gaunt, with fangs, usually partially naked, wearing a tiger skin and a necklace of human heads. She is propitiated by blood sacrifices of animals, birds, and even human beings.

Kali is depicted as black, with four arms, two of which hold severed heads, her tongue dripping with blood. She represents the dark, abysmal void above time, space, and causation. There are many temples dedicated exclusively

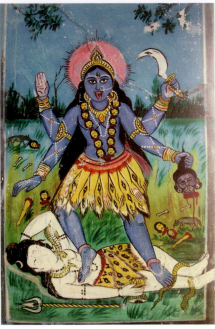

Sujit Kumar/Wikimedia Commons

Figure 2.18. Kali, the Hindu Goddess associated with Shakti (feminine empowerment), who uses her power to annihilate influential evil forces

to Kali, and she is not all bad; Kali is credited with decapitating a host of demons and thus helping to maintain dharma.

Among the consorts of Vishnu is Lakshmi (Sanskrit, *Lakṣmī,* "sign"), the personification of goodness and beauty. She is depicted with four arms, holding a lotus. Her arms represent the four directions and also symbolize her omnipotence and omnipresence. Her four hands represent the four goals of life: dharma (righteousness, religious duty), **kama** (genuine desires), **artha** (wealth), and *moksha* (liberation from death and rebirth). She often accompanies Vishnu on his incarnations—for example, she appears to Sita in the Ramayana. Regardless of her appearances, Lakshmi is associated with good fortune and fertility. Perhaps the most widely revered consort of Brahma is **Sarasvati**, the patron Goddess of education and the arts, particularly of music. She is often worshiped at the beginning of the school year and attracts the devotion of students. Sarasvati is depicted as fair-skinned, elegant, and beautiful, holding a musical instrument (*vina*) and riding on a peacock (*vahana*). Tradition records that Sarasvati created the sacred language of Sanskrit and that she appears in the Rig Veda as Vac (speech), which is the personification of sacred utterance. It is important to keep in mind that the followers of Devi, the great Goddess, are called Shaktas. Worshipers of specific Goddesses, such as Parvati and Durga, are devotees of Devi.

Alongside the Gods and Goddesses, there are secondary deities loosely connected to Vishnu, Shiva, or Devi, but they maintain their own identities. For instance, Ganesha, the elephant-headed God, would be considered a secondary deity, and people make offerings to him before any new undertaking. There are also countless regional and village deities who protect specific villages. These types of Goddesses are usually represented in non-pictorial form, such as by a tree or a rock covered in paint or a pot of water. Additionally, local deities can be human beings who have been divinized, heroes, or ghosts. Heroes are those who have lived extraordinary lives, for instance, by following their dharma well. Ghosts can be the spirits of people who have died prematurely or from a bad accident. Angry ghosts can be hungry and linger near the living, causing misfortune, until they are placated with offerings.

Puja: *Worship as Offering to a Deity*

Our brief tour of the Vedas, Upanishads, Epics, Puranas, and Yogasutras illuminates the immense diversity within the Hindu religious tradition. As I stated at the beginning of the chapter, Hinduism is not a neatly defined set of practices, doctrines, or beliefs. Rather it is best understood as a living tradition whose broad parameters are quite inclusive, even of other religious traditions. The immense diversity within Hinduism is also reflected in its worship. **Puja** (Sanskrit, *pūjā*, "respect, homage, worship") connects the human domain with that of the divine and often focuses on the invocation of a God as a royal guest. The worship of deities (*devapuja*) is a fundamental part of the bhakti tradition and involves offering food and flowers to a God, the consumption of the offering by the God, and the act of receiving the goodwill (*prasad* or *prasada*) of the deity. *Prasada* is the free action of favor or grace of a god that helps devotees advance toward liberation (*moksha*, release).

This *ātman* [i.e., the recognition *tat twam asi*—"Thou art that"] cannot be attained by instruction, or by intellect, or by learning. He can be attained only by the one whom he chooses: to such a one that *ātman* reveals his own nature.

Katha Upanishad 2.23

When favored by Brahman, the self (*ātman*) attains immortality.

Shvetashvatara Upanishad 1.6

Modern Movements

The Republic of India was founded in 1947, the product of Hindu and Indian nationalism in the face of British domination and colonialism. From the seventeenth century onward, however, social and political developments had caused major changes in Hindu religious life, eventually introducing revival and reform movements into the tradition to define it in relation to other world religions and modernism.

One of the most enduring cultural legacies on the Indian subcontinent was left by the Mughal Empire. The Mughal Empire, a Turko-Persio-Mongol Islamic dynasty that dominated most of the Indian subcontinent (1526–1857), began with Emperor Babur (1526–30) and ended with Emperor Aurangzeb (1658–1707). The Mughal emperors left magnificently beautiful palaces and tombs, such as Shah Jahan's (1627–58) Taj Mahal, built as a tomb for his wife Mumtaz Mahal after she died during the birth of their fourteenth child.

Charles E. Farhadian

Figure 2.19. The Taj Mahal in Agra, India. This building is a white marble mausoleum built by Mughal emperor Shah Jahan in memory of his third wife, Mumtaz Mahal, beginning in 1632. The calligraphy on the Great Gate reads, "O Soul, thou art at rest. Return to the Lord at peace with Him, and He at peace with you."

The Mughal emperors were uneven in their toleration of non-Islamic religions, particularly of Hinduism and scattered pockets of Sikhism and Christianity. The appointment of Warren Hastings in 1773 as the first governor-general of India represented the British extension of political power over India. While the **British Raj** (Hindi, "rule"), known as the period of British India, colonized the Indian subcontinent from 1858 to 1947, British presence began in 1608, when the British East India Company (1600–1874) first arrived to India, in today's Gujarat, to establish trade links there. Within a short period of time, the company established trading posts in several major cities, such as Madras (today's Chennai), Bombay (today's Mumbai), Calcutta (today's Kolkata), and Gujarat, and traded opium, spices, textiles, and other items that could benefit Britain and its colonies. British traders needed the permission of Mughal leaders to engage in their businesses.

The British Raj

By the time Britain entered the Indian subcontinent, Islam as a political force had declined, although the number of its adherents continued to grow, and the Mughal Empire was less unified. In response to the Indian mutiny (1857), when Indians rebelled against the colonial power of the British East

Figure 2.20. Tomb of the Mughal emperor Humayun, commissioned by his first wife, Bega Begum, in 1570. Humayun's tomb was the first garden-tomb on the Indian subcontinent (New Delhi, India).

India Company, Britain withdrew the British East India Company and replaced it with direct rule by Britain, thus initiating the period known as the British Raj. Under the dominion of Queen Victoria of England, also known as the empress of India, the British Raj brought a degree of unity to the Indian subcontinent and aimed to modernize the region. Indian identity, religion, and culture were profoundly challenged by the presence of British rule.

The Indian National Congress, led by Mahatma Gandhi and Pandit Jawaharlal Nehru, led India to its independence from the British Raj on August 15, 1947. The Muslim League, a political party in the British Raj, sought the

Christianity in India

Beginning in 1820, the British East India Company permitted Christian missionaries to travel on their ships to the Indian subcontinent. Yet the British East India Company's policy on Christian missionaries was uneven, varying from region to region. The Indian subcontinent has a long history of Christian presence, beginning with the probable arrival of Thomas, Jesus's disciple, whom church tradition records as arriving in southwest India after the death and resurrection of Jesus and eventually establishing the first Christian church in India. The Christian church in India was called the Indian Orthodox Church, the Orthodox Church of the East, or the Malankara Orthodox Church.

creation of a separate state for the subcontinent's Muslims. When India became independent, Pakistan was also created as an Islamic nation-state for Indian Muslims. This great division of South Asia, known as the "partition," separated the Indian subcontinent into the independent nations of India and Pakistan and led to strife resulting in the deaths of tens of thousands.

CHANGES INTRODUCED BY THE BRITISH RAJ

The British Raj introduced several changes to the Indian subcontinent. First, it sought to blend Christianity and modernization into Indian culture, which communicated the confidence and superiority of Western culture and Christianity. For example, British colonial administrators and missionaries were often critical of what they believed to be harmful Hindu practices, such as child marriage, caste distinctions, temple prostitution, and the practice of sati (or suttee; wife immolation), where the surviving widow followed her dead husband onto the funeral pyre and thus was burned alive. The last well-documented case of sati occurred in 1987, when the eighteen-year-old widow Roop Kanwar immolated herself. Although rare, wife immolations have purportedly occurred as late as 2008 in India.

Second, the British Raj introduced a British nationalism in which British civilization was considered superior to Indian civilization. From the 1860s onward, Indians responded to this sort of British nationalism with their own nationalism, which sought political independence from Britain.

Third, the British Raj communicated the secular ethos of the colonial administrators, which was not necessarily dependent on God or other notions of the divine, Hindu or otherwise. For instance, religion was left out of the political realm as a source of knowledge or policy making.

Fourth, the colonial powers established a new economic system, a modified form of capitalism, that threatened and often devastated indigenous cottage industries, such as cloth making and cotton spinning. The new economic system was supported by the construction of a massive railway network that linked larger cities and factories.

Fifth, the British Raj introduced Western forms of higher education, particularly in the larger cities, such as Calcutta (Kolkata), Bombay (Mumbai), and Madras (Chennai), which encouraged the separation of religion from the social sciences. Following the Enlightenment pattern, religion was something to be "studied" objectively, to be critiqued like other domains of knowledge.

Finally, the British colonial powers introduced a worldview based on modern, Western science that had contributed to the development of Western nations.

The legacy of the British Raj left a permanent mark on Indian culture and society. How do people respond to being oppressed by an outside group? The options are fairly limited. Simply put, the dominated (1) will wholeheartedly accept the values, traditions, and political and religious systems of the outsiders; (2) they will reject wholeheartedly all foreign imposition, even to the point of death; or (3) they will respond in countless ways to selectively accept and reject elements of foreign influence. This is one of the most intriguing and relevant questions for the history of religions and our understanding of religions in our contemporary world.

Hinduism under Conditions of Colonialism

Conditions of domination and subjugation force people to reflect on their own identities. The sources of identity found in religion can be one of the most potent forms of identity construction and maintenance. When people are oppressed or hindered from fully expressing their religion, history, and power, it is not unusual for them to reach back into their religious traditions, where they find resources to respond to the new ideas, values, and influences of others. The fact that colonized people are able to respond reminds us that human beings are not completely passive even in the face of being dominated. We see a similar pattern among all believers (and even secularists)—people demonstrate their ability to act even in small ways that reflect their dignity, agency, and power.[16]

Following Ainslee T. Embree's categorization of modern Hindu tradition, I will conclude this chapter with a brief introduction to the various Hindu responses to the British Raj. This summary will lead us into a discussion of the contemporary world and the current challenges Hindus face in modern India. Embree employs the categories of (1) acceptance and reform and (2) rejection and revival to outline the responses of Hindu reformers to the experience of being subjugated by the British Raj.

Rammohan Roy and Swami Vivekananda

Among those Hindus who accepted much of the British Raj, while reforming the Hindu religious tradition itself, are **Rammohan Roy** (1772–1833), who appealed mostly to Brahmins rather than ordinary people, and the great Hindu missionary to the West, **Swami Vivekananda** (1863–1902). Rammohan Roy and Swami Vivekananda both selectively accepted what they believed were the positive contributions of the British Raj and reformulated their understandings of Hinduism to make it more relevant to the modern Indian subcontinent.

Figure 2.21. Statue of Rammohan Roy at Green College in Bristol, England

Rammohan Roy was from a Bengali Brahmin family; however, he was educated at a Muslim university and served the British East India Company in Calcutta until he retired in 1815. His significance in part is that he established the first Indian reform movement, called the Brahmo Samaj ("Society for Brahmin Worship" or "Society of Worshipers of the One True God"), founded in 1823, which would eventually inspire major Bengali social reforms.

The Brahmo Samaj was quite egalitarian. It opposed the caste system by arguing that all people were equal before the divine and that the caste system was not religious; the group also supported monotheism, the worship of Brahman alone. Among the social reforms advocated by the Brahmo Samaj were the establishment of a Hindu college in Calcutta and the use of Western education; the movement even argued that instruction ought to be in English rather than Sanskrit. Furthermore, Rammohan Roy vigorously supported women's access to education and fought fiercely against the practice of sati and polygamy. He believed the Upanishads and the Brahma Sutras to be the highest form of wisdom and sought to purify Hinduism of the accumulated practices that were not essential to the tradition, such as idol worship and polytheism. Rammohan Roy's self-introduction sounds similar to Paul's introduction from Philippians 3:5:

> From considerations like these, it has been that I, (although born a *Brahmin*, and instructed in my youth in all the principles of that sect,) being thoroughly convinced of the lamentable errors of my countrymen, have been stimulated to employ every means in my power to improve their minds, and lead them to the knowledge of a purer system of morality. Living constantly among the *Hindoos* of different sects and professions, I have had ample opportunity of observing the superstitious puerilities into which they have been thrown by the self-interested guides; who, in defiance of the law as well as of common sense, have succeeded but too well in conducting them to the temple of Idolatry; and while they hid from their view the true substance of morality, have infused into their simple hearts a weak attachment for its mere shadow.[17]

Rammohan Roy was a strong Indian nationalist who campaigned against social injustices, such as heavy taxes levied on peasant farmers, that Indians suffered under the British Raj. Rammohan Roy's ideas and the Brahmo Samaj influenced the development of the Indian National Congress, which would eventually spearhead the political independence of India.

Swami Vivekananda was the famous disciple of **Sri Ramakrishna** (1834–86), a Bengali Vaishnava Brahmin who served as a priest in a temple devoted to the Goddess Kali near Calcutta. Although many Westerners may be unfamiliar with Ramakrishna, most are familiar with his ideas, for he suggested that behind all religious practices, and behind all the particular religions themselves, stands the one God. Ramakrishna arrived at the conclusion of the essential unity of all religions through his experience of deep meditative practice, where he had visions of many deities, including Jesus

Ramakrishna Mission Delhi/Wikimedia Commons

Figure 2.22. Vivekananda in Jaipur, India

Christ and Allah. What is crucial to note is that the basis for Ramakrishna's insights was the religious experience of deep meditation, which he felt gave him access to the one divine unity inside all people's hearts and the unity of existence itself, a philosophy based on Advaita Vedanta—that is, the belief that the divine is all-pervasive and that the spiritual goal of human beings is to realize their identity with that divinity.

While Ramakrishna was an early visionary of the unity of everything, it would be his most renowned disciple, Swami Vivekananda, who would popularize this vision, promoting it throughout much of the Western world. Swami Vivekananda had a tremendous impact on the modern understanding of Hinduism, particularly in the West. Swami Vivekananda visited the United States to address the World Parliament of Religions in Chicago in 1893. For about three years he toured the United States and England, delivering lectures advocating Vedanta philosophy and the insights of his guru, Ramakrishna.

Swami Vivekananda's speech at the World Parliament of Religions became the basis for the Western understanding of Hinduism for the next several generations. Even today his legacy remains. Because of Swami Vivekananda's lectures in the West, Hinduism was accorded respect as an insightful world religion instead of being dismissed as an inferior tradition. During his tour

Vedanta philosophy varies from non-dualistic to dualistic perspectives. The most popular Vedanta philosophy, Advaita Vedanta ("non-dualistic" unity), developed by Adi Shankara (c. 788–820) and based mainly on the Upanishads, is a monistic perspective identifying the atman (self, soul) with the Divine (Brahman): "Brahman is the only truth, the world is illusion, and there is ultimately no difference between Brahman and the individual self." Another Vedanta philosopher, Ramanuja (1017–1137), advocated Visistadvaita Vedanta, which maintains some distinction between Brahman and Atman, though Brahman "transcends the sum of its parts and yet fully inheres within them."

R. King, *Indian Philosophy*, 222

of the United States and England, Swami Vivekananda established several chapters of the Ramakrishna Mission, which continues today in its philanthropy, social service, and religious meditation and education.

Dayananda Sarasvati

Another category of Hindu response to the British Raj is one of rejection and revival, which emphasized the harsh repudiation of any non-Hindu influence. One of the most outspoken opponents of non-Hindu religions was **Dayananda Sarasvati** (1824–83), a *sannyasi* from boyhood who argued that Hinduism was corrupt because it had strayed from the ancient wisdom of the Vedas. According to Sarasvati, the only truth is found in the Vedas—he was a Vedic fundamentalist who advocated strict adherence to the unquestionable authority of the Vedas to the point of abandoning the Upanishads altogether.

His most significant legacy was the founding of the Arya Samaj ("Society of Nobles") to rid Hinduism of false and fictitious beliefs and practices, including idol worship, temple offerings, the caste system (including untouchability), discrimination against women, and child marriages, none of which were based on the Vedas. Likewise, women were seen as having equal rights as men. However, Sarasvati's scathing critique of Christianity and Islam demonstrated his aggressive defense

Christian Reflections

Swami Vivekananda was not the only major early contributor to the West's understanding of India in the nineteenth century. The Hindu convert to Christianity Pandita Ramabai (1858–1922) visited the United States and England a decade earlier than Swami Vivekananda. Pandita Ramabai's reflections on her visits to the West, and particularly her thoughts on the church, remain controversial. Pandita Ramabai was a brilliant Brahmin woman who had memorized thousands of Hindu texts, and she was able to debate respected Hindu scholars at the University of Calcutta, who gave her the title "Pandita," the feminine form of "Pandit" (Hindi, "scholar"). Pandita Ramabai became a Christian and worked tirelessly defending Brahmin widows in India, establishing a girls' school (Mukti Mission), criticizing some of the traditional Hindu practices such as polygamy and child marriage, and translating the Bible into her indigenous language, Marathi.

of the Hindu tradition, since he considered non-Hindu religions to have corrupted the purity of Hinduism.

Presently the Arya Samaj has chapters throughout the Western world. Some scholars argue that the ideas of Dayananda Sarasvati and the Arya Samaj planted the seeds that gave rise to the Hindutva movement of the twentieth century. Hindutva (Hinduness) advocates Hindu nationalism and has espoused a violent right-wing ideology responsible for legitimating religious conflicts against non-Hindu Indians. India's former ruling party, the Bharatiya Janata Party (BJP), indirectly promoted Hindutva ideology through the Sangh Parivar, a family of Hindu organizations advocating Hindu nationalism. In May of 2014, Narendra Modi, the Hindu nationalist from the BJP, was elected as prime minister of India.

> *I realized after reading the fourth chapter of St. John's Gospel, that Christ was truly the Divine Saviour he claimed to be, and no one but He could transform and uplift the down-trodden women of India. . . . Thus my heart was drawn to the religion of Christ.*
>
> Ramabai, *Testimony*, 25–26

Today's Hindu population is as diverse as ever. As Indians have immigrated across the globe, they, like others, have found meaning and guidance through Hindu belief and practice. As Indians in the West have achieved significant economic status, Hindu worship is moving out of rented halls and into well-established permanent Hindu temples funded by Western Hindus. And while, according to some, non-Indians cannot fully enter the tradition of Hinduism

Figure 2.23. Hindu temple in Malibu, California, USA, built in 1981. The temple is for the Hindu deity Venkateswara and contains a separate shrine for Shiva.

since they are not ethnically Indian, there is a steady stream of non-Indian converts who have made Hinduism their religious home.

Self-Realization Fellowship

Many of these non-Indian converts have joined the Self-Realization Fellowship (SRF), an international group that offers weekly meditation and provides opportunities for spiritual fellowship. Founded in 1920 by Paramahansa Yogananda (1893–1952) for the purpose of introducing Westerners to the meditative practices of Hinduism, the SRF has more than five hundred meditation centers worldwide through which men and women seek inner stillness and the awareness of the presence of the divine through yoga methods and teachings based on the writings of Yogananda.

> *Self-realization is the knowing in all parts of body, mind, and soul that you are now in possession of the kingdom of God; that you do not have to pray that it come to you; that God's omnipresence is your omnipresence; and that all that you need to do is improve your knowing.*
>
> Paramahansa Yogananda, quoted in Walters, *Essence of Self-Realization*, 197

In an era when new religious movements are proliferating, sometimes broadly and incorrectly referred to as "New Age movements," it is important to remember that some new religious movements, such as the SRF, are genuine expressions of historic world religions. Such new movements reflect the dynamism in which a world religion moves across cultural boundaries, being reformulated to make sense to people who are not from the religion's place of origin. Despite the ongoing debates about the identity of being Hindu, the traditions of Hinduism appear to remain robust and vitally important to hundreds of millions of believers worldwide. In significant ways, Hinduism established the foundation for many religions that emerged from South Asia, including the one we will consider in the next chapter, Buddhism.

Christian Reflections

It is not unusual to find members of the SRF who were once members of a Christian church, even leaders such as church deacons and elders, but who have left Christianity because of its perceived lack of spirituality and the church's overemphasis on reason and rationality. Today many Christians are seeking more experiential dimensions of their faith. Pentecostalism, which emphasizes the personal experiences of God, healings, spiritual deliverance, and the power of the Holy Spirit, is the fastest growing segment of the Christian church worldwide. Perhaps one appealing feature of Pentecostalism is its emphasis on the experience and power of God in the believer's life, rather than stressing rational, systematic doctrines and creeds.

Timeline

c. 3500–1800 BCE	Indus Valley civilization in northwestern South Asia
c. 2000–1400 BCE	Migrations of the Aryans, the people speaking Indo-European languages, into the subcontinent
c. 1500 BCE	Indus city populations migrate to Ganges plains
c. 1500–900 BCE	Early Vedic period; composition of earliest Vedas
c. 1500–500 BCE	Growth of Indus Valley civilization
c. 1400 BCE	Early version of Mahabharata
c. 1000–400 BCE	Composition of the Upanishads
c. 900–500 BCE	Composition of later Vedas, the Brahmanas, and the early Upanishads
c. 500 BCE–1000 CE	Composition of Epics (Ramayana and Mahabharata) and early Puranas
5th century BCE	Buddhism and Jainism founded in India
c. 320–185 BCE	Mauryan Dynasty founded by Chandragupta
c. 100 BCE–200 CE	Patañjali's Yogasutras
c. 100–500 CE	Expansion of Hinduism into Southeast Asia
c. 320–500 CE	Gupta Empire
c. 400–500	Vyasa's commentary on the yoga aphorisms; origins of Tantrism
c. 500–650	Gupta Empire divides into several kingdoms
788–820	Life of Shankara, Vedanta school advocate of Advaita Vedanta
c. 600–1600	Rise of devotional movements and *puja* rituals
1025–1137	Life of Ramanuja, philosophical defender of bhakti faith
1200–1757	Muslim rule of north India; decline of Buddhism in South Asia
1336–1565	Kingdom of Vijayanagara, the last Hindu empire in India
1420–1550	Period of devotional saints often venerated for their devotional bhakti song (e.g., Mirabai, Ravidas, Kabir, Chaitanya, Surdas)
1469–1539	Life of Nanak, founder of the Sikh tradition
1526–1707	Mughal Dynasty; Muslims rule most of South Asia; both support and oppose non-Muslim religions (Buddhism, Jainism, Sikhism)
1526–1757	Mughals rule north India; destruction of most Hindu temples
1542	Jesuit missionary Francis Xavier arrives in Goa
1651	British East India Company opens first factory in Bengal

1757–1857	British colonial governance in India
1815	Christian missionaries present in many Indian towns
1828	Rammohan Roy, Hindu reformer, founds Brahmo Samaj
1834–86	Life of Ramakrishna, guru with universalist teaching
1857	Indian mutiny; British expelled from India for nearly two years
1858–1922	Life of Pandita Ramabai, Indian social reformer, convert to Christianity
1858–1947	British Raj; British rule of most of Indian subcontinent
1863–1902	Life of Swami Vivekananda, Ramakrishna's disciple who popularized Ramakrishna's ideas and established the Ramakrishna Mission
1875	Founding of Arya Samaj by Swami Dayananda Saraswati
1893	Swami Vivekananda speaks at World Parliament of Religions, Chicago, inspiring interest in Hindu tradition
1920	Mahatma Gandhi begins his All-India Civil Disobedience Movement, leads civil disobedience campaigns
1923	Founding of the Rashtriya Svayamsevak Singh (RSS), a Hindu nationalist and fundamentalist movement
1947	India's independence; partition into India and Pakistan; Prime Minister J. Nehru declares India a secular state
1948	Mahatma Gandhi assassinated by Hindu fundamentalist; Pandit Nehru elected first prime minister of independent India
1992	Hindus demolish Babri mosque in Ayodya, leading to Hindu-Muslim riots throughout South Asia
1998–2004	Hindu nationalist party Bharatiya Janata Party (BJP) forms and wins parliamentary majority for first time; rules India until 2004
2004	Bharatiya Janata Party loses national parliamentary elections but retains control of ten states across India; Congress Party wins elections; Manmohan Singh becomes prime minister
2007	India has its first female president, Pratibha Patil
2008	Bombings and shootings in Mumbai by militants from Pakistan
2014	Election of Narendra Modi, of the national Bharatiya Janata Party, as the prime minister of India

Key Terms

Agni
Aranyakas
artha
Aryan
ashrama
Atharva Veda
atman
avatar
Bhagavad Gita
bhakti
Brahma
Brahman
Brahmanas
Brahmins
British Raj
Dalit
Deva
dharma
Durga
Gandhi, Mahatma (Mohandas Karamchand)
Ganesha
guru
Harappa

Harijans
Indra
Indus River Valley
jati
Kali
kama
karma
Krishna
Kshatriyas
Mahabharata
mantra
maya
Mohenjodaro
moksha
monism
Orientalism
Parvati
puja
Puranas
Purusha
Ramakrishna, Sri
Ramayana
Rammohan Roy
Rig Veda
Sama Veda

samsara
sannyasi
Sanskrit
Sarasvati
Sarasvati, Dayananda
Shakti
Shiva
shmriti
shruti
Shudras
Soma
Swami Vivekananda
Trimurti
Upanishad
Vaishyas
varna
Varnashrama-dharma
Varuna
Vedanta
Vedas
Vishnu
Yajur Veda
yoga
Yogasutras

Further Reading

Bharati, Swami Dayanand. *Living Water and Indian Bowl*. Pasadena, CA: William Carey Library, 2003.

Buck, William, trans. *Mahabharata*. Berkeley: University of California Press, 2012.

Burnett, David. *The Spirit of Hinduism: A Christian Perspective on Hindu Life and Thought*. Oxford, UK: Monarch Books, 2006.

Doniger, Wendy. *Hindu Myths: A Sourcebook Translated from the Sanskrit*. New York: Penguin Books, 1975.

Eck, Diana L. *Darsan: Seeing the Divine Image in India*. New York: Columbia University Press, 1998.

———. *India: A Sacred Geography*. New York: Three Rivers Press, 2012.

Embree, Ainslee T. *The Hindu Tradition: Readings in Oriental Thought*. New York: Vintage Books, 1972.

Flood, Gavin D. *An Introduction to Hinduism*. New York: Cambridge University Press, 1996.

Hawley, John Stratton, and Vasudha Narayanan. *The Life of Hinduism*. Berkeley: University of California Press, 2006.

King, Richard. *Indian Philosophy: An Introduction to Hindu and Buddhist Thought*. Washington, DC: Georgetown University Press, 1999.

Kinsley, David R. *Hindu Goddesses: Visions of the Divine Feminine in the Hindu Religious Tradition*. Berkeley: University of California Press, 1988.

Radhakrishnan, Sarvepalli, and Charles A. Moore, eds. *A Sourcebook in Indian Philosophy*. Princeton, NJ: Princeton University Press, 1957.

three

Buddhism

Contemporary Snapshot

On the last day of 2004, the *San Francisco Chronicle* ran an article, "Buddha Arrives in the Mission," which noted that a German Lutheran church built in the 1900s in the Mission District of San Francisco now serves a growing Buddhist community. The accompanying photo shows a massive twenty-one-foot Buddha statue, draped in a red robe, towering over the Hua Zang Si temple, in the former Saint John's Evangelical Lutheran sanctuary on Twenty-Second Street, flanked by stained-glass windows on either side.

> Inside an old German Lutheran church in San Francisco, Chinese nuns sit on the glossy wooden floors, wearing headphones, listening to Buddhist mantras on portable CD players.
>
> Gone are the pews and the church piano, but the organ pipes and stained glass windows remain—a backdrop to giant Buddha statues at the Hua Zang Si temple, which opened its doors this week in the Mission District. . . .
>
> On Dec. 26 [2004], Hua Zang Si began three days of ceremony to celebrate its opening and the birthday of Amitabha Buddha, one of many Buddhas, who is believed to reside in the land of ultimate bliss.

Saint John's Evangelical Lutheran Church had served many in the immigrant German community of San Francisco in the early twentieth century. But after World War II, German, Italian, and Irish families moved out of the Mission District, leaving the small congregation to serve a growing Latino population in a new location nearby. In 2002 the United International World Buddhist Association purchased the abandoned German Lutheran church for $2.5 million. The Lutheran church has been reborn as a Chinese Buddhist temple that now serves the growing Buddhist community of the city.

As the number of Christians has declined in the North Atlantic region, followers of other religious traditions and businesspersons are buying up abandoned or defunct church properties and transforming them into new worship spaces, commercial properties such as restaurants and bookstores, and personal residences. In the past century the North Atlantic region has become home to followers from every world religion, and they have greater

Christian Reflections

What is the relationship between worship spaces and the identity of a religious community? With the massive de-Westernization of Christianity, reflected in the substantial decrease in the numbers of Christians in Europe and North America, a loss of approximately fifty-four thousand church attendees weekly, how should Christians perceive the purchasing of abandoned or defunct Christian church buildings by members of other growing religions in the region? The emptying of worship spaces by Christian congregations whose numbers have severely dwindled and the concurrent purchasing of those spaces by other religious communities raise significant questions about Christian identity and the future shape of Christian faith in the West.

As defunct churches have abandoned their properties, leaving them to be purchased by other communities and transformed into spaces such as restaurants, bookstores, or Buddhist temples, how should Christians perceive the relationship between space and identity? What is the relationship between Christianity as a religious *movement*, where Christ calls his disciples to "go," and the sedentary nature of Christianity that has found its home in the well-established institutional life of the church? Many modern churches consist of buildings that appear more like campuses, replete with bookstores, gyms, and coffee dispensers, than houses of prayer (Matt. 21:13). Should Christians be concerned when Christian churches are transformed into non-Christian spaces or commercial businesses? Why or why not? The assertion that the *body of Christ* only entails the gathering of believers, where a particular building is unnecessary, may ignore the implications of the massive changes occurring in the religious landscape of Europe and North America in part reflected by the transformation of property.

wealth than in past decades. Today there are approximately 375 million Buddhists worldwide, making the tradition among the most popular religions in the world. Christians need to understand Buddhism because of the large number of Buddhists worldwide, the great attention the religion pays to the concept of suffering, and its missionary tradition, which seeks to convert others. In fact, Buddhism is the earliest of the three so-called missionary religions, along with Christianity and Islam. One could argue that any religion that claims to possess universal truth is a missionary religion when followers of those religions seek to share their religious commitments in order to convince hearers of the truth of those religions. That said, it is generally accepted that Buddhism, Christianity, and Islam are the great missionary religions.

Challenging the Brahmin Tradition

Buddhism is a South Asian religious shramanic movement. A shramanic movement (Sanskrit, **shramana**, "wandering monk," "one who strives") describes monks (*shramana*) or nuns (**shramani**), wandering ascetics responsible for their own actions as they work toward liberation. The South Asian shramanic religions include Hinduism, Buddhism, and Jainism. While the shramanic traditions focus on ascetic practices, each tradition has a different degree of austerity. Lord **Buddha** himself regarded extreme asceticism (e.g., pulling out hair, starving oneself) to be unnecessary for liberation and therefore advocated the **Middle Way**, discussed later in this chapter. Although Buddhism is a complicated and paradoxical tradition, it began formally with a specific person rather than Hinduism, which developed as a compilation of local religions without a founder.

Emerging at a time (sixth century BCE) when Upanishadic texts were challenging the control that Brahmins had over sacrificial rites, Buddhism was part of a nonconformist movement that questioned the Brahmanical tradition. As such, Buddhism sought new avenues of gaining liberation, including meditation, insight, and rigorous asceticism (e.g., **sannyasi**). The historic Buddha grew up within the cultural and religious world of Hinduism, yet it was a religious world that was being questioned by new interpretations of the older Vedic tradition. The religion that would eventually become known as Buddhism employed several of the same key theological concepts as its predecessor, Hinduism, but redefined them.

Defining the Tradition

Buddhism is often divided into two major branches, **Theravada** and **Mahayana**, with what seem to be countless subdivisions.

The earliest Buddhist scriptures were in **Pali**, an Indo-European language that, while sharing similar words with Sanskrit, nevertheless was not derived from Sanskrit. Sanskrit flourished in the northwest part of the Indian subcontinent as a high-caste sacred language, whereas Pali, from the **Prakrit** (Sanskrit, "original," "usual," "vernacular") language group, was a vernacular language. The issue of language is significant. The fact that the Buddhist scriptures were communicated in Pali, a vernacular language, rather than the largely inaccessible sacred language of Sanskrit, meant that Buddhist truths were more easily accessible to all people, regardless of caste.

The Two Major Vehicles of Buddhism

Theravada (Pali, "teaching of the elders") is one of the earliest schools of Buddhism and is sometimes referred to as the Southern School. Theravada Buddhism is the predominant religion in much of mainland Southeast Asia (e.g., Thailand, Cambodia, Laos, and Myanmar) and Sri Lanka, where about 70 percent of the population identify themselves as followers

SIDEBAR 3.1

Main Branches of Buddhism

	Theravada	Mahayana
Location	Mainland Southeast Asia (e.g., Thailand, Myanmar, Laos, Cambodia), Sri Lanka; also known as the Southern School	East Asia (e.g., China, Tibet, Japan, Korea, Taiwan, Mongolia), some parts of Southeast Asia (e.g., Singapore, Vietnam, and parts of South Asia, such as Bhutan); also known as the Northern School; subset of Mahayana is Tibetan Buddhism
Buddha	Historical Buddha (Gautama Siddhartha) and past Buddhas (Enlightened Ones)	Gautama Buddha, Amitabha, and others
Scriptures	Pali Canon (also known as the **Tipitaka**, or Theravada Canon)	Pali Canon and Mahayana sutras (e.g., *Perfection of Wisdom*, *Lotus Sutra*, *Heart Sutra*)
Bodhisattvas	Maitreya (the future Buddha)	Maitreya, Avalokiteshvara, Jizo, Manjusri, Santideva, Skanda
Original Language	Pali; the Tipitaka is studied in Pali, with some supplemental material in local languages	Sanskrit; Mahayana sutras are translated into local languages
Religious Path	**Arhat**	Buddhahood through bodhisattva path

Charles E. Farhadian

Figure 3.1. Buddhist monks collecting alms in northern Thailand

of Theravada Buddhism. Theravada has been referred to pejoratively as **Hinayana** (Sanskrit, "small vehicle") because of its preoccupation with self-reliance as a means of gaining liberation—a narrow view of attaining liberation. Mahayana (Sanskrit, "great vehicle") is by far the more popular branch of Buddhism.

Mahayana is the form of Buddhism prominent in East Asia (i.e., Korea, China, Japan, Tibet, Mongolia, and Vietnam). Mahayana takes several forms, many of which have become quite successful in the West, such as **Zen**, and is open to a variety of techniques to attain enlightenment. Tibetan Buddhism is a subset of the Mahayana variety, with enough variation that many scholars suggest it should be understood as a third major branch of Buddhism. **Vajrayana** (Sanskrit, "diamond vehicle") refers to Tibetan Buddhism, which is predominant in northern India, Tibet, Bhutan, Nepal, and southwestern China. It emphasizes mystical practices and the use of visualizations and verbalizations (e.g., mantras, chants) that practitioners employ to seek complete unity with a deity. Tibetan Buddhism is unique because it combines elements of Mahayana and the indigenous Tibetan religion, called Bön. A second form of Vajrayana Buddhism is Shingon Buddhism,

Paul Turgeon/Wikimedia Commons

Figure 3.2. American Zen Buddhist monk Claude Anshin Thomas

found primarily in Japan; it includes the use of Japanese **mandalas** (i.e., anthropomorphic representations), mantras, and visualizations to seek total identification with reality.

> Whenever you see any sentient beings,
> Regard them as your parents or your children.
> Don't befriend those who act in harmful ways;
> Instead rely on true spiritual friends.
>
> From Tibetan Buddhism, "The Bodhisattva's
> Garland of Jewels," in *Lojong Texts*, p. 9

It is worthwhile to note that the original terminology used in Buddhism is translated into the local languages, such as Japanese, Chinese, or Korean. Names for Lord Buddha, for instance, may be different in each country, yet the terms refer to the same concepts. Furthermore, we will see that the same Buddhist celestial beings can be represented in either male or female forms. Given the fact that terms and genders are easily translated into local languages, it is important to keep a close eye on the linguistic variations so that one can appreciate both the local and more universal aspects of the religion.

For reasons of convenience and clarity, I have chosen not to provide an exhaustive list of various Asian names for deities. Instead, I will remain close to the early tradition, using in this case Pali and Sanskrit terms. The Pali language is a result of the homogenization of several dialects in which the teachings of Lord Buddha were recorded and transmitted orally. Readers may want to consult a dictionary or encyclopedia of religion for a more complete list of variations in terminology within the Asian religious traditions.

Origins and Concepts

Narrative of Lord Buddha

Let us begin with the life of Lord Buddha. Who was Lord Buddha? When we approach the story of Lord Buddha, we ask a modern question: "Who was that man?"

When we attempt to carry out the search for Lord Buddha, we soon find that we are looking at him through many veils, and we try to remove the veils in order to see him more clearly. To attempt to

Wikimedia Commons

Map 3.1. Bodh Gaya, Bihar State, India

120

Asimilar question is faced by Christians who grapple with the comparison between the *Jesus of history* and the *Christ of faith*. Jesus walked on the earth as a human being, feeling the same hunger and thirst and sadness and joy that all human beings experience. Yet Jesus was Christ, being one with the Father, and one who is available to all people through time. In whom do Christians believe? The human Jesus of history or the divine Christ of faith? When do Christians emphasize one aspect of Jesus Christ over another? Is it justifiable to do so? How should we understand the relationship between the historical Jesus, who lived and breathed on earth, and the cosmic Christ, who transcends time and space as a member of the Godhead? What is the drawback for our faith, as Christians, were we to emphasize Jesus Christ's humanity over his divinity? Or, vice versa, what problems emerge in our theology and engagement with the world as Christians if we emphasize his divinity over his humanity? Similar challenges characterize the search for Lord Buddha, where differing answers have given rise to numerous legitimate Buddhist perspectives.

remove the veils to find the "real" Buddha is similar to what happens when we peel back the layers of an onion—we find nothing. Just emptiness. We should remember, however, that the veils themselves tell us important information, not necessarily about Lord Buddha himself, but about the way the Buddhist community viewed him and about what the community thought was significant in the image of the founder of the Buddhist tradition.

How then should we approach the story of Lord Buddha? We can approach the life of Lord Buddha in two ways. On the one hand, we can look for the historical kernel, the historical figure, which lies behind the stories of Lord Buddha. There is little doubt about the existence of the historical figure of Lord Buddha, but there is scant information about that history. On the other hand, we can look at the veils to see what they tell us about the Buddhist tradition as the tradition itself interprets Lord Buddha and makes the Buddhist tradition meaningful. Events in the life story of Lord Buddha can be connected to

PHG/Wikimedia Commons

Figure 3.3. Mahayana statue of an Indian Buddha from the eleventh century

important Buddhist virtues. One of the tensions within the Buddhist community revolves around the question of the relationship between the events of Lord Buddha's life (and lives) and the ideals and values those lives communicate to believers.

As you read this chapter, I encourage you to keep in mind the challenge of history (e.g., "Who really was Lord Buddha?") and the more universal claims (e.g., the pervasiveness of Buddha nature). Furthermore, it is wise to keep in mind the usefulness of **emic/etic** distinctions (insider/outsider perspectives), since emic perspectives give access to how Buddhists themselves make the tradition meaningful, while etic viewpoints can provide helpful observation from outside the tradition. Let us begin with the historical narrative of Lord Buddha's life.

The Story of Siddhartha

JATAKA TALES

The historical Buddha is thought to have passed through several existences prior to being born as a human being, called Shakyamuni Gautama **Siddhartha**.[1] Unlike the historical Jesus Christ, Lord Buddha had existed as many figures in the past, yet knowledge of Buddhism is based on the historical Buddha, whose legends are recorded in the **Jataka Tales**. The Jataka Tales are a set of 547 poems that provide a record of the former lives of Lord Buddha, which are considered to have been written during the time of the historical Buddha.

The Jataka Tales recount edifying stories of previous existences of Lord Buddha, such as when he was a human, a deity, a hare, and a snake. Furthermore, they serve a didactic function as a source of instruction in social and religious life with their accounts of Lord Buddha's life and his compassion for his followers. While it is hard to get at

Anonymous/Wikimedia Commons

Figure 3.4. Bhutanese painted Jataka Tales (18th–19th century, Bhutan)

the "historical Buddha," most scholars believe that Siddhartha (563–483 BCE) was born into the **Kshatriya** class near the Ganges River in northeast India. Siddhartha, who would later become "the Buddha," was born into a people called the Sakyas, and his father, Suddhodana, was a ruler. His mother, Queen Maya, was described as a pure human who was "free from all deceit." The Jataka Tales note that Siddhartha was born outside sexual relations and grew up in luxury as a prince. Suddhodana protected his son Siddhartha from the sight of suffering. But after he married Yashodhara and had a son, Rahula, Siddhartha yearned to meet his subjects beyond the confines of his father's palace. However, King Suddhodana continued to work to prevent Siddhartha from gaining knowledge of suffering.

> The king [Suddhodana], having learned the character of the wish thus expressed by his son [Siddhartha], ordered a pleasure-party to be prepared, worthy of his own affection and his son's beauty and youth. He prohibited the encounter of any afflicted common person in the highroad: "heaven forbid that the prince with his tender nature should even imagine himself to be distressed." Then having removed out of the way with the greatest gentleness all those who had mutilated limbs or maimed senses, the decrepit and the sick and all squalid beggars, they made the highway assume its perfect beauty. Along this road made beautiful, the fortunate prince with his well-trained attendants came down one day at a proper time from the roof of the palace and went to visit the king by his leave. Then the king, with tears rising in his eyes, having smelt his son's head and long gazed upon him, gave him his permission, saying, "Go"; but in his heart through affection he could not let him depart.
>
> Ashvaghosha, *Buddhascarita* (3:3–7)[2]

Four Sights of Suffering

Prince Siddhartha left his father's palace, accompanied by his chariot driver, and what Siddhartha saw would change his life forever and eventually sow the seed that would give rise to the religion called Buddhism. Siddhartha entered the road, on which scattered flowers and garlands had been laid. Then the deities created images of suffering for Siddhartha to encounter.

> But then the gods, dwelling in pure abodes, having beheld that city thus rejoicing like heaven itself, created an old man to walk along on purpose to stir the heart of the king's son. The prince having beheld him thus overcome with decrepitude and different in form from other men, with his gaze intently fixed on him, thus addressed his driver with simple confidence: "Who is this man that has come here, O charioteer, with white hair and his hand resting on a staff, his eyes hidden beneath his brows, his limbs bent down and

hanging loose,—is this a change produced in him or his natural state or an accident?"

Ashvaghosha, *Buddhascarita* (3:26–28)[3]

The driver explained that the sight was of old age—the "ravisher of beauty, the ruin of vigor, the cause of sorrow, the bane of memories." With great surprise, Siddhartha exclaimed, "What! will this evil come to me also?" The driver confirmed Siddhartha's fear—"Old age thus strikes down all alike."

Then the same deities created another man with his body all afflicted by disease; and on seeing him the son of Suddhodana addressed the charioteer, having his gaze fixed on the man: "Yonder man with a swollen body, his whole frame shaking as he pants, his arms and shoulders hanging loose, his body all pale and thin, uttering plaintively the word, 'mother,' when he embraces a stranger,—who, pray, is this?" Then the charioteer answered, "Gentle Sir, it is a very great affliction called sickness, that has grown up, caused by the inflammation of the (three) humors, which has made even this strong man no longer master of himself."

Ashvaghosha, *Buddhascarita* (3:40–42)[4]

The charioteer told Siddhartha, "O Prince, this evil is common to all," which deeply distressed Siddhartha's mind. The sights of suffering continued.

But as the king's son was thus going on his way, the very same deities created a dead man, and only the charioteer and the prince, and none else, beheld him as he was carried dead along the road.

Ashvaghosha, *Buddhascarita* (3:54)[5]

Noticing that Siddhartha was troubled by the sight of the dead man, the charioteer said, "This is the final end of all living creatures; be it a mean man, a man of middle state, or a noble, destruction is fixed to all in this world."[6] With that, Prince Siddhartha told his charioteer to turn back the chariot; this was no time or place for a pleasure trip—how can a rational being remain the same after seeing such sights of suffering? But the charioteer did not turn back the chariot, and as Siddhartha considered the troubling sights he had just encountered, a beggar (*sannyasi*) approached the chariot. Inquiring why the man begged, the ascetic answered the prince:

I, being terrified at birth and death, have become an ascetic for the sake of liberation. Desiring liberation in a world subject to destruction, I seek that happy indestructible abode,—isolated from mankind, with my thoughts unlike those of others, and with my sinful passions turned away

> from all objects of sense. Dwelling anywhere, at the root of a tree, or in an uninhabited house, a mountain or a forest,—I wanted without a family and without hope, a beggar ready for any fare, seeking only the highest good.
>
> Ashvaghosha, *Buddhascarita* (5:17–19)[7]

Prince Siddhartha, twenty-nine years old at the time, had seen four sights of suffering, (1) a very old man, (2) a sick person, (3) a corpse, and (4) an ascetic (*sannyasi*). When he returned to his father's palace, Siddhartha prostrated himself before his father and said, "Grant me graciously thy permission, O lord of men,—I wish to become a wandering mendicant [*sannyasi*] for the sake of liberation; since separation is appointed for me."[8] Within a few days, Siddhartha left his father's palace in search of answers to the origin and cure of suffering. He took on the life of a wandering ascetic, seeking liberation.

Prince Siddhartha Becomes Lord Buddha

After following different meditation gurus (teachers), such as Arada Kalama and Udraka Ramaputra, but not achieving the liberation he sought, Prince Siddhartha set out alone and eventually adopted an extreme ascetic practice combining severe fasting, long hours in seated meditation, and rigorous breath control, yet without success. Buddhist tradition says that in his sixth year of being a severe ascetic he sat under a fig tree near the northern Indian town of Gaya and overheard a musician teaching his student how to play the sitar, a traditional Indian stringed instrument. The teacher said that tightening the strings too tightly will snap them, while leaving them too loose will not produce the right sound. Tradition says that at that time Siddhartha was awakened to recognize the uselessness of practicing severe austerities. While sitting under the fig tree (some say it was a rose-apple tree), later called the *bodhi* tree (the tree of awakening), he determined to walk the Middle Path (**Majjhima Patipada**).[9]

At that point, Prince Siddhartha had direct experience of the reality of all things. He was awakened to "the unconditioned,"

Charles E. Farhadian

Figure 3.5. Statue of Buddha as an ascetic in northern Thailand

to the origin and elimination of suffering itself, and became known as "the Buddha" ("the Enlightened One")—fully awakened, experiencing **nirvana** (liberation), freed from any contaminants of the mind and no longer subject to suffering. Technically, to be enlightened is like awakening from a dream. Lord Buddha is "the awakened one" who knows reality. All other beings remain as in a sleep, until they are awakened—enlightened. The Middle Way represents the path of the spiritual life lived between the extremes of severe asceticism and hedonism, thus appealing to a wide variety of ordinary people.

LORD BUDDHA'S FIRST SERMON

After seven weeks of enjoying liberation near the *bodhi* tree, Lord Buddha went to Deer Park near **Varanasi** (Benaras), the sacred city on the banks of the Ganges River, and preached his first sermon, "The Sermon of the Turning of the Wheel" (of dharma), to his five former *sannyasi* companions, who became his first disciples. The dharma wheel (Pali, **dhamma**) refers to Lord Buddha's teaching of the way to enlightenment. In his first sermon, Lord Buddha expounded on the Middle Path.

Sacca/Wikimedia Commons

Figure 3.6. Buddha's Sermon of the Turning of the Wheel (Deer Park, Varanasi)

> There are these two extremes that are not to be indulged in by one who
> has gone forth. Which two? That which is devoted to sensual pleasure with
> reference to sensual objects: base, vulgar, common, ignoble, unprofitable;
> and that which is devoted to self-affliction: painful, ignoble, unprofitable.
> Avoiding both of these extremes, the middle way realized by the Tathagata—
> producing vision, producing knowledge—leads to calm, to direct knowledge,
> to self-awakening, to Unbinding.
>
> *Dhammacakkappavattana Sutta* (**56.11**)[10]

Lord Buddha also taught his followers the **Four Noble Truths**, the foundation of Buddhism, which are discussed below. His first disciples formed
the first Buddhist *sangha* (Pali and Sanskrit, "community," "assembly,"
"congregation"), the monastic order of ordained Buddhists. (Incidentally,
while Lord Buddha ordained both monks and nuns, in some predominately
Theravada countries today, such as Thailand and Sri Lanka, there are currently no ordained Buddhist nuns because of legal prohibitions.) Lord Buddha traveled and preached for forty-five years, encouraging his enlightened
disciples (arhats), and establishing his community, until he "died" at eighty
years old. Lord Buddha preached according to the capacity of his listeners,
which would give rise to a variety of interpretations of his words. To comfort
his cousin, the monk Ananda, who wept as he saw Lord Buddha weakening,
Lord Buddha exclaimed to his disciple not to be upset.

> Do not grieve, Ānanda, do not be depressed! You have served me well,
> with body, speech, and mind, in ways that were loving, unparalleled,
> immeasurable, helpful, and pleasing. All the completely enlightened Buddhas
> of the past also had attendants who served them, just as you have served
> me. So do not grieve, Ānanda, do not be depressed! For how could it be that
> something born, living, fashioned, karmically constituted, . . . dependently
> arisen, should not be subject to decay, to change, decline, destruction?
>
> *Mahāparinivanānasūtra*[11]

REACHING "FINAL NIRVANA"

Lord Buddha left this earthly life in Kushinagar. His body was cremated,
the remains divided into eight parts, preserved in the **stupas** (relic mounds)
that would become pilgrimage sites for Buddhist devotees. Lord Buddha's
leaving of this earthly life is called his "final nirvana" (***parinirvana***, "real
transformation"), since he had obtained complete awakening (*bodhi*, enlightenment). The veneration of relics thought to be from Lord Buddha or his early
disciples, housed in stupas, is a major part of Theravada worship. For instance, a tiny chip believed to be a relic from Lord Buddha is enshrined at Doi

Figure 3.7. Buddhist stupas in Tibet

Figure 3.8. Theravada monks circumambulating a stupa in northern Thailand

Figure 3.9. Doi Suthep Temple in Chiang Mai, Thailand

Suthep Temple in Chiang Mai, Thailand. Today in Chiang Mai, Buddhist pilgrims and tourists ascend the 290 steps to the temple and pray for blessings by lighting incense, offering flowers, prostrating themselves before Buddha images, and pressing squares of gold leaves onto an image of Lord Buddha. Such veneration of religious relics is common to many other faith traditions.

THE THREE BUDDHIST REFUGES

Following Lord Buddha's *parinirvana*, his disciples committed themselves to Three Refuges, also known as Three Jewels, which summarize the basic Buddhist orientation to life. The Trisarana (Sanskrit, "Threefold Refuge" or "Three Protections") means taking refuge in the Three Jewels (**Triratna**), the three most valuable commitments: Lord Buddha, the dharma, and the *sangha*, in that order. Taking refuge in these three is considered a single commitment—one unit: "*Buddham śaranam gacchāmi; adharmam saranam gacchāmi; sangham saranam gacchāmi*"—"I take refuge in the Buddha; I take refuge in the dharma; I take refuge in the *sangha*." The first refuge, "I take refuge in the Buddha," affirms that protection comes from the Enlightened One, who out of compassion taught the principles (Sanskrit, *dharma*; Pali, *dhamma*). Theravada Buddhism honors Lord Buddha as a real, historical person, who fought ignorance and delusion, becoming awakened to how the world really is.

The second refuge, "I take refuge in the dharma," affirms the truth to which Lord Buddha was awakened. The dharma literally means "what holds together" and is the basis of all order, whether social or moral. While dharma is a central concept in the Indian religious traditions, in Buddhism the term means cosmic order, the natural law, and, particularly,

Christians affirm the uniqueness of Jesus's birth. The biblical story records that Jesus Christ, the anointed one (Messiah), was born of a virgin (Matt. 1:23). How do the births and early lives of the historic Buddha and the historic Jesus compare? What seems similar and dissimilar? First, the families into which they were born were quite different. The historic Buddha, Siddhartha, was born in a wealthy setting and into a noble family of the Kshatriya class, whereas Jesus was born in a relatively humble setting of an animal stable and into a middle-class carpenter's family.

Siddhartha was initially protected from the suffering in the world, whereas Jesus walked among common people and religious leaders alike, such as fishermen, farmers, and Pharisees. Never claiming to be more than an ordinary person, Siddhartha became enlightened after struggling hard to understand the profound misery of the world and the human condition, eventually achieving enlightenment after an act of surrender. Siddhartha awoke to the truth of how the world really is, and his message was understood as universal truth, an insight that offered liberation for all sentient beings. Siddhartha invited people to follow principle truths. The truths of Buddhism were not revealed but rather were principles of which he became conscious. Lord Buddha never claimed to be anything other than a man—perhaps an extraordinary man, but just a man, not a supernatural being.

✗ Jesus, on the other hand, never claimed to find any truth but rather declared himself to be truth incarnated (John 14:6). His call is an invitation to follow him, which means to follow both a person and a principle for which he lived and died. Following the *parinirvana* of Lord Buddha, the community was to live according to truths articulated by the Buddha. The possibility of liberation lay in the hands of the individual practitioners. Prior to Jesus's death, he told his followers that he would send the Comforter (i.e., the Holy Spirit), who would guide them in the world. The early Christian community was not left alone but became animated by the Spirit of God, who gave them power to speak and act on his behalf in the world. Jesus Christ was the truth. Christians affirm that God's Spirit is in them, transforming their self-understanding and making possible deep communion between human beings and the Creator God.

the teachings of Lord Buddha.[12] Dharma refers to things, thoughts, anything that is happening, and the way things are thought to have happened, the pattern of the world, and the way of the universe.

Simply put, for Theravada Buddhists, dharma is the teaching of Lord Buddha. Lord Buddha taught his own version of how one should live in the world in order to be released from the bondage of **samsara**—existence itself. The third refuge, "I take refuge in the *sangha*," was revolutionary since the Buddhist community, the custodians of his teaching (dharma), accepted people from all castes and did not recognize the superiority of the Brahmins and the Vedas. This point alone distinguished the Buddhist and Jain communities as non-Hindu.

The Four Noble Truths

Lord Buddha made no claim for himself other than "I am awake," and that he was a teacher of the fact of suffering—its origin and remedy. Regarding the universality of suffering, the tradition notes that it is more difficult to comprehend the universality of suffering than to split a single hair into a

Christian Reflections

Roman Catholic theologian Hans Küng reflects on the similarities and differences between Siddhartha and Jesus. Küng proposes that Siddhartha and Jesus shared the following *ethical dimensions*: (1) both were wandering preachers; (2) both used a common vernacular (Pali/Aramaic), rather than an inaccessible sacred language (Sanskrit/Hebrew) to make their messages intelligible to ordinary people, using proverbs and parables from listeners' everyday world, rather than systematized, abstract discourse; (3) both said that greed, power, and delusion were the great temptations; (4) both started a new religious movement that reinterpreted earlier religious ideas (Hinduism/Judaism); (5) both, having gathered disciples around them, started missionary movements sending followers beyond the region of the religion's origin; (6) both delivered messages of urgency (dharma/gospel) that demanded changed perspectives (conversion); and (7) both advocated a "middle way," which proved to be an accessible practice, between the extremes of hedonism and asceticism.

Küng submits that differences between Siddhartha and Jesus include Jesus's turn toward the poor and burdened, calling them blessed. Jesus's ministry lasted about three years, until he was crucified on the cross. Siddhartha's ministry lasted for decades, until he died from a trivial cause (perhaps from poisonous mushrooms). The lack of emphasis on Lord Buddha's *parinirvana* points to the fact that Lord Buddha's "death" is of no significance in itself to Buddhists. It is striking to think that Siddhartha became the Enlightened One (the Buddha), whereas Jesus became the Suffering One. Siddhartha discovered the way to transcend suffering. Jesus entered suffering deeply, thus offering a path for humanity to make sense of suffering, becoming the Crucified One who was later glorified, raised into heaven.[a]

a. See Küng, *Christianity and World Religions*, 321–25.

hundred strands. Let us remember that Lord Buddha was deeply moved by the four sights of suffering he saw after he left his father's palace grounds. Seeing suffering compelled Prince Siddhartha to leave his father's compound to seek an answer to its origin and cure. When he became enlightened, Lord Buddha recognized the nature of all things, which he summarized in the Four Noble Truths, the mainstream Buddhist doctrines.

The First Noble Truth: Suffering Exists

The First Noble Truth, called **dukkha**, is about the nature of suffering. Life is full of suffering. But what is suffering? Lord Buddha's understanding of *dukkha* is broader than just physical or emotional pain, for it involves everything. I prefer to use the Sanskrit term "*dukkha*," because it is new to most readers and therefore can carry more of the exact Buddhist meaning of "suffering," rather than confusing a typically Western understanding of the word. Generally *dukkha* means unsatisfactoriness, frustration, unhappiness, transience, impermanence, pain, sorrow, and dis-ease.[13]

There are three modes of *dukkha*. (1) **Dukkha-dukkha** is obvious physical or mental pain, the kind we are all aware of. Any kind of physical pain is *dukkha-dukkha*. (2) **Virparinama-dukkha** ("pain of alteration" or "pain of change") is losing something that is valuable to you. We have all experienced loss, whether the keys to our car, our favorite toy (iPhone), or a loved one; we suffer because of loss. It is in part because of our suffering that we recognize that the happiness we experience is only momentary. (3) **Samkhara-dukkha** is the ignorance of thinking that cravings for anything (e.g., people, ideas, material items) can be fully satisfied. According to Lord Buddha, believing that we will be permanently happy *if* _____ (e.g., "I have a huge house," "I have a college degree," "I am married," "I have children") will leave us dissatisfied, suffering. Nothing can satisfy our cravings permanently—we will always be left feeling unsatisfactory. Happiness itself testifies to suffering since happiness is never permanent. "Hey, my girlfriend changed." "I wish my car hadn't gotten that scratch." "I thought I'd be happy if I got that job." Buddhism attempts to provide an answer to why human beings are never permanently satisfied.

The Three Marks of Existence

Buddhism teaches that the universality of *dukkha* is tied to three marks of existence itself, giving us a wider context to consider this fundamental concept. *Dukkha* is tied to the notion that everything is impermanent (Pali, **anicca**; Sanskrit, *anitya*) and that everything lacks an abiding, enduring, persistent self (Pali, **anatta**; Sanskrit, *anātman*), that there is no permanent

131

substance, no abiding self (negation of self).[14] The doctrine of *anicca* posits that everything is in flux, changing, without permanency, no matter how things appear to be. In order for one to be liberated, one must overcome the appearance of permanency; one has to see beyond the world of what appears.

The appearance of permanency is just an illusion (Sanskrit, **maya**) that makes the unreal appear real. There are some images that might help us envision this concept. "Swinging a torch around at a rapid rate creates an illusion of a circle of light hanging in the air."[15] Or think about watching a film. Movies consist of individual still images that rapidly move from one image to the other (at a rate of usually more than twenty-four frames per second). Seeing these images in quick succession gives the appearance of continuous action. But if we could stop the film, we would notice that the film itself is made up of many individual images. Stopping the film allows us to investigate each image more thoroughly.

Buddhist Detachment

The goal of Buddhist perception is to penetrate beyond the realm of illusion. *Anatta* means there is no abiding self or soul that permanently transmigrates through samsara, the cycle of death and rebirth. The experience of unsatisfactoriness and dis-ease are indications that the "self" has attempted to attach itself to something permanently. Here it is in a nutshell: since there is no abiding self and nothing is permanent, *dukkha* (of all kinds) will result whenever one tries to attach the self to something in order to be happy and satisfied. There are two reasons why the attempt to attach oneself will always result in unhappiness. First, there is no abiding self that can permanently attach to anything. Second, there is nothing permanent to be attached to! Everything is changing. All is in flux. Nothing remains the same. Buddhist psychology teaches that we are deceived if we believe that something will satisfy us permanently. Incidentally, the denial of an abiding self is another Buddhist feature that distinguishes Buddhism from the Brahmanical philosophy of the permanent atman.

What Gets Transmigrated?

Lord Buddha adopted the key Hindu concepts of samsara (reincarnation), **atman** (permanent self), **karma** (action), and liberation (Pali, *nibbana*; Sanskrit, *nirvana*), having been awakened to the true nature of these concepts. What then transmigrates, traveling through samsara, if there is "no self" (*anātman*)? You will recall that in Hinduism, the permanent self (atman) transmigrates through samsara, existence, but not so in Buddhism. According to Buddhism, there are **Five Aggregates** (Sanskrit, *skandhas*; Pali, *khandha*) composed of bodily and physical states, divided into (1) body

Time and perception are conceived of differently by Lord Buddha and Jesus. For Lord Buddha, who inherited the conceptual constellation of cyclical history, karma, dharma, and samsara, the automatic law of samsara was a major motivating factor to do good (karma) in order to better one's next life. Jesus is eternal, hence outside and above "linear" time; "before Abraham was, I am" (John 8:58). Yet Christians affirm that God breaks into real time and space in Jesus Christ, who proclaims that he himself is the way, the truth, the life, announcing that the beginning of the end of time has come. For Jesus, then, the world and time itself were not futile and empty but rather something created good, yet fallen and spoiled by human beings. Consequently, for Christians the real world of time and space is the arena for the struggle of the religious life. For the Buddhist, the mind and psychological processes become the essential battleground and therefore the focus of intense concentration in an effort to rid oneself of impure karma in order to achieve enlightenment.

(*rupa*), (2) feelings (*vedana*), (3) perceptions (*sanna*), (4) predispositions from past impressions (*samskara*), and (5) consciousness (*vijnana*).

These Five Aggregates (*skandhas*) constitute an individual person but do not constitute a soul or self, since the *skandhas* have no essence of themselves.[16] These are the particular ways that human beings tend to be attached to the world. Likewise, there are the elements that need to be overcome if one is going to be liberated. According to Richard King, "Buddhists have generally accepted that there is causal *continuity* throughout our physical and mental lives but deny that this means that there is an underlying *identity* holding the process together. . . . There are no unchanging substrata, only a stream of causally connected qualities (*dharma*)."[17] That is, what appears to constitute a human being is merely causally related, but nonetheless there is no permanent self. The fundamental Buddhist perception is that there is no subsistent reality underlying appearances, but the *skandhas* flow together and give us the impression of identity and persistence through time.[18]

Blowing Out the Flame

If this is hard to imagine, you can think of *skandhas* as resembling the sparklers that are so popular during Fourth of July ceremonies in the United States. You light the end of the sparkler, then watch as the sparkles travel down the shaft until they end, and everyone sighs as the light goes out. Similarly, the *skandhas* are like the light that sparkles along the shaft of the sparkler. Let us say that each burst of sparkle consists of five elements. At

Figure 3.10. The role of a Buddha: to enlighten the path for other people to follow, so they too can cross the stream of samsara and reach nirvana. Wallpainting in a Laotian monastery.

each moment, there are numerous bursts of light, as though at every particular moment each of the five elements recombine to create another unique splash of light. As the light moves down the shaft of the sparkler, it gives us the appearance of continuity. Yet the light has been remade each time through a recombination of the five elements. At the end of the sparkler, the light is extinguished. Likewise, the Buddhist goal is to "blow out the light."

Ultimately, the use of terms that express individual selves (e.g., "I," "he," "she") is necessary; Lord Buddha distinguished between conventional language that employed pronouns and the philosophical (ultimate) language that denied the self as a permanent, independent entity. Remember that nothing is fixed or substantial in the *skandhas*—there is no "it" that can be named, but only a flow, a process, a being-ness. One way to imagine this is to think about streams that flow as a river. The streams

---

SIDEBAR 3.2

The Four Noble Truths

First Noble Truth *Dukkha* = Suffering	Life is filled with all kinds of suffering, transience, unsatisfactoriness, dis-ease.
Second Noble Truth *Dukkha samudaya* = Suffering's origins	Suffering is caused when we desire (*tanha*) and crave, because the origin of suffering is attachment.
Third Noble Truth *Dukkha nirodha* = Suffering's cessation	Suffering can end if we stop thirsting for things. The end of suffering is attainable.
Fourth Noble Truth *Dukkha nirodha gamini patipada magga* = The path leading to the cessation of suffering	There is a path to the cessation of suffering. This is the way to stop craving things; it is known as the Eightfold Path: (1) do not say anything to hurt others (Right Speech); (2) respect life, morality, and property (Right Action); (3) work at a job that does not injure anything (Right Livelihood); (4) try to free your mind from evil (Right Effort); (5) be in control of your thoughts and feelings (Right Mindfulness); (6) practice proper concentration (Right Concentration); (7) try to resist evil (Right Thought); (8) know the truth (Right Understanding).

flow as a "river," but the river itself cannot be captured as a simple solid thing since it is always moving and changing. What appears to be constant is actually always in flux.

THE SECOND NOBLE TRUTH: THE ARISING OF SUFFERING

The Second Noble Truth, called *dukkha samudaya* (Sanskrit, "rising of suffering") concerns the origin and cause of *dukkha*. How does *dukkha* arise? Lord Buddha taught that *dukkha* comes from craving, which in turn comes from ignorance (Sanskrit, *avidyā*) of the nonself. We are ignorant of reality (e.g., impermanence) and so we suffer. The term that Buddhists use to describe craving is "*tanha*" (Pali, *taṇhā*; Sanskrit, *tṛṣṇā*, "desire," "craving," "thirst"), which means thirsting after the objects of the senses and the mind. *Tanha* is the root cause of all suffering (*dukkha*). Craving sets off a chain reaction that always leads to dissatisfaction. I may work hard to get things (e.g., camera, house, friendship), thinking that those things will satisfy. But in the end those things change, and I am left feeling quite unsatisfied.

In fact, nirvana (Sanskrit, "extinction," "liberation") is synonymous with the extinction of all craving. Why? According to Lord Buddha, when we crave permanence—thirst for that which passes away (as all things do)—the satisfaction that comes in things that necessarily pass away is transient. What is known as the "chain of dependent origination" (Pali, *paticca samuppāda*) is universally accepted within Buddhism. After Lord Buddha gained enlightenment, he saw that the process of "becoming" (i.e., birth, youth, old age, death) consisted of links, each conditioned on the previous link, giving rise to *dukkha*.[19] This chain of dependent origination (i.e., existence) needs to be broken. Otherwise one will continue to be bound to samsara—existence itself. Suffering arises because of ignorance and craving. Since karma is a part of consciousness (one acts consciously), one needs to stop craving attachments; one needs to stop the process of "becoming."

THE THIRD NOBLE TRUTH: DESTRUCTION OF SUFFERING

The Third Noble Truth, *dukkha nirodha* (destruction of suffering) concerns the cessation of suffering. Although *dukkha* arises because of a thirst for attachment and existence itself, *dukkha* can nevertheless be brought to cessation by eradicating *tanha* (thirst, craving). The goal, then, is not to desire, not to crave, by "blowing out" the flame of craving and finally of the personality itself—which leads to freedom from samsara and entrance into nirvana. Nirvana (Sanskrit, "extinction"; Pali, *nibbana*) means "blowing out," "cooling," and "perfection," which etymologically comes from the verb root *vā* = "blow out" + *nir* = "out." According to Theravada Buddhism, nirvana is the eradication of the cravings that cause rebirth, overcoming the wheel of death and rebirth (samsara), and the final exit from the world of becoming.[20]

In classical Buddhist theory, there are two moments of nirvana: nirvana with residues (i.e., the moment of awakening) and nirvana without residues (i.e., the moment of death: *parinirvana*). At the first moment, one realizes that one is no longer feeling the fire of existence, allowing one to continue in the world and at the same time to be completely detached from it. Here one lives the life of a serene, peaceful, free, and perhaps even compassionate Buddha. At the second moment, the lingering traces of one's previous actions completely burn out, and the transmigration of *skandhas* completely stops. The second moment (*parinirvana*) is a radical cessation of the energies of existence. No more craving, no more becoming, no more birth; only nirvana.

THE FOURTH NOBLE TRUTH: THE PATH TO THE CESSATION OF SUFFERING

The Fourth Noble Truth, ***dukkha nirodha gamini patipada magga*** (Sanskrit, "the path to the cessation of suffering"), lays out the specific way to extinguish suffering (*dukkha*). Put simply, the *magga* (means) of destroying suffering, unsatisfactoriness, and misery is the destruction of desire. Lord Buddha not only taught about the origins of *dukkha* and the possibility of stopping suffering, but he concluded his teaching with the path to enlightenment, called the **Noble Eightfold Path** (Sanskrit, *arya astanga-marga*; Pali, *atthangika-magga*), which embodies the way that leads to the ending of sorrow, unhappiness, and unsatisfactoriness—*dukkha*. The path (*marga*), as a practical guide to end *dukkha*, is divided into eight elements within three categories.

The overall goal of the Eightfold Path is to become at once sensitized and calm. One cannot even start with the basic morality (*sila*) of the Eightfold Path of Buddhism unless one has a certain understanding that this life is not what it should be and a certain notion that Buddhism might be a good help.

SIDEBAR 3.3

The Path

1. ***Sila*** (Sanskrit and Pali, "conduct," "good behavior," "morality"), which reflects ethical conduct: (1) right speech, (2) right action, (3) right livelihood.
2. ***Samadhi*** (Sanskrit and Pali, "one-pointedness," "concentration," "unifying concentration"), which is delineated as (4) right effort, (5) right mindfulness, (6) right concentration.
3. ***Prajna*** (Pali, *panna*, "wisdom," "intuitive wisdom," "knowledge of nonself"), which entails (7) right thoughts, (8) right understanding.

So there is a circular relationship, with one first recognizing that something in the world is wrong. And each step along the Eightfold Path helps the other—for example, if you do not drink alcohol, you can concentrate better; if the mind is calm from better concentration, the sensations are felt more clearly in the body; if the sensations are clear, the law of impermanence and impersonality of all physical and mental phenomena becomes evident.

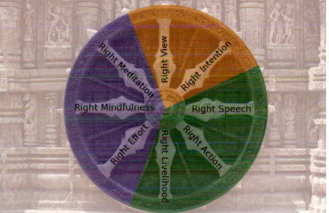

Figure 3.11. *Dharmachakra* ("wheel of dharma"): a symbol of the Buddha's teaching of the path of enlightenment

Krisse/Wikimedia Commons

Early Buddhism

Not much is known about the details of the early history of the Buddhist community because no written records exist. Yet the religion of Buddhism kept spreading to every social class, to men and women. Soon each group of followers developed its own version of what Lord Buddha taught. The earliest disciples of Lord Buddha traveled widely to advance the Buddhist mission by teaching Buddha dharma and being engaged in charitable works. During the rainy season, usually for roughly three months, July to October, the Buddhist monks remained in a single location, such as a temple. Known as the "rain retreat" (Pali, *vasso*, "rain"), the disciples' time there enabled them to engage in meditation and be spiritually reinvigorated.

The ideal situation was that of full-time practitioner—that is, the wandering ascetic—but the Indian monsoon rains forced devotees to stay in a dry place, where they would gather with fellow believers. Gradually, they decided that wandering was not necessary all the time, so they kept up the rain retreat places permanently, some of which became monasteries. Once monasteries were established, monks (Pali, *bhikku*) and nuns (Pali, *bhikkhuni*) established sects, rules, and codes of behaviors. Subsequently, Buddhist monks and nuns of the *sangha* received land and buildings.

Lord Buddha's first disciples were organized into the Buddhist monastic order, probably modeled on the Jain communities. Lord Buddha developed a complex code of rules, called the **Vinaya** (Sanskrit, "discipline," "that which separates"), by which members of the *sangha* lived their lives. He also explained his teachings in a series of talks to his disciples. These talks are collectively referred to as the **Sutras** (Pali, *Sutta*; Sanskrit, "thread"),

The seriousness with which Buddhism recognizes and addresses *suffering* makes it an eminently appealing tradition for many. Everyone suffers. What is striking about Buddhism is the acute attention the tradition pays to analyzing and providing a cure for the universality of suffering. The all-encompassing nature of the Buddhist notion of suffering might be compared to the all-encompassing nature of the Roman Catholic and Protestant notion of the fall, whereby everything (e.g., human beings, natural environment) fell from its original state of perfection and now needs redemption. Is the Buddhist notion of impermanency similar to themes within Christianity? According to Buddhism, everything is transitory; nothing is permanent. Even the Four Noble Truths of Buddhism are only provisional, since they too are dependent on other forces. What aspects of the Buddhist theology of suffering can Christians affirm? Christianity also makes claims about what is permanent and impermanent. Both the Old and the New Testaments tell of the fleeting nature of things, yet affirm the imperishability of the Word of God:

> A voice says, "Cry out!"
>   And I said, "What shall I cry?"
> All people are grass,
>   their constancy is like the flower of the field.
> The grass withers, the flower fades,
>   when the breath of the Lord blows upon it;
> Surely the people are grass. (Isa. 40:6–7)

The New Testament use of this Isaiah passage begins with the following statement: "You have been born anew, not of perishable but of imperishable seed, through the living and enduring word of God" (1 Pet. 1:23).

While both Lord Buddha and Jesus taught that the world is transient and temporary, Jesus's teaching affirmed permanency in the midst of change. From a Christian perspective, there is a firm foundation of life—that is, the Word of God. Although the world will pass away and is, we can say, transitory in nature,

aphorisms that, since they are so cryptic and brief, are open to conflicting interpretations. The Vinaya and the Sutras, along with a third group of texts, the **Abhidharma** (Pali, *Abhidhamma*; Sanskrit, "philosophic discussion" or "philosophical texts"), make up the sacred scripture of early Buddhism, known collectively as the Pali Canon or Tipitaka (Sanskrit, **Tripitaka**), which are considered canonical texts by Theravada Buddhists.

empirical reality (matter, nature, world) is not an illusion. The writers of the New Testament and the early church fathers contended against the worldview of gnosticism, which raised spirit over matter, making Jesus himself like a mere appearance of light (see *Gospel of Thomas*) rather than the fleshly incarnation of the living God in time and space, bound to the same physical, linguistic, and cultural limitations under which human beings exist in their particularities. Buddhism and Christianity are both "earthly" religions in that they present a realistic view of the profound suffering (uneasiness, disquietude) of the world. Yet Christianity claims that underneath and beyond the material world, God exists and loves the world. And in some ways, Christians and Buddhists recognize that the followers of their traditions continue to live in the world of suffering.

Lord Buddha himself, for example, did not immediately enter nirvana but taught his disciples. Likewise, the disciples of Christ suffered horribly after the death and resurrection of Jesus. Jesus promised the same to all his followers. Paul's address to the Romans entails an immediately palpable sense of suffering in the world combined with assurance that we are not alone.

> Who will separate us from the love of Christ? Will hardship, or distress, or persecution, or famine, or nakedness, or peril, or sword? As it is written: "For your sake we are being killed all day long; we are accounted as sheep to be slaughtered." No, in all these things we are more than conquerors through him who loved us. For I am convinced that neither death nor life, nor angels, nor rulers, nor things present, nor things to come, nor power, nor height, nor depth, nor anything else in all creation, will be able to separate us from the love of God that is in Christ Jesus our Lord. (Rom. 8:35–39)

What is striking about this biblical passage is not only the all-encompassing nature of God's love, which cannot be separated from us by death, principalities, supernatural powers, or highest distances, but that Christians are victors in the midst of suffering.

The Tipitaka contains the 547 Jataka Tales about the previous lives of Lord Buddha. *Pitaka* means "baskets," so the "three-baskets" (Tipitaka) of the Pali Canon consist of the Vinaya Pitaka, the Sutra Pitaka, and the Abhidharma Pitaka. The core of the Sutras and the Vinaya comes from the time of Lord Buddha, with later additions representing attempts to clarify certain passages and to explain the implications of the early scriptures. The texts were

Figure 3.12. Buddhist novices walking in Thailand

memorized and passed down to students orally. The Tipitaka was written down beginning in the third century BCE, with the oldest copies written in Pali, the language of the common people.

BUDDHIST COUNCILS

After Lord Buddha left his earthly existence, several Buddhist councils gathered to discuss the meaning and mission of Lord Buddha and his followers. These meetings, much like the early Christian ecumenical church councils, sought to formalize the tradition. The First Buddhist Council (c. 400 BCE), consisting of five hundred Buddhist monks, met at Rajagriha (Bihar state, India) soon after the *parinirvana* of Lord Buddha in order to stabilize the Buddhist scriptures by agreeing which sayings (i.e., sutras) were spoken by Lord Buddha. The council also sought to begin the collection and preservation of the Sutras and the Vinaya (monastic rules). Tradition says that Lord Buddha's close disciple Ananda recited the Sutras, while Upali, another of Buddha's early disciples, recited the Vinaya. Although there was agreement on the basic message of Lord Buddha, there was none on particular details.

He, truly is supreme in battle,
Who would conquer himself alone,

Rather than he who would conquer in battle
A thousand, thousand men.

Dhammapada 8:103[21]

The Second Buddhist Council was held at Vaisali in northwest Bihar state about a century after the first council (c. 350 BCE) to discuss the Vinaya, since the monks of Vaisali had a more flexible interpretation of the monastic rules. During this council meeting the assembled monks were split on the interpretation of the Vinaya Pitaka, with some advocating a more relaxed, open interpretation while others advocated a stricter interpretation. The more conservative group was referred to as the followers of the "Way of the Elders" (i.e., **Sthaviravadins** or Sthaviras), while the more liberal interpreters were the "great order of monks" (i.e., **Mahasanghikas**). A majority of the monks voted against the Vaisali rules and thus were more conservative in their interpretation of the Vinaya Pitaka, leaving the minority of defeated monks to form the Mahasanghika (Sanskrit, *Mahāsanghika*, "great order of monks").

The second Buddhist council sowed the seeds for the major division within Buddhism—that is, between Theravada (i.e., Sthaviravadins; "way of the elders") and Mahayana (greater vehicle). Furthermore, the Mahasanghikas believed in multiple Buddhas that were accessible at any given moment, the historical Buddha being only one of a plurality of Buddhas. Mahasanghika Buddhists affirmed the three bodies (*trikaya*) of Lord Buddha: his human body, his eternal teaching, and his transcendent body.[22] Another major disagreement between the Sthaviravadins and the Mahasanghikas was whether an arhat (Sanskrit, "worthy one," "enlightened one," "holy one"; Pali, *arahant*) could still be subject to human uncertainties and frailties, which the Mahasanghikas affirmed and the Sthaviravadins rejected. The two groups failed to resolve their conflict, so they went their separate ways, eventually becoming the Theravada and the Mahayana traditions.

The Third Buddhist Council was convened by Emperor Asoka, who would eventually be

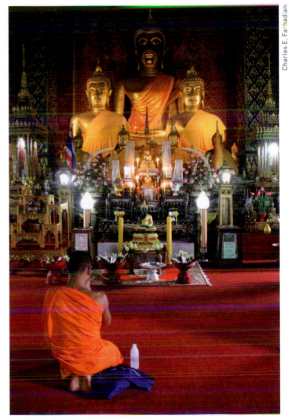

Charles E. Farhadian

Figure 3.13. Buddhist monk worshiping Buddha

a major proponent of Buddhism throughout the Indian subcontinent. The council was held at Pataliputra (c. 300 BCE) and resulted in the great schism between the "Way of the Elders" (Sthaviravadins) and the "Great Assembly" (Mahasanghikas). The "Elders" fought for the doctrinal purity of Lord Buddha's teachings and the centrality of monasticism, while the Mahasanghikas sought doctrinal innovation, were open to accepting indigenous religious beliefs and practices into the tradition, and allowed a greater role for the laity.

A Split in the Buddhist Community

The Mahasanghikas also emphasized Lord Buddha's supernatural qualities, while the Sthaviravadins denied these since in their view Lord Buddha was an extraordinary person, his nature essentially human. The Mahasanghikas emphasized the doctrine of "*lokottara*" (Sanskrit; Pali, *lokuttara*), an Indian religious term that refers generally to the transcendental and supramundane. Within Buddhism particularly, *lokottara* applies to Lord Buddha as a transcendent being of limitless power and wisdom. His supramundane nature expresses the possibility of moving beyond the craving (*tanha*) for attachment toward nirvana. The debate about the essential nature of Lord Buddha would contribute to the great schism between the two early divisions within the Buddhist community.

The same debate, over the essential nature of the founder of the religious tradition, is repeated in all religious traditions founded by a human being and often leads to major divisions within the religious community. Along with the schism that occurred, another significant legacy of the Third Council meeting was Emperor Asoka's dispatch of Buddhist missionaries to nine countries, including Sri Lanka, where Theravada Buddhism was firmly established.[23] Subsequent Buddhist councils did not have the same impact on the overall tradition as that of the earlier meetings. Therefore, from the fourth century BCE onward, different interpretations of the teachings of Lord Buddha led to different schools, and especially to the major differences between Theravada and Mahayana, with the latter's innumerable styles and divisions that reflect its eclectic assimilation of other religious practices and beliefs.

Emperor Asoka

During the reign of Emperor Asoka (c. 268–239 BCE), Buddhism spread widely throughout much of the Indian subcontinent. Emperor Asoka ruled over most of the region of modern India, excluding the furthest southern part of the subcontinent. In 258 BCE Asoka celebrated a major festival of Buddhism in his vast capital of Pataliputra, the largest city in the world at the time. Asoka had been converted, at least nominally, to Buddhism by 260

Wikimedia Commons

Figure 3.14. King Asoka rock inscription. The inscription records Asoka's sixth edict (c. 238 BCE).

BCE and had adopted its social ethics, particularly the Buddhist notion that leaders were to preserve social harmony. Emperor Asoka was concerned about the moral development of his subjects and sent out dharma officials to promote Buddhist virtues. He ordered them to "look after old people and orphans, and ensure equal judicial standards throughout the empire . . . he abolished torture and, perhaps, the death penalty. . . . Released prisoners were given some short-term financial help, and encouraged to generate karmic fruitfulness for their future lives."[24]

Instead of hunting trips, Asoka encouraged pilgrimages to Buddhist sites. Although the emperor gave Buddhism a central place in his kingdom, he also supported other religious devotees, such as Hindus and Jains. Tradition notes that Asoka established ten stupas (relic monuments holding an object of Buddhist devotion), which attracted Buddhist pilgrims and popularized the devotional cult. One way that Asoka encouraged people to learn Buddhist virtues was through the numerous rock inscriptions he had made throughout his kingdom, and which covered a wide variety of civic and

SIDEBAR 3.4

The Purpose of Construction

Along roads I have had banyan trees planted so that they can give shade to animals and men, and I have had mango groves planted. At intervals of eight //krosas// [a measurement], I have had wells dug, rest-houses built, and in various places, I have had watering-places made for the use of animals and men. But these are but minor achievements. Such things to make the people happy have been done by former kings. I have done these things for this purpose, that the people might practice the Dhamma.

http://www.cs.colostate.edu/~malaiya/ashoka.html#PREFACE

SIDEBAR 3.5

Dharma Blessings

Now due to Beloved-of-the-God, King Piyadasi's [a title of King Asoka] Dhamma practice, the sound of the drum has been replaced by the sound of the Dhamma. The sighting of heavenly cars, auspicious elephants, bodies of fire and other divine sightings has not happened for many hundreds of years. But now because of Beloved-of-the-Gods, King Piyadasi promotes restraint in the killing and harming of living beings, proper beings, proper behavior towards relatives, Brahmans and ascetics, and respect for mother, father and elders, such sightings have increased.

http://www.cs.colostate.edu/~malaiya/ashoka.html#PREFACE

SIDEBAR 3.6

Dharma in the Kitchen

Formerly, in the kitchen of Beloved-of-the-Gods, King Piyadasi [a title of King Asoka], hundreds of thousands of animals were killed every day to make curry. But now with the writing of this Dhamma edict only three creatures, two peacocks and a deer, are killed, and the deer not always. And in time, not even these three creatures will be killed.

http://www.cs.colostate.edu/~malaiya/ashoka.html#PREFACE

religious topics. Asoka's edicts were written not in Sanskrit but rather in the vernacular language, Prakrit.

Asoka sent out Buddhist missionaries, preferring "conquest by dharma" rather than by military force. The most famous Buddhist missionary sent by Asoka was his own son in the mid-third century BCE, the arhat monk Mahinda, to Sri Lanka, where he was well received, planting a form of Buddhism that would become Theravada. Asoka became a model of a just ruler for Buddhists. Under his authority, Buddhism flourished, and with it the development of stupas and new ritual acts.

Buddhism's Decline in South Asia

The reason for Buddhism's decline, and indeed virtual disappearance, remains an academic dispute, with arguments ranging from the deliberate Hindu assimilation of some of Lord Buddha's ideas, along with clarification and defense of the ritual practices Lord Buddha attacked, to the Muslim conquest and its general aggression against non-Muslim religious traditions. The Hindu assimilation of Buddhism is exemplified in the fact that Hindus claimed that Lord Buddha was an avatar of the great Hindu God Vishnu beginning in the seventh century CE. And the Muslim threat is exemplified in the tenth century, when Mahmud of Ghazni defeated the Hindu Shahis of eastern Afghanistan and northern Pakistan, ending Hindu and Buddhist influence across central Asia, in part by destroying Hindu and Buddhist statues and stupas.

Simply put, the decline of Buddhism in the Indian subcontinent was due in part to a combination of the inability of Buddhist regions to withstand invasion— for instance, by the central Asian nomadic White Huns (fifth to eighth centuries)—and the outright destruction of Buddhist monasteries and stupas by Muslim forces. By the tenth century, Buddhism had declined substantially. According to one scholar, the combination of Buddhist pacifism and its identifiable *sangha* contributed significantly to the demise of Indian Buddhism in the face of the Muslim advance.

By the nineteenth century, the religion was nearly extinct in India. Long before its decline, Buddhism had begun to expand in different geographical directions, in part due to Emperor Asoka's launching of Buddhist missionaries and embassies, eventually establishing Buddhism north into Tibet; east into China, Korea, and Japan; and southeast into Sri Lanka, Myanmar, and Thailand, where vastly different visions of Buddhism would burgeon.

> *The Muslim invasions were the worst blow, however, for Buddhism had few royal defenders, and, unlike Hinduism with its Kshatriya warrior class, it lacked a soldierly spirit. The Sangha, whose survival is essential for the flourishing of Buddhism, was an easily identifiable and thus vulnerable institution.*
>
> Harvey, *Introduction to Buddhism*, 196

Worship and Practice

The two major branches of Buddhism, called Theravada and Mahayana, present different emphases on the nature of liberation. Historically, Tibetan Buddhism is an outgrowth of Mahayana and so affirms many of the insights of the Mahayana traditions. How one is liberated is a complicated matter that each major branch of Buddhism helps illuminate. Is one entirely self-reliant on one's spiritual and religious journey? Or does one rely on an "other" for help? Is it entirely egotistical to rely on one's own efforts for liberation? Or is it irresponsible to rely on a semidivine being who claims to have crossed the sea of suffering and is therefore able to free individuals today from their human conditions of distress? The fundamental distinction between self-reliance and reliance on an "other" separates the Theravada, Mahayana, and Tibetan forms of Buddhist practice and belief.

What is important to note is that Buddhism involves being awakened to the way the world really is. Buddhist worship, then, ought to be seen not simply as a separate act but rather as the countless ways in which a Buddhist practitioner strives to see, think, and feel differently throughout life's journey. That said, it is also true that there are several different types of Buddhist worship that do in fact function as distinct sets of practices geared toward the goal of enlightenment. Buddhist worship is often more about showing respect to the insights and virtues of Lord Buddha and Buddhism than it is about worshiping a divine being. The Theravada tradition emphasizes self-reliance in the religious path, while Mahayana and Tibetan forms encourage practitioners to rely on quasi-savior Buddhas for their liberation. Worship is a fundamental part of these religious paths.

Theravada Buddhism

Theravada is viewed as a single major lineage dating back to Lord Buddha himself.[25] They hold to the oldest collection of Buddhist scripture, the Pali Canon (Tipitaka), claiming they have preserved the precise words of Lord Buddha and that the followers of Mahayana have made unwarranted additions to the words of Lord Buddha. Theravada is the oldest surviving form of Buddhism. Early Buddhism is divided into eighteen lineages on the basis of scholarly disputes about the nature of all three of the Three Jewels (Trisarana), but none except for Theravada can be identified in later Buddhism. We know, for instance, that since the third century BCE Sri Lanka

Charles E. Farhadian

Figure 3.15. Wat Chai Watana Ram, a Buddhist temple in Ayuthaya, Thailand

has followed the tradition that would become Theravada. The *Dhammapada*, from the Tipitaka, records the essential goal of Buddhist life:

> Not to do any evil,
> To cultivate good,
> To purify one's mind,
> This is the teaching of the Buddhas.

BUDDHIST VIRTUES

On a practical level, Buddhists follow particular principles that aid their worship and journey toward enlightenment, and which function as a moral code for human interaction. All Buddhists, whether monks, nuns, or lay-persons, cultivate five Buddhist virtues (Pali, *sīla*), known as the Five Virtues (Pali, *pañca-sīlāni*), which are in the form of the following abstentions:

1. Harming living beings (e.g., no killing)
2. Taking what is not given (e.g., no stealing)
3. Misconduct concerning sense-pleasures (e.g., no sexual misconduct)
4. False speech (telling lies)
5. Unmindful states due to alcoholic drinks or drugs (e.g., no intoxicating drinks and drugs that would cause negligence)

In Buddhist societies, these five virtues are expected of its citizens and are not to be considered a heavy burden, but rather are internalized as a way to achieve control and purity of mind. In addition to these five precepts, five additional precepts (restraints) are added for monks and nuns, and for more-devoted laypersons who follow the precepts as a guide on their spiritual journeys, such as during Buddhist festivals (e.g., birth of Lord Buddha and his *parinirvana*):

6. Taking untimely meals (i.e., no eating after noon)
7. Singing, dancing, playing music, or attending entertainment programs (i.e., no participating in performances)
8. Wearing perfume, cosmetics, and garlands (i.e., no decorative accessories)
9. Sitting on high chairs and sleeping on luxurious, soft beds (e.g., no thick mattresses or soft pillows)
10. Accepting money (i.e., no touching gold or silver or any other kind of money)

Novice monks and nuns are required to follow all ten training rules. Beyond these universally accepted Buddhist precepts, several features of Theravada distinguish it from the larger Buddhist branch, Mahayana.

First, the Theravada school adheres to the Tipitaka, which is the monastic code (Vinaya Pitaka), the word of Lord Buddha (Sutra Pitaka), and the philosophical analyses and discussions of the prior pitakas (Abhidharma Pitaka). Monastic disciplines, which are a subset of the larger Vinaya, are referred to as the *patimokkha* (Pali; Sanskrit, *prātimokṣa*), consisting of 227 rules of restraint for *bhikkhus* (monks) and 311 for *bhikkhunis* (nuns), divided into eight major categories. Here are some examples, not in any particular order:

- No accepting or eating food from an unrelated *bhikkhuni*.
- No accepting or eating food from a family living in a dangerous location, unless the monk is sick.
- No keeping an extra robe for more than ten days after receiving a new one.
- No owning a blanket or rug made of silk.
- No making or accepting a sitting rug without incorporating at least one old piece of felt twenty-five centimeters square, for the sake of discoloring it.
- No lying about one's mental state, such as falsely claiming to be an arhat (enlightened).
- No lustful bodily contact with a woman, including kissing or holding hands.
- No criticizing the justice of one's own banishment, even after having been rebuked three times.
- No making unfounded charges about another *bhikkhu* in the hopes of having him disrobed.
- No buying or selling goods.

The Vinaya, "that by which one is led out [from suffering]," consists of training rules and regulations for the communal life of *bhikkhus*. The rules are seen less as prohibitions than as encouraging spiritual training in order to be "ever mindful." Breaking these codes of conduct incurs karmic repercussions and thus can have both immediate and future implications. The Sutra Pitaka contains more than ten thousand sutras (discourses) conveyed by Lord Buddha and his early disciples, with some additional verses by others in the *sangha*. Theravada Buddhists study the Sutra Pitaka, which is divided into five major collections (*nikayas*).

Here are some excerpts from the Sutra verses.

This was said by the Blessed One [Lord Buddha], said by the Arahant [arhat], so I have heard: "Abandon one quality, monks, and I guarantee you non-return. Which one quality? Abandon greed as the one quality, and I guarantee you non-return." This is the meaning of what the Blessed One said. So with regard to this it was said:

> The greed with which
> beings go to a bad destination,
> coveting:
> from rightly discerning that greed,
> those who see clearly
> let go.
> Letting go,
> they never come to this world
> again.

Itivuttaka 1.1.1[26]

This was said by the Blessed One [Lord Buddha], said by the Arahant, so I have heard: "Monks, one who had not fully known and fully understood the All, whose mind has not been cleansed of passion for it, had not abandoned it, is incapable of putting an end to stress. But one who has fully known and fully understood the All, whose mind has been cleansed of passion for it, has abandoned it, is capable of putting an end to stress."

> Knowing the All
> from all around,
> not stirred by passion
> for anything at all:
> he, having comprehended
> the All,
> has gone beyond
> all stress.

Itivuttaka 7.1.7

The third part of the Tipitaka is the Abhidharma Pitaka, the philosophical discussions of the Sutra and the Vinaya, which is divided into seven sections (books). The Abhidharma presents a systematic analysis of all phenomena, including human experiences, personality types, psychological processes, the mind, material phenomena, the five *skandhas* (aggregates), and causal conditioning (how all things are dependent). Theravada communities give the Abhidharma different statuses within their communities, with some, such as Sri Lankan and Burmese Buddhists, placing it on the same level as the Vinaya and the Sutras, while others, such as Thai Buddhists, considering it of secondary importance.

MONASTIC LIFE

A second distinguishing feature of Theravada is the central place of monastic life. The vast majority of Theravada adherents believe that liberation is only possible for those who have been ordained as monks (*bhikkhus*), even in those regions that deny the possibility of ordaining Buddhist nuns. Generally there are two broad kinds of Theravada monks: the urban-based monks and the forest-dwelling ones. Urban-based monks emphasize studying the Tipitaka and often study at universities, particularly Buddhist institutions if such universities are present. Buddhist universities and monasteries contribute significantly to the social uplift of communities by providing subsidized education and residences for the ordained. It is not uncommon for boys without means to receive financial assistance from a Buddhist educational foundation, even through university level. Such charity has a direct social impact.

Forest-dwelling monks focus on meditation, maintaining a vigorous schedule of sitting and walking meditation throughout the day. As the name implies, forest-dwelling monks live away from urban and suburban centers, often in remote locations surrounded by the natural environment. The goal of all Theravada Buddhists is to gain discernment (Pali, *pañña*; Sanskrit, *prajñā*)—that is, wisdom of the Four Noble Truths. Meditation, study of the Pali Canon, and pilgrimages to stupas aid that journey. Theravada practices often focus on cleansing the mind from impurities—as the mind is the gateway to wisdom—and being fully present in the moment, being entirely "mindful" of all things, even to an extreme degree.

The following passage from a Theravada meditation text discusses how to be mindful of the body, feelings, mind, and mental qualities. Here is a short selection, addressed to Theravada monks, from a longer passage on the body.

> Monks, there is one road, one path for beings to purify themselves, to transcend sorrow and grief, to overcome suffering and melancholy, to attain the right way, to realize nirvana: that is the fourfold establishment of mindfulness. What are the four mindfulnesses? They are the mindful contemplation of the body, the mindful contemplation of the feelings, the mindful contemplation of thoughts, and the mindful contemplation of the elements of reality.
>
> How does a monk practice the mindful contemplation of the body? In this way: he goes to the forest, or to the foot of a tree, or to an empty room, and he sits down, cross-legged, keeps his back straight, and directs his mindfulness in front of him. Mindfully, he breathes in, mindfully, he breathes out; breathing in a long breath, he knows "I am breathing in a long breath"; breathing out a long breath, he knows "I am breathing out a long breath"; breathing in a short breath, he knows "I am breathing in a short breath";

breathing out a short breath, he knows "I am breathing out a short breath."
He should be like a lathe operator who knows that "I am making a long turn"
when he is making a long turn and that "I am making a short turn" when he
is making a short turn. Thus a monk practices mindfully contemplating his
body.

Furthermore, when a monk is walking, he knows "I am walking," and
when he is standing, knows "I am standing," and when he is sitting, knows "I
am sitting," and when he is lying down, knows "I am lying down." Whatever
posture his body may take, he knows that he is taking it. Thus a monk
practices mindfully contemplating his body.

Majjhima-Nikaya, Sattipatthanasutta 10:1–2[27]

The scriptural passage continues with a discussion of mindfully contemplating the body by advising monks to be mindful of what they are doing, where they are going, and where they are looking. The passage on the mindful contemplation of the body ends with the contemplation of the impermanent nature of the body—that all the elements that make up the body are changing, and eventually our bodies will perish and become a corpse, a skeleton, and finally dust—"This body of mine is just like that; it has the same nature, and it will not escape this fate." Notice the kind of single-minded concentration required to be fully present, mindful of just the body. Through meditation, Buddhists attempt to apply this same mindful concentration to all areas of life, being fully present in any given moment.

The Four Noble Truths and Nothing More

A third aspect of Theravada is its affirmation of the verbatim words of the Four Noble Truths, which are considered true in a literal sense. According to Theravada there is no greater, deeper truth than what is outlined in the Four Noble Truths. They are the very words of the historic Buddha. Much effort is spent in meditation, following guidelines presented in the Noble Eightfold Path, in order to train the mind to overcome the desire for "becoming," which begins with a thirst (*tanha*) for attachment. Since Lord Buddha was awakened to the truth of how things are, there is no need to look elsewhere or to rely on any other doctrine or person for insight. Although both Theravada and Mahayana affirm the historicity of Lord Buddha, Theravada asserts the necessity for individual Buddhists to strive to achieve enlightenment on their own, without outside help. As such, the path of enlightenment and liberation is an individual path requiring a great deal of effort, such as meditation, concentration, and study, in order to inculcate the virtues, train the mind, and anticipate enlightenment. Self-reliance becomes the mode of operation, for each individual is responsible for achieving liberation.

MAKING MERIT

Fourth, Theravada Buddhists focus on specific worship practices and virtues that will help them gain merit for their current and future lives. "Making merit" (***punya***) is a form of self-sacrifice and charity, generating good karmic consequences. *Punya* means meritorious acts that produce happiness and, therefore, good karma. Having a pure motive in the process of giving generates better merit and strong positive karma. Although a large gift, such as a donation to construct a monastery, is auspicious, the key factor is one's purity of heart, which makes even small gifts a significant matter. Those who cannot give any material item for financial reasons (e.g., they may not have anything to give) can say the ritualized chant, "***sadhu***" (Pali, "it is good"), when others give. It is often repeated three times, "*sadhu, sadhu, sadhu*," meaning something like, "Welcome, yes, we agree."

Traveling through Theravada communities, one notices devotees "making merit" in innumerable large and small ways, such as bowing to a passing monk, throwing coins into a collection bowl at a temple, or giving food to a monk. Any performance of a good deed generates good karma. Even good thoughts can have a positive effect in one's life. Merit making is undertaken with great seriousness, since one's intention and purity of heart are the determining factors in the cultivation of good merit.

As already mentioned, the Theravada tradition holds that only the ordained have the potential of achieving liberation. Because of the religious requirement to be ordained, most boys or young men in Theravada communities do in fact get ordained, even if ordination lasts only several days. Even short-term ordination requires that the ordinand follow the monastic vows. Ordination generates merit for both the ordained individual and his family, whose generosity is demonstrated by "giving over" their son to the *sangha*.

While some are ordained for a short time, maybe even just as long as they study at a university, others have a long-term commitment to their vows and remain Buddhist monks to the end of their lives. There is no shame in leaving

SIDEBAR 3.7

Three Kinds of Merit Making from the Pali Canon

1. Giving (*dānamayam puññakiriyavatthu*: "*dana*").
2. Virtue (*sīlamayam puññakiriyavatthu*: "*sīla*"), which entails living ethically, calmly, with tranquility.
3. Mental development (*bhāvanāmayam puññakiriyavatthu*: "*bhavana*"), which entails cultivation of charity, loving-kindness, mental discipline of purity.

one's ordination (being disrobed), unless of course disrobing was due to the commitment of a moral infraction. What about laypeople? What is their role in Theravada communities? The relationship between monks and laypersons of the community can be described as one of mutual dependence, for monks literally depend on the food, clothing, and other necessities offered by lay Buddhists to sustain themselves, while laypersons need the monks as moral exemplars and for opportunities to make merit by serving them.

Charles E. Farhadian

Figure 3.16. Forest monks walking to a village to collect alms in northern Thailand

Theravada monks begin each day by waking just before sunrise. Then they walk quietly, each with an alms bowl hanging from a strap around his neck, toward the residences of the faithful to receive food offerings from those who have awakened early to prepare the food. The faithful wait eagerly for the opportunity to make merit by placing the food in the alms bowls. The monks who receive the food respond to this act by praying for the generous laypeople of the community. Thus, the encounter between monk and laity is a mutually enriching and dependent relationship. Consequently, laypersons can always become monks (and nuns in some countries), but most choose to remain in their normal lives, still participating in the tradition by affirming its truths and making merit (*punya*), which is the path laid out for laypersons. The harmony between the *sangha* and the lay community is that of two halves of a single entity, and is the reason why Buddhist monasteries are often at the center of villages and open for people to come and go.

Mahayana Buddhism

The Mahayana branch of Buddhism is by far the largest form of Buddhism today, marked by so many varieties that it can be misunderstood as an entirely different religion. No other religious tradition seems as paradoxical as Mahayana, yet in its seeming contradictions are new insights on Buddhism that push believers beyond notions of reason and rationality toward states of intuitive knowledge and direct experience. The goal of the Mahayana tradition and its worship practice is the same as the Theravada tradition: liberation

153

from samsara. Because of its diverse nature, it is nearly impossible to speak of a unified Mahayana school. However, there are a few common themes that, while general, can help us consider the distinctive character of Mahayana.

The great schism between what would later become the Theravada and the Mahayana traditions, as you recall, was in part based on differing interpretations of the monastic codes and the status of the arhat (Pali, *arahant*), with the early Theravada adherents advocating a stricter interpretation of the monastic codes and the idea that the enlightened (arhat) remain sinless on earth, while the Mahayana Buddhists were more liberal in their interpretation and believed that the enlightened remain susceptible to human frailties until their death and *parinirvana*. Perhaps most significantly, Mahayana followers criticized the Theravada emphasis on personal effort in achieving liberation. Central to Lord Buddha's insight was the realization that release from the cycle of death and rebirth (samsara) comes from personal effort. There is no God who can save a practitioner, no teacher who can present him with the truth. It is only through personal effort that the nature of reality can be understood and samsara be broken. Reaching nirvana requires disciplining the mind and the body—and being self-reliant—which to the Mahayana tradition seems egocentric, ironically. In the final analysis, the ideal of the serene arhat, or Theravada saint, is regarded by the Mahayana tradition as selfish and focused entirely on the individual necessity to save oneself.

Beginning around 100 BCE, Mahayana Buddhism developed as a movement, rather than a single school of thought, emphasizing the distinction between monastics (monks) and common people, with new scriptures that took a more liberal approach designed to encompass everybody, giving everyone an opportunity to follow and attain liberation. Mahayana Buddhists honor the Pali Canon but contend that there are more-advanced teachings of Lord Buddha. The Mahayana Sutra (scriptures) emphasize the importance of religious experience. The scriptures themselves are secondary to the experience of dharma (the teaching of Lord Buddha, righteousness, law, duty). Mahayana adherents suggested that dharma is not embodied in the scriptures, and therefore enlightenment can be achieved in a variety of ways outside the bounds of what is recorded in the texts, even the sacred sutra. Given this openness to going "beyond" the scriptures, the Mahayana tradition offers special methods to attain awakening. In contrast to the uniformity of the Theravada, the Mahayana tradition is quite varied, but most Mahayana schools hold a few characteristics in common.

Sunyata

First, Mahayana Buddhism affirms the doctrine of *sunyata* (Sanskrit, **sunyata**; Pali, *suññatā*, "emptiness," "voidness")—that is, that everything is "void" and "empty" of independent substance. Nothing has a permanent, absolute identity, since all things are mutually dependent. The doctrine of *sunyata* is one of the most challenging concepts in the study of religion—and it is meant to be challenging since only the enlightened can truly comprehend it. Actually, *sunyata* is a logical extension of the idea that human beings do not possess an enduring soul (*anātman*) and that all things are affected by preexisting conditions. That is, nothing is independent. Everything is interconnected and contingent on prior conditions.

The doctrine of *sunyata* was elaborated by **Acharya Nagarjuna** (c. 150–250 CE), who argued, based on the Mahayana sutra called "The Perfection of Wisdom," that there is no such thing as a self-essence of any kind.[28] According to Nagarjuna, everything arises and passes away in a process of events that are dependent on other events, having no independent reality. What becomes mind-boggling, at least to an outsider, is that the Mahayana tradition applies *sunyata* to everything within Buddhism itself, including the Four Noble Truths and Lord Buddha! The Four Noble Truths are essentially empty of substance. In the material sense they, like all things, are empty of enduring "substance." All things are dependent, passing, temporary. Even Lord Buddha is void. Likewise, knowledge and reason are without substance. While the Theravada tradition had an idea of nonself and the transitory nature of all things, it was Nagarjuna who applied the doctrine of *sunyata* to all things.

In the words of the Mahayana text, the *Heart Sutra*:

> Form is emptiness, emptiness is form. Form is not other than emptiness, and emptiness is not other than form. That which is form equals emptiness, and that which is emptiness is also form. . . . All *dharmas* bear the marks of emptiness, which are: not to have arisen nor to have been suppressed, neither to be corrupt nor pure, and to be neither finished nor complete.[29]

This insight is, according to Mahayana Buddhism, the perfection of wisdom: "form is emptiness, emptiness is form" (*rupan shunyata shunyataiva rupan*). The idea of *sunyata* in the Mahayana tradition is applied to everything; even the Four Noble Truths are empty—they are *provisional*. Even nirvana is empty in the sense that it is a thought construct, entirely dependent on conditions, and not an eternal reality. Nirvana is literally "blowing out the flame." Ultimate reality is *sunyata* because it transcends all thought constructs, relationships, and contingencies.

THE BUDDHA'S DEATH WAS AN ILLUSION

Second, followers of the Mahayana tradition believe that Lord Buddha's *parinirvana* was an illusion. Usually Buddhists do not refer to the end of

Lord Buddha's earthly life as his "death." Lord Buddha referred to himself as *tathagata* (Sanskrit, "thus gone"). "***Tathagata***" is a paradoxical term that means "one who has gone" and "one who has thus come." It conveys that Lord Buddha arrived as "suchness." Therefore, Lord Buddha is beyond the transitions of coming and going (e.g., beyond life and death, samsara, and suffering), beyond all transitory phenomena. As such, Lord Buddha remains accessible to suffering humanity. His spiritual self is still available for consultation to everyone. From the first century onward, a new collection of sacred literature arose claiming to be the direct word of Lord Buddha, which the Theravada tradition denied. The texts claimed to have deeper insights into the tradition and represented for the Mahayana community the second "turning of the dharma wheel."

The turning of the dharma wheel refers to the teaching and disseminating of Buddhist insights. While the Theravada tradition believes in only one turning of the wheel, referring to the first sermon of Lord Buddha, Mahayana schools distinguish between the first and subsequent turnings. The Mahayana "turnings" referred to new sutras, which were more accessible to lay Buddhists and claimed to surpass the earlier teachings (i.e., the Pali Canon), leading to a further distancing between the Theravada and the Mahayana branches of Buddhism since the new sutras claimed to contain true dharma. Buddhist cults arose around each of these new sutras, which had little connection beyond the belief that the sutras contained the words of Lord Buddha. Adherents to these new texts felt themselves to be in direct contact with Lord Buddha, either through the new sutras or through meditation.

One of the most popular new sutras of this kind was the *Lotus Sutra*, recorded in the first century CE, but claiming to be a discourse of the historical Buddha. Around 200 CE, the *Lotus Sutra* laid out the fundamental Mahayana concept of skillful means (*upaya*), one of the most significant concepts in Mahayana Buddhism. *Upaya* (Sanskrit, "skillful means," "technique," "expedient means," or "means of liberation") is a way or device to persuade individuals to move toward liberation. Lord Buddha used *upaya* (skillful means) whenever he said or did anything that encouraged an aspirant's progress toward liberation. According to the doctrine of *upaya* a devotee may use almost any technique or method to stop *dukkha* and teach about dharma. Expediency connotes that a believer may be awakened quickly, even suddenly, through the use of various means of enlightenment. Each school of Mahayana promotes its own techniques of *upaya*, such as meditation, calligraphy, or word riddles. Anything that can awaken a practitioner is useful. The doctrine of *upaya* has enabled the Mahayana branch of Buddhism to proliferate into innumerable schools, each one practicing different techniques for achieving liberation.

THE BODHISATTVA IDEAL

Third, the Mahayana tradition claims that the highest goal of the religious life was not self-seeking enlightenment, such as was practiced by the followers of Theravada, but that individuals would become like Lord Buddha by seeking enlightenment for the sake of saving others. Here Mahayana Buddhism is a radical departure from the Theravada tradition, since the Mahayana affirms that liberation needs to come from an "other" rather than being gained by oneself. One could reach Buddhahood (enlightenment) and remain accessible to other human beings in order to help all people achieve liberation. This was the bodhisattva ideal. A **bodhisattva** (Sanskrit, "an awakened person," "one who has attained the essence of wisdom") is a "Buddha-to-be," a being who has achieved enlightenment but has taken a vow to remain accessible to others until all beings are saved. Bodhisattvas have dedicated themselves to helping others reach enlightenment, and they exist for the good of all. There are earthly and transcendent bodhisattvas; the earthly ones continue to be reborn into the world, while the transcendent bodhisattvas remain in some region between earth and nirvana, not having entered nirvana but not remaining on earth.

Bodhisattvas introduce a new element into Buddhism—faith in an "other," with the vigorous challenge to the efficacy of self-sufficiency. Many Buddhists were dissatisfied with the ideal of the arhat, those already enlightened on earth. If one were truly spiritual, one would be filled with compassion for all other creatures who suffer in samsara. Bodhisattvas render spiritual and material aid to those who call on them. As such, bodhisattvas are the focus of popular devotion, influenced by the Hindu bhakti tradition. Bodhisattvas are quasi saviors whose vow not to enter nirvana unless all beings join them impels them to be actively engaged in the world.

Notice the patterned nature of the Four Great Bodhisattva Vows: (1) Beings are infinite in number; I vow to end them all; (2) the obstructive passions are endless in number; I vow to end them all; (3) the teachings for saving others are countless; I vow to learn them all; (4) Buddhahood is the supreme achievement; I vow to attain it. Each bodhisattva has a specific attribute of the eternal Buddha, and they are all compassionate beings to whom people offer fervent prayer for aid. The task of these heavenly savior-beings is to skillfully help beings awaken, uncover, and know their own Buddhaness—their own Buddha nature. According to the tradition, chanting the name of the bodhisattva provides peace, protection, better rebirths, and even liberation.

One of the earliest cult bodhisattvas is Maitreya, the bodhisattva of the future who currently lives in Tusita Heaven, where he responds to prayer

Miguel A. Monjas/Wikimedia Commons

Figure 3.17. Carving of the future Buddha, Maitreya, in Feilai Feng Caves at Hangzhou, China

and worship. Maitreya is unique since he is the only bodhisattva accepted by both Theravada and Mahayana followers. The faithful believe that Maitreya is the next historical Buddha, who will be incarnated into the world when dharma has significantly diminished or been forgotten.

Manjushri (Sanskrit, *Mañjuśrī*, "Sweet Glory") is the bodhisattva of supreme wisdom and eloquence, with the ability to destroy ignorance and awaken spiritual understanding. Manjushri often appears in dreams, and he carries a sword to cut the bonds of delusion, thus aiding devotees toward enlightenment. The Japanese bodhisattva Jizo (also known as Kṣitigarbha) is another popular Buddha-to-be, with the ability to save people from the tortures of hell. Jizo is known as the guardian of children who have died prematurely—from abortions, stillbirths, or miscarriage—and his statue is often placed near children's graves, since he actively works for the rescue of those unborn in hell. According to Buddhist thinking, hell (Sanskrit, ***naraka***) is a world of greatest suffering.

First, it is important to remember that no God sends a person to *naraka*. Instead, it is one's accumulated karma that determines whether one will spend time in hell. Second, one does not stay in *naraka* forever. The time in hell is finite. One's stay there, while usually long, depends on how long it takes for one's karma to be depleted. As such, *naraka* is similar to the Christian notion of purgatory. Jizo also acts as the guardian of travelers and women, and his statue is placed on the side of rural roads and mountain paths.

The most popular bodhi-sattva is Avalokiteshvara (Sanskrit, *Avalokiteśvara*, "Lord who looks down" or "one who listens to the cries of the world"), who is the embodiment of the compassion of all Buddhas. There is a chapter in the *Lotus Sutra* dedicated to him ("Avalokiteshvara Sutra," chap. 25), where it is said, "True regard, serene regard, far-reaching wise regard, regard of pity, compassionate regard, ever longed for, ever looked for! Pure and serene in radiance, wisdom's sun destroying darkness . . . law of pity, thunder quivering,

Figure 3.18. Avalokiteshvara cast-iron statue from the tenth or eleventh century

compassion wondrous as a great cloud, pouring spiritual rain like nectar, quenching the flames of distress!" There are around 130 different depictions of Avalokiteshvara, each highlighting a different aspect of his compassionate nature. Bodhisattva Avalokiteshvara is the all-seeing, all-knowing one, as the bodhisattva of love and mercy who can grant people liberation. Often portrayed as having a thousand eyes to see the troubles of the world and a thousand arms to relieve them, Avalokiteshvara is omnipresent, omnipotent, and omniscient, and appears in the world in different forms.

> Though he sees that in all phenomena there is no coming and going,
> He strives solely for the sake of being:
> To the sublime teacher inseparable from Avalokitesvara, the Protector of Beings,
> I pay constant homage with respectful body, speech, and mind.
>
> The perfect buddhas—source of happiness and ultimate peace—Exit through
> having accomplished the sacred Dharma,
> And that, in turn, depends on knowing how to practice it;
> This practice of the bodhisattvas I shall therefore now explain.
>
> Now that I have this great ship, a precious human life, so hard to obtain,
> I must carry myself and others across the ocean of *samsara*.
> To that end, to listen, reflect, and meditate
> Day and night, without distraction, is the practice of a bodhisattva.[30]

In China Avalokiteshvara is called Kuan-yin (or Guanyin), the Chinese female bodhisattva of compassion, while in Japan he is known as Kannon. Avalokiteshvara is the chief attendant to Amitabha (Infinite Light), known in Japan as Amida and in China as O-mit'o, a celestial Buddha who promises to help one's quest for liberation. Amitabha resides in the Western Paradise, better known as Pure Land (Sukhavati). Thus, Pure Land Buddhism refers to the worship of Amitabha Buddha, with the central feature of faith in Amitabha as savior. The *Sukhavati-vyuha Sutra*, the sacred text of the devotees of Amitabha, promises that whoever calls on Amitabha will be saved, born into a blissful state. Pure Land Buddhism is particularly popular in Japan, where people worship Amida Buddha.

Figure 3.19. Statue of Kuan Yin from the Ming Dynasty, China

One of the unique aspects of Mahayana Buddhism is its affirmation that enlightenment can occur outside the use of scripture and rationalized creeds, such as through mind-to-mind transmission and direct experience alone. At first sight it may seem impossible that one can be awakened without following the exact words (sutra) of Lord Buddha, a perspective established by Theravada tradition. Yet there is a historical precedent for the Mahayana assertion that awakening can occur outside the knowledge of formal scriptures, rituals, and even the words of Lord Buddha.

At the end of his life, Lord Buddha gathered his disciples and preached one of his last sermons, called his Flower Sermon. One of Lord Buddha's closest disciples, Mahakashyapa (Sanskrit, *Mahākāśyapa*, "The Great Kāśyapa"; Pali, *Mahākassapa*), was present to listen to his words. His disciples sat around him silently. Lord Buddha too was silent. He reached into the mud, picked a lotus flower, and held it silently before them. Although his disciples were confused, they attempted to make sense of the symbolism of the flower in the context of Lord Buddha's message. When Lord Buddha approached his disciple Mahakashyapa, the disciple immediately smiled, then laughed, and Lord Buddha handed the lotus flower to Mahakashyapa with the words, "What can be said I have said to you, and what cannot be said, I have given to Mahakashyapa." Mahakashyapa understood—he was awakened. Thus the tradition of awakening by direct experience was established. Mahakashyapa summoned the First Buddhist Council and is the first of the Zen patriarchs, with Ananda being the second.

> I possess the true Dharma eye, the marvelous mind of Nirvana, the true form of the formless, the Subtle Dharma Gate that does not rest on words or letter but is a special transmission outside of the scriptures. This I entrust to Mahākāśyapa.
>
> Lord Buddha to Mahakashyapa [31]

Tibetan Buddhism

Let us look briefly at some of the more popular forms of Mahayana Buddhism and their worship practices, keeping in mind that Mahayana itself is so diverse that these are only representatives of the larger, more expansive tradition. Tibetan Buddhism stands in its own right as an independent school of Buddhism and deserves more of an introduction than this brief summary.[32]

The spiritual and aesthetic heartland of Tibetan Buddhism was at Lhasa, Tibet, set nearly twelve thousand feet high in the Tibetan mountains. Today the seat of the Tibetan government is Dharamsala, in northern India, where the Dalai Lama resides. Tibetan religion consists mainly of Vajrayana Buddhism (a variant of Mahayana) and the indigenous Bön (pronounced "pern") tradition. Buddhism arrived in Tibet significantly in the seventh century CE,

---

Religious conversion features as a prominent part of both Buddhism and Christianity.[a] Followers of each tradition believe they are following the truth—it is a truth that is universally applicable and needs to be offered to others. Conversion to Buddhism involves turning inward, seeking to exchange perception (Pali, *sañña*; "label," "evaluation") with wisdom (Pali, *pañña*; "discernment," "insight") in every encounter and action, both mental and physical. Buddhism's intense analysis of psychological (mental) states and the attending ways that human beings should purify the mind put the work of salvation on the shoulders of the believer. In contrast, Jesus called his disciples to reshape the world according to the kingdom of God, following Jesus's prayer, "Your kingdom come. Your will be done, on earth as it is in heaven" (Matt. 6:10). And he promised to send the Holy Spirit as a guide and comforter.

a. See Rambo and Farhadian, *Oxford Handbook of Religious Conversion.*

Christian Reflections

Figure 3.20. Tibetan woman praying with prayer wheel in Lhasa, Tibet

when the Tibetan king Srong-bstan-sgam-po (known as Songtsan Gampo; 616–650 CE) was converted to the tradition by his two wives, who were from Nepal and China. The early growth of the tradition resulted mostly from Buddhist influences from India, China, and central Asia.

The indigenous Tibetan Bön religion centered on spirit possession, magic, exorcism of demons, and the cult of dead kings.[33] Despite occasions of violent conflict between followers of Buddhism and Bön, the traditional Tibetan religion influenced Tibetan Buddhism considerably, synthesizing the two traditions yet allowing space for Bön to continue to also exist independently. Tibetan Buddhism utilizes tantra, which are complicated, esoteric meditational systems aimed to produce deep religious experience that can lead to enlightenment faster than the path of the bodhisattva. Tantrism exists throughout several Indian religious traditions, yet its origins are obscure. Tantric language expresses profound religious insights that are obscure, requiring explanation by a spiritual teacher. Tantric texts range from magic to sophisticated philosophy.

By the eleventh century, Buddhism was firmly established in Tibet, reflecting its own unique style of blending between Mahayana and Bön traditions. By the fourteenth century, the Tibetan canon was complete, consisting of over three hundred volumes, with its esoteric knowledge recorded in the tantric texts. Tibetan Buddhism is divided into four major schools (Nyingma, Sakya, Kagyu, and Geluk), focusing on different scriptures, meditational

Luca Galuzzi – www.galuzzi.it

Figure 3.21. Tibet Potala

techniques, and ways of communicating the tradition. The distinction between "Red Hats" and "Yellow Hats," terms employed by early Western observers to distinguish between Tibetan Buddhist practitioners, is not used by Tibetans themselves. Before 1949, Tibet was an independent state, ruled by its own religion, a Buddhocracy based in Lhasa. However, in 1950 tens of thousands of Chinese troops invaded Tibet and later incorporated it into China's national boundaries, in a violent clash that many argue was based on the illegitimate claim that Tibet had been a part of Chinese territory several hundred years earlier. Today part of Tibet is the Autonomous Region of China. Tibetans claim that over one million Tibetans have died as a result of China's control.

Tibetan Buddhism is quite diverse in its worship practices and beliefs, yet there are common features of tradition distinguishing it from other forms of Mahayana Buddhism.

THE IMPORTANCE OF RITUAL

First, Tibetan Buddhist worship prioritizes ritual over meditation. As in all other Buddhist schools, meditation is seen as a major help in the quest for liberation. But Tibetan Buddhists believe that enlightenment can be achieved through the power of ritual as well. Meditation is still essential, but the dual approach of using both ritual and meditation sets Tibetan Buddhism apart from other Buddhist schools, which contend that ritual is always subordinate to meditation. Tibetan Buddhists suggest that enlightenment can be achieved in one lifetime, if one is prepared to take certain risks, such as learning Tantrism—that is, undergoing initiation by a guru (teacher) into the particular rituals and sacred texts to gain esoteric knowledge. Sometimes tantric initiates engage in forbidden practices, such as meat eating or sexual intercourse, to help rise "beyond morality" and therefore beyond the world itself. Through the guidance of a guru, the Tibetan Buddhist practitioner seeks unity between different aspects of the individual life, the cosmos, and the deities. This is known as the Vajrayana (Diamond Vehicle), which affirms the eternal Buddhahood resident in all beings, unsplittable, and achieved through the cutting edge of wisdom. Spiritual exercises and rituals of tantra aim at gaining identification with Buddhahood in the here and now.

MANDALAS

Second, Tibetan Buddhist worship employs magical diagrams called mandalas (Sanskrit, "circle"), which are symbolic pictorial representations of the universe, visualized during tantric rituals. Practitioners chant mantras (Sanskrit, "instrument of thought") while internalizing the mandala. By imagining a deity, such as a bodhisattva, a practitioner gains unity with the deity, a nondual identification sometimes symbolized by the sexual bond—two bodies become fused. The sacred chant is the mantra of Avalokiteshvara—*"Om mani padme hum"* ("Oh, the Jewel is in the Lotus"), which are invocation syllables. Technically, the mantra suggests a female deity, called Manipadma, but there is no known record of such a deity.[34]

The origins and exact meaning of the *Om mani padme hum* remain obscure. According to some scholars, mantras are mostly meaningless syllables or strings of syllables whose sound nevertheless possesses great potency when they are said the right way and one is "tuned

Anonymous/Wikimedia Commons

Figure 3.22. Painting of four Tibetan mandalas from the fourteenth century

in" to what is being visualized.[35] Furthermore Tibetan Buddhists are famous for their sand mandalas (Tibetan, *kilkhor*), used to show the transient nature of all things. The sand mandala may take weeks to construct, as Tibetan monks create a symbolic replica of the cosmos replete with deities using colored sand or stone. Following its creation, the colorful mandala, which can be several feet in diameter, is destroyed ceremonially to illustrate the impermanence of everything.

Anonymeus/Wikimedia Commons

Figure 3.23. *Om Mani Padme Hum* mantra, Tibetan script

PRAYER WHEELS

Third, Tibetan Buddhist worship utilizes prayer wheels containing scrolls on which the mantra of Avalokiteshvara and other texts can be found. The prayer wheels can be small and handheld, or large, perhaps twenty feet tall. They may be individual or arranged in rows, where practitioners can turn the wheels and thus generate the mantra. Some prayer wheels are turned by the force of water or electric motors.

Finally, a well-known feature of Tibetan Buddhism is the leadership role of the Dalai Lama. "Lama" is an honorific title, equivalent to the Sanskrit term "guru," conferred generally on anyone accepted as a spiritual leader, but more specifically on the one who has completed a particular regime of scholastic and yogic training. *Dalai* means "Ocean" and refers to the highest level of spiritual teacher-leader. There have been fourteen Dalai Lamas in Tibetan Buddhism; the present one, Tenzin Gyatso (b. 1935), has been in exile in Dharamsala, India, since the Chinese invasion of Tibet in 1959. To Tibetan Buddhists the Dalai Lama is an emanation of the bodhisattva Avalokiteshvara. In 1989 the Dalai Lama was awarded the Nobel Peace Prize for his work defending Tibetans by employing Buddhism's nonviolent principles.

Henryart/Wikimedia Commons

Figure 3.24. Tibetan sand mandala ritual in Kitzbuehel, Austria

Luca Galuzzi – www.galuzzi.it

Figure 3.25. Prayer wheels in Tibet

Zen Buddhism

One of the best-known forms of Buddhism in the West is Zen. What we know as Zen began in China in the fifth century CE when Bodhidharma, a south Indian Buddhist monk, traveled from southern China to a monastery in northern China. Reportedly, Bodhidharma spent nine years "wall-gazing"—sitting "facing the wall"—eventually becoming the first patriarch of the radical path called Ch'an (meditation) Buddhism in China. The word "Ch'an" derives from the Sanskrit word *"dhyana"* (meditation) and thus focuses on meditation as a way to realize the Buddha nature within one's self. Ch'an is better known in the West in its Japanese variant, Zen, which has been imported to the West quite successfully.

Figure 3.26. Zen Buddhist priest in Kyoto, Japan

> The Great Way is not difficult
> for those who have no preferences.
> When love and hate are both absent
> everything becomes clear and undisguised.
> Make the smallest distinction, however,
> and heaven and earth are set infinitely apart.[36]

Zen worship places great importance on meditation and the possibility of an immediate awakening (**satori**, "individual enlightenment," "flash of sudden awareness"). A major Japanese interpreter of Zen for a Western audience, D. T. Suzuki, suggests that Zen seems illogical, absurd, beyond ordinary reasoning for the untrained mind, for understanding requires a new way of observation "whereby we can escape the tyranny of logic."[37]

Suzuki quotes the fifth-century Zen practitioner Fudaishi (Fu-tai-shih) to illustrate the paradoxical nature of Zen as the means to acquire an entirely new point of view, since the ordinary process of reasoning is powerless to satisfy our spiritual needs.

> Empty-handed I go, and behold the spade is
> in my hands;

> I walk on foot, and yet on the back of an ox
> I am riding;
> When I pass over the bridge,
> Lo, the water floweth not, but the bridge doth flow.[38]

Zen claims to preserve the essence of Lord Buddha's teachings through direct experience, as illustrated in Lord Buddha's Flower Sermon. It dismisses scriptures, Buddhas, and bodhisattvas in favor of training for direct intuition of cosmic unity, of the Buddha nature or what is sometimes referred to as the void. Zen employs an empty circle to depict the nature of reality—it is empty. In Zen there is no concept or idea of a Buddha; there is only the Buddha for those who do not know the Buddha. In the words of Japanese Zen Master Kobare, "There is Buddha for those who do not know what he is really, there is no Buddha for those who know what he is really."[39] Zen worship uses two methods to directly experience Buddha nature and thus enlightenment. First is sitting meditation (*zazen*), a rigorous practice involving sitting in an upright position and not moving for long periods of time in order to avoid mental distractions. Skillful means (*upaya*) are applied to make the mind singularly focused and lucid, with the belief that when the mind is calmed and stopped, actions are spontaneous and natural in every domain, with one being able to experience the "thus-ness" of life, the unconditioned reality. A second skillful means employed by Zen practitioners is the use of word puzzles (koans), which are questions that boggle the mind, like "throwing sand into the eyes of the intellect" and forcing one to experience the answer intuitively, rather than rationally. "What is the sound of one hand clapping?" "What is your face before your parents' birth?" "Does a dog have Buddha nature?" Koans are designed to shock practitioners into enlightenment, since they have an opportunity to reflect directly on the nature of things as they are.

> *To meditate, a man has to fix his thought on something; for instance, on the oneness of God, or his infinite love, or on the impermanence of things. But this is the very thing Zen desires to avoid. If there is anything Zen strongly emphasizes it is the attainment of freedom; that is, freedom from all unnatural encumbrances. Meditation is something artificially put on; it does not belong to the native activity of the mind.*
>
> Suzuki, *Introduction to Zen Buddhism*, 41

Tendai Buddhism

Japanese Tendai Buddhism has major religious and historical significance, since it influenced the development of several other popular Buddhist schools, including the Japanese Buddhist schools of Pure Land, True Pure Land, Rinzai Zen, Soto Zen, and Nichiren. Today the number of Tendai Buddhists

Christian Reflections

How do religious people receive sustenance from their tradition as well as be fully engaged with the world? Does one discover the greater truth of a tradition when one is sedentarily meditating in a quiet place or robustly active in the world? Will one pattern be right for all believers? One of the most interesting and relevant topics in the religions of the world is the way that people practice and grow into the tradition. Buddhism and Christianity affirm both sedentary meditation and active engagement. Zen takes time—and it can entail long hours of deep meditation and focused concentration. By calming the mind, the practitioner of Zen can stop mental actions (karma) and capture a glimpse of enlightenment and the fundamental identity of all things.

Christianity too connects the practice of being still with knowing God: "Be still, and know that I am God" (Ps. 46:10), an idea that is taken up in the New Testament to refer to giving over control of oneself to God rather than relying on one's own efforts. For a Christian, the call to "be still" is an invitation not to seek the truth within but to know that God is God—that is, there is Someone to trust entirely with one's life. The Gospels tell of Jesus's calming all kinds of powers and principalities, such as demons and storms: "Be still" was his command under conditions where his power would be revealed. Some forms of Christianity, in particular Roman Catholicism, Orthodoxy, and Quakerism (Protestantism), seem more open to the way of meditation and silence.

These older Christian traditions have a long history of sacramental theology that enables the use of icons and sacraments as means of gaining and sustaining awareness of God. On the other hand, Protestants tend to be more verbal—rather than heavily sacramental—because of the centrality of preaching the Word of God. In any case, both Buddhism and Christianity do not end their calls with sedentary solitude, but rather they emphasize that followers should be active in the world, demonstrating charity and compassion, promising equal access to salvation. Recall that both Buddhism and Christianity democratized earlier traditions (i.e., Hinduism, Judaism) by taking their messages to wider, more diverse linguistic and cultural audiences.

has been dwarfed by the Zen and the Nichiren movements. Tendai Buddhism was established in the sixth century CE in China and subsequently was introduced to Japan in the ninth century by the Japanese monk Saicho. Tendai teaches the superiority of the *Lotus Sutra* over all other scriptures, believing this text to contain the most profound communication of Lord Buddha's dharma, particularly the concept that all beings possess Buddha nature.

Monk Saicho learned Tendai in China in 804 CE, then returned to Japan to establish his temple, Enryaku-ji, on Mount Hiei, near Kyoto. Saicho combined Buddhist teachings with several esoteric doctrines and practices distinctly Japanese, such as Shingon (True Word), the secrets of the body, speech, and mind. According to Tendai worship practices, the secrets of the body include special hand positions (*mudrās*), the secrets of speech include chanting verses and syllables of divine origin (mantras), and the secrets of the mind include special teacher-to-pupil oral transmission of teachings. Together these three secrets (body, speech, mind) are used in esoteric rituals, since the ultimate nature of Buddhahood is ineffable and cannot be communicated verbally.

Nichiren Buddhism

Figure 3.27. Tendai Buddhist priest in Hawaii, USA

Nichiren Buddhism is another Japanese sect that in worship follows the teachings of the *Lotus Sutra* above all others, believing that the *Lotus Sutra* contains the essence of Buddhism. Nichiren (1222–82) was a Tendai monk who believed that the only true form of Buddhism was that taught by Saicho, who had founded the Tendai sect. Nichiren, following the *Lotus Sutra*, preached that all beings can be enlightened by faith and the chanting of the sacred mantra *"namu myōhō renge kyō"* ("I take refuge in the Lotus of the Wonderful Law Sutra"). Nichiren fiercely condemned all other Buddhist sects, proclaiming them to be demonic, and denounced the Japanese government for disallowing his form of Buddhism. Nichiren was arrested, later to be pardoned, by the Japanese government and eventually exiled to an isolated island in the Sea of Japan. He died in the home of one of the sect's followers.

One of the legacies of Nichiren was his creation of the Object of Worship (Gohonzon), a calligraphic inscription on wood with the invocation *"namu myōhō renge kyō."* Although there is some debate about the location of the original Gohonzon, whether it is enshrined at their headquarters at Mount Minobu or at Taisekiji, modern worshipers chant the invocation in front of a replica of Gohonzon, usually in the form of a scroll, claiming that faith in the Gohonzon's power enables one to recognize one's Buddha nature.

Modern Movements

The reasons for Buddhism's increasing popularity in the West are multifaceted, but it is in part due to its focus on the elimination of suffering (*dukkha*), meditation techniques that promise to calm the mind, and its psychological perspective that makes sense of the impermanence of things. While Buddhism has borrowed salient concepts from Hinduism, its reinterpretation of those ideas has made Buddhism an attractive religious path, illustrated by the fact that many people around the world are converting to the tradition. Buddhism is a missionary religion, for its adherents believe it has access to universal truth. For centuries what Westerners knew about Asian Buddhism came from the letters and records of European colonial officials and Western Christian missionaries. During the World Parliament of Religions held in Chicago in 1893, Western audiences heard significant representatives of various world religions speak for the first time in North America.

World Parliament of Religions

The World Parliament of Religions introduced several significant religious leaders of Asian religious traditions, such as Vivekananda, the so-called Hindu missionary to the West. At that meeting the Buddhist leader Anagarika Dharmapala (1864–1933), who represented Theravada Buddhism, introduced a Western audience to the virtues of Buddhism, particularly Buddhist psychology, meditation, and doctrine. Anagarika Dharmapala, whose name means "homeless Guardian of the Dharma," is credited with being the first to formally introduce Theravada Buddhism to the United States, as well as being the first to preach Buddhism on three continents: Asia, North America, and Europe.

The immigration of Asian Buddhists to North America, beginning in large numbers in the mid-nineteenth century, led to the construction of hundreds of Buddhist temples along the West Coast of the United States. Following the Second World War, the increased number of Asian immigrants enabled the proliferation of Buddhist temples, schools, universities, and social service agencies throughout North America.

American Buddhist Universities and Meditation Centers

Some American Buddhist universities include the Dharma Realm Buddhist University, located in the small town of Ukiah, California, which boasts the largest Chinese Zen Buddhist temple in the United States, the City of Ten Thousand Buddhas; Won Institute of Graduate Studies (Glenside, PA); the University of the West (Hsi Lai University) (Rosemead, CA), the first Buddhist-funded university in the United States; and the Institute of Buddhist Studies (Berkeley, CA), which is a member of the Graduate Theological Union.

Ultimately, anyone prepared to follow Lord Buddha or Jesus Christ has to have faith—that is, trust that their message and who they claim to be are true, leading to salvation. There is much that Buddhism can offer Christians. The Buddhist emphasis on the impermanency of all things reminds Christians that life is fleeting, and that our identity should not be tied too closely to our attachments, such as the things we own, the degrees we accumulate, or our family and friends. If we are honest, many of us Western Christians need to be reminded that life on earth is not eternal. Even with the best medicine, material comforts, and therapies, our lives will end one day. The human mortality rate has always been 100 percent.

Buddhism can also help remind Christians not to take things too seriously or personally. The truth is that we are all suffering at some level. Why not train the mind to be less judgmental about things? What appeals to me about Christianity, in part, is its affirmation of the material world, as neither comprehensive nor ultimate reality, but as a fundamental part of the existence that also needs redemption, rather than as an impediment to be overcome in order to be enlightened. Liberation itself is conceived differently by Buddhists and Christians, one conception promising nirvana and the other eternal life. Their founders differed as well: one claimed to be an ordinary man who became enlightened, the other the incarnation of the Creator God who suffered on behalf of the world and rose from the dead. There is also a time-space dimension to each: the Buddha was multiplied—there are several Buddhas within Buddhism—whereas the Christ-event was so fundamentally bound to concrete history that the notion of multiplying Christ into multiple abstractions (e.g., cosmic Christs) is unthinkable and belies his historicity in real time and space, an event never to be repeated again.

Furthermore, there are countless Buddhist meditation centers of all kinds throughout North America, with the Hsi Lai Temple in Hacienda Heights, California, being one of the largest Buddhist temples in the Western Hemisphere. Today all major forms of Buddhism are present in North America and are followed by Asians and non-Asians alike. As generations of Asian Buddhists have become economically successful Americans, their resources finance the construction of Buddhist worship and social spaces. Mahayana's enormous flexibility enables all kinds of people to engage it faithfully, regardless of their gender or cultural or social background.

Timeline ....

c. 563 BCE	Birth of Lord Buddha in Kapilavastu, present-day Nepal (some traditions suggest 463 BCE)
c. 528 BCE	Enlightenment of Siddhartha, the Buddha; creation of the *sangha*
c. 483 BCE	End of Lord Buddha's earthly life (some traditions suggest 383 BCE)
c. 400 BCE	First Buddhist Council
c. 350 BCE	Second Buddhist Council
c. 300 BCE	Buddhism arrives in Southeast Asia
c. 272 BCE	Emperor Asoka converts to Buddhism, takes throne, and spreads Buddhism throughout India and beyond (i.e., Sri Lanka, Afghanistan, Myanmar)
c. 250 BCE	Third Buddhist Council, resulting in great schism between Theravada and Mahayana Buddhism
c. 247 BCE	Mahinda introduces Buddhism to Sri Lanka
c. 100 BCE	Formal beginnings of Mahayana branch of Buddhism
80 BCE	First written canon, beginning with Vinaya Pitaka
1st century BCE	Theravada Buddhist canon (Tripitaka) completed in Sri Lanka
c. 85 CE	Composition of *Lotus Sutra*
150–250 CE	Life of Nagarjuna, the most influential Mahayana philosopher
220–589	Buddhist missions to Southeast Asia (Vietnam, Java, Sumatra) and East Asia (Korea, Japan)
4th century	Emergence of Vajrayana Buddhism
c. 300	Emergence of Pure Land school in India
372	Chinese monks take Buddhism to Korea
c. 500	Rise of Vajrayana Thunderbolt school in India, which would shape Buddhism in northeastern India, Nepal, and Tibet
520	Bodhidharma arrives in China
527	Korea accepts Buddhism
6th century	Burma adopts Theravada Buddhism
c. 600	Formation of Ch'an school in China inspired by Bodhidharma
609–50	Life of Songtsan, who declares Buddhism the national religion of Tibet
700–1270	Buddhist kingdom of Sri Vijaya on Sumatra and Java; building of Borobodur stupa in central Java
1000–1400	Establishment of Buddhism in Burma
1192	Muslim rule of northern India; destruction of Indian Buddhist monasteries
1193–1227	Formation of new Buddhist schools in Japan (Zen, Pure Land, and Shinran)

1200–53	Life of Dogen, who spread Zen Buddhism in Japan
1222–82	Life of Nichiren
c. 1200–1500	Buddhism declines in northern India; then declines in southern India
1871–76	Meiji persecution of Buddhism in Japan, with destruction of 70 percent of Buddhist monasteries
1905	Zen Buddhism enters the United States
1959–present	Chinese Communists annex Tibet and repress Buddhism; exile of fourteenth Dalai Lama from Tibet; center of Tibetan Buddhism moves with Dalai Lama to Dharamsala, northern India
1998	Ordination taken by Theravada nuns in Chinese monasteries
2007	Monks lead democracy protests in Myanmar, resulting in harsh government repression of Buddhist monks

Key Terms

Abhidharma
Acharya Nagarjuna
anatta
anicca
arhat
atman
avidyā
bodhisattva
Buddha
dhamma
dukkha
dukkha-dukkha
dukkha nirodha
dukkha nirodha gamini patipada magga
dukkha nirodha marga
dukkha samudaya
emic
etic
Five Aggregates
Four Noble Truths
Hinayana
Jataka Tales

karma
Kshatriya
Mahasanghikas
Mahayana
Majjhima Patipada
mandala
maya
Middle Way
naraka
nirvana
Noble Eightfold Path
Pali
parinirvana
Prakrit
punya
rupa
sadhu
samkhara-dukkha
samsara
samskara
sangha
sanna
sannyasi

satori
shramana
shramani
Siddhartha
skandhas
Sthaviravadins
stupa
sunyata
Sutras
tanha
tathagata
Theravada
Tipitaka
Tripitaka
Triratna
Vajrayana
Varanasi
vedana
vijnana
Vinaya
virparinama-dukkha
Zen

Further Reading

Dalai Lama. *Ethics for the New Millennium*. New York: Riverhead Books, 1999.

———. *The World of Tibetan Buddhism: An Overview of Its Philosophy and Practice*. Somerville, MA: Wisdom Publications, 1995.

Gombrich, Richard, and Gananath Obeyesekere. *Buddhism Transformed*. Princeton: Princeton University Press, 1990.

Harvey, Peter. *An Introduction to Buddhism: Teachings, History, and Practices*. Daryaganj, New Delhi: Cambridge University Press, 2004.

King, Richard. *Indian Philosophy: An Introduction to Hindu and Buddhist Thought*. Washington, DC: Georgetown University Press, 1999.

Learman, Linda, ed. *Buddhist Missionaries in the Era of Globalization*. Honolulu: University of Hawaii Press, 2005.

McMahan, David L. *The Making of Buddhist Modernism*. Oxford: Oxford University Press, 2008.

Merton, Thomas. *Mystics and Zen Masters*. New York: Farrar, Straus & Giroux, 1961.

Nhat Hanh, Thich. *Living Buddha, Living Christ*. New York: Penguin Group, 1995.

———. *The Miracle of Mindfulness: An Introduction to the Practice of Meditation*. Translated by Mobi Ho. Boston: Beacon, 1975.

Prebish, Charles S., and Martin Baumann, eds. *Westward Dharma: Buddhism beyond Asia*. Berkeley: University of California Press, 2002.

Rahula, Walpola. *What the Buddha Taught*. New York: Grove Press, 1959.

Strong, John S. *The Experience of Buddhism: Sources and Interpretations*. Belmont, CA: Wadsworth/Thompson Learning, 2002.

Suzuki, Daisetz Teitaro. *An Introduction to Zen Buddhism*. New York: Grove Press, Inc., 1964.

Wangyal, Geshe. *The Door of Liberation: Essential Teachings of the Tibetan Buddhist Tradition*. Boston: Wisdom Publications, 1995.

Watson, Burton. *The Essential Lotus: Selections from the Lotus Sutra*. New York: Columbia University Press, 2002.

Williams, Paul. *Mahayana Buddhism: The Doctrinal Foundations*. New York: Routledge, 2001.

four

Jainism

Contemporary Snapshot

In 2008 a massive $6 million temple was completed in Los Angeles, California, close to the Knott's Berry Farm amusement park. Known as the Jain Center of Southern California, the temple serves about one thousand Jain families who attend weekend prayers at the facility. Inside the Jain Center there are twenty-four white marble figures representing twenty-four liberated souls who exemplify nonviolent, simple lives. The figurines were paraded through several city blocks, past Korean and Salvadoran markets, before being installed in the center's temple. The center features a library containing more than eight thousand books, a temple, a children's room, and study rooms.

The Jain Center of Southern California is the result of decades of influence of a growing number of generally well-educated and affluent Jains in the region who started meeting for prayer in the home of Dr. Manibhai Mehta, a retired urologist and fellow Jain. Jainism is considered the most rigorously vegetarian of the world religions, and Jains honor even the most microscopic sentient beings and attempt to avoid harming any life form. In Mehta's words,

Figure 4.1. Siddhachalam Jain center in New Jersey, USA

"We don't want to kill any living beings. We don't eat any meat, we don't eat fish—none of the living things. . . . Though we believe vegetables also have life, that is the least conscious level of life."[1] Its motto, "Live and Let Live," communicates the Jain ideal of living peaceably with all living things. But who are the Jains, and what makes them unique compared to other South Asian religionists?

The Jain community, numbering roughly six million worldwide, has had a far greater impact on the world than its relatively small number might suggest. Mahatma Gandhi's work was influenced by the Jain concept of nonviolence, which has been famously attached to Gandhi's legacy in inspiring movements of nonviolent resistance worldwide. Jainism is a distinct religion of India that has adopted and reinterpreted the key concepts of its predecessor, Hinduism.

Like Hinduism and Buddhism, Jainism attempted to address the central problem of Indian life—that is, how to find release from karma and the continual round of rebirths entailed in **samsara**. Jainism provides one answer to this important question. Both Jainism and Buddhism are South Asian religions with founders and organized doctrines. They each have organized rituals, including worship, prayer, a special set of scriptures, a monastic tradition, particular ideas of orthodoxy and heterodoxy, and even conversion. Jainism's founder lived around the time of the Buddha, in the sixth century BCE.

Today Jains live throughout the world but have a large presence in pockets of India, such as Mumbai and Gujarat, with diaspora Jain populations in the United States and other countries, particularly Kenya and Belgium. While there are fewer than fifty Jain temples in North America, the Jain population in the North Atlantic region since the late 1960s has grown to more than fifty thousand.

Europeans have been aware of the Jains since the beginning of the sixteenth century, describing them as "merchants" because of their involvement in the gem industry. Western travelers and missionaries were more interested in the outward aspects of the Jain tradition and the appearance of Jain ascetics than in the details of Jain doctrines, practices, and beliefs. The first formal Western attempt to understand Jains as a historical and social phenomenon took place during the British Raj beginning in the sixteenth century, when British observers recorded observations about the distinctive nature of the Jains without consulting Jain literature itself, leading to the misconception that Jainism was a variant branch of Hinduism rather than a distinct religion in itself.

Ranveig/Wikimedia Commons

Jainism, like Buddhism, rejected the traditional Brahmanical control of the sacrificial ritual and its power over sacred knowledge. As followers of an anti-Brahmanical movement, most Jains affirmed the possibility that anybody could be liberated, with one Jain denomination believing liberation was limited just to men. As a movement opposed to the class system (**varna**) and considered heterodox by some early Hindus, Jainism had the potential to appeal to a wide variety of people, although its strict asceticism would make it less attractive to others.

The term "*jaina*," from which we get the word Jain, is derived from the term "***jina***," a general name for the supreme souls that are totally free from all defilements. A *jina* is a spiritual conqueror, a title given to twenty-four great teachers, or **fordfinders**, known as ***tirthankaras*** (Sanskrit, "builders of the ford"), who have discovered the way across the sea of suffering to the realm of liberation. As human teachers, *tirthankaras* have overcome the passions and obtained enlightenment, having taught the true doctrine of nonviolence and the way to attain freedom from rebirth. At a basic level, Jains are those who credit these spiritual conquerors with total authority and

Figure 4.2. *Tirthankara* Rishabhadeva, considered the first *tirthankara* of Jainism

therefore act according to the *tirthankaras'* teachings. *Jinas* have overcome the passions, thus becoming great examples of spiritual strength.

Origins and Concepts

The Life

The religion of Jainism was initiated by Vardhamana **Mahavira** (599–527 BCE).[2] Mahavira, which means "Great Man" or "Great Hero," was part of an anti-Brahmanical group in northern India that rejected Brahmanism. Like the historical Buddha, Siddhartha Gautama, Lord Mahavira was from a Kshatriya family in north India (Bihar), and was the son of King Siddhartha and Queen Trishala, at about the same time as the Buddha. Jain tradition says that while in his mother's womb, Lord Mahavira followed the doctrine of non-violence (***ahimsa***), causing his mother no pain. Reared in luxury as a member of a high Hindu caste, Lord Mahavira had five nurses: a wet nurse, a nurse to bathe him, one to dress him, one to play with him, and one to carry him.

Figure 4.3. Statue of Mahavira at Shravanabelagola Temple in Karnataka, India

Tradition notes that Mahavira grew up enjoying the fivefold joys of sound, touch, taste, sight, and smell, the five sense pleasures he would later renounce. Some Jain communities believe Mahavira married a princess, Yashoda, who bore him a daughter, Priyadarshana, while other Jain communities argue that Mahavira never married.

After his parents had gone to the worlds of the gods and he had fulfilled his promise, he gave up his gold and silver, his troops and chariots, and distributed, portioned out, and gave away his valuable treasures (consisting of) riches, corn, gold, pearls, etc, and distributed among those who wanted to make presents to others. Thus he gave away during a whole year. In the first month of winter, in the first fortnight, in the dark (fortnight) of Mâgasiras, on its tenth day, while the moon was in conjunction with Uttaraphalguní, he made up his mind to retire from the world.

Acaranga Sutra 2.15.17–20[3]

Jains affirm that at around thirty years of age Mahavira renounced the world, became a wandering ascetic, and followed the ascetic rule of **Parshva**, a yogi (practitioner of yoga) from the ninth century BCE, later known as the twenty-third *tirthankara*—a Jain master who found a way across the sea of suffering. Parshva was a fordfinder, a prince from Benares (Varanasi) who attained enlightenment at the age of thirty. Jain tradition holds that for twelve years Mahavira followed a path of extreme asceticism, practicing severe fasting, silence, meditation, and pulling out his hair, while highly respecting all living beings, including plants and insects, without harming them. His practice was intense. In his own words, "I shall neglect my body and abandon the care of it; I shall with equanimity bear, undergo, and suffer all calamities arising from the divine powers, men, or animals."[4]

On the difficulty of his practice, Jain tradition records,

For some it is not easy (to do what he did), not to answer those who salute; he was beaten with sticks and struck by sinful people.

Disregarding slights difficult to bear, the Sage wandered about, (not attracted) by story-tellers, pantomimes, songs, fights at quarter-staff, and boxing-matches. . . .

For more than a couple of years he led a religious life without using cold water; he realized singleness, guarded his body, had got intuition, and was calm.

Thoroughly knowing the earth-bodies and water-bodies and fire-bodies and wind-bodies, the lichens, seeds, and sprouts,

He comprehended that they are, if narrowly inspected, imbued with life, and avoided to injure them; he, the great Hero. . . .

Practicing the sinless abstinence from killing, he did no acts, neither himself nor with the assistance of others.

Acaranga Sutra 1.8.7–8, 10–12, 16[5]

Lord Mahavira was often treated violently.

When he who is free from desires approached the village, the inhabitants met him on the outside, and attacked him, saying, "Get away from here."

He was struck with a stick, the fist, a lance, hit with a fruit, a clod, a potsherd. Beating him again and again, many cried.

When he once (sat) without moving his body, they cut his flesh [or mustaches], tore his hair under pains, or covered him with dust.

Throwing him up, they let him fall, or disturbed him in his religious postackground postures; abandoning the care of his body, the Venerable One humbled himself and bore pain, free from desire.

Acaranga Sutra 2.1.9–12[6]

The wandering ascetic Lord Mahavira was said to have plucked out with his right and left hands his hair in five handfuls. Never staying more than one night in a village or more than five in a town, Lord Mahavira, according to tradition, never formed attachments to any place or people that might bind him to the world. Finally, the gods themselves awoke "the best of *Jinas*," referring to Lord Mahavira, with the injunction, "'*Arhat*'! Propagate the religion which is a blessing to all creatures in the world!"[7]

LORD MAHAVIRA ACHIEVED PERFECT KNOWLEDGE

After following such austere practices, Lord Mahavira achieved a state of purity, achieving omniscience (***kevala jnana***; Sanskrit, *kevala jñāna*), supreme and perfect knowledge, the omniscience that Jains regard as defining enlightenment. He had become a spiritual victor (Sanskrit, *jina*). "*Kevala jnana*" is a technical term referring to one having been cleansed of karmic matter—that is, of being detached from the bondage of samsara and now freed to ascend to the top of the universe in complete isolation. *Kevala jnana* is a state of painless omniscience, much like Hindu *moksha* or Buddhist nirvana.

After achieving a state of *kevala jnana*, liberation, at around the age of forty-three, Lord Mahavira traveled throughout northeast India for thirty years, teaching by his words and actions the path of purification of the soul. As the twenty-fourth *tirthankara*, a supreme leader who had discovered the passage across the ocean of suffering and existence, Lord Mahavira was recognized as the final supreme ford-finder. Parshva's fourfold restraint included ***ahimsa*** (noninjury), ***asatya*** (not lying), ***asteya*** (not taking anything not given), and ***aparigraha*** (nonattachment

Figure 4.4. Mahavira statue in Mumbai, India

180

to people, places, or things), with Mahavira later adding the fifth restraint, *brahmacharya* (chastity), which would form the Five Great Vows undertaken by Jain ascetics. Beyond Rishabha (considered the first *tirthankara*), Parshva, and Mahavira, almost nothing is known about the other *tirthankaras*, except that Jain scriptures note that all *tirthankaras* are from Kshatriya families and most of them were born in **Ayodhya**, located in the northeastern Indian state of Uttar Pradesh. Parshva's death place in the state of Bihar has become a major cultic center for Jains today.

Lord Mahavira's Death

Mahavira died by following the rite of **sallekhana**, voluntary self-starvation, after teaching about his insights for thirty years. Jains note that *sallekhana*, the Jain ritual death by fasting, should be seen as distinct from suicide, which implies spontaneity, impulse, and self-initiative due to one's depression or isolation, aimed to eliminate one's life. *Sallekhana* is interpreted as the "holy death" through gradual fasting in a peaceful, meditative manner, usually practiced at the end of life to demonstrate one's final act of renunciation. Today, Jains still practice *sallekhana* as a sign that they have conquered the material world. Controlling the desire for food is crucial to the spiritual life since eating anything has karmic repercussions, given that no food can be consumed without harming some form of life. Eliminating the craving for food can empower one to use that same control to eliminate all passions and attachments.

Jain Philosophy

The Law of Karma

Like Hinduism and Buddhism, Jainism affirms the existence of **karma** and the necessity to overcome karma in order to be released from the cycle

What do you make of the fact that Lord Buddha, Lord Mahavira, and Jesus Christ all had "enlightenment" experiences around the age of thirty? Is there something universal about the development of human beings that would allow for greater insight around that age? Siddhartha Gautama and Lord Mahavira both had wives, were from the Kshatriya warrior class, and led movements that eliminated Brahmanical control of the sacrificial system, Siddhartha Gautama by advocating the Middle Way and Lord Mahavira by following the extreme path of asceticism. Jesus led a democratizing movement that gave all people, Jew and gentile, access to God. It is striking to consider that Jesus promised fullness of life on earth, even within the fallen world in which we live and act daily.

Christian Reflections

of death and rebirth. The word "karma" is among the most salient terms in the Indian religious traditions. Karma is commonly employed by the Indian religious traditions, but it nevertheless is interpreted in a variety of ways, at least regarding which aspects of the term are emphasized over others. Karma means "action." And there are all kinds of actions, physical and mental. According to the theory of karma, every action has a consequence in one's current or future life to such a literal extent that one's current condition, positive or negative, is explained by reference to one's past actions.

> *The cause of the soul's embodiment is the presence in it of what is called karmic matter. The self is never separated from matter until its final release.*
>
> Radhakrishnan and Moore, *Sourcebook in Indian Philosophy*, 251

That is, karma is the perfect law of cause and effect. Actions done today will come to fruition. Each Indian religious tradition emphasizes a different aspect of action, physical or mental, and offers corresponding ways to achieve liberation. Jainism conceives of karma as a kind of subtle weight that binds to the ***jiva*** (Sanskrit, *jīva*, "living being," "soul"), weighing it down like pressure on a helium balloon. Any action (karma), good or bad, will weigh down the originally light and buoyant embodied soul. One's deeds are literally deposited in and on the *jiva*, like layers or incrustations of foreign substance that may form as many as five sheaths around the soul. Whenever the *jiva* is moved by desire or passion, it becomes, as it were, sticky, covering itself with or permeated by karmic matter. Lord Mahavira himself compared karma to the coats of clay that weigh down a *jiva*.

Unlike Hinduism and Buddhism, Jainism interprets karma in almost exclusively physical terms, as a physical substance that holds the soul prisoner. One needs to completely renounce action and adopt the extreme ascetic practice envisioned by Lord Mahavira and other *tirthankaras* to achieve liberation. Karmic clusters must be worn off by the process of living an ascetic lifestyle, since a *jiva* is pure consciousness trapped in the body.

The Nature of the Soul

Every *jiva* is in itself omniscient, but due to karmic defilement it loses this knowledge. Jains often use the metaphor of a diamond to express the idea about the physical blockage created by karma: it is like dust accumulated on a diamond that prevents it from shining brilliantly. One needs to rid oneself of karmic dust in order to see clearly again. As mentioned earlier, prior, current, and future karmic debt can be paid off speedily through extreme ascetic practices. Karmic debt can be relieved through increasing the heat (***tapas***) generated through Jain asceticism. Once the physical body, including desires and passions, is overcome, the *jiva* becomes a ***paramatman*** (Sanskrit, "supreme self"), freed from all impediments of action (karma)—this is the fully realized *jiva* that is disembodied, purified, and omniscient.

The *paramatman* is revered by Jains, for it is what distinguishes the *tirthan-kara* from the still-embodied spiritual aspirant. Once liberated, the *paramat-man* (the supreme **atman**) enters **moksha** (also referred to as **kevala** and **nirvana**). There are two distinct phases in the process of liberation. The first is enlightenment (*kevala jnana*), when karmic obstructions have been eliminated and the *jiva* is isolated and pure, remaining embodied until the moment of death. The second phase is when liberation itself (*kevala*, *moksha*, nirvana) occurs, marked by permanent freedom of the soul.

Nine Fundamentals

The Jain theory of karma is known as the Nine Fundamentals (Sanskrit, **Nav Tattvas**), the so-called nine reals, which illustrate the detailed focus on the nature of karma and the elimination of karmic buildup on the soul, which leads to the path of liberation.[8] An acceptable Jain tradition is to describe the Nav Tattvas in terms of a popular Jain analogy, with each fundamental related to a scene in a story about a farmhouse.

> There lived a family in a farmhouse. They were enjoying the fresh cool breeze coming through the open doors and windows. The weather suddenly changed, and a terrible dust storm set in. Realizing it was a bad storm, they got up to close the doors and windows. By the time they could close all the doors and windows, lots of dust had entered the house. After closing the doors and windows, they started clearing the dust that had come in to make the house clean.[9]

Interpreting this analogy using the Nav Tattvas gives us insight into the Jain path of liberation. First, the *jiva* (sentient soul) is represented by the people in the house. The *jiva* is described as blissful, self-contained, potent, and peaceful. Although it is similar to the atman (Sanskrit, "breath," "soul," "self"), the *jiva* is the embodied self, whereas atman is the self or soul freed from the bondage of existence. That is to say, the *jiva* is the atman in bondage and the atman is the *jiva* liberated. The body is merely a home for the soul (*jiva*). Jainism divides *jivas* into five categories according to how many senses these beings possess.

Second, **ajiva** (Sanskrit, *ajīva*, "not *jiva*," "not living," nonliving matter, insentient nonsoul) is represented by the house itself. Anything that does not have a soul (*jiva*) is called *ajiva*, which has no consciousness and, like *jiva*, is divided into five categories.[10] Third, **punya** ("merit," "result of good deeds," "action that produces happiness"), as a meritorious form of karma,

The heresy of gnosticism in the ancient world challenged Christian orthodoxy, provoking the New Testament writers to address its beliefs in their writings. Gnosticism was a broad range of perspectives that shared common features, rather than a narrowly defined movement. Gnostics (from Greek, *gnosis*, "knowledge" or "wisdom") claimed to have secret knowledge about the true nature of the world. Although each gnostic group had its own history and theological perspective, the feature common to most gnostic groups was a belief in a sharp contrast between the soul, which they argued was the true self that endured through many lifetimes, and the body, which trapped the soul.[a]

Gnostics believed that they were originally spiritual beings who had come to live in souls and bodies. Originally dwelling in the spiritual world above, they had been made to fall into this world of sense and sin. Now, thanks to their self-knowledge, they were reborn into the spiritual world. Gnosticism was professed to be universal, with dualism between pure and good spirit, impure and evil material reality, as a central theme. Subsequently, gnostics believed that an individual's true self, the spiritual self, needs to be freed from entrapment in the cycle of rebirths in evil bodies. Theologically, they posited the notion that since the world contains a blending of good and evil (i.e., bad matter and pure spirit), the world could not have been created by a good God. So gnostics denied the goodness of their bodies and all empirical reality, believing that matter (e.g., bodies) is not a part of one's true self. This dualism between matter and spirit led them to affirm that the highest spiritual path meant purifying the soul by denying bodily pleasures.

is represented by the enjoyment resulting from the nice cool breeze, suggesting that by undertaking healthy activities, one acquires good karmas. *Punya* results when, for instance, individuals perform acts of charity, propagate the teachings of Jainism, or act piously.

The self's (*jiva*) essence is life, the capacity of being liberated, and the incapacity of becoming liberated. . . .
The distinctive characteristic of self is attention.
Selves are [of two kinds]: worldly and liberated.

Tattvarthadhigama Sutra 2:7–8, 10[11]

Fourth, *pap* ("result of bad deeds," demeritorious form of karma) is represented by the discomfort resulting from the storm, which brought

Combined with certain elements of Christianity, gnosticism proved attractive to many early Christians. While statistics are unavailable on how many Christians were influenced by gnosticism in the ancient world, scholars suggest there was a time in early Christianity when the majority of Christians adhered to one or another of its forms. These gnostic Christians, and their scriptures, such as the *Gospel of Thomas* and other so-called gnostic gospels, presented Jesus as the savior who revealed secret wisdom about how to escape this evil world.[b] Jesus himself was depicted in the gnostic gospels as an angel of light. And his physical crucifixion was denied since gnostic Christians denied that Christ had a body.[c]

Indirectly, gnosticism proved a positive influence on Christianity because it forced early Christians to define the parameters of Christian orthodoxy in response to the threat of gnostic beliefs. There is a tinge of the legacy of gnosticism in some Christian communities today, at least to the degree that certain Christian groups may affirm the ultimate significance of the spirit over matter. While the Christian "battle" is not between flesh and spirit, Christians do affirm that we were created to live *in this world* as active agents that give testimony to God's kingdom on earth. Our ultimate destination may be heaven, but we live and have our being here on earth. Christians are, as some have suggested, resident aliens.[d]

a. See Placher, *History of Christian Theology*, 45.
b. For a general overview, see Pagels, *Gnostic Gospels*; Meyer, *Gnostic Gospels of Jesus*; and Layton, *Gnostic Scriptures*.
c. See Placher, *History of Christian Theology*, 46–47.
d. See Hauerwas and Willimon, *Resident Aliens*.

dust into the house. *Punya* eventually gives rise to happiness and calm. *Pap* is the result of undertaking bad activities, which, according to karmic law, incur bad *karmas*. *Pap* activities can range from being violent toward any living being, being angry, or showing disrespect to authorities such as parents or teachers. *Pap* eventually gives rise to suffering, unhappiness, sorrow, and despair.

Fifth, *asrava* (influx of karmic matter) is represented by the influx of dust through the doors and windows of the house, which is similar to the influx of karmic particles to the soul. This process of karmic incursion known as *asrava* is caused by physical, mental, or verbal activities such as wrong belief, strong passions, negligence, or failing to observe the fundamental Jain vows. *Asrava* functions as a conduit through which karma may enter the soul. Technically, Jainism accounts for forty-two types of such channels.

The Nine Nav Tattvas

1. *Jiva*: sentient soul
2. *Ajiva*: "not *jiva*," "not living," nonliving matter, insentient nonsoul
3. *Punya*: "merit," "result of good deeds," "action that produces happiness"
4. *Pap*: "result of bad deeds," demeritorious form of karma
5. *Asrava*: influx of karmic matter
6. *Samvar*: stoppage of karmic influx
7. *Bandha*: bondage of the soul by karmas
8. *Nirjara:* eradication of karmas
9. *Moksha:* liberation

Christian Reflections

Like the Jain tradition, Christianity also affirms the utter importance and eternal nature of the spirit (i.e., soul). Yet a difference between Christianity and Jainism is that Christianity maintains a distinction between the self (soul) and God. German Catholic theologian Karl Rahner (1904–84) wrote that

> [a human being] is a *Christ-centered* being, i.e., his being possesses an ontic and spiritual-personal capacity for communicating with Jesus Christ in whom God has forever made the countenance of a man his own and has opened the reality of man, with an unsurpassable finality, in the direction of God; only thus was the real possibility of a direct communication of all men with God established with finality. Hence . . . we can only speak ultimately of God by engaging . . . in anthropology; and ultimately any information about anthropology . . . can be given only when we engage in theology about God and from God.[a]

According to Rahner, human beings are inherently capable of communicating with God—but only through Jesus Christ, who opens us to God. Likewise, the Christian tradition teaches that human beings are created by God, and that God loves his creation immensely: "He who did not withhold his own Son, but gave him up for all of us, will he not with him also give us everything else?" (Rom. 8:32).

A Christian anthropology affirms that God created human beings for God's enjoyment. There is fellowship between the human and the divine, but not total immersion that leads to the emancipation of self from material reality. God's creation is a reflection of God's good and generous nature. What is remarkable is that God created human beings in God's image (Gen. 1:26),

Sixth, *samvar* (stoppage of karma influx) is the process of reversing the flow of material (karma) particles that bind the *jiva* (individual). In the house analogy, *samvar* is represented by closing the doors and windows to stop the dust from entering the house, which is similar to the stoppage of the influx of karmic particles to the soul. Blocking the continuing influx of karmic contact on the *jiva* requires one to observe *samiti* (Sanskrit, "moderation," "carefulness") in walking, speaking, bodily desires, handling of objects, and disposal of excreta (e.g., urine, mucus).

Seventh, *bandha* (Sanskrit, "lock," bond, bondage of the soul by karmas) is illustrated by the accumulation of dust in the house, which is similar to the bondage of karmic particles to the *jiva*. In fact, according to Jains, this is the actual binding of karmic particles to the *jiva*. In Jainism, the bondage of karma to the *jiva* is caused by activities of the body-mind complex influenced

which gives human beings a special relationship with God. As such, human beings are conscious of worshiping God, rather than a form of divinity within themselves, like Jainism suggests. In the words of French mathematician, writer, and Christian philosopher Blaise Pascal (1623–62), referring to a person seeking happiness, "he in vain tries to fill from all his surroundings, seeking from things absent the help he does not obtain in things present[.] But these are all inadequate, because the infinite abyss can only be filled by an infinite and immutable object, that is to say, only by God Himself."[b] Hence the Christian tradition teaches that there remains a distinction between Creator and created (including material reality), with the knowledge that peace and joy can be experienced only in relationship with God through Jesus Christ.

The possibility that human beings can be in communion with God and yet distinct from God can only be described as a mystery, where communion and distinction embrace one another in mystery. Christians experience the tension between living *in the spirit* and living *according to the flesh* (see Paul's inner conflict, Rom. 7), yet the Bible affirms that in the post-fall world human beings are unable to rid themselves of inherited sin, no matter how hard they try. God's creation is good, yet fallen and in need of redemption. The Christian tradition affirms the coexistence of spirit and matter, with the fallenness of all things to be redeemed in Christ. Redemption happens in real time and space, within the confines of the material world, with its consummation in heaven.

a. Rahner, *Theological Investigations*, 2:240–41.
b. Pascal, *Pensées*, 425.

by human passions (Sanskrit, *kasāya*) that make the *jiva* vulnerable to the accumulation of karmic buildup. *Bandha* occurs when individuals react to any situation with a sense of attachment or aversion—any strong attachment or passion—that leads to the interpenetration of karmic matter and soul, described like the blending of milk and water. According to a Jain monk, "The entire universe is thickly stuffed with it [karmic matter]."[12]

The Jain theory of karma recognizes four causes of bondage, which require the cultivation of opposite qualities for their removal. These causes are **mithyatva** ("delusion," "perversion of faith"), meaning lack of spiritual reflection; **avirati** (nonrestraint), meaning lack of control and enjoyment of worldly pleasures; **pramada** (carelessness, negligence), meaning spiritual lethargy regarding virtuous acts; **kasaya** (passions), meaning passions like anger and greed; and **yoga** (activities, disciplines), meaning negative activities of the mind, speech, and body. In the words of Jain monk Muni Shri Nyayavijayaji,

> Water enters a boat through holes and when those holes are filled with some proper substance water stops entering the boat. Similarly, activities of mind, speech, and body are the entrances through which karmic matter enters the soul, and when these entrances are shut, the karmic matter stops entering the soul. It is a common experience that when we shut windows and doors, the dust does not enter a room and settle on clothes hanging in it. Similarly, when the activities that serve as doors for the entry of the karmic matter are completely arrested, no karmic matter at all enters the soul and sticks to it.[13]

The one who is able to "shut the windows and doors" of his mind, speech, and body is called the one who is liberated-while-living-in-the-world—that is, **jivanmukta** (Sanskrit, "liberated while living"). That individual lives in the world but is not of it. According to the tradition, liberation is so literal that once one has achieved the state of *jivanmukta* it doesn't matter whether one has a body or not; one is liberated even while embodied.

Eighth, **nirjara** (eradication of karmas) is the destruction of karmas, represented by the cleaning up of accumulated dust from the house, which is similar to shedding accumulated karmic particles from the soul. In this process of shedding karmic matter called *nirjara*, karmic matter can be shed either passively or by active efforts. That is to say, one can wait for karmas to mature and to give their results in due time (*akama nirjara*) or actively strive to destroy karmas even before their enjoyment is finished (*sakama nirjara*). The aggressive process of shedding karmic matter highlights one of the most distinctive features of Jainism—that is, the ability to purify one's *jiva* (soul) of past, present, and future karmas even before the karma (act) is complete.

On a practical level, *sakama nirjara* can be achieved by such practices as performing penance, following a strict ascetic lifestyle, asking for forgiveness for the discomfort one may have caused someone, or engaging in meditation.

Finally, the ninth Nav Tattvas is *moksha* (liberation, nirvana), represented by the cleaned house; it is similar to shedding all karmic particles from the soul. If one rids oneself of all karmas, one will attain *moksha*. Release from samsara, the cycle of death and rebirth, is the highest state of isolation, in which one is freed from all bonds of karmic particles.

Jain Teaching

THE INTERNALIZATION OF SACRIFICE

Jainism emerged, along with Buddhism, toward the end of the Vedic period of Hinduism, a time of great social transformation in northern India.

Jain theory of karma and *jiva* is highly detailed, reflecting the seriousness with which Jains approach the relationship between action and soul. Just as when we study different religions and their sacred texts, learning what is important in the tradition in part by the frequency and specificity with which particular concepts are discussed, so too we learn that Jains put great effort into purifying the soul (*jiva*) so that it will be released into a liberated state of omniscience. The religious path is the path of purification. And the effort to purify lies in the hands of the devotee, without the assistance of a god or deity. And according to Jainism, the achievement of purification is indeed possible even on earth. What does Christianity say about purity? Are Christians required to be pure? How pure?

Vigorous theological debates throughout the history of the church about purity have given rise to significant theological variety within Christianity today, with some claiming that purity (i.e., entire sanctification) is possible within the spans of our earthly lives while others claim that purity will be obtained only in heaven. Regardless, we cannot deny that the Bible admonishes Christians—and Jews before them—to be pure (e.g., Job 15:14–15; Hosea 8:5; Pss. 19:9; 51:10; 2 Cor. 6:6, Phil. 2:15; 1 Tim. 4:12; 5:2; 1 Pet. 3:2).

Yet it is not our purity that provides liberation or salvation. Recall that the North African early church father Augustine (354–430) confronted the ascetic monk Pelagius (c. 354–c. 420), who contended that the biblical command for perfection (Matt. 5:48: "Be perfect, as your heavenly Father is perfect") implies that perfection is possible. Pelagius's famous statement, "the obligation implies the ability," was built entirely on the notion that we are totally responsible for our actions and that we can be "without sin" if we continue to choose (cf. karma) the good.

Christian Reflections

The Vedic sacred texts of Hinduism were written in Sanskrit, outside the intellectual reach of common people, which was one reason why the Vedic religion eventually lost support. By contrast, Jain sacred literature was more accessible, because it was written in Prakrit, a language of the common people in northern India. As mentioned above, Jainism shares many similarities with Hinduism and Buddhism. For instance, Hinduism, Jainism, and Buddhism all affirm samsara (the cycle of death and rebirth), the practice

Figure 4.5. Mahavira accepting alms (Digambara Temple, Mumbai, India)

Anishshah/Wikimedia Commons

n his letter "On the Grace of Christ," Augustine confronts the central issues of Pelagius's thinking about perfection, launching a frontal attack on Pelagius's theological anthropology:

> In his system, [Pelagius] posits and distinguishes three faculties, by which he says God's commandments are fulfilled,—*capacity, volition,* and *action*: meaning by "capacity," that by which a man is able to be righteous; by "volition," that by which he wills to be righteous; by "action," that by which he actually is righteous. The first of these, the capacity, he allows to have been bestowed on us by the Creator of our nature; it is not in our power, and we possess it even against our will. The other two, however, the volition and the action, he asserts to be our own; and he assigns them to us so strictly as to contend that they proceed simply from ourselves. In short, according to his view, God's grace has nothing to do with assisting those two faculties which he will have to be altogether our own, the volition and the action, but that only which is not in our power and comes to us from God, namely the capacity; as if the faculties which are our own, that is, the volition and the action, have such avail for declining evil and doing good, that they require no divine help, whereas that faculty which we have of God, that is to say, the capacity, is so weak, that it is always assisted by the aid of grace.[a]

Augustine argued that we possess neither the *capability* nor the *power* to save ourselves. None of our efforts, actions, or intentions can save us. According to John Calvin (1509–64) even our reliance on "religious efforts" to reach God demonstrates "that man's nature, so to speak, is a perpetual factory of idols." Karl Barth (1886–1968) borrowed Calvin's language to argue that human beings were, without the revelation of God, "idol factories."[b]

of nonviolence, the possibility of liberation from life through the practice of asceticism, the ordination within the monastic community, and the struggle to eliminate karma.

The two most important ideas, samsara and karma, were central to Indian religious traditions. Jains, along with Buddhists and Hindus, accepted the idea of samsara and karma, with the necessity to shed karma. The concept of karma was originally connected to the correctly performed sacrificial action (*karman*) in the context of Vedic Hindu religion. Jains also focused on sacrifice but reinterpreted it to refer to both internal and external actions.

There is a well-known story that illustrates the fundamental difference between the notion of sacrifice in the Jain tradition and in Buddhist traditions through the narrative of the encounter of a Jain monk and a group of Hindu Brahmins. According to a story recorded in Jain scriptures, the Jain monk Harikesha silently approached some Brahmin priests who were performing a sacrifice. On being violently attacked by them, Harikesha was saved by a tree

Calvin's perspective on the relationship of *spirit* and *matter* profoundly affected his theological insights on a vast range of topics, such as the use of icons, stained-glass windows, and musical instruments. Calvin inherited Ulrich Zwingli's (1484–1531) conviction that material objects, such as icons and clerical vestments, were incapable of communicating the spirit of grace. In fact, Zwingli was an iconoclast, an advocate of destroying images and stained-glass windows since they could lead to idolatry and could in no way communicate God's grace; only the Bible could do this, as the sole authority for the Christian. In the Reformation debates about the relationship between *spirit* and *matter*, Martin Luther (1483–1546) upheld the view that matter could mediate the Spirit of God, whereas Zwingli maintained a strict dichotomy between *spirit* and *matter*, arguing forcefully that material objects could not mediate the Spirit.

What is important for us is not the details of the debate, which are quite fascinating in themselves, but the fact that the early Reformers, while they disagreed about the relationship between *spirit* and *matter*, nevertheless affirmed that *spirit* and *matter* coexist in human beings and that salvation does not involve the separation of the two.[c] Even Zwingli, and later Calvin, despite his contempt of the view that matter could mediate spirit, did not repudiate the material world as something apart from which one was saved.

a. This original selection comes from Augustine's letter "On the Grace of Christ" (year 418), chap. 4, quoted in Placher, *Readings in the History of Christian Theology*, 1:115–16.

b. Calvin, *Institutes of the Christian Religion*, 1:108.

c. For instance, see Placher, *History of Christian Theology*, 188–90; and González, *History of Christian Thought*, 3:70–85.

spirit that intervened on his behalf. The climax of the episode is Harikesha's explanation to the Brahmins of the nature of the true, internal sacrifice of a Jain monk. Notice the vivid description Harikesha uses to compare the elements of the Brahmin's sacrificial fire to that of the Jain monk.

> Austerity is my sacrificial fire, my life is the place where the fire is kindled. Mental and physical efforts are my ladle for the oblation and my body is the dung fuel for the fire, my actions my firewood. I offer up an oblation praised by the wise seers consisting of my restraint, effort, and calm.
>
> *Uttaradhyayana Sutra* 12:44–45[14]

Thus, according to Harikesha, purity has nothing to do with birth (i.e., class or caste) or ritual purity, but comes about through steadfast adherence to Jain principles. By comparison, the heat (*tapas*) generated by the Brahmin's sacrificial fire is insignificant compared to the heat generated by the austerity (*tapas*) produced by the Jain monk through his intense ascetic practices.[15] *Tapas* (Sanskrit, "heat"), meaning "austerity," "penance," "energy," and "to heat up," is a spiritual force of concentrated energy generated by a spiritual devotee that is instrumental to the acquisition of spiritual power and liberation.

SEVERE ASCETIC PRACTICES

More broadly among the Indian religious traditions, *tapas* is the power underlying all manifestations—so much so that the Hindu scriptures note that cosmic order (**rita**) and truth (**satya**) were created from it (Rig Veda 10.190). The Indian religious traditions recognize that while this cosmic force cannot be created by the Gods, it could be created in the fire sacrifices performed by Brahmin priests, who manifest *tapas* by sweating. Eventually severe ascetic practices, such as fasting, celibacy, and meditation, were adopted by priests to increase their *tapas* (heat) for the performance of sacrificial rituals.[16] There is a direct correspondence between the purification of the body and the purification of the soul, with the necessity to purify everything that pollutes. The Jain practice of *sallekhana* (self-starvation) is an example of the tremendous effort to generate *tapas* and to withdraw from the world.

Consequently, spiritual authority is vested not in the ritual technician, such as the Brahmin priest, but in the individual who generates *tapas* through ascetic practices—that is, the fire of austerity. No longer would individuals need to follow the long process of ritual sacrifice. Now they could quickly destroy karmic buildup by increasing the heat produced by austerity. Jain asceticism is known for being the most rigorous of all forms of asceticism in the Indian religious traditions.

Can we see that Christ's death affected a kind of *tapas* (heat) sufficient for salvation? Is it helpful to propose that instead of leading toward his own bodily purification and spiritual enlightenment, Christ's death satisfied the penalty of sin that marks human existence? How should we understand the relationship between *tapas* and suffering, not *dukkha* but the kind of suffering biblical writers refer to as part of the Christian life? "Whoever does not take up the cross and follow me is not worthy of me" (Matt. 10:38); "Then [Jesus] said to them all, 'If any want to become my followers, let them deny themselves and take up their cross daily and follow me'" (Luke 9:23).

Since the time Christ called his first disciples, his followers have suffered, sometimes paying with their lives for their witness. The history of the Christian church, beginning with the biblical witness, is a story of followers of Christ who were sent out to proclaim in word and deed the presence of the kingdom of God and new life in Christ. They were called to be witnesses (Greek, *martyres*), where the English equivalent, "martyr," means to seal one's commitment through suffering. It is far too tempting in some Christian communities to have an overly spiritualized, otherworldly orientation to life, where the religious path entails looking beyond the world of the material realm rather than looking at it. Yet regardless of one's spiritual orientation, Christians should anticipate suffering experienced as a result of being witnesses to the kingdom of God, which may entail confronting the powers and principalities that lead to unrighteousness and injustice of all kinds. This world is not what God intended (Isa. 5:1–7; Luke 13:6–9). The Christian tradition promises not that one will be free from suffering, but that in all things, through Jesus Christ, we will have power to overcome our circumstances.

COSMOLOGY

Cosmology is the reflection on the world and the universe as a meaningful whole, whether the universe is understood as being an independent organism or the expression of a transcendent being or beings. Cosmologies necessarily communicate knowledge about the origins and nature of the world and the universe (the cosmos). As such, cosmologies are linked to cosmogony, the theory of the origin of the universe, and cosmography, the mapping of the world and the cosmos, typically including the use of astronomy, geography, and geology.[17] According to Jain cosmology, the universe runs on its own cosmic laws, with no creator deity who initiated the creative act. According to Jain tradition, the belief that the cosmos was created by a god is a false and "evil doctrine."

Some foolish men declare that Creator made the world. The doctrine that the world was created is ill-advised, and should be rejected.

If God created the world, where was he before creation? If you say he was transcendent then, and needed no support, where is he now?

No single being had the skill to make this world—

For how can an immaterial god create that which is material?

How should God have made the world without any raw material? If you say he made this first, and then the world, you are faced with an endless regression.

If you declare that his raw material arose naturally you fall into another fallacy, for the whole universe might thus have been its own creator, and have arisen equally naturally.

If God created the world by an act of his own will, without any raw material, then it is just his will and nothing else—and who will believe this silly stuff? If he is ever perfect and complete, how could the will to create have arisen in him? If, on the other hand, he is not perfect, he could no more create the universe than a potter could.

If he is formless, actionless, and all-embracing, how could he have created the world? Such a soul, devoid of all modality, would have no desire to create anything.

If he is perfect, he does not strive for the three aims of man, so what advantage would he gain by creating the universe?

If you say that he created to no purpose, because it was his nature to do so, then God is pointless. If he created in some kind of sport, it was the sport of a foolish child, leading to trouble.

If he created because of the karma of embodied beings [acquired on a previous creation] he is not the Almighty Lord, but subordinate to something else. . . .

If out of love for living things and need of them he made the world, why did he not make creation wholly blissful, free from misfortune?

If he were transcendent he would not create, for he would be free; nor if involved in transmigration, for then he would not be almighty.

Thus the doctrine that the world was created by God makes no sense at all.

And God commits great sin in slaying the children whom he himself created. If you say that he slays only to destroy evil beings, why did he create such beings in the first place? . . .

Good men should combat the believer in divine creation, maddened by an evil doctrine.

Know that the world is uncreated, as time itself is, without beginning and end, and is based on the principles, life and the rest.

Uncreated and indestructible, it endures under the compulsion of its own nature, divided into three sections—hell, earth, and heaven.

Mahapurana 4.16–31, 38–40[18]

Jains affirm the existence of blissful, perfected souls (*jiva* or atman) who are omniscient and omnipotent, but not a distinct god who created the universe. As such, there are many gods in Jainism, and their numbers are increasing as living beings gain liberation and enter the realm of *moksha*. No creator God is necessary or possible for creation, since the universe consists of mental and material factors that have been and will be in eternity. All natural forces exist without the intervention of a deity.

Yet within these natural forces some are purer than others, which explains the movement of upward mobility of individual *jivas* to higher levels of heaven. Space itself is devoid of any sensory potential, so it is without sight, sound, taste, touch, and smell. Jain thinkers speak of the insignificance of human beings in comparison to the vastness of the universe: "The universe is very vast. We are very small. We are nothing when compared to the stupendous universe. In it we are like an atom. We are insignificant. This makes us humble and dissolves our pride."[19]

The Jains adopted the notion of the hierarchical ***triloka*** (Sanskrit, "three worlds") from Indian cosmology, often depicted in the shape of an hourglass. According to Jainism, the universe is shaped roughly in the form of a human being, with the earth situated at waist level. The three worlds of existence consist of a series of heavens or celestial worlds (Sanskrit, *urdhvaloka*); the middle world (Sanskrit, *mahhyaloka*), which is populated by earthbound living beings, such as human beings, animals, and insects; and the lower world (Sanskrit, *adholoka*).

Wikimedia Commons

Figure 4.6. Jain cosmology depicted as a cosmic man, Loka-Purusha (Samghayanarayana manuscript, India, c. 16th century)

Jains think of the cosmos less as a compilation of distinct domains than as a graded progression of heavens and hells that join in the middle ground of earth. The heavens consist of many heavens of increasing brightness, culminating at the very top, the highest place in the cosmos (Sanskrit, *iśatpragbhara*) in a region populated by entirely purified, disembodied souls. At the top of the celestial heavens, in the region of the head of the imaginary cosmological human body, dwell the perfected, liberated souls. The world below consists of seven layers of increasingly horrible hells (purgatories) populated by those still possessing karmic matter, with the most evil beings in the worse hells, and out of which people are reborn with further opportunities to purify their souls.

When liberated, the soul rises through the universe and comes to dwell in the top, in the area known as the *siddha-sila* (Sanskrit, "the home of the perfected ones"), where they become a *siddha* (Sanskrit, "perfected one," "complete one"). This region lies far above the stars, a gradually purer

Christian Reflections

The Christian (and Jewish and Muslim) affirmation is that God created the heavens and the earth. God created the world out of nothing—*creatio ex nihilo*—rather than out of preexisting matter (*creatio ex materia*) or out of God (*creatio ex deo*). Into nothingness, God breathed existence into being, which turns out to be a demonstration of God's divine integrity. What God said, appeared. By God's *ruaḥ* (Hebrew, "spirit," "breath," "air," "wind")—the breath of God—God created the world. That is to say, while God is distinct from creation, God's spirit was still present in God's creation. The Bible declares, "By the word of the Lᴏʀᴅ the heavens were made, and all their host by the breath of his mouth" (Ps. 33:6). According to theologian Hans Küng, *ex nihilo* is

> a theological formula for the belief that the world and humanity, space and time, have no other cause but God for their existence. And since God is the origin of each and every thing, he faces no competition from an evil or demonic counterprinciple (as he would in Mazdaism or Manichaeism): According to the biblical account of creation, the world in general and in particular, including matter, the human body, and sexuality—is fundamentally good.[a]

Consequently, according to Christian tradition, the world is neither the emanation of God—which is the denial of monism, or the idea that God is identical to the world—nor strictly and entirely separate from God (complete dualism). Christian theology "ascribes to God a basic relationship with the world, and to the world a basic *participation in the divine Being*, in the dynamic Being that is God."[b] So the world is not autonomous from God, the Creator, but instead is relative, finding its existence as substantial beings to the extent that creation shares in the Being itself (God). That is, God remains both inside and outside creation, which remains a paradox.

a. Küng, *Christianity and World Religions*, 205. Mazdaism refers to Zoroastrianism, a religion that acknowledges the divinity called Ahura Mazda, proclaimed by Zoroaster in Persia. Manichaeism was a dualistic religion from Persia whose prophet Mani denied the existence of a good and perfect God, and whose theology focused on the conflict between the spirit (good) and the body (bad).

b. Ibid., 206.

counterpart to the earthly, lower world. The surest way to reach liberation is through the power accumulated from the practice of asceticism or austerities (*tapas*), which aims at the purification of all desires for dependence on the world and any of its matter.

REALITY

The principle elements of reality are simple. All reality consists of either *jiva* (soul, spirit) or *ajiva* (all matter, everything that is not *jiva*). All *jivas* have equal value regardless of the *ajiva* they inhabit, human or otherwise. All living beings consist of a *jiva* and an *ajiva*—embodied souls. It is important to note that the Jain understanding of living beings is quite broad and includes human beings, animals, insects, vegetation, and even earth, stones, fire, water, and air. Even the universe is seen as being animated by *jivas*. Through contact with *ajiva* and the accumulation of karma, the originally pure, omniscient, and blissful *jiva* is now bound to the samsara. Some *jivas* are minute while others are enormous, but all *jivas* correspond to the actual dimensions of the *ajiva*. For instance, the soul of a human being actually fills the human body, having the same shape as that particular human body. Likewise, the soul of an insect fills the insect with the same size.

McKay Savage/Wikimedia Commons

Figure 4.7. Ranakpu Jain temple in Udaipur, India

The larger the body (*ajiva*), the larger the soul (*jiva*) that fills it. Damaging living beings of any kind is a serious matter, resulting in bad karmic consequences. Furthermore, Jainism classifies all living beings according to the number of senses they possess, with the highest-sensed being on top and the lowest-sensed being on the bottom. The highest category of living beings is the five-sense beings, which have all five senses (sight, hearing, taste, touch, smell), such as human beings, animals, gods, and hell beings. The second category consists of four-sense beings such as larger insects, bees, flies, and butterflies. The third contains three-sense beings, such as moths and smaller insects, without sight and hearing. The fourth category consists of two-sensed beings, such as worms, shellfish, leeches, and minute creatures. And the fifth category, that of one-sense beings, consists of such living beings as vegetables, trees, seeds, wind bodies, water bodies, and fire bodies. All living beings, whether large or small, great or humble, need to be respected.

Earth and water, fire and wind,
    Grass, trees, and plants, and all creatures that move,
Born of the egg, born of the womb,
    Born of dung, born of liquids—

These are the classes of living beings.
    Know that they all seek happiness.
In hurting them men hurt themselves,
    And will be born again among them. . . .

The man who lights a fire kills living things,
    While he who puts it out kills the fire;
Thus a wise man who understands the Law
    Should never light a fire.

There are lives in earth and lives in water,
    Hopping insects leap into the fire,
And worms dwell in rotten wood.
    All are burned when a fire is lighted.

Even plants are beings, capable of growth,
    Their bodies need food, they are individuals.
The reckless cut them for their own pleasure
    And slay many living things in doing so.

He who carelessly destroys plants, whether sprouted or full grown,
    Provides a rod for his own back.
He has said, "Their principles are ignoble
    Who harm plants for their own pleasure."

Sutrakritanga 1.1–9[20]

Karma and Living Beings

The higher the life form, the heavier the karmic burden of its destruction. Given that living beings are in wind, water, and fire, it is impossible to live without harming some living being. It is better to liberate one's soul from this life, which is fraught with the constant killing of living beings. Each breath inhales and destroys living bodies. When one walks, each step has the real potential of destroying some minute life form, thereby adding to one's karmic weight.

Jain tradition teaches that every centimeter is filled with living beings—for instance, each drop of water contains at least three thousand living beings. The intense focus on eliminating all forms of violence to all living beings has required various practices aimed at lessening the impact on living beings. The necessity of honoring all life remains an essential commitment of Jain devotees, though not all Jains share the same practices to avert violence to living forms (such as covering the mouth with cloth, straining all water, or sweeping the path before walking to move aside all living beings).

As you may recall, Jainism is a part of that great constellation of Indian religions and philosophies that have inspired millions of people worldwide, yet it interprets the fundamental Indian philosophical terms differently than do Buddhism or Hinduism. For instance, Hinduism posits that Brahman, the unspeakable essence behind everything, is absolutely permanent, motionless, while everything else is ultimately illusory. Buddhism, on the other hand, suggests that reality consists of a series of discrete elements (i.e., origination and destruction, like cause and effect), perpetually changing such that appearances of being static or permanent are illusory since everything is always in flux. Distinct from these other two Indian religious traditions, the Jain perspective on reality affirms a triple nature of origination (i.e., cause, destruction, and persistence), so that reality is both permanent and changing.

A Jain ideal is to recognize the impermanency of the material world while affirming the permanency and the necessity of purifying the soul. In the words of Lord Mahavira,

On account of its permanent aspect, the thing is called permanent (unchanging, static). And on account of its impermanent aspect, it is regarded as undergoing origination and destruction (i.e., as constantly changing). When we pay attention to one aspect alone, we find the thing either absolutely permanent or absolutely impermanent. But when we pay attention to both the aspects, we know the thing in its entirety, as it is.

Nyayavijayaji, *Jaina Darśana,* 336–37

By hurting these [living] beings, people do harm to their own souls, and will repeatedly be born as one of them.

Sutrakritanga 1.7.2[21]

Ahimsa

Given the pervasive nature and presence of living beings, it is crucial to recognize that the severe ascetic practices advocated by Jainism are a logical extension of the Jain understanding of the most fundamental aspects of life. The central virtue of Jainism is *ahimsa* (Sanskrit, "noninjury," "nonviolence"), the law of compassion in the body, mind, and spirit. Considered negatively, *ahimsa* refers to restraining oneself from causing any injury to any living being and thus preventing karmic accumulation.

Positively, the concept enjoins devotees to show love, compassion, benevolence, and affection to all beings. Since every living thing has a soul, Lord Mahavira opposed killing and took unusual precautions not to injure any living being, directly or indirectly. Put simply, the Jain challenge is to refrain from violence and to engage in life-affirming activities. Refraining from doing harm to living things is insufficient, since karmic defilement of the soul needs to be counterbalanced by doing good to living beings.

Referring to Lord Mahavira, the Jain scriptures note,

More than four months many sorts of living beings gathered on his body, crawled about it, and caused there pain. For a year and a month he did not leave off his robe. Since that time the Venerable One, giving up his robe, was a naked, world-relinquishing, houseless sage. Then he meditated (walking) with his eye fixed on a square spaced before him of the length of a man. Many people assembled, shocked at the sight; they struck him and cried.

Acaranga Sutra 1.8.2–4[22]

Without ceasing in his reflections, and avoiding to overlook them, the Venerable One slowly wandered about, and, killing no creatures, he begged for his food. Moist or dry or cold food, old beans, old pap, or bad grain, whether he did or did not get such food, he was rich (in control). And Mahavira meditated (persevering) in some posture, without the smallest motion; he meditated in mental concentration on (the things) above, below, beside, free from desires. He meditated free from sin and desire, not attached to sounds or colors; though still an erring mortal (*khadmastha*), he wandered about, and never acted carelessly. Himself understanding the truth and restraining the impulses for the purification of the soul, finally liberated, and free from delusion, the Venerable One was well guarded during his whole life.

Acaranga Sutra 1.8.12–16[23]

On the point of nonviolence (*ahimsa*), Jainism is quite practical. Since it is impossible not to kill a life form, given that people need water to drink, dig up the earth to build houses, and so on, lay Jains vow, "I shall not kill with determined intention," thereby maintaining the Jain's promise to uphold non-violence. Added to the statement is another phrase, "when they are innocent," which becomes a limiting factor: Jains recognize times when they need to kill—for instance, in self-defense—but unbridled killing is unwarranted on any grounds.

The possible kinds of violence are divided into four categories: (1) intentional violence (*sankalpi himsa*), (2) violence undertaken by ordinary daily actions of a householder (*arambhi himsa*), (3) violence perpetuated through one's occupation (*udyogi himsa*), and (4) violence as self-defense (*virodhi himsa*). The only type of violence lay Jains need to relinquish is *sankalpi himsa*—that is, intentional violence—while the other three are considered the result of the daily acts of most Jains. The lay Jain devotee may kill living beings daily, but that kind of "violence" is, or should be, unintentional. With the presence of innumerable living bodies, no action is free from violence. But violence done to lesser sense-beings and without being intentional carries fewer karmic repercussions. The opening verses of *The Book of Sermons* summarize Jain teaching on the central themes of nonviolence and karma:

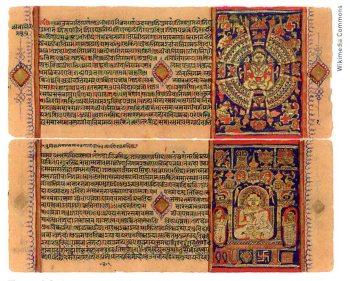

Figure 4.8. Suryaprajnapti Sutra, Jain scripture (c. 1500, western India)

> One should know what binds the soul, and, knowing, break free from bondage. What bondage did the Hero declare, and what knowledge did he teach to remove it? He who grasps at even a little, whether living or lifeless, or consents to another doing so, will never be freed from sorrow.
>
> If a man kills living things, or slays by the hand of another, or consents to another slaying, his sin goes on increasing.
>
> The man who cares for his kin and companions is a fool who suffers much, for their numbers are ever increasing.
>
> All his wealth and relations cannot save him from sorrow. Only if he knows the nature of life, will he get rid of karma.
>
> *Sutrakritanga* 1.1.1.1–5[24]

Worship and Practice

Practices of Liberation

As you might imagine by the discussion of nonviolence and the impossibility of following the doctrine absolutely and literally, there are different strategies to gain liberation as well as different levels of commitment to a life of nonviolence. *Moksha-marga* (path of liberation) is for all Jains, lay or monk or nun. Ultimately, however, the Jain devotee is alone in his or her struggle for liberation: "When the monk realizes that he is alone, that he has no connection with anyone and that no one has any connection with him, in the same way he should realize that his self is also alone."[25]

The path to liberation (Sanskrit, *moksha-marga*) is summarized in Jainism as the **Triratna** (Sanskrit, "Three Jewels"), which consists of **right knowledge** (*samyag-jñana*), which is specialized knowledge of the essence of the self (*jiva*), **right vision** (*samyag-darshana*), the fundamentally important faith in the

Christian Reflections

How would Christians live their lives differently were they to affirm the sacredness of all living beings? The Christian tradition believes that God gave human beings stewardship over creation. Abuse of that privilege has led to all kinds of destructive activities that do not uphold the goodness of creation. Christianity too has a tradition of nonviolence—or, at least, a theological perspective on the conditions under which a Christian can use force.

The patristic father Augustine (354–430) articulated what has become known as the just war theory, which has had immense impact on religious and political discourse in the West. What similarities exist between the Jain categories of violence and the Augustinian notion of a just war (Latin, *bellum justum*)? The Just War theory, initiated by Cicero (106–43 BCE) but developed by and credited to Augustine, required that certain criteria must be met prior to engaging in the use of force. All criteria need to be met for war or the use of force to be justified.

Augustine's just war theory was divided into two major divisions, *jus ad bellum* (right to war) and *jus in bello* (justice in war), or that which justifies entrance into war and how combatants are to act in war, respectively. The theory attempted to answer two questions for Christians: "When can I justify using force?" and "How do I use that force?" The just war theory staked out a middle ground between a pacifist attitude and a crusade spirit, where pacifism says, "You can never enter war," and the crusade spirit says, "We can use unlimited power and unrestrained violence."

"reals" of *jiva*, *ajiva*, *bandha*, *samvara*, *nirjara*, and *moksha*, and **right conduct** (*samyak-caritra*), the practice of beneficial activities that lead to liberation and abstinence from harmful activities that bind the individual, leading to a pure life free from moral vices. The *ajiva* binds the *jiva*. The goal of Jainism is to liberate one's *jiva* that has been enmeshed and weighed down by karma. The Three Jewels provide a practical guide to achieving that liberation.[26] Therefore, an individual can save herself (*jiva*) by discovering her own perfect, unchanging nature, transcending the miseries of earthly life.

Dineshkarnambadi/Wikimedia Commons

Figure 4.9. Jain Narayana temple in Karnataka, India

Jus ad bellum included having a *just cause*—for instance, to regain something wrongfully taken, to punish evil, or in defense against planned or actual aggression. *Jus ad bellum* also requires a *lawful authority*, which means that the use of force must be an organized activity of a state, or proper authority, such as the king, queen, or president, rather than individuals or groups who do not constitute an authority sanctioned by the state. Third, it requires *just intent*, which means that the goal of war must be to promote or secure peace, not merely to obtain revenge, wealth, or personal glory. Fourth, a just cause requires that war be fought as a *last resort*, which calls states to avoid using force if reasonably possible, through negotiations and diplomacy. And fifth, there must be a *reasonable hope of success*, since a hopeless war is deemed pointless and irresponsible.

The conditions of *jus in bello* (justice in war) include *discrimination*, which means that warring parties are obligated to discriminate between an enemy's armed forces and its civilian population, upholding noncombatant immunity, unless civilians shield legitimate military targets; and *proportionality*, which means that the amount and type of force to be utilized in war should be the minimum necessary to end war and secure peace. Similarly, given that Jains recognize the inevitability of doing some kind of violence to living beings, there are nevertheless limitations on the use of violence.

Moksha, then, results when the *jiva* has been cleansed of all karmas, when nothing remains except the purified *jiva*. Needless to say, the life of Lord Mahavira is regarded as an ideal model. It is interesting to note that while Lord Mahavira was depicted as living in solitude, Jain monks and nuns today ordinarily live in a "company" (**sangha**) where they receive support from fellow Jains, much like Buddhist monks receiving alms from lay Buddhists as a means to accrue merit. In the Jain perspective, the path of liberation leads ultimately to the elimination of all passions and culminates in omniscience as a pure self (atman), being liberated from matter. This state has been described as possessing infinite perception, infinite knowledge, infinite power, and infinite bliss. A Jain text describes the liberated, perfect souls:

> [The liberated soul] is not long nor small nor round nor triangular nor quadrangular nor circular; he is not black nor blue nor red nor green nor white; neither of good nor bad smell; not bitter nor pungent nor astringent nor sweet; neither rough nor soft; neither heavy nor light; neither cold nor hot; neither harsh nor smooth; he is without body, without resurrection, without contact (of matter), he is not feminine nor masculine nor neuter; he perceives, he knows, but there is no analogy (whereby to know the nature of the liberated soul); its essence is without form; there is no condition of the unconditioned. There is no sound, no color, no smell, no taste, no touch— nothing of that kind. Thus I say.
>
> *Acaranga Sutra* 1.5.4[27]

It would not be far off the mark to suggest that the Jain description of the liberated soul (atman) sounds similar to the portrayal of Brahman in Hinduism. A liberated soul has no karma. That state is beyond explanation. The text ends here, leaving the matter to rest. We know no more.

Lord Mahavira's ascetic practices summarized in the Five Great Vows for Jain devotees are the heart of Jainism's radical asceticism. The Five Great Vows are *ahimsa* (noninjury), *asatya* (not lying), *asteya* (not taking anything not given), *aparigraha* (nonattachment to people, places, and things), and *brahmacharya* (chastity). Jain monks and nuns have an even stricter set of duties, such as sweeping the path before them, wearing cloths over their mouths, and filtering water to avoid injuring living beings. They live by collecting alms and should have no possessions. Ideally, they should follow the doctrine of *sallekhana* (self-starvation), the so-called wise man's death, thus annihilating karmic matter. Although mental training is important, as it is in Buddhism, physical austerities are of utmost importance, since karma is conceived of as a physical substance.

Any threat to one's religion is usually defended by either redefining or clarifying one's own religion. This process can be seen even in the New Testament, where the biblical writers contended against gnosticism. For instance, Paul referred to a gnostic group that worshiped invisible orders of thrones, sovereignties, authorities, and powers, admonishing, "See to it that no one takes you captive through philosophy and empty deceit, according to human tradition, according to the elemental spirits of the universe, and not according to Christ" (Col. 1:16; 2:8).[a]

In his Gospel, John also counters gnostic claims about Christ when he writes that "the Word became flesh and lived among us" (1:14). By the third century, most Christians affirmed what became orthodoxy: that Jesus Christ was both fully human and fully divine. In the fourth century, the great Egyptian theologian Athanasius (c. 293–373) battled with a fellow Egyptian, the Alexandrian priest Arius (c. 250–336), over the relationship between Jesus Christ the Son and God the Father. Just how much was Jesus Christ a part of God? Athanasius employed the Greek term *"homoousios"* (of the same substance) to communicate the absolute unity of Christ the Son with God the Father: "Jesus is *of the same substance* as the Father." The Son was of the exact same essence as the Father.

The affirmation of sameness stood in opposition to Arius's language, *homoiousios* (of like substance), regarding Jesus's relationship to the Father. That is to say, Arius's theology led him to argue that although Jesus Christ was of similar substance, he was not of the exact same substance as the Father. In Arius's view, Jesus Christ was "*homoiousios* with the Father." Furthermore, in Arius's own words, "There was a time when the Son was not." So Arius claimed that Christ was the first created being, but not fully God himself.

Being "of *like* substance" with the Father and depicting Christ as being *born in time* has serious soteriological (salvific) implications, for a being who is not God would be incapable of saving human beings, including creation itself. Even the most purified, first creation could not impart salvation, since that being would have neither the authority nor the power to do so. Just like Jesus Christ is affirmed as both fully human and fully divine, we too as modern Christians are called to embrace a similar tension of being fully in the world and fully animated by the Spirit, which raises a salient question: How is one to be *in the world* as a Christian? This question begs a further set of questions about theological anthropology, such as, "What does it mean to be a human being?" and "What makes a human being?" More specifically, "How much of a human being is 'spiritual' and how much is 'material'?" Or is the distinction between spirit and matter a false dichotomy, unhelpful to a sensible Christian anthropology?

a. See Placher, *History of Christian Theology*, 48.

Figure 4.10. Jain worship in Santhu, Rajasthan, India

Jain laypeople need to uphold the Five Great Vows as well, which means they cannot engage in activities that promote violence such as military service, farming, fishing, or any work that kills animals, produces weapons, or distributes intoxicants. Devotees are strict vegetarians and abstain from alcohol, gambling, and illegal drugs. Perhaps there are so few Jains worldwide today because of Jainism's severe ascetic practices. Yet, despite their relatively small numbers, Jains continue to have significant impact in the broader society. Ironically, even with restrictions on so many activities, Jains tend to be among the wealthiest groups in India today, for they are quite active in banking, law, and real estate. Additionally, they have been vocal opponents to the development of weapons of massive destruction.

1. The vow is to be free from injury (*ahimsa*), falsehood, theft, unchastity, and worldly attachment. . . .
2. Vows [are of two kinds]: lesser vow and greater vow.
3. For fixing of these five vows in the mind, there are five meditations for each.
4. The five meditations [for the vow against injury] are carefulness of speech, carefulness of mind, care in walking, care in lifting and laying down things, and thoroughly seeing to one's food and drink.
5. And the five meditations [for the vow against falsehood] are giving up anger, greed, cowardice and frivolity, and speaking in accordance with scriptural injunctions.
6. The five meditations [for the vow against theft] are residence in a

206

solitary place, residence in a deserted place, residence in a place where one is not likely to be interfered with by others, purity of alms, and not disputing with disciples of the same faith as to "mine" and "thine."

7. The five meditations [for the vow against unchastity] are renunciation of hearing stories inciting attachment for women, renunciation of seeing their beautiful bodies, renunciation of remembrance of past enjoyment of women, renunciation of aphrodisiacs, and renunciation of beautifying one's own body.

8. The five meditations [for the vow against worldly attachment] are giving up of love and hatred for the pleasing and displeasing objects of the senses. . . .

11. And one must meditate upon compassion for all living beings, delight at the sight of beings more advanced than ourselves [on the path of liberation], pity for the afflicted, and indifference toward those who mistreat you.

Tattvarthadhigama Sutra 1.1–8, 11[28]

THE DAILY PRAYER

Practicing Jains rise before dawn and pray the daily prayer, called the **Namaskar Mantra**. The daily prayer invokes the five classes of superior beings, which are the spirits, patriarchs, ascetic leaders, living saints, and all ascetics. At night Jains again invoke these five classes of superior beings. Jain worship falls within the larger set of requirements called the Six Obligatory Duties (*sadavashyaka*). The six duties include (1) worship of the supreme soul (*devapuja*), (2) serving the elders (*guru-upasti*), (3) studying the Jain scriptures (*svadhyaya*), (4) self-control (*samyama*), (5) austerities (*tapas*), and (6) charity (*dana*).

In their prayers, Jains do not ask for favors or material benefits from the perfected souls or the *tirthankaras*. They do not even address these souls or *tirthankaras* individually. Rather, they seek guidance and inspiration from the perfected souls to help them follow the right path to happiness and total liberation from the suffering of life.

The Sanskrit term *"puja"* is used throughout the Indian religions to refer to "worship," "honor,"

Matthew Logelin/Wikimedia Commons

Figure 4.11. Making liquid offering on Jain Shravanbelgola Gomateshvara head in Karnataka, India

"adoration," and "ritual." *Pujas* can be small or large, simple or complex, but they are performed to receive the deity's blessing and to develop the divinity within each devotee. Usually *pujas* are marked by three actions: devotees present offerings to the deity, the devotees see (***darshana***) the deity, and the deity gives grace (***prasad***) to the devotees through a material object offered to the deity. Devoted Jains worship three times a day for forty-eight minutes, called *samayika* (Sanskrit, "attaining equanimity"), reciting scriptures and praying. *Samayika*, considered the highest form of spiritual discipline, is usually practiced at dawn and dusk. Forty-eight minutes is significant because it is the standard Indian unit of time used for ritual purposes (*mahurta*).

THE OBJECT OF WORSHIP

According to many Indian religious traditions, the offerings blessed by the deity are believed to purify the spiritual pollution in the objects presented in worship. Jain worship focuses not on just any "supreme soul"—although even the virtuous individual is worshiped—but specifically on its pure qualities, thus meditating on the pure virtues that animate the virtuous individual and the supreme soul. Jains often use the term "supreme soul" (***devapuja***) to refer collectively to all *tirthankaras*.

SIDEBAR 4.2

The Namaskar Mantra Prayer

Namo Arihantanam
 I bow down to Arihanta
Namo Siddhanam
 I bow down to Siddha
Namo Ayriyanam
 I bow down to Acharya
Namo Uvajjhayanam
 I bow down to Upadhyaya
Namo Loe Savva-sahunam
 I bow down to Sadhu and Sadhvi.
Eso Panch Namokaro
 These five bowing downs
Savva-pavappanasano
 Destroy all the sins
Manglananch Savvesim
 Amongst all that is auspicious
Padhamam Havei Mangalam
 This Navkar Mantra is the foremost.

   http://www.jainworld.com/education/juniors/junles01.htm

By worshiping the "supreme soul," Jains have an opportunity to purify their own souls and thoughts of defilement. Any soul manifesting pure qualities can be worshiped, since these pure qualities comprise the Jain ideal. One of the most important Jain prayers begins, "I bow down before the Destroyer of (internal) enemies," referring to enemies such as hatred, attachment, pride, deceit, and violence. Through prayer Jains cultivate friendship with all living beings:

> I forgive all beings;
> may all beings forgive me.
> All living beings are my friends;
> I have malice towards none.[29]

Although no "one God" exists in Jainism, the many gods addressed and venerated in worship are the pure souls that have attained liberation. They are remembered in prayer. Summarizing the Jain ideals, a common prayer for Jains ends with

---

Cessation of sorrow
Cessation of karma
Death while in meditation
Attainment of enlightenment.
O holy Jina [conquering one]! friend of the entire universe,
let these
be mine,
For
I have taken refuge at your feet.

Nityanaimittika-pathavali, 89[30]

Jains fast regularly, confess their sins to priests, and accept penances to eliminate karmic matter produced by the transgression.

Modern Movements

Around the fourth century BCE, the Jain community divided into two sects or denominations called **Shvetambara** (white-clothed) and **Digambara** ("clothed in air" or "sky-clad"). Later several subsets of these major denominations emerged, including the **Sthanakavasi**. While the origins of the split between these sects are obscure and warrant more research, the major division is not just doctrinal. The major denominational division is between the Shvetambara and the Digambara. Shvetambara monks and nuns wear white and are located primarily in western India, whereas the Digambaras are more strict, clothed by heaven (i.e., naked), and adhere to Lord Mahavira's words that women are "the greatest temptation in the world." The Digambaras are located predominately in southern India.

There are five major differences between these two major sects. First, Shvetambara monks and nuns wear clothes; Digambara monks do not. The Digambaras argue that Lord Mahavira himself and his followers walked around naked to model renunciation of the world, but that it was in the fifth century CE that images of the *tirthankaras* are clothed. Second, the Shvetambaras use a bowl for begging and for eating; Digambara monks do not. The Digambaras suggest that using cupped hands instead of an alms bowl is closer to being purified from the need for food. Third, the Shvetambaras believe that the **kevalin** (fully omniscient being) still requires food, whereas the Digambaras do not affirm this. Thus the Shvetambaras make no issue over the use of alms bowls for collecting food.

Fourth, the Shvetambaras believe that women can attain liberation; the Digambaras believe women must first be reborn as men before having the opportunity to be liberated. The Shvetambaras argue that Lord Mahavira's holy people (Sanskrit, *tirtha*) consisted of twice as many women ascetics as men, therefore Lord Mahavira thought gender was irrelevant to achieving liberation. To the contrary, the Digambaras argue that nudity was essential for devotion and women could not walk around naked because of safety concerns. For the Digambaras, the impossibility of women being naked corresponds to their inability to be liberated.

Fifth, the Shvetambaras accept the ancient writings as scripture (Sanskrit, *agama*). Both major denominations affirm sacred texts, but the Digambaras believe that the original texts were lost and that the truth of the tradition is communicated orally to disciples.[31] Among the movements that indirectly rose out of the Shvetambara sect is the Sthanakavasi. The Sthanakavasis practice the high ideals of purity, tolerate no idols, and have no temples. Emerging in the early eighteenth century, the Sthanakavasis, perhaps influenced by Muslim conquest, repudiated what they believed was the worship of idols of Lord Mahavira and other *tirthankaras*. Thus the Sthanakavasis, who make up the largest denomination of Jains today, are free to worship anywhere, such as in simple buildings (*sthanakas*) and in their own homes,

Figure 4.12. Acharya Mahapragya, Jain sect leader

and they emphasize meditation and introspection. All Jains are vegetarians and uphold the value of all sentient beings, even if there are various degrees of the ascetic lifestyle.

Beyond the Jain denominations, which help to organize Jain worship and meditation, it is worthwhile to note several influential Jain leaders who have steered the Jain tradition in the modern period. The first major event in the West where Jain and other South Asian religionists addressed Western audiences was the 1893 World Parliament of Religions in Chicago. This was the same parliament where the Hindu representative Vivekananda spoke so compellingly about Hinduism, prompting a new appreciation for the Hindu tradition. The Jain tradition was represented at the World Parliament of Religions by twenty-nine-year-old Sri Virchand Gandhi (1864–1901).

The Jain Sri Virchand Gandhi was perhaps the first Jain to visit North America. The choice to send Gandhi, the first honorary secretary of the Jain Association of India, was propitious since he made a lasting positive impression and demonstrated sophistication and intellectual ability that many Westerners did not expect from Indians.

Christian Reflections

The Jain commitment to nonviolence is a strong reminder to Christians of the sacredness of creation—that creation itself is a gift from God, and rather than possessing and dominating it, we are to be stewards of that gift. Jainism adopted several of the most important theological elements of other Indian traditions, yet redefined them in unique ways in order to overcome the human predicament, characterized by karmic buildup, accumulation of karmic weight, and the heavy burden of samsara, the cycle of death and rebirth. It can be easy for Christians, or any outsider to Jainism, to see Jain life and practices as the "exotic other," something entirely different from one's own experience.

While some of the ascetic practices are quite extreme, even for the committed Jain, it seems that there is much in Jainism that Christians can learn from, such as its central doctrine of nonviolence toward any living being, its egalitarian spirit (in most Jain denominations), and its sense of connectedness with all living things. Faithful Jains follow a daily spiritual regimen of prayer, yogic meditation, and the cultivation of virtues such as self-control and charity. Although the severe practices of Jainism can seem to demonstrate an otherworldly orientation to life, the reverse seems true as well. That is to say, the Jain path of liberation can be seen as affirming at once earthly life as well as the purified states of heaven.

Another influential Jain intellectual was Champat Rai Jain, a brilliant, multilingual barrister-at-law whose writings in the early twentieth century communicated Jain principles to Western audiences by employing concepts from modern psychology and science. Champat Rai Jain's *Fundamentals of Jainism*, *The Key of Knowledge*, and *The Science of Thought* contain, among other topics, his thoughts on comparative theology and the scientific method of self-realization.

Indirectly, one of the most influential Jains in the modern period was Srimad Rajchandra (1867–1901), the Jain philosopher whose legacy includes being the spiritual guru and guide to Mahatma Gandhi, to whom he is credited with

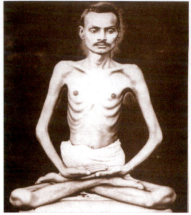

Figure 4.13. Srimad Rajchandra, spiritual guru of Mahatma Gandhi

teaching the values of nonviolence. Known as one of Gandhi's best friends, Srimad Rajchandra committed himself to a life of rigorous asceticism in his late twenties, claiming at that time, "My soul has attained complete knowledge of its nature."

These and other Jain leaders continue to provide guidance to the Jain community today. Although Jainism is a numerically smaller tradition when compared to other world religions, its influence on the social, ethical, economic, and political life of India is disproportionate to the number of its adherents, and it continues to be a vitally important source of guidance for millions worldwide.

Timeline

877–777 BCE	Life of Parshva, the twenty-third *tirthankara*
599–527 BCE	Life of Mahavira, the last *tirthankara*
507 BCE	Death of Ganahar Sudharma Swami, the group leader of the *sangha* and primary disciple of Mahavira
357 BCE	Death of Acharya Bhadrababu, a spiritual leader and author famous for his dedication to Jain principles at any cost
78 BCE	Division between Digambara and Svetambara Jains
2nd century CE	Life of Kundakunda, Digambara philosopher

454	Council of Valabi; Devardhigani compiles the Jain Agams (Jain canon) based on Mahavira's teachings
800	Massacre of eight thousand Tamil Jains at Madurai, India
9th century	Tirumalai (the holy mountain) temple is established in Tamil Nadu, India
10th century	Formation of Svetambara (white-clad) sect, one of two main sects of the Jain tradition
1089–1172	Acharya Hemachandra, a Svetambara monk, becomes tutor of King Siddharaja of Gujarat
1451	Lonka Sah, who opposed the use of images in worship, initiates Jain schism, creating Lonka Gacch, a Sthanakvasi movement
1760	Terapanthi Gacch, a reformist movement, splits off from Sthanakvasis
18th–19th centuries	Decline of use of images in worship among ascetic communities
21st century	Revival of Jain asceticism; development of Jain mystical sects; increased Jain immigration to Britain, east Africa, and North America

Key Terms

ahimsa

ajiva

aparigraha

asatya

asrava

asteya

atman

avirati

Ayodhya

bandha

darshana

devapuja

Digambara

fordfinders

jina

jiva

jivanmukta

karma

kasaya

kevala

kevala jnana

kevalin

Mahavira

mithyatva

moksha

moksha-marga

Namaskar Mantra

Nav Tattvas

nirjara

nirvana

pap

paramatman

Parshva

pramada

prasad

puja

punya

right conduct

right knowledge

right vision

rita

sallekhana

samsara

samvar

sangha

satya

Shvetambara

siddha

siddha-sila

Sthanakavasi

tapas

tirthankara

triloka

Triratna

varna

yoga

Further Reading

Babb, Lawrence A. *Absent Lord: Ascetics and Kings in a Jain Ritual Culture*. Berkeley: University of California Press, 1996.

Chapple, Christopher Key, ed. *Jainism and Ecology: Nonviolence in the Web of Life*. Delhi: Motilal Banarsidass, 2006.

Dundas, Paul. *The Jains*. New York: Routledge, 2002.

Granoff, Phyllis, ed. *The Forest of Thieves and the Magic Garden*. New York: Penguin Classics, 2007.

Jacobi, Hermann, trans. *Jaina Sūtras*. Richmond, UK: Curzon Press, 2001.

Long, Jeffery D. *Jainism*. New York: I. B. Tauris & Co., 2009.

Rankin, Aidan D., and Kanti V. Mardia. *Living Jainism: An Ethical Science*. Hants, UK: Mantra Books.

Shah, Bharat S. *An Introduction to Jainism*. New York: The Setubandh Publications, 2002.

Shanta, N. *The Unknown Pilgrims: History, Spirituality, and Life of the Jaina Women Ascetics*. Delhi: Sri Satguru Publications, 1997.

Tobias, Michael. *Life Force: The World of Jainism*. Fremont, CA: Jain Publishing Company. 1991.

five

Sikhism

Contemporary Snapshot

In 2008 a local Sikh high school student in New Jersey was assaulted by a fellow student who set fire to the Sikh student's turban in an unprovoked attack that outraged New Jersey's Sikh community. Other incidents of violence have been directed toward Sikh students in schools in the United States in large part because they wear the Sikh turban, a sacred piece of attire and an essential part of the Sikh faith. Prejudice and misunderstanding of the Sikh community are not limited to incidents within North America. In many places around the world, Sikhs have been mistakenly identified as either Hindu or Muslim, leading some Sikhs to be victims of discriminatory conduct such as physical violence.

While there were many instances of prejudice prior to the terrorist acts of September 11, 2001, the incidents of violence and discrimination against Sikhs in the post-9/11 period have increased dramatically in several Western nations as non-Sikhs have equated the Sikh turban with the head covering of radical Islamists opposing the West.[1] Because of the rise in discriminatory conduct in the United Kingdom, a conference was held in Berkshire, England, in August 2009 to discuss where the Sikh community fits within the Western world and how to communicate to others that the turban is a Sikh symbol of spiritual wisdom, dignity, and integrity, rather than of violence. The topic of religious dress is a complicated one in the West, where the balance between religious freedom and the values of mutual respect and civil society are not easily achieved. For instance, in an increasingly security-sensitive world, the wearing of the Sikh turban has raised several legal and ethical questions about the freedom of religion in the public sphere. Should Sikhs be able to wear their turbans for passport, driver's license, or ID photos? Should the Transportation Security Administration (TSA), which provides airport security screening of luggage and carry-on baggage, be permitted to search turbans for concealed weapons or explosive devices? Or is such an examination an infringement on civil liberties? These are important issues that both provide the opportunity to reflect on the nature of religion in the public sphere and compel us to learn about Sikhism as a distinct religion.

The term "Sikhism" is derived from the Pali term "*sikha*" ("learner," "disciple"). Sikhs are disciples of ten **Gurus** (Sanskrit, *gurūs*, "teachers"), beginning with Guru Nanak (b. 1469 CE) and ending with Guru Gobind Singh (d. 1708), the final human Sikh Guru. The eleventh Guru, considered the last Guru, is the **Adi Granth**, the Sikh Holy Scripture. A Sikh then is one who believes in the ten Gurus and in the Adi Granth, also called the **Granth Sahib**.

In Indian traditions, "guru" can apply to any religious teacher or guide, but for Sikhs "Guru" is restricted to God as **Sat Guru** (True Teacher), the ten Gurus from Guru Nanak to Guru Singh, and to the Adi Granth, the "Lord Teacher Granth" (book). Today, there are approximately twenty-five million Sikhs worldwide, with the majority living in India's Punjab region. The largest Sikh diaspora, about three hundred thousand people, lives in the UK.[2] Together Sikhs make up the *panth* (Punjabi, "path," "way"), the entire Sikh community worldwide, in which it is believed that the guidance of the Gurus is also present. Fully committed and initiated Sikhs belong to the **Khalsa** (Punjabi, *khālsā*; "pure"), a classless body of Sikhs distinguished by their vows and dress, the details of which will be discussed later in the chapter.

Charles E. Farhadian

Figure 5.1. Sikh in Amritsar, Punjab, India

216

Charles E. Farhadian

Figure 5.2. Golden Temple in Amritsar, Punjab, India

From an **etic** perspective—that is, from an outsider's viewpoint—Sikhism appears as a combination of Hindu devotion and Muslim, and more specifically Sufi (Islamic mystic), ideas and practices, "the fruit of hybridization between Islam and Hinduism."[3] From an **emic** perspective—that is, from a Sikh viewpoint—the religion is independent of Hinduism and Islam, standing on its own two feet, given to the Gurus as a separate act of revelation, even if straddling two countries with massive Hindu and Muslim populations, India and Pakistan, respectively. Sikhism's home is the Punjab in northern India, where the spectacularly beautiful **Golden Temple** (Punjabi, *Harimandir Sāhib*; "temple of God") at Amritsar is located, on whose walls are inscribed the verses of the sacred Adi Granth.

Origins and Concepts

Vaishnava Ramanandi

We can trace the early background of Sikhism to the fifteenth century CE, with the famous *sannyasi* (renunciant) **Ramananda** (c. 1360–c. 1470), a Vaishnava Hindu, famous **bhakti** saint, social reformer, and follower of

Map 5.1. Punjab, northern India and eastern Pakistan

Ramanuja. Ramanuja was the eleventh-century CE Hindu theologian who advocated the idea of the unity and distinction of Brahman with **atman**—that is, the divine essence was unified with the individual self (atman) yet the self was not identical to Brahman entirely. Ramananda had preached Hinduism in several locations throughout the Indian subcontinent, yet on one occasion when he tried to eat with fellow disciples, he was rejected and told to sit apart from them for fear that his journey and possible contamination by lower-class Hindus had polluted him. This experience affected Ramananda so profoundly that he started his own sect, the **Vaishnava Ramanandi** sect, which advocated a classless equality of all people. Ramananda called for radical equality, even between genders. Although Ramananda did not condemn the multiple gods of Hinduism, he stressed the need to worship the one God, Rama, through bhakti (warm devotion) commitment.

Today, the Vaishnava Ramanandi sect is known as the most egalitarian Hindu sect and one of the largest monastic orders in India, with about one million disciples in northern India. Besides being a renunciant, Ramananda was a strong devotional poet, who included ecstatic Sufi poetry in his works. Ramananda's poetry combines stories of his physical journeys, spiritual insight about divine unity, and the unparalleled role of the Guru.

Members of the Vaishnava Ramanandi sect are deeply devoted to Rama and Sita of the great Ramayana story, and the devotion of a sect member is marked by intense religious fervor. Members of the Vaishnava Ramanandi sect often burn the name Rama into their skin and add the name *dasa*

(Sanskrit, *dāsā*, "slave") to their names. Gender equality is often demonstrated by male followers wearing women's clothing and jewelry.

AYODHYA

The headquarters of the Vaishnava Ramanandi sect is **Ayodhya**, the birthplace of Rama, in the northeastern Indian state of Uttar Pradesh. Ayodhya has been the locus of terrible conflict between Muslims and Hindus over the history and ownership of the city, with both groups contesting that the site is sacred to their particular religious tradition. Hindus argue that Ayodhya is the birthplace and capital city of the revered Hindu deity Lord Rama of the epic Ramayana, while **Babur**, the first emperor of the Islamic **Mughal** Empire of South Asia, built the Babri mosque in the sixteenth century CE on that same site.

Hindu fundamentalists of the twentieth century argue that the Mughal rulers destroyed the Ram Mandir (Temple of Rama) and replaced it with the Babri mosque. On December 6, 1992, approximately 150,000 militant Hindus demolished the Babri mosque, giving rise to one of India's bloodiest religious conflicts, which left at least 2,000 people dead. Ayodhya was also the birthplace of five of the Jain *tirthankaras* (fordfinders), so its sacredness is affirmed by Sikhs, Muslims, and Jains for different religious and historic reasons, as well as by Buddhists since it contains several ancient Buddhist temples and monuments. Thus, Ayodhya is a major pilgrimage site for many Indian religionists.

KABIR

Ramananda's most famous disciple was **Kabir** (1440–1510), the son of a high-caste Vaishnava Brahmin and one of the best-known Hindi poets of northern India, although the

Where I went
I met only water and stone –
but You remain
all-pervasive
and forever unchanging.
I read and searched
all the Vedas
and the Puranas;
I go to them
if I do not find Him here.

O my true Gurū,
I am your handmaid,
your living sacrifice,
for you have cut away
all my hardened doubts,
all my great fears.
Ramananda's lord
is the all-pervasive Brahma –
a Gurū's word
can destroy a million sins.

Ramananda, in Dass,
"Raga Basant," 162–63

Figure 5.3. People worshiping at Gurdwara Sri Guru Singh Sabha in Bangkok, Thailand

Ddalbiez/Wikimedia Commons

> *He is one, there is no second.*
> *Rama, Khuda, Sakti, Shiva, are all one.*
> *Tell me, pray, how can ever you tell them apart?*
> *By the One Name I hold fast!*
>
> Ramananda, in Keay, *Kabir and His Followers*, 69

> *Hari [God] is like sugar spilled in the sand*
> *that an elephant cannot pick up.*
> *Says Kabir: The Gurū gave me the hint:*
> *Become an ant and eat it!*
>
> Kabir, in Vaudeville, *Kabir*, 1:331

details of his life are unclear, and in fact some even doubt his existence at all. Kabir was unconcerned about what he believed were the superficial differences between Hindus and Muslims, since in his view "Allah" and "Rama" were but different names for the same deity. Like Ramananda, Kabir opposed class and caste distinctions.

It is important to consider the source of Kabir's knowledge about the divine. Naturally, he was influenced by Guru Ramananda's view of the One Name behind the many names. But Kabir claimed to have derived spiritual awareness of the One Name from direct experience of the **shabad** (Punjabi, "word"), the divine word and mystical sound that give authority to the Vedas and yogic practices. According to the tradition, *shabad* is the verbal description of the nature of God, known also as the "Message of the Teacher." In Sikhism, *shabad* can also mean a hymn or selection of the Sikh holy scriptures, the Adi Granth. Kabir sought to express and experience the love of God through mystical songs, some of which were later recorded in the Adi Granth. Composing hymns in the vernacular, Kabir chose words that were animated with images from ordinary life.

Kabir employed the terms "Hari" or "Allah" or "Rama" not in a sectarian way but as distinct names for the same God, whom he often referred to as the *satGuru* or Sat Guru (Supreme Gurū), the true Guru who illumines human hearts. Kabir is credited with the words,

> I am neither Hindu nor Muslim.
> [The One] Allah-Ram is the breath of my body.
>
> Adi Granth, 1136[4]

Nanak employed the term "Sat Guru" (Supreme Guru, i.e., "God") more than three hundred times in the Adi Granth. Similarly, the Hindu bhakti tradition taught that God (i.e., Brahman) is the one and only reality, the rest being maya—illusion. As such, the best way to worship and serve God is by absolute submission to his will, found best through the teaching of a spiritual mentor (guru) who teaches one to approach God through meditation on the name of God and singing hymns to God.

Historical Background

At the end of the twelfth century CE, Persian-speaking Muslim Mughals from northwestern India began occupying the Indian subcontinent, at least superficially and formally, converting some to Islamic culture and religion and establishing the Mughal Empire (1526–1857). "Mughal" is the Persian word for "Mongol," and the first Mughal emperor was a descendant of the Mongol emperor Genghis Khan. By the early sixteenth century, the Mughal Empire controlled most of the South Asian subcontinent, except for the most southern parts of the subcontinent and Sri Lanka. Eventually, there would be a succession of six major Mughal emperors, each characterized by a different approach to non-Islamic religions, including Hinduism, Jainism, Buddhism, Sikhism, and Christianity. The major emperors included Babur (r. 1526–30), **Humayun** (r. 1530–39, 1555–56), **Akbar** (r. 1556–1605), **Jahangir** (r. 1605–27), **Shah Jahan** (r. 1628–58), and **Aurangzeb** (r. 1659–1707).

There is a massive corpus of literature on the Mughal period and, for that matter, on the history of the South Asian subcontinent. But for our purposes, I want to introduce just a few of the more notable Mughal emperors to illustrate the ways in which the Islamic Empire engaged Indian cultures and religions. Generally, the farther a community was located from a Mughal capital, the less the Mughal rulers were concerned with control and domination, and religious minorities, such as Sikhs, thus experienced greater independence.

The Mughals, who were Turkic-Persians from central Asia, introduced many Persian words into the languages of the South Asian subcontinent. Founded by Zahir ud-Din Muhammad (called Babur)—a descendant of the famous Mongol Genghis Khan, the founder of an empire that eventually dominated most of Asia—the Mughal Empire left in its wake numerous significant influences in the South Asian subcontinent, including Mughal architecture, food, arts and crafts, and literary and pictorial works, as well as Muslim conversions.

How many names are there for God? Where do they come from? Do the names for God arise out of local culture, or are they introduced from a world religion? Who decides which name(s) to use in worship? Should there be limits on the number of names for God or the metaphors about God?[a]

a. For a fruitful introduction to the theological possibilities and pitfalls of using metaphors to speak about God, see McFague, *Metaphorical Theology*; Bevans, *Models of Contextual Theology*, 103; Nida, *Signs, Sense, and Translation*; Nida, *Message and Meaning*.

Christian Reflections

Babur was a physically strong and talented military leader who succeeded in capturing immense territories, sometimes being greeted as a liberator by those he conquered; yet some Sikh leaders, including the great Guru Nanak, noted Babur's brutal treatment of and terror against South Asians, including his hacking princes to death and trampling them into the dust.

Jalal ud-Din Muhammad (aka Akbar the Great) was considered one of the greatest Mughal emperors, with a reputation for being quite tolerant of non-Muslim religions. Akbar the Great was "great" for many reasons, such as creating a strong central government and extending the Mughal Empire into Afghanistan, abolishing the *jizya* (Arabic, "reward"), the Islamic poll tax levied on non-Muslims in Muslim regions (see Qur'an 9:29), and permitting non-Muslims, such as Sikhs, to flourish in their own religious traditions.

One of the best-known Mughal emperors, at least for the architectural legacy he left behind, was Shahabuddin Muhammad Shah Jahan (aka Shah Jahan), who ruled during the period known as the golden age of Mughal arts—a period that owes this title to Shah Jahan's robust support of Mughal architecture. The great **Taj Mahal** in Agra, just south of Delhi, was built as a mausoleum in memory of his favorite wife, Mumtaz Mahal, on the occasion of her death while giving birth to their fourteenth child; its construction took over seventeen years.

If Akbar was "great" in part because of this tolerance for non-Muslims, his great-grandson, the son of Shah Jahan, Muhi-ud-Din Muhammed Aurangzeb Alamgir (aka Aurangzeb), could be described as his mirror opposite. Aurangzeb, the sixth Mughal emperor, was exceedingly restrictive, prohibiting non-Muslim rituals, establishing not only the *jizya* poll tax but also extra taxes on non-Muslims, and imposing **sharia** (Islamic law), which forbade gambling and drinking alcohol, as well as instituting Islamic law courts with harsh punishments in the Mughal Empire. In response to Emperor Aurangzeb's harsh policies, resistance grew to such an extent that by the time he died the Mughal Empire was coming to an end, even if it would take another 150 years to fully reach its demise under the burgeoning British domination of the subcontinent.

The strengths and weaknesses of the Mughal legacy are vigorously debated by contemporary scholars, and the record of the Mughal influence remains uneven, with some positive and negative aspects.[5] Although the empire continued for another 150 years after the decline of Emperor Aurangzeb, it was weakened greatly, and within a matter of a few decades the empire was so enervated that the political vacuum left in the wake of Aurangzeb's death was fairly easily filled by British powers, whose presence dated back to the early seventeenth century with the British East India Company.

When studying religions, it is important to keep in mind the social and historical contexts out of which the religions emerged, since the context provides the seedbed for new ideas, conflicts, and opportunities of the new religion. Since its inception, Sikhism was a minority religion in the midst of large numbers of Hindus and Muslims. Occupying a geographic region between Pakistan and India has made Sikhs conscious of their own status as members of a unique religion, and they have exerted great effort to defend themselves against onslaughts from both the Hindu and the Muslim communities. How influential are specific contexts to the development of a religion? Contexts determine to a large extent the types of theological issues, communication styles, and linguistic and cognitive frames of reference of the religions.

Christianity too inherited and redefined theological notions from its immediate surroundings. Although early Christians did not have to deal with concepts of karma, atman, and samsara, they did have to make sense of such topics as sacrifice, salvation, and law. While the impact of contexts should not be seen as overly deterministic, it is crucial that we strike a balance between understanding a religion as emerging from the soil of local cultures and seeing it as somehow sui generis (independent of its context), unique in itself.

The early conflicts between the Sikh community and Mughal leaders gave way to the creation of the Sikh army and later the special order of initiated Sikhs, known as the Khalsa, with the explicit purpose of defending Sikhism and fighting against injustice. In large part, Sikh identity, theology, and practice surfaced in response to the various political, religious, and economic forces surrounding the *panth* (Sikh community). Even the installation of the Sikh sacred scriptures, the Adi Granth, could be interpreted as a move to maintain the Sikh community after a series of its human Gurus had been assassinated by Mughal emperors. The commitment to make the sacred scripture the permanent and final teacher helped to sustain the *panth* through the often difficult days of Mughal rule.

There are several reasons for the ultimate decline of the Mughal Empire, and the reasons themselves are contested. But there seems to be some agreement that the decline was due in part to a combination of Aurangzeb's intolerant religious policies, which led to social instability; a series of incompetent leaders who lacked the character, ethics, and intelligence to rule justly; and the burgeoning of all kinds of corruption throughout the empire.

Following the Battle of Plassey (1757), in which the British East India Company defeated the Mughal provincial governor of Bengal and his French allies, the **British Raj** (i.e., the British Empire in India) was established, dominating South Asia for the next two centuries. A series of revolts produced social unrest, culminating in the famous Indian mutiny of 1857, otherwise known as the Sepoy mutiny. "Sepoy" was a term used to describe indigenous Indian soldiers in the service of the British forces in India, usually at the level of the lowest enlisted rank.

The Ten Gurus

The role of the Guru in Sikhism is of central importance. Having laid out a general background of the significant forerunners to the Sikh tradition as well as the historical context of the Mughal Empire, we now turn our attention to the specific human Gurus and the Adi Granth, as the eleventh Guru, on which the Sikh tradition is based. It is worthwhile to note that all Gurus were from the same mercantile caste (Punjabi, *zat*; Sanskrit, *jati*), the Khatri *zat*, which was originally the Kshatriya caste in the Punjab.

Guru Nanak

The first Sikh Guru was **Guru Nanak** (1469–1539). Nanak was born in the Punjab; he was known for being Punjab's chief advocate of Hindu bhaktism and was deeply influenced by the **Sant** tradition, as Nanak was raised at a time and in a region in which the Sant tradition had developed. The Sant tradition emphasized not only bhakti devotion to an avatar (divine descent) of the Hindu God Vishnu but called specifically for the engendering of an emotional love commitment to that God. Coupled with the valorization of love as the modus operandi of the devotee's dedication was the prominence of the role of the Guru to guide the devotee and, perhaps more telling, be the voice of the God. The Sants declared that the way to union with God was open to all people regardless of class, caste, or gender, providing that devotees adhered to the teaching of the Guru and performed certain rituals, pilgrimages, and sacrifices.

The Sikh forerunner **Kabir** was firmly rooted in the Sant tradition and was himself recognized as a Sant. Scholars note that the trace of Sufi (Islamic mystic) influences appearing later in the Sikh concept of divine immanence—that is, the presence of God in the world and in persons—are already found in the writings of Nanak's Sant predecessors and were thus transmitted to him via the Sant tradition.[6] Crucial to Nanak's perspective on society and religion, then, was his intense disapproval of asceticism, captured in his saying, "Be in the world but not worldly." Instead Nanak advocated a tradition of the householder, even refusing to meet with audiences unless they first shared a meal in the Sikh community kitchen, demonstrating the social equality of Sikhism.

Tradition records that Guru Nanak was from the Kshatriya (warrior) class; he received elementary education in the Sanskrit, Persian, and Punjabi languages but had a fervent interest in religion. Married at the age of thirteen, he had two sons. Although he followed his father's occupation and worked as an accountant, Nanak remained deeply attracted to the spiritual quest. His spiritual outlet was writing and singing hymns, accompanied by his Muslim companion, Mardana, who was of simple Muslim origins. Tradition records that Mardana played a stringed instrument (*rabab*), while Nanak sang. The two were known for organizing community meetings, where they performed together. This episode of Nanak's friendship with Mardana illustrates his openness to other religious traditions.

Nanak's Mystical Awakening

Around 1499, when he was approximately thirty years old, Nanak had a mystical experience that would profoundly shape his understanding of religion. While bathing in the River Bein in the small district of Sultanpur in Uttar Pradesh, Nanak disappeared for three days and was given up as drowned. According to the **Janamsakhi** (Punjabi, Janamsākhī; "birth testimony," "life stories"), a collection of hagiographies—that is, uncritical biographies of the saints—during his disappearance Nanak was offered the nectar of immortality (Punjabi, *amrit*; "undying," "ambrosia"), symbolizing an initiation ceremony of baptism and suggestive of immortality and sweetness resulting from meditation on God. Punjabi tradition also notes that *amrit* has healing properties. After offering him *amrit*, God gave Nanak a mission:

> Nanak, I am with thee. Through thee will my name be magnified. . . . Go in the world to pray and to teach mankind how to pray. Be not sullied by the ways of the world. Let your life be one of praise of the word [*nām*], charity [*dān*], ablution [*ishnan*], service [*seva*], and prayer [*simran*].[7]

Nanak appeared on the fourth day, announcing, "There is no Hindu; there is no Muslim," and exclaiming that the new religion, Sikhism, is a distinct tradition from Hinduism and Islam. His call to mission set Nanak on a new life trajectory, where he abandoned worldly pursuits and, accompanied by his Muslim companion Mardana, took several journeys around South Asia, beginning in the Punjab and including Sri Lanka, the Arabian Peninsula, Mecca and Medina, as well as Baghdad and Basra, Iraq. As Nanak visited different places, singing, teaching, and discussing religion with his listeners, he established a **dharmasala** (Sanskrit, *dharmasālā*, "place of worship," "village hospice") that functioned as a religious asylum, a place set apart so that believers could meet regularly for worship. *Dharmasalas* were predecessors of the Sikh **gurdwara** (Punjabi, *gurdwārā*, "gateway of the Guru"; Sikh worship space). In the 1520s, Nanak founded the town of Kartarpur (God's City) in Pakistan and built a *dharmasala* where his disciples congregated and chanted the hymns he had composed. He would later die in that same village.

Neither Hindu nor Muslim

As one may well imagine, the message that Nanak was neither Hindu nor Muslim implied that followers of these traditions were not entirely faithful believers—that there was a better way. The notion that the vast majority of South Asians were unfaithful raised the indignation of many. Furthermore, Nanak accorded considerable respect to women, exclaiming, "Why denounce her, who even gives birth to kings?" Tradition says that Nanak's own sister, Bibi Nanaki, was the first to recognize her brother's spiritual power and became his first disciple. Nanak spent the rest of his life as a Sikh preacher throughout the region until his return to India, where he died on September

---

SIDEBAR 5.1

Sikh Morning Prayer

There is one God.
He is the supreme truth.
He, the creator,
Is without fear and without hatred.
He, the omnipresent,
Pervades the universe.
He is not born,
Nor does he die to be born again.
By his grace shalt thou worship him.

Before time itself
There was truth.
When time began to run its course
He was the truth.
Even now, he is the truth,
And evermore shall truth prevail.

Khushwant Singh, *Hymns of Guru Nanak*, 14

22, 1539, at the age of seventy. Nanak's concept of God was formalized in the opening lines of the **Japji** (Punjabi, Japjī, "recitation"), the Sikh morning prayer. The Japji prayer is recited, not sung, every morning and during the Khalsa initiation ceremony.

Nanak accepted the doctrine of samsara, the cycle of death and rebirth, so fundamental and burdensome to the followers of the Indian religious traditions. In Nanak's words, "Just as the pots of a Persian wheel go down, fill with water as they come up, empty and go down again, so is this life—a pastime of our Lord."[8] Liberation from the cycle of death and rebirth comes to those who merge with God—that is, those who find union with the One Name through meditation and charitable actions.

Spiritual Levels of Maturity

Generally, Sikhs recognize that all human beings are on one of four spiritual levels. A person on the first level is called **Manmukh** (Punjabi, "person guided by inclination"), an ego-centered, perverse, self-willed individual who is controlled by human impulses rather than the truth of the Gurus. The Adi Granth calls such individuals ignorant of the name of God (**Nam**), a condition that will bind them to samsara and misery since they cannot obtain union with God. Those on the second level of spiritual maturity are called Sikh, those disciples who submit to the Ten Gurus and the Adi Granth without reservation. They are on the path of righteousness and union with God, attempting to displace self-centeredness with meditation on and devotion to the Nam. All Sikhs are members of the *panth*.

Along the journey toward liberation, an individual is encouraged to control the five human impulses of pride, anger, lust, greed, and worldly attachment. The third level of spiritual maturity is the Khalsa (initiated Sikhs), consisting of more fully committed Sikhs. We will consider the Khalsa in greater detail later in this chapter.

The final level of spiritual maturity is called **Gurmukh** (Punjabi, "person oriented toward the Guru"), a term describing one who has obtained the status of *mukhti* (Sanskrit, "release," "liberation"), liberation from successive rebirths and therefore the achievement of peace through the

Figure 5.4. Adi Granth worship, Sri Guru Granth Sahib

ultimate union with God. The Gurmukh is believed to embody the living teachings of the Adi Granth and therefore is highly venerated by the Sikh community. No wonder the Gurus, those who have attained liberation, are so highly regarded, their voice being equal to the voice of God.

> The Gurū is the ladder, the dinghy, the raft by means of which one
>   reaches God;
> The Gurū is the lake, the ocean, the boat, the sacred place of
>   pilgrimage, the river.
> If it pleases Thee I am cleansed by bathing in the Lake of Truth.
>
> Adi Granth, 9[9]

Without the Guru as guide, one cannot attain liberation, for the Guru keeps his disciple on the straight path, like an elephant trainer keeping an elephant on the right path by gently leading it here or there, rather than allowing the follower to run in all directions. Having noted the immense respect and central role of the Guru in the Sikh tradition, we should be mindful that the Guru is not in the end seen as a God. The Guru should be consulted and honored, but not worshiped.

Sikhism has endured because of the teachings of Nanak, which were canonized in the Adi Granth, the establishment of the office of Guru, and the institution of the Khalsa, the order of initiated Sikhs. Nanak, like the Sikh forerunners Ramananda and Kabir, asserted that God was a single, omnipotent, and omniscient being—the True One behind the countless names ascribed to that name. According to Nanak, while it is impossible to define God, the attributes of God can be named, and they include Father (**Pita**), the Lover (**Pritam**), the Master (**Khasam**, Malik, Sahib), and the Great Giver (**Data**). God is known as **Sat Nam** (the True Name).

Nanak even selectively employed terms from the ancient Hindu Vedas to describe God as "without quality" (i.e., without attributes) before creation, but manifesting characteristics subsequent to creation, frequently using the term "*ek*" (meaning the number one) to refer to the one God. As noted earlier, *shabad* is revelation through the spoken word. Liberation is obtained through meditation on the name of God, which serves to displace the ego and enables union with the one God.

Within the Sikh tradition, the Guru himself is almost literally the Word of God, as the voice of God itself. Who is God? In Nanak's own words, "One, True Name, Creator, Without Fear, Without Hate, Beyond Time, Unborn, Self-existent, the Gurū's Gift of Grace" (*Mul Mantra*, Adi Granth).[10] In the following passage Nanak relates the Nam (Name) and *shabad* (word), which

Christian Reflections

To say that any particular image is literally God is tantamount to idolatry. No major world religion affirms a literal and permanent parity between God and the sign, symbol, or even residence of God on earth. *That* thing, be it a stone, pillar, or picture, is not God in a literal sense but rather points to God as a sign of something larger than itself. Given this fact, do all signs of Gods point to the same God? Christian missionaries have a history of wrestling with the challenging questions about the relationship between the universal God affirmed in the Bible with vernacular names of God from local cultures worldwide.

Using a variety of names to refer to God dates as far back as biblical times, when Paul sought to communicate to the Hellenistic world—areas influenced by Greek culture and philosophy outside Greece—that something new had happened with God's breaking into the world in Jesus Christ. Paul had to use Greek words and thought patterns to communicate a tradition that emerged out of a Jewish context, for instance using the term "Theos" (Greek, "God") to refer to God. Likewise, the writer of the Gospel of John used the Greek philosophical term "Logos" (divine reason, Word) to refer to the incarnation of God in Jesus Christ. The biblical writers claimed to know the name of the living God in a way that others could not apprehend fully (Acts 17:16–31), because of the revelation of Jesus Christ.

The orthodox Christian formulation is that we can know God only through the particular phenomenon of God's self-disclosure in Jesus Christ. We know in particulars first. Paul's dialogue with the philosophers of Athens at the Areopagus begins with an affirmation that his interlocutors are exceptionally religious people, and that God is not far from each one of us:

> Then Paul stood in front of the Areopagus and said, "Athenians, I see how extremely religious you are in every way. For as I went through the city and looked carefully at the objects of your worship, I found among them an altar with the inscription, 'To an unknown god.' What therefore you worship as unknown, this I proclaim to you. The God who made the world and everything in it, he who is Lord of heaven and earth, does not live in shrines made by human hands, nor is he served by human hands, as though he needed anything, since he himself gives to all mortals life and breath and all things. From one ancestor he made all nations to inhabit the whole earth, and he allotted the times of their existence and the boundaries of the places where they would live, so that they would search for God and perhaps grope for him and find him—though indeed he is not far from each one of us. For 'In him we live and move and have our being'; as even some of your own poets have said, 'For we too are his offspring.'" (Acts 17:22–28)

appear as nearly synonymous terms, situating Sikhism vis-à-vis Hindu and Muslim ideas:

> By listening to the Word,
> The seeker becomes equal to Shiva, Brahma, and Indra;
> By listening to the Word,
> The seeker becomes praiseworthy;
> By listening to the Word,
> One learns the secrets of Yoga;
> By listening to the Word,
> One learns the wisdom of the Shāstra, the Smriti, and the Veda;
> Nānak says: Devotees find bliss,
> By listening to the Word, sorrow and sin are destroyed.
>
> Japji, 9, Adi Granth[11]

Liberation can be attained by listening to the word, which involves inner awareness of the soul, struggling to live selflessly and unencumbered by human impulses. Nanak believed that by repetition of the Nam one can conquer the greatest of sins—the self, the ego—enabling the aspirant to attain salvation even while still living. The openness to God has been described as like having an extra bodily orifice that opens, receiving God's voice and permitting union with God. The attainment of inner purity—neither caste or class purity nor asceticism—is central to the spiritual quest.

Guru Angad Dev

The second Sikh Guru was **Guru Angad Dev** (1504–54), a close disciple of Guru Nanak who so impressed Nanak that he told Angad that he would be Nanak's successor. Angad himself, like Nanak, had been a Hindu, a devotee of Durga, but after hearing the recitation of one of Nanak's hymns he was fascinated with what he had heard and visited Nanak in the village of Kartarpur, where Nanak had established a *dharmasala*. After spending about seven years as Nanak's disciple at Kartarpur, Nanak died, and Angad carried on the new Sikh religion, beginning with the introduction of a new alphabet known as Gurmukhi script, a simplified script used among Punjabis.

Angad was the first to gather information on the earlier life and travels of Nanak. He also began the compilation of the Sikh hymnal, the seed of which would later develop into the Adi Granth. Like his Guru, Angad traveled widely, establishing hundreds of new centers of Sikhism. Angad died in 1554; his accomplishments include establishing a new town and a new alphabet, and recording the first authorized biography of Guru Nanak (1544), thus solidifying the new religion through his preaching, hymn writing, and consolidation of faithful teachings of Guru Nanak. For Angad, the ultimate guide to liberation was Guru Nanak himself, rather than the inner voice of God.

Guru Amar Das

Guru Amar Das (1479–1574) became the third Guru, chosen by Guru Angad himself. Amar Das, born in the Amritsar district, was raised a devout Vaishnava Hindu. Like his predecessor, Guru Angad, Amar Das heard the singing of the hymns of Guru Nanak one day; he had grown increasingly interested in the hymns when he met Guru Angad. Amar Das, however, was over sixty years old before he became a Sikh.

Amar Das, like Guru Nanak, had high regard for women. For instance, he condemned the Hindu ritual of sati (wife immolation) and fought for the widow's right to remarry. And, in a critique of Islam, he believed that veiling women was humiliating. Amar Das sent Sikh missionaries throughout India, dividing the Sikh community into twenty-two *manjis* (districts, dioceses), each led by a pious Sikh *masand* (Punjabi; "minister," "tithe collector") who served as a territorial deputy, preached Guru Nanak's words, and collected the tax (Punjabi, *dasvandh*; "the tenth"), a contribution of one-tenth of one's earnings given in the name of the Guru used for the common resources of the Sikh community.

The notion of a common financial pool enabled Amar Das to strengthen the role of the Guru; provide charitable gifts to the Sikh community; enlarge Sikhism through the founding of new cities, including Ramdaspur, which would later become the Sikh holy city of Amritsar; and expand the Sikh community's free kitchens (*langar*). The *langar* was a significant symbol in the community, for it demonstrated the equality of all people, regardless of caste or gender. Started by Guru Nanak himself at the *dharmasala* in Kartarpur as a free kitchen to serve vegetarian food to wandering holy people, the *langar* became a robust means of social reform, demonstrating the unity of all people. At the *Guru ka langar* (refectory of the Gurū), as it is formally called, people sit on the floor in a group or in lines (called *pangat*) to share in the simple, yet nourishing, free community meal. The *langar* continues to be a significant Sikh social institution worldwide, providing free food and hospitality to guests, Sikh and non-Sikh.

Finally, Amar Das compiled an anthology of writings and hymns of the two previous Gurus, Nanak and Angad, including his own contributions. Amar Das died in 1574 at ninety-five years old, after appointing his son-in-law, Jetha, as his successor, rather than either of his own sons, Mohan and Mohri. Jetha was renamed Ram Das.

Guru Ram Das

Guru Ram Das (1534–81) became the fourth Guru of Sikhism. He had already purchased the town of Ramdaspur in 1577, where he dug a sacred pool that would later lead to renaming the city **Amritsar** (literally, nectar + pool; "pool of the nectar of immortality"). Ram Das then began the construction of the famous Golden Temple at Amritsar, known as the **Harmandir Sahib** (the Abode of God), the sacred city and capital of Sikhism. The Golden Temple is open on all sides and open at all times, reflecting the openness of God. The town developed into the most important trading center in the Punjab.

Among the most important contributions made by Ram Das was making the office of the Guru hereditary, thereafter limiting the lineage to the Sodhi clan, a subdivision of the Khatris Punjabi class. There may have been several reasons for Ram Das's insistence on ensuring that future Gurus remained within the Sodhi family group. The personal reason could have been that Ram Das himself was an outsider to the bloodline of the Guru that preceded him and thus wanted to maintain control over the lineage. The practical reason for his decision may have been simply to protect the heritage from splinter groups. As it turned out, with the death of Guru Ram Das, who had appointed his younger son, Arjan Dev, as successor, his elder son, Prithi Chand, declared himself the Guru, establishing a separate sect of Sikhs that was discontinued by the last human Guru in the seventeenth century.

Guru Arjan Dev

The fifth Guru, **Arjan Dev** (1563–1606), the first Guru to be born in a Sikh family, made one of the most important contributions to Sikhism: the final compilation in 1604 of the Adi Granth, the collection of writings and hymns of the first five Gurus and a few early bhakti poets. Arjan Dev's addition of 2,216 hymns forms the largest contribution to the Adi Granth. He formally installed the Adi Granth as the sacred Sikh scriptures in the vernacular language of the Punjab, in the Gurmukhi script created by Guru Angad Dev in the sixteenth century. Arjan Dev led the Sikhs during the rule of Mughal emperor Akbar the Great (1556–1605). Tradition says that when Akbar received a copy of the Adi Granth, he was so pleased with its universal message that he offered a gift of gold to the book.

In 1595, on the birth of his son **Hargobind** (World Lord), Guru Arjan Dev composed a work that became part of the Adi Granth. His words celebrate both the birth of his son after a long period of childlessness and God's provision for a future successor to the Sikh tradition.

> The True Guru has sent the child. The long awaited child has been born by destiny. When he came and began to live in the womb his mother's heart was filled with gladness. The son, the world-lord's child, Gobind, is born. The one decreed by God has entered the world. Sorrow has departed, joy has replaced it. In their joy Sikhs sing God's Word.
>
> Adi Granth, 396[12]

Furthermore, Arjan Dev was responsible for the immense growth of the Sikh religion, while also encouraging trade with Afghanistan, Persia, and Turkey for Indian spices, textiles, and horses, which in turn procured greater wealth for the Sikh *panth*. Arjan Dev stressed the unique identity of the Sikhs apart from Hindus and Muslims, even introducing the special Sikh dress.

Suspected of supporting Prince Khusrau, the seditious son and rival of the Mughal emperor Jehangir (r. 1605–27), Arjan Dev was imprisoned because the emperor would not permit his apparent alliance with the rebellious prince. Jehangir also resented Arjan Dev's increasing power and influence. Arjan Dev was later tortured to death by Emperor Akbar's son, by being made to sit in a red-hot cauldron while his naked body was bathed in boiling water until he died. Before his arrest, Arjan Dev named his son, Hargobind, the sixth Sikh Guru, giving him two swords that represented spiritual and temporal power (*piri* and *miri*). Sikh tradition declares that Arjan Dev calmly meditated on God as he was tortured with boiling water, becoming the first Sikh martyr. The Adi Granth records his tribute, idealizing the great Guru.

> *I do not keep the Hindu fast nor the Muslim Ramadan.*
> *I serve Him alone who is my refuge.*
> *I serve the one Master, who is also Allah.*
> *I have broken with the Hindu and the Muslim,*
> *I will not worship with the Hindu, nor like the Muslim go to Mecca;*
> *I shall serve Him and no other.*
> *I will not pray to idols nor heed the Muslim's azan;*
> *I shall put my heart at the feet of the one Supreme Being,*
> *For we are neither Hindus nor Muslims.*
>
> Guru Arjan Dev, in Kitagawa, *Religious Traditions of Asia*, 117

> Grasping him by the arm, the Guru lifts them up and out, and carries them across to the other side.
>
> Adi Granth, 1204[13]

By the time of the fifth Guru, relations between the Sikh community and the Mughal authorities had begun to deteriorate rapidly. With Arjan Dev's death, interpreted as martyrdom, a new era of Sikhism emerged, one in which Sikhs armed themselves for defense against the Mughals. From this point onward, Sikhs took measures to protect themselves and at times defend the vulnerable of all religious traditions against oppression.

Guru Hargobind

The sixth Sikh leader was Guru Hargobind (Har Gobind) (1595–1644), the son of Guru Arjan Dev. Hargobind was born in Amritsar, where he later built a fortress (called Lohgarh) and the Akal Takht (Punjabi, "immortal throne"), the chief Sikh shrine located in the Golden Temple, which served both spiritual and military purposes, since it received the sacred Adi Granth nightly and housed the weapons of previous Sikh Gurus and martyrs. Hargobind was imprisoned for a year on account of his father's unpaid fine, gaining the title Holy Liberator (Punjabi, *Bandī Chhor'*) for his successful negotiation with Mughal rulers to release fifty-two fellow captives. After his release, Hargobind raised a Sikh army and became an important military leader in the Punjab, teaching people to defend their religion.

Most notably, Hargobind fought and won four separate battles against the Mughals (1628–34), which raised his prestige immensely. Hargobind traveled widely, appointing *masands* and both establishing new and restoring older *gurdwaras*. Unlike Gurus before him Hargobind did not compose hymns. He was instead oriented toward martial arts and military defense. However, his legacy consisted in the exercise of both spiritual and temporal power (*piri* and *miri*), and he even wore two swords at his waist. Hargobind's father was the first Sikh martyr, and Hargobind was the first to militarize the Sikh tradition and engage in warfare. Since Hargobind's three sons had died and his eldest grandson, Dhir Mal, had turned against his grandfather, the sixth Guru appointed another grandson, **Har Rai**, as the seventh Guru.

Figure 5.5. Golden Temple Akal Takht and Harmandir Sahib in Amritsar, Punjab, India

234

Guru Har Rai

Guru Har Rai (1630–61) was the grandson of Guru Hargobind from Hargobind's deceased son Gurditta (d. 1638); he became the seventh Sikh Guru. It is worth noting that the seventh and eighth Gurus maintained peace with Mughal authorities, never using their armies against the Mughals. Har Rai was known for his compassion for all living beings and his peaceful heart. He established an herbal-medicine hospital and a zoo in the city of Kiratpur, and although he maintained the hunting tradition of his grandfather, he would take the animals to the zoo rather than kill them. About extending hospitality, Guru Har Rai declared,

> Do service in such a way that the poor may not feel he is partaking of some charity but as if he had come to the Gurū's house which belonged to all in equal measure. He who has more should consider it as God's trust and share it in the same spirit. Man is only an instrument of service: the giver of goods is God, the Gurū of us all.[14]

Although he was known for his compassion toward living things, Har Rai also maintained well over two thousand mounted soldiers. He was known for instituting 360 Sikh *manjis*, appointing devout Sikhs as *masands*, since by that time the *masand* system itself had become corrupt. Regarding the religious life, Har Rai recognized the ineffable nature of the Word, maintaining that with time God helps everyone to understand the Gurus' truth.

Har Rai supported Emperor Shah Jahan's eldest son, Dara Shikoh, which provoked the anger of the emperor's youngest son, Aurangzeb. After Aurangzeb himself became Mughal emperor (r. 1658–1707), he summoned Har Rai directly. In response to the summons, Har Rai sent his own son, Ram Rai, to meet Aurangzeb. Sikh history regards Ram Rai as an apostate in part because he changed one verse of Guru Nanak's hymn in the Adi Granth to read more acceptably to Aurangzeb while Ram Rai was detained. The verse in the Adi Granth originally read, "The Muslim's clay comes under the potter's power," but Ram Rai substituted the word "faithless" for "Muslim" to avoid raising Emperor Aurangzeb's displeasure. Given Ram Rai's apparent apostasy, it is not surprising that Guru Har Rai would overlook him as the next successor and instead proclaim Ram Rai's younger brother, **Har Krishan**, as the eighth Sikh Guru. According to tradition, Guru Har Rai died from a broken heart due to Ram Rai's surrender to Mughal influence.

Guru Har Krishan

Guru Har Krishan (1645–64 CE), the eighth Sikh Guru, also maintained a peaceful relationship with Mughal authorities. He was installed as Guru at the age of five and died only three years later. Referred to as the Child Guru, Har Krishan was said to possess spiritual powers. For instance, tradition says that with water from a well he healed people suffering from cholera; he recognized a queen who had dressed as a slave to test him; and after touching a poor, deaf, speech-impaired Sikh water carrier with his cane, the water carrier immediately expounded the subtleties of the Bhagavad Gita.

Emperor Aurangzeb summoned the young Guru Har Krishan to Delhi, where he died of smallpox. Before his death, Guru Har Krishan indicated that his successor would be an older man from Bakala. A merchant discovered the next Guru by vowing secretly to offer five hundred coins to the Guru, then offered just a few coins to several Sodhis to see how each would respond. When **Tegh Bahadur**, the youngest son of Guru Hargobind, was approached by the merchant with a few coins, Bahadur exclaimed, "You promised five hundred coins," thus demonstrating his guruship.

Guru Tegh Bahadur

The ninth Sikh Guru, Tegh Bahadur (1621–75), whose name means "hero of the sword," was born in Amritsar. A poet and a Sikh missionary leader, he was eventually martyred by Emperor Aurangzeb for defending Hindus in Delhi. Tegh Bahadur lived during the time when Emperor Aurangzeb was Islamizing South Asia, exemplified in his closure of Hindu schools (1672), demolition of temples—sometimes replacing them with mosques—and imposition of the *jizya* (poll tax) (1679) on non-Muslims.

The groups of Sikhs that had splintered off from the mainstream tradition because they believed Dhir Mal, Ram Rai, and other Sodhis were rightful heirs to guruship then rejected the guruship of Tegh Bahadur, even preventing him from entering Harimandir, Amritsar. In response, Tegh Bahadur founded Anandpur. Then, because of further harassment, he fled through Bengal to Assam, a northeastern state in India. Upon learning from Kashmiri Hindu pundits (Sanskrit, "teachers," "intellectuals," "philosophers") that Hindus were being forcefully converted to Islam by the Mughal viceroy of Kashmir and being invited by the Hindu pundits to intervene on their behalf, Tegh Bahadur relayed a message assuring Emperor Aurangzeb that the Hindus would enthusiastically embrace Islam if Tegh Bahadur himself could be convinced to be converted to Islam.

The emperor wanted revenge on the Sikhs who had supported the emperor's brother, Dara Shikoh. With that in mind, Tegh Bahadur prepared to visit the emperor in Delhi, declaring that his son **Gobind Singh** should be installed as the subsequent Guru if Tegh Bahadur were not to survive. Soon afterward, Tegh Bahadur and his entourage were arrested by Aurangzeb, but they refused to become Muslims, even under the threat of torture and death. After his arrest, Tegh Bahadur wrote words on a piece of paper and strung it around his neck. In November 1675, Tegh Bahadur was beheaded before a crowd of thousands. After the execution the paper was opened. It read, "I gave my head but not my faith."

Guru Gobind Singh

The tenth and final (human) Guru was Gobind Singh (1666–1708). He was born in Patna, which is located in Bihar state in eastern India. After his father's execution by Aurangzeb, Gobind Singh received his father's severed head. As a young boy, Gobind Singh excelled in martial arts, hunting, and swordsmanship. Educated in the Hindi, Sanskrit, Punjabi, and Persian languages, he composed several poems that were included in the Dasam Granth, a semicanonical Sikh text.

Gobind Singh left three important legacies. First, he abolished the succession of (human) Gurus, who had all been identified originally with Guru Nanak. Because some previous Gurus had been executed, Gobind Singh eliminated the human institution of Guru to protect the heritage and the future of the tradition. Second, in a related move Gobind Singh installed the Adi Granth as the next and final Guru, the perpetual Guru of the Sikhs (the Sri Guru Granth Sahib),

Wikimedia Commons

Figure 5.6. Guru Gobind Singh meets Guru Nanak, eighteenth-century painting

This is an important illustration of the role of the Guru within Sikhism, for while the human Gurus may have been different, the "divine light" was always the same. The Adi Granth notes, "The divine light is the same, the life form is the same. The king has merely changed his body" (Adi Granth, 966).[15] Since Gobind Singh instituted the Adi Granth as the final Guru, Sikhs have believed that all spiritual wisdom to live one's life is found in the Guru Granth. Third, Gobind Singh created the Khalsa, transforming the religious community into a militant brotherhood. It is worthwhile to note that while the Punjabi term "*khālsā*" means "pure," Khalsa also refers to the community of the Guru's own people, so we would be mistaken to think of the Khalsa in militaristic terms exclusively.

Figure 5.7. Adi Granth, Sri Guru Granth Sahib Nishan, Lahore, Pakistan, from the late seventeenth century

Yet for Gobind Singh there was an undeniable connection between the Khalsa and the Guru. According to Gobind Singh, "wherever five Sikhs gather together in the presence of their sacred scripture, the Adi Granth or Guru Granth Sahib, there too is the eternal Guru."[16]

Khalsa

While Guru Hargobind maintained a small standing army, it was Guru Gobind Singh who established a distinct army with sole allegiance to the Guru. The fifth and ninth Gurus, Arjan Dev and Tegh Bahadur, had been executed, but Gobind Singh created a means by which the tradition could maintain itself through the eternal Guru (Adi Granth) and defend the community (Khalsa). Tradition says that in 1699 a group of Sikhs congregated at Anandpur to listen to Gobind Singh's invitation for volunteers willing to be obedient to the Guru, in contradistinction to the rival *masands* who challenged the Guru, even to the point of offering their heads as a sacrifice: "My sword wants today a head. Let any one of my Sikhs come forward. Isn't there a Sikh of mine who would be prepared to sacrifice his life for his Guru?" Daya Ram was the first of five to step forward. Gobind directed each one individually into his tent, emerging from the tent each time with blood on his sword. What happened? Gobind was testing the commitment of his followers. After emerging from his tent the fifth time, with blood dripping from his sword, all five volunteers appeared with him. These five, because of their great courage in sacrificing to the Guru, became known as the "five beloved ones" (Punjabi, *Panj Piare*), the nucleus of the Khalsa.

Gobind Singh had initiated the "five beloved ones" through the ritual of *khanda di pahul* (Punjabi, "rites of the two-edged sword"). Gobind Singh did not invent the ceremony but rather added to a ritual action begun by Guru Nanak called *charan amrit*, initiation by water that had touched the Guru's toe or foot. Early Sikh disciples sipped water poured over the Guru's large toe. However, Gobind Singh introduced the ceremony called Amrit Pahul to baptize Sikhs into the Khalsa, a transformative ritual that marked their new identity.

The ceremony itself is rather straightforward. A mixture of water and a sweet substance, the nectar of immortality (*amrit*), is stirred with a two-edged sword (*khanda*), while hymns are recited. The Khalsa baptism ceremony involves drinking the *amrit* mixture, which is the sugar water stirred with a dagger, in the presence of five Khalsa Sikhs as well as the Adi Granth.

Beyond following the four codes of conduct (see sidebar 5.2), the initiated were to adorn themselves at all times with the five emblems of the Khalsa, often referred to as the "five Ks," each having a literal and spiritual meaning: (1) **Kesh**—long, uncut hair and beard. No hair may be removed from the body since this interferes with God's will. In contrast to the matted hair of the Hindu ascetics (e.g., *sannyasi*), Sikh hair must be kept clean and tidy. Having the *kesh* identifies one as part of the Khalsa—for one is easily recognized by his or her long, uncut hair. The spiritual connotation is that a member of the Khalsa accepts God's will. (2) **Kangha**—comb. This small comb is usually

SIDEBAR 5.2

Sikh Rules of Conduct

1. You shall never remove any hair from any part of your body.
2. You shall not use tobacco, alcohol, or any other intoxicants.
3. You shall not eat the meat of an animal slaughtered the Muslim way.
4. You shall not commit adultery.

Charles E. Farhadian

Figure 5.8. Sikh devotee with *dastar* and symbols of the Khalsa at the Golden Temple in Amritsar, Punjab, India

made of wood or ivory. As one may imagine, its purpose is to keep the hair neat and tangle free at all times. Members of the Khalsa should wash their hair regularly as a matter of self-discipline. The spiritual meaning of the comb is that it symbolizes spiritual control. (3) ***Kirpan***—sword. This ceremonial sword can be five to ninety centimeters long. It can be worn at the waist or neck or in the *kangha*, representing quick defense of truth and the prevention of violence. The *kirpan* is primarily a religious symbol rather than a weapon. Spiritually, the *kirpan* connotes the Sikh struggle against injustice and the power of truth to cut through untruth. (4) ***Kara***—steel bangle bracelet. Worn on the right wrist, the *kara* reminds the wearer of his or her unity with God and other Sikhs in bondage to the Guru, restraining the wearer from evil action. (5) ***Kaccha***—short trousers, undershorts. Used practically during the period of the human Gurus to enable quick action in war, especially if a Sikh was surprised by an enemy, the *kaccha* is worn as an undergarment to symbolize self-restraint and self-control of sexual desires, like lust.

Khalsa men replace their family name with "**Singh**" (Punjabi, "lion") and Khalsa women with the name **Kaur** (Punjabi, "princess"). Anyone, regardless of class or gender, can receive initiation provided that he or she follows the vows and codes of conduct and wears the five Ks. Furthermore, members of the Khalsa are required to follow the *rahit maryada* (code of discipline), which provides cohesion to Sikh identity by prescribing particular conduct that should characterize faithful Sikhs. These include, for instance, the study of scripture, meditation on God, living according to the Guru's teaching, and serving all humanity.

Finally, most Sikhs are visibly recognizable by their head covering, called *dastar* (Persian for turban). The *dastar*, while not formally a part of the five Ks, is commonly worn by Sikh men and sometimes by Sikh women. Unlike the use of hats in the Western world, the *dastar* (turban) in central and South Asia connotes royalty and dignity. Historically, the turban has been held in high esteem in Asian and Middle Eastern cultures. Guru Gobind Singh transformed this cultural symbol into a religious requirement of Sikhs so that members of the Khalsa would always have high self-esteem. In fact, the *dastar* is mandatory for all Sikh men and optional for Sikh women. The *dastar* cannot be covered by any other headgear or replaced by a hat or cap.

Sikh Teaching

Sikhism teaches strict monotheism, that God is the creator, spaceless, timeless, unborn. There are no **avatars** (divine descent), as in Hinduism, but God can be known through the grace of the Guru and the scripture. Sikhs

---

Christian Reflections

Sikhism sees a unity underlying the various religions of the world. All names for God refer to the same being. That being can be called by a multitude of names—for example, Allah, Rama, Hari, Shiva, Yahweh, Dios, Creator of the Universe, the One Who Receives Sacrifices, Father, Jupiter, Mighty One, Baal. Do all names for God refer to the same being? Is there One behind the many names worshiped around the world? From a Christian perspective, how important are the names of God? In the Bible, God is called by a vast number of names that reflect various aspects of God's character (see sidebar 5.3). Can nonbiblical names, such as Guru or Nam, equally carry the sense of the biblical God? Do they refer to the same qualities, attributes, and characteristics?

Naturally, there are significant differences between concepts of God throughout religions, such as the understanding of God's personality, relationship with the created order, requirements for salvation, accessibility, and changeability, and how God communicates with human beings. And the image of God varies quite dramatically in the world religions, with some depictions of God being considerably frightening and others peaceful and serene.

must worship one God, believe in the oneness of all the Gurus, and raise their children to believe the same. The major focus of Sikhism is on loving devotion to the one God, who is worshiped by countless names worldwide. One of the best ways to worship God is to recite his name, whether that be Hari, Ram, Khuda, Sahib, or others.

It is believed that the light of God shines through the Guru, thus underscoring the central role of the Guru in Sikh life. Since God is not separate from the world but actually pervades the cosmos and can be found within everything, Sikhs generally do not try to convert others to their religion.

Simply put, the purpose of life is to recognize God within the world and treat all people equitably. The hallmarks of social action for Sikhs are their hospitals, leprosariums, and free kitchens (*langar*). Sikhs are famous for providing free communal hostels where visitors are received, lodged, and fed for three days without charge no matter what religion they follow. As one might imagine, guests in such Sikh hostels are required to follow Sikh rules, such as refraining from smoking, shaving, begging, or providing tips. However, Sikh hostels do commonly receive "contributions" from guests. In

---

SIDEBAR 5.3

Biblical Names for God

Abhir ("Mighty One," Gen. 49:24)

Adonai ("Lord," Gen. 15:2)

Despotes ("Lord," Luke 2:29)

El ("mighty," "strong," "prominent," Gen. 33:20)

El-Berith ("God of the Covenant," Judg. 9:46)

El Elyon ("Most High," Gen. 14:19, 20)

El-Gibbor ("God the warrior," Isa. 9:5)

Elohim (plural noun for God, Gen. 17:7)

El-Olam ("Everlasting God," Gen. 21:33)

El Roi ("God of seeing," Gen. 16:13)

El Shaddai ("God all sufficient," Gen. 17:1)

Eyaluth ("Strength," Ps. 22:20)

Goel ("Redeemer," Job 19:25)

Hypsistos ("Highest," Matt. 21:9)

"I am" (preexistent, living, personal God, John 8:58)

Jehovah, Yahweh ("Lord"; "I am who I am," Exod. 3:14)

Jehovah Elohim ("Lord God," Gen. 2:4)

Jehovah-Jireh ("The Lord will provide," Gen. 22:14)

Jehovah-M'Kaddesh ("The Lord who sanctifies," Lev. 20:8)

Jehovah-Nissi ("The Lord our banner," Exod. 17:15)

Jehovah-Ro'i ("The Lord our shepherd," Ps. 23)

Jehovah-Rophe ("The Lord who heals," Exod. 15:22–26)

Jehovah-Shalom ("The Lord our peace," Judg. 6:24)

Jehovah-Shammah ("The Lord is there," Ezek. 48:35)

Jehovah-Tsidkenu ("The Lord our righteousness," Jer. 23:5, 6)

Kadosh ("Holy One," Ps. 71:22)

general, then, Sikhs emphasize social service and meditation on the name of God, with their three duties summed up as keeping God continually in mind (*nam japna*), earning a living by honest means (*kirt karna*), and giving to charity (*vand chakna*).

The Adi Granth is 1,430 pages long, with scriptural references noted by page number. Originally ordained by Guru Arjan Dev in the Harimandir and completed by Guru Gobind Singh, it was installed as the final, eternal Guru in October of 1708. The Adi Granth is seen as the embodiment of divine light, consisting of *shabads* (hymns) organized in thirty-one ragas (ancient Indian musical notes and melodies), arranged by the order of Sikh Gurus whose words are contained therein.

The Adi Granth opens with the Japji section, a set of verses recited every morning by faithful Sikhs. *Jap* means to recite, and *ji* is an honorific, so the term "Japji" communicates respect for the recitation. At the center of Sikh theology is the Mool Mantra (Root Mantra), which forms the basis for the proceeding verses, hymns, and prayers of the Adi Granth. The Mool Mantra was composed by Guru Nanak himself and summarizes Sikh theology,

Kanna ("Jealous," Exod. 20:5)

Kyrios ("Lord," appears about 600 times in the New Testament)

Logos ("Word," John 1:1)

Magen ("Shield," Ps. 3:4)

Melekh ("King," Ps. 5:3)

Palet ("Deliverer," Ps. 18:3)

Pantokrator ("Almighty," 2 Cor. 6:18)

Shophet ("Judge," Gen. 18:25)

Soter ("Savior," Luke 1:47)

Tsaddiq ("Righteous One," Ps. 7:9)

Theos ("God," appears about 1,000 times in the New Testament)

Theotes ("Godhead," Col. 2:9)

Tsur ("God our rock," Deut. 32:18)

Yesha ("Savior," Isa. 43:3)

Furthermore, the names for Jesus are numerous in the New Testament:

   Advocate

   Ancient of Days

Branch

Chief Apostle

Christ ("the anointed one")

Daystar

Deliverer

Firstborn

Great High Priest

Immanuel

Jesus ("Joshua")

Lamb of God

Lord of lords

Perfector of our Faith

Physician

Rock

Root of Jesse

Second Adam

Shepherd

Slain Lamb

Stone

even while being quite philosophically challenging to understand. The Mool Mantra states, "One Universal God, the Name Is Truth, Creative Being Personified, No Fear, No Hatred, Image of the Timeless One, Beyond Birth, Self-Existent, By Guru's Grace." Sikh scholars and laypeople suggest that the Mool Mantra is the fundamental building block of all Sikh theology.

Figure 5.9. A *langar* (Sikh community kitchen)

The Adi Granth is installed in the *gurdwara*, the Sikh worship space or Sikh temple, the most important and holiest being the Harmandir Sahib in Amritsar in the Punjab. Although everyone has access to the Adi Granth, it is typical in large *gurdwaras* for men and women to sit apart, leaving a path in the middle leading to the Adi Granth. When entering a *gurdwara*, one must show respect by removing one's shoes before the worship space, dressing conservatively but comfortably enough to sit on the floor, and abstaining from alcohol and tobacco. Everybody needs to cover his or her head, but not with a baseball cap.

Sikhism has a fairly open form of worship, led by men and women. Worship can be public or private. There are no images and statues. Prayer and hymn singing, in praise of "His Name," and distribution of *karah parshad* (a consecrated sweet vegetarian pudding) form the central focus of Sikh worship practice. Before and after the service, the Adi Granth is ceremoniously brought out into public viewing, where someone will read portions, after which it is rewrapped and taken to its special location. The Adi Granth should be placed, when not being read, in the highest position in the room.

Worship and Practice

According to the Sikh code of conduct, "A Sikh should wake up in the ambrosial hours (three hours before dawn), take a bath and, concentrating his or her thoughts on One Immortal Being, repeat the name Waheguru (Wondrous Destroyer of Darkness)." The main purpose of Sikh worship is to praise God and remember the teachings of the ten Gurus. Sikh worship focuses on honoring God in the abstract, rather than through the use of images or statues. And, as noted above, there are countless names for God.

The **Christian tradition affirms** what theologians call *general* and *special revelation*. *General revelation* refers to the belief that all people have some insight into God through observation of the natural world, reason, philosophy, and personal conscience. *Special revelation* refers to the explicit knowledge of Jesus Christ. Special revelation can take many forms within Christianity—for example, personal experience, Scripture (i.e., the Bible), prophecy, miracles, and the life of Jesus Christ. Christians recognize that there is no greater knowledge of God than through Jesus Christ. Special revelation gives us the fullest knowledge of God.

> Long ago God spoke to our ancestors in many and various ways by the prophets, but in these last days he has spoken to us by a Son, whom he appointed heir of all things, through whom he also created the worlds. He is the reflection of God's glory and the exact imprint of God's very being, and he sustains all things by his powerful word. When he had made purification for sins, he sat down at the right hand of the Majesty on high, having become as much superior to angels as the name he has inherited is more excellent than theirs. (Heb. 1:1–4)

The Sikh scriptures use beautiful poetic and tactile language to communicate the greatness of God and the passionate commitment followers have to God (i.e., Nam), yet God remains veiled in mystery:

> The believer's bliss cannot be described.
> If one tries to do so, he repents in the end.
> There is no paper or pen nor any scribe to do so.
> None can understand the state of mind of the believer.
> The name of the Lord is immaculate.
> He who would know must have faith. (Japji 12, Adi Granth)[a]

One of the strengths of the Sikh view of God is the profound mystery encompassing the divine. No one can comprehend divinity. Our minds cannot conceive the grandeur of God. A Christian perspective can indeed affirm the same, for who can understand fully the ways of God? Yet the radical assertion of orthodox Christianity is that God can be known, even in mystery, because God stooped into earthly time and space to reveal himself.

a. Bhagat Singh, *Japji*, 43.

Sikh prayer is seen as a way to spend time with God, and even though the Sikh God is portrayed as intangible, that God is understood as one who has affection for his followers. Honoring the name of God has primacy over all

Christian Reflections

There is a striking similarity between Hinduism and Sikhism, in that Hindus affirm the existence of nearly countless Gods and Sikhs of nearly countless names for God. Both stress the one and the many: the one divinity with many emanations (Hinduism) or names (Sikhism). The Sikh perspective on God enables Sikhs to be open and generous in their orientation to others, illustrated by their *langars* and charitable works.

The Sikh diaspora in the United States has created greater awareness of their traditions and practices. The first Sikh *gurdwara* in the United States was built in Stockton, California, in 1912. Today there are hundreds of *gurdwaras*, many of which can hold hundreds of Sikh worshipers, serving Sikh communities in most major cities of the United States as well as in several rural areas. Sikhs in the diaspora sustain their identity in large part through their commitment to communal worship in the *gurdwara* and the celebration of festivals of the tradition. According to Sikh tradition, their wealth is one of faith in righteousness, one that seeks truth and sincerity. The Sikh ideal has been summarized by Bhai Gurdas (1551–1636), a Punjabi Sikh companion of four of the Gurus, missionary, historian, and the first interpreter of the Adi Granth:

> At dawn a Sikh wakes up and practices meditation,
> charity and purity.
> A Sikh is soft-spoken, humble, benevolent, and grateful to
> anyone who asks for help.
> A Sikh sleeps little, eats little, and speaks little, and adopts the
> Gurū's teachings.
> A Sikh makes a living through honest work, and gives in charity;
> though respected a Sikh should remain humble.
> Joining the congregation morning and evening to participate in
> singing hymns, the mind should be linked to the *gurbani* [Adi Granth] and
> the Sikh should feel grateful for the Gurū.
> A Sikh's spontaneous devotion should be self-less for it is
> inspired by the sheer love of the Gurū.[a]

a. These words come from Bhai Gurdas's Var 28, 15 (Ballad 28, 15), quoted in Cole, "Sikhism."

other aspects of worship. In the words of Guru Arjan, "The praising of his Name is the highest of all practices. It has uplifted many a human soul. It slakes the desire of restless mind. It imparts an all-seeing vision."[17] There are private and public forms of Sikh worship. Private worship entails following the Sikh code of conduct by striving to wake early, bathe, and begin the day by worshiping God.

> O brother, you worship gods and goddesses. What can you ask of them and what can they give to you? O brother, the stones/idols you wash with water sink in water (in other words how could these stones help you cross the ocean of worldly temptations).
>
> Adi Granth, 637[18]

While it is permissible for Sikhs to worship privately and pray at any time and in any place, public worship is a special time of communal worship when it is believed that God is present in the congregation (**Sangat**). While there is no formal set day to worship, Sikhs are encouraged to visit the *gurdwara* as frequently as possible. In Western countries, most Sikh communities have decided to worship on Sundays, since that is the day many people do not work. Congregational worship (**diwan**) occurs in a *gurdwara* and, since there are no ordained priests in Sikhism, can be led by any Sikh, male or female, who has demonstrated Sikh faith, knowledge of the tradition, and competence in reciting the Adi Granth. These leaders are called Granthi, and they are responsible for organizing services and reading from the Adi Granth. Worshipers focus their attention on the Adi Granth, since it is the living word of the Guru. Reading the Adi Granth is a sacred practice.

> *My Lord Pervades all places, all*
> *hearts;*
> *By the Guru's Grace, I found Him*
> *(also) within myself.*
> *Now, single-mindedly, I Meditate on*
> *Him.*
> *And, by the Guru's Grace, Merge in*
> *True One.*
>
> Guru Amar Das, Majh, 126, quoted in *Sri Guru Granth Sahib 1*, 117

The *gurdwara* itself can be a simple or elaborate building, but all *gurdwaras* fly the Sikh flag (**Nishan Sahib**), a triangular cloth that displays the symbol of Sikhism, a double-edged sword (**khanda**) and two single-edged swords (*kirpans*). The Nishan Sahib is located in the most prominent spot on every *gurdwara* property.

As the "doorway to the Guru," the *gurdwara* is considered to be the very residence of God. The four doors of the *gurdwara* are called the Door of Peace, the Door of Livelihood, the Door of Learning, and the Door of Grace, communicating the hospitality and openness of Sikh worship to include all people, even those from the different Hindu castes. *Gurdwara* architecture communicates an egalitarian spirit of the religion. And it is said that the doors of the *gurdwara* are always open.

Prior to entering the *gurdwara*, worshipers remove their shoes and wash their feet, and men and women cover their heads as a sign of respect. Upon entering the *gurdwara*, Sikhs will first bow before the Adi Granth, demonstrating their submission to the living

Figure 5.10. A Nishan Sahib (Sikh flag) in Amritsar, Punjab, India

Jasleen Kaur/Wikimedia Commons

teacher by touching their foreheads to the floor. Then a worshiper quietly states, "The Khalsa owes allegiance to God; sovereignty belongs to God alone." Although there is no official liturgy for Sikh worship in the *gurdwara*, Sikh worship usually consists of singing, a sermon, prayers, and readings from the Adi Granth. Sometimes after the service, worshipers and visitors share *karah parshad*, considered a blessing from the Guru.

Modern Movements

In the modern period, several Sikh reform movements, social institutions, and individuals have helped guide the *panth* through the challenges and opportunities it has encountered. Sikh reform movements, like other religious reform movements, emerged primarily as a response to the Sikhs' experience of being subjugated by colonial powers. Recognizing that they were unable to drive the British forces out of the Punjab in the late nineteenth century, the Sikhs employed their faith as a source of solace and guidance to reform Sikh cultural, religious, and intellectual processes to revitalize them under the conditions of British colonialism.

Among the more influential Sikh reform movements beginning in the late nineteenth century was the **Singh Sabha Movement**, which sought to protect Sikhism from outside influences, including those from Hindu, Christian, and Muslim sources. Upholding the dignity of Sikhism, the Singh Sabha Movement sought to combat Sikh illiteracy and the conversion of Sikhs to Hinduism, Christianity, and Islam by producing religious literature that would communicate the virtues and truths of Sikhism while providing the foundation of education and literacy. Thus the Singh Sabha Movement was essentially a reformist movement seeking to reconvert Sikhs during a time when some were converting to other religions.

An important *gurdwara* reform movement that emerged in the early twentieth century was the **Akali Dal Khara Sauda Bar**, which worked to liberate Sikh shrines from control by the dominating Udasi and Nirmala priests, who considered the shrines and lands associated with them as their personal property. Some Udasi and Nirmala priests earned income from the use of the *gurdwaras* under their control, while other priests actually sold *gurdwara* properties. Today this organization is called the **Shiromani Gurdwara Prabandhak Committee**, or the Parliament of the Sikhs, and is responsible for preserving Sikh places of worship in northern India by managing the religious, financial, and security facets of *gurdwaras*.

Modern Sikh social institutions include educational, research, political, and voluntary organizations. Although the Sikh tradition is a nonmissionary religion, in that it does not seek to convert non-Sikhs, a Sikh educational institution called **Shahid Sikh Missionary College** in Amritsar trains Sikh preachers in Sikh sacred texts, philosophy, music, and preaching, and is distinguished by the fact that prominent Sikh theologians are associated with the college. Additionally, the **Panjabi Pracharni Sabha**, also known as the Society for the Promotion of Punjabi Language, requires that the Punjabi language, spoken by the indigenous inhabitants of the historical Punjab (southern Pakistan and northwest India), be the official language for all government business in the Punjab and that the Punjabi language should be the medium of instruction in government schools.

With a focus on promoting the values of Sikhism among young people, the **Sikh Students Federation** (SSF) emphasizes the political representation of Sikhs in Pakistan and India. In the mid-1960s, the SSF organized student marches to pressure the Indian government to establish a Sikh state within India. Today the headquarters of the SSF are located adjacent to Punjabi University, in Punjab, India.

Alongside the various Sikh social institutions, there are numerous outstanding Sikh political leaders, businesspersons, and intellectuals whose influence impacts countless persons throughout the world. For instance, **Manmohan Singh** (b. 1932), best known worldwide as the first Sikh prime minister of India, is also a renowned economist credited with instituting economic reforms as prime minister that dramatically reduced regulations, thus stimulating the Indian economy. Another important Sikh politician is **Rajinder Kaur Bhattal** (b. 1931), the first woman chief minister of the Punjab, with a reputation for being a strong

Figure 5.11. Manmohan Singh, prime minister of India, 2004–14

Richardo Stuckert/Wikimedia Commons

leader. In terms of business, Sir **Sobha Singh** (1890–1978) was a prominent real-estate owner of Delhi, referred to as "the owner of half of Delhi," having constructed a large number of commercial, residential, governmental, and educational properties throughout the area and earning the reputation of being the single largest builder and real-estate owner of New Delhi.

Considered the father of fiber optics, **Narinder Singh Kapany** has fundamentally shaped the world of technology and communications through his research in fiber-optic communications, biomedical instrumentation, and solar energy. Also known for his work as a philanthropist, art collector, artist, and farmer, Kapany is arguably one of the greatest contributors to the world of telecommunications.

The diaspora Sikhs have done a remarkable job maintaining their traditions in contexts where its adherents are a clear numerical minority. Like the examples mentioned above, many members of the Sikh diaspora in the West have become quite successful in education, business, and the arts, and there is no reason to believe that this pattern will change as Sikhs continue to thrive while preserving their social, cultural, and religious traditions.

Timeline

1479–1574 CE	Life of Guru Amar Das
1504–52	Life of Guru Angad
1534–81	Life of Guru Ram Das
1563–1606	Life of Guru Arjan; construction of Darbar Sahib; completion of Adi Granth
1595–1664	Life of Guru Hargobind
1621–75	Life of Guru Tegh Bahadur
1666–1708	Life of Gobind Singh; formation of the Sikh Khalsa
1790–1839	Life of Ranjit Singh; Sikh rule of the Punjab
1849	British conquer Duleep Singh and end Sikh control of Punjab
1897	Publication of *We Are Not Hindus* by Kahn Singh Nabha
1925	Gurdwaras Act of 1925 gives control of all *gurdwaras* in the Punjab to Shiromani
1984	Operation Bluestar; Indira Gandhi assassinated by her two Sikh bodyguards
2004	Manmohan Singh becomes first Sikh prime minister of India

Key Terms

Adi Granth
Akali Dal Khara Sauda Bar
Akbar (the Great)
amrit
Amritsar

atman
Aurangzeb
avatar
Ayodhya
Babur
bhakti

Bhattal, Rajinder Kaur
British Raj
dasa
dastar
Data
dharmasala

diwan
emic
etic
Golden Temple
Granth Sahib
gurdwara
Gurmukh
Guru
Guru Amar Das
Guru Angad Dev
Guru Arjan Dev
Guru Gobind Singh
Guru Hargobind
Guru Har Krishan
Guru Har Rai
Guru Nanak
Guru Ram Das
Guru Tegh Bahadur
Harmandir Sahib
Humayun
Jahangir
Janamsakhi
Japji
jizya

Kabir
kaccha
kangha
Kapany, Narinder Singh
kara
Kaur
kesh
Khalsa
khanda
Khasam
kirpan
langar
manji
Manmukh
masand
Mughal
mukhti
Nam
Nishan Sahib
Panjabi Pracharni Sabha
panth
Pita
Pritam
Ramananda

Sangat
sannyasi
Sant
Sat Guru
Sat Nam
shabad
Shahid Sikh Missionary College
Shah Jahan
sharia
Shiromani Gurdwara Prabandhak Committee
sikha
Sikh Students Federation
Singh
Singh, Manmohan
Singh, Sobha
Singh Sabha Movement
Taj Mahal
tirthankara(s)
Vaishnava Ramanandi

Further Reading

Brown, Judith M. *Global South Asians: Introducing the Modern Diaspora*. New York: Cambridge University Press, 2006.

Grewal, J. S. *History, Literature, and Identity: Four Centuries of Sikh Tradition*. Delhi: Oxford University Press, 2011.

Mann, Gurinder Singh. *The Making of Sikh Scripture*. New York: Oxford University Press, 2001.

———. *Sikhism*. Upper Saddle River, NJ: Prentice Hall, 2004.

McLeod, W. H. *Exploring Sikhism: Aspects of Sikh Identity, Culture, and Thought*. New Delhi: Oxford University Press, 2000.

———. *Sikhs and Sikhism: Comprising Guru Nanak and the Sikh Religion, Early Sikh Tradition, the Evolution of the Sikh Community, and Who Is a Sikh?* Delhi: Oxford University Press, 2004.

Shackle, Christopher, and Arvind-pal Singh Mandair, trans. and ed. *Teachings of the Sikh Gurus: Selections from the Sikh Scriptures*. New York: Routledge, 2005.

Singh, Gopal. *A History of the Sikh People, 1469–1988*. Mumbai, India: World Book Centre, 1988.

Singh, Nikky-Guninder Kaur, ed. *The Name of My Beloved: Verses of the Sikh Gurus*. San Francisco: HarperSanFrancisco, 1995.

Singh, Pashaura, ed. *Sikhism in Global Context*. New York: Oxford University Press, 2012.

six

Taoism and Confucianism

Contemporary Snapshot

Four days a week in Montgomery, Alabama, senior citizens gather at a down-town building to practice a Chinese exercise program called **tai chi**, an ancient Chinese method of slow meditative physical exercise and martial arts that practitioners claim increases *chi* (life energy). These elderly practitioners state that tai chi leads to enhanced physical, emotional, and spiritual health, the reduction of tension, improvement in circulation, and increase in phys-ical strength and flexibility. Images of Kuan Yin, considered by the Chinese Buddhist tradition to be the goddess of mercy, and a large Taoist shrine, reflecting a blending of health and spirituality, feature prominently on the website of the Taoist Tai Chi Society of the USA.

The Taoist Tai Chi Society of the USA is a part of the International Tao-ist Tai Chi Society, headquartered in Orangeville, Ontario, Canada, with centers in more than twenty-five countries worldwide. The International Tai Chi Society, whose "internal arts and methods" were developed by founder Master Moy Lin-shin, is deeply rooted in the spiritual tradition of Taoism.[1] Worldwide people are practicing tai chi for purposes of general physical and mental health. In some parks in Beijing, China, over a thousand people prac-tice tai chi daily. Others practice tai chi in parks, beaches, and community centers in vastly different countries, such as Aruba, Denmark, Costa Rica, and the Slovak Republic. And the Chinese internal art of tai chi is growing in popularity in urban, suburban, and rural areas across the United States as people gather to seek new avenues to holistic health.

Chinese Religion and American Popular Culture

The influence of Chinese philosophy and religion on popular culture in the United States stretches beyond the parameters of the physical practice of tai chi. Consider other Chinese practices that have been well received in the United States. The principles of **feng shui**, for instance, which discerns the proper harmony of vital energies, is a popular topic in magazines found in many bookstores, in articles educating people about achieving the right balance in architecture, room decoration, cooking, and even relationships. What does it say about the widespread impact of the concept of feng shui when books about it are found on bookstore shelves for categories as diverse as cooking, architecture, religion and spirituality, psychology, and health?

Chinese herbal medicine and acupuncture have also been accepted enthusiastically by many Westerners seeking physical, mental, and spiritual health benefits from these forms of historically non-Western medicines. What does it say about a tradition that so effortlessly blends spirituality, health, and architecture? Can Christianity make the same claims—is there such

Jakub Hałun/Wikimedia Commons

Figure 6.1. Practicing tai chi in Kowloon Park, Hong Kong

a thing as "Christian architecture" or "Christian medicine"? The foundation of all Chinese religions lies neither in practicing the physical movements of tai chi nor in believing in the vital forces of feng shui. Rather, the essential nature of Chinese religious traditions begins with and is based on the concept of the "Way," also known as the **Tao**. And it is to the Way that we turn our attention in his chapter.

Figure 6.2. Tai chi demonstration in Chattanooga, Tennessee, USA

The Tao [Way] that can be told of is not
   the eternal Tao [Way];
The name that can be named is not the
   eternal name.
The Nameless is the origin of Heaven
   and Earth;
The Named is the mother of all things.

Therefore let there always be non-
   being, so we may
   see their subtlety,
And let there always be being, so we
   may see their outcome.
The two are the same,
But after they are produced, they have different names.
They both may be called deep and profound.
Deeper and more profound,
The door of all subtleties.

Tao Te Ching 1[2]

Confucius said, "When the Way [Tao] prevails in the Empire,
the rites and music and punitive expeditions are initiated by the
   Emperor.
When the Way does not prevail in the Empire, they are initiated by
the feudal lords. When they are initiated by the feudal lords, it is
surprising if power does not pass from the feudal lords within
five generations. When the prerogative to command in a state is in the
hands of officials of the Counsellors it is surprising if power does not
pass from the Counsellors within three generations. When the Way
prevails in the Empire, policy does not rest with the Counsellors.
When the Way prevails in the Empire, the Commoners do not express
critical views."

Confucius, Analects 16.2

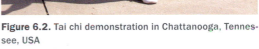

255

In this chapter we leave the South Asian subcontinent, the birthplace of Hinduism, Buddhism, Jainism, and Sikhism, and turn our attention to the two most prominent religio-philosophical traditions that emerged out of East Asia: Taoism and Confucianism. The classic Chinese texts of these two traditions introduce readers to the Way—called the Tao—that forms the basis for all interactions and relationships; the path to longevity, prosperity, and posterity; the three recurring Chinese divinities; and the practical goals of life. Understanding Taoism and Confucianism provides great insight into East Asian (and more generally, Asian) people and society. To this point we have considered the South Asian religious traditions, a world populated by gods, bodhisattvas, and the divine essence, and where the constellation of theological concepts of **karma**, **samsara**, and self are the elemental ingredients of the world of the religious aspirant.

In the two passages quoted at the beginning of this chapter, the common element in both is the centrality of the concept of the Tao. And the traditions that have developed from the essential concept are distinct yet intimately connected. As we concentrate on Taoism and Confucianism, we will learn that both traditions are based on the same fundamental concept, the Tao. And rather than contending against karmic matter, followers of Taoism and Confucianism speak of a force that animates all reality. The force itself is nonpersonal but nevertheless profoundly affects all of life, from the highest heaven to the spices one adds to food, the color of the sky, the breaking of the ocean waves, disease and health, and even to one's own personality.

The standard scholarly perspective on Chinese religiosity is that Chinese people tend to be pragmatically oriented. That is, many Chinese people traditionally look for what works. If a particular God or religion seems to be effective, then a Chinese person will follow that God or religion. The idea is, "If a particular God or religion doesn't work for me, I'll move on." That is why, according to some scholars, "Chinese religion" consists of Taoism, Confucianism, Buddhism, and indigenous Chinese traditions, with additional followers of Christianity and Islam, and there is no dominant system. It is important to recognize that all these neologisms (e.g., Taoism, Confucianism, Buddhism) were never in use before the nineteenth century.

From an outsider's (**etic**) perspective, it is far too easy to see Chinese and Western religiosity as entirely distinct from each other, whereas I would suggest that the difference is of degree rather than of kind. What strikes the attention of many first-time visitors to East Asia is seeing a single religious complex populated by several different worship spaces, each representing a different religious tradition. It is not uncommon to see a Buddhist temple and a Taoist temple located on the same property, surrounded by many vendors selling food and gifts, with the same individuals and family groups moving

Christian Reflections

Comparatively, it would likely seem strange to see a Christian church and a Muslim mosque occupying the same property, where the faithful benefit from both on the same day. A reason for this difference is that **monotheistic** traditions (e.g., Judaism, Christianity, Islam) are generally more exclusive in their orientation toward nonbelievers than the Asian religions.

One illuminating difference between the monotheistic religions and Asian religious and philosophical traditions (e.g., Hinduism, Buddhism, Taoism, Confucianism) is that monotheistic religions account for their people by keeping membership records, whereas membership is less important for the religions originating in Asia. Hindu, Buddhist, Taoist, and Confucian places of worship do not typically carry membership rolls. The monotheistic religions were, by definition, founded in part on their exclusive commitment to one God, stated clearly throughout their respective religious texts: for example, "Now if you are unwilling to serve the LORD, choose this day whom you will serve, whether the gods your ancestors served in the region beyond the River or the gods of the Amorites in whose land you are living; but as for me and my household, we will serve the LORD" (Josh. 24:15). Although the various monotheistic religions debate among themselves about the role of human agency in establishing a relationship with the one God, Judaism, Christianity, and Islam affirm the primacy of the one God, even beyond the world of the spirits.

from one space to another, offering worship and seeking answers, without feeling any internal contradiction.

Religious demographer David Barrett uses census data to come up with figures of 2,654,514 Taoists and 6,298,597 Confucians, with 384,806,732 "Chinese folk-religionists."[3] At best these figures give us a general perspective on the numbers of adherents to these two major Chinese traditions, since the line between Taoism/Confucianism and Chinese indigenous religions is blurry, and most Chinese religionists do not formally worship exclusively within one tradition. Regardless of the flexible nature of Chinese religiosity, there are very real and distinct traditions that emerged in China and have made their way throughout the world.

Defining the Tradition

Religions are intimately connected to society and as such are not simply a composite of beliefs and affirmations. Religions are made real by people living the tradition. Religions deal with real-life problems and many kinds of questions: "How do I make sense of the world?" "How do I escape the suffering of the human condition?" These sorts of questions have plagued people in all places and in all times. Taoism and Confucianism offer specific answers to the problems that all people face. What is unique about these traditions, at least in view of the South Asian traditions we have already covered, is that they do not posit the notion of a God or a personal force that directs the activities of the world and that must be placated or relied upon for salvation. As such, it is quite fair to see Taoism and Confucianism as philosophies rather than religions. And these traditions can just as well be taken up in a philosophy course as in a religion course.

Nevertheless, they can be viewed as religions as well, or at least as religio-philosophical systems, since they exhibit many of the characteristics of religions, such as possessing a symbol system, sacred texts, founders, community worship, myths and legends, and ritualized actions. Taoism and Confucianism are intimately connected; they emerged at roughly the same time and addressed the same set of struggles that emerged at that historical moment.

Four Seasons of Chinese Religion

Traditionally, religion in China has been divided into four "seasons" dating to the fourteenth century BCE. During the spring season of Chinese religion (c. 1100–206 BCE), the Six Ways developed. These ways refer to the six major philosophical traditions, including Taoism and Confucianism, that emerged together to tackle similar problems of the human condition of the period. The summer season of Chinese religion (206 BCE–900 CE) saw the introduction of Buddhism into China and the blending of Buddhism with indigenous Chinese religions, leading to a mutual enrichment of Buddhism and early Chinese traditions.

SIDEBAR 6.1

Common Terms for "Religion"

chiao, meaning "teaching," "guiding doctrine" (as in *fo-chiao*, the religion of the Buddha)

ju-chiao, the way of Confucius

tao-chiao, (religious Taoism), usually in combination with *tsung*, "ancestral, traditional," "devotion, faith"

tsung-chiao, the nearest equivalent to "religion"

Bowker, *Oxford Dictionary of World Religions*, 211

Studying world religions presents helpful challenges to our own perspective on Christianity. Can we separate "religion" from "Christianity"? Is there such a thing as a "religionless Christianity"—a kind of Christianity that seamlessly encompasses all spheres of life rather than just the "religious" domain? Should Christians aim to make faith so integral to their lives that there is no distinction between religious and secular realms, as we see in some of the Chinese religious-philosophical traditions?

If so, what are the social, political, and economic implications of such a vision? Or is it necessary, in fact, that Christianity not be wholly a part of every life domain, instead maintaining a separation that allows it to critique and affirm aspects of culture and society that need to be transformed? If one believes that Christianity should somehow be separate from culture, then just how much distance between Christianity and culture is necessary? And to what end? Because Taoism and Confucianism are intimately connected to all of life, they are totally encompassing visions.

The autumn season of Chinese religion (900–1912 CE) is marked by attempts to restore the earliest forms of Chinese religion. The winter season of Chinese religion (from the early twentieth century to the present) saw the adoption of Communism, thus signaling a decline, subjugation, and persecution of religionists. In spite of its best efforts, though, the apparent success of Communism has not led to the demise of religions in China. Nearly all religions are growing, with some showing signs of significant revival. Even smaller religions, known as new religious movements such as the **Falun Gong**, which claim to have millions of adherents in China, are on the rise.

Religion as the Way

Although Chinese languages have no specific term equivalent to "religion," there are many terms that function in nearly the same way as the so-called Western understanding of religion. For instance, *men* means "door," referring to the door that leads to long life, enlightenment, and immortality. Tao means "way." Accordingly, while there may not be an exact equivalent term in Chinese for the English word "religion," there are many Chinese words that communicate what is important about Chinese religiosity.

In the end, there are so many overlapping features of the "Chinese religions" (i.e., Taoism, Confucianism, Buddhism, indigenous traditions) that expressions such as "Taoism" and "Confucianism" are actually artificial constructions of Western scholars.[4] It is important to note that this chapter introduces Taoism and Confucianism rather than "Chinese religions" generally. Nevertheless, our task here is to tease out the unique features of Taoism and Confucianism, while keeping in mind that they too belong to a wider assemblage of religions that mutually act upon and influence one another. Furthermore, Taoism, Confucianism, Buddhism, and Chinese indigenous religions are not monolithic but rather have undergone significant transformations throughout Chinese history. This is due in part to the ways each has engaged Chinese culture and cultures around the world, the historical moment from which each emerged, and the political regime changes under which each has existed.

Origins and Concepts

The Axial Age

Asia and Europe experienced massive religious and philosophical changes between 800 and 200 BCE. The German philosopher Karl Jaspers coined the term *"Achzenzeit"* (**Axial Age**) to describe the profound and lasting influence of particular individuals and their ideas on the world during this period.[5] In Jaspers's view, the ideas that began in the Axial Age formed the foundations upon which human beings since have lived, the lens through which most human beings see the world. Indeed, it is quite astounding to think of the prominent persons and philosophies that emerged in this period: **Siddhartha Gautama** (Buddhism), **Laozi** (Taoism), **Mahavira** (Jainism), **Confucius** (Confucianism), Plato, Zoroaster, Homer, Socrates, Heraclitus, Parmenides, Archimedes, Elijah, Jeremiah, and Isaiah.

The Axial Age, according to Jaspers, was a pivotal period that ushered in a new era of universal religions and philosophies. The religions were instrumental in

Ding Yunpeng/Wikimedia Commons

Figure 6.3. Laozi, Confucius, and the Buddha talking (Ming Dynasty, Palace Museum, Beijing)

affecting great changes in history, with the innovations of the great religious leaders establishing the basis of major world civilizations, at least until this pattern of civilization was disrupted by the European Enlightenment and the expansion of trade and empire into Asia. In significant ways, the world would never be the same after the era of European colonialism, not only because of the new systems of thought introduced by Europeans but also because of the cultural, social, and (eventually) religious influence of Asians on European ways of life.

Needless to say, the changes that burgeoned in the Axial Age were connected to social, economic, political, and technological changes that occurred throughout Asia and the West. The vast changes that came about during the Axial Age highlight the innate connections between various domains of life (religion, politics, economy, culture) and remind students of the world religions not to see religions as disconnected from wider realities of the human order. Changes in the economy, environment, culture, and so on do in fact impact religious perspectives.

CHINESE DYNASTIES

Much of East Asian history unfolded and is named according to the ruling family dynasties. Early Chinese history is divided into the following dynasties:

- Xia Dynasty (c. 2070–1600 BCE)
- Shang Dynasty (c. 1600–1046 BCE)
- Zhou Dynasty (1122–256 BCE)
- Qin Dynasty (221–206 BCE)
- Han Dynasty (206 BCE–220 CE)

Many Chinese people consider the Han Dynasty to be one of the greatest periods of Chinese history, to such a degree that the majority of ethnic Chinese today refer to themselves as "Han people." Han designation is quite powerful, laden with overtones of idealized Chinese identity. The Han make up about 92 percent of the total Chinese population, and because of their sheer number nearly 20 percent of the total human population.

It is important to dispel two myths about the Chinese. First is a myth of homogeneity in China, which assumes that all Chinese are ethnically and linguistically the same, when in fact there are fifty-six recognized ethnic groups in China, not including the nine unrecognized ethnic minority groups, along with twenty-four different Taiwanese ethnicities ("aborigines"). Second, and a related point, is the myth of linguistic homogeneity. Referring to *the* Chinese language really means a complex of languages, with Mandarin

Chinese having the largest number of speakers in the world (c. 850 million). Other Chinese people speak Wu (c. 90 million), Min (c. 70 million), Cantonese (c. 70 million), and Hakka (c. 34 million), along with numerous other languages and dialects. That said, we need to remember that Chinese religions, ethnicities, and languages are complex, making universal statements that apply to all Chinese impossible to sustain.

During the Axial Age in Asia, simple feudal orders were breaking down. Feudal orders are systems of political organization whereby a lord provides land to a vassal who in turn pays a fee, gives homage, and provides service to the lord. The Chinese feudal states were not always contiguous but rather were scattered, located at strategic points for defense against potentially hostile outsiders. Therefore, the feudal states consisted of fortified cities, functioning as quasi-independent principalities, controlled by feudal lords.

The Middle Kingdom

Generally, at least in the Zhou period (1046–256 BCE), split between Western Zhou (c. 1100–771 BCE) and Eastern Zhou (771–256 BCE), these scattered feudal territories maintained stability among themselves, with small skirmishes against some intruders in the interior and on the northern frontier. Since the Zhou territories were located in the middle of the region, China was later referred to as the Middle Kingdom. The Zhou dynasty enjoyed relative peace and stability through its hegemonic system, whereby Zhou kings appointed hegemons (powerful leaders) (Chinese, *Ba*) to dominate the subjugated peoples by consent rather than by force. During the Eastern Zhou period, hegemons imposed Zhou policies throughout their appointed regions and thus increased their own prestige, until the entire hegemon system collapsed with the demise of the Zhou dynasty in 256 BCE.

China's Axial Age was a time of unprecedented political instability and social unrest. People wondered whether three thousand years of culture and relative harmony would be lost in anarchy as simple feudal orders collapsed. Troubles were particularly bad during the **Warring States Period** (475–221 BCE), which eventually ended in the unification of China under the Qin Dynasty (221 BCE). The Warring States Period was a 254-year period of violent civil disorders when smaller states disappeared and seven larger states remained to fight ruthlessly for supremacy. Finally, in 221 BCE, Duke Cheng of the State of Qin conquered all his rivals and, as the great **Emperor Shi Huang Di**, completely unified China under his rule. As you may recognize, the English word "China" is derived from the word "Ch'in," the Wade-Giles transliteration of Qin (see sidebar 6.2), the name of the dynasty that ruled China at this time (221 BCE–206 CE).

Figure 6.4. The Great Wall of China near Jinshanling

When Emperor Shi Huang Di, also referred to as Qin Shi Huang, defeated the six other states (Han, Zhao, Chu, Qi, Yan, Wei), he became the first emperor in Chinese history to entirely unify China. With the establishment of the Qin Dynasty, the emperor of China was called the Son of Heaven and considered the descendent and representative of heaven on earth, whose rule was blessed and legitimated by the Mandate of Heaven, requiring him to rule from a "directive from above" since he was considered divinely appointed.[6]

EMPEROR SHI HUANG DI

Emperor Shi Huang Di used aggressive reforms to unify China, including extending China's boundaries southward, starting the Great Wall of China to protect China's northern and western border areas from invasion, constructing an expansive national (often tree-lined) road system, nationalizing Qin laws, instituting uniform systems of weights and measures, and perhaps most significantly, outlawing Confucianism. Emperor Shi Huang Di's legacy is mixed, for his policies and development strategies cost many thousands of lives. To some he was seen as a brutal tyrant, to others a great hero of Chinese history. It is thought that his fear of death motivated him to build a massive mausoleum, measuring three miles across, constructed with 700,000 military recruits, and protected by his eternal guards, the famous Terracotta Army. It is striking to think that for nearly two thousand years, until 1974, no one knew of the emperor's burial ground and the 8,099 life-size clay soldiers protecting him.

During the massive disruptions of China's Axial Age and the Warring States Period, there were violent reactions against many of the philosophers, including organized book burnings and the burial of scholars while still alive. People looked everywhere for answers to this time of dis-ease and dishar-mony. Changes were not only massive but widespread, with social, cultural, economic, and religious repercussions. This was the beginning of the Iron Age, when new modes of production aided the creation of more and innova-tive items. New forms of production enabled the increase of cultivation and production of rice, a fundamental part of the Chinese diet. Increased rice enabled larger populations to be sustained in concentrated centers, which encouraged the construction of more roads and larger villages to permit travel and provide housing for people.

Additionally, new modes of production increased the difference in classes because of the ability of some to produce luxury goods. Wars with larger infan-try armies and mass killings by foot soldiers became common. Many positive developments occurred in this period, yet all the changes in social mobility, technology, and food production created what moderns would call "ontological insecurity." That is, people attempted to make sense of the changes going on around them and yearned for answers to regain social stability and personal security. Six major Chinese philosophical schools provided answers in this tumultuous time. Each proposed a way to regain lost harmony, instilling peace, prosperity, and longevity. Each dealt with real problems in society, such as the problems of identity and self-understanding, social dislocation, and fear. How should one live in such a world?

ANCIENT CHINESE SCHOOLS OF PHILOSOPHY

The first philosophical school that emerged from this period was Taoism, which suggested that disharmony resulted when people had lost touch with the Tao. Their spontaneity and simplicity were lost. Taoism provided the answer: return to a *simple life*, having nothing to do with the feudal system or development strategies. The second school, Confucianism, argued that China's decay was due to the disappearance of formal politeness. People had forgotten behavioral protocols and ritual formality. Propriety needed to be retrieved, based not on individual wishes but on mutual reciprocity of responsibilities. The third school, that of **Mozi** (Teacher Mo), a Chinese phi-losopher who once followed Confucius but who later became fiercely critical of Confucianism because of Confucius's emphasis on ritual and antagonism toward heaven (*t'ien*), sought the recovery of universal love (*ai*) toward all beings, not just in a reciprocal pattern, as advocated by Confucius, but rather without anticipation of any return. To Mozi, the practice of loving others was personalizing the will of *t'ien*. Against the social hierarchy advanced by Confucianism, the followers of Mozi advocated brotherly and sisterly love to mend the social disharmony.

Fourth, the **Yin-Yang Cosmologists** sought to live their lives according to the natural rhythms of the universe, doing the correct actions at the proper cosmological times. Thus they studied the nature of the cosmos and sought to discover how all things could follow the fundamental principles of **yin** and **yang**, the two great forces of life. They forwarded a theory of opposites (yin and yang) that was rejected by some cultivated Chinese elites as superstitious but was later subsumed into all Chinese thought. Under the Later Han Dynasty, the cosmologists were an important feature of Han Confucian thought (around the tenth century).

Fifth, the **Legalists** argued that a rigid code of laws, with an elaborate system of punishments and rewards rather than ritual actions, would restore a state of harmony. Opposed to Taoism and Confucianism, the Legalists argued that morality must be the basis for the government. As the government fostered moral development, people would inevitably adopt the same principles. Finally, the Logicians believed that disharmony could be overcome by thinking positive thoughts and correcting language. Seeing a relationship between language and reality, the Logicians argued for the proper use of language, recognizing that language shapes human behavior and interaction.

The Tao

According to Chinese tradition, the world began with the Tao. Pictured as an empty circle, the world began as nothing. Then chaos emerged. In the midst of that chaos, yin and yang developed as two balancing forces inherent in all things. Therefore, creation begins with this basic split between yin and yang but evolves and holds together in a world without any fundamental divisions. That is, the cosmos and the world are of one substance—a monism.

Consequently, Taoism and Confucianism see that cause and effect are of the same essence, which differs from the so-called Western understanding of dualism, where cause and effect are two moments, and differing actions. The universe unfolds by division of yin and yang, with continuity between these two forces. Rather than being a normative quality, where, for instance, one side is deemed bad and the other good, yin and yang are complementary; both are needed. Balance between these two fundamental complementary forces guarantees long life and success of all kinds. Unbalance between the two brings heartache, disease, and all kinds of suffering. Everything in the

Unlike monotheistic and theistic perspectives, in which religion involves worshiping one God, Chinese religion balances all of life in an overall monistic worldview—in a union of opposites. Rather than seeing the world as a competition between good and evil, however those may be defined, Chinese religions tend to see the world as a single whole with two complementary forces that need to be held in balance.

One of the greatest hurdles in speaking constructively about Christianity to followers of Chinese religions is addressing the dualism within Christianity. That is to say, Christianity asserts that there *is* a spiritual battle between God and the forces of evil. But this perspective of a fundamental battle between good and evil can too easily create a worldview in which God appears only in the light, whereas evil presents itself in the forces of the dark. At worst, such a view of good and evil, light and dark, can unnecessarily eliminate God's presence from certain domains of life since it is a denial of God's lordship over all.

Many great models of Christian spirituality, such as Saint John of the Cross (1542–91) and Mother Teresa (1910–97), made this same point when they wrote of the "dark night of the soul," a period of extremely difficult desolation plagued by feeling abandoned by God. Regardless of the length of this "dark night," Christian mystics have taught that spiritual rewards and purity await those who remain faithful to God. Can God also be in the dark? The psalmist writes, "Yea, though I walk through the valley of the shadow of death, I will fear no evil; for You are with me; Your rod and Your staff, they comfort me" (Ps. 23:4 KJV).

world and the universe is a result of the balance between the forces of yin and yang.

HARMONY AND BALANCE OF YIN AND YANG

If one wants to apply the terms "good" and "evil" to the constellation of Taoism and Confucianism, it would be appropriate to say that what is good is balance and what is evil is imbalance. Everything depends on the Tao, and all things reflect the balance or imbalance of yin and yang (e.g., the flavors in cooking, choosing the right time and location to move, deciding when to start a job or when to get married). Religion involves every activity. No activity is outside the realm of religion. As such, religion is not just what happens on a particular festival day or the ritual activities at a temple or church. Religion entails all of life, every day. Consequently, the role of religion in ethical reflection and action is significant.

The unbounded Tao is the basis of all things, the supreme and ultimate source, and in particular the foundation of both Taoism and Confucianism. The Tao is described as impersonal and **nonanthropomorphic**—it does not resemble human form. Most conceive of the Tao as an impersonal and unconscious force that is at once transcendent and immanent. If united with the eternal Tao, one participates in its eternity.[7] However, the Tao is never known directly; rather, it is manifested in the unfolding creation of myriads of forms through the complementarities of yin and yang, the two opposite energies in Chinese thought.

STABILITY AND CHANGE OF YIN AND YANG

All oppositions can be mapped using yin and yang. From their interaction and fluctuation, the universe and all forms emerge. Yang represents the force of light, brightness, heat, maleness, strength, above, heaven, sunny, day, south. Yang is the masculine, hard, active, red, the sun, and odd numbers. Yin represents the balancing force of opposites, such as darkness, coldness, femaleness, heaviness, weakness, below, earth, shady, night, north. Yin is the feminine, yielding, receptive, moon, water, clouds, and even numbers.

To explain the tension between stability and change, the Chinese thought in terms of balancing yin and yang. Changes in the relationship between yin and yang account for the changes in the seasons, the moon's phases, and tides. The key to stability is not one side (yin or yang) winning over the other, but rather a balance between the two. And the role of culture is to preserve this balance. Furthermore, yin and yang are not totally isolated from each other. Both are present in a small amount in the other. Inside the dark yin is a small dot of light yang, and inside the light yang is a dot of dark yin.

The ancient Chinese stressed harmony with nature's functioning, following a preestablished pattern into which all things ought to fall if they are to be in their proper place to do their proper work. For those who desire to be right, superior, and happy, and to have lives marked by longevity, prosperity, and posterity, one must follow the pattern—the Way—of the Tao. Since the way of the Tao is the path of harmony, then following the Tao will make heaven, earth, and humankind harmonious.

Figure 6.5. Yin-Yang symbol

How would it be possible to compare Jesus Christ with the Tao? Some Asian Christians have had to wrestle with understanding Christianity through Asian categories, aiming to move Christianity out of a predominately Greek way of thinking. For instance, the biblical book of Acts refers to Christianity as *hodos*, which in Greek means "way," "path," "road," "route," "journey" (see Acts 9:2; 19:9; 22:4).[a]

Quoting Herbert Fingarette, Korean theologian Heup Young Kim suggests, "Jesus Christ as the *Tao* means 'the right Way of life, the Way of governing, the ideal Way of human existence, the Way of the cosmos, the generative-normative Way (pattern, path, course) of existence as such.'"[b] How might Jesus Christ be seen as the paradigm of humanity? What opportunities for Christian dialogue, or challenges to Christianity, exist were we to understand Jesus Christ as the incarnation of the Tao, since Jesus referred to himself as "the way, the truth, and the life" (John 14:6)? As you read the description of the Tao, ask yourself how those characteristics may be similar and dissimilar to the characteristics of Jesus Christ.

a. See the innovative theological insights of Heup Young Kim, *Christ and the Tao*, 32.
b. Ibid., 33.

Taoism

The Sages of Philosophical Taoism

When we consider the term "Taoism," we might think of one religious or philosophical system. Taoism refers to at least two systems: a philosophy and a religion. The two systems of Taoism are related to each other, but they developed into distinct streams within the larger tradition of Taoism. Philosophical Taoism, the older of the two streams, begins with the writings of two **sages**, Laozi and **Zhuangzi**, which formed the backbone for the development of religious Taoism. Because of his profound influence on the tradition, we will spend more time on Laozi than on Zhuangzi. While the tradition dates back to these individuals, their own histories are highly debatable, and they may not even have been real people. However, for our purposes we will consider both Laozi and Zhuangzi to be historical figures, in part because the tradition itself believes it began with these two sages. However, even the relationship between Laozi and Zhuangzi is questionable.

Laozi is considered the first sage of Taoism: *Lao* means "old age," and *tzu* is an honorific term meaning "gentleman," "scholar," and "master." So "Laozi" means "Old Master." Virtually everything about Laozi is debatable, including his name, place of birth, date of birth, occupation, and even his existence. There are many legendary accounts of Laozi, which include stories of him visiting India, where he taught Siddhartha Gautama (the Buddha).

Most importantly, Laozi was credited with writing the **Tao Te Ching** (The Way and Its Virtue), the immensely popular basic writings of philosophical Taoism. Some scholars suggested that Laozi lived sometime between the sixth and fourth centuries BCE, arguing that he was a contemporary of Confucius and that the two knew each other. But neither the Tao Te Ching (Taoism) nor the **Analects** (Confucius) mentions that they were contemporaries or that they even knew of each other. Laozi was born in the state of Zhou, and he worked as a curator of archives at Loyang, the capital of Zhou, in today's Henan State. It is accepted by Taoists as part of the early history that while working as a curator Laozi began to question the wisdom of having any sort of government. He believed that the search for knowledge was in vain, leading only to perversion of the simplicity by which human beings were to pattern their lives. Laozi resigned as an official because his work was false and, according to tradition, returned "to his own house."

> *The relationship of the two [i.e., Laozi and Zhuangzi] is so enigmatic that it is hard to decide whether Chuang Tzu [i.e., Zhuangzi] is in effect writing an exegesis upon texts of Lao Tzu [i.e., Laozi], or Lao Tzu is a reduction to provocative aphorisms of Chuang Tzu—or whether, upon close examination, they represent two basically different outlooks.*
>
> Thompson, *Chinese Way in Religion*, 46

Figure 6.6. Statue of Laozi in Quanzhou, China

Tom@HK/Wikimedia Commons

Map 6.1. Provinces of China

Driven by an unceasing desire for escape into the unknown, leaving everything behind, Laozi, the Old Master philosopher, decided to go west. In a two-wheeled carriage drawn by black oxen he set out, prepared to leave the world of deluded, society-corrupted human beings behind him. As he arrived at the Western Gate (we have no specific details about this location), the keeper of the gate persuaded Laozi to write down his philosophy before letting him pass through.

Tradition notes that Laozi lingered at the gatehouse long enough to compose the Tao Te Ching, then departed over the pass, never to be seen or heard from again. Scholars suggest that the Tao Te Ching expresses an attitude toward life and nature that presupposes a rather advanced disintegration of the Chinese feudal order, and therefore the Tao

Figure 6.7. Laozi on ox going west

How important is the historicity of a religion's founder? Likewise, how important is the historicity of the religious tradition itself? That is to say, is it important that religious traditions be founded by a historically identifiable human being? Some religious traditions that originated in Asia offer a distinct vision of history and myth, contending that truth need not be based on real historical events and personages but rather is carried in myth. Some say, then, that truth does not need history to be valid, for truth itself is a different matter entirely that stands apart from empirical history. Christianity claims that its founder, Jesus Christ, is in fact a historical person whose life, death, and resurrection his followers and antagonists alike bore witness to.

It is remarkable that given Christianity's two-thousand-year history, many documents still exist that were written by the hands of contemporary witnesses of Jesus's life on earth. Although the identity of Jesus may be debated, whether he was just a man, a prophet, or the Son of God, there is exceptional data about his human existence and many of his words and actions.

Te Ching may have been written later than the time of Laozi. However, we will give Laozi credit for being the author; at least, his name appears on the cover of the book in its many translations!

THE TAO TE CHING

The Tao Te Ching was written perhaps around 250 BCE. The title is usually translated as "The Book of the Way and Its Power" (*Tao* = "Way"; *Te* = "virtue," "power"; *Ching* = "classic," "book"). The book contains eighty-one short chapters, with no systematic ordering. With more than one thousand commentaries and more than fifty English translations, the Tao Te Ching is one of the most popular books in the world. Its impact on Western popular cultures is also quite evident in such diverse areas as architecture, design styles, therapies, cuisine, art, and relationships.

The Tao Te Ching advises that when things are allowed to take their natural course, they move with perfection and harmony—since the Tao would not be hindered in its smooth operation. The Tao Te Ching argues that human society is overly dominated by yang (Confucian) traits, so it emphasizes counterbalancing yin values (e.g., feminine, darkness, passivity) to provide a countervailing force to society and culture.

If Confucianism can be described as emphasizing cultural sophistication and governmental bureaucracy, the balance provided by Taoism focuses on doing things the natural way, without sophistication and massive bureaucracies. It has been said that a Confucian will ask, "What should I do?" whereas a Taoist will ask, "What kind of person should I be?" And both are founded on the Tao. Let's delve into the Tao Te Ching to learn what it says about the Tao.[8] What is the Tao?

Mysterious and Unknowable

The first chapter of the Tao Te Ching opens with the following verses:

> The Tao that can be told is not the eternal Tao.
> The name that can be named is not the eternal name.
> The nameless is the beginning of heaven and earth.
> The named is the mother of ten thousand things.
> Ever desireless, one can see the mystery.
> Ever desiring, one can see the manifestations.
> These two spring from the same source but differ in name;
>   this appears as darkness.
> Darkness within darkness.
> The gate of all mystery.
>
> Tao Te Ching 1

Most chapters of the Tao Te Ching consist of just a few lines of text. The first chapter of the Tao Te Ching communicates the ineffability of the Tao—it is the transcendent natural principle that works in and through all things. The Tao is empty of attributes, yet possesses character and effect.[9] It is behind countless names that have emerged from it. We cannot say much about the Tao, except that it is mysterious and the mother of all things.

> There is something,
> an undifferentiated whole,
> born before sky and earth,
> silent and solitary,
> unique and unchanging,
> going everywhere without danger,
> thereby being a mother for the world.
> I do not know its name, but label it the Way.
> Imposing a name on it, I call it great. . . .
> Humans derive laws from earth,
> earth derives laws from the sky,
> the sky derives laws from the Way,
> the Way derives laws from Nature.
>
> Tao Te Ching 25[10]

"I know not its name"—the Tao cannot be understood as a tangible or concrete "thing." The Tao is inaccessible to human reason, since it is eternal. Comparatively, anything that can be named will ultimately die. The Tao is portrayed as the natural rhythm and as the pattern of the universe. All named things emanate from the Tao. So the key practice for Taoists is to discern the Tao, the primordial source of order and the guarantor of the stability of all appearance—the origin of all things. The Tao is the unproduced Producer of all that is.

> The Tao begot one.
> One begot two.
> Two begot three.
> And three begot the ten thousand things.
>
> The ten thousand things carry yin and embrace yang.
> They achieve harmony by combining these forces.
>
> Tao Te Ching 42

To live in accord with the Tao is to realize this order and nature and stability in one's own life and society. Laozi recognized that noninterference with the natural order of things (the Tao) would give longevity to life and stability to society. Furthermore, the Tao is a cosmic force that created the first thing, giving rise to all other created things.

QUIETNESS

Although it is impossible to describe the Tao perfectly, its characteristics can be described generally. The Tao is quiet, so quiet that its presence goes easily undetected, except by intuition.

> Express yourself completely,
> then keep quiet.
> Be like the forces of nature:
> when it blows, there is only wind;
> when it rains, there is only rain;
> when the clouds pass, the sun shines through.
>
> If you open yourself to the Tao,
> you are at one with the Tao
> and you can embody it completely.
> If you open yourself to insight,
> you are at one with insight
> and you can use it completely.
> If you open yourself to loss,

> you are at one with loss
> and you can accept it completely.
>
> Open yourself to the Tao,
> then trust your natural responses;
> and everything will fall into place.
>
> Tao Te Ching 23

Living according to the Tao does not mean "going after" the Tao but rather "being open" to the quiet presence of the Tao. "Empty yourself of everything. Let the mind rest at peace" (Tao Te Ching 16).

LOW POSITION

The characteristics of the Tao are all related to one another, overlapping in significant ways. The quiet nature of the Tao is related to the quietness of being a female (a yin quality), whose ascendancy in human affairs is accounted for by the fact that she is never aggressive (a yang quality) and yet accomplishes all things. Quietness and femaleness (both yin values) are compared frequently to the position of a valley, and give rise to everlasting life. An example of the low position of the Tao is presented in one of the most frequently quoted verses in the Tao Te Ching.

> The valley spirit never dies;
> It is the woman, primal mother.
> Her gateway is the root of heaven and earth.
> It is like a veil barely seen.
> Use it; it will never fail.
>
> Tao Te Ching 6

According to Taoism, there is power in passivity and in a low position. The low position of the female quality is powerful. Rather than bombarding the other with strong words or actions, the female quality aims toward negotiation, gentle prodding, and diplomacy. The female quality leads indirectly and through nuance. The valley is powerful in its low position. Because of its low position, the valley collects water from the rain, and can hold rivers and lakes that give life to the natural world. In contrast, the Confucian (yang), as some would interpret, can be exemplified in the mountains—a strong, robust, male quality of aggression. It should be pointed out that the female (Taoist) and the male (Confucian) qualities do not necessarily correspond to gender; not all Chinese men are Confucian, and not all women are Taoist. Plenty of men will have "female" qualities; many women will have "male" qualities.

Dmitry A. Mottl/Wikimedia Commons

Figure 6.8. The passivity and power of the valley, Altay Mountains, Kazakhstan

Know the strength of man,
But keep a woman's care!
Be the stream of the universe!
Being the stream of the universe,
Ever true and unswerving,
Become as a little child once more.

Know the white,
But keep the black!
Be an example to the world!
Being an example to the world,
Ever true and unwavering,
Return to the infinite.

Know honor,
Yet keep humility.
Be the valley of the universe!
Being the valley of the universe,
Ever true and resourceful,
Return to the state of the uncarved block.

When the block is carved, it becomes useful.
When the sage uses it, he becomes the ruler.
Thus, "A great tailor cuts little."

Tao Te Ching 28

The Tao Te Ching calls people to follow the subtle, mysterious, profound, unfathomable Tao, "Yielding, like ice about to melt. Simple, like uncarved blocks of wood. Hollow, like caves. Opaque, like muddy pools" (Tao Te Ching 15). The cardinal virtue of Taoism is described as "giving birth and nourishing, having without possessing, acting with no expectations, leading and not trying to control: this is the supreme virtue" (Tao Te Ching 10). To lead, but not dominate. To work, but not take credit. To bear, yet not possess.

REVERSION

Connected closely to the Tao's quality of low position is its quality of reversion. People who do not follow the Tao may have temporary success, but there is an inevitable law in all things—everything returns to its original state.

> Better to stop pouring than to keep on overflowing.
> Forge a blade with a thousand blows;
> Its sharpness still will not last long.
> Gold and jade may fill your house,
> But how long can they be kept?
> Pride in wealth and rank will bring you only curses.
> To retire after winning success and establishing a reputation
>   Is the way of Heaven.
>
> Tao Te Ching 9[11]

The mind itself needs to be at peace rather than seeking to amass wealth, fulfill ambitions, and seek others' approval. An open mind is related to an open heart, so being empty without desire for more gives peace.

> Empty yourself of everything.
> Let the mind rest at peace.
> The ten thousand things rise and fall while the Self watches their
>   return.
> They grow and flourish and then return to the source.
> Returning to the source is stillness, which is the way of nature.
> The way of nature is unchanging.
> Knowing constancy is insight.
> Not knowing constancy leads to disaster.
> Knowing constancy, the mind is open.
> With an open mind, you will be openhearted.
> Being openhearted, you will act royally.
> Being royal, you will attain the divine.
> Being divine, you will be at one with the Tao.

Being at one with the Tao is eternal.
And though the body dies, the Tao will never pass away.

Tao Te Ching 16

All things have a natural position in their created order, since there is an invariable law in all things. If any movement occurs, particularly to its extreme of development, it necessarily has to "return" or "revert" to its common origin.

Look, it cannot be seen—it is beyond form.
Listen, it cannot be heard—it is beyond sound.
Grasp, it cannot be held—it is intangible.
These three are indefinable;
Therefore they are joined in one.

From above it is not bright;
From below it is not dark:
An unbroken thread beyond description.
It returns to nothingness.
The form of the formless,
The image of the imageless,
It is called indefinable and beyond imagination.

Stand before it and there is no beginning.
Follow it and there is no end.
Stay with the ancient Tao,
Move with the present.

Knowing the ancient beginning is the essence of the Tao.

Tao Te Ching 14

The ancients said, "Yield and overcome." To follow the Tao one must yield.

Yield and overcome;
Bend and be straight;
Empty and be full;
Wear out and be new;
Have little and gain;
Have much and be confused.

Tao Te Ching 22

Taoism is marked by a seeming weakness, humility, yielding, passivity, and reversion—but of a kind that does not seek its own extinction but through these qualities becomes virtuous and pure.

> In the pursuit of knowledge,
> every day something is added.
> In the practice of the Tao,
> every day something is dropped.
> Less and less do you need to force things,
> until finally you arrive at non-action.
> When nothing is done,
> nothing is left undone.
> True mastery can be gained
> by letting things go their own way.
> It can't be gained by interfering.
>
> Tao Te Ching 48

That is to say, there is nothing to be gained by adding things to one's life. Noninterference is the way to peace. In a nutshell, just accept the way things are—let it be.

SIMPLICITY

Related to quietness, reversion, and passivity, the Tao is said to be utterly simple.

> The Tao cannot be perceived.
> Smaller than an electron,
> it contains uncountable galaxies.
> If powerful men and women
> could remain centered in the Tao,
> all things would be in harmony.
> The world would become a paradise.
> All people would be at peace,
> and the law would be written in their hearts.
> When you have names and forms,
> know that they are provisional.
> When you have institutions,
> know where their functions should end.
> Knowing when to stop,
> you can avoid any danger.
> All things end in the Tao
> as rivers flow into the sea.
>
> Tao Te Ching 32

The Tao remains undefined—it cannot be grasped because of its profound simplicity. Its simplicity seems insignificant, but none can master it. The Tao is easily overlooked, yet it gives rise to all of creation.

LONGEVITY

If one lives according to the Tao, one is promised a long life, interpreted by some to mean eternal life.

> Going out is life, entering in is death.
> The followers of life are three in ten; the followers of
>   death are three in ten; the lives of people who tend
>   to go to grounds of death are also three in ten.
> Why? Because of the richness of their living life.
> It is said that one who is good at taking care of
>   Health
> may travel on land without encountering tigers
>   and rhinos,
> and go into the army without donning armor or
>   wielding weapons.
> Rhinos have nowhere to gore,
> tigers have nowhere to maul,
> weapons have nowhere to wound.
> Why is that? Because they have no death spot.
>
> Tao Te Ching 50[12]

Long life was an ideal among Chinese religionists. Eventually, longevity was defined literally to mean eternal life, which later would give rise to various and strange attempts to practice this doctrine among religious Taoists. We will consider some of these practices below under the discussion of religious Taoism.

CONTENTMENT

All people seek contentment. China's Axial Age was an unprecedented period in which people were seeking stability, comfort, and guidance. The Tao Te Ching notes that contentment comes when one follows the Tao. Otherwise, discontentment reigns.

> When the Tao is present in the universe,
> The horses haul manure.
> When the Tao is absent from the universe,
> War horses are bred outside the city.
> There is no greater sin than desire,
> No greater curse than discontent,
> No greater misfortune than wanting something for oneself.
> Therefore he who knows that enough is enough
> will always have enough.
>
> Tao Te Ching 46

Contentment was a major theme in Laozi's teaching. According to tradition, Laozi was dissatisfied with his work as an archivist and recognized the foolishness of gaining knowledge, advancing culture, and aggressive leadership styles.

Nonbeing

If the Tao is so difficult to know because it precedes all created forms, labels, names, and categories, how does the Tao operate in the realm of being—that is, the realm of empirical existence? Followers of the Taoist tradition seek to gain the fullness of life through harmony with the Tao, but where is the Tao? The "**nonbeing**" nature of the Tao illustrates brilliantly a difference between Taoism and Confucianism, for Taoism focuses on "nonbeing," while Confucianism strives for "being."

Taoism's concept of nonbeing is one of the most fascinating concepts in religious studies and philosophy. Focusing on what is "not there," rather than what "is there," Taoism invites an entirely different perspective that sees value and utility in the "nonbeing" aspects of reality. According to Taoism, it is the nonbeing space that actually enables functionality and usefulness. The Tao Te Ching illustrates the point perfectly.

> Thirty spokes share the wheel's hub;
> It is the center hole that makes it useful.
> Shape clay into a vessel;
> It is the space within that makes it useful.
> Cut doors and windows for a room;
> It is the holes which make it useful.
> Therefore profit comes from what is there;
> Usefulness from what is not there.
>
> Tao Te Ching 11

In a passage replete with the themes of reversion, passivity, and nonbeing, the Tao Te Ching notes that nonbeing is the foundation of being itself.

> Returning is the motion of the Tao.
> Yielding is the way of the Tao.
> The ten thousand things are born of being.
> Being is born of not being.
>
> Tao Te Ching 40

Think about it. When looking at a bicycle wheel, a clay pot, a doorway, or a window, we would normally "see" the material (empirical reality) of those items: for example, spokes, tires, bicycle frame, ceramic pot, ornate door and frame, windowpane and frame, and so on. In the Taoist worldview, these elements entail the "being-ness" of what we see. However, the utility of these items, whether a bicycle, a pot, a door, or a window, relies ultimately on the "nonbeing" space of each. That is, the functionality of the bicycle depends on the center, the empty hole around which the bicycle wheel turns.

Without the empty, "nonbeing" space, it would be impossible for the wheel to turn. Likewise, it is the empty, "nonbeing" space of the pot, the window, and the door that enables the usefulness of each thing. We "use" the empty space of the pot: "there is an active space in the pot." We "use" the empty, nonbeing space of windows and doors as we see through and walk through those spaces. Without the emptiness of a room, we could not study in a classroom environment. A house is valuable and useful because of the space inside it. We could not inhabit a house without the empty, nonbeing space of our rooms. Likewise, the margin on a page or the space between letters on a page illustrates that emptiness allows us to see and give meaning to the words and characters on the page. Even the Tao is compared to emptiness.

> Tao is a whirling emptiness,
>   yet when used it cannot be exhausted.
> Out of this mysterious well
>   flows everything in existence.
> Blunting sharp edges,
> Untangling knots,
> Softening the glare,
> Settling the dust,
> It evolves us all and
>   Makes the whole world one.
>
> Something is there, hidden in the deep!
> But I do not know whose child it is—
> It came even before God.[13]
>
>   Tao Te Ching 4[14]

Wu-wei

How does one engage the empty, "nonbeing" space that provides such great utility? One does so by taking no action. That key Taoist concept is called **wu-wei** (Chinese, "not doing/nondoing" or "actionless-action"), and it is related to "nonbeing," being a fundamental principle of the tradition. The Chinese term "*wu*" denotes the absence of qualities perceivable by the senses—but it does not mean "nonexistent." Rather than meaning "nothingness," *wu* refers to pure form—and, as such, it can give life. So the wise person learns to act according to the Tao, "going with the grain," not against it. *Wu-wei* can be translated as "nonaction," "doing nothing," "going with the flow," and "acting through nonacting."

This concept correlates with nonbeing since individuals do not act as a reflection of nonbeing itself. Taoism employs at least three illustrations for this idea. First, the valley is a metaphor for the power of *wu-wei*: "The valley spirit never dies; It is the woman, primal mother. Her gateway is the root of heaven and earth. It is like a veil barely seen. Use it; it will never fail."[15] The valley symbolizes the Tao's inclination toward the lowly rather than the prominent. The valley fills with water because it does not resist it—it does not "act," yet the space itself becomes active. The valley is active through nonacting—that is, active through nonbeing.

Second, the female as a metaphor communicates the power of passivity, yielding, and adaptability. The quality of feminineness influences not by assault but by indirection, nuance, and suggestion. Thus, "nonaction" proves in the end to be quite active. Finally, Taoism illustrates *wu-wei* through the "uncarved block," the ideal condition of human nature before society and culture limit it.

> The softest thing in the universe
> Overcomes the hardest thing in the universe.
> That without substance can enter where there is no room.
> Hence I know the value of non-action.
> Teaching without words and work without doing
> Are understood by very few.
>
> Tao Te Ching 43

Since an equivalence exists between one's self and the Tao, scholars note that to "understand the emptiness of character of the Tao which nevertheless is its truth is to be drawn into becoming an expression of the same in one's own life, through active inactivity (*wu-wei*)."[16] It is important to note that *wu-wei* does not advocate a kind of "couch potato" mentality, where one just sits comfortably all day long, with a total lack of activity.

Instead *wu-wei* calls for "active inactivity" that enables the Tao to be expressed. Go with the grain of life, not against it. Try not to upset the natural way. When you climb a mountain, do so slowly and calmly. Don't rush. "The world is ruled by letting things run their course, not by interfering" (Tao Te Ching 48).

TAOIST LEADERSHIP

Although it is true that Taoism values the practice of getting back to nature and going with the flow and the natural grain, the tradition does not reject society entirely. In fact, Taoism directly encourages the proper leadership of

How knowable are the attributes of God? As Christians we affirm that God is knowable, through his Word (Scripture) and the Word (Jesus Christ). But in what ways does God remain mysterious? How might God be seen as possessing "low position" or "quietness," like the Tao? How profitable might it be to compare the characteristics of God to those of the Tao? Some Asian Christian theologians have even gone so far as to argue that for East Asians Jesus Christ is best seen as the incarnation of the Tao (the "Way"), the great primordial force shrouded in mystery.

These theologians argue that the Tao can be known fully only in Jesus Christ, who was the Tao in the flesh. When addressing a Greek audience, biblical writers stated that Jesus was the Logos (Greek, "Word") made flesh (John 1:1). When writing to a Jewish audience, biblical writers used the metaphor of "lamb" to refer to Jesus as the "lamb" of God who takes away the sin of the world (John 1:29, 36). Likewise, some Asian theologians suggest that when communicating to East Asian cultures, Jesus should be interpreted as the Tao made flesh.[a]

For instance, in the Chinese and Korean translations of the Bible, Jesus states, "I am the *tao* (way) and the truth and the life" (John 14:6). However one feels about using Asian metaphors to communicate meaningfully the identity of Jesus Christ in Asian contexts, were one to compare God to the Tao some of the characteristics of the Tao, such as humility, nonaction, and passivity, could illuminate biblical themes about God that may be overlooked by Western Christians. In that sense, the comparison might be beneficial.

a. See Kim, *Christ and the Tao*.

sages, teachers, and even government authorities. It is striking to think that following the Tao makes one somewhat invisible and forgettable, since the truth of the Tao is what is remembered. For instance, if leaders implement *wu-wei* in society, followers will cherish their teaching but forget the teacher. In the same way, a good referee in a football game is not "visible." Likewise, the skill of a dynamic actor or teacher calls attention not to his or her own skill but to the message, role, or lesson.

> When the Master governs, the people
> are hardly aware that he exists.
> Next best is a leader who is loved.
> Next, one who is feared.
> The worst is one who is despised.
> If you don't trust the people,

you make them untrustworthy.
The Master doesn't talk, he acts.
When his work is done,
the people say, "Amazing:
we did it, all by ourselves."

Tao Te Ching 17

Ruling well, teaching well, and leading well reflect the natural way and do not focus on the communicator. The sage can achieve greatness because he does not act: "Therefore the sage goes about doing nothing, teaching no-talking" (Tao Te Ching 2). The Tao Te Ching directly addresses the attributes of governmental leaders.

If you want to be a great leader,
you must learn to follow the Tao.
Stop trying to control.
Let go of fixed plans and concepts,
and the world will govern itself.
The more prohibitions you have,
the less virtuous people will be.
The more weapons you have,
the less secure people will be.
The more subsidies you have,
the less self-reliant people will be.
Therefore the Master [sage] says:
I let go of the law,
and people become honest.
I let go of economics,
and people become prosperous.
I let go of religion,
and people become serene.
I let go of all desire for the common good,
and the good becomes common as grass.

Tao Te Ching 57

Taoist thought emphasizes qualities of not-acting, naturalness, spontaneity, passivity, peace, and meditation, resulting in inner stillness.

Act without doing;
work without effort.
Think of the small as large
and the few as many.
Confront the difficult

while it is still easy;
accomplish the great task
by a series of small acts.

The Master never reaches for the great;
thus she achieves greatness.
When she runs into a difficulty,
she stops and gives herself to it.
She doesn't cling to her own comfort;
thus problems are no problem for her.

Tao Te Ching 63[17]

Knowledge is passed on without an attitude of self-aggrandizement or posturing for first place: "Therefore the sage works without recognition. He achieves what has to be done without dwelling on it. He does not try to show his knowledge" (Tao Te Ching 77). The Taoist theory of government is one of laissez-faire noninterference by government in the lives of its citizens, thus letting people live in their natural state, avoiding all kinds of sophisticated cultural and bureaucratic developments, permitting the enjoyment of life without aggression.

Summarily, Laozi advocated (1) noninterference with the natural order, (2) that the presumed progress of morality was really regress, (3) that one should respond to change without acting, (4) the application of the Tao in the world as virtue rather than erudition, (5) that the golden age of harmony could be reclaimed if people lived in accord with the Tao, (6) that social disharmony and overall decline result through cultural sophistication, (7) that the reversal of disharmony is achieved through simplicity and meditation, exemplified by following a simple lifestyle and possessing a pure mind, and (8) that all should be open to practicing *wu-wei* (nonaction) to become sages, animated by the Tao.

SAGE ZHUANGZI

Having reflected on the insights of Laozi, let us turn our attention briefly to his famous disciple Zhuangzi, who is credited with reinterpreting and carrying on the tradition of philosophical Taoism. Just about everything in the history of Zhuangzi (Master Zhuang) (c. 370–286 BCE), like Laozi, is debatable. But there is more historical evidence for the existence of Zhuangzi than for Laozi.

Tradition says that Zhuangzi was a fierce critic of Confucianism. In fact, much of Zhuangzi's writing is ironic propaganda against Confucianism. Zhuangzi is credited with writing *Zhuangzi*, a collection of thirty-three chapters of prose of which scholars believe the first seven chapters are his own,

Chinese Transliterations

There are two major systems for transliterating traditional Chinese into English, Wade-Giles and Pinyin. So it is important to remember that any name can have more than one transliteration. Here are some examples:

Wade-Giles	Pinyin
Lao Tzu	Laozi
Mencius, Meng Tzu	Mengzi
Chuang Tzu, Chuang Chou	Zhuangzi
K'ung Fu Tzu	Kung Fu Zi
Mo Tzu	Mozi
I Ching	Yijing
Chou	Zhou
Chu Hsi	Zhu Xi
Mao Tse-tung	Mao Zedong
Teng Hsiao-peng	Deng Xiaoping
Ch'in	Qin
Ch'ing	Qing
Peking	Beijing
Nanking	Nanjing
Shantung	Shandong
Tao	Dao

whereas the remaining chapters were written by his pupils. Zhuangzi suggested that the Tao is present equally in all things, making human beings on par with all other forms of creation rather than creation's pinnacle.

All religions have popularizers, those who successfully articulate the ideas of the founder to a wide audience. While Zhuangzi shares much with Laozi, his writing goes further than the Tao Te Ching, displaying greater idealism and criticism of his contemporary society. For instance, Zhuangzi argued that none of the forms and institutions of social life under the Zhou Dynasty (1050–265 BCE) did anything but confuse people about their natural equality and thus corrupt their native integrity. With social institutions, Zhuangzi contended, "gangsters appear."

Some of the salient emphases in Zhuangzi's work are the following: First, Zhuangzi spoke of the relativity of the Tao—that is, that every creature has its own Tao. Each person follows his or her own Tao. There is no standard way of doing anything, no ultimate, all-encompassing truth or right path to which all creatures must conform. Philosophical Taoism never refers to a transcendent God or Gods but only to the eternal and numinous unity of the Tao that underlies and sustains all things.

Each creature should be true to its own Tao, not to another's. A woman does not sleep in a tree, a monkey does. Each thing needs to follow its Way. Zhuangzi's relativism is illustrated by the fact that he rejects anything that elevates one life over another, since all are equal.[18] *The Book of Chuang-tzu* records a story of Po Yi, a former king, and Robber Chih, who depicts greed and ruthlessness.

> Po Yi died for the sake of fame at the bottom of Shou Yang mountain, Robber Chih died for gain on top of the Eastern Heights. These two both died in different ways but the fact is, they both shortened their lives and destroyed their innate natures. Yet we are expected to approve of Po Yi and disapprove of Robber Chih—strange, isn't it?
>
> Zhuangzi, *Book of Chuang-tzu*, xxii

Second, Zhuangzi believed in seeking the eternal Way (Tao) rather than being distracted by material forms of the material world. For instance, he taught Chinese artists which direction to look for truth in their art—for his antagonism against all social institutions, such as art, was mitigated when he turned toward nature. Addressing Chinese artists, Zhuangzi trained them not to focus on outward forms of the material world (the being-ness) but to seek to discover the eternal Way within its nature. Zhuangzi was not satisfied looking at the outward forms of nature, since that is not where their reality lies. Zhuangzi's most famous words capture this sense of form and reality: "Once upon a time, I Chuang Tzu, dreamt I was a butterfly, fluttering hither and thither, to all intents and purposes as a butterfly. . . . Suddenly, I awakened. . . . Now I do not know whether I was then a man dreaming I was a butterfly, or whether I am now a butterfly dreaming I am a man."[19]

A third and related feature of Zhuangzi's teaching was that reality must be seen not as a duality—as matter versus spirit—but as a

I say, "There is nowhere where it is not." You say, "Where does the spirit come from? Where does enlightenment emerge from?" "The sage brings them to be and the king completes them, and the origin is the One."

The one who is not cut off from his primal origin is known as the Heavenly man. The one not cut off from the true nature is known as the spiritual man.

The one who is not cut off from the truth, is known as the perfect man. The one who views Heaven as the primal source, Virtue as the root and the Tao as the gate, and sees change and transformation as natural, such a one we call a sage.

Zhuangzi, *Book of Chuang-tzu*, 296

Figure 6.9. Traditional Chinese painting (Chen Minglou, 2008)

Poemandpainting/Wikimedia Commons

resolved unity: "The universe is the unity of all things. If one recognizes his identity with this unity, then the parts of his body mean not more to him than so much dirt, and death and life, end and beginning, disturb his tranquility no more than the succession of day and night."[20]

It is the sage who blends apparent dualities and divisions into complete harmony.

> The sage has the sun and the moon by his side. He grasps the universe under his arm. He blends everything into a harmonious whole, casts aside whatever is confused or obscured, and regards the humble as honorable. While the multitude toil, he seems to be stupid and non-discriminative. He blends the disparities of ten thousand years into one complete purity. All things are blended like this and mutually involve each other.
>
> Zhuangzi[21]

> What is, is, what is not, is not.
> The Tao is made because we walk it,
> things become what they are called.
> Why is this so? Surely because this is so.
> Why is this not so? Surely because this is not so.
> Everything has what is innate,
> everything has what is necessary.
> Nothing is not something,
> nothing is not so.
> Therefore, take a stalk of wheat and a pillar,
> a leper or a beauty like Hsi-shih,
> the great and the insecure,
> the cunning and the odd:
> all these are alike to the Tao.
> In their difference is their completeness;
> in their completeness is their difference.
>
> Zhuangzi, *Book of Chuang-tzu*, 13

Thus, Zhuangzi sought to recover harmony through the realization of the limits of knowledge and the oblivion of classification. Therefore, put away knowledge and conscious categories, letting the mind flow with whatever may happen in order to experience the spontaneity of the Way (Tao). Do not analyze intensely, but seek simplicity and tranquility. Such harmony with the Way gives rise to a true human being, free and easy, full of perfect happiness. Zhuangzi says that the sage is a truly natural person.

Fourth, Zhuangzi's work was directed more toward the individual practitioner rather than to the ruler, unlike Laozi's writing. Yet Zhuangzi's writing is more mystically and philosophically oriented than that of Laozi. Zhuangzi tends to be more contemplative than Laozi. In the end, Zhuangzi and Laozi share similar ideas about the Tao, but Zhuangzi's emphases make his writing more intense, reflecting a higher-stage philosophy.

> *The perfect man has no self;*
> *The spiritual man has no merit;*
> *The holy man has no fame.*
>
> Zhuangzi, Book of Chuang-tzu, 3

Confucianism

CONFUCIUS

Confucius (K'ung Fu Tzu, Master Kung, 551–479 BCE) presented another way to retrieve the lost sense of social harmony in China. Whereas Laozi's analyses emphasized the yin side of the Tao, Confucius's thoughts stressed the yang forces of the Tao. Tradition says that Confucius was born into a minor aristocratic family in Shandong province, on the northeast coast of China. Confucius's father, Kong He, a general, died when his son was three years old, leaving Confucius to be brought up in poverty by his mother. Confucius was perturbed by the chaotic state of political and social life in China and constructed a religio-philosophical system that sought to regain harmony not by the use of physical force but by moral persuasion. Confucius paid much attention to rites and ceremonies, believing them to inculcate right behavior and loyal service, the kinds of attitudes and relationships that would secure the social harmony that had been lost.

THE *JUNZI* IDEAL

Confucius's idea was that of the scholar as administrator, which he described as **junzi**—a noble, superior person dedicated to virtue. A *junzi* was a scholarly gentleman, a perfect human being, capable of ruling by moral example, knowledge, and love for his subjects. Scholar-administrators would be placed at various levels of China's massive bureaucracy and thus be examples of virtue, kindness, and knowledge, demonstrating good etiquette, trustworthiness, and maturity.

What was remarkable about Confucius was that he believed all people should have equal

Wikimedia Commons

Figure 6.10. "Confucius and his disciples Yanzi and Huizi at the 'Apricot Altar'": etching from the mid-seventeenth-century Edo period, Japan

opportunity to become a *junzi*. Rather than affirming that governmental leaders should acquire those positions through heredity, Confucius argued that the best leaders were the most noble and morally virtuous people. Although Confucius's ideas were not eagerly adopted during his lifetime, they became state orthodoxy beginning with the Han Dynasty (206 BCE–220 CE) and served as the norm of the Chinese ideal for two thousand years.

What does it take to become a *junzi*? Confucius advocated the mastery of two major sets of books, the Six Classics of Confucianism and the Confucian Canon, on which people would be tested in order to obtain a position of civic leadership. The system of advancement was so open that a boy from a rice-growing family in rural China could conceivably study the Six Classics and the Confucian Canon, score high points on the examination, and then be placed in a leadership position in China.

Mastery of the Six Classics and the Confucian Canon helped to create what some Westerners have called the "renaissance person," one talented in several spheres of human endeavor, rather than being an expert in just one life domain. A renaissance person possesses many diverse skills, such as knowledge of science, art, music, history, and philosophy, and is interested not in self-serving ambition but in the betterment of society.

THE SIX CLASSICS OF CONFUCIANISM

It is said that Confucius did not write the Six Classics of Confucianism, but that he edited them, passing judgment and adding commentary on them. The Six Classics include the following:

1. **Shih Ching** (Classic of Poetry), a collection of folk songs that recount the myth of the founding of the Shang Dynasty (1600–1200 BCE). Although the myths idealize this early Chinese dynasty, they also give us insight into ancient Chinese society.

Wikimedia Commons

Figure 6.11. Imperial portrait of Noble Consort Hui Xian of Qing Dynasty, China

2. **I Ching** (Classic of Changes) is a divination classic of the Zhou Dynasty (c. 1050–256 BCE). Divination is the act of divining that which is unknown, for instance to discover something in the future, to identify a culprit, to find lost items, or to locate the best partner for marriage. The I Ching was a diviner's manual, built on the symbolism of yin and yang forces. This book is still readily available in many bookstores in Western nations.

3. **Shu Ching** (Classic of History) is purported to have been compiled around 800 BCE and contains stories of mythical emperors of China. Among the most influential ideas of the Shu Ching is ***T'ien ming*** (Mandate of Heaven; *T'ien* = Chinese supreme source of power and order, heaven). *T'ien ming* is similar to a power or blessing given to an emperor to animate his rule. It is assumed that an emperor lacking virtue or the ability to rule justly has forfeited the right to rule—that is, the *T'ien ming* has moved from the ineffective ruler to the next dynastic leader.

4. **Li Qi** (Book of Ritual) is a set of codes of behavior for the privileged classes, with emphasis on morality, geared toward regulating human conduct.

5. **Ch'un-ch'iu** (Spring and Autumn Annals) provides a detailed history of various Chinese states.

6. **Yueh Ching** (Classic of Music) maintains that a Confucian *junzi* should be adept at music, since music is calming and harmonizes the mind.

FOUR CONFUCIAN CLASSICS

In addition to the Six Classics of Confucianism, Confucians came to admire four additional works as canonical expressions of the wisdom of Confucius himself, known collectively as the Confucian Canon. Tradition says that these works contain the words of Confucius and his disciples. The Confucian Canon includes the following books:

1. **Lunyu** (Analects) is the most important text in the history of Confucianism, since it contains the words of Confucius himself organized in twenty chapters. The Analects teaches the cardinal Confucian virtues of humanity, propriety, respect for parents, and how to become a superior person. The Analects is significant in part because it describes the way people should behave in specific, concrete situations.

2. **Da Xue** (Great Learning) argues that the cultivated person can contribute to the right ordering of society. Children in China still study this book.

3. **Zhung Yung** (Doctrine of the Mean) is a philosophical text reasoning that the moral person occupies the center of the universe, since a moral person follows the underlying moral order of the universe (the Tao).

4. **Mengzi** (Book of Mencius) is a collection of the words of Confucius's most famous disciple, Mengzi, who was the first to create a systematic presentation of Confucian teachings.

Here is a sampling of Confucius's words as recorded in the Analects:

> The Master said, "The gentleman seeks neither a full belly nor a comfortable home. He is quick in action but cautious in speech. He goes to men possessed of the Way to be put right. Such a man can be described as eager to learn."
>
> Analects 1:14

> Confucius said, "When in attendance upon a gentleman one is liable to three errors. To speak before being spoken to by the gentleman is rash; not to speak when spoken to by him is to be evasive; to speak without observing the expression on his face is to be blind."
>
> Analects 16:6

> Confucius said: "By nature men are pretty much alike; it is learning and practice that set them apart."
>
> Analects 17:2

> Confucius said: "A youth, when at home, should be filial, and away from home he should be respectful to his elders. He should be earnest and truthful. He should overflow in love to all, and cultivate the friendship of good people. When he has time and opportunity, after the performance of these things, he should employ them in the arts."
>
> Analects 1:6

Confucius emphasized the qualities of a "perfect human being," often contrasting such a person with the "inferior person":

> Tzu-kung asked about the gentleman [i.e., *junzi*]. The Master said, "He puts his words into action before allowing his words to follow his action."
>
> Analects 2:13

> The Master said, "Wealth and high station are what men desire but unless I got them in the right way I would not remain in them. Poverty and low station are what men dislike, but even if I did not get them in the right way I would not try to escape from them.
>
> "If the gentleman forsakes benevolence, in what way can he make a name for himself? The gentleman never deserts benevolence, not even for

292

as long as it takes to eat a meal. If he hurries and stumbles one may be sure that it is in benevolence that he does so."

Analects 4:5

The Master said, "In his dealings with the world the gentleman is not invariably for or against anything. He is on the side of what is moral."

Analects 4:10

Confucius said, "The gentleman stands in awe of three things. He is in awe of the Decree of Heaven. He is in awe of great men. He is in awe of the words of the sages. The small man, being ignorant of the Decree of Heaven, does not stand in awe of it. He treats great men with insolence and the words of the sages with derision."

Analects 16:8

Confucian Virtues

It is important to note that the *junzi* not only has mastered the Six Classics and the Confucian Canon, but the scholar-administrator also needs to exhibit the Confucian virtues. The Confucian virtues include **jen** (fellow-feeling, love, benevolence), **yi** (righteousness), **li** (moral actions, propriety), *chi* (wisdom), and **xin** (faithfulness).

Jen, as the central virtue in Confucianism, is the root of all other Confucian values. Generally, *jen* embraces both *yi* and *li* and emphasizes the internal nature of the perfect person out of which all other virtues are to emanate. *Jen* develops and is perfected within the context of human relationships, rather than as an autonomous virtue. *Li* (rituals of formality) emphasizes external actions and appropriate concrete be-haviors, manners, or ceremonies that bind human beings together.

The goal of a *junzi* is to have *jen* ani-mate *li*, which, according to the Confu-cian tradition, makes living artful and sacramental. The Confucian Golden Rule is "Do not do unto others what you would not have them do unto you." The Confucian ideal entails making the human life alive with both *jen* and *li*. Confucius said: "If a man lacks the vir-tues proper to humanity [*jen*], what has he to do with the rites of propriety [*li*]?" Confucius said: "*Li* performed without

Wikimedia Commons

Figure 6.12. Confucian temple in Nagasaki, Japan

reverence, the forms of mourning observed without grief—how can I bear to look on these things?" It is striking to note that Confucius was the first to suggest the possibility of the refinement of an inner moral force (*te*), maintaining that everyone possessed such an inherent inner moral force, but that this force needed to be cultivated.

The challenge was to put aside self-interest in one's home, village, province, state, and nation, for the sake of the larger group. Every civil servant needed to cultivate the inner moral force for the "great family"—that is, Chinese society. Today, followers of the Confucian tradition aim to inculcate Confucian virtues, seeking harmony within relationships, marked by respect for elders, responsibility for younger people, and desire to live a balanced life squarely within the human community.

Equal and Hierarchical Social Relationships

Based on Confucian virtues, Confucian society was strictly hierarchical—yet individuals possessed equality of rights guided by reciprocity of duties. The principal Confucian relationships are those between father and son, older sibling and younger sibling, friend and friend, husband and wife, and ruler and subject. According to Confucius, if these primary relationships are based on mutual reciprocity and equality of rights, social harmony will result. For instance, in the father-and-son relationship, the father has the duty to protect his son (or daughter), feed and clothe him, and provide for his education. But the son has greater duties: to obey his father as a youth, support his father in later life, and honor his father after death. One of the greatest family virtues is **filial piety** (***xiao***)—a respect for parents, grandparents, and ancestors.

Practically, filial piety is the basis of good relationships between children and parents, demonstrated by honoring parents, taking care of parents, performing duties required of the son or daughter, and performing sacrifices to parents after their death. Filial piety holds the entire family together. Likewise, in the relationship between the older sibling and the younger sibling, the older sibling shares the responsibility to provide for the younger sibling, while the younger sibling has enduring responsibility to obey her elder sibling in family matters. Between friends, the older friend has greater responsibility to guide and be an example to the younger friend, even if that younger friend is only slightly younger. Regarding husbands and wives, the husband has to provide for the support of his wife and widow, but her duty is greater—she has to obey and serve him and his sons.

Finally, in terms of the relationship between ruler and subject, the emperor is seen as the earthly form of the Son of Heaven, on which the Mandate of

Figure 6.13. Aberdeen Chinese Permanent Cemetery in Hong Kong

Heaven (*T'ien ming*) has fallen, so he needs to be an example of virtue and humaneness to his subjects, providing for and protecting them. On the other hand, subjects are to obey their rulers, in part because rulers have a closer connection to heaven.

Worship and Practice

Given the acceptance of the Tao as the preexistent fountainhead of all creation, how do those influenced by Confucian and Taoist thought practice their respective traditions? Remember that the Tao is *the Way*—the patterned way of living that moves with the cosmos. And Taoist thought emphasizes the patterned relationship between human beings and nature, while Confucianism stresses the relationships between human beings. Generally, those who follow Taoist and Confucian thought seek to align themselves with the force of the Tao, but attempt to do so in different ways.

Together, traditional Chinese society encapsulated both yin and yang forces—that is, both Confucian and Taoist forces. Some say that younger people traditionally tended to follow Confucianism, with its detailed guidance about structuring human relationships, and upon retirement turned toward

But the spirit of Neo-Confucian rationalism is diametrically opposed to that of Buddhist mysticism. Whereas Buddhism insisted on the unreality of things, Neo-Confucianism stressed their reality. Buddhism and Taoism asserted that existence came out of, and returned to, non-existence; Neo-Confucianism regarded reality as a gradual realization of the Great Ultimate. . . . Buddhists, and to some degree, Taoists as well, relied on meditation and insight to achieve supreme reason; the Neo-Confucians chose to follow Reason.

Chan, *China*, 268

Things are what they are (men, women, dogs, cats, rocks, and the like) because of the abstract form, of li, that combines with and shapes the matter, or ch'i, that embodies them, and things of any one category have their individual particularities because of the particular complexities of cosmic forces that happened to govern the combining of form and matter in their particular instances.

Zhu Xi, quoted in Hucker, *China's Imperial Past*, 367

Taoism, retreating to more simple, spontaneous living. Both Taoism and Confucianism are necessary to maintain harmony within traditional Chinese society. Laozi and Confucius taught their respective ways to align with heaven's way (Tao).

Neo-Confucianism

Beginning in the middle of the ninth century, a revival of Confucian philosophy led to new emphases within the tradition, which had a significant impact on China, Korea, and Japan for hundreds of years. These new developments gave rise to what was called **Neo-Confucianism**. Neo-Confucianism reinterpreted Confucianism, using insights of both Buddhist and Taoist thinking, at a time when Buddhism and Taoism dominated Chinese philosophy. Generally, Neo-Confucianism resulted in a more complex and sophisticated Confucian metaphysics. Neo-Confucian thought emphasized *rationalism*, which stressed objective reason as the foundation of learning and behavior, and *humanism*, which focused on the relationships between human beings rather than between humans and the divine. Neo-Confucianism is divided into two major schools, the School of Principle and the School of Heart/Mind.

THE SCHOOL OF PRINCIPLE

The **School of Principle** and the School of the Heart/Mind both agree that all elements of the universe are manifestations of a single principle (*li*) and that this principle was the essence of morality. The School of Principle was shaped by Chinese Neo-Confucian scholar **Zhu Xi** (aka Chu Hsi) (1130–1200), who was hugely influential in the development of the reinterpretation of Confucian thinking. Zhu Xi was a Confucian scholar during China's Song Dynasty (960–1279). He played a major role in synthesizing the fundamental Confucian ideas such as chi (also *ch'i* or *qi*, "vital force") and *li* (principle), which he believed operated together in mutual interdependence. The School of Principle saw knowledge as a cultivation or preparation for action, whereas the rival school, the School of Heart/Mind, saw knowledge as inseparable from action.

THE SCHOOL OF HEART/MIND

Wang Yangming (1472–1529) was influential in the creation of the **School of the Heart/Mind**. Wang Yangming argued that one should look to one's own heart or mind (*xin*) to understand principle (*li*; i.e., morality), since principle is the essence of human nature. So, according to Wang Yangming, it is better to look to the heart or mind rather than to some external principle or standard. Wang Yangming sought to unify knowledge with action. Furthermore, according to Wang, everyone possesses innate knowledge (*liangzhi*), which is not acquired by learning but rather is intuitive, perfect, and worth trusting as a guide to moral knowledge.

> *My own nature is, of course, sufficient for me to attain sagehood. And I have been mistaken in searching for the li [principle] in external things and affairs [shiwu].*
>
> Tu, *Neo-Confucian Thought in Action*, 120

KOREAN NEO-CONFUCIANISM

During Korea's Joseon Dynasty (1392–1897), Neo-Confucianism was the primary ideological system among Korea's leaders. It also helped shape social relations and the moral system in Korea. With King Sejong (r. 1418–1450), Neo-Confucian thinking guided all educational systems, based on about fifteen Korean Confucian works. Throughout the Joseon Dynasty, Korean Neo-Confucian thought impacted the governmental administration, development of the patrilineal lineage system that gave priority to the eldest son, and the sagelike qualities of the ruling classes.

Neo-Confucianism was the primary system of belief among the scholarly *yanban* classes (nobles) and military leaders in Korea, which meant that Neo-Confucianism was encouraged among the ruling classes, while shamanism, where practitioners reach altered states of consciousness, was maintained in rural areas. In contemporary Korea, Korean art, ceremonies (such as those for weddings, deaths, and births), and social relations continue to be influenced by Neo-Confucian thinking.

> *Wang's legacy in Neo-Confucian tradition and Confucian philosophy as a whole is his claim that the fundamental root of social problems lies in the fact that one fails to gain a genuine understanding of one's self and its relation to the world, and thus fails to live up to what one could be.*
>
> Youngmin Kim, Seoul National University, South Korea, http://www.iep.utm.edu/wangyang/

Today the legacy of Confucian thought remains a crucial part of Korean, Chinese, and Japanese societies. Confucian values continue to have an immense influence on East Asian societies and are still prevalent to a large degree in the daily administrative governance, social organization, and interpersonal and familial relationships of Asian societies, even though Confucianism has been removed from the educational curricula in these regions. In fact, Neo-Confucian thought became the basis for the standard educational curriculum for the civil service examination system until it was abolished in 1905. Yet within the important rituals of East Asian Confucianism, such as marriages, funerals, and the anniversaries of the death of loved ones, Confucianism remains a significant part of the life of people throughout East Asia.

Religious Taoism

Early Taoist thought, through the works of the sages Laozi and Zhuangzi, became an ingredient of religious Taoism. Whereas the philosophical Taoism of Laozi and Zhuangzi emphasized spiritual immortality, religious Taoists emphasized literal and physical immortality through the use of various technologies that sought to prolong life. Although its origins are unclear, and the practices used in religious Taoism most likely preceded the beginnings of religious Taoism itself, religious Taoism is concerned mainly with longevity—prolonging life in the here and now. In the fourth century BCE, some believed that immortals were living on islands off the coast of China, so a mission was sent to obtain their elixir of immortality.

Religious Taoism notes that Chang Ling (second century CE) formally started the tradition; it was then carried on by his grandson, Chang Lu (second and third century), who established a rigorously governed religious state in northern Szechwan. Since many Chinese people of the period believed there was a connection between disease and sin, Chang Lu required strict moral observance, with offenders required to make practical restitution by, for instance, paying a fine or repairing a public building. Chang Lu called himself **T'ien Shih** (Celestial Master or Heavenly Lord), and introduced the role of **Taoshi** (Taoist priests), the scholars and ritual functionaries of religious Taoism who organize Taoist communities and are sometimes marked by a monastic lifestyle. These early Chinese leaders of religious Taoism were considered rebels by many, since they also sought to establish a semi-independent state in China.

Eventually, the religions that developed out of the notions within philosophical Taoism challenged—some say corrupted—Taoist philosophy, particularly in terms of the idea of letting things take their natural course. Yet early religious Taoism appealed to commoners who wanted practical things, rather than philosophical reflection. Their lives were filled with daily concerns about long life, harvesting rice and good crops, raising healthy children, and divination (e.g., foretelling the future), palm reading, and astrology.

The goal of religious Taoism was to gain physical immortality, an idea presented in the Tao Te Ching since Laozi himself wrote about the possibility of long life (e.g., Tao Te Ching 6, 33, 50, 59). Logic affirmed that death should be avoided for a truly perfect human being because one would have eternal powers if animated by the Tao. It was not long before people were using the Tao Te Ching as a manual for the preservation of life. And some of the techniques used to extend life are quite unimaginable today.

ALCHEMY

First, **alchemy** (magical formula) was utilized in the attempt to prolong life. Although longevity was considered a blessing received by many, immortality was an achievement available to just a few.[22] Ko Hung (c. 280–340 CE), the author of *Pao-p'u-tzu* (*Book of the Master Who Embraces Simplicity*), enumerated the procedures for attaining immortality on earth, the nature and practice of alchemy, and a system of merit whereby actions increase or decrease one's days on earth.[23] According to Deborah Sommer, a scholar of Chinese religions, Ko's alchemy recipes were based on earlier scriptures, such as the *Scripture of the Yellow Emperor's Divine Cinnabar of the Nine Tripods*,

---

SIDEBAR 6.3

Ko Hung on Alchemy and Longevity

I have investigated and read books on the nourishment of human nature and collected formulas for everlasting existence. Those I have perused number thousands of volumes. They all consider reconverted cinnabar [turned into mercury] and gold fluid to be the most important. Thus these two things represent the acme of the way to immortality. . . . The transformation of the two substances are the more wonderful the more they are heated. Yellow gold does not disintegrate even after having been smelted a hundred times in fire, and does not rot even if buried in the ground until the end of the world. If these two medicines are eaten, they will refine our bodies and therefore enable us neither to grow old nor to die. . . . If we smear copper on our feet, it will not deteriorate even if it remains in water. This is to borrow the strength of the copper to protect our flesh. Gold fluid and reconverted cinnabar, however, upon entering our body, permeate our whole system of blood and energy and are not like copper which helps only the outside.

Ko Hung, *Inner Chapters of the Master Who Embraces Simplicity*, 4:1a–3a, quoted in Coward, Neufeldt, and Neumaier, *Readings in Eastern Religions*, 315–16 which "cites the effectiveness of an elixir consumed by the Yellow Emperor himself, a legendary figure associated with various curative powers."[24]

Ko Hung outlines the proper attitude one should exhibit before concocting the elixir of immortality. "First maintain a vigil of a hundred days, and bathe and scent yourself until you are purified; keep away from unclean things and avoid common people. Do not let people who do not believe in the Way know what you are doing. If you should desecrate the divine elixir, it cannot be completed; when done, however, not only you but your entire family can become immortal."[25] Ko Hung was the most influential philosophical Taoist who influenced religious Taoism in the last several centuries.

YOGIC BREATHING

Second, one of the best religious Taoist techniques for immortality is **yogic breathing**, which aims to harmonize the spirits of yin and yang on which all harmony depends. Since human beings are the microcosm of the universe, the point of yoga is to attain the Tao, letting the Tao animate the individual. Yoga itself is a means to an end. As a practice of quiet sitting, meditative breathing was adopted from Buddhist (Ch'an/Zen) meditation. Even the Tao Te Ching recommends breathing exercises (Tao Te Ching 10), where Laozi advocates keeping the mind in the quietude of nonaction in order to "concentrate your vital force."[26] Ko Hung sees the complementary nature of concentration and alchemy. The goal of religious Taoist yoga is to "get behind" one's thoughts, transcending the self to the point of attaining the Tao. If the Tao can be attained by other means, that is well and good. Yogic breathing controls *chi*, the Chinese term that means "air," "breath," "strength," and "spirit," the vital energy that animates all things—including heaven, earth, gods, humans, animals, plants, and minerals. Practitioners of yogic breathing attempt to ingest and circulate *chi* in one's body. According to Ko Hung, those who master yogic breathing can withstand all kinds of disease:

> A person resides in the midst of pneumas [*chi*]; pneumas reside in a person. From Heaven and Earth to the myriad creatures, there is none that does not need pneumas to live. He who excels at circulating pneumas nourishes the body within and dispels malignancy without, yet common people make use of them without even realizing it. . . . Those who know the method can enter plague-stricken areas and even lie down beside its sufferers without becoming infected.[27]

FENG-SHUI AND SEXUAL TECHNIQUES

Third, religious Taoists used feng shui (wind-water), the skill of reading topography, to divine auspicious locations and directions animated with good energy. Geomancers are those who could decipher various forces that embody yin and yang forces by identifying those topographical spots where yin and yang come together to produce good energy that benefits human beings. Underlying the practice of geomancy is the belief that the earth is a whole organism, like an integrated conscious system, not a lump of matter.

By analyzing the forms of earth, topography, shape of the earth, and direction, with the recognition that each part has its own energy, a geomancer can help determine good places and auspicious times for nearly everything. Yin is shady (north); yang is sunny (south)—a building should follow the natural contours of the earth. One has to be careful where one builds one's house: a hill may look like a cat's tail or claws, a row of hills like the scales of a dragon. Geomancers might suggest refraining from putting a building on a dragon's nose or mouth, but encourage construction on the dragon's side to benefit the living being.

The vital energy (breath) that circulates throughout the landscape is called *chi* energy, which embodies both yin and yang forces. *Chi* is the vital energy in Chinese religion, medicine, and philosophy. Pervading and enabling all things, *chi* is harnessed and manipulated through breathing and all sorts of traditional Chinese medicine, such as acupuncture, with the goal not to escape the human condition but to harness the forces of nature into one's body. Incidentally, some of the most expensive real estate and cemetery plots in Asia are those regions with good *chi*.

Fourth, religious Taoists advocated sexual techniques to gain immortality, including holding the semen in during intercourse to rejuvenate the brain, with belief that withholding ejaculation recirculates the sperm internally, feeding the brain. Regardless of the technique, religious Taoism sought longevity, not transcendence: "If you do not obtain gold or cinnabar, but only ingest medicinals from herbs and trees and cultivate other minor arts, you can lengthen your years and postpone death, but you cannot attain transcendence."[28]

Practicing Confucianism

The practice of Confucianism can be described as a combination of sacrifice, self-cultivation, and veneration of Confucius. First, Confucianism is inherently ritualistic, stressing various ceremonies geared toward obtaining peace and harmony within oneself, society, and the nation. Central to Confucian ritual life is sacrifice. Confucians perform sacrifices to ancestors, as laid out in the Confucian Six Classics. According to the Book of Rites, "Of all the methods for the good ordering of men, there is none more urgent than the use of ceremonies [rituals]. Ceremonies are of five kinds [auspicious, mourning, hospitality, military, and festive], and there is none of them more important than sacrifices."[29]

What is important in Confucian rituals is that sacrifices be motivated by an inner sincerity (i.e., *jen*), rather than by external pressure from an outside authority. Ideally, Confucian sacrifice is done without desire for gain, but rather to perfect one's moral virtues, such as showing reverence toward the spirits and human-heartedness toward fellow human beings, thus reflecting a humanistic orientation to ritual activity. Traditionally only the morally perfect are entitled to perform sacrifices, which communicates how crucial it is for people to seek moral perfection. Sacrifices to ancestors include not only food and material objects but also a demonstration of reverence toward ancestors and the past, exemplifying the close connection between sacrifice and the perfection of moral virtues.

Second, Confucianism emphasizes practices that lead to self-cultivation. Education was a crucial feature of personal transformation. State examinations were given to see who had mastered the Confucian texts, while one's future, including marriage possibilities and social prestige, was in part determined by how well one was educated. Quiet meditation is aimed at perfecting the self, and it is practiced not to forget the world but to be a better, more spiritual person.

Many followers of Confucianism and Taoism also practice **tai chi chuan** (power of the Great Ultimate), an old form of physical and mental exercise that promotes good health, longevity, and mental discipline. Tai chi chuan seeks to balance yin and yang forces (i.e., Taoist and Confucian emphases), attempting to fuse these fundamental forces into a single person. While there are dozens of tai chi chuan styles, most are practiced using slow, methodical physical postures and flowing movements.

Finally, Confucians venerate Confucius and his ideals, though Confucius himself never claimed to be more than an ordinary person who simply communicated the ways and traditions of the ancestors to his disciples. Nevertheless, his disciples believed that Confucius had achieved the greatest virtues in the world. Several temples dedicated to him are located throughout China, functioning as places where sacrifices to Confucius are performed and where his birthday (the twenty-seventh day of the eighth month in the Chinese calendar) is celebrated. Confucius's own sayings never mention his own deification, but both ancient and contemporary disciples recognize him to be nearly divine, possessing spiritual powers. Today Confucius is seen in a variety of ways, as a great man, a deity, or a wise teacher.

Modern Movements

Since both Taoism and Confucianism are all-encompassing religious philosophies that focus more on harmony of vital life forces rather than adherence to strict creeds and doctrines, these traditions lend themselves to being somewhat portable.[30] Taoism and Confucianism are enjoying increased popularity in the West as these traditions flourish in new forms among those seeking new insights into cosmic reality (e.g., Tao), mental-physical connections, and social and behavioral protocols that help give people meaning and guidance in relationships with nature and with other human beings.

Scholars Robert Neville and John Berthrong, of Boston University, and Tu Wei-ming, of Harvard University, argue that Confucianism does not have to be closely tied to Chinese culture and is therefore transportable to other cultural contexts. Neville and Tu have introduced what is informally called **Boston Confucianism** as an attempt to formulate Confucian ideals for a Western audience, showing how Confucianism has been and can be adapted in the West.

Neville reflects on the challenge of incorporating Chinese Confucianism into the social realities of contemporary Boston:

> Where Chinese Confucianism as well as Western Aristotelianism have emphasized equality as a condition for true friendship, that condition cannot obtain in a society with the late-modern conditions of Boston. Even egalitarianism means that people are to be treated with equal respect who are vastly different in age, talent, interests, and background. With rare exceptions, true friendships in the Boston situation will have to be possible among "unequals," among people of different gender, different ages, different talents and intelligence, and different positions in social hierarchies.[31]

Boston Confucianism falls within a twentieth-century movement broadly known as New Confucianism, based on the publication of the essay "A Manifesto on Chinese Culture to the World" (aka "New Confucian Manifesto"), which argues in part that the West would be enriched if it combined its knowledge of science, technology, and democracy with the spirituality of the Confucian tradition. The so-called New Confucians represent primarily a scholarly movement that aims to make Confucian ideals compatible with the West.

Taoist themes have thrived particularly well in the popular culture and medicine of the West. If books and magazines are any indication of the popularity of Taoist ideas in the West, then this Chinese tradition is making good headway. For instance, perusing the shelves of a local bookstore one can find titles such

Boston Confucians then need to point out that at the heart of true friendship are the social habits or rituals for enduring through a long time. Friendships are formed only through long endurance of changes in relations among the friends; gender roles change as people age, social positions change with age, talents and responsibilities change, as well as offices in hierarchies. Friends are those who learn to love, respect, and defer to one another through a long period of changes.

Neville, Boston Confucianism, 17–18

as *The Tao of Pooh*, *The Tao of Piglet*, *The Tao of Health*, *The Tao of Physics*, *The Tao of Love and Sex*, and, of course, the Tao Te Ching, the foundational text of philosophical Taoist thought. Increasingly, interior designers and architects in the West are employing concepts of feng shui to find the right balance within rooms and larger spaces. There are movements that combine feng shui with green architecture to create living and work spaces that are both spiritually balanced and environmentally friendly. Furthermore, Taoist temples, priests, and monasteries can be found in several large Western cities, along with many tai chi societies, which serve as centers of meditation and learning.

Timeline

1122–221 BCE	Zhou Dynasty in China
551–479 BCE	Life of Confucius
372–289 BCE	Life of Mencius
221–206 BCE	Qin Dynasty in China; Legalism adopted as state ideology; Confucianism persecuted
136 BCE	Han emperor Wu decrees that Confucian Classics be adopted as the basis for China state examination
24–220 CE	Eastern Han Dynasty in China; beginnings of religious Taoism
372	King Sosurim of Koguryo establishes a national academy for the study of Confucianism on the Korean peninsula
404	Introduction of Confucianism to Japan
440	State support of Taoism
918–1392	Koryo Dynasty in Korea; establishment of civil examination following Chinese model
932	Printing of Confucian Classics in China
1019	State-sponsored printing of Taoist scripture
1127–1279	Southern Song Dynasty in China; Neo-Confucianism revival
1130–1200	Life of Zhu Xi, famous exponent of Neo-Confucianism
1313	Mongol Yuan government adopts civil-service examination system based on Confucian Classics; Zhu Xi's system declared state orthodoxy
1403–25	Reign of Emperor Chengzu; Taoism receives imperial support; compilation of a new Taoist scripture
1392–1910	Yi Dynasty in Korea; Confucianism declared state ideology
1472–1529	Life of Wang Yangming, famous exponent of Neo-Confucianism

1917	May Fourth Movement begins in China; some attempt to eradicate Confucianism
1947	Communist Revolution in China led by Mao Zedong; Nationalists defeated, with some escaping to Taiwan; beginning of religious persecution in mainland China
1966–76	Mao's Cultural Revolution in China; widespread religious persecution and destruction of religious sites
1973–74	Anti-Confucius campaign in China
1986	Chinese government allows annual sacrifice to Confucius to be performed

Key Terms

alchemy

Analects (Lunyu)

Axial Age

Boston Confucianism

chi

Ch'un-ch'iu

Confucius

Da Xue

etic

Falun Gong

feng shui

filial piety

I Ching

jen

junzi

karma

Laozi

Legalists

li

Li Qi

Lunyu (Analects)

Mahavira

men

Mengzi

monotheistic

Mozi

Neo-Confucianism

nonanthropomorphic

nonbeing

sages

samsara

School of Principle

School of the Heart/
    Mind

Shih Ching

Shi Huang Di, Emperor

Shu Ching

Siddhartha

tai chi

tai chi chuan

Tao

Taoshi

Tao Te Ching

t'ien

T'ien ming

T'ien Shih

Wang Yangming

Warring States Period

wu-wei

xiao

xin

yanban

yang

yi

yin

Yin-Yang Cosmologists

yogic breathing

Yueh Ching

Zhuangzi

Zhung Yung

Zhu Xi

Further Reading

Chan, Wing-Tsit. *A Source Book in Chinese Philosophy*. Princeton: Princeton University Press, 1969.

Giles, Herbert A., trans. *Teachings and Sayings of Chuang Tzu*. Mineola, NY: Courier Dover Publications, 2001.

Kim, Heup Young. *Christ and the Tao*. Eugene, OR: Wipf & Stock, 2010.

Kim, Sung-hae. *The Gourd and the Cross: Daoism and Christianity in Dialogue*. Cambridge, MA: Three Pines Press, 2014.

Kohn, Livia. *The Taoist Experience: An Anthology*. SUNY Series in Chinese Philosophy and Culture. Albany: SUNY Press, 1993.

———. *Zhuangzi: Text and Context*. Cambridge, MA: Three Pines Press, 2014.

Komjathy, Louis. *The Daoist Tradition: An Introduction*. New York: Bloomsbury Academic, 2013.

Neville, Robert Cummings. *Boston Confucianism: Portable Tradition in the Late-Modern World*. Albany, NY: SUNY Press, 2000.

Palmer, Martin, and Elizabeth Breuilly, trans. *The Book of Chuang-tzu*. New York: Penguin Books, 1996.

Rainey, Lee Dian. *Confucius and Confucianism: The Essentials*. Malden, MA: Blackwell Publishing, 2010.

Sommer, Deborah. *Chinese Religion: An Anthology of Sources*. New York: Oxford University Press, 1995.

Thompson, Laurence G. *The Chinese Way in Religion*. Belmont, CA: Wadsworth, 1973.

Tu, Wei-ming. *Neo-Confucian Thought in Action. Wang Yang-ming's Youth (1472–1509)*. Berkeley: University of California Press, 1976.

Yao, Xinzhong. *An Introduction to Confucianism*. Cambridge: Cambridge University Press, 2000.

seven

Judaism

Contemporary Snapshot

A small but radical movement has emerged. Its members brandish neither swords nor guns, for its weapons consist merely of prayer shawls and sacred scriptures. But this movement has caused quite a stir among many in one of the most religiously contested cities in the world, Jerusalem. Deemed illegal by traditionalists, about 150 Jewish women in December 2009 have donned prayer shawls, reserved only for Jewish men, and gathered at the **Western Wall** of the Jewish temple in the Old City of Jerusalem to pray. Known also as the **Wailing Wall** (or **Kotel**) among Jews, and al-Buraaq Wall to Arab speakers, the Western Wall dates back to the end of the Second Temple period (516 BCE–70 CE), and is what remains of the temple that was once the center of Jewish worship and identity.

The Wailing Wall was and continues to be a prominent site of Jewish mourning over the destruction of the temple and a place where

Figure 7.1. Western Wall, with separation between men and women in Jerusalem, Israel

Jewish lamentations are lifted up daily. Considered a sacred space by faithful Jews, the Western Wall has endured a history of control by the Ottomans, the British, and the Jordanians. After Israel's victory during the 1967 Six-Day War, the Western Wall came under the control of Israel.

Women and the Western Wall

Today the Western Wall is partitioned off, so that only Jewish men can pray directly at the wall, leaving women to pray on the other side of a dividing screen in a reserved area to the extreme right of the Western Wall. But the new movement that emerged in 1988, calling itself Women at the Wall, has sought to challenge the limitations imposed on them by an ultraorthodox Judaism that discriminates by gender, denying women access to the Western Wall for purposes of prayer. The restriction against these mostly Conservative Jewish women was also supported by a ruling of the Supreme Court of Israel, which rejected a petition submitted by the Women at the Wall to have their religious freedom defended.

Instead of permitting them access, the Supreme Court granted the women a separate place of prayer in a garden away from the immediate vicinity of the wall. The conflict involving the Supreme Court, Orthodox Jewish men who uphold the traditional gender separation at the Western Wall, and Conservative Jewish women who want to hold organized prayer at the wall, illustrates the complex relationship between different understandings of sacred space, gender, theology, and religious tradition. What is at stake for some in the contest at the wall is nothing less than the control of Jewish identity and the survival of its traditions.

Of the world's religions that we have considered so far, Judaism stands closest to Christianity, since in significant ways the history, sacred texts, practices, and theology of early Judaism form the basis for New Testament Christianity. Currently, there are approximately fourteen million Jews worldwide, making it the smallest of the world religions, yet Judaism formed the foundation of what would later become the largest religion in the world, Christianity. Although its numbers are small, Judaism is a broad tradition that encompasses both religious and secular viewpoints. To be Jewish, or a member of the Jewry (a community of Jews), may mean being of a particular ethnicity or having a particular set of religious beliefs and practices.

Religious Jews and Ethnic Jews

It is important to recognize that being Jewish today does not necessarily mean following a particular religion, since the vast majority of Jews today would claim that they are Jewish because of birth. However, it is equally crucial to note that there is a Jewish religion and that for many Judaism is the source of their group identity that binds Jews together and gives them meaning and sustenance in life. It would be misleading to think of the term "Judaism" as implying a uniformity of belief and practice among all Jews, when in fact significant variation exists throughout the Jewish community.

That is to say, a distinction is sometimes drawn between "secular" or "cultural" Jews, who accept the history and some values of Judaism, and "religious" Jews, who accept the **Torah**, even with major differences of opinion about the ways in which it is applied in daily life. These divisions of religious Jews are manifested in the main branches of Judaism—Orthodox, Reform, Conservative, and Reconstructionist Judaism—which will be discussed toward the end of this chapter.

Today, about half of all Jews living in Israel would identify themselves as "secular" because they do not believe in God. Similarly, many Jews in the United States today do not belong to a synagogue, a worshiping community of Jews. While Judaism is not normally considered a missionary religion, like Buddhism, Christianity, and Islam, most branches of Judaism are open to receiving people into the tradition, which usually means joining a people as well as adopting a particular faith. As such, belief is secondary to belonging, and Jewishness springs primarily from birth rather than from personal belief in a set of doctrines. Needless to say, being Jewish can mean quite different things depending on which community or historical moment one considers.

According to Jewish law, one is Jewish either by birth or by choice. Being Jewish by birth is typically traced through the mother's lineage, with children of Jewish mothers considered Jewish. Today a small group of liberal Jews argue that Jewish identity can come equally through the father's lineage, so if the father is Jewish then his children will be Jewish by birth. A non-Jew can become Jewish by submitting an application to a court of three rabbis (i.e., teachers or official leaders of Jewish congregations), by studying, by being baptized, and, for males, being circumcised. For instance, it is possible for a non-Jew who marries a Jew to enter Judaism by choice.

Modern Jewry

Modern Jewry consists of a people scattered throughout the world, with the largest demographic concentration in the United States (roughly 6 million Jews), then the State of Israel (over 3.5 million), then the countries of Eastern Europe (roughly 2.2 million). Others live mostly in sizable communities in Britain, Canada, France, and South America. Jews who migrated to central Europe, Russia, Hungary, Poland, and Lithuania are called **Ashkenazic Jews** (also known as Ashkenazim); they share the Yiddish language, which consists of words from German, Hebrew, and Slavic languages, written with Hebrew script. The Ashkenazim live mostly in Christian lands and have been quite influential in the establishment of the modern state of Israel.

Another main ethnic branch of modern Jewry consists of those originating from the Iberian Peninsula (i.e., Spain and Portugal), known as the **Sephardic Jews** (also known as Sephardim). Sephardic Jews lived mostly in Islamic countries and were relatively isolated until the twelfth century.

In the nineteenth century, most Jews lived either in countries dominated by Christians (Ashkenazim), and spoke **Yiddish**, or in Muslim lands (Sephardim), and spoke Arabic. During the era of European colonialism, there were different patterns of acceptance and constraint of Jews according to each particular European nation. For instance, Spain and Portugal prevented Jews from settling in their colonial territories, thus constraining their movements, while Jews were allowed open access to territories under English, Dutch, or French rule.

Since the beginning of the Jewish tradition, Jews have been an immigrant people. Over the past two hundred years, however, a significant feature of Jewish life has been migration and displacement, illustrated by the fact that most Jews today do not live in the towns where their grandparents were born. Today the Jewish population worldwide is predominately urban, with over half of modern Jewry living in English-speaking countries. Given the history of Jewish populations worldwide, different Jewish immigrant groups have developed their own institutions, which center on synagogues. Despite the differences between Ashkenazic and Sephardic communities, mostly because of the differing contexts in which they lived (Christian and Muslim, respectively), these two groups share in common the basic elements of Judaism that began to emerge in the Second Temple period, before the temple was destroyed by the Romans in 70 CE.

Origins and Concepts

Early History and Covenants

The Hebrew people in the Bible shared some of the cultural and linguistic features of other Semitic groups, such as the Arabs. Hebrews, who were also known as Israelites, were monotheistic, worshipers of one God, while others in the ancient Near East (i.e., Mesopotamia, Persia, Anatolia, ancient Egypt, and the Levant) were polytheistic, worshipers of many gods. Around 2000 BCE, Hebrews, along with other Semitic peoples, venerated certain stones

Map 7.1. World of Genesis

International Mapping

and pillars and other unusually shaped natural objects that they believed had sacred character. Yet, beyond the various spirits they acknowledged, the early Hebrews recognized one God (Eloah), which in comparison made the other gods appear as non-gods (Hebrew, *elilim*).

The story of the Hebrews begins with the creation of the world and all that is in it by the breath of God. Adam and Eve were progenitors of humankind, but their disobedience of God in the garden of Eden (Gen. 1–2), enacted when they ate from the tree that God had forbidden them, created enmity between God and human beings, along with the suffering of all creation. In response to human disobedience, and because of God's faithfulness to his creation, God made a covenant (legal promise) with Abraham, telling him that he would be the father of many nations. Because of the covenant, the Jews believed they were chosen by God to fulfill a role in God's salvation history.

> Now the LORD said to Abram, "Go from your country and your kindred and your father's house to the land that I will show you. I will make of you a great nation, and I will bless you, and make your name great, so that you will be a blessing. I will bless those who bless you, and the one who curses you I will curse; and in you all the families of the earth shall be blessed."

So Abram went, as the LORD had told him; and Lot went with him. Abram was seventy-five years old when he departed from Haran. Abram took his wife Sarai and his brother's son Lot, and all the possessions that they had gathered, and the persons whom they had acquired in Haran; and they set forth to go to the land of Canaan. When they had come to the land of Canaan, Abram passed through the land to the place at Shechem, to the oak of Moreh. At that time the Canaanites were in the land. Then the LORD appeared to Abram, and said, "To your offspring I will give this land." So he built there an altar to the LORD, who had appeared to him. From there he moved on to the hill country on the east of Bethel, and pitched his tent, with Bethel on the west and Ai on the east; and there he built an altar to the LORD and invoked the name of the LORD.

Genesis 12:1–8

On that day the LORD made a covenant with Abram, saying, "To your descendants I give this land, from the river of Egypt to the great river, the river Euphrates, the land of the Kenites, the Kenizzites, the Kadmonites, the Hittites, the Perizzites, the Rephaim, the Amorites, the Canaanites, the Girgashites, and the Jebusites."

Genesis 15:18–21

A COVENANT PEOPLE

Covenants were not new among Semitic peoples. In the ancient Near East covenants were made between individuals, marriage partners, states, kings and subjects, and, in the case of the people of Israel, between God and human beings. Covenants were usually accompanied by signs, such as the biblical notion of the Sabbath rest (weekly day of rest) or male circumcision. Crucial to a covenant between God and the people of Israel was the idea of relationship between the two parties, which is fundamental to the Jewish religion, exemplified by the biblical words, "I will walk among you, and will be your God, and you shall be my people" (Lev. 26:12).

THE COVENANTS

God would eventually make several covenants with human beings to demonstrate God's love for human beings. There was the Edenic covenant (Gen. 1:26–31), whereby Adam and Eve were created in God's image (*imago Dei*), given permission to partake of and have stewardship over creation. After the fall of humankind, represented by Adam and Eve eating of the tree of the knowledge of good and evil, God made a covenant with Adam (Gen. 3:16–19), called the Adamic covenant, whereby God declared the curses invoked upon the failure of the Edenic covenant, yet established a promise of grace and showed God's redeeming care of Adam and Eve. Following the covenant with Adam, there was the covenant with Noah (Noahic covenant) (Gen. 9), whereby God promised Noah that God would never again destroy the world by flood.

Then there was the Abrahamic covenant (Gen. 12:1–3, 6–7), whereby God promised to make Abraham's name great and that the people of the world would be blessed through the lineage of Abraham (Gen. 12:3; 22:18), referring to the Messiah, who would be from the line of Abraham. After that the Mosaic covenant (Exod. 19–24) introduced the Ten Commandments (Exod. 20) and over six hundred instructions, and God promised to make the people of Israel God's special possession.

The Palestinian covenant (Deut. 29:1–29) was another covenant between God and the people of Israel, whereby God called them to return to a relationship with him and be devoted to the Mosaic law—the 613 ethical principles contained in the Torah, often referred to as the "Law of Moses." In the Davidic covenant (2 Sam. 7:8–16) God promised that the **Messiah** (Savior, Liberator) would come from the physical lineage of David. Christians believe that this anticipated Messiah was Jesus (Luke 1:32–33).

A New Covenant

Finally, God gave the people of Israel a new covenant (Jer. 31:31–34), whereby God reaffirmed the forgiveness of sin and made the knowledge of God accessible for all people, rather than just the Jews: "No longer shall they teach one another, or say to each other, 'Know the Lord,' for they shall all know me, from the least of them to the greatest, says the Lord; for I will forgive their iniquity, and remember their sin no more" (Jer. 31:34). In many respects, the history of the people of Israel can be summarized as a history of broken covenants with God, with God making an overture to reestablish the wrecked relationship through the institution of another covenant, like a person wooing his lover to return to him. God set the terms of the covenantal relationship:

> Speak to all the congregation of the people of Israel and say to them: You shall be holy, for I the Lord your God am holy. You shall each revere your mother and father, and you shall keep my sabbaths: I am the Lord your God. Do not turn to idols or make cast images for yourselves: I am the Lord your God.
>
> When you offer a sacrifice of well-being to the Lord, offer it in such a way that it is acceptable in your behalf. It shall be eaten on the same day you offer it, or on the next day; and anything left over until the third day shall be consumed in fire. If it is eaten at all on the third day, it is an abomination; it will not be acceptable. All who eat it shall be subject to punishment, because

they have profaned what is holy to the Lord; and any such person shall be cut off from the people.

When you reap the harvest of your land, you shall not reap to the very edges of your field, or gather the gleanings of your harvest. You shall not strip your vineyard bare, or gather the fallen grapes of your vineyard; you shall leave them for the poor and the alien: I am the Lord your God.

You shall not steal; you shall not deal falsely; and you shall not lie to one another. And you shall not swear falsely by my name, profaning the name of your God: I am the Lord.

You shall not defraud your neighbor; you shall not steal; and you shall not keep for yourself the wages of a laborer until morning. You shall not revile the deaf or put a stumbling block before the blind; you shall fear your God: I am the Lord.

You shall not render an unjust judgment; you shall not be partial to the poor or defer to the great: with justice you shall judge your neighbor. You shall not go around as a slanderer among your people, and you shall not profit by the blood of your neighbor: I am the Lord.

You shall not hate in your heart anyone of your kin; you shall reprove your neighbor, or you will incur guilt yourself. You shall not take vengeance or bear a grudge against any of your people, but you shall love your neighbor as yourself: I am the Lord.

You shall keep my statutes. You shall not let your animals breed with a different kind; you shall not sow your field with two kinds of seed; nor shall you put on a garment made of two different materials.

If a man has sexual relations with a woman who is a slave, designated for another man but not ransomed or given her freedom, an inquiry shall be held. They shall not be put to death, since she has not been freed; but he shall bring a guilt offering for himself to the Lord, at the entrance of the tent of meeting, a ram as guilt offering. And the priest shall make atonement for him with the ram of guilt offering before the Lord for his sin that he committed; and the sin he committed shall be forgiven him.

When you come into the land and plant all kinds of trees for food, then you shall regard their fruit as forbidden; three years it shall be forbidden to you, it must not be eaten. In the fourth year all their fruit shall be set apart for rejoicing in the Lord. But in the fifth year you may eat of their fruit, that their yield may be increased for you: I am the Lord your God.

You shall not eat anything with its blood. You shall not practice augury or witchcraft. You shall not round off the hair on your temples or mar the edges of your beard. You shall not make any gashes in your flesh for the dead or tattoo any marks upon you: I am the Lord.

Do not profane your daughter by making her a prostitute, that the land not become prostituted and full of depravity. You shall keep my sabbaths and reverence my sanctuary: I am the Lord.

> Do not turn to mediums or wizards; do not seek them out, to be defiled by them: I am the Lord your God.
>
> You shall rise before the aged, and defer to the old; and you shall fear your God: I am the Lord.
>
> When an alien resides with you in your land, you shall not oppress the alien. The alien who resides with you shall be to you as the citizen among you; you shall love the alien as yourself, for you were aliens in the land of Egypt: I am the Lord your God.
>
> You shall not cheat in measuring length, weight, or quantity. You shall have honest balances, honest weights, an honest ephah, and an honest hin: I am the Lord your God, who brought you out of the land of Egypt. You shall keep all my statutes and all my ordinances, and observe them: I am the Lord.
>
> Leviticus 19

Jewish Books

The Jewish religion emphasizes the written text, and sacred books are highly valued as containing God's word. As such, the sacred books of Judaism profoundly shape the lives of religious Jews. There are several important books in Judaism, but those most commonly found in a Jewish home are the Hebrew Bible, known as "God's Word," and a prayer book. In addition to these books, the massive collection called the Talmud is another source of Jewish identity and guidance.

The Hebrew Bible

The Hebrew Bible is the primary text of the Jewish religion, and it consists of many of the same books that are recognized by Christians and appear in the Old Testament. The Hebrew Bible contains twenty-four books divided into three sections. First is the Torah ("teaching," "guidance," "instruction"), otherwise known as the Pentateuch ("five books"; i.e., the first five books of the Hebrew Bible—Genesis, Exodus, Leviticus, Numbers, and Deuteronomy). The Torah sets out the teachings of the written law of the Jewish people, which is the source of Jewish oral law. It also contains the history of the Jewish people from the creation of the world until the death of Moses. Since it is both history and a large body of laws, the Torah is the ultimate source of many Jewish religious practices.

Secondary to the Torah is the second section of the Hebrew Bible, the **Nevi'im**. The Nevi'im (Prophets) is a collection of eight books that recount the history of the Jews from their entrance into the land of Canaan (the promised land) to the Babylonian exile, along with various teachings of individual prophets. They are divided into two sections, the Former Prophets and the Latter Prophets.[1]

The third section of the Hebrew Bible, called the **Ketuvim** (scriptures), the Writings, is divided into four sections: (1) poetical books (Psalms, Proverbs, and Job), (2) the Scrolls (Song of Solomon, Ruth, Lamentations of Jeremiah, Ecclesiastes, and Esther), (3) prophecy (Daniel), and (4) history (Ezra, Nehemiah, and Chronicles). Together the Torah, Nevi'im, and Ketuvim are referred to as the **Tanakh**, an acronym made up of the first letters of the three sections of the Hebrew Bible.

For religious Jews, reading the biblical texts is inseparable from interpretation. Between the third and eleventh centuries, a massive collection of interpretations, sermons, and lectures on the biblical books was compiled. These compilations are referred to collectively as **midrash** (interpretation). As a method of biblical exegesis, midrash is not considered as authoritative as the Torah, but midrash does influence religious authority, the interpretation of the biblical texts, and Jewish preaching. Generally, there are two types of midrashim (midrash literature). The **halakhic midrashim** focus on commentaries on the Tanakh (Hebrew Bible), and therefore investigate and interpret Jewish laws. And the **Aggadic midrashim** provide commentary on the nonlegal portions of the Hebrew Bible.

Jewish Prayer Book

In addition to the Hebrew Bible, Jews use a prayer book, which contains Hebrew prayers, many of which were codified in the ninth century. Today's Jewish prayer books are markedly different in part because of the diversity within the Jewish community, with some incorporating additional meditative or instructional prayers. Most Jewish prayer books consist of the **siddur**, which contains the Sabbath and daily prayers, and the **mahzor**, which contains prayers used during festivals such as **Rosh Hashanah** (Jewish New Year) and **Yom Kippur** (Day of Atonement). Mahzor means "to return," communicating the fact that the mahzor prayers are to be performed annually. Since each major Jewish group has its own prayer book, Orthodox, Conservative, Reform, and Reconstructionist Jews will have their own collections that are used throughout the year at home and in the synagogue. Because Jews do not have many definitive creeds, prayer books constitute an important way that Jews learn about Jewish theology and life.

The Talmud

The **Talmud** ("learn," "study," "teach") is the third major text used in the Jewish community. Written in a mixture of Hebrew and Aramaic, the Talmud is fairly inaccessible to laypeople because of its languages and difficult style. While the Talmud consists of the **Babylonian Talmud** and **Jerusalem**

Talmud, the Babylonian Talmud is considered more authoritative, dating back to Babylon in the fifth century CE. The Talmud consists of two parts: the **Mishnah** (teaching), a compilation of Jewish oral law, and the **Gemara** (completion), the discussions of rabbis (teachers).

In addition to the Hebrew Bible, the prayer book, and the Talmud, which form the most important sources of Judaism, a few other books have helped to shape the tradition. Among the medieval texts are **Rashi**'s (1040–1105) commentary on the Hebrew Bible and the Babylonian Talmud, **Moses Maimonides**'s (1135–1204) *Mishneh Torah*, a systematic presentation of the oral law, and his *Guide for the Perplexed*, a philosophical treatise that sought to demonstrate to "the perplexed" how scripture could be interpreted spiritually and literally. Considered one of the greatest medieval Jewish philosophers, Maimonides produced works that influenced Christians such as Thomas Aquinas, Duns Scotus, and Meister Eckhart.

In the late Middle Ages, **Rabbi Joseph Caro** (1488–1575) wrote a code of Jewish law and ritual, the *Shulkhan Arukh* (Prepared Table), which incorporated customs of Spanish and Asian Jews. **Rabbi Moses Isserles** (1525–72) later added to the text some of the customs of Central and Eastern European Jews, thus expanding the code of Jewish law and ritual and impacting Jewish communities worldwide. While normally the Hebrew Bible and prayer book would be found in the homes of religious Jews, the other works are chosen according to the particular emphasis that a community may uphold, since each Jewish movement (e.g., Orthodox, Reform) has produced its own works.

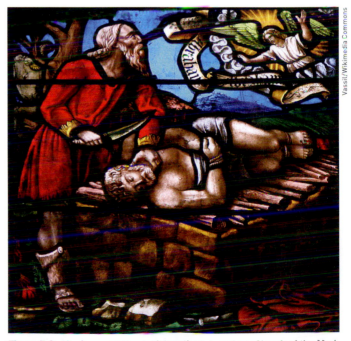

Vassil/Wikimedia Commons

Figure 7.2. Abraham and Isaac, sixteenth century, from Church of the Madeleine, Troyes, France

Basic Teachings of Judaism

Jews trace their history back to the biblical characters of Adam and Abraham, whose wife Sarah gave birth to Isaac. Among Isaac's progeny was Jacob, the grandson of Abraham, who became the father of the Israelites. Early biblical accounts refer to Abraham as "Abram the Hebrew" (Gen. 14:13). It is notable that one definition of the term "Hebrew" means "the other side" and communicates that Abraham came from the other side of the Euphrates River.

Usually the terms "Hebrews" and "Israelites" refer to the same people, with the term "Hebrew" used to describe them before the conquest of the land of Canaan, and the term "Israelite" afterward. The term "Jews" (Hebrew, *Yehudim*) describes an ethnic and religious group originating from the Israelites and Hebrews of the ancient Near East. Given that there were originally twelve tribes of Israel, Judah being one of them that survived, the term "Jews" is directly related to "Hebrews." The term "Jew" refers to the descendants of the tribe or kingdom of Judah (see Jer. 32:12; 34:9). After the Babylonian exile, when the "Hebrews" were taken into exile in Babylon, the term "Jew" came to describe God's covenant people.

NAMES FOR GOD

Jewish belief affirms the existence of one God who created heaven and earth: "the earth was a formless void and darkness covered the face of the deep, while a wind from God swept over the face of the waters" (Gen. 1:2). A crucially important name for God is **Yahweh** (YHWH), the God who demanded that people worship God alone. Yahweh means, "I will be what I want to be" or "I am that (or who) I am," or simply, "I am," as in "I AM WHO I AM" (Exod. 3:14). For many early followers, and even today's strongly Orthodox Jews, God's name was so holy that verbalizing it was considered a sin. Only the high priest, according to Jewish law, could pronounce the Tetragrammaton, the four-letter word "YHWH" (Yahweh), once a year on Yom Kippur, the most important holiday set aside in the Jewish calendar to repent for the sins of the past year.

God is so unique that a depiction of God cannot be made (Exod. 20:4). The Hebrew Bible describes God as all-knowing (omniscient) (Job 28:23), all-powerful (omnipotent) (Job 42:2), and present everywhere (omnipresent)

SIDEBAR 7.1

Hebrew Names for God

The Hebrew Bible (Old Testament) notes several names for God, such as Elohim (plural form of "strength"), the earliest biblical name for God, which is found in Genesis 1:1—"In the beginning Elohim created the heavens and the earth." According to Judaism and the Hebrew Bible, there are many names for the one God—for example, El (God), which was also used by the Canaanites; El Elyon (God most high); El 'Olam (the everlasting God); El Shaddai (God Almighty); El Berit (God of the Covenant); and Adonai (the Lord).

(Ps. 139:7–12). God is eternal (Isa. 40:6–8) and unchangeable (Isa. 41:4). As its Creator, nature reveals the glory of God (Ps. 19:2), even while God remains distinct from and involved in creation itself.

A Chosen People

Furthermore, Israel is a people chosen by God, whose identity is bounded by adherence to Torah and the practice of male circumcision. The Torah is considered divinely inspired, and the oral teachings of Judaism are believed to be rooted in the revelation

Figure 7.3. YHWH in Hebrew (Num. 18:27–30)

given to Moses (Torah). According to Judaism, the connection between God and the Jews is a special one marked by mutual love and embodied in a covenantal relationship. The Hebrew concept of "covenant" means binding legal agreement, similar to a marriage contract. And the biblical story tells of a God whose love for the chosen people is demonstrated by God's faithful commitment even in the midst of being forgotten and dishonored by the people of Israel. Love is the only response to God, as stated in the **Shema Yisrael** ("Hear, O Israel"), the words from the Torah that are the foundation of the morning and evening Jewish prayer services.

> Hear, O Israel: the Lord is our God, the Lord alone.
>
> You shall love the Lord your God with all your heart, and with all your soul, and with all your might. Keep these words that I am commanding you today in your heart. Recite them to your children and talk about them when you are at home and when you are away, when you lie down and when you rise. Bind them as a sign on your hand, fix them as an emblem on your forehead, and write them on the doorposts of your house and on your gates.
>
> Deuteronomy 6:4–9

Ancient Near Eastern Religions

One way to understand the uniqueness of the religion of Israel is to compare it briefly with the religions of the surrounding nations of the ancient Near East. First, other Near Eastern religions were based on a reenactment, repetition, and remembrance of the past. For example, ancient Near Eastern deities were appeased and cajoled in rituals for their abilities to provide for the eternal cycle of harvest and fertility and help with universal rites of passage, such as birth and death. Ancient Near Eastern gods or goddesses guaranteed that the world would function, but they did not create anything new.

Yet God (Yahweh) did something new, not just reenacting old patterns of the agricultural cycle. Yahweh led the Israelites into the land of Canaan, made a covenant (legal promise) with them, demonstrating that history is the arena of God's activity, directing it in a purposeful way: "Then God spoke all these words: I am the LORD your God, who brought you out of Egypt, out of the house of slavery; you shall have no other gods before me" (Exod. 20:1–3).

Second, God, the Creator and Sustainer of life, promised to be with God's people. Just as God had been present in the past with Abraham, Isaac, and Jacob, God promised to be present in the future. Third, God elected Israel as a people to serve marginalized people, such as orphans, widows, strangers, and the poor. The chosen people of Israel were obligated to care for victims of society. Fourth, ethical monotheism characterized the God of the Jews. The Jews of the ancient Near East were said to have worshiped the one true God, even while acknowledging the existence of other gods. Whereas the Romans and the Greeks worshiped many gods, the Jews worshiped Yahweh alone, who provided a moral framework that guided the Israelites' life together as well as their relationships with those outside the covenant community. In fact, Judaism was successful at winning many converts to its ethical monotheism.

Finally, some believe that the biblical account tells of an apocalyptic hope that raised the anticipation for the appearance of the Messiah, the anointed one who would be the king of Israel from the lineage of King David. The biblical drama, beginning in Genesis, tells a story of human disobedience in the chosen people's covenantal relationship with God and God's faithful commitment to them. For many Jews, the hope of a messiah is part of how they view the future of the world, looking forward to a savior who will establish peace and justice.

Moses Maimonides (1135–1204), one of the greatest medieval Jewish philosophers, wrote the "thirteen fundamentals" of Jewish belief, which have been accepted as an unofficial Jewish creed. A major contribution of Maimonides was his belief that spirituality could be integrated with reason. Maimonides argued that God has no attributes, and so can only be understood through his actions, which the biblical account records. While the thirteen fundamentals originated in the medieval period, Jewish belief and practice are today still influenced by these convictions. Maimonides outlined the fundamentals of Jewish belief as follows:

1. God is the creator of all that is.
2. God is one.

Who is the Messiah? Jews, Christians, and Muslims employ the term "messiah," yet with different meanings. In the Jewish religion, messiah means "anointed one" or "anointed king," and carries a political meaning since it refers to the future king of Israel who will establish peace and justice in the world. Given the tumultuous social context of the Greco-Roman world at the time of the birth of Jesus and the subjugation experienced by Jews of the day, most Jews were looking for a messiah who would liberate them from the oppression of Roman authorities—thus they anticipated a messiah with social and political strength. Some first-century Jews of the Greco-Roman world did in fact recognize Jesus Christ as the Messiah as prophesied in the Hebrew Bible (Old Testament).

According to the Christian faith, Jesus Christ was God's self-disclosure, the revelation of God in human flesh, the anticipated Messiah promised by God to bring peace on earth. Jesus interpreted himself using the phrase "Son of Man," rather than as a supernatural being like an angel or as light (cf. *Gospel of Thomas*). Jesus was subject to death, yet he demonstrated the power of God, for he himself is God. Jesus was a descendent of King David (Matt. 1:1–16): "A shoot shall come out from the stump of Jesse [David's father], and a branch shall grow out of his roots" (Isa. 11:1).

Furthermore, Christians cite other Old Testament prophecies that they believe attest to Jesus as Messiah: for instance, his virgin birth (Isa. 7:14), birth in Bethlehem (Mic. 5:2), sacrificial death (Isa. 53:5), crucifixion (Ps. 22:14–18), and physical resurrection (Ps. 16:10), noting the early church affirmation that "Jesus is the Messiah, the Son of God" (John 20:31). Christians believe that Jesus was sacrificed and was raised from the dead as the perfect God-man for the sins of humankind, inherited from the disobedience of Adam and Eve.

3. God is incorporeal.
4. God is eternal.
5. God alone is to be worshiped.
6. God communicates to humanity through the medium of prophecy.
7. Moses was the greatest of the prophets to whom God communicated most directly.
8. Torah (the Pentateuch) was revealed to Moses by God.
9. Torah will not be supplanted by another revelation from God.
10. God knows the actions of human beings and is concerned about them.
11. God rewards and punishes people for their good or evil ways.

The identity of the "anointed one" remains a mystery to most Jews today, but herein lies one of the major theological points of difference between Jews and Christians, and more generally between Christians and followers of other religious traditions. While some first-century Jews recognized Jesus Christ as the Messiah, others rejected him. The Bible notes that while the person and work of Jesus Christ is a "stumbling stone" and "foolishness" to people without faith, he is nevertheless called the Son of God (Mark 1:1), God incarnate (John 1:1–14; Col. 2:9), without sin (1 Pet. 2:22), and the giver of eternal life (John 10:28):

> Where is one who is wise? Where is the scribe? Where is the debater of this age? Has not God made foolish the wisdom of the world? For since, in the wisdom of God, the world did not know God through wisdom, God decided, through the foolishness of our proclamation, to save those who believe. For Jews demand signs and Greeks desire wisdom, but we proclaim Christ crucified, a stumbling block to Jews and foolishness to Gentiles, but to those who are the called, both Jews and Greeks, Christ the power of God and the wisdom of God. For God's foolishness is wiser than human wisdom, and God's weakness is stronger than human strength. (1 Cor. 1:20–25)

The affirmation that Jesus Christ is fully human and fully divine is a crucial component of Christian faith and practice. Muslim perspectives are correct to imply that were Jesus only a prophet, Christian faith would be misplaced. Christians, though, view Jesus—as the only God-man—as the sole reconciler between God and human beings, extending an invitation to abundant life (John 10:10). The early ecumenical church councils affirmed scriptural insights about the identity of Jesus and his relationship to the Father. The ecumenical First Council of Nicaea (325), initiated by the Roman

12. The Messiah (anointed one), a descendent from the lineage of David, will establish the messianic age.
13. The dead will be resurrected.

On the topics of prophetic revelation, inspiration of the Bible, the concept of the Messiah, and the resurrection of the dead, vigorous debate exists among the various branches of Judaism, with, for instance, Reform Judaism accepting higher critical perspectives (such as literary or historical criticism) of the biblical texts and rejecting the notion of an individual person ushering in the messianic age—a time of peace and justice on the earth and among human beings.

emperor Constantine, declared that Jesus was "begotten, not created" and "of the same substance (**homoousios**) as the Father." Jesus was not *of similar substance* (**homoiousios**) to the Father, but of the very same substance, reflected in the Nicene Creed's (381) statement,

> We believe in one God, the Father Almighty, Maker of heaven and earth, and of all things visible and invisible. And in one Lord Jesus Christ, the only-begotten Son of God, begotten of the Father before all worlds, Light of Light, very God of very God, begotten, not made, being of one substance with the Father.

The Council of Chalcedon (451) provided a clear statement on the human-divine nature of Jesus Christ:

> Following the holy Fathers, we unanimously teach and confess one and the same Son, our Lord Jesus Christ: the same perfect in divinity and perfect in humanity, the same truly God and truly man, composed of rational soul and body; consubstantial with the Father as to his divinity and consubstantial with us as to his humanity; "like us in all things but sin." He was begotten from the Father before all ages as to his divinity and in these last days, for us and for our salvation, was born as to his humanity of the virgin Mary, the Mother of God.
>
> We confess that one and the same Christ, Lord, and only-begotten Son, is to be acknowledged in two natures without confusion, change, division, or separation. The distinction between natures was never abolished by their union, but rather the character proper to each of the two natures was perceived as they came together in one person and one hypostasis [i.e., "being"].

Therefore, the Christian perspective on Jesus Christ is that he is the self-disclosure of God, at once fully human and fully divine, and a full member of the Trinity—the Godhead consisting of Father, Son, and Holy Spirit.

The Jewish religion, like other religions, is not solely an affirmation of particular beliefs and abstract concepts. Jewish beliefs are expressed through worship and what are called **halakhah** rituals. Halakhah (Hebrew, "he went") refers both to a particular Jewish practice and the entire Jewish legal system. Composed of the written law (613 commandments from the Pentateuch), the oral law (including the interpretations of the written law), and additional statements from earlier generations, the halakhah (Jewish practices), according to many Jews, began with Moses. The presence of the halakhah illustrates that Judaism is not simply a set of doctrines, but a practice guided by the wisdom of faithful followers of God and the word of God revealed in the Hebrew Bible. Indeed, the term communicates that law and practice are closely connected in Judaism. Today, some Jews see halakhah as the center of their faith and practice. Given the significance of the halakhah, let us look at some of the major Jewish religious practices.

Worship and Practices

Jewish Rituals

JEWISH YEAR

All world religions emphasize particular dates and events on the calendar that help remind the faithful of their past and serve as a way to bind the current generation together. Most follow either a lunar or a solar calendar. The Jewish year is no different, for it communicates what is important within the tradition.

ROSH HASHANAH

The Jewish religious calendar follows a lunar year of twelve months, which is about eleven days shorter than the solar year. The Jewish year begins in late September or early October with Rosh Hashanah (Hebrew, "New Year"), the New Year festival. According to Judaism, Rosh Hashanah is the day on which all people are judged, so it is a time when Jews repent for their sins. Jewish tradition notes that on Rosh Hashanah the completely evil ones are inscribed in the Book of Death, while the completely righteous ones are written in the Book of Life. Those in between wait until Yom Kippur (Hebrew, "Day of Atonement") to be judged.

On Rosh Hashanah the **shofar** (ram's horn) is blown, which, according to Maimonides, has the purpose of declaring, "Awake from your slumbers, you who have fallen asleep, and reflect on your deeds." During Rosh Hashanah it is customary to greet one another with the statement, "May you be inscribed [in the Book of Life] for a good year." A day of fasting (**Tzom Gedaliah**) follows Rosh Hashanah.

YOM KIPPUR

Ten days after Rosh Hashanah, the Day of Atonement (Yom Kippur) occurs, marked by a twenty-four-hour fast beginning at daybreak and lasting until the nightfall on the following day. Yom Kippur is the most solemn day of the Jewish year, for it is on this day that atonement is made: "on this day atonement shall be made for you, to cleanse you; from all your sins you shall be clean before the Lord" (Lev. 16:30). On this day, the faithful are to "deny" themselves (Lev. 23:27) by abstaining from food and drink, from wearing leather shoes (i.e., comfortable shoes), from sexual intercourse between husband and wife, and from washing. During Yom Kippur, it is common for synagogues to be full as worshipers seek forgiveness from God.

Sukkoth

Only five days after Yom Kippur, **Sukkoth** (Hebrew, "Festival of Booths" or "Festival of Tabernacles") occurs, the Jewish autumn festival lasting eight days. Commemorating the time when the Jewish people wandered through the wilderness after the exodus from Egypt, protected by God, Sukkoth recalls the passage from Leviticus:

> You shall live in booths for seven days; all that are citizens in Israel shall live in booths.
>
> Leviticus 23:42

In the past, Jews were to construct a booth, making it their principal residence during Sukkoth. Today, Jews who follow the tradition may build a *sukkah* (little hut, booth) at home and at the synagogue, without a strict obligation to sleep in it. During the first day of Sukkoth, Jews may not work, but on the following days minimal work is permitted, with the last day given to rejoicing and celebration accompanied by singing and dancing in the synagogue.

Hanukkah

About two months later, Jews celebrate **Hanukkah**, an eight-day festival commemorating the rededication of the Jerusalem temple after the Maccabean revolt against the Seleucids. Hanukkah (Hebrew, "dedication") is the Jewish Festival of Lights. According to tradition, Judas Maccabee purified the temple after the Hellenistic desecration and rededicated it. In response to the purification of the temple, the Jews celebrated for eight days. A central part of the story is that one day's supply of the holy oil lasted for eight days. Thus, during the celebration of Hanukkah, it is customary to display Hanukkah lights outside the entrance of homes or set them on a windowsill on the street side of the

Figure 7.4. Hanukkah display in Chicago, Illinois, USA

Turelio/Wikimedia Commons

325

house. There are eight lights (usually candles), and each night a successive light is lit, and a short prayer is said. The candlesticks are usually placed in a **menorah** (Hebrew, "candelabrum"), which is a symbol of Jewish identity. According to Jewish scriptures, the menorah was a significant furnishing in the temple in Jerusalem and the tabernacle in the wilderness.

> You shall make a lampstand of pure gold. The base and the shaft of the lampstand shall be made of hammered work; its cups, its calyxes, and its petals shall be of one piece with it; and there shall be six branches going out of its sides, three branches of the lampstand out of one side of it and three branches of the lampstand out of the other side of it; three cups shaped like almond blossoms, each with calyx and petals, on one branch, and three cups shaped like almond blossoms, each with calyx and petals, on the other branch—so for the six branches going out of the lampstand. On the lampstand itself there shall be four cups shaped like almond blossoms, each with its calyxes and petals. There shall be a calyx of one piece with it under the first pair of branches, a calyx of one piece with it under the next pair of branches, and a calyx of one piece with it under the last pair of branches—so for the six branches that go out of the lampstand. Their calyxes and their branches shall be of one piece with it, the whole of it one hammered piece of pure gold.
>
> Exodus 25:31–36

In regions where Christmas is celebrated, Hanukkah has become a Jewish equivalent, with gift exchanges on each night of the lighting ceremony. During Hanukkah, it is common for children to spin the **dreidel** (a four-sided spinning top) and play other games. Hanukkah is a great time of celebration, since it recalls God's saving acts during Jewish history.

Purim

Continuing with the Jewish year, the next festival is **Purim** (Hebrew, "lots"), a feast commemorating the deliverance of the Jews from the wicked Haman by Mordecai and Esther, recorded in the biblical book of Esther. Esther is read in the synagogue in the evening and during the day, and members of the congregation stomp their feet and make noise with a **Purim** *gragger* (noisemaker) in disapproval whenever the name of Haman is mentioned. Purim (i.e., "lots") is a reference to when Haman cast lots to decide the day on which to exterminate the Jews.

Passover

Following Purim is one of the most important Jewish festivals, **Passover**, which commemorates the events of the Israelites' exodus from slavery in

Egypt. Also known as the "Festival of Unleavened Bread," Passover celebrates God's mercy when God "passed over" the houses of the Hebrews during the tenth plague of Egypt (Exod. 12), sparing them when every other first-born in Egypt was killed as a sign of God's presence with the Hebrews and judgment on Egypt. Crucial to Jewish festival life is the remembrance of God's provision, blessings, and protection.

Figure 7.5. Passover Seder aboard the *USS Nimitz* in the Arabian Gulf

Tradition notes that since they had to flee quickly, the Hebrews had no time to wait for their bread to rise; thus, **matzo** (unleavened bread) is a significant symbol of Passover. A **Passover seder** (Hebrew, "order") meal, consisting of matzo, *maror* (bitter herb), *charoset* (mixture of apples, cinnamon, nuts, and wine), *beitzah* (roasted egg), *karpas* (parsley or celery), *zeroah* (roasted lamb shank-bone), and wine, is served to remind Jews of God's faithfulness to deliver them from subjugation.

Religious or liturgical calendars are immensely important ways to celebrate and remember the crucial events of a religious tradition. Most of the world's religions follow a religious calendar, whether based on a solar model (e.g., Christianity) or lunar model (e.g., Islam). And within each religion there is often significant difference regarding which dates, events, and persons are included.

Within Christianity, some churches celebrate only a few Christian events, such as the birth of Christ (Christmas) and his resurrection (Easter), while other church calendars are filled with daily events, fast and feast days, and personages to be remembered and celebrated. Christians follow the Julian calendar, which was reformed by Pope Gregory XIII in 1582. Specific dates of the Christian liturgical calendar vary according to Christian tradition, such as Roman Catholic, Anglican, and a host of Eastern Orthodox traditions, with each date including theological and scriptural emphases.

Following the church calendar can be quite meaningful to Christians, for the dates serve to remind them of the fundamentals of their faith, which have encouraged, uplifted, and guided Christians throughout the centuries. Christians worldwide find enormous hope through the remembrance of Christ's birth, death, and resurrection, as well as the saints who have gone before them.

Christian Reflections

> You shall tell your child on that day, "It is because of that which the LORD did for me when I came forth out of Egypt."
>
> Exodus 13:8

During Passover no leaven can be in the home. The Passover is such a major festival that even secular Jews tend to celebrate it.

The next festival is Pentecost, which is a one-day celebration of Moses receiving the Ten Commandments on Mount Sinai. Known as **Shavuot** (Hebrew, "weeks"), Pentecost is a time when congregations read the biblical book of Ruth and the Ten Commandments, and many Jews stay up the entire night reading the Torah. About five weeks after Pentecost, there is a three-week period of remembering and mourning the destruction of the first (sixth century BCE) and second temples (first century CE) in Jerusalem. This time of intense mourning begins with the Shiva Asar Be-Tammuz fast in the daytime and ends with the Tisha Be-Av twenty-five-hour fast. During this period, weddings are prohibited. Around September, the Jewish ritual year ends with the month of Elul, the twelfth month of the lunar calendar, when Jews throughout the month prepare for the New Year by repenting and being mindful of the coming Day of Judgment (Rosh Hashanah) and Day of Atonement (Yom Kippur).

Shabbat

The other major festival that occurs weekly is the **Sabbath (Shabbat)**, observed on the seventh day of the week, when Jews abstain from work, following the biblical account of God working for six days to create the world, then resting on the seventh day. According to the biblical narrative, God blessed the seventh day, making it holy:

> Thus the heavens and the earth were finished, and all their multitude. And on the seventh day God finished the work that he had done, and he rested on the seventh day from all the work that he had done. So God blessed the seventh day and hallowed it, because on it God rested from all the work that he had done in creation.
>
> Genesis 2:1–3

The Sabbath begins each Friday evening at sunset and ends at nightfall on Saturday. Since God rested on the seventh day, Jews are to rest on that day as well. Throughout the Hebrew Bible, the Sabbath is recognized as a holy day on which work is not permitted (e.g., Exod. 20:8–11; Deut. 5:14–16; Ezek. 20:12; Neh. 10:31–32).

Along with abstaining from work, Jews are to attend the synagogue for prayers and reading from the Pentateuch. The Sabbath's paramount importance in the life of the Jewish community is summarized aptly by the saying, "More than the Jews have kept the Sabbath, the Sabbath has kept the Jews."

RITES OF PASSAGE

Jews follow rituals that mark major transitions in their lives, from birth to death, usually referred to as rites of passage. Usually rites of passage are accompanied by a ceremony marking a new status of the individual. Generally a child is considered Jewish if his or her mother is Jewish. The male child is circumcised on the eighth day after his birth, representing his entrance into the covenant relationship. Male converts to Judaism, even if they are adults, are expected to undergo circumcision. A

> *The rabbis emphasized the sacredness of the Sabbath, noting, "If Israel keeps one Sabbath as it should be kept, the Messiah will come. The Sabbath is equal to all other precepts in the Torah."*
>
> Tudor, *Jews of Ethiopia*, 195

Christian Reflections

Christians also celebrate the Sabbath, beginning in the first century when they were first called "Christians" in Antioch (Acts 11:26). Early first-century Christians, most of whom were Jewish followers of the Messiah (Jesus), worshiped in the synagogue and observed the Sabbath. They believed that Christianity was continuous with Judaism, since Jesus was the fulfillment of Jewish messianic expectations as foreshadowed in the Hebrew Bible. After the failed Jewish revolt against Roman authorities in 70 CE, rabbinic Judaism distanced itself from the new religion that recognized Jesus as Messiah. It was at this time that the celebration of the Lord's Supper moved to Saturday evening, then to Sunday morning in the fourth century.

The notion of a "Christian Sabbath" dates back to the twelfth century, but was articulated more forcefully by the early Reformers, such as Martin Luther, John Calvin, and John Knox, who insisted that the Sabbath was a day of rest. With the evangelical revivals of the eighteenth century, which sought a renewal of Christian commitment at a time when the Christian church had lost some vitality and relevance, came greater reinforcement of the Sabbath, or Sabbatarianism, whereby Sunday would be reserved solely for worship and rest. Today, large segments of Christianity worldwide have experienced an erosion of Sabbath observance, which in part has given rise to the Seventh-Day Adventist movement, which asserts that Christ's second coming (i.e., advent) is delayed because of the failure to observe the Sabbath.

Chesdovi/Wikimedia Commons

Figure 7.6. Circumcision ceremony, called Brit Milah, in fulfillment of the covenant of Abraham

girl is considered a minor until she reaches the age of twelve, a boy until he reaches thirteen.

As minors, Jewish boys and girls learn the Jewish rituals, Hebrew, and how to read and translate verses from the Hebrew Bible. When a minor is recognized as an adult, he or she is expected to keep the Jewish practices outlined in the halakhah. When a boy is considered an adult, he goes through a **bar mitzvah** ceremony; at the comparable time, the girl goes through a **bat mitzvah** ceremony. At a bar mitzvah (Hebrew, "son of the commandment") ceremony, the boy attains religious adulthood, and the father ceases to be responsible for the actions of his son. During the bar mitzvah ceremony, the boy is called up in the **synagogue** to read from the Torah scroll and sections from the Prophets. Traditionally, this ritual is followed by a party in which family and friends celebrate the boy's new status as a young man.

Similarly, a girl of about twelve years of age will go through a bat mitzvah (Hebrew, "daughter of the commandment") ceremony, and, while more common among Reform and Reconstructionist Jewish congregations, she follows a Jewish liturgy and her status changes from girl to young woman.

The next major rite of passage is marriage. Although it is expected that a Jew will marry another Jew rather than a gentile, intermarriage between Jews and gentiles occurs frequently. The ceremonies for these unions, however, are not supposed to be performed in the synagogue, and such marriages are often regarded as a disastrous circumstance by religious Jews.

According to Judaism, marriage is instituted by God.

Figure 7.7. Bar mitzvah celebration

> Then the Lord God said, "It is not good that the man should be alone; I will make him a helper as his partner."
>
> Genesis 2:18

A significant motive for marriage is to have children, for Jews believe this to be a biblical commandment, while being single is typically discouraged. It is not uncommon for gentiles to convert to Judaism within the context of marriage to a Jewish partner. The marriage ceremony is performed under a **huppah** (Hebrew, "canopy"), where blessings are recited over glasses of wine and either a rabbi or an expert on halakhah officiates. Although divorce is discouraged, it is permissible, especially if both husband and wife agree to dissolve the marriage.

Figure 7.8. Bar mitzvah Torah

Death is another major rite of passage, and duties and rituals accompany this last transition in the Jewish community. It is customary for Jews to have their own burial grounds, which must be consecrated (i.e., made sacred or set apart), although

Figure 7.9. Orthodox Jewish wedding in Vienna, Austria

nowadays it is not uncommon to find Jewish sections in gentile cemeteries. The burial of the deceased typically takes place immediately. Mourners will often throw a small amount of earth from Israel onto the coffin. Customarily, men are buried wrapped in their Jewish prayer shawl (Hebrew, **tallit**) and a special prayer, called the mourner's **kaddish**, is recited (see sidebar 7.2). This kaddish is recited for thirty days and then at every anniversary of the death.

The mourner's kaddish is a prayer of praise since, according to Jewish tradition, people should give praise for the evil that befalls them even as they give praise for the good. Alongside the influence of the various rites of passage that help to provide meaning, remembrance, and guidance to Jewish life, are the synagogue, home, and family, which play crucial roles in the maintenance of Jewish identity. Together, these three institutions constitute

SIDEBAR 7.2

Mourner's Kaddish

Leader:
   May His great Name grow exalted and sanctified
Congregation:
   Amen
Leader:
   in the world that He created as He willed.
   May He give reign to His kingship in your lifetimes and in your days,
   and the lifetimes of the entire Family of Israel,
   swiftly and soon. Now say:
Mourners and Congregation:
   Amen. May His great Name be blessed
   for ever and ever.
Leader:
   Blessed, praised, glorified, exalted, extolled,
   mighty, upraised, and lauded be the Name of the Holy One
Mourners and Congregation:
   Blessed is He
Leader:
   beyond any blessing and son, praise
   and consolation that are uttered in the world. Now say:
Mourners and Congregation:
   Amen
Leader:
   May there be abundant peace from Heaven
   and life upon us and upon all Israel. Now say:
Mourners and Congregation:
   Amen
Leader:
   He Who makes peace in His heights, may He make peace,
   upon us and upon all Israel. Now say:
Mourners and Congregation:
   Amen

the foci of Judaism in the world and represent the Jewish community and how it functions as both public and private spheres of living.

The Jewish Community

THE SYNAGOGUE

Synagogue means "house of assembly," or sometimes "school," referring more particularly to the assembly and education of the community of Jews. A synagogue is a Jewish meetinghouse of prayer and worship, perhaps dating back to the time of the Babylonian exile (586 BCE). The Babylonian exile began when the northern kingdom of Israel was conquered by Assyria in the eighth century BCE, which led to the deportation of ten northern Hebrew tribes to other parts of the Assyrian Empire. By the sixth century BCE, the kingdom of Judah was part of the Babylonian Empire, and all except the poorest inhabitants in Judah were transported to Babylon (2 Kings 24–25).

Yet Jews continued to worship even while in exile in Babylon in what some scholars have called a "proto-synagogue."

Figure 7.10. Synagogue in Prague, Czech Republic

> You have killed many in this city, and have filled its streets with the slain.
>
> Ezekiel 11:16

The Talmud notes that this "little sanctuary" was in fact the synagogue. The Talmud also mentions 480 synagogues in Jerusalem before the destruction of the temple in 70 CE. With the destruction of the Jerusalem temple, the synagogue became the central focus of Jewish religious life, functioning as a house for assembly prayers, reading of the Pentateuch, instruction in Jewish teachings, and community activities.

It is worthwhile to note that the synagogue used to play a somewhat less significant role compared to

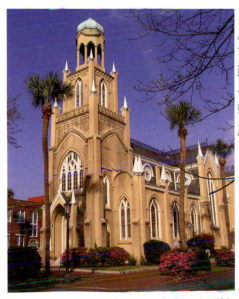

Figure 7.11. Synagogue in Savannah, Georgia, USA

the home for Jewish community building and identity maintenance. However, in the modern period, marked by increased secularization of society and home life, the synagogue plays a more crucial role than in the premodern period.

Architecturally, according to the halakhah, a synagogue should have twelve windows and be oriented toward Jerusalem. Jews face Jerusalem when praying. Inside the synagogue copies of the Torah scrolls are housed in the holy ark (Hebrew, *aron kodesh*), in front of which typically is placed a reader's desk. A **bimah** (Hebrew, "elevated place"), a synagogue platform on which the Torah reading stand is placed, is customarily located in the middle of the building. It is from the bimah that the sermon is preached and the Torah is chanted.

The theological differences between the branches of Judaism are in part reflected in the design and priorities of the architecture of the synagogues in which each group worships. For instance, Orthodox Jewish congregations forbid gossiping, sleeping, or frivolous actions in the synagogue, and separate men and women into different seating areas, whereas Reform synagogues have no special sections dividing genders. Hasidic congregations, which focus on extreme scrupulousness in fulfilling ritual duties, worship in unadorned synagogues. Furthermore, in all Orthodox and Conservative synagogues the male congregants wear either a hat or a skullcap during worship, whereas in Reform synagogues, head coverings are not mandatory for either men or women.

SIDEBAR 7.3

Examples of Prayers Said in the Synagogue

You, O Lord, are the endless power that renews life beyond death; You are the greatness that saves. You care for the living with love. You renew life beyond death with unending mercy. You support the falling and heal the sick. You free prisoners, and keep faith with those who sleep in the dust. Who can perform such mighty deeds, and who can compare with You—a king who brings death and life, and renews salvation. You are faithful to renew life beyond death. Blessed are You Lord, who renews life beyond death. (*Forms of Prayer*, 1977)

It is our duty to praise the Lord of all, to recognize the greatness of the creator of first things, who has chosen us from all people by giving us his Torah. Therefore we bow low and submit, and give thanks before the King above the kings of kings, the Holy One, blessed be He. He extends the limits of space and makes the world firm. His glory extends through the universe beyond, and the presence of his strength into farthest space. He is our God; no other exists. Our king is truth; the rest is nothing. It is written in His Torah: "Realize this today and take it to heart—it is the Lord who is God in the heavens above and on the earth beneath; no other exists." (*Forms of Prayer*, 1977)

Selections taken from translation in De Lange, *Introduction to Judaism*, 133–34

In terms of synagogue polity, each synagogue is autonomous, and there may be many in a city, yet several can be grouped together under a single organizational structure, such as the United Synagogue of America. Synagogues are administered by a council and honorary officers, such as chairperson, secretary, and treasurer.

The first generation of Christians worshiped in synagogues and followed many of the rituals and practices that were part of Jewish tradition. The word for "church" (Greek, *ekklesia*) occurs only twice in the Gospels (Matt. 16:18; 18:17) and infrequently outside the Gospels (e.g., 1 Cor. 16:1; Col. 1:18). "Church" refers to an institution of Christianity (e.g., the church building), the universal body of Christ (e.g., Christians worldwide and through time), and to particular denominations (e.g., the Methodist Church, the Roman Catholic Church).

Orthodox Christians believe the church is constituted by "apostolic succession"—the affirmation that the authority of the ordained ministry is protected by the continuous transmission dating back to the apostles. Catholic Christians affirm apostolic succession and also emphasize the church as "one, holy, catholic, and apostolic." Broadly, Protestant Christians recognize the church as either a single, visible body, but divided because of sin, or an invisible body whose membership is dependent on one's personal faith commitment to God through Jesus Christ. In a dramatic biblical episode where Jesus angrily turns over the tables of vendors who have set up shop in the synagogue, we overhear Jesus's own understanding of the purpose of the gathering of God-fearers:

> Then they came to Jerusalem. And he entered the temple and began to drive out those who were selling and those who were buying in the temple, and he overturned the tables of the money changers and the seats of those who sold doves; and he would not allow anyone to carry anything through the temple. He was teaching and saying, "Is it not written, 'My house shall be called a house of prayer for all the nations'? But you have made it a den of robbers."
>
> And when the chief priests and the scribes heard it, they kept looking for a way to kill him; for they were afraid of him, because the whole crowd was spellbound by his teaching. And when evening came, Jesus and his disciples went out of the city. (Mark 11:15–19)

Regardless of the various understandings of the church, which have given rise to many denominations and movements throughout history, the fact that Jesus makes prayer so paramount to the gathering of believers, rather than the exchange of goods and services, gives Christians worldwide insight into the nature of the church. Notice that Jesus was considered a teacher—that is, a rabbi.

A Jewish priest is considered an inherited role based on its lineage from Aaron, the brother of Moses, who in the book of Exodus helped Moses lead the Hebrews out of slavery in Egypt to the promised land. The Jewish priest's duties are to perform the religious ceremonies and prepare the ritual objects, and perhaps most importantly, he should be called up first to read the Torah. Although a priest is not a rabbi, the priest may become a rabbi.

THE RABBI

A **rabbi** (Hebrew, "my master") is a Jewish learned man (or woman, in some congregations) who has been ordained. The term "rabbi" was used around the time of **Hillel**, a Jewish scholar who lived in Rome during the reign of King Herod, to describe interpreters and teachers of the scriptures and oral law, who had no sacramental role. Hillel noted, "What is hateful to thee, do not unto thy fellow man: this is the whole Law; the rest is mere commentary."[2]

> *A rabbi exclaimed, "Whenever the Holy One, blessed be He, comes into a Synagogue and does not find ten persons [a minyan] there, He becomes angry at once. For it is said: Wherefore, when I came, was there no man? When I called was there no answer?"*
> Babylonian Talmud, *Berakhot* 6b, available at http://www .come-and-hear.com /berakoth/berakoth_6.html

Rabbinic Judaism reflected a diversity of interpretations of the written Torah, thus becoming a sort of "second" Torah (oral Torah), which produced halakhah (Jewish law and practice). In the modern period the role of the rabbi varies according to the Jewish community, with Reform rabbis functioning similarly to Christian pastors and Orthodox rabbis as teachers and legal consultants. A **minyan** refers to a quorum, or number of persons, necessary to make up a congregation for a public Jewish service. The Talmud notes that if ten men pray together, the divine Presence is with them. For instance, a minimum of ten adult male Jews is required for the recitation of the kaddish prayer. In fact, in the past a minyan was so crucial that there was a "minyan man," typically a poor Jewish man who was paid to attend worship in order to increase the numbers. It is important not to overlook the significance of a minyan, for it distinguishes between public and private worship.

THE FAMILY AND HOME

The Jewish home is a crucial site for practicing Jewish faith within relationships of the family. Within this private domain, observant Jews live out the ideals of the faith. Like any family, Jewish families reflect the intellectual and cultural influences within their broader contexts. Karl Marx (1818–83), Jewish by birth, challenged what he claimed was Judaism's encouragement of bourgeois society—the oppressive society of influential, affluent individuals that he felt needed to be overthrown. Marxism attacked the family since Marx believed that this social unit perpetuated the kinds of religious, social, and economic values that blocked the revolutionary liberation of the masses from their economic subjugation. Nevertheless, despite the debates about the Jewish family, many faithful Jews still highly value the family and its prominent role in teaching Jewish traditions, celebrating Jewish rituals, and learning the Jewish religion.

The Jewish home is often separated from the outside world by external signs that mark it as a special place. Most conspicuous is the mezuzah (Hebrew, "doorpost"), a parchment scroll with the first two paragraphs of the Shema Yisrael ("Hear, O Israel") on it that is placed in a case attached to the doorposts of Jewish homes. The Bible instructs Jews to write the words of God on the doorposts of their houses (Deut. 4:6–9; 11:13–21), and attaching these handwritten parchments to the right-hand doorpost of every room in the home serves as a reminder of the words of the Torah.

> Bind them as a sign on your hand, fix them as an emblem on your forehead, and write them on the doorposts of your house and on your gates.
>
> Deuteronomy 6:8–9

The verses above are the basis for a traditional Jewish practice of tying leather boxes (phylacteries) containing handwritten scriptures to the forehead and upper arm with leather straps.

Dietary laws are influenced by food taboos (i.e., restrictions); therefore, kitchen arrangements also help define a Jewish home. Separation is a major theme within the kitchen—and strict separation is made between milk and meat as well as between the utensils that come into contact with either milk or meat products. While it is permissible to eat meat and milk, observant Jews cannot partake of these products together. Rather, they need to wait for some time after eating a meat product before partaking of a milk product. "Kosher" refers to food that is ritually pure for consumption.

According to Deuteronomy 14:6, animals that have a cloven hoof and chew the cud (e.g., ox, sheep, and goat) are kosher. Others are considered unclean—such as the pig or the camel—and thus forbidden to eat (Deut. 14:7–8). There are also restrictions on some birds and fish. Food unfit to eat is called *terefah* (Hebrew, "torn flesh"), and it is believed that *terefah* food contaminates other food. Slaughtering animals for food follows ritual customs as well, with a goal of avoiding as much as possible the infliction of pain on the animal.

Friday is the highlight of the week, in part because it anticipates the Sabbath, in keeping with the command, "Remember the sabbath day, and keep it holy" (Exod. 20:8). Jewish families gather for Sabbath and festivals in homes to share meals, typically accompanied by prayers and hymns.

The Holocaust

No event in the modern period has impacted the self-understanding of the Jewish people as much as the **Holocaust** (Greek, "burnt" or "destruction"), the systematic destruction of European Jewry between 1933 and 1945. In a broad sense of the term, the Holocaust refers to the systematic extermination by Nazi Germany of approximately twelve million Jews, Catholics, homosexuals, Jehovah's Witnesses, Slavs, Gypsies, and other religious and political minorities of Nazi Germany.

Led by **Adolf Hitler** (1889–1945), the German leader of the Nationalist Socialist German Workers Party (Nazi Party) and chancellor of the German state, Nazi anti-Semitic ideology fueled an ultranationalist German pogrom to eliminate Jews from European society. This genocide of the Jews, by which roughly six million Jews were exterminated ruthlessly in concentration camps in Europe, was committed with the compliance of the German government, leading one scholar to note that the Nazi state had become a "genocidal state."[3]

Figure 7.12. Holocaust clothes

Aldo Ardetti/Wikimedia Commons

> *Love. How did one show it? How could God Himself show truth and love at the same time in a world like this?*
>
> *By dying. The answer stood out for me sharper and chiller than it ever had before that night: the shape of a Cross etched on the history of the world.*
>
> Corrie ten Boom, *The Hiding Place*, 92

While some Jews were saved, some at the hands of courageous German and Dutch citizens, such as **Oskar Schindler** (1908–74) and **Corrie ten Boom** (1892–1983), the horrendous destruction of the Jews has echoed through generations of Jewish people.

Where was God during the Holocaust? Why did God allow this horrendous event to occur? Why did God abandon "God's chosen people"? And where is God now, for those of Jewish faith? These are vitally important questions that resonate with any human community that has experienced genocide or other severe trauma.

Today, given that more than six decades have passed since the Holocaust, relatively few Jewish Holocaust

Jongleur100/Wikimedia Commons

Figure 7.13. Oskar Schindler's enamel factory, where many Jews were saved, Krakow, Poland

survivors remain. Yet Jewish consciousness of the Holocaust remains a vital part of the memories of both Jewish and non-Jewish people worldwide. It is worthwhile to note that within the Jewish community, a distinction is often made between the terms "Holocaust" and "**Shoah**" (Hebrew, "destruction"), since Holocaust carries the meaning of a burnt sacrifice offered at the temple while Shoah means desolation and destruction not for priestly and sacrificial purposes. Jews are conscious of interpreting the Holocaust not as a form of sacrificial burnt offering at the hands of the Nazi regime but as their very desolation.

With this in mind, there are several responses to the Holocaust, ranging from seeing Jewish suffering as a punishment for sin demanded by God to affirming that God is dead and thus absent from historical forces and the human community. It is important to note that genocide has always been a theme in Jewish thinking, from the stories of the Exodus, Esther, and the Passover feast. Yet as Jewish scholar Nicholas De Lange notes,

> *I knew that people who worked for me [were to be executed]. . . . When you know people, you have to behave towards them like human beings.*
>
> Oskar Schindler, quoted in Walters and Jarrell, *Blessed Peacemakers*, 118

Where was God during the Holocaust? Where were the churches? Although many non-Jews did help save the lives of Jews during the Nazi regime, in general the Christian churches, including the Vatican, did little to prevent the Nazi pogroms. In a post-Holocaust world, where human beings have witnessed the use of modern technology combined with anti-Semitic ideology to destroy massive numbers of people like never before, we are confronted with the problem of evil, even in a period in which we claim to be enlightened moderns.

What role should the Christian church have played during the Holocaust? What theological, social, or political forces disabled the church from acting? And how might the church today respond differently to current human atrocities brought about by structures and systems that perpetuate evil? Conversely, what resources exist within the church that can serve as the guide for social and political engagement so that its worldwide witness balances word and deed? It is worthwhile to note that the Holocaust is not just a Jewish problem. Rather, it is an event that compels us to confront our understanding of the nature of the church in society, with the recognition that the church's role in society is in part to confront oppressive principalities and powers (Eph. 6:12).

Always it is tempered by the belief that God intervenes to protect and save his people. It is certainly possible to argue that this happened in the Nazi Holocaust, that though six million were killed twice as many were saved; but that is not an argument that is usually advanced, and the universal attitude to the Holocaust is that it was an actual destruction, not a threat of destruction that was averted.[4]

Sadly, there has been a recent upsurge of **anti-Semitism** in Europe and elsewhere, making the importance of remembering the historicity of the Holocaust even more critical.

Modern Movements

Beginning in the early nineteenth century, Jewish communities, which up to that point had been led primarily by rabbis, underwent several reforming movements and experienced some of the greatest changes since the destruction of the second temple in 70 CE. Scholars note that the new ideas manifested themselves at first in liturgical rather than legal or theological reforms. Influenced by pressures from Christian worship, some Jews began to argue that prayers be recited using the vernacular, for the introduction of sermons and music, and for shortening the worship service.[5] Eventually, several modern movements appeared that coalesced into the divisions commonly known as Orthodox Judaism, Reform Judaism, Conservative Judaism, and Reconstructionist Judaism.

Orthodox Judaism

In 1795 a distinction emerged between traditional Judaism, which accepted the written and oral law (Talmud) as divinely inspired, and those who identified themselves with the Reform movement. **Samson Raphael Hirsch** (1808–88), a German rabbi considered to be the founder of modern **Orthodox Judaism**, argued against biblical criticism and advocated faith in the divine inspiration and authority of the Hebrew Bible, the oral law (Talmud), and rabbinic law. Adherents of Orthodox Judaism claim to continue the ancient traditions of premodern rabbinic Judaism, and that God's revealed Torah and its laws are immutable, and their authority or interpretation cannot be challenged by biblical criticism.

Figure 7.14. Ultraorthodox Jews in Brooklyn, New York, USA

One of the major issues separating Orthodox from Reform Jews is whether God acted in changing history or whether God was revealed solely in the eternal covenant given at Mount Sinai (Exod. 19). Reform Jews believe that God does in fact continue to work through an ever-changing history, while Orthodox Jews affirm the unchangeable covenant communicated at Mount Sinai. Orthodox Jews call for submission to the demands of the halakhah as encapsulated in the written and oral law. Today, Orthodox Judaism remains a vocal presence among world Jewry, but it shows signs of disarray in part because of its insistence on a rigid doctrine of revelation that makes it resistant to change and to engaging wider cultures and societies.

Figure 7.15. A man prays at the Western Wall in Jerusalem

Reform Judaism

In the nineteenth century, a set of new ideas initiated by the German rabbis **Samuel Holdheim** (1806–60) and **Abraham Geiger** (1810–74) gave rise to a movement called Reform or Liberal Judaism. As a modern post-Enlightenment interpretation of Judaism, **Reform Judaism** attempted to make Judaism, beginning with its liturgy, more relevant to its context in Europe. For instance, early Reform Judaism introduced choral singing and vernacular prayers into worship.

While it was unclear how far the modernizing movement in Judaism would go to make Judaism resonate with post-Enlightenment Europe, Reform Judaism became one of the most liberal and secular formulations within nineteenth-century Judaism. As it developed in Europe, Reform Judaism sought to eliminate aspects of the law that divided Jews and gentiles, encouraged a commitment to social justice as illuminated by the biblical prophets, and embraced the equality of men and women.

The Talmud voices the convictions of its times, and from that standpoint it is right. I voice the convictions of my time, and from that standpoint, I am right.

Samuel Holdheim, quoted in Baron, *Treasury of Jewish Quotations*, 252; also in Holdheim, *Das Ceremonialgesetz in Messiasreich*, 50

Samuel Holdheim represented the extreme trend in Reform Judaism—for example, holding Sabbath services on Sunday, defending the right of uncircumcised male children to be considered full Jews, and contending that the Talmud must be adaptable to changing times. He had no problem eliminating many of the religious Jewish festivals, and he was known to officiate at marriages between Jews and gentiles.

An equally influential voice of early Reform Judaism was that of Abraham Geiger, who was less radical than Holdheim but nevertheless contributed significantly to the movement. According to those within the Orthodox and Conservative movements, Geiger's ideas remain unorthodox, for he maintained that Judaism should assimilate itself into the national life and be characterized by freedom of inquiry based on one's God-given reason. Geiger believed that the Hebrew Bible and the Talmud reflected an earlier, primitive stage in an ongoing series of revelations that continues throughout human history. When modern sensibilities are incompatible with earlier revelations, it is permissible to reinterpret those revelations. Thus, Geiger was known for his attempt to "dethrone the Talmud" by employing higher-critical methods of studying the Hebrew Bible and the Talmud.

Although Reform Judaism began in Europe, in 1885 some members of the rabbinate announced a reform platform in Pittsburgh that initiated the movement in the United States. The Pittsburgh Platform stated, "We recognize in Judaism a progressive religion, ever striving to be in accord with the postulates of reason. . . . We accept as binding only the moral laws and maintain only such ceremonies as elevate and sanctify our lives, but reject all such as are not adapted to the views and habits of modern civilization."[6]

In 1937 the United States Reform rabbis met at the Central Conference of American Rabbis in Columbus, Ohio, and issued the Columbus Platform (1937). The Columbus Platform declared that

> Judaism is the historical religious experience of the Jewish people. Though growing out of Jewish life, its message is universal, aiming at the union and perfection of mankind under the sovereignty of God. Reform Judaism recognizes the principle of progressive development in religion and consciously applies this principle to spiritual as well as cultural and social life. Judaism welcomes all truth, whether written in the pages of scriptures or deciphered from the records of time. The new discoveries of science, while replacing the older scientific views underlying our sacred literature, do not conflict with the essential spirit of religion as manifested in the consecration of man's will, heart, and mind to the service of God and humanity.[7]

There have been important theological changes within Reform Judaism, especially as Reform rabbis have grappled with making Judaism relevant to ever-changing intellectual, social, and cultural contexts. In 1972 the first woman was ordained by the Reform movement. Today the Reform movement claims to be the largest Jewish religious movement in the United States.

Conservative Judaism

A third major division within Judaism is called **Conservative Judaism** or "traditional" Judaism, which lies between the extremes of Orthodoxy and Reform. Noted for being mostly an American movement, associated with the Jewish Theological Seminary in New York, Conservative Judaism sought to blend pluralism and traditional Judaism, attempting to conserve Jewish tradition rather than reform it. The intellectual roots of Conservative Judaism go back to **Solomon Schechter** (1847–1915), an English rabbi and scholar who was founder and president of the United Synagogue of America, the Jewish Theological Seminary of America (New York), and the American Conservative Jewish movement.

Conservative rabbis influenced by Schechter founded the Jewish Theological Seminary, whose aim was to preserve, in the words of the seminary's articles of incorporation, "the knowledge and practice of historical Judaism as ordained in the Law of Moses, expounded by the prophets and sages in Israel in Biblical and Talmudic writings." Schechter was persuaded that halakhah evolves, rather than being stagnant, in the context of the life of the people. Schechter did not advocate an all-out assimilation of Judaism but rather argued that halakhah should change and develop when faithful Jews agreed by consensus, a process he referred to as "catholic Israel." Several decisions by Conservative Judaism, such as rulings on divorce, the ordination of women, and conversion are rejected by adherents of Orthodox Judaism.

While Conservative Judaism generally accepts Orthodox Judaism's perspective on halakhah, it upholds relevant interpretation and application of halakhah as the most authentic expression of Jewish law and practice. Today, about 30 percent of Jews in the United States belong to Conservative synagogues. Despite the differences between Orthodox, Reform, and Conservative Jews, each of these major divisions within Judaism believes in a single God and the authority of scripture and affirms the synagogue and rabbinate.

Reconstructionist Judaism

An outgrowth of the Conservative movement is a more radical orientation known as **Reconstructionist Judaism**, founded by the Conservative **Rabbi Mordecai M. Kaplan** (1881–1983), a Lithuanian rabbi ordained at the Jewish Theological Seminary of America, who then served as an Orthodox rabbi in New York. Kaplan eventually left his Orthodox congregation and taught at Jewish Theological Seminary.

In 1922 Kaplan broke with the Conservative movement and initiated the Reconstructionist movement, defining Judaism as "the evolving religious civilization," marked by specific beliefs and practices, as well as culture, ethics, language, art, symbols, and history. Contending that Judaism ought to incorporate the ideals of democracy and equality, Kaplan set the Reconstructionists in the middle ground between religious and secular Judaism, abandoning belief in a personal God while placing high value on the embodiment of the ideals of preserving Jewish identity and civilization.

Stating that the halakhah is not binding, Reconstructionists reject revelation and seek instead to base religious practices on their historical status reflecting the corporate identity of the Jews. Basing itself on the experience of the Jewish people, Reconstructionist Judaism recognizes the faith as continually evolving, its actions of seeking justice and morality founded on God's revelation through the Torah and the Talmud. Reconstructionist Judaism was formalized in New York with the founding of the Society for the Advancement of Judaism in 1922. The Reconstructionist conception of the synagogue emphasizes the space as a community center rather than as a place for the performance of religious rituals. Today, both Reform and Reconstructionist movements ordain women as rabbis.

Kabbalah

Alongside these major divisions within modern Judaism, there is the mystical component of the religious tradition that seeks to have direct experience of the divine. Known as **kabbalah** (Hebrew, "received" or "handed down"),

Religions are naturally reforming. Since they are not static, but instead are constantly engaging with social, cultural, and religious contexts, religions need to continually reform themselves in order to make sense of new information, while maintaining their identity through time. There is an inherent conservativeness to religions, in the sense that religionists always look back to past traditions, earliest revelations, and words of the founders to make sense and meaning of their current conditions. And all faithful people are required by their circumstances to negotiate the demands of living in a changing world by using the wisdom of their religious tradition to interpret their current conditions. The wisdom may not change, but it does need to be adapted and made relevant to contemporary questions and ethical dilemmas.

Although in Christianity we often think of the Protestant Reformation, in its various divisions, as the chief example of reform within the Christian tradition, it is important to recognize that Christianity has always been reforming as a result of its engagement in mission. Encountering new philosophies, languages, and lifeways requires that Christians through history make sense of Christianity within changing social and cultural realities. New movements within Christianity were stimulated in part by movements within wider social, cultural, and intellectual movements.

Just like Judaism, Christianity is not a monolithic movement, but rather confronts many of the same dilemmas that Judaism does regarding how to maintain its foundational beliefs and practices in the face of an ever-changing environment. As an indication of the robust life of Christianity, reform is part and parcel of the ongoing nature of Christian life engaged in the world. Christian reformations lead to an articulation of new perspectives that can powerfully refashion Christian faith so that, in the best case, these transformations give rise to a proliferation of Christianities that resonate meaningfully with local cultural ways while remaining unified worldwide by a common faith in Christ and the biblical witness. In the worst case, Christian diversity can lead to a fragmented condition where church divisions lose sight of their overall unity and the local church becomes an end in itself rather than being recognized as a part of one body of Christ on earth.

Jewish mysticism evolved around the time of the second temple (70 CE), but became more formalized during the Middle Ages. Minimizing the legal aspects of Judaism, kabbalah seeks immediate experience of God through contemplation. Kabbalists believe in the presence of secret aspects of the oral law.

The central work of the kabbalists is the **Zohar** (Hebrew, "Book of Radiance"), a collection of several commentaries on the Torah attributed to Simeon ben Yohai (second century CE), written partly in Hebrew and partly in Aramaic. The *Zohar* contends that the universe emerged from a pure, spiritual reality, a divine unity from which come ten active divine powers (*sefiroth*)—for example, love, beauty, intelligence—that are each paired to a color. The *sefiroth*, or ten emanations, are the attributes through which the divine will reveals itself. The ten *sefiroth* are a step-by-step process of understanding the divine will revealed in creation. Many commentaries have been written on the *Zohar*, the most influential being Simeon Labi of Tripoli's *Ketem Paz* (1570). Kabbalists assert that there is a hidden structure of the universe and that the Pentateuch contains coded language that could be interpreted only by those familiar with the code. Deciphering the code enables practitioners to know God's will and to experience the divine directly.

Zionism

A particularly potent issue among Jews and non-Jews is the debate about a Jewish nation-state and the maintenance of Jewish identity. Will Jewish religious or ethnic identity be assimilated into majority cultures or religions? There have been many ways that Jews, as religious and cultural minorities, have sought to maintain their identity, particularly when they lived as minorities. One way that Jews have sought to maintain their identity is to advocate **Zionism**. The term "Zion" refers to Jerusalem. Zionism, then, is a movement that seeks to resettle Jews in what they believe to be their ancestral homeland.

Many times throughout their history, the Jews have been a **diasporic people**, living mostly outside the land of Israel (Palestine). In 586 BCE, the Babylonians destroyed the first temple and expelled Jews from Jerusalem. Then in the first and second centuries, the Romans expelled the Jews from Judea. For centuries, Jews longed to return to Israel, particularly because they experienced anti-Semitism throughout much of Europe. For the most part, Jews in the nineteenth and early twentieth centuries in Europe were not accepted as equals, however much they tried to downplay their Jewish identity. Furthermore, the Holocaust in Germany brought the challenge of Jewish identity to a head. What would happen to the Jewish survivors? What role would memory play in the post-Holocaust period to maintain Jewish identity as a religious and ethnic minority?

Influenced by nationalist movements in central Europe beginning in the late nineteenth century, Jewish thinkers started to advocate Jewish nationalism, emphasizing Jewish ethnicity based on common culture and shared memory. It is important to recognize that Jews in nineteenth-century Europe were experiencing severe prejudice and anti-Semitism. One Jewish response was to encourage Jewish migration into Ottoman Palestine, which was later called Israel. Most of these nationalists would later be known as Zionists.

The most significant Zionist leader was **Theodor Herzl** (1860–1904), known as the founder of Zionism as a political movement. Herzl had experienced anti-Semitism firsthand during the Dreyfus affair in Paris in the 1890s. The Dreyfus affair involved a Jewish captain in the French army who was falsely accused of espionage, and it became a political scandal that divided France. The term "Zion" has many meanings, but what is common to all Zionists is the determination to make the state of Israel the national homeland of the Jews. That is, Zionists link the Jewish people and identity to the land of Israel.

SIDEBAR 7.4

Selection from the Jerusalem Declaration on Christian Zionism

We affirm that all people are created in the Image of God. In turn they are called to honor the dignity of every human being and to respect their inalienable rights.

We affirm that Israelis and Palestinians are capable of living together within peace, justice and security.

We affirm that Palestinians are one people, both Muslim and Christian. We reject all attempts to subvert and fragment their unity.

We call upon all people to reject the narrow world view of Christian Zionism and other ideologies that privilege one people at the expense of others.

We are committed to non-violent resistance as the most effective means to end the illegal occupation in order to attain a just and lasting peace.

With urgency we warn that Christian Zionism and its alliances are justifying colonization, apartheid and empire-building.

God demands that justice be done. No enduring peace, security or reconciliation is possible without the foundation of justice. The demands of justice will not disappear. The struggle for justice must be pursued diligently and persistently but non-violently.

"What does the Lord require of you, to act justly, to love mercy, and to walk humbly with your God." (Micah 6:8)

Available at http://imeu.net/news/article003122.shtml

Palestinians

On May 14, 1948, the Jewish People's Council announced the establishment of the State of Israel, following a vigorous Zionist campaign to create a homeland for the Jewish people. Today, over 40 percent of the world's Jews live in Israel. The current **Israel-Palestine conflict** began in the early twentieth century, and some of its key issues are the borders between Israel and Palestine, mutual recognition of the two groups, security, water rights, and the control of Jerusalem. Both Israelis and Palestinians have been victims and perpetrators of horrendous violence in recent years as Israel has sought to maintain and extend its national borders, while Palestinians have sought a Palestinian Arab state.

Christian Reflections

Christian Zionism is the belief among some Christians that the return of the Jews to the Holy Land and the establishment of the State of Israel (1948) are prerequisites to the second coming of Christ, in accordance with biblical prophecy. Many Christian Zionists continue to believe that the people of Israel remain the chosen people of God and that God literally will gather his chosen people to the land of Israel prior to the second coming.

Some Christians who reject Christian Zionism do so for the following reasons. First, Christian Zionism is not based on sound Christian theology. That is to say, the argument that the State of Israel has a particularly significant role to play in salvation history under the new covenant of Jesus Christ fails to recognize that God has extended his grace and the promise of being heirs to all people who follow Christ and receive his forgiveness, regardless of culture, gender, class, or national citizenship. The new covenant has had a leveling effect on all cultures, ethnicities, and religions.

Second, Christian Zionism is not based on the biblical message. The New Testament teaches that under Christ no geographic region, no language, no culture is given prominence in salvation history. Christ provided a means to become a new community, a new creation whereby exceptionalism—that is, making one people more important than another—is no longer the order of the day.

Third, Christian Zionism tends to subordinate the rights of Muslims to the rights of Jews in the State of Israel. Thus, it may foster fear and hatred of Muslims in the Middle East, leading to forms of dehumanization, exclusion, and marginalization of Muslims at a time when Christians can advocate for peace and justice in the region.

Twenty years after Israel's annexation of the West Bank, East Jerusalem, the Sinai Peninsula, and the Gaza Strip during the **Six-Day War** in 1967, the Palestinians responded with the First **Intifada** (Arabic, "shaking off," "uprising," "resistance") from December 1987 to 1993. An intifada is a popular resistance to oppression. During the First Intifada, Palestinians used primarily nonviolent civil disobedience such as boycotts and general strikes against Israeli businesses as well as graffiti, refusal to pay taxes, erection of barricades, and rock throwing. The Second Intifada, which lasted from September 2000 to 2005, was sparked in part by Israeli Prime Minister Ariel Sharon's visit to the **Temple Mount**, the location of the **Al-Aqsa Mosque**. This site is considered sacred by both Jews and Muslims, since the Temple Mount is believed to have been the location of the holy temple of the ancient Jews as well as the third most holy mosque for Sunni Muslims (Al-Aqsa). Needless to say, the Temple Mount is a powerful symbol and representative of Jewish and Muslim identities. Palestinian frustration with Ariel Sharon's Temple Mount visit combined with the failure of Israel to deliver a Palestinian state resulted in what is often called the Al-Aqsa Intifada, leading to years of violence that left hundreds of Israelis and Palestinians dead or imprisoned.

Messianic Jews

Another modern Jewish movement is that of the **Messianic Jews**. Highly controversial because they combine many Jewish practices with belief that **Yeshua** (Jesus's Hebrew name) is the Messiah, Messianic Jews in many respects bridge traditional Judaism and Christianity. They do not deny their Jewish identity and, in fact, claim they are the most Jewish of the Jews. This assertion is based on their recognition that Jesus himself was thoroughly Jewish. Yeshua was a descendent of Abraham and King David. He was raised in a Jewish home and went to the synagogue. And he followed Torah. Messianic Jews believe that the Sinai Covenant, which forms the basis of much rabbinic Judaism, is broken since no religious ritual, no temple, no sacrifice can bring people near to God without God providing the sacrifice. So Messianic Jews accept the new covenant established by Yeshua's death and resurrection.

Many Messianic Jews would say that they are not different from Christians. In fact, they contend that their origins begin during the time of Yeshua himself, when some Jews did recognize him as the Messiah. Messianic Jews see themselves in continuity with the promises given to Abraham that through him all the nations of the earth would be blessed (see Gen. 12:1–3). They feel the urgency to proclaim the good news to fellow Jews and gentiles. Through their mission work, Messianic Jews have seen many people become followers of Yeshua (Jesus). Like Paul of the New Testament, Messianic Jews suggest not that they have converted out of their Jewish faith, but rather that Yeshua is the fulfillment of their own traditions anticipated in the Hebrew Bible and the Jewish writings. Therefore, Messianic Jews see a continuity between Yeshua and their own unfolding story.

Timeline

922 BCE	Kingdom of Israel divided between north and south
722 BCE	Assyrian invasion of northern kingdom
587 BCE	Babylonian invasion of southern kingdom
200–100 BCE	Tanakh canonized
164 BCE	Judas Maccabee controls Jews
63 BCE	Judea becomes a Roman province
66–70 CE	Jewish revolt; destruction of Jewish temple and fall of Jerusalem
132–35	Revolt led by Simeon Bar Kokhba; mass dispersion of Jews (diaspora)
200	Mishnah compiled
450–600	Jerusalem and Babylonian Talmuds compiled
900–1090	Golden age of Jewish culture in Spain
1135–1204	Life of Maimonides, the leading rabbi of Sephardic Judaism (Jews from Iberian Peninsula)
1492	Jews expelled from Spain
1700–1760	Life of Ba'al Shem Tov, founder of Hasidic Judaism
1820–60	Development of Orthodox Judaism and Reform Judaism
1897	Theodor Herzl argues for the creation of an independent Jewish state in Palestine
1915	Yeshiva College and its Rabbi Isaac Elchanan Rabbinical Seminary established in New York City
1938–45	Nazi Holocaust
1947	The United Nations approves creation of a Jewish state and an Arab state in the British mandate of Palestine
1948	State of Israel becomes an independent Jewish state hours before the British Mandate is due to expire
1968	Rabbi Mordechai Kaplan creates separate Reconstructionist Judaism movement by establishing Reconstructionist Rabbinical College in Philadelphia
1983	American Reform Jews accept patrilineal descent, creating a new definition of who is a Jew

| 2000 | Senator Joseph Lieberman becomes first Jewish American to be nominated for national office (vice president of the United States) |
| 2005 | Government of Israel recognizes the Bnei Menashe, a people of northeastern India who were previously Christian, as one of the Ten Lost Tribes of Israel, enabling thousands of people to immigrate to Israel |

Key Terms

Aggadic midrashim
Al-Aqsa Mosque
anti-Semitism
Ashkenazic Jews
Babylonian Talmud
bar mitzvah
bat mitzvah
beitzah
bimah
Caro, Rabbi Joseph
charoset
Christian Zionism
Conservative Judaism
covenant
diasporic people
dreidel
Geiger, Abraham
Gemara
halakhah
halakhic midrashim
Hanukkah
Herzl, Theodor
Hillel
Hirsch, Samson Raphael
Hitler, Adolf
Holdheim, Samuel
Holocaust
homoiousios
homoousios
huppah
intifada
Israel-Palestine conflict

Isserles, Rabbi Moses
Jerusalem Talmud
kabbalah
kaddish
Kaplan, Rabbi Mordecai M.
karpas
Ketuvim
Kotel
mahzor
Maimonides, Moses
maror
matzo
menorah
Messiah
Messianic Jews
midrash
minyan
Mishnah
Nevi'im
Orthodox Judaism
Passover
Passover seder
Purim
Purim *gragger*
rabbi
Rashi
Reconstructionist Judaism
Reform Judaism
Rosh Hashanah
Sabbath

Schechter, Solomon
Schindler, Oskar
sefiroth
Sephardic Jews
Shabbat
Shavuot
Shema Yisrael
Shoah
shofar
siddur
Six-Day War
Sukkoth
synagogue
tallit
Talmud
Tanakh
Temple Mount
ten Boom, Corrie
terefah
Torah
Tzom Gedaliah
Wailing Wall
Western Wall
Yahweh
Yeshua
Yiddish
Yom Kippur
zeroah
Zionism
Zohar

Further Reading

Ariel, David S. *What Do Jews Believe? The Spiritual Foundations of Judaism*. New York: Schocken Books, 1995.

Baron, Joseph L., ed. *A Treasury of Jewish Quotations*. Northvale, NJ: Jason Aronson, Inc., 1999.

Cohn-Sherbok, Dan. *Judaism: History, Belief and Practice*. Philadelphia: Psychology Press, 2003.

De Lange, Nicholas. *An Introduction to Judaism*. New York: Cambridge University Press, 2000.

———. *Judaism*. New York: Oxford University Press, 2003.

Deutsch, Yaacov. *Judaism in Christian Eyes: Ethnographic Descriptions of Jews and Judaism in Early Modern Europe*. New York: Oxford University Press, 2012.

Halbertal, Moshe. *People of the Book: Canon, Meaning, and Authority*. Cambridge, MA: Cambridge University Press, 1997.

Heschel, A. J. *The Sabbath*. New York: HarperCollins, 1979.

Neusner, Jacob. *Do Jews, Christians, and Muslims Worship the Same God?* Nashville: Abingdon Press, 2012.

Schoen, Robert. *What I Wish My Christian Friends Knew about Judaism*. Chicago: Loyola Press, 2004.

Tudor, Parfitt. *The Jews of Ethiopia: The Birth of an Elite*. London, UK: Routledge Press, 2005.

eight

Christianity

Contemporary Snapshot

The Rwandans have a mission to save North America. The Most Reverend Emmanuel Mbona Kolini is archbishop of the Province of the Anglican Church of Rwanda and bishop of Kigali, Rwanda. He is also the leader of the Anglican Mission in the Americas (AM), established in 2000 in Pawley's Island, South Carolina, as a missionary outreach of the Anglican Church of Rwanda to the United States and Canada in response to what the Anglican Church of Rwanda believed was the theological liberalism of the Episcopal Church in the United States and the Anglican Church of Canada regarding the Episcopal Church's election and ordination of an openly gay, noncelibate bishop in the United States. Focusing its work not on African or Asian nations but rather on planting churches throughout North America, the Anglican Church of Rwanda reports on average one new congregation every three weeks in the United States and Canada. Its goal is to reach for **Christ** the 130 million "unchurched" in the United States and 20 million in Canada.

The Rwandans are not the only ones succeeding in converting North America. There is a 550-acre compound in Texas that serves as continental headquarters of the Redeemed Christian Church of God, which started in a Nigerian shantytown and now has millions of converts in Nigeria and

Ferdinand Reus/Wikimedia Commons

Figure 8.1. Christian baptism in Benin, Africa

mission representatives in more than one hundred nations. While Pastor Daniel Ajayi-Adeniran's home office is in a storefront church in the Bronx, where he orchestrates the North American expansion of his Nigerian Christian movement, the church he leads extends worldwide by being empowered by the Holy Spirit to invite all people, regardless of ethnicity, gender, or education, to the saving knowledge of Jesus Christ.

The United States, which remains the largest mission-sending country in the world, has been receiving missionaries on its own soil from Africa, Asia, Latin America, and Oceania. There is a revolution going on in Christianity. It is a movement that started with twelve followers of Jesus, a first-century **Jew** from Palestine, to become the world's largest religion. A faith that for years was an export tradition of mostly white missionaries from Europe and America to Africa, Asia, South and Central America, and Oceania, is now gaining its strength from the peoples of the global southern world, who are fundamentally changing the face of Christianity around the world.[1]

Origins and Concepts

The Christian Story

The Christian story begins with God's creation of the cosmos, filling the earth with flora and fauna and being pleased with his creation. Life began, the Bible says, in the Garden of Eden, where Adam and Eve lived and enjoyed a relationship with God, with few limitations from God except that they were not to eat from the tree of the knowledge of good and evil. Eventually, Adam and Eve disobeyed God by eating fruit from the tree, an event Christians call "the **fall**," the act of disobedience of Adam and Eve that resulted in the condition of pain, suffering, and death in the entirety of creation (Gen. 2–3).

The fall broke the harmonious relationship between God and human beings, but its effects also impacted the created order. Everything fell—our minds, bodies, souls, and everything in the natural realm. And all need redemption—that is, healing and restoration—in order to be complete again. **Sin**, then, is "missing the mark" of what God intended; it is related to disbelief (John 9:41) and is anything that separates human beings from God (Rom. 3:23). Therefore, sin separates human beings from a covenantal relationship with God. As a result of the fall, sin not only is an "action" (e.g., disbelief, disobedience) but also an inheritance that all human beings have received because of Adam and Eve's disobedience.

> The person who sins shall die. A child shall not suffer for the iniquity of a parent, nor a parent suffer for the iniquity of a child; the righteousness of the righteous shall be his own, and the wickedness of the wicked shall be his own.
>
> Ezekiel 18:20

To be human is to be a sinner. Sin, then, is at once subjective, exemplified by human decisions to do and think "bad actions," and objective, inherited from the original disobedience of humanity against God. Thus, the "original sin" committed by Adam and Eve is inherited by all human beings. Christians assert that no matter how hard one tries to perfect oneself, by doing all the "right things," no amount of effort can make restitution for the objective sin that is a fundamental part of our human nature. Hence, we need a savior who can do the work of redemption on our behalf. But since the offense against God is so great, no human being can pay the price. And only a human can pay for it, since human beings disobeyed God. Christians recognize that the God-man, Jesus Christ, is necessary to restore the **covenantal** relationship between God and human beings. Jesus Christ (c. 1–33 CE) was the "good news" (**gospel**), the glad tidings of God's redemption of creation through

While the majority of Christians worldwide, Catholic and Protestant, affirm the inherited nature of sin—that is, that human beings inherited the sin of Adam and Eve, thus marking their human condition—Eastern Orthodox Christianity rejects the idea that the guilt of original sin is passed down generationally. Based in part on its understanding of Ezekiel 18:20, Eastern Orthodoxy teaches that human beings are born with a tendency to sin because of their fallen condition. Therefore, Adam and Eve's sin is seen as a prototype of all human sin; each human being bears the responsibility for his or her own sin.

Christian Reflections

PawelS/Wikimedia Commons

Figure 8.2. Gdansk Jesus and apostles (Gdansk, Poland)

his substitutionary offering for the broken relationship between God and creation due to human disobedience.

The story of Christianity, then, is a narrative of personal and communal transformation into a restored relationship with God that reaches across cultures and times, beginning with Jesus's own disciples.

Jesus gathered a band of a dozen ordinary people in first-century Palestine, starting a movement that has expanded to become the largest religion in the world, with more than two billion adherents today. Christianity emerged from a dynamic first-century Greco-Roman religious and social setting marked by a variety of cultural, religious, and philosophical perspectives. The field was rife with rival authorities, including Romans, Greeks, and Jews. The theme of continuity and discontinuity was key—just how would Christianity be similar to the surrounding cultures, and how would it be dissimilar? How would early Christians balance acceptance of local culture while at the same time defining their own religion apart from local cultures and philosophies? Christianity was influenced deeply by the Jewish and Greco-Roman environment out of which it materialized. Also a part of the first-century Roman Empire were the religions of the ancient Near East, a broad category of religions that were mostly polytheistic, focusing generally on magic, purification rituals, sacrifice, and divination.

> *In speaking of "the gospel," I am, of course, referring to the announcement that in the series of events that have their center in the life, ministry, death, and resurrection of Jesus Christ something has happened that alters the total human situation and must therefore call into question every human culture.*
>
> Newbigin, *Foolishness to the Greeks*, 3

Jewish and Greco-Roman Influences

Jewish Influences

Christianity began with the birth of Jesus of Nazareth in the Roman Empire. He was born into a Jewish family, circumcised according to Jewish law, and raised and educated in a Jewish culture. Jesus was thoroughly

Jewish, worshiping at the temple and the synagogue, and choosing all his disciples from among his fellow Jews. Jesus was born into a Jewish group that longed for the end of Roman rule.

First-century Judaism was distinct from the Near Eastern religions that surrounded it. First, the religion of Israel affirmed "ethical monotheism," which was the belief in one God (**monotheism**). The Jews of the ancient Near East did not deny the existence of other deities, but they worshiped the one true God, known as **YHWH** (Yahweh). God provided a moral framework for their lives, which stood in stark contrast to the religious life of the Romans and Greeks, who worshiped the Roman emperor and Greek gods. Jews worshiped God alone. YHWH communicates through ethical principles rather than through doctrine alone, since the worship of YHWH is based on practice rather than on philosophical argument. God directly revealed to the Jews how to act, giving them knowledge of right and wrong.

Second, YHWH created new things, unlike the Near Eastern gods, which were believed to simply perpetuate a cycle of life, such as the agricultural round of planting and yielding. Jews believed that YHWH played an active role in history, directing and guiding his people.

Third, the religion of Israel offered apocalyptic hope—that is, an expectation that a Messiah would appear in the future to bring peace and justice. The **Messiah** (Hebrew, "anointed one" or Christ) would bring justice to the Jews and a new social order based on the kingdom of God. It is significant, then, that the first words of Jesus Christ recorded in the Gospel of Mark

Map 8.1. Roman provinces, first century CE

Although Christianity began as a movement of Jews for Jews, its greatest growth came not among Jews, but among gentiles. Because Christians claimed to be the rightful inheritors of the tradition of ancient Israel and believed on the basis of the Hebrew prophets that Jesus of Nazareth was the Messiah (Christ), conflict with Jews who did not become Christian—the majority of Jews—was inevitable. As the new movement constituted itself and established new practices, such as baptism in place of circumcision, the Christian communities were marked off as distinct from the synagogue.

Wilken, *First Thousand Years,* 125

were "The time is fulfilled, and the kingdom of God has come near; repent, and believe in the good news" (Mark 1:15), where Jesus identifies himself as the bearer of the kingdom of God, which many Jews eventually would reject.

Greco-Roman Influences

Greco-Roman influences also deeply impacted early Christianity and, some would say, left an indelible mark on Christianity as it spread across the globe. Alexander the Great (356–323 BCE) had unified a massive territory, after his father, King Philip of Macedonia, defeated several small Greek cities, thus uniting numerous people, cultures, and lands. Alexander had been tutored by the Greek philosopher Aristotle, and he promoted Greek culture and philosophy throughout the lands he conquered, his brilliance in part being that he created a fairly unified common culture and language in what would become the Roman Empire. "**Hellenism**," a term that refers to the influence of Greek culture and philosophy outside Greece, dominated the Roman Empire before and during the life of Jesus. Jesus, in fact, was born at the time of the so-called **Pax Romana** ("Roman Peace," 27 BCE–180 CE), when Greek and Roman culture and religion, along with administrative power, spread throughout the empire.

Particular factors helped immensely to fuel Greco-Roman expansion. In terms of government, Rome became an empire ruled by an emperor, with full-time administrators who carried out his policies, and a common law that was established to govern the entire empire. Massive Roman aqueducts carried water from the mountains directly to Roman cities, and expansive Roman roads unified the region. And language was key, as the Roman alphabet spread widely and became the basis for the alphabets used in Western languages (such as French, Italian, Spanish, and English). At the time of Jesus's birth, the Romans, with their strong military, controlled much of the Mediterranean world, borrowing many aspects of Greek culture and philosophy to unify their empire. The fusion of Greek and Roman culture is referred to as "Greco-Roman."

Hellenistic religions prevailed in the Greco-Roman world, and though they were quite diverse, they did share some common features. Hellenistic religions were private, with certain religious practices connected to the home. Worship in these private religions focused on deities expected to protect the family from harm and help with economic needs. Private Hellenistic religions employed astrology, the belief that stars determined the fates of individuals. According to the Hellenistic religions, practicing astrology helped one discover one's fate. Shrines memorializing heroes served as places where people could ask for success in relationships or business or for physical healing. Beyond the private religions, there were state cults, which served the interests of the state. Included in Hellenistic state cults was imperial worship—for instance, accepting the divinity of Caesar, because the emperor was the most powerful person alive and he controlled the destinies of his people. Consequently, throughout the Roman Empire, people offered sacrifices to Caesar, a practice to which the Jews strongly objected since it pitted their commitment to YHWH against loyalty to the empire.

Finally, **mystery religions** were part of the broad category of Hellenistic religions. Mystery religions were the most popular form of Hellenistic religion and are perhaps better seen not as a single tradition but as a set of religious perspectives and practices. The details of the mystery religions are still not entirely known, but most of them shared a few similar emphases. First, there were secret initiations, where *mystery* was a central theme—for example, a secret that devotees were pledged to keep, such as a myth underpinning ritualistic practices of the tradition. These secret initiations took many forms such as sharing a meal with a deity.

> I am now rejoicing in my sufferings for your sake, and in my flesh I am completing what is lacking in Christ's afflictions for the sake of his body, that is, the church. I became its servant according to God's commission that was given to me for you, to make the word of God fully known, the mystery that has been hidden throughout the ages and generations but has now been revealed to his saints. To them God chose to make known how great among the Gentiles are the riches of the glory of this mystery, which is Christ in you, the hope of glory.
>
> Colossians 1:24–27

Second, mystery cults focused on the worship of "saviors" who could be contemporaries of the devotees. In a process called **apotheosis**, whereby a person becomes divine—exalted to a divine level—to the point where that person is worshiped by others, certain individuals were seen as divine living beings. Some scholars have called these "savior cults." Third, mystery cults promised salvation to their followers. The assurance of salvation and eternal life assuaged personal fears at a time of significant social and cultural change. Finally, and perhaps most interestingly, the mystery cults contained stories of gods who died and rose again, not in a concrete historical sense but rather in a cyclical and vague way. The dying and rising of the "savior" occurred not in actual time and space, not in real history in which you and I live, but in mystical and mythical time.

Jesus in Greco-Roman Context

Jesus was born as a Jew into this dynamic Greco-Roman context. Reaction to him was mixed, with some Jews outright rejecting him and others recognizing him as the Messiah foretold in the Hebrew Scriptures (Old Testament), a fulfillment of Hebrew prophecies.

Who has believed what we have heard?
    And to whom has the arm of the LORD been revealed?
For he grew up before him like a young plant,
    and like a root out of dry ground;
he had no form or majesty that we should look at him,
    nothing in his appearance that we should desire him.
He was despised and rejected by others;
    a man of suffering and acquainted with infirmity;
and as one from whom others hide their faces
    he was despised, and we held him of no account.

Surely he has borne our infirmities
    and carried our diseases;
yet we accounted him stricken,
    struck down by God, and afflicted.
But he was wounded for our transgressions,
    crushed for our iniquities;
upon him was the punishment that made us whole,
    and by his bruises we are healed.
All we like sheep have gone astray;
    we have all turned to our own way,
and the LORD has laid on him
    the iniquity of us all.

He was oppressed, and he was afflicted,
    yet he did not open his mouth;
like a lamb that is led to the slaughter,
    and like a sheep that before its shearers is silent,
    so he did not open his mouth.
By a perversion of justice he was taken away.
    Who could have imagined his future?
For he was cut off from the land of the living,
    stricken for the transgression of my people.
They made his grave with the wicked
    and his tomb with the rich,
although he had done no violence,
    and there was no deceit in his mouth.

Yet it was the will of the LORD to crush him with pain.
When you make his life an offering for sin,
    he shall see his offspring, and shall prolong his days;
through him the will of the LORD shall prosper.
    Out of his anguish he shall see light;

> he shall find satisfaction through his knowledge.
>   The righteous one, my servant, shall make many righteous,
>   and he shall bear their iniquities.
> Therefore I will allot him a portion with the great,
>   and he shall divide the spoil with the strong;
> because he poured out himself to death,
>   and was numbered with the transgressors;
> yet he bore the sin of many,
>   and made intercession for the transgressors.
>
> Isaiah 53

Jesus was recognized by some as the Messiah (John 4:25–26); the Savior (John 3:16–17; 11:25); the Son of God (Matt. 4:3; 14:33; Mark 15:39; Luke 4:3); everlasting (John 8:58); the only way to God, the truth, and the life (John 14:6); the judge of the world (Matt. 24:27–30; 25:31–33; Mark 14:61–62; John 5:22); the forgiver of sins (Luke 5:20–21; 7:48–49); and the one to die for our sins (Matt. 26) and rise from the dead (Luke 18:31–33; John 10:17; 12:32–33). Around the age of thirty, Jesus began his public ministry, gathering twelve male disciples whom he taught and sent out. Women too followed Jesus but were not formally counted among the Twelve. Christian tradition, based in part on the biblical witness, notes that he performed many miracles, and while he was misinterpreted by his own disciples early on as being a Jewish political liberator against the oppression of Roman authorities, Jesus was eventually recognized as the Messiah, the anointed one (Christ), by his disciples and others after his death and resurrection.

Following his resurrection and appearance among the Twelve and other followers, Jesus sent his disciples into the wider world to bear witness to God's kingdom, to make disciples of Jesus, teaching, baptizing, and seeking justice empowered by the Holy Spirit. According to his followers, Jesus was both message and messenger of God's kingdom on earth, and Christians recognize that in Jesus Christ something new happened in the world that fundamentally changed our general orientation to God and one another.

Christians and the Roman Empire

The term "Christian" was probably first used to describe followers of Jesus Christ in Antioch (Acts 11:26), referring to the Jewish messianic sect that followed Jesus. The Bible mentions that early Christians were persecuted for following Jesus, and there were significant tensions over whether the Christian movement was a fulfillment of earlier Judaism and the religion of Israel or an entirely new tradition. In the first century of Christianity (roughly the years 33–100 CE), the followers of Jesus consisted mainly of Jewish believers who recognized him as the Messiah and therefore a continuity of Jewish traditions, the fulfillment of the Hebrew Scriptures. The relationship between Christians and the Roman Empire was quite tenuous, since Christians were frequently blamed for conflicts within the empire. In fact, the first time the term "Christian" is used outside the Bible was when Nero blamed "Christians" for the great fire of Rome in 64 CE. The first three centuries of Christianity were a torturous time as Christians were martyred for a variety of reasons, some of which were outright misunderstandings.

They were called atheists since Christians did not depict God in statue form, whereas the Greeks and Romans had deities for every aspect of living and represented them in various physical forms. Christians worshiped an unseen God, which appeared to be belief in no God at all. Christians also encountered problems with the empire because theirs was an unrecognized religion. Roman law permitted legal (state-recognized) religions but did not permit them to spread outside their land of origin. Christianity was an unrecognized religion that spread quite rapidly throughout the Roman Empire, even though it was an oppressed, minority religion. Furthermore, some viewed Christians as cannibals, eating the body and drinking the blood of their leader—for instance, Jesus broke bread and said, in celebrating what became known as the Lord's Supper, "This is my body broken for you," and some observers believed that babies were being eaten during the service of communion (**Eucharist**). According to an ancient commentator, "They kill a Jewish child, they take his blood, they cook it in bread and they proffer it to them as food. They mix the menstrual blood of a nun who prostitutes herself with their wine, and they give it to them in a chalice to drink."[2]

Christians were seen as incestuous, since they called each other "brothers and sisters," thus establishing a new common fellowship. These new Christian fellowships, which often met in house churches, appeared to threaten the empire and the status quo maintained by it. Christianity gathered people from all walks of life, regardless of their social rank, and even gender was no longer an obstacle to fellowship: "There is no longer Jew or Greek, there is no longer slave or free, there is no longer male and female; for all of you are

> *On July 17, 180 CE, twelve Christians from the small settlements of Scilli near Carthage stood in the chambers of the governor of North Africa in Carthage. Carrying with them the letters of a just man named Paul, they were arraigned for being Christians. That was the only charge leveled against them. They insisted that they had never done any wrong, but being a Christian was enough in a Roman's eyes to condemn them to beheading. They went joyfully to their execution.*
>
> Doran, *Birth of a Worldview*, 9

one in Christ Jesus" (Gal. 3:28). Such challenges to followers of Jesus as the Messiah and the Son of God marked the first three centuries of Christianity.

Defining Moments

Christianity is one of the great missionary world religions, with Buddhism and Islam being the other major missionary traditions. The term "**mission**" refers to sending, and missionary religions assert that they possess universal truth, and that communicators of that truth (sometimes known as "**missionaries**," people sent out) teach and work toward that truth. As a missionary movement, Christianity has found a home in disparate cultures throughout the world with astonishing relevancy to its recipients. One of the most fruitful challenges to understanding Christianity, and the one that reveals one's perspective on the relationship between Christianity and culture, is grasping the way that Christianity has engaged cultures as it has expanded throughout the world.

> Go therefore and make disciples of all nations, baptizing them in the name of the Father and of the Son and of the Holy Spirit, and teaching them to obey everything that I have commanded you. And remember, I am with you always, to the end of the age.
>
> Matthew 28:19–20

Figure 8.3. Christian missionaries, with the highest numbers coming from the United States

> And he said to them, "Go into all the world and proclaim the good news to the whole creation."
>
> **Mark 16:15**

> But you will receive power when the Holy Spirit has come upon you; and you will be my witnesses in Jerusalem, in all Judea and Samaria, and to the ends of the earth.
>
> **Acts 1:8**

Christians by province, 2010

Percent Christian

0 2 5 10 40 60 75 85 90 95 100
☐ = Few or none

1910
Christians by country

Rather than rehearsing the history of Christianity's expansion, it would be more illustrative for our purposes to consider its initial movement from its Jewish background into the gentile community, and then, most significantly, the early church's defining of Christianity, which would impact followers of Christ and the church for the entire history of Christianity.

> *They carry a message of salvation: a new consciousness, a liberation of spirit through a centredness in love and truth; a man believed to be at one with a transcendent Godhead. This is the "good news" which, they believe, is for everyone.*
>
> Burridge, *In the Way*, 4

In order to understand the shape of early Christianity, and concomitantly the emergence of the church, I will discuss three topics: (1) the Bible, Christianity's sacred text; (2) the breakthrough of Christianity out of its Jewish context into the gentile world, which gives us insight into the way that Christianity engages diverse cultures; and (3) the early church councils, which established the parameters of Christian **orthodoxy** (right belief), thus laying the foundation for the common life of faith in the church worldwide.

The Bible: Establishing the Christian Canon

Christians believe that truth is revealed or unveiled by God and that the Bible is a sacred text that helps to encourage, guide, and teach the church. "All scripture is inspired by God and is useful for teaching, for reproof, for correction, and for training in righteousness" (2 Tim. 3:16). Christians recognize that the Bible, consisting of the Old and the New Testaments, was

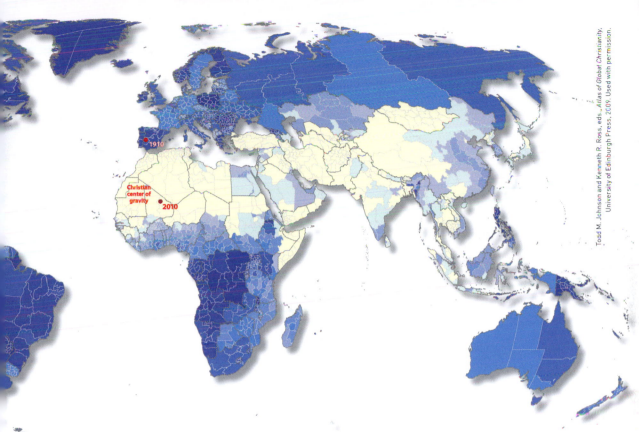

Todd M. Johnson and Kenneth R. Ross, eds., *Atlas of Global Christianity*, University of Edinburgh Press, 2009. Used with permission.

Map 8.2. Christians 1910–2010

revealed by God over centuries. The New Testament was canonized around the fourth century.[3] By the mid-second century, the Old Testament and the Gospels were being read in Christian assemblies in Rome since they were already considered authoritative.

The question of **canonicity**—that is, which documents should be included in the **sacred corpus** (sacred collection)—was a topic of debate for decades within the church, with the Western and the Eastern branches eventually endorsing somewhat different collections of writings. The **canon** (Greek, "rule," "authoritative list," or "scripture") of any religious tradition refers to the list of scriptures accepted as authoritative in the religion. The process of canonization is quite fascinating since it affords us a glimpse into the debates within the early church. What should be included in the canon? How would you decide?

Three major criteria guided the early church in deciding the canonicity of scriptures. First, the writing had to have **apostolic authority**, meaning that it had to be written by an **apostle** (one sent forth) of the gospel or by someone under the authority of an apostle, such as Mark or Luke. Second, the content of the writing had to display theological consistency with other apostolic writings. Such theological consistency was crucial as the only way to distinguish **heresy** (false doctrine) from truth, even if that writing had the name of an important follower of Jesus attached to it, such as the *Gospel of Peter*, *Gospel of Thomas*, *Gospel of Judas*, or *Gospel of Mary*, all of which turned out to be gnostic and therefore heretical based on their theological inconsistency with authentic apostolic writings.

Third, scriptural usage helped determine the canonicity of a book. Was the book used in the prominent Christian churches throughout the Roman Empire? For instance, the Gospel of Matthew was endorsed by Christians in Antioch, the Gospel of John and the Gospel of Luke were important in Asia Minor, and the Gospel of Mark was significant in churches in Rome. Although some books were accepted fairly unanimously, vigorous debates ruled the day as church leaders argued over which books to include on the "list" that we know today as the Bible.

The first list of books that was accepted as canon appeared in a letter written by Bishop Athanasius of Alexandria in 367 CE, though that list of twenty-seven books was not universally accepted. Indeed, contention over the canon continued even into the sixteenth century as Martin Luther (1483–1546) fiercely opposed the inclusion of Hebrews, James, Jude, and Revelation, even calling James "a right strawy epistle,"[4] because it appeared to emphasize works over faith in the Christian life.

Although there is significant overlap, the books of the Bible are listed differently in the biblical canons of **Catholic**, **Orthodox**, and **Protestant** churches, the main branches of Christianity. But even within these major branches—for instance, within the Orthodox traditions (e.g., Greek, Armenian, Coptic, Russian, Serbian, Syrian)—different books are accepted in the biblical canon. The Roman Catholic and Orthodox canons include a variety of books from the **Apocrypha** (e.g., Tobit, Judith, Wisdom, Ecclesiasticus, Baruch, 1 and 2 Maccabees, and Additions to Esther and Daniel), books

SIDEBAR 8.1

Biblical Canon

Protestants, Catholics, and Eastern Orthodox Christians share the same Bible, with some variations. For instance, compared to the Protestant canon (Bible), Eastern Orthodox Christians affirm the books of 1 Esdras, 1–4 Maccabees, Prayer of Manasseh, Baruch, Wisdom, Sirach, and Letter of Jeremiah. Roman Catholics include Tobit (Tobias), Judith, 1 and 2 Maccabees, Wisdom, Sirach (Ecclesiasticus), and Baruch.

with uncertain authorship or writings considered "hidden" because of their contested value to the church. Although the Roman Catholic and Orthodox churches accept different portions of the Apocrypha, Protestant churches reject these as authoritative for Christian life.

Gentile Breakthrough: Demonstrating the Universal Mission of God

Christianity began as a movement within the Jewish tradition. And the Jewish tradition began with God making a covenant (contract) with Abraham, promising that Abraham would be "father of a multitude of nations."

> When Abram was ninety-nine years old, the LORD appeared to Abram, and said to him, "I am God Almighty; walk before me, and be blameless. And I will make my covenant between me and you, and will make you exceedingly numerous." Then Abram fell on his face; and God said to him, "As for me, this is my covenant with you: You shall be the ancestor of a multitude of nations. No longer shall your name be Abram, but your name shall be Abraham; for I have made you the ancestor of a multitude of nations. I will make you exceedingly fruitful; and I will make nations of you, and kings shall come from you. I will establish my covenant before me and you, and your offspring after you throughout their generations, for an everlasting covenant, to be God to you and to your offspring after you."
>
> Genesis 17:1–7

What would mark followers of the Abrahamic covenant as distinct from other Near Eastern peoples was male circumcision, an outward sign of being a follower of YHWH (Yahweh) and adherence to the **Torah** (Law). In fact, circumcision as an identity marker was so crucial that the biblical writers note, "Any uncircumcised male who is not circumcised in the flesh of his foreskin shall be cut off from his people; he has broken my covenant" (Gen. 17:14). And the Torah, which communicated the covenant and law of God, instilled confidence and delight in its followers.

> See, just as the LORD my God has charged me, I now teach you statutes and ordinances for you to observe in the land that you are about to enter and occupy. You must observe them diligently, for this will show your wisdom and discernment to the peoples, who, when they hear all these statutes, will say, "Surely this great nation is a wise and discerning people!" For what other great nation has a god so near to it as the LORD our God is whenever we call to him? And what other great nation has statutes and ordinances as just as this entire law that I am setting before you today?
>
> Deuteronomy 4:5–8

Circumcision and the Torah, then, reflected the unique relationship between God and God's people, a boundary marker setting apart followers of God from other Near Eastern religionists, sometimes referred to as "**heathens**" or "**pagans**." Adding strength to the boundary between the Jews and other religious people of the Near East was the fact that the God of the Jews was a jealous God, and while Near Eastern gods were territorial—that is, related just to particular places—YHWH was not territorial because he was everywhere (omnipresent).

It is striking that the boundary established in the Old Testament setting apart the people of God was not to be permanent, since the covenant of God was to encompass a multitude of nations (peoples, ethnicities). But the Old Testament boundary became a wall restricting their understanding of God's mission in the world and God's covenant that was to encompass all nations, since God had intended to establish a new covenant that would in fact enlarge the notion of covenant people. The New Testament notes that Jesus Christ was the end of the law, which subverted the Old Testament identity markers of circumcision and law.

A New Covenant

According to the New Testament, Jesus Christ was the author of a **new covenant** that reconstituted the people of God by redefining the boundaries that marked off the people of God. Specifically, because of the life, death, and resurrection of Jesus Christ, the older margins ruptured and were redrawn more broadly, whereby the people of God were those with shared faith in Jesus Christ rather than the common factors of ethnicity, circumcision, and adherence to Torah. This new Christ-centered covenant resulted in immediate social and cultural change, with a new sociology of difference that defined the people of God as any faithful follower of Christ regardless of cultural or ethnic background.

Simply put, falsely conceived differences nullify the gospel, because any attempt to create artificial boundaries negates the power of the gospel message to bring unity to those sharing a common faith in Christ. The Old Testament attests to God's preparation of the Jews to communicate the gospel to the entire world, that God loves his people and redeems them. The **Great Commission** texts of the New Testament recount Jesus's last commission to his disciples—statements calling Jesus's followers to communicate in word and deed the good news of God's new covenant (Matt. 28:16–20; Mark 16:14–20; Luke 24:44–47; John 20:19–23). The biblical account narrates the early church council, known as the **Council of Jerusalem** (Acts 15), where tensions broke out among early Christians over the question of which practices new converts should embrace to demonstrate their new faith in Christ.

Gentiles as Fellow Heirs

During the Council of Jerusalem, some leaders argued that **gentile** (non-Jewish) followers of Christ should follow Jewish practices: "Unless you are circumcised according to the custom of Moses, you cannot be saved," they said (Acts 15:1). The conflict over the underlying question, "what must one do to be saved?" was so severe that Paul, Barnabas, and others were appointed to go to Jerusalem to deal with this great debate. It is not ironic that on their way to Jerusalem, they met gentiles who had converted to Christ. Upon their entry to the meeting, Paul and the others were told, referring to the new believers, "It is necessary to circumcise them and to order them to keep the Law of Moses" (Acts 15:5 ESV). But Paul rebuked Peter publicly (Gal. 2), opposing him to his face.

> But when I saw that they were not acting consistently with the truth of the gospel, I said to Cephas before them all, "If you, though a Jew, live like a Gentile and not like a Jew, how can you compel the Gentiles to live like Jews?"
>
> We ourselves are Jews by birth and not Gentile sinners; yet we know that a person is justified not by the works of the law but through faith in Jesus Christ. And we have come to believe in Christ Jesus, so that we might be justified by faith in Christ, and not by doing the works of the law, because no one will be justified by the works of the law.
>
> Galatians 2:14–16

Furthermore, Paul argued, "I do not nullify the grace of God; for if justification comes through the law, then Christ died for nothing" (Gal. 2:21). After the debate, Peter attested,

> "My brothers, you know that in the early days God made a choice among you, that I should be the one through whom the Gentiles would hear the message of the good news and become believers. And God, who knows the human heart, testified to them by giving them the Holy Spirit, just as he did to us; and in cleansing their hearts by faith he has made no distinction between them and us. Now therefore why are you putting God to the test by placing on the neck of the disciples a yoke that neither our ancestors nor we have been able to bear? On the contrary, we believe that we will be saved through the grace of the Lord Jesus, just as they will."
>
> Acts 15:7–11

What some scholars call "**the gentile breakthrough**" demonstrated that the grace of God, exhibited in the Abrahamic covenant, was intended not just for the Jews but for all people, beginning with the gentiles. The breakthrough of the gospel into the gentile community demonstrated that Christianity was eminently flexible, with a final destination that lay not with a particular ethnic group but with all peoples scattered throughout the world. Consequently, the breakthrough of cultural, ethnic, and religious boundaries separating Jews and gentiles, and that in effect opened the door for gentile inclusion in the history of salvation, demonstrated the inherent plurality of Christianity, whereby all people with their particularities are invited as full participants in the story of God's redemption of the world (Eph. 2; Rev. 7; 21). Yet as Christianity expanded out of its location of origin in Palestine/Israel into the eastern Mediterranean, where Christians encountered robust Greek culture and philosophy, the parameters of Christian orthodoxy would have to be established.

Early Church Councils: Setting the Parameters of Orthodoxy

Christianity has never been a monolithic tradition, for even in its early years it displayed great variety, stimulated in part by conflicts within the household of faith as well as debates with outside forces. Questions of "orthodoxy"—that is, which beliefs were correct—were raised early on and engendered some of the most fruitful discussions, debates, and decisions that have profoundly shaped the understanding of Christianity ever since.

As Christianity expanded out of its Jewish and Greco-Roman context, it contended with the threat of "**syncretism**," a broad term that refers to the merging of religious beliefs and practices in such a way that the original elements of the religion (e.g., Christianity) are obscured. One of the most vigorous challenges of syncretism to early Christianity came in the form of gnosticism, the beliefs and practices of an amorphous series of emergent groups that emphasized "secret knowledge" (*gnosis*) transmitted only to the "enlightened" who recognized that matter (i.e., material reality) is evil. Many **gnostics** believed in the distinction between a distant, supreme God and an inferior creator god responsible for the imperfect and impure material world. Gnostics emphasized knowledge of the spiritual world and stressed that salvation was a freeing of the spirit from matter. They saw Jesus as the emissary of the supreme God, yet only known by secret knowledge.

Early Gentile Christianity went through a period of amnesia. . . . What was their relation to the Greek past? Some of them (some indeed in the first generation, as the New Testament indicates) solved the problem by pretending their Greek past did not exist, by pretending they were Jews, adopting Jewish customs, even to circumcision. Paul saw this coming and roundly condemned it. You are not Jews, he argues in Romans 9–11; you are Israel, but grafted into it.

Walls, *Missionary Movement in Christian History*, 13–14

SPIRIT VERSUS MATTER

By positing a sharp distinction between spirit and matter, claiming that physical bodies consisted of evil matter, the gnostics aimed to free the pure spirit from evil matter. Gnosticism proved attractive to some early Christians, and its highly syncretistic nature is addressed frequently throughout the New Testament. According to the **gnostic gospels**, which were texts written from a gnostic perspective with names of early followers of Jesus attached to give them a sense of authenticity, Jesus was a "righteous angel" and a "wise philosopher" but not a real, physical human being. Likewise, his disciples came from "the light." Gnostic ideas would influence the church for centuries and, some would argue, may have left residues in the church today.

The Patristic Period (c. 100–500 CE), in which the **church fathers** (Latin, *pater*, "father") developed distinctive ideas that would profoundly shape Christianity, was one of the most exciting and creative periods in the history of Christian thought. Every mainstream Christian tradition, such as Roman Catholic, Anglican, Eastern Orthodox, Reformed, Lutheran, and Anabaptist, regard the Patristic Period as the definitive time in the development of the church, and they all trace their histories back to this period and the theological commitments that were affirmed.

THE APOLOGISTS

While the first century of Christianity was centered in Jerusalem and was dominated by Jewish followers of the Messiah Jesus, toward the middle of the second century, a number of Christian writers set out to defend their faith in the face of false accusations that had justified Christian persecution throughout the Roman Empire. These "defenders of the faith" (**apologists**) confronted syncretistic movements, such as gnosticism, and engaged Greek philosophical traditions, communicating Christianity in new ways that would resonate with Hellenistic thought. Among the better known church fathers and apologists were Justin Martyr (c. 100–c. 165), Clement of Alexandria (c. 150–215), Origen of Alexandria (c. 185–c. 254), and Tertullian (c. 160–c. 220). The first three of these fathers represented what would become known as the Eastern church, located in the eastern Mediterranean, while Tertullian represented the Western (i.e., Latin) church. Given the geographic proximity of the Eastern church to Greece, the home of Hellenistic culture and philosophy, church fathers of the Eastern church had to

> *Yet when one looks more closely at the writings of the early apologists, it is apparent that Christian thinkers had seen something in Christ and the Scriptures that would not yield easily to conventional philosophical reasoning.*
>
> Wilken, *Spirit of Early Christian Thought*, 13

communicate Christian faith in ways that were relevant to Greek traditions. Long embitterment between the Western and the Eastern churches came to a head in 1054, in an event known as the **Great Schism**, when the single church formally divided into Western and Eastern branches.

Justin Martyr

Justin Martyr, who came to Christianity after an intellectual journey, wrote to show unbelievers that Christianity is rational and that traces of Christian truth can be found in great philosophical (even non-Christian) traditions. In his *First Apology*, Justin uses the term *"**Logos spermatikos**"* (Greek, "seed-bearing word"), borrowing from Greek (e.g., Platonic) philosophy, to demonstrate that the divine **Logos** (Word, truth) has been sown as a seed throughout human history, known only in part by non-Christians until Christianity unearthed and fulfilled these hints of truth. So, according to Justin, the Word (truth) known partly by Greek philosophers is revealed in its entirety in Christ. Justin's perspective asserted that God prepared the way for his final revelation of Christ.

Clement of Alexandria

Clement of Alexandria also wrote for nonbelievers, emphasizing the value of philosophy for the Christian life. In his *Exhortation to the Heathen*, in which he affirms that truth can be found in ancient philosophers, Clement urges readers to accept the Christian faith. Like Justin, Clement believed that partial truth can be found in Greek philosophy, even while he ridiculed Greek gods—since God, Clement claimed, can only be known fully through the Logos, the Word, an early Greek concept meaning the source of the cosmos, which Clement and other early church leaders identified as Jesus Christ. Greek philosophy, Clement argued, was given to the Greeks with the same purpose that the law was given to the Jews—to serve as a guide to lead them to Jesus Christ. Despite his understanding that the Jews were to bear the good news, Clement was strongly anti-Semitic.

Origen

Clement's most famous student, **Origen**, wrote *On First Principles*, the first systematic, complete statement of the Christian faith. As a prolific writer with a brilliant mind, Origen developed a theory of Scripture interpretation that posited three levels of meaning: the literal, the moral, and the spiritual. The literal meaning referred to the straightforward, common, on-the-surface interpretation that even the less-educated interpreter can understand. The moral meaning referred to the ways in which Scripture instructs and edifies believers. And the spiritual meaning was the deepest sense, hidden from a literal reading of the text but revealed by God to the discerning reader.

Tertullian

Finally, **Tertullian**, from the North African city of Carthage (in today's Tunisia), wrote stridently oppositional essays antagonizing those who attempted to allow Hellenistic culture and philosophy into the matter of Christian faith. Arguing in Latin that heresies and false beliefs stem from acceptance of philosophy, Tertullian leveled sharp criticism against any who added philosophy to the necessity of faith, since faith and philosophy could not mix. Tertullian is credited with asking, "What has Athens to do with Jerusalem?"[5] noting in his view the incompatibility of reason (e.g., philosophy) and faith (i.e., Christianity), since Athens represented the seat of philosophy and Jerusalem the origin of Christian faith. Consequently, there were different perspectives on the relationship between Christianity and culture in the Western and Eastern churches, which in part has fueled ecclesiastical and theological diversity ever since. The church fathers not only wrote to articulate Christian faith and defend it against its opponents but were also active in church councils that had permanent results for Christianity.

The Ecumenical Church Councils

Ever since the beginning of the church, representatives of the church have met to discuss crucial issues of belief and practice impacting Christian life. One noteworthy example is the Council of Jerusalem, recorded in Acts 15 and considered the first church council. Councils continue to be convened today, gathering thousands of church representatives from around the world to determine church policies, debate ethical issues, and share Christian fellowship. The first four **ecumenical** Christian councils met to determine church doctrines that would later become the building blocks for Christian theology. The term "ecumenical" refers to "the whole household of God," thus indicating a broad gathering of Christian representatives who seek unity. An ecumenical Christian meeting, then, means a gathering of Christian leaders from a wide variety of churches representing the whole church.

> *Christian theology is a series of footnotes to St. Paul.*
>
> Ahlstrom, *Theology in America*, 23

COUNCIL OF NICAEA

Needing to hold the Roman Empire together, and under growing threat of division in part because of contention within the church, **Emperor**

Constantine (c. 288–337) called for the first ecumenical church council, which met in Nicaea (325), to resolve conflict within the church about the relationship between God and Jesus. The priest **Arius** (c. 250–c. 336), a well-respected theologian, argued that Jesus was the first created being but was not the same as God, even though he was "of similar substance" (*homoiousios*) to the Father. Bishop **Athanasius** (c. 296–373) argued that Jesus was in fact "of the same substance" (*homoousios*) with the Father and therefore God incarnate rather than just a creation of God. At the **Council of Nicaea**, Arius was declared a heretic, since he rejected Jesus as being of the same substance as the Father and was therefore unable to provide salvation. **Arianism** had spread into Europe—for example, among Germanic tribes, such as the Visigoths, Ostrogoths, Lombards, and Vandals, who invaded the Roman Empire, leading to its fall in 476.

Cara Denney

Figure 8.4. Russian Orthodox Christian Church in Kyiv, Ukraine

COUNCIL OF CONSTANTINOPLE

The second ecumenical meeting was the **Council of Constantinople** (381), where church representatives focused on the triune nature of God (Father, Son, and Holy Spirit). What was the identity of the triune God? Debates about the nature of God pitted the modalists against the tritheists. The modalists, in trying to safeguard the absolute unity of the Godhead, contended that God was known through different self-revelations throughout history, and thus there were different modes of God's expression in time: God as "Father" is revealed as the creator and lawgiver; God as "Savior" is revealed as Jesus Christ, the Son; and God as "Holy Spirit" is revealed as the sanctifier after Christ ascended to heaven. The problem with modalism is that it presented one supreme God without distinction, as though the Godhead were only distinct in its chronological expression, rather than in its being itself.

The **tritheists** ("three gods") argued that the Godhead consists of three equal, independent, autonomous parts, each of which is divine. The problem with the tritheists' argument is that they viewed the Godhead as consisting of distinct parts and failed to address the unity of the Godhead. The **Cappadocian fathers**, consisting of Basil (c. 330–379), Gregory of Nyssa (c. 330–c. 395), and Gregory of Nazianzus (329–389), resolved the issue of the Trinity in what came to be called the Cappadocian Formula. The Cappadocian approach defended the unity of the Godhead with the recognition that the one Godhead exists simultaneously in three different persons: "one substance [*ousia*] in three persons [*hypostases*]." In the fourth century, the Councils of Nicaea and Constantinople defined the orthodox understanding of the relationship between the Son and the Father and the nature of the Godhead; the chief end of the third council was to determine the identity of Jesus Christ.

COUNCIL OF EPHESUS

During the third ecumenical church meeting, the **Council of Ephesus** (431), which focused on the topic of **Christology**—the nature of Jesus Christ—church representatives had to confront two heresies about Jesus Christ that to us may appear to be hair-splitting distinctions. First, Bishop **Apollinarius** (c. 310–390) of Laodicea argued that God infused Jesus with God's spirit (i.e., Logos), thus replacing Jesus's human spirit. The problem, according to the majority of representatives at the council, was that Christ would then not be fully human, since he could not have experienced normal human moral development, but instead was imbued with God's spirit.

Second, the archbishop of Constantinople, **Nestorius** (c. 386–451), proposed that Jesus Christ consisted of two distinct persons, human and divine. As such, Nestorius argued, when Christ suffered he experienced that suffering only through his humanity, not his divinity. Likewise, when Christ felt hunger, for instance, he only experienced that hunger through his human nature. Nestorius had political opponents and was charged with suggesting that there are two *distinct* natures of Jesus Christ, human and divine, but did not say how these two were joined. He believed that a union between the human and the divine aspects was impossible. It was as though Jesus Christ had two personalities within him—like a split personality—with no unity.

The ideas of Apollinarius and Nestorius were condemned as heretical at the Council of Ephesus. It is important to note that today the **Nestorian Church**, which is also called the "Church of the East," was the ancient church of the Persian Empire, and had established itself in India and China around

The Father was neither made nor created nor begotten; the Son was neither made nor created, but was alone begotten of the Father; the Spirit was neither made nor created, but is proceeding from the Father and the Son. Thus there is one Father, not three fathers; one Son, not three sons; one Holy Spirit, not three spirits. And in this Trinity, no one is before or after, greater or less than the other; but all three persons are in themselves, coeternal and coequal; and so we worship the Trinity in unity and the one God in three persons.

Selection from the Athanasian Creed, available at http://www.elca.org/What-We-Believe/Statements-of-Belief/The-Athanasian-Creed.aspx

Every place in the city is full of them: the alleys, the crossroads, the forums, the squares. Garment sellers, money changers, food vendors—they are all at it. If you ask for change, they philosophize for you about generate and ingenerate natures. If you inquire about the price of bread, the answer is that the Father is greater and the Son inferior. If you speak about whether the bath is ready, they express the opinion that the Son was made out of nothing.

Gregory of Nyssa on the theological debate throughout Constantinople, *Oration on the Deity and the Son and the Holy Spirit*, in Migne, *Patrologia Graeca*, col. 558; also found in Placher, *History of Christian Theology*, 68

the seventh century, before the commencement of the Roman Catholic mission effort in those regions. The Nestorian church still exists.

COUNCIL OF CHALCEDON

The fourth ecumenical church gathering, the **Council of Chalcedon** (451), met in response to a doctrinal letter from Pope Leo I (c. 400–461), who declared that Jesus Christ has two distinct natures, one divine and one human, existing inseparably in one person. The key was that these two natures coexist in one person (**hypostasis**), and the oneness of the person makes it appropriate to apply the qualities of each nature to the other. The Christology affirmed at the fourth council showed that mutual interchange between the aspects of Jesus Christ was genuine. This **Chalcedon Definition**—that Jesus Christ has two natures in one person—became the orthodox position among Western (Latin) churches. Some of the Eastern Orthodox churches (non-Chalcedonian) argued that the two natures of Christ were combined into a third new being, a single nature referred to as the **Monophysite** tradition. These churches are called Oriental Orthodox and form a subset of the larger designation, Eastern Orthodox Church.

Oriental Orthodox churches include the Armenian Apostolic Church, the Coptic Orthodox Church, the Ethiopian Orthodox Church, the Eritrean Orthodox Church, the Syriac Orthodox Church, and the Indian (Malankara) Orthodox Syrian Church. It is striking to note that neither Arianism nor Nestorianism was completely eradicated in the universal church—these became some of the earliest forms of Christianity that spread outside the Roman Empire. It was one thing for the church to spread out of its Jewish background into the gentile world, but it was quite another for the Christian faith to move outside the Roman Empire entirely, making its home in cultures around the world. As the Christian faith expanded

Matthew E. Cohen/Wikimedia Commons

Figure 8.5. Armenian Apostolic Church in Fresno, California, USA

376

worldwide, it encountered a wide range of cultural, social, philosophical, and religious issues that would force it to decide what it deemed was orthodox on each account, thus profoundly shaping Christian faith.

Christianity's Worldwide Expansion

While there are several significant histories of the church and Christianity, for our purposes I will introduce the historic periodization of the church presented by Andrew Walls, a scholar of Christian mission history who has influenced the way contemporary scholars understand the relationship between the gospel and culture as Christianity moved across the world.[6] Walls presents five periods of Christian expansion to illustrate the identity of the church and Christian faith through history. By considering these periods, we gain insight into Christianity as a movement as well as a better understanding of Christianity itself. Imagining a space visitor who drops into human history at various points to study Christianity, Walls provides basic contours of Christianity at each point of major geographic change in the Christian faith.

> Declare his glory among the nations,
> his marvelous works among all the people.
>
> 1 Chronicles 16:24

JERUSALEM, 37 CE

The first phase of the transmission of Christianity worldwide began in 37 CE, when Jerusalem was the center of the faith and Christians were mostly Jewish. Worship remained within the confines of the temple, the language of worship remained Hebrew, and followers of the Messiah (i.e., Jesus) read the old law books of the Old Testament. This was a tightly knit social group that in part found its solidarity in its shared ethnicity. They spoke of Jesus the Messiah as the "**Son of Man**" and the "**Suffering Servant**," expressions used in the Old Testament that identify the anticipated Messiah. This predominantly Jewish group recognized Jesus as the promised Messiah. Some of the questions that needed to be resolved for these early Christians were the following: What is the relationship between the religion of Israel and the gospel of Jesus Christ? How will Christianity be seen as continuous and discontinuous with Jewish culture and religion? How can Christianity affirm the Jewish religion while at the same time inviting gentiles into fellowship and equal partnership with Jewish followers of the Messiah? How does the older covenant of the Old Testament relate to the newer covenant articulated in the New Testament?

Nicaea, 325 CE

The second major shift in Christianity occurred in 325 CE, at the time of the Council of Nicaea. Walls notes that the space visitor would see that there were hardly any Jewish followers of the Messiah and that the main center of Christian growth was in the eastern Mediterranean. Greek was the language of worship, rather than Hebrew, and in fact, the space visitor would notice hostility between followers of Christ and the Jews. Christians described Jesus as the "Son of God" and "Lord," terms borrowed from Greek culture and religion. In this period, which roughly covers the Patristic Period, the most important Christian affirmations were established.

For instance, who is Jesus Christ, and what is his relationship to God, the Father? What is the Godhead, and how do the three persons of the triune nature of God relate to one another? What are the **sacraments**, which **Augustine** suggested were an outward and visible sign of an inward and spiritual grace, and do they work by the power and perfection of the priest, or are they performed as a transaction between God and the community regardless of the state of the priest? And what about human agency and its role in the Christian life? That is, does God choose human beings to follow him, or do human beings choose God? Who takes the initiative in the divine-human relationship? How does grace, as God's unmerited favor, work? What is the nature of grace? What is the relationship between free will and sin? Is grace based on human perfection, or is it strictly an act of God's love for human beings? Under what conditions are Christians justified in using physical force (i.e., just war theory)? All these questions, and many others, were discussed in the medieval period of the church.

> *As the Son and the Logos of God, Christ was the revelation of the nature of God; in the formula of Irenaeus, "the Father is that which is invisible about the Son, the Son is that which is visible about the Father." If, in a phrase that Irenaeus quoted from an even earlier source, "the Son is the measure of the Father," one would expect that the Christian definition of the deity of God would be regulated by the content of the divine as revealed in Christ. In fact, however, the early Christian picture of God was controlled by the self-evident axiom, accepted by all, of the absoluteness and the impassibility of the divine nature.*
>
> Pelikan, *Christian Tradition*, 1:229

Ireland, 600 CE

The third phase of the growth of Christianity began in roughly 600 CE, when, as Walls notes, the balance of Christianity shifted westward out of the Mediterranean region and into the lands of the northern and western tribal and semitribal peoples of Europe. What we now call Ireland was the center of Christian growth, and Christianity had taken on a particularly ascetic perspective as monks engaged in practices of harsh self-discipline, such as whipping themselves for failing to say "Amen" at the right time. In this twelve-hundred-year period, Europe became thoroughly Christian, with a Lithuanian group being the last to enter the faith in the year 1386.

The growth of Christianity was marked by several crucial theological discussions. Some of the major theological issues with which Christian faith struggled during the Middle Ages until the era of European colonialism (roughly the fifth to the nineteenth century) include the following: How exactly does Jesus save humanity? Attempts to answer this question have been called theories of the **atonement**. "Atonement" is an English term coined to mean the action of "making one"—that is, making reconciliation between human beings and God through the sacrificial death of Jesus Christ. How can one talk about God, which raises the issue of language, since even our best language cannot exhaustively capture the notion of God? How does one balance the ability to know God with the mystery of God? Who are saints, and what role do they play in Christian life—as intercessors or exemplars? What is the relationship between faith and reason? Should faith and reason be mutually exclusive or integrated? How should Christians engage with philosophy?

The Protestant Reformation

Martin Luther

During this period the Protestant Reformation occurred, giving rise to several new Christian denominations. The Protestant Reformation, a reform movement out of the Roman Catholic Church, consisted of three different movements (the earliest being Lutheran, Reformed, and Anabaptist). **Martin Luther** (1482–1546), a German Catholic monk who emphasized faith alone (***sola fide***), Scripture alone (***sola scriptura***), Christ alone (***solus Christus***), grace alone (***sola gratia***), and glory to God alone (***soli Deo gloria***), began the Protestant movement. In the face of strong pressure from Emperor Charles V, who adamantly supported the Roman Catholic Church, Martin Luther appealed to Scripture alone, rather than, for instance, the pope, to justify his understanding of the Christian life.

> *Unless I am convinced by the testimony of Scripture by clear reason, for I do not trust either in the pope or in councils alone, since it is well known that they have often erred and contradicted themselves, my conscience is captive to the Word of God. I cannot and will not retract anything. . . . I cannot do otherwise, here I stand, may God help me. Amen.*
>
> Martin Luther, "Luther at the Diet of Worms," in *Luther's Works*, 32:112–13

Ulrich Zwingli

Another branch of the Protestant Reformation was led by **Ulrich Zwingli** (1484–1531), whose ideas gave rise to the Reformed tradition. Zwingli was in substantial agreement with Luther on matters of salvation by faith alone and the importance of Scripture alone. However, Zwingli and Luther fiercely debated the role of reason in faith. Luther did not see reason as completely authoritative in the Christian life, while Zwingli contended that we must apply reason to make sense of God and Scripture.

Luther and Zwingli also disagreed fundamentally on the relationship between spirit and matter. Zwingli believed in a sharp distinction between spirit and matter, arguing, for instance, that musical instruments, stained-glass windows, and clerical garments could not mediate the spirit of God, while Luther disagreed. Better known in the Reformed tradition is **John Calvin** (1509–64), considered one of the greatest Protestant theologians, a second-generation reformer following in the tracks of Zwingli, employing his gifted mind to write a theology, the *Institutes of the Christian Religion*, that became the basis for Reformed churches worldwide (e.g., Presbyterian, Christian Reformed Church, Reformed Church in America).

Anabaptist

The third major branch of the Protestant Reformation was the **Anabaptist** movement, which had a militant and a moderate side. The radical Anabaptists were led by **John of Leiden** (c. 1509–36), **Melchoir Hoffman** (c. 1500–1543), and **Thomas Münster** (c. 1490–1525), who led quasi-communistic congregations in preparations to overthrow what they believed was the current ungodly and corrupted world. Many were martyred by other Reformers as heretics. Moderate Anabaptists distanced themselves from the more radical movement, seeking a more pacifistic faith. Leaders of the early moderate Anabaptists, who held a rather strict social ethic, included **Menno Simons** (1492–1545)

Pasteur/Wikimedia Commons

Figure 8.6. Amish girls at the beach in Chincoteague, Virginia, USA

and **Michael Sattler** (c. 1495–1527). They encouraged, among other tenets, nonviolence (pacifism) and the strict separation of church and state.

The Enlightenment

This period of Christian growth also witnessed the age of the **Enlightenment** (eighteenth and nineteenth centuries), a time of massive intellectual and philosophical development that in effect replaced God with human beings as the final source of knowledge, thus unseating God and the church as ways to validate truth. The Enlightenment made human beings the center of knowing rather than God, with reason supplanting faith as the beginning of knowledge. The Enlightenment left an indelible mark on Western Christianity,

United States president Thomas Jefferson introduced a moral vision based on the life and teachings of Jesus Christ as the way Jefferson wished Christianity would be practiced. Beginning in 1804, Jefferson published works on philosophy and morals that sought to strip away the miracles of Jesus, leaving Jesus as a moral exemplar for humanity. Found posthumously was Jefferson's Bible, from which he cut out the miracles of Jesus. Said one scholar,

> Jefferson did not hesitate to cut off a biblical verse in the middle of a sentence if it proved to be awkward to his religious sensibilities. What he retained was a completely demystified Jesus. It was a kind of non-miraculous biography of Jesus gleaned from Luke and Matthew. All references to miracles, Holy Spirit, and any instances which highlighted Jesus exercising authority were excluded. [Jefferson] ended his construal of Jesus with Jesus' death and left out narratives related to resurrection. For the teaching of Jesus, he focussed mainly on the milder admonitions, especially in the Sermon on the Mount and his most memorable parables. The result was a reasonably coherent and oddly truncated biography.[a]

The impact of the Enlightenment on Christianity has reverberated throughout the centuries, deeply impacting biblical scholarship and thus our understanding of our lives as Christians. Are there ways that contemporary Christians eliminate portions of Scripture that are unappealing? What is lost when the body of Christ worldwide fails to learn biblical insights from other Christians around the world—for example, if American Christians do not learn from Nigerian Christians or Chinese Christians? How might other perspectives on the Bible help us correct, broaden, and refine current understandings?

a. Sugirtharajah, *Bible and Empire*, 15.

Christian Reflections

including the emphasis on the autonomous individual, rather than human reliance on God or the church; the affirmation of the scientific worldview, which was promised to provide all answers to human and environmental problems; the notion that progress was inevitable with the employment of new technologies and economic advancements; and the belief that the mysteries of the Bible, such as miracles, would eventually be explained through scientific investigation.

GREAT BRITAIN, 1840

The fourth major historical movement of Christianity emerged in the 1840s, when Great Britain had become a powerful Christian kingdom and embarked on a massive program of colonization in Africa and Asia. Andrew Walls imagines the space visitor overhearing discussions in a great university hall in London about promoting Christianity and planting cotton at the same time, while also talking about stopping the African slave trade. This group promoted the three Cs: Christ, commerce, and civilization. These three Cs were advanced famously by missionary **David Livingstone** (1813–73), a Scottish Congregationalist medical missionary who served with the London Missionary Society in Africa. By this time, Europe had become "Christianized," and with the region's massive technological and scientific advantage over other nations, European nations, often animated by Christianity, gained control over much of the world as their colonizing forces set a course that changed the world. In the nineteenth century, many crucial Christian affirmations were reconsidered and rearticulated in a context much different from when they were first enshrined.

National Portrait Gallery, London/Wikimedia Commons

Figure 8.7. David Livingstone

Liberal Protestantism

Out of the context of a heavily rational understanding of Christian faith, where the human being occupied the center of knowledge making, **Friedrich Schleiermacher** (1768–1834), a German liberal Protestant theologian, argued that religion is about feelings, a "deep abiding disposition," an emotional posture to the world, a "sense and taste for the Infinite." He followed a group called the Romantics, consisting mostly of cultured, radical young men (e.g., poets, painters) who explored the depths of emotion and reacted against the emphasis on reason. For Schleiermacher, then, religion was the "feeling of absolute dependence" on God.

Liberal Protestantism, which was influenced deeply by Enlightenment notions, was open to new ways of envisioning God and salvation. Liberal Protestantism had a broader interpretation of the Bible (not affirming at the outset that it was divinely inspired), questioned the authority of Scripture, and emphasized Jesus as a moral exemplar rather than his central role in salvation.

Fundamentalist Protestantism

By the 1880s, an American phenomenon called **fundamentalism** emerged, presenting an open attack against **liberalism**, seeking to argue for the historicity and literal interpretation of the Bible. Fundamentalism contended that the Bible is without error in all instances of geography, science, and history, as though the Bible contained a record of history and science, whereas its relative, **evangelicalism**, is more open to seeing that the Bible is without error within the scope of its purpose. That is to say, most evangelicals would argue that the Bible reflects a prescientific worldview, combining, for instance, history, theology, and poetry to tell the story of God's love for human beings.

Nigeria, 1980

The fifth significant shift of Christianity worldwide occurred around 1980, when Africa became the continent most notable for its profession of Christianity, marking a massive numerical shift of Christianity southward into the nations of the Global South. Christians were certainly present throughout many parts of the Global South prior to the late twentieth century; however, numerically the tide turned sometime in the late twentieth century when there was a greater number of Christians in the Global South than in the Global North. The space visitor, Walls says, watched as white-robed Christian Nigerians danced and chanted in the streets on their way to church, inviting people to experience the power of God and be healed. This group of Nigerians, representing the experience of African Christians more generally, was concerned with spiritual power—that is, the power to heal miraculously, receive personal visions, and preach boldly. In the

We who are involved in the theological enterprise in Africa must also take a critical look at the churches' stance vis-à-vis the political, economic, and social changes around us. We are duty-bound to call attention to the theological roots of the Christian role in humanization and in the struggle for justice and peace. These are universal issues, of course, for it is not only in Africa that "Christianity lived" does not measure up to "Christianity preached."

Oduyoye, *Hearing and Knowing,* 9

twenty-first century, the perspectives and questions coming from around the world may serve as a necessary corrective to a narrow theological vision, reshaping our understanding of Christianity, the church, and one another.

Twentieth-Century Protestant and Roman Catholic Theologians

Among the great Western theologians of the twentieth century were the Protestant **Karl Barth** (1886–1968), the Roman Catholic **Karl Rahner** (1904–84), and the Roman Catholic **Hans Urs von Balthasar** (1905–88). Each wrote numerous volumes attempting to provide a faithful response to the modern West, but with different approaches and emphases. Barth was known for his "neoorthodox" position, which argues that the gospel judges culture and should never be co-opted by any human institution, culture, or thought system ("the gospel is a bombshell from above").

Rahner's work emphasizes the triune nature of God, the nature of grace, and the provocative idea that even among non-Christians there may be "anonymous Christians" if they have accepted the grace of God, though they may never have heard the gospel. And Balthasar, focusing on Christology (the nature of Christ), soteriology (the nature of salvation), eschatology (the nature of end times), and especially aesthetics, emphasizes how God is revealed in beauty and mystery rather than just in truth and righteousness.

Figure 8.8. Entoto Mariam Church in Addis Ababa, Ethiopia

Southward Shift of World Christianity, Mid-1980s

In the mid-1980s, scholars recognized that numerically Christianity had shifted dramatically to the Global South, where explosive growth was occurring in Africa, Asia, and Latin America. While Christianity in the North Atlantic region (i.e., North America and Western Europe) was declining rapidly, Christianity in Africa, Asia, and Latin America showed signs of robust vitality. Christianity began as a religion of the Middle East, moved into northern Europe, then throughout much of Asia, Africa, and South and Central America, often being carried on the ships of colonial governments.

Figure 8.9. Evangelical Christian preacher in Cambodia

Today Christianity is receding in the Global North, as the Global North has become post-Christian and Christianity has become non-Western. The emerging changes occurring in worldwide Christianity today are reshaping Christianity as missionaries from the Global South are making their way to nations of the Global North and as Christians from the Global South are raising different questions about their faith out of social, cultural, religious, and political contexts quite distinct from those in the Global North.[7]

Figure 8.10. The Church of San Jacinto, constructed in 1524 in Salcaja, Guatemala

Common Features of Christianity Worldwide

These historical moments of Christianity's growth appear quite disparate, exhibiting immense variety in relation to culture, politics, and society. Given its diverse expression within cultures, how can one make sense of its common features? Is it even possible to identify common features of Christianity across time and space? Andrew Walls argues that the coherence of Christianity worldwide is in its affirmation that Jesus is of ultimate significance and that the Bible is normative for the life of the community of faith. The continuity of the transmission of the gospel united observant Jewish followers of the Messiah (c. 37 CE), Greek theologians (c. 325), Irish ascetic monks (c. 600), zealous Victorian supporters

Figure 8.11. Cathedral of Christ the Light, Roman Catholic Diocese of Oakland, California, USA

Figure 8.12. The translated Bible is used in a jungle area of West Papua, Indonesia

of Christian missions (c. 1840s), and white-robed Nigerian congregations chanting in the streets about the power of the Spirit (c. 1980).[8]

Christianity is a single phenomenon with countless expressions, perhaps illustrated most dramatically in its varied forms of worship and practice. As Christianity continues to be made meaningful in various contexts around the world, the unforeseen future of Christianity may be quite distinct from the past. Christianity at the beginning of the twenty-first century is post-Western, with its most vigorous growth occurring in Africa and Asia. **Pentecostalism**, which emphasizes the Holy Spirit's manifestation through speaking in tongues and other gifts of the Spirit, is burgeoning so dramatically worldwide that it has caught the attention of secular and religious scholars from all over the world. Forms of Christianity are proliferating around the world, making this one of the most exciting periods to learn and experience Christian faith.

Our observer [space visitor] is therefore led to recognize an essential continuity in Christianity: continuity of thought about the final significance of Jesus, continuity of a certain consciousness about history, continuity in the use of the Scriptures, of bread and wine, of water. But he recognizes that these continuities are cloaked with such heavy veils belonging to their environment that Christians of different times and places must often be unrecognizable to others, or indeed even to themselves, as manifestations of a single phenomenon.

Walls, *Missionary Movement in Christian History*, 7

Worship and Practice

Worship

On any given Sunday, Christians around the world will be worshiping in such diverse ways and locations that from observation alone it would seem almost impossible to make sense of the religion as a single movement.[9] What is common to all Christians, regardless of their denominational stripes, is that they worship God, revealed in Jesus Christ. Before we launch into a discussion of Christian worship and practice, it would be helpful to note some of the basic theological affirmations of Christian orthodoxy that guide worship and practice.

TRANSCENDENCE AND IMMANENCE

First, Christians claim that God is both transcendent and immanent. The transcendent aspect means that God is entirely holy, independent, "other" than his creation (2 Chron. 2:6). However, God is also immanent, meaning that God manifested himself in the material world, for example, becoming Jesus Christ, the God-man (Phil. 2:6–8). In Christian worship, these two qualities of God, transcendence and immanence, interrelate and give rise to a wide spectrum of worship styles and emphases from highly liturgical worship (i.e., with a prescribed order) to informal worship. Second, depending on the theological tradition of the church, Christian worship varies significantly based on how a denomination or individual church views the relationship between spirit, matter, and grace. Grace is God's unmerited favor. It is because of God's

Christian Reflections

Worship is central to Christian experience. It is the pulse of the Christian church. In the Lutheran World Federation Nairobi Statement on Worship and Culture (1996), four challenges and opportunities for contemporary Christian worship were outlined. We can understand these characteristics as marks of the best Christian practices, and thus they can serve as guides for Christian worship in the contemporary world. The Nairobi Statement suggests the following four themes of Christian worship. First, Christian worship is *transcultural*: worship transcends and is beyond any particular culture. Second, Christian worship is *contextual*: the mystery of Christ's incarnation is the model and mandate for contextualization of Christian worship. "A given culture's values and patterns, insofar as they are consonant with the values of the Gospel, can be used to express the meaning and purpose of Christian worship." Third, Christian worship is *countercultural*: worship calls us not to conform to the world but to be transformed by it (Rom. 12:2). There is a challenge to transform cultural patterns that idolize the self or establish false gods, which can be unseated through countercultural worship. Fourth, Christian worship is *cross-cultural*: there is one church, and that church can celebrate the sharing of hymns, arts, and other elements of worship across cultural barriers to enrich the whole church worldwide.[a]

a. The Lutheran World Federation Nairobi Statement on Worship and Culture is available at http://www.elca.org/Growing-In-Faith/Worship/Learning-Center/LWF-Nairobi-Statement.aspx.

Figure 8.13. Catholic Church procession in Chichicastenango, Guatemala

grace that human beings, according to the Christian tradition, can be in right relationship to God despite human fragility, finitude, and imperfection.

COMMUNICATING GRACE

But just how does God communicate grace? Can grace be communicated through material elements, such as the Eucharist (Lord's Supper) of bread and wine, or through music or art? Or is grace only communicated via the Spirit? As I mentioned above, during the Protestant Reformation, Lutherans and Calvinists disagreed on this subject. Lutherans believed that God's grace could be mediated through matter (e.g., stained-glass windows), while Calvinists argued vehemently against the idea that grace is communicated through any material thing. That is why early followers of Zwingli were iconoclasts, destroyers of religious symbols, and as such even destroyed stained-glass windows and statues in churches. They believed these elements distracted from faith in God. The Catholic and the Eastern Orthodox churches affirm, along with Lutherans, that grace can be expressed through matter.

Worship is not a mere memory or a matter of looking back to a historic event (that is an Enlightenment notion). Rather, worship is the action that brings the Christ event into the experience of the community gathered in the name of Jesus. Three implications to this understanding of worship are: (1) worship recapitulates the Christ event, (2) worship actualizes the church, and (3) worship anticipates the kingdom.

Webber, Worship Old and New, 67

While this discussion may sound abstract, the topic of the relationship of grace to spirit and matter has immediate implications for Christian worship. Broadly speaking, worship spaces, whether they are ornate cathedrals or warehouse churches, will, to a great extent, indicate the church's perspective on how grace is communicated to the assembly. For instance, churches with many icons, symbols, and clerical vestments would communicate that God works through these items, even if mysteriously. Churches with fewer items may suggest a de-emphasis on material items as means of communicating grace.

There is a "scandal" of worship, where non-Christians often wonder why there are so many "Christianities"—Catholic, Orthodox, Protestant, Anabaptist. Some worship in the near dark, using just candles. Some use rock bands and encourage dancing. Some use jumbo screens hung above the heads of thousands of worshipers. By recognizing that worship in part entails combining the notion that God is both transcendent and immanent and that grace may be communicated through matter or through the Spirit, we gain a sense of why Christian worship is so extremely diverse worldwide.

Grace and Works

For by grace you have been saved through faith, and this is not your own doing; it is the gift of God—not the result of works, so that no one may boast. For we are what he has made us, created in Christ Jesus for good works, which God prepared beforehand to be our way of life.

Ephesians 2:8–10

For some Christians a dilemma exists that involves the relationship between "grace" and "works." If Christians are saved based on the grace of God, not by anything that they do, then what role do "works" play in the Christian faith? Although Christians affirm that salvation is by grace through faith, many Christians also understand the announcement of the good news to mean that followers of Christ ought to seek being transformed by God, because we are forgiven our sins, and pursue bringing justice and reconciliation to the world. Since Christians recognize that something is fundamentally wrong with the world (e.g., sin), they are empowered by the Holy Spirit to seek the kingdom of God on earth; as the Lord's Prayer proclaims, "Thy [God's] Kingdom come, Thy will be done on earth as it is in Heaven."

Many Christian practices, then, have something to do with improving oneself (or being improved by God—"sanctification") and being in the world as Jesus Christ was in the world—that is, to be people who invite others into a relationship with God, who conquered sin so that human beings would have peace with God and with one another.

What practices are required? Prayer and reading the Bible devotionally help Christians maintain an ongoing commitment to God and provide opportunities for God to speak through those encounters. Believing that the Holy Spirit, the third person of the Godhead, does in fact enter the life of a believer, Christians anticipate that prayer and Scripture reading can guide and comfort them, particularly within the gathering of fellow believers.

> But be doers of the word, and not merely hearers who deceive themselves. For if any are hearers of the word and not doers, they are like those who look at themselves in a mirror; for they look at themselves and, on going away, immediately forget what they were like. But those who look into the perfect law, the law of liberty, and persevere, being not hearers who forget but doers who act—they will be blessed in their doing.
>
> James 1:22–25

Sacraments

Sacraments are also a part of Christian practice, as they form crucial elements of Christian worship. The word "sacrament" does not appear in the Bible, but the term carries the meaning of "oath" and "mystery," and it is used to refer to God's saving work in general. Augustine's famous definition was that sacraments were the "visible form of invisible grace," or as the Anglican catechism states, "an outward and visible sign of an inward and spiritual grace . . . ordained by Christ himself."

A sacrament, then, is a ritual or ritual object in which God is uniquely active. Roman Catholics and Protestants recognize a different set of sacraments. Roman Catholics affirm the sacraments of baptism (christening), confirmation (chrismation), Eucharist (Holy Communion, Lord's Supper), confession (penance), anointing the sick (sacrament of the sick), holy orders (ordination for ministry), and marriage (matrimony). Generally, Protestants, rather than recognizing these seven sacraments, acknowledge baptism and communion (Lord's Supper) and usually marriage.

BAPTISM

Baptism is practiced by all Christian denominations, even if it is done quite differently, with some sprinkling water on the forehead of the candidate and other churches requiring full immersion, whereby the body of the candidate needs to be submerged fully underwater in a symbolic act of purification and new life. Jesus underwent baptism at the hands of John the Baptist (Mark

1:9), and the Bible contains many instances of baptism, which has a Jewish background. In the Bible, the practice of baptism meant washing away someone's sins (Acts 2:38), dying with Christ (Rom. 6:4), being "born again" (John 3:5), and receiving the gift of the Holy Spirit (1 Cor. 12:13). The history of Christianity displays some variety of perspectives on baptism, and churches today continue to hold various views on the topic.

Figure 8.14. Christian baptism in Cambodia

It is important to note that even sacraments are practiced differently around the world as local cultural elements are incorporated into these traditions. For instance, what meaningful substances can be used to celebrate the Lord's Supper in a given culture? Protestant churches in the West typically use wine or grape juice to represent Christ's blood and unleavened bread or cracker for his body. The fact that Christianity is a movement of translation means that even aspects of its sacraments are translatable in particular contexts. In some Pacific Island churches, kava, an indigenous plant from which a drink is made, is used instead of wine. Coconut milk is used in other

Figure 8.15. Russian Orthodox Church baptism in St. Petersburg, Russia

places. Pushing the parameters of translation raises some interesting dilemmas: can Coca-Cola be used meaningfully in the Global North as a substitute for wine? Soda drinks may be popular in the Global North, and increasingly to people in the Global South, but they represent multinational corporations and convey unintended messages about the relationship between the church and corporate culture.

THE LORD'S SUPPER

Furthermore, there are three significantly different perspectives about the elements used in the Lord's Supper. The Roman Catholic and the Orthodox churches affirm the doctrine of **transubstantiation**, which means that the elements (wine and bread) in fact are

Figure 8.16. Roman Catholic ordination in Schwyz, Switzerland

SIDEBAR 8.2

Whiteman on Contextualization

One of the most important issues in Christianity, theology, and worship is contextualization. Indeed, contextualization has been a part of the church since its beginning. Contextualization is a debated term, but most simply it refers to the attempt to communicate the gospel meaningfully in cultures; that is, contextualization implies a certain relationship between gospel and culture. According to anthropologist and mission scholar Darrell Whiteman, contextualization attempts "to communicate the Gospel in word and deed and to establish the church in ways that make sense to people within their local cultural context, presenting Christianity in such a way that it meets people's deepest needs and penetrates their worldview, thus allowing them to follow Christ and remain within their own culture." Thus, says Whiteman, there is "good contextualization" and "bad contextualization." Good contextualization offends "but only for the right reasons, not the wrong ones." Bad contextualization is poor contextualization, since people are offended for the wrong reasons: for example, "the garment of Christianity gets stamped with the label 'Made in America and Proud of It,' and so it is easily dismissed as a 'foreign religion' and hence irrelevant to their culture." Good contextualization exposes people's sinfulness and "the tendency toward evil, oppressive structures and behavior patterns within their culture." Indeed, this would be offensive for some, because it would challenge the powers that be and the patterns that oppress.

Whiteman, "Contextualization," 3–4

transformed (transubstantiate, "change in substance") into the real blood and body of Christ during the celebration of the Eucharist based on a literal reading of the biblical passage "this is my body" (e.g., Matt. 26:26). Some Protestant churches, such as the Lutherans, believe in **consubstantiation**, where the bread and wine *and* the real body and blood of Christ exist together. Other Protestant churches, such as those from the Zwingli/Calvin Reformed, Wesleyan, and Anabaptist traditions, hold a *memorial* view that sees the elements of bread and wine as only signifying and representing the blood and body of Christ, but not literally becoming or sharing in those realities.

Figure 8.17. Benediction during Eucharistic Adoration, during holy hour at St. Ignatius Roman Catholic Church in Hicksville, New York, USA

Ed Casey Jr.

Tithes and Offerings

Another practice that seems nearly universal is the giving of tithes and offerings, which are voluntary contributions given to the church for its ministries among the congregation, the wider community, and the world. The Bible distinguishes between "tithes," often considered a tenth of what one earns or produces, and "offerings," the gifts given to God that go beyond tithes; yet both are encouraged as a reflection of one's gratitude for God's provisions. The Old Testament presents several instances where tithes were given, noting that Abram gave a tithe to Melchizedek, king of Salem (Gen. 14:18–20) and that a tithe of 10 percent was required by their religious law (Lev. 27:30; Num. 18:26; Deut. 14:23; 2 Chron. 31:5).

The New Testament addresses offerings as contributions to support the church but does not suggest a particular percentage of one's earnings or produce (1 Cor. 16:1–2). Offerings can consist of cash or stocks, but they can also be of agricultural products, literally, the "first fruits" from one's crop yield. The Bible mentions that persons who give tithes should not be compelled to do so, but the practice should emanate from a cheerful heart because "God loves a cheerful giver" (2 Cor. 9:7).

> *I have decided to give priority to indigenous response and local appropriation over against missionary transmission and direction, and accordingly have reversed the argument by speaking of the indigenous discovery of Christianity rather than the Christian discovery of indigenous societies.*
>
> Sanneh, *Whose Religion Is Christianity?*, 10

Modern Movements

As mentioned previously, the demographic center of gravity of Christianity has moved southward to the Global South.[10] By the 1980s, Christians in the Global North were ceasing to practice their faith at a rate of 7,600 a day (53,200 weekly). None of the mainline, historic churches (e.g., Lutherans, Methodists, Presbyterians, Episcopalians) have experienced positive numerical growth in the West for decades. By 2010, Christians in the Global North made up only 40 percent of the world's Christians, so that 60 percent of Christians now live in Africa, Asia, Latin America, and the Pacific. Christian growth in the Global South is exploding. It has been reported that out of a worldwide increase of 77,000 Christians every day, 70,000 (i.e., 91 percent) can be found in Africa, Asia, and Latin America.[11]

With the massive numerical decline in the historic churches in the West, new Christian movements are emerging that are rearticulating Christianity in ways that make Christian life more relevant to both Christians and non-Christians in the West and elsewhere. And in the Global South, Christianity is also being reconceptualized in the postcolonial period, when Christians are understanding their faith on their own cultural and social terms rather than through a perspective adopted solely from Western Christian missionaries.

Given that approximately 60 percent of the world's Christians live in the Global South, many Christians today are struggling with levels of poverty, illiteracy, health concerns, and unstable political orders incomparable to those of the Global North. While these new Christian movements have not easily been accepted in all cases by older Christian churches and denominations, they reflect an aspect of the growing edge of Christianity worldwide—the dynamic charismatic-Pentecostal movements.

To introduce some of the main modern influences on Christianity, let us look briefly at three categories: individuals, megachurches, and new movements. While not an exhaustive treatment of modern Christianity, these three categories represent some of the major powerhouses that have shaped the church in the contemporary world.

Preachers, Activists, and Prophets

Beginning in the eighteenth and nineteenth centuries, outdoor meetings, often called tent revivals, revival crusades, or evangelistic rallies, became a popular way for Christians to worship. Preachers at these revival meetings often preached a "fire and brimstone" message that called listeners to repent and be saved from the fires of hell. With intense, charismatic performance styles, these tent revivalists were among the nation's most popular speakers, animated by dramatic rhetorical flair. These multiday revivals emphasized an energetic presentation of the gospel (evangelism) and often involved healings from illnesses and emphasized speaking in tongues (**glossolalia**).

> When the day of Pentecost had come, they were all together in one place. And suddenly from heaven there came a noise like the rush of a violent wind, and it filled the entire house where they were sitting. Divided tongues, as of fire, appeared to them, and a tongue rested on each of them. All of them were filled with the Holy Spirit and began to speak in other languages, as the Spirit gave them ability.
>
> Acts 2:1–4

Revivalist preachers used whatever technology was available to communicate the power of God. With the introduction of television, these popular preachers became a significant part of the American religious landscape,

Figure 8.18. Billy Graham (right) and his son Franklin Graham (left), at a Stadium Crusade in Cleveland, Ohio, USA

influencing hundreds of thousands of people throughout the years. With increased international travel, evangelists took their messages around the world. It is important to note the power of technology in promoting religions that take advantage of multinational communication technologies.

Among the well-known early North American revivalists are the following persons: **William J. Seymour** (1870–1922), the leader of the Azusa Street Revival, was an early leader of American "Pentecostalism." **Aimee Semple McPherson** (1890–1944) founded the Pentecostal church called the Foursquare Church. **Oral Roberts** (1918–2009), a Pentecostal tent-revival preacher, helped spur the founding of Oral Roberts University. **Billy Graham** (b. 1918), considered by some to be one of the greatest evangelists ever, preached to more people around the world than any other Protestant. Other popular preachers and church leaders were **Bill Bright** (1921–2003), founder of Campus Crusade for Christ, and **Jerry Falwell** (1933–2007), founder of the fundamentalist movement called the Moral Majority, and the fundamentalist university Liberty

[Aimee Semple McPherson's] own experience with tongues had begun near the small Canadian mission where she met Robert [her husband]. Following her conversion, she began pleading with God to grant her this most coveted gift. She eventually received her wish. The process began as she shouted, "Glory to Jesus! Glory to Jesus! Glory to Jesus!!!" With each repetition, she recalled, the words "seemed to come from a deeper place . . . until great waves of 'Glory to Jesus' were rolling from my toes up; such adoration and praise I had never known possible."

Sutton, *Aimee Semple McPherson*, 39

University. Christianity has never been a monolithic tradition, and its inherent diversity has fueled the immense variety of its expression worldwide.

Modern Christian priests, pastors, and intellectuals, some of whom have straddled the fence between teaching and activism, include Bishop **Lesslie Newbigin**, **John Stott**, **Martin Luther King Jr.**, Archbishop **Oscar Romero**, and **Mother Teresa**.

LESSLIE NEWBIGIN

Lesslie Newbigin (1909–98), a Cambridge graduate and outstanding missiologist, theologian, and ecumenical statesman who spent decades in southern India, first as a village evangelist, then as a church bishop, was fiercely committed to the unity of the church worldwide. Newbigin started the Gospel and Our Culture movement that sought to re-evangelize an increasingly secularized modern West.

JOHN STOTT

John Stott (1921–2011), a London-born Christian who helped spearhead the ecumenical evangelical movement of the Lausanne Commission in 1974, was a prolific evangelical Anglican writer and church leader who was curate at All Souls Church, London (1945–50). Stott's work was primarily geared toward broadly conservative evangelical circles of the worldwide church, but he is read and respected by members of a wide variety of Christian churches.

MARTIN LUTHER KING JR.

One of the most recognized names in modern American Christianity, whose reputation and influence span the globe, is that of the pastor-activist Martin

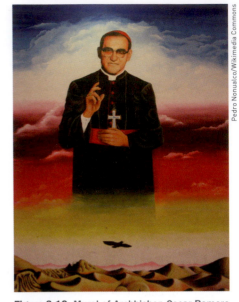

Pedro Nonualco/Wikimedia Commons

Figure 8.19. Mural of Archbishop Oscar Romero (Gioranni Ascencio and Raul Lemus, University of El Salvador, 1991)

Dick DeMarsico/Wikimedia Commons

Figure 8.20. Martin Luther King Jr.

Luther King Jr. (1929–68). Born in Atlanta, King was an African American minister, writer, and civil rights activist. He was deeply influenced by Protestant theology and Mahatma Gandhi's philosophy of nonviolent protest. He started a movement of blacks and whites that challenged the legal racial oppression in the United States, and he received the Nobel Peace Prize in 1964. King was assassinated in Memphis, Tennessee, on April 4, 1968. On the evening before his assassination, just as he had arrived in Memphis, King said:

> We've got some difficult days ahead. But it doesn't matter to me now. Because I've been to the mountaintop. And I don't mind. Like anybody, I would like to live a long life. Longevity has its place. But I'm not concerned about that now. I just want to do God's will. And He's allowed me to go up to the mountain. And I've looked over. And I've seen the promised land. I may not get there with you. But I want you to know tonight, that we, as a people, will get to the promised land. And I'm happy, tonight. I'm not worried about anything. I'm not fearing any man. Mine eyes have seen the glory of the coming of the Lord.[12]

Oscar Romero

Archbishop Oscar Romero (1917–80) was a Roman Catholic native of, and bishop in, El Salvador. Archbishop Romero had a reputation of being spiritually oriented and morally strict, and he spoke out against the murder of hundreds of the poor, including some of his own priest friends. He believed that the church's crucial task of mission and evangelism was tied to its struggle for justice for all peoples.

Because of the threat he posed to existing social and economic structures in El Salvador, and his message that the church's assignment is to transform society, particularly being on the side of the poor, Archbishop Romero was martyred while celebrating Mass on March 24, 1980. A few days before his martyrdom, Archbishop Romero told a reporter, "You can tell the people that if they succeed in killing me, that I forgive and bless those who do it. Hopefully, they will realize they are wasting their time. A bishop will die, but the church of God, which is the people, will never perish."[13]

A church that suffers no persecution but enjoys the privileges and support of the things of the earth—beware!—is not the true church of Jesus Christ. A preaching that does not point out sin is not the preaching of the gospel. A preaching that makes sinners feel good, so that they are secured in their sinful state, betrays the gospel's call.

Archbishop Oscar Romero, quoted in Schmidt, *Becoming a Storyteller*, 39

Mother Teresa

Mother Teresa (1920–97), the recipient of the Nobel Peace Prize (1979) for her nearly half-century of work among the poorest of the poor of India, was born in Albania and founded the Catholic order called the Missionaries of Charity in Kolkata (Calcutta), India. Mother Teresa established several homes for the destitute and dying throughout India, and she guided her Missionaries of Charity through its gradual expansion to cities around the world. In 2003 Mother Teresa was beatified, which is recognition by the Roman Catholic Church that she can intercede on behalf of individuals who pray in her name. Beatification is the third of four steps in the process of canonizing a saint. For beatification the Vatican requires proof of a miracle attributed to Mother Teresa. A second miracle attributed to Mother Teresa must occur after the beatification process. Several miracles attributed to her have been reported since her beatification.

Figure 8.21. Mother Teresa

Africa

On the African continent, Christian prophet-pastors have initiated major Christian movements that still exist, making Christianity thoroughly African by its blending with aspects of African traditional religions and cultures. Combining roles of spiritual leadership, prophecy, healing, and power, these pastor-prophets give Christian leadership a particularly African flavor. While not always formally ordained into the pastorate, these African leaders nonetheless function as a combination of pastor and prophet to their communities, making Christianity meaningful in indigenous African contexts.

Figure 8.22. The rooftop of Mother Teresa's Home for the Sick and Dying Destitute in Old Kolkata, India

Among the many pastor-prophets in Africa are **Isaiah Mdliwamafa Shembe**, **William Wade Harris**, **Simon Kimbangu**, **Samuel Ajayi Crowther**, **Garrick Sokari Braide**, and Bishop **Festo Kivengere**. Isaiah Shembe (1870–1935), a Zulu religious leader considered a "black Messiah" by some, founded the Zulu Nazareth Baptist Church, the largest independent Christian

I was only twelve years old then. It was then that I first knew that I had a vocation to the poor, in 1922. I wanted to be a missionary, I wanted to go out and give the life of Christ to the people in the missionary countries. . . . I've never doubted even for a second that I've done the right thing; it was the will of God. It was His choice.

Mother Teresa, *Mother Teresa*, 14

movement among the Zulus. After an initial career as an itinerant evangelist, Shembe started an annual pilgrimage to the sacred mountain of Nhlangakazi. Fellow Zulus recognized Shembe's ability to perform dramatic healings, write Christian hymns following Zulu musical traditions, and introduce Christian Zulu dancing. Some believed Shembe to be an incarnation of God.

William Wade Harris (c. 1860–1929), who was also considered a prophet, was the leader of a massive West African Christian movement that eventually became the Church of the Twelve Apostles in Ghana and the Harrist Church in Ivory Coast. Born in Liberia, Harris became a lay preacher, seeing himself as a black Elijah preaching in the last days before Christ's return. Harris wore the garments of an African prophet, carried a Bible, a calabash rattle, and a baptismal bowl, preaching the power of God and calling for repentance.

Simon Kimbangu (c. 1889–1951), born in Zaire, was another African church leader. Kimbangu received some Baptist missionary education before being rejected by missionaries who refused to accept Kimbangu's ministry as legitimate. Preaching against the usefulness of African traditional ways of protection, Kimbangu sought the intervention of God, rather than relying on missionary or governmental support. Kimbangu was considered a threat to the government and public security and was sentenced to life in prison. Today, the Kimbanguist Church has nearly five million believers.

Samuel Ajayi Crowther (c. 1807–91), a Yoruba who had been born in Nigeria, was taken as a slave by the Fulani Muslims, who sold him to Portuguese traders. Crowther was liberated by the British and sent to Sierra Leone. He later taught at Fourah Bay Institution, studied in London, returned to Yorubaland to help open a mission there, and helped to produce the translation of the Yoruba Bible. Crowther eventually became bishop over large sections of the church in West Africa.

Garrick Sokari Braide (c. 1880–1918) was another church leader, considered the first Nigerian Christian prophet. In 1915 Braide led a mass revival with baptisms and preaching against traditional African religions. Known as a prominent healer, Braide was eventually imprisoned, in part because of the complaints by

In Africa a person's name is the carrier of hope for his or her future. Our names oftentimes tell of the experiences of our parents, families, clans, ancestors, and so on. . . .

Names confer identity and personality on us and allow for the possibility of entering into a relationship with other people, other names. God reveals the divine names so that we too might know God as a personal God, and call God by name, just as God calls us by name. One of the key implications of professing faith in God is that it involves a personal commitment. The declaration "God is" does not merely announce the logical conclusion to a brilliantly crafted theological or philosophical argument. To say "God is" implies to know, love, and worship God.

Orobator, *Theology Brewed in an African Pot*, 17

religious traditionalists and also the economic threat due to his denunciation of the consumption of alcohol.

A final example of influential African leaders in contemporary Africa is Bishop Festo Kivengere (1919–88), "the Billy Graham of Africa," who gained a reputation as an evangelist and Anglican bishop of the Church of the Province of Uganda, Rwanda, Burundi, and Boga-Zaire. Born in Uganda, Kivengere was a leader in the East African revival movement and worked among rural pastoralists of Uganda. Serving as bishop during the brutal reign of President Idi Amin, who was responsible for the murder of hundreds of thousands of Ugandans, Kivengere voiced his opposition directly against Amin, proclaiming, "On the cross, Jesus said, 'Father, forgive them, because they don't know what they are doing.' As evil as Idi Amin was, how can I do less toward him?"[14]

Today African missionaries are dispersed throughout much of the world, and African pastors are leading some of the largest churches in the Global North. The history of Christianity is replete with examples of Christian leaders from around the world, be they lay, pastor, or priest, engaged in teaching, healing, baptizing, and paying with their lives for speaking and acting in ways that seek to reflect God's kingdom on earth. Christianity has burgeoned on the continent of Africa these past several decades: "By 1985 there were over 16,500 conversions [per day], yielding an annual rate of over 6 million."[15] There is good reason to believe that in the near future Africa will have the largest number of Christians of any continent.

Asia

Christianity has its origins in Asia. Jesus spent his earthly life in Palestine. The early church had its strongest congregations in Asia Minor (modern Turkey). Asians were a significant part of the day of Pentecost, when early followers of Jesus were filled with tongues of fire (i.e., languages) in order to spread the good news of Christ to all people.

> When the day of Pentecost had come, they were all together in one place. And suddenly from heaven there came a sound like the rush of a violent wind, and it filled the entire house where they were sitting. Divided tongues, as of fire, appeared among them, and a tongue rested on each of them. All of them were filled with the Holy Spirit and began to speak in other languages, as the Spirit gave them ability.
>
> Now there were devout Jews from every nation under heaven living in Jerusalem. And at this sound the crowd gathered and was bewildered, because each one heard them speaking in the native language of each. Amazed and astonished, they asked, "Are not all these who are speaking

Galileans? And how is it that we hear, each of us, in our own native language? Parthians, Medes, Elamites, and residents of Mesopotamia, Judea and Cappadocia, Pontus and Asia, Phrygia and Pamphylia, Egypt and the parts of Libya belonging to Cyrene, and visitors from Rome, both Jews and proselytes, Cretans and Arabs—in our own languages we hear them speaking about God's deeds of power." All were amazed and perplexed, saying to one another, "What does this mean?"

Acts 2:1–12

Asians were part of the beginning of the church. Following this dramatic event of speaking new tongues, Asians were among those who returned to their homes with the message of the gospel.

Some of Jesus's apostles traveled widely to introduce the good news. According to tradition, in 52 CE Thomas traveled to the region near what is known today as Chennai, India, to preach the gospel. Thomas preached in Kerala; the descendants of these followers of Christ became known as Saint Thomas Christians, known today as Syrian Christians or Nasrani. Thaddeus and Bartholomew, both disciples of Jesus, spread the good news of Jesus Christ to Syria, Iraq, and Armenia. Years later, in the year 301, Armenia would become the first nation to adopt Christianity as a state religion after Gregory the Illuminator led King Tiridates of Armenia to Christ. The disciples Simon and Andrew preached to people in the nation of Georgia. As such, the church in some places in Asia can boast of beginning as a result of direct witness by the apostles.

CHINA

Nestorian Christians visited China during the Tang dynasty (618–907), translating portions of Scripture, such as the Sermon on the Mount, into Chinese. Nestorians also converted some Mongols in the sixth century, leaving Christian influence on Mongol tribes. Despite opposition from Buddhists and Taoist communities, Christianity received support from the Chinese emperor for 150 years in China, beginning in the eighth century.

Although the current number of Christians in China is impossible to verify, in part because of the Chinese government's policies, official government estimates say there are 25 million Christians. Most observers believe that figure is hugely underestimated, with most suggesting a conservative estimate of 60 million Christians. Protestants are divided into registered and unregistered churches. The registered church is called the **Three-Self Patriotic Movement**. The unregistered church is sometimes called the "underground church" or "house church." Within the Catholic Church, the official Catholic Patriotic Association appoints its own bishops and does not allow official dealings with the Vatican. Despite the challenges and, at times, outright persecution of Christians in China, the church continues to grow.

KOREA

Tradition notes that Korea was self-evangelized, after a Korean diplomat, **Yi Gwang-jeong**, returned from Beijing in 1603 with Chinese translations of theological books written by **Matteo Ricci**, a Jesuit missionary to China. Several Korean scholars (e.g., Silhak) became Christian as a result. However, in 1758 King Yeongjo of Joseon outlawed Roman Catholicism, beginning a long period of persecution of Korean Christians. During the Joseon Dynasty (1392–1897), Korean leaders persecuted and killed over eight thousand Catholics and nine French Catholic missionaries in 1866.

The first Protestant missionary to Korea was **Robert Jermain Thomas** (1839–66), of the London Missionary Society, who was martyred in Korea. In 1884 **Horace Allen** (1858–1932), a Presbyterian, was the first American missionary to arrive in Korea. Other influential early Protestant missionaries who worked in Korea include **Horace G. Underwood** (1859–1916), of the Northern Presbyterian mission, who received financial support from his brother, John Underwood of the Underwood Typewriter Company. **Henry G. Appenzeller** (1858–1902), of the Northern Methodist mission, helped establish the first Methodist churches and actively supported Korean independence from Japan.

Born in Massachusetts, **Mary F. Scranton** (1832–1909), from the Methodist Episcopal Church, was the first Woman's Foreign Missionary Society representative in Korea. Scranton founded Ewha Girls School, which is today Ewha Womans University, one of Korea's most prestigious universities. Today Christianity is the largest religion in Korea, with nearly one-third of the population professing some form of Christian faith.

Likewise, Korean Christians grapple with their own context, which includes a history of ancestor veneration, shamanism, and various forms of oppression. Beginning in the 1970s, an indigenous theology, called ***minjung sinhak*** (theology of the people), has emphasized how Christian faith gives hope to the dispossessed. ***Minjung*** (people) theology proclaims that *minjung* are proper subjects of history—that they are subjugated people and need liberation. **Sung-Bum Yun** (1916–80), a Korean theologian who studied with Karl Barth, wrote in support of Korean Confucianism as a lens through which to understand Christian ethics. Sung-Bum Yun was a controversial figure who sought to create an indigenous Korean Christian theology—for instance, interpreting the Christian notion of the Godhead through the ancient Korean mythologies of divine figures. He was appointed to the faculty at Korea Methodist Theological Seminary (1946) and served as the seminary's president until his death in 1980.

Another important Korean Christian theologian is **Heup Young Kim** (b. 1949), who was a professor of systematic theology at Kangnam University in South Korea. After graduating from the engineering college of Seoul National University, he earned an MDiv and ThM from Princeton Theological Seminary and a PhD from the Graduate Theological Union in Berkeley, California. Kim's books focus on theology of religions, interfaith dialogue, science and religion, and constructive theology. In his book *Christ and the Tao*, he seeks to construct a theology in which the figure of Christ and his message are contextualized in a Confucian milieu. For example, Christ, as the great Sage, is presented as the incarnation of the Tao (Way). Korean theologians are contributing innovative insights to understanding Christian faith and identity.

JAPAN

In Japan, **Kanzo Uchimura** (1861–1930), a Japanese author and Christian evangelist, founded Mukyokai, or **Nonchurch Christianity**, to promote a notion of church as unorganized meetings rather than as a particular denomination. Uchimura stressed the importance of affirming what were

Percentage and Number of Christians in Some Asian Countries

Country	Total Population	Christian Population	Percentage of Christians
Armenia	3,299,000	3,256,113	98.7%
Timor-Leste	1,108,777	1,087,601	98%
Philippines	92,681,453	83,876,714	90.5%
Georgia	4,636,400	4,107,850	88.6%
Cyprus	792,604	628,535	79.3%
Lebanon	3,971,941	1,549,057	39%
South Korea	49,232,844	14,375,990	29.2%
Kuwait	2,596,561	259,656	10%
Indonesia	230,512,000	20,746,080	9%
India	1,147,995,226	26,403,890	2.3%
Iran	70,472,846	300,000	0.4%
Turkey	74,724,269	149,449	0.2%

http://en.wikipedia.org/wiki/Christianity_in_Asia

called the two Js: "Japan and Jesus." Another Japanese Christian leader was **Nitobe Inazo** (1852–1933), an author, economist, and diplomat. Nitobe studied at Johns Hopkins University in the United States, then received a doctorate in agricultural economics from Halle University in Germany. Nitobe was founding president of Tokyo Women's Christianity University.

It is wrong to say that we must produce an indigenous theology. It is not necessary to produce one. It is there.

Kosuke Koyama, *Water Buffalo Theology*, 60

Toyohiko Kagawa (1888–1960), a pacifist and labor activist, employed Christian principles to reform Japanese society. Kagawa was an action-oriented Christian who moved to Kobe, Japan, to serve as a missionary and social worker. Eventually, Kagawa was imprisoned for his labor activities during strikes, but that did not deter him from his social activism. Kagawa believed that the church should be a cooperative movement, and he advocated what he called "brotherhood economics." Kagawa was a prolific writer, publishing over 150 books.

The crucified mind, not the crusading mind, must be the mind of all missionaries, indeed of all Christians.

Kosuke Koyama, *Water Buffalo Theology*, 159

The influential Japanese Christian **Kosuke Koyama** (1929–2009) was born in Tokyo and studied at Drew Theological Seminary and Princeton Theological Seminary, where he earned a PhD. Koyama taught at several theological schools in Asia, then was appointed as John D. Rockefeller Jr. Professor of World Christianity at Union Theological Seminary, New York. One of the leading Japanese theologians of the twentieth century, Koyama argued that theology needs to be made accessible to uneducated persons rather than being limited to academic discourse.

India

Indian Christianity dates back to the days of Thomas. Contemporary Christianity in India, while its followers represent a small percentage of the Indian population, remains a thriving and vital part of Indian society. Perhaps because of the multireligious context of India, Indian Christian theologians have had to articulate their faith in ways that are meaningful to Indian Christians as well as Hindus, Buddhists, Jains, Sikhs, Muslims, and within secular contexts. A particularly challenging issue that Indian theologians engage is the uniqueness of Christ in the midst of a religiously diverse world.

Among the important twentieth-century Indian Christian leaders are Michael Amaladoss, M. M. Thomas, and P. D. Devanandan. Jesuit theologian Father **Michael Amaladoss** (b. 1936), director of the Institute for Dialogue with Cultures and Religions in Chennai and a professor at Vidyajyoti College of Theology, Delhi, has written several books about Christianity's encounter with South Asian religions and cultures. **M. M. Thomas** (1916–96) was a renowned Indian Christian theologian and governor of the Nagaland, India. Thomas was born in a Mar Thoma family and, after opening an orphanage in Kerala, became chairman of the Central Committee of the World Council of Churches (1968–75). A strong supporter of the ecumenical movement, Thomas actively promoted mission and evangelism in India and throughout the world.

P. D. Devanandan (1901–62), an Indian Protestant theologian, was a pioneer in interreligious dialogue in India. Born in Chennai, India, Devanandan studied in India, taught in Sri Lanka, then earned his PhD in comparative religion at Yale University in 1931. He was ordained in the Church of South India and directed the Center for the Study of Hinduism (later called Christian Institute for the Study of Religions and Society, Bangalore). Devanandan's writing focused on Christian attitudes toward non-Christian religions, the Christian understandings of Hinduism, and religion and nationalism in India, among other topics.

Contemporary Asian theologians and church leaders are wrestling with what it means to be a Christian both in their local contexts and in an increasingly globalized world. Since Asia is the birthplace of nearly all the major world religions, the region presents unique challenges to Christian faith and identity. Asia is unique in part because it is home to many religious scriptures from the various world religions, has immense linguistic and cultural variety, possesses the oldest forms of Christianity, and has massive national populations (e.g., China, India, Indonesia).

The presence of Christians throughout Asia today is quite uneven, with Christians making up less than 2 percent in many nations (e.g., Japan, North Korea, Cambodia, Thailand, and the Muslim countries of Turkey, Afghanistan, the Maldives, Oman, Saudi Arabia, and Yemen), while in other nations they constitute the

Many Indian disciples of Jesus, whether Hindu or Christian, have considered him as their guru. Christians stress the uniqueness of Jesus by calling him sadguru (true guru).

Amaladoss, *Asian Jesus*, 69–70

The real problem in Hindu India is to effect a synthesis between the traditional world-view and contemporary secularism . . . it is in relation to this concern that the good news of God incarnate in Jesus Christ will have to be spelled out.

P. D. Devanandan,
Preparation for Dialogue, 38

At best we can only confess our inability to understand God's ways with us men; at worst, we must blame ourselves for our blindness in refusing to believe that God is equally concerned with the redemption of people other than us, people who may not wholly agree with our understanding of God's being and His purpose for the world of His making.

P. D. Devanandan, *Preparation for Dialogue*, 188

majority (e.g., Armenia, Timor-Leste, the Philippines, Georgia, Cyprus, and South Korea). In some Asian countries, Christians make up a sizable minority group. For instance, there are over twenty million Christians in Indonesia. Today almost all forms of Christianity can be found in Asia, from Eastern Orthodoxy to Pentecostal expressions.

Megachurches: Bigger, Better

Christianity is the world's largest religion, with more than two billion adherents. The sizes of local churches today stand in stark contrast to those of the first century, when the first followers of Jesus met mostly in small homes. Since the mid-twentieth century, large churches have emerged, often called "**megachurches**" since they have more than two thousand attendees. Roughly 80 percent of North American megachurches are categorized as the following: nondenominational (34 percent), Southern Baptist (16 percent), Baptist (10 percent), Assemblies of God (6 percent), United Methodist (5 percent), Calvary Chapel (4.4 percent), and Christian (4.2 percent). In a 2005 survey of the theology of 403 United States megachurches, one study categorized their theological orientation as follows: evangelical (56 percent), charismatic (8 percent), Pentecostal (8 percent), moderate (7 percent), traditional (5 percent), seeker (7 percent), fundamentalist (2 percent), and other (7 percent), showing that members of megachurches overwhelmingly define themselves as "evangelical."[16]

Puzzlet Chung/Wikimedia Commons

Figure 8.23. Yoido Full Gospel Church in Seoul, South Korea

The term "megachurch" is usually applied to Protestant churches rather than Roman Catholic churches. Among these megachurches are the largest churches in the world, such as the Yoido Full Gospel Church, in Seoul, South Korea, with nearly 850,000 members, over 500 pastors, and 100,000 deacons. While it is impossible to provide an exhaustive summary of all aspects of megachurches, such churches are usually characterized by a high number of believers, conservative evangelical theology, Pentecostal or charismatic worship and preaching styles that emphasize relevant messages, high value placed on the use of modern technology, and contemporary worship music played by a band, with electric guitars, bass, keyboard, and drums. The theology that undergirds some megachurches is known as the prosperity gospel—that is, the emphasis that God promises to bless with material wealth those who give to him (i.e., to the church).

Examples of North American megachurches include Lakewood Church in Houston, Texas, and Willow Creek Community Church in South Barrington, Illinois, which host over 50,000 and 23,000 attendees respectively each Sunday. Saddleback Church, in Lake Forest, California, led by Pastor **Rick Warren**, has 20,000 in weekly attendance, and The Potter's House, in Dallas, has 30,000 attendees. One of the largest churches in the United Kingdom, which happens to be led by Pastor **Matthew Ashimolowo**, a Nigerian,

Wikimedia Commons

Figure 8.24. Universal Church of the Kingdom of God in Mercado de las Flores, Buenos Aires, Argentina

boasts 12,000 attendees. Some of the megachurches located outside the North Atlantic region include Hillsong Church (Australia), with 20,000 members; City Harvest Church (Singapore), with over 23,000 attendees; the Reformed Millennium Cathedral (Jakarta, Indonesia), with 4,500 attendees; and the Universal Church of the Kingdom of God (Brazil), which boasts dozens of congregations throughout the world, including Latin America, Europe, North America, Africa, and Asia. There are more than 5,000 Universal Church of the Kingdom of God churches in Brazil alone, and approximately 12,000 people weekly attend the main church in Rio de Janeiro. Since the average congregational size of North American churches is about 250 attendees, these megachurches stand out in local communities, sometimes receiving the critical description of being "big-box churches," which have dominated the market share of Christian membership, leaving smaller churches with fewer attendees, akin to the "big-box stores" that have put smaller commercial enterprises out of business.

Politically, megachurches have become quite powerful, since by their sheer numbers they have the potential to shape local and national elections, even if megachurches claim to be politically neutral, such as when Rick Warren of Saddleback hosted President George W. Bush and presidential hopeful Barack H. Obama on the Saddleback Church campus during the 2008 presidential campaign.

New Movements: Beyond the "Confines" of the Church

In the late twentieth and early twenty-first centuries, a new church movement appeared that was broadly referred to as the **emerging church** ("emergent church" or "emerging movement"). The emerging movement has been described as postliberal, postevangelical, post-Christendom, postmodern, and even postdenominational, emphasizing narrative and personal story as carriers of truth rather than cold, abstract propositions.

These new communities of faith seek to provide a fresh interpretation of Christianity that is meaningful in modern Western culture, engaged politically, highly relational, and action oriented. The emerging movement, according to Scot McKnight, combines five major themes: (1) prophetic rhetoric that aims to be consciously provocative; (2) a postmodern stance that rebuffs propositional truth in favor of "faith seeking understanding"; (3) a praxis orientation that seeks to live out Christian faith rather than just speaking about it or assuming it simply means mental assent to a set of doctrines (McKnight suggests that the emerging church focuses on worship that is creative and sensory, and also missional, by participating with God in acts of holistic redemption); (4) postevangelical, rejecting the "in versus out" or "us and them" mentality that characterizes some traditional evangelical churches that draw a hard line between Christians and non-Christians; and (5) politically engaged, leaning toward the left (i.e., Democratic) on the political spectrum.[17]

Emerging churches meet in a wide variety of spaces, such as homes, businesses, empty warehouses, skateboard parks, and church buildings refashioned to meet their needs. Worship assemblies vary with some sitting in circles, some on soft-cushioned sofas, and others in a coffeehouse-like atmosphere with attendees gathered around small tables. Emphasizing the relationality of the community, emerging churches boast of the freedom to explore new ways of enhancing community in part by utilizing worship spaces creatively, engaging in modern technology and forms of communication (e.g., Twitter, Facebook, blogs) to enhance face-to-face and virtual communities both locally and worldwide.

The communitarian nature of the emerging church, where focus is more on building personal relationships rather than institutions, has its appeal in modern Western contexts, which sometimes lack the warmth of interpersonal relationships. Furthermore, there are new groups that combine emerging church commitments in the context of alternative communities, such as the New Monasticism movement, which emphasizes social justice, environmental stewardship, and simple living, while inserting those intentional communities into residential neighborhoods as intentional bodies of Christian witness.

> *Emerging churches are communities that practice the way of Jesus within postmodern cultures. This definition encompasses nine practices. Emerging churches (1) identify with the life of Jesus, (2) transform the secular realm, and (3) live highly communal lives. Because of these activities, they (4) welcome the stranger, (5) serve with generosity, (6) participate as producers, (7) create as created beings, (8) lead as a body, and (9) take part in spiritual activities.*
>
> Gibbs and Bolger,
> *Emerging Churches*, 45

Conclusion

Since the beginning of the church, Christians have assembled to share fellowship, worship, and discuss and debate theological doctrine, to be sent back into the world as bearers in word and deed of the good news of the kingdom of God. More recently, three large ecumenical movements have gathered most of the Christian church: the **World Council of Churches** (WCC), the mainline Protestant movement consisting of approximately 347 denominations spanning over 110 countries, and including many Orthodox Christians; the Lausanne Movement, started in 1974 by American evangelist Billy Graham and others, and including over 4,000 evangelical Christian leaders and numerous evangelical denominations; and the Roman Catholic

Church, which has over 1 billion adherents and meets as a large body to discuss timely theological issues, with the **Second Vatican Council** (1962–65) being a significant example.

Today these ecumenical groups frequently extend invitations to members of the other assemblies to join their gatherings, even if visitors are not given the privilege to vote. While there have always been independent churches apart from these three major ecumenical movements, it appears that with the emergence of megachurches and the emerging church movement a new style of ecumenism may arise in the future. Or will there be increasing division within the church worldwide, which would negatively impact its witness? In other words, will older patterns of ecumenism, which sought visible unity and common vision for ministry, give way to a new ecumenism based not on narrow theological commitments but rather on the broadest theological affirmations of Christian faith?

Herein lies both the strength of Christianity and a major challenge, since as a movement of translation Christianity enables and embraces new forms of cultural expression and theological articulation, and at the same time it seeks unity in the midst of such diversity. As Christianity engages particular cultures, it also is often reformulated to make it meaningful to local people. Still, a major criticism of Christianity has been its lack of unity. In contexts where Christianity is a minority tradition, it is not unusual for people to ask some variation of "What religion are you, Lutheran, Methodist, Catholic, or

Charles E. Farhadian

Figure 8.25. Jesus in yoga position at a Christian ashram in Tamil Nadu, India

Assemblies of God?" The fact is that the division between Christian churches (e.g., denominations) around the world has been a poor witness to Christian unity.

It is important to keep in mind that Christianity, like other religions, cannot be separated from the social, cultural, political, and personal (e.g., psychological, emotional) contexts in which it thrives. As such, being the largest religion in the world brings with it challenges to remain meaningful in numerous contexts while at the same time demonstrating continuity with its past.

Timeline

c. 4 BCE	Jesus born
c. 26 CE	John the Baptist begins his ministry
c. 27	Jesus begins his ministry
c. 30	Crucifixion of Jesus
c. 35	Conversion of Saul (becomes Paul)
c. 36	Martyrdom of Stephen
c. 46–48	Paul's first missionary journey
c. 49	Council of Jerusalem
c. 50–52	Paul's second missionary journey
c. 53–57	Paul's third missionary journey
c. 59–62	Paul imprisoned in Rome
c. 68	Martyrdom of Paul
70	Fall of Jerusalem
325	Council of Nicaea
380	Christianity made official religion of Roman Empire
381	Council of Constantinople
451	Council of Chalcedon
1054	Great Schism between East and West
1200	Bible available in twenty-two languages
1383	Bible translated into English from Latin by John Wycliff
1415	Council of Constance
1453	Constantinople falls to the Muslim Ottoman Turks; Islamic service of thanksgiving is held in the church of Saint Sophia
1496	First Christian baptisms in the New World, on island of Hispaniola
1517	Martin Luther posts *Ninety-Five Theses*
1536	John Calvin's *Institutes of the Christian Religion* published

1542	Francis Xavier goes to Portuguese colony of Goa, India
1584	Matteo Ricci and a Chinese scholar translate a catechism into Chinese
1605	Roberto de Nobili traveled to India
1611	King James (Authorized) Version of the Bible produced
1644	John Eliot begins ministry to Algonquians in North America
1706	Bartholomaeus Ziegenbalg, pietist missionary, arrives in Tranqubar, India; establishes first Protestant church in India
1738	John Wesley, founder of Methodism, feels his "heart strangely warmed"
1810	American Board of Commissioners for Foreign Mission (ABCFM) established, the first American Christian missionary organization
1869	First Vatican Council
1885	Horace Grant Underwood (Presbyterian) and Henry Appenzeller (Methodist) arrive in Korea
1906	Azusa Street Revival; early Pentecostalism
1910	World Missionary Conference, Edinburgh
1948	Founding of World Council of Churches
1962–65	Second Vatican Council
1973	Billy Graham attracts 4.5 million people to his services in six Korean cities
1974	Lausanne Covenant is written and ratified
1989	First woman ordained in an apostolic-succession church (Episcopal Church)
2001	Armenia marks 1,700th anniversary of Christianity as its state religion
2008	Conservative Anglicans plan to split from liberal Anglicans in the "Jerusalem Declaration"
2013	Pope Francis, an Argentinean, became first non-European pope

Key Terms

Allen, Horace	apostolic authority	atonement
Amaladoss, Michael	apotheosis	Augustine
Anabaptist	Appenzeller, Henry G.	Balthasar, Hans Urs von
Apocrypha	Arianism	Barth, Karl
Apollinarius	Arius	Braide, Garrick Sokari
apologists	Ashimolowo, Matthew	Bright, Bill
apostle	Athanasius	Calvin, John

Further Reading ....

Amaladoss, Michael. *The Asian Jesus*. Maryknoll, NY: Orbis, 2006.

Bediako, Kwame. *Jesus and the Gospel in Africa: History and Experience*. Maryknoll, NY: Orbis, 2004.

Burridge, Kenelm. *In the Way: A Study of Christian Missionary Endeavors*. Vancouver: University of British Columbia Press, 1991.

Gutiérrez, Gustavo. *A Theology of Liberation*. Maryknoll, NY: Orbis, 1988.

Jenkins, Philip. *The Next Christendom: The Coming of Global Christianity*. New York: Oxford University Press, 2007.

McFague, Sallie. *Metaphorical Theology: Models of God in Religious Language*. Minneapolis: Augsburg Fortress, 1982.

Newbigin, Lesslie. *The Finality of Christ*. Richmond, VA: John Knox Press, 1969.

Nida, Eugene A. *Message and Meaning: The Communication of the Christian Faith*. Pasadena, CA: William Carey Library, 1990.

Oduyoye, Mercy Amba. *Hearing and Knowing: Theological Reflections on Christianity in Africa*. Maryknoll, NY: Orbis, 1986.

Pelikan, Jaroslav. *The Christian Tradition*. Vol. 1, *The Emergence of the Catholic Tradition (100–600)*. Chicago: University of Chicago Press, 1971.

Placher, William C. *A History of Christian Theology: An Introduction*. Philadelphia: Westminster Press, 1983.

Robert, Dana Robert. "Shifting Southward: Global Christianity since 1945." *International Bulletin of Missionary Research* 24, no. 2 (April 2000): 50–58.

Sanneh, Lamin. *Whose Religion Is Christianity? The Gospel beyond the West*. Grand Rapids: Eerdmans, 2003.

Sugirtharajah, R. S. *The Bible and Empire: Postcolonial Explorations*. New York: Cambridge University Press, 2005.

Walls, Andrew F. *The Missionary Movement in Christian History: Studies in the Transmission of Faith*. Maryknoll, NY: Orbis, 2007.

Wilken, Robert Louis. *The Spirit of Early Christian Thought: Seeking the Face of God*. New Haven: Yale University Press, 2005.

nine

Islam

Contemporary Snapshot

It is 4:23 a.m., with the dark night just now beginning to give way to the morning sun on the horizon. The streets are quiet; only two shop owners are sweeping away the dust that had gathered in front of their stores earlier that night. It's been a warm evening in the tropics, so windows are open, letting the cool air of the night skies circulate through the rooms made hot by the sun throughout the day. As cows and chickens begin to stir, and a rooster readies itself to broadcast its first crow, a Muslim crier (**muezzin**) named Bilal, having ritualistically washed himself thoroughly with water only moments before, ascends the long steps taking him to the top of the prayer tower (**minaret**) of the **masjid** (i.e., **mosque**). Once at the top, Bilal offers a brief prayer stating his intention to offer prayer, then purposely raises his cupped hands to his mouth, as though he is positioning himself to speak to the world, readying himself to make an important announcement. He breaks the quiet of the night by exclaiming loudly and melodiously, so that the entire village hears every word:

415

God is the greatest
I bear witness that there is no god except God
I bear witness that Muhammad is the Messenger of God
Make haste toward worship
Come to the true success
Prayer is better than sleep
God is the greatest
There is no deity except God

It is early in the morning, and Bilal's voice is the first that villagers will hear that day. From this Indonesian village, Muslim faithful will face northwest, toward the **Qa'abah** (cube) located in the middle of the Great Masjid in **Mecca**, Saudi Arabia. All Muslims throughout the world, no matter where they are located, will be directing their prayers toward the large black cube (Qa'abah) of the Great Masjid in Mecca. Some, then, will be facing north, others south, some east, and some west. "Prayer is better than sleep." Not everyone in the village will rise to pray, but those within earshot of the call to prayer will begin their day thinking about God ("God is the greatest"), even if just for a fleeting moment. Committed Muslims will pray five times daily: **Fajr** (dawn prayer), **Zuhr** (noon prayer), **Asr** (afternoon prayer), **Maghrib** (sunset prayer), and **Isha** (night prayer). Muslims pray for many reasons, but one of the most important reasons is that prayer reminds believers of their reliance on God and God's compassion and mercy.

Origins and Concepts

Swift Spread of Islam

It will surprise some to learn that the vast majority of the world's Muslim population lives in South Asia and Southeast Asia, with Indonesia being the most populous Muslim country in the world. Numerically, then, Islam is

Figure 9.1. Muslim men praying

Figure 9.2. Grand Mosque in Mecca, Saudi Arabia

Charles E. Farhadian

Ali/Wikimedia Commons

Figure 9.3. Interior of Cordoba Mosque in Cordoba, Spain

heavily Asian, with the number of South and Southeast Asian Muslims far surpassing the number of Middle Eastern Muslims. Although the history of Islam began in the Arab world, its center of gravity is in South and Southeast Asia. Large Muslim populations also inhabit central Asia and China.

Islam began in the western Arabian Peninsula town of Mecca in the seventh century and rapidly spread north into Syria and Palestine, east into central Asia, and west into Egypt, Libya, Tunisia, Algeria, Morocco, Spain, and Portugal. The swift expansion of Islam was possible partly because the religion had a single founder (Prophet Muhammad), a foundational document (**Qur'an**), and some say it contained within it a political blueprint enabling rapid decision making about organization, legal matters, and relationships among Muslims and between Muslims and non-Muslims. Today Islam is the second largest religion in the world, with approximately 1.3 billion adherents spread throughout almost every region of the world.

THE LIFE OF PROPHET MUHAMMAD

Since it is impossible to underestimate the place of **Prophet Muhammad** (i.e.,

Figure 9.4. Sufi Mosque at Ladysmith in KwaZulu-Natal, South Africa

417

Map 9.1. Arabian Peninsula

the Prophet) in Islam, let us examine the life of Muhammad (c. 570–632 CE), considered the final in a long line of prophets who witnessed to the reality of the one God. Muhammad was born in Mecca, in the Hejaz region of the Arabian Peninsula, around 570 CE, in a tribe called the **Quraysh**, who were custodians of the Qa'abah, the large cube in Mecca, whose base measures 34 feet by 40 feet with a height of 43 feet, toward which certain rituals were directed by the vast numbers of Meccan tribes.

At the time of Muhammad's birth, Mecca was a prosperous place whose economy was based primarily on trade, thanks to its strategic location at the intersection of trade routes from the eastern Mediterranean to ports that served trade with India and Sri Lanka. Various other religions were present in pre-Islamic Arabia, including Christianity, Judaism, and Zoroastrianism, the indigenous religion of Persia. Although some scholars note that these religions influenced Muhammad and Islam, it is unclear to what extent there was a cross-fertilization of ideas.

Muhammad grew up in a period when young boys had no future without having items to trade and engage the wider economy. By the age of six, both of Muhammad's parents had died. Were it not for **Abu Talib**, Muhammad's uncle, the Prophet may have been left an unprotected orphan. Abu Talib raised and sheltered Muhammad, along with Abu Talib's son, **'Ali** ibn Abi Talib (otherwise known as 'Ali). Mecca's social and religious worlds were interconnected; each tribe identified itself by its local deity, which was portrayed in the form of a statue or other depiction. The Qa'abah contained the idols with which Meccan tribes identified themselves. Although Meccan tribes engaged in intertribal conflicts, going close to the Qa'abah during religious rituals required that warring peoples disarm themselves, thus creating an atmosphere of peace around the Qa'abah. Therefore, Muhammad was raised in a religious and cultural environment that recognized several gods.

418

Muhammad and the Recitations

As a young man, Muhammad did not possess the resources to engage in trade, but a wealthy widow, **Khadijah**, employed him. After his successful leadership of a trade caravan to Damascus, Khadijah, who was fifteen years older than Muhammad, married him in 595 CE. The Qur'an, the Muslim holy book, says that Muhammad grew up in poverty (Qur'an 93:6–7) and was perhaps illiterate (Qur'an 29:51). Tradition says that Muhammad was spiritually sensitive and began his career accepting the religious affirmations of his community, which included in part the belief in jinn (fiery spirits), good and evil, omens, and Satan. As Muhammad grew to maturity, he became increasingly critical of the polytheistic religions and the quarreling within Mecca between the various Meccan tribes. In 610, at about the age of forty, Muhammad visited a cave near the base of Mount Hira, outside Mecca, where he prayed. As Muhammad was praying, tradition says that the angel Gabriel (i.e., Jibra'il) appeared to him suddenly, exclaiming, "*Iqra!*" (Arabic, "Recite/read"), demanding that Muhammad recite the words that the angel Gabriel would deliver from God.

Figure 9.5. The Prophet Muhammad (figure without face) on Mount Hira. Ottoman miniature painting from the Siyer-i Nebi (from the Topkapi Sarayi Müzesi, Istanbul, Turkey).

The words from the angel Gabriel are accepted as the earliest recitation that appears in the Qur'an:

> Proclaim! [or Read!] in the name of your Lord and Cherisher,
> who created, Created man, out of a leech-like clot. Proclaim!
> And your Lord is Most Bountiful, He Who taught (the use of) the Pen,
> Taught man that which he knew not.
>
> Qur'an 96:1–5

According to Yusuf 'Ali, whose modern English translation of the Qur'an is the most popular among English-speaking Muslims, Gabriel's imperative message started Islam's worldwide mission.[1] At first Muhammad rejected Gabriel's word, but then he felt the words driven through him. Muslim tradition says that Muhammad remembered the whole recitation and afterward told others. Muhammad continued to receive recitations from Gabriel until his death in 632 CE. Furthermore, Muhammad's wife 'Aisha was said to have seen a recitation come down on Muhammad on one occasion: "I saw revelation coming down on him in the severest cold, and when that condition was over, perspiration ran down his forehead."[2]

Muhammad became the Prophet. For the first three years after his encounter with Gabriel, Prophet Muhammad told those closest to him about the recitations, which led to the acceptance of the messages by, among others, Khadijah (his first wife), 'Ali (his first cousin), and Zayd ibn Haritha (later called Zayda ibn Muhammad, a freed slave and adopted son of Prophet Muhammad). After three years, Prophet Muhammad went public with the recitations he was receiving, which raised the indignation of Meccan tribes that perceived the recitations as a threat to their social, economic, and moral lives. And the challenge to Meccan social, economic, and moral lives was genuine, based on the content of the recitations.

Early Recitations Received by Prophet Muhammad

The early recitations can be summarized in three parts. First, and most importantly, the early recitations focused on the affirmation that Allah is one, known as *tawhid* (Arabic, "doctrine of oneness" or "divine unity"), where God is understood as an indivisible being, nonanthropomorphic, impossible to depict through pictures or images of any kind. *Tawhid* challenged the rampant polytheism in Mecca, directly confronting the economic livelihood of those who depended on Meccan shrines and making idols used in pre-Islamic Meccan worship. Second, the early recitations revealed that all human beings would face a judgment day when everyone would appear before God. Neither the judgment day nor the concept of eternal life was recognized by pre-Islamic Meccan tribes, but the influence of Jews, Christians, and Zoroastrians, who did have a notion of a final judgment day, heaven, and hell, is recognized by non-Muslims as impacting the Prophet's message.

The fact that Prophet Muhammad's recitations included judgment was tantamount to pronouncing an ethic that defied the moneymaking policies of the wealthy merchants of Mecca, since their moral actions would be adjudicated by none other than God, which provided quite an incentive to be morally honest when dealing with neighbors and trade partners. Finally, Prophet Muhammad revealed to the Meccans that he was the final prophet, the channel through which God would reveal God's word, the Qur'an. The message was clear and simple: there is only one God, all creation is derived from him, and all human beings should submit to God in corresponding unity—a simple message with profound social and religious implications.

THE FIRST MUSLIMS

The early recitations and the emerging community of faith, consisting of about fifty persons, met with strong resistance by fellow Meccan tribes, which eventually led to the flight of the small group of adherents from Mecca to another important trade city, **Yathrib**, in 622 CE. Leaders in Yathrib—a place not unlike Mecca in its composition of various tribal groups that occasionally fought and identified with local deities—invited Prophet Muhammad to adjudicate intertribal conflicts and teach them about the recitations. Consequently, in 622 CE, the small group of Prophet Muhammad's followers left Mecca for Yathrib, with Prophet Muhammad and **Abu Bakr**, the Prophet's father-in-law, following behind.

The migration of early followers, referred to as the **Companions** (of the Prophet), was immensely significant, for this was the first time that this group identified itself not according to tribal or clan affiliations but rather as people who submit to God—that is, **Muslims**. In Yathrib, Prophet Muhammad arbitrated tribal and Jewish conflicts successfully, through the Constitution of **Medina**, and introduced the recitations, which were quickly received as revealed truth. Yathrib was renamed Medina, "the City of the Prophet," where Prophet Muhammad established the first masjid (place of Muslim worship).

Prophet Muhammad's leadership combined the roles of politician, religious prophet, and military general. In 630 CE, Prophet Muhammad and ten thousand Medinan Muslims conquered Mecca in what scholars note was a relatively bloodless coup, in which only a few Meccans were killed. By the time of his death in 632 CE, Prophet Muhammad had united the majority of the Arabian Peninsula, as tribal representatives negotiated truces with him and submitted to Islam.

THE RIGHTLY GUIDED SUCCESSORS

Following the death of Prophet Muhammad, four **Rightly Guided Caliphs** (Arabic, "successors," "stewards," "guardians") led Islam in succession, but not without fierce disagreement. The Rightly Guided Caliphs included Abu Bakr (632–34), Umar (634–44), **Uthman** (644–56), and 'Ali (656–61).[3] Each caliph extended Islam further outside the Arabian Peninsula, each bringing his own gifts to bear on his rule. However, Uthman's **caliphate**

Figure 9.6. Umayyid Mosque in Damascus, Syria

(i.e., government) left an indelible mark on Islam, for it was Uthman who led the task of gathering the recitations of Prophet Muhammad that had made their way across the Islamic world through writings on branches, leaves, leather, bones, and different sorts of parchment, deciphering which ones were authentic and fraudulent and destroying all inaccurate compilations. Uthman's compilation, which is considered a miracle by Muslims, was known as the Uthmanic Codex and was established as the true recitation given to Prophet Muhammad, otherwise known as **al-Qur'an** (literally, "the recitation").

Allah

The central focus of the Qur'an is **Allah**. The Arabic term "Allah" comes from the conflation of the Arabic *al-ilah*, meaning "the God" (*al* is the definite article, and *ilah* is "god"). Crucial to understanding this Arabic term is the fact that *al-ilah* cannot be pluralized. In Arabic there is no such thing as "al-ilahs," even though grammatically the English does allow for the terms "Gods" or "gods." The Arabic exclamation ***Allahu Akbar*** ("Allah is greater" or "God is greatest") is known as the ***Takbir***, a common Muslim expression used in various contexts such as prayer, celebration, or times of distress. Since Arabic is a Semitic language, like Hebrew and Aramaic, it should not be surprising that there are many similarities between the names for God in this language family.

The Qur'an proclaims that Allah is creator, sustainer, judge, and ruler of the material, human, and spiritual realms, guiding history through a long line of prophets, such as Adam, considered the first prophet, Noah (**Nuh**), Abraham (**Ibrahim**), Moses (**Musa**), Jesus (**Isa**), and finally Prophet Muhammad. Allah is worshiped at the Qa'abah in Mecca as the "high god" over all pre-Islamic gods.

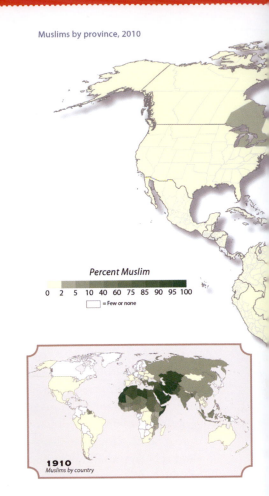

Muslims by province, 2010

Percent Muslim

0 2 5 10 40 60 75 85 90 95 100

☐ = Few or none

1910
Muslims by country

Figure 9.7. Arabic script for "Allah"

2010

1910

Muslim center of gravity

Map 9.2. Muslims 1910–2010

God, there is no god but He—the Living, the Self-subsisting, Eternal. No slumber can seize Him nor sleep. His are all things in the heavens and on earth. Who is he that can intercede in His presence except as He permitteth? He knoweth what (appeareth to His creatures as) before or after or behind them. Nor shall they compass aught of His knowledge except as He willeth. His Throne doth extend over the heavens and the earth, and He feeleth no fatigue in guarding and preserving them for He is the Most High, the Supreme (in glory).

Qur'an 2:255

The Old Testament presents several names for God, including El (God, "strong"), Elohim (plural form of God), El Shaddai ("God Almighty"), El Elyon ("Most High"), El-Olam ("Everlasting God"), El-Berith ("God of the Covenant"), and El-Gibhor ("Mighty God").

http://www.myredeemerlives .com/namesofgod /el-compound.html

Prophet Muhammad told Muslims to believe only in Allah to the exclusion of all other gods, for associating anything with Allah would be to commit *shirk* (association; comparing any-thing to the divine). While there are more than ninety-nine names for Allah, the Qur'an mentions only ninety-nine, such as merciful (**al-Rahman**), compas-sionate (**al-Rahim**), the Preserver (al-Hafiz), the Real (al-Haqq), the Powerful (al-Qadir), and the Director (al-Rashid). For our purposes in this chapter, and to follow the English translation, I will use the terms "God" and "Allah" interchangeably.

Christian Reflections

Are the God of the Bible and Allah of the Qur'an the same God? What similarities and dissimilarities mark their identities? How would you compare the characteristics of God and Allah? What do such characteristics reveal about the respective notions of the divine and human beings? What difference would it make to say that Christians direct their worship to Allah? Or that Muslims direct their prayers to God? On what basis does one decide? Since "Allah" is the Arabic term for God, is it acceptable for Christians to employ the same term for the biblical notion of God? If a Christian does not employ the term "Allah" when speaking to an Arab-speaking person, then what word should be used? Arabic-speaking Christians use the name Allah.

Christianity is a religion that translates itself into local terms, even using the most sacred names for the divine. Would it not be bad Christian mission practice to invite non-English speakers to follow "God," when they have never heard of such a being as "God"? For purposes of communication one is compelled to employ local terms and idioms to speak about the divine. That is to say, God would be called by different names in different languages and cultures, such as Dios (Spanish), Engkai (Maasai), Y'wa (Karen), Tao (Chinese), Brahmin (Sanskrit), and Allah (Arabic), each term signifying the highest principle, the source of life and creation.

Hence, one can argue that there are countless names for God, given the vast number of cultures around the world. The discrepancies between the biblical notion of God and, say, the Qur'anic notion of Allah raise a set of additional questions: for example, is it profitable, even necessary, to employ the local term for God, then fill it with Christian meaning, thus changing the concept of the indigenous notion of God? How else can one speak meaningfully about God if one does not use meaningful terms? Many Christian missionaries have done just that—they have utilized local terms for God, but introduced a "full" understanding of God as presented in the biblical witness. In fact, in many regions of the world influenced by Islam and Arabic, Bible translators have translated the Hebrew and Greek terms for God into the Arabic "Allah." The Indonesian Bible reads, "Karena begitu besar kasih Allah akan dunia ini" ("For God so loved the world"; John 3:16).

Division within the Ummah

In the early decades after the death of Prophet Muhammad, there was great division among the Muslim community (***ummah***), with a minority of Muslims arguing all along that 'Ali should have been promoted to caliph since he was Prophet Muhammad's cousin, the first male convert, and later Prophet Muhammad's son-in-law, for 'Ali had married Prophet Muhammad's daughter, **Fatimah**. 'Ali eventually accepted the decision of the *ummah*, as did his followers. Those who sided with 'Ali were called the "Partisans of 'Ali" (Arabic, *Shi'a*), which sowed the seeds of major division within Islam—that is, between **Shia** and **Sunni** Muslims.

Shia (or Shiites) believe that the caliph should be a descendent of 'Ali and Fatimah's lineage, whereas Sunni argue that leaders can be chosen from a descendent of Prophet Muhammad's tribe, which is a wider social designation. The *ummah* (worldwide Muslim community) consists of roughly 10 percent Shia and 90 percent Sunni, with a majority of Shia residing in Iran and Iraq. Although Muslims stress the indivisibility of the *ummah*, it is important to note that there is enormous diversity within the tradition.

Shia and Sunni Islam vary according to the different kinds of religious authorities they follow, illustrated by their respective understandings of the person called **imam** (Arabic, "one at the front," "the one who leads"). An imam is the person who leads the congregation in prayer during Islamic gatherings. Often an imam is available to answer questions about Islamic practices and belief. Most importantly, an imam leads the prayer prostrations, as a model of good practice for the community. While both Shia and Sunni accept the notion of the imam, the Shia also recognize particular historical *Imams* who were chosen by God as perfect examples of submission to God and were sinless. Generally, Shia are divided between **Twelver** and **Sevener** (or Isma'ili) Islam, which reflects the number of historical imams they each accept as God's appointed.

Second, Shia and Sunni vary in terms of religious authority, which directly impacts the interpretation and practice of Islam. Since within the Shia tradition, the imam's words are infallible, and the number of imams is finite (either twelve or seven), Shia authority can appear more potent, as immense spiritual and temporal power is believed to reside in these few individuals and their writings. This more concentrated power contrasts with the authority structure within the Sunni tradition, which affirms that decisions are made through judicial consensus or through the use of reason and analogy and a host of other interpretive strategies that have given rise to significant variety within the Sunni branch of Islam.

For Shia, then, the Islamic leader (imam) is more than just a guardian of Prophet Muhammad's recitation. Rather, Shia assert that Prophet Muhammad bequeathed 'Ali with his *wilaya* (Arabic, "spiritual abilities"), enabling 'Ali and his descendants (i.e., imams) to interpret the Qur'an and lead the Islamic community. The majority of Shia believe that the *wilaya* cycle will end with the return of **al-Mahdi** (Arabic, "the Guided One," "the Awaited One"), a messianic-like redeemer who is the twelfth imam, who had gone into hiding, only to come again to restore justice on earth.

Finally, each major branch of Islam accepts different sets of secondary sacred texts, called the **hadith** (Arabic, "narrative"), the records of the words and actions of the Prophet, which thus serve as the basis for faithful Islamic action and jurisprudence (*fiqh*). Indeed, the hadith are accepted by all Islamic schools of law as significant instruments for guiding Muslim decision making, second only to the Qur'an itself. Shia and Sunni each recognize different hadith collections, named after the person who is believed to have collected the narratives.[4] Much of Islamic preaching during Friday congregational prayers (Arabic, *jumu'ah*) is based on a blending of Qur'anic and hadith injunctions, making the hadith extremely valuable and indispensable guides to Muslim daily life.

Guides to Muslim Life

Every day we are required to make decisions, from simple ones about food and clothing preferences, to major ones about changing residences or jobs or getting married. Some choices impact just the individual, while others involve groups of people, the environment, or the spiritual world. Whether decisions entail the mundane events of life ("I think I'll vacation in Hawaii") or significant actions ("Will you marry me?"), many people find comfort and guidance in their respective religions. Can a Muslim marry a Christian? What are Muslims prohibited from eating? When is it justified to use physical force? How should Muslims view genetic engineering or stem-cell research? How should Muslims strive to introduce Islam to non-Muslims? How should Muslims purify themselves and seek to submit to God?

The larger question is, how do Muslims make decisions? What should guide their lives? It is important to resist making simple generalizations about any group (especially one that contains well over one billion people). Even if no single individual will make his or her decisions in exactly the same manner as another individual, since each person processes information differently (we are biological, cultural, psychological, and spiritual beings), it is still helpful to ponder what guides the lives of Muslims, while also recognizing that each Muslim, like other believers, will process information differently. Muslims worldwide find guidance in four complementary sources: the Qur'an, Prophet Muhammad and hadith, **sharia**, and Islamic jurisprudence.

The Holy Qur'an

Muslims consider the Holy Qur'an (al-Qur'an, "the recitation") the absolute, perfect revelation of God's word through the angel Gabriel to Prophet Muhammad beginning in 610 CE. Since Muslims value it so highly, the Qur'an should not be placed directly on the ground or in a location in which it may get dirty. Likewise, prior to handling or reading the Qur'an, one must purify oneself through formulaic washing called **wudu**, an obligatory cleansing ritual that will be discussed later in this chapter. The Qur'an consists of 114 chapters (**surah**) arranged from the longest to the shortest, except for the first chapter, *al-Fatihah* ("The Opening").

In the Name of God, the Merciful, the Compassionate

Praise belongs to God, the Lord of all Being,
the All-merciful, the All-compassionate,
the Master of the Day of Doom.

Thee only we serve; to Thee alone we pray for succour.
Guide us in the straight path,
the path of those whom Thou hast blessed,
not of those against whom Thou art wrathful,
nor of those who are astray.

Qur'an 1

Surahs

The Qur'an, compiled by Caliph Uthman, has remained the most authoritative word for 1,400 years in its original Arabic. It contains God's commandments, claiming to cover all domains of human life, applicable to all places, times, and peoples. Many non-Muslim scholars divide the contents of the Qur'an into two parts, volume 1 and volume 2. Volume 1 covers chapters 1–22, containing the recitations revealed to Prophet Muhammad while he lived in Medina and reflecting a state where the Muslim community was more developed and required guidance about various laws and religious practices pertinent to a rapidly growing group; thus, these chapters are often referred to as the "Medinan *surahs*." Volume 2, chapters 21–114, described as short, more trumpet-like and staccato, contains the recitations revealed in Mecca, known as the "Meccan *surahs*." It is clear from the Meccan *surahs* that something brand new was happening to the community; it is as though an announcement were being made to get the attention of listeners and change their course of action. Muslims assert that the Qur'an was sent down (**tanzil**), being the exact duplicate of the preexisting Qur'an in heaven: "With the truth We have sent it down [*tanzil*] and with the truth it has come down" (Qur'an 17:105).

Most religions have some notion of descent. That is, most religions posit the existence of a God, divinity, or essence *out there* that enters human time and space *here, in the now* to communicate truth, whether that be a relational truth, such as Jesus Christ, or a principled truth, such as a pattern to live by (e.g., Hinduism's dharma principle or Taoism's Tao). For our purposes, a fruitful question is "what descends?" Muslims view *tanzil* (to send down) as the transmission of divine guidance for humanity culminating in the mission of Prophet Muhammad, rather than considering God himself to be the subject of the descent.

In Islam, God does not descend; rather, God's guidance does. Prophets, then, are messengers and exemplars, but God's revelation of the Qur'an remains unquestionable and unchallengeable, without equal. One of the goals of Muslim living is to align oneself with God's revealed will, the religion (Islam) revealed by God. To some Christians, that kind of statement sounds quite similar to Christianity. But the similarities are only surface deep.

The fundamental difference between Islamic and Christian conceptions of following the will of God is between following "categorically" versus following "ontologically." "Categorical following" means patterning one's life—in actions, deeds, thoughts, and even appearances—on the one being followed, for example, Jesus Christ. By contrast, "ontological following" means pursuing the subject, Jesus Christ, based on the relationship that has arisen out of a changed existence. That is to say, followers of Jesus Christ are changed beings (ontologically different) and are, because of the guidance of the Holy Spirit, empowered to live differently in the world.

The path that followers of Christ are to follow is not a categorical way—we do not follow Jesus Christ categorically as though we do exactly and literally everything that Jesus did. Christianity involves an ontological transformation; we are changed inside-out to be different people. Christians affirm that what descended was Jesus, who in Karl Barth's words was "God's self-disclosure." God descended. And the Word became flesh and dwelled among us (cf. John 1:1–14).

According to Islam, the word of God descended and became a book—the law of God. For comparative purposes, then, it is illustrative to match the Qur'an with Jesus, rather than with the Bible. Since the written word in each religion functions differently, it should give Christians some pause when thinking about the role of the Qur'an in a Muslim's life. Recall that for the Protestant Reformers, such as Martin Luther and John Calvin, the words of the Bible reveal the Word (Jesus Christ). In contrast, the Qur'an *is* the very word of God for Muslims, like Jesus *is* the very word of God for Christians. Therefore, harming the Qur'an by tearing, sullying, or burning it is anathema to Muslims, tantamount to doing such things to Jesus.

Figure 9.8. Great Mosque of Djenne, Mali

The Nontranslatability of the Qur'an

Muslims claim that nothing compares to the beauty of reading the Qur'an in its original Arabic language. Since the Qur'an cannot be translated from Arabic without losing its validity as a sacred text, committed non-Arabic speaking Muslims are encouraged to learn Qur'anic Arabic and Arabic prayers. To Muslims, the Qur'an is God's divine speech, his divine law incarnated in words dictated verbatim by Gabriel. Any translation of the Qur'an from its original Arabic language is considered an "interpretation" and immediately loses its authority as the sacred word of God.

As Islam spread out of the Arabian Peninsula, north into western Asia and east into North Africa and South Asia, Arabic was employed increasingly as the language of various domains of life, such as commerce, education, and religion, helping to further unify the Islamic world. "The author of the Qur'an, which is God, thus came to be associated with its speech, so that the very sounds of the language are believed to originate in heaven."[5]

In fact, all Islamic law schools (i.e., **Shafi'i**, **Malik**, **Hanbal**, and **Hanafi**) enshrine the ban on using vernacular languages for prayer. Instead, there is a firm obligation to use Arabic. The power of the untranslatability of the Qur'an is that theological and linguistic corruptions are prevented from entering the sacred text—the text is locked up, solidified in Arabic, and transported through cultures without the possibility of alterations that lead to falsehoods and untruths, as has occurred, according to Islam, in the Christian and Jewish traditions.

"In the Name of God, the Merciful, the Compassionate"

The Qur'an contains all that is necessary for life. Almost every *surah*, except *surah* 9, opens with the expression **Bismallah al-Rahman al-Rahim** ("In the

Christian Reflections

What are the **implications** of a sacred text that can be translated out of its original language into any number of vernaculars, or mother-tongue languages? What social, cultural, personal, and religious difference does it make if a sacred text is translatable or untranslatable, according to the religious tradition itself? Most Western Christians take it for granted that they have access to Bibles in English. Beginning with the Venerable Bede (c. 672–735), an English monk, then more notably with John Wycliff (mid-1320s–1384), who based his translation of the English Bible (1382) on the Vulgate, a fifth-century translation of the Bible in Latin popular in Christianity during the Middle Ages, the Bible has been translated into thousands of English versions.

The Authorized King James Version (1611) was commissioned by the Church of England and was known as the Great Bible for many subsequent decades. Several scholars argue that the nature of Christianity is its translatability, illustrated most poignantly in the translation of God into the humanity of Jesus Christ.

When God became "enfleshed" in the God-man Jesus Christ, divinity was translated into humanity, having entered into a particular historical moment and cultural and linguistic context. As Christianity has been promulgated worldwide, it has done so fueled by the necessity to translate its most salient affirmations into local languages. There is such an intimate connection between language and culture that when one learns a language, one also learns that culture. One cannot learn Mandarin without learning Chinese culture. Christianity makes the radical claim that *my* language (e.g., Korean, Spanish, Zulu, Tagalog) can carry divine truth about God, without my needing to abandon my language to learn another one.

The history of Christianity throughout the world is replete with instances where Christians have gained a renewed sense of themselves and their culture because they hear God's Word in their own languages.[a] Likewise, one can argue that the Muslim view of the nontranslatability of the Qur'an and concomitant valorization of Arabic grants Arabic language and culture a privileged position in the face of other languages and cultures.

a. For example, see Sanneh, *Translating the Message*; Sanneh, *Whose Religion Is Christianity?*; Walls, *Missionary Movement in Christian History*; Jenkins, *New Faces of Christianity*; Richardson, *Eternity in Their Hearts*.

name of God, the Merciful, the Compassionate"), establishing at the start the relationship between human beings and the divine. The only response to a God who is merciful and compassionate, all-powerful, and all-knowing is to submit to his revealed law. *Bismallah* means something like "with the blessings of God" or "under the guidance of God," with *al-Rahman al-Rahim* referring to God's attributes as marked by the utter tenderness of one who protects, nourishes, and comforts. Indeed, the Qur'an states that God is the most compassionate (e.g., Qur'an 1:1; 2:207; 3:30; 16:07; 22:65; 24:20) and merciful (e.g., Qur'an 2:163; 3:31; 4:100; 5:3; 5:98; 11:41; 12:53; 12:64; 26:9; 30:5; 36:58) one.

> Say, "Call upon Allah or call upon the Most Merciful, Whichever name you call—to Him belong the best names." And do not recite too loudly in your prayer or too quietly but seek between that an intermediate way.
>
> Qur'an 17:100

> And of men there is he who would sell himself to seek the pleasure of Allah; and Allah is compassionate to his servants.
>
> Qur'an 2:207

> And your god is one God. There is no deity worthy of worship except Him, the Entirely Merciful, the Especially Merciful.
>
> Qur'an 2:163

SIDEBAR 9.1

Prophets Mentioned in the Qur'an

Adam	Musa (Moses)
Idris (Enoch)	Harun (Aaron)
Nuh (Noah)	Dhul-Kifl (Ezekiel)
Hud	Daud (David)
Saleh	Sulayman (Solomon)
Ibrahim (Abraham)	Ilyas (Elijah)
Lut (Lot)	Al-Yasa (Elisha)
Isma'il (Ishmael)	Yunus (Jonah)
Isaac	Zakariya (Zechariah)
Yaqub (Jacob)	Yahya (John the Baptist)
Yusuf (Joseph)	Isa (Jesus)
Ayyub (Job)	Muhammad
Shoaib (Jethro)	

> Say, O Muhammad, "If you should love Allah, then follow me, so Allah will love you and forgive you your sins. And Allah is Forgiving and Merciful."
>
> Qur'an 3:31

Many biblical figures are mentioned in the Qur'an. In many cases, when biblical figures are mentioned, the Muslim perspective is that the Qur'an provides corrections to the corruptions of the Old and the New Testaments. As such, the Qur'an does not present entire stories, as we would find in the biblical account, since its job, when overlapping with the biblical narrative, is to correct falsehoods that have crept into the Bible.

Wikimedia Commons

Figure 9.9. Medieval Persian manuscript showing Muhammad leading prayer for Abraham, Moses, and Jesus

Isa (Jesus) in the Qur'an

The Qur'an presents Jesus (Isa) as one of the most important prophets, a messenger (like Prophet Muhammad), born of a virgin (Qur'an 3:47; 19:16–21), a miracle worker (Qur'an 5:110); yet he was not God (Qur'an 9:30), not the Son of God (Qur'an 112:1–4), and neither crucified (Qur'an 4:156) nor raised from the dead (Qur'an 4:157). However, according to Islamic tradition, Jesus is expected to return to help judge the world.

> And when the angels said, "Mary, God has chosen thee, and purified thee; He has chosen thee above all women. Mary, be obedient to thy Lord, prostrating and bowing before Him." (That is of the tidings of the Unseen, that We reveal to thee; for thou wast not with them, when they were casting quills which of them should have charge of Mary; thou wast not with them, when they were disputing.) When the angels said, "Mary, God gives thee good tidings of a Word from Him whose name is Messiah, Jesus, son of Mary; highly honored shall he be in this world and the next, near stationed to God. He shall speak to men in the cradle, and of age, and righteous he shall be." "Lord," said Mary, "how shall I have a son seeing no mortal has touched me?" "Even so," God said, "God creates what He will. When He decrees a thing He does but say to it 'Be,' and it is. And He will teach him the Book, the Wisdom, the Torah, the Gospel, to be a Messenger to the Children of Israel saying, 'I have come to you with a sign from your Lord. I will create

for you out of clay as the likeness of a bird; then I will breathe into it, and it will be a bird, by the leave of God. I will also heal the blind and the leper, and bring to life the dead, by the leave of God. I will inform you too of what things to eat, and what you treasure up in your houses. Surely in that is a sign for you, if you are believers. Likewise confirming the truth of the Torah that is before me, and to make lawful to you certain things that before were forbidden unto you. I have come to you with a sign from your Lord; so fear God, and obey you me. Surely God is my Lord and your Lord; so serve Him. This is a straight path.'"

Qur'an 3:42–51

Notice that the quotation above mentions Jesus's ability to give life to clay birds, which was recorded hundreds of years earlier than the compilation of the Qur'an in a "gospel" called the *Gospel of Thomas*, a noncanonical text deemed heretical by the early church (see also Qur'an 5:110).

According to the Qur'an, Jesus is a messenger of the one God.

The Messiah [Jesus], son of Mary, was not more than a Messenger before whom many Messengers have passed away; and his mother adhered wholly to truthfulness, and they both ate food [as other mortals do]. See how We make Our signs clear to them; and see where they are turning away.

Qur'an 5:75

The Qur'an states that Jesus spoke from his cradle.

Then she [Mary] pointed to him. They said: "How can we talk to one who is a child in the cradle?" He [Jesus] said: "Verily! I am a slave of God, He has given me the Scripture and made me a Prophet."

Qur'an 19:29–30

According to the Qur'an, Jesus is not God, and there is no Trinity (Father, Son, and Holy Spirit).

People of the Book [Jews and Christians]! Do not exceed the limits in your religion, and attribute to God nothing except the truth. The Messiah, Jesus, son of Mary, was only a Messenger of God, and His command that He conveyed unto Mary, and a spirit from Him. So believe in God and in His Messengers, and do not say: "God is a Trinity." Give up this assertion; it would be better for you. God is indeed just One God. Far be it from His glory that He should have a son. To Him belongs all that is in the heavens and in the earth. God is sufficient for a guardian.

Qur'an 4:171

Isa (Jesus) as Messiah

It is important to distinguish between the terms "**al-Masih**" (Arabic, "the anointed one," "savior," "Messiah") and "al-Mahdi" (Arabic, "the Divinely Guided One"). The term "al-Masih" is applied to Jesus (Isa). That is, Muslims view Jesus as Messiah (al-Masih), which is usually interpreted as a prophet or messenger. However, neither the Qur'an nor the hadith link Jesus with traditional messianic expectations. Therefore, Jesus is usually not referred to as al-Mahdi, understood as an eschatological figure who Muslims believe will usher in an era of justice and true belief prior to the end of time.

According to Islam, Jesus will return to earth at the end of time, but not as al-Mahdi. Al-Mahdi will appear at the end of time in order to establish the domination of Islam over all people. Al-Mahdi will defeat the enemies

Christian Reflections

Christians affirm both the divinity of Jesus (as fully human and fully divine) as well as Jesus's membership in the triune nature of God, the Godhead composed of Father, Son, and Holy Spirit. With regard to the triune nature of God, the Cappadocian formula, adopted at the ecumenical Council of Constantinople (in 381), enshrined the orthodox, mainstream understanding of the relationship between Jesus and the other two members of the Godhead.

The Cappadocian fathers consisted of Basil, his brother Gregory of Nyssa, and their friend Gregory of Nazianzus. They played a pivotal role in resolving the issue of Jesus as fully divine and in establishing the full divinity of the Holy Spirit at the Council of Constantinople. The Cappadocian fathers are held in high esteem by Eastern Orthodox churches today. The Cappadocian solution resolved the challenge of the Godhead, making sense of the relationship of the Father, the Son, and the Holy Spirit.

The Cappadocian approach to the triune nature of God is best understood as a defense of the unity of the Godhead, coupled with recognition that the one Godhead exists in three different "modes of being." The Cappadocian fathers expressed the mystery of the Godhead with the formula "one substance (*ousia*) in three persons (*hypostases*)," thus affirming one indivisible Godhead common to all three persons of the Trinity. This orthodox formulation held that the Godhead exists simultaneously in three different "modes of being"—Father, Son, and Holy Spirit.

Some theologians, such as Karl Rahner and Jürgen Moltmann, emphasize the inherently social beingness of God, called "social trinitarianism." That is,

of Islam and restore Islamic faith. About the identity of al-Mahdi, Muslims assert that he will be neither Christian nor Jewish, but rather an Arab from the tribe of Prophet Muhammad. Jesus's role will be as al-Mahdi's assistant on the day of judgment, encouraging others to submit to God.

According to the famous fourteenth-century Muslim historian Ibn Khaldun (1332–1406):

> It has been (well known) by all Muslims in every epoch, that at the end of time a man from the family of the Prophet will, without fail, make his appearance, one who will strengthen the religion [Islam] and make justice triumph. The Muslims will follow him, and he will gain domination over the Muslim realm. He will be called the Mahdi.[6]

Furthermore, the Qur'an does not recognize Jesus as the Son of God.

God exists in three persons, each part of which loves the others and whose unity is defined by that love. Intrinsically, then, the Christian notion of the Godhead exhibits plurality of persons (i.e., Father, Son, and Holy Spirit) within the complex unity of the one God.

Finally, we must recognize that beliefs nearly always have social and cultural implications. The way that people see God profoundly impacts culture, society, and self-understanding. Muslims believe that, just as God is one (*tawhid*; the doctrine of oneness of God), the human community ought to be one in submission to God, unified in part through use of the sacred Arabic.

The oneness of God is mirrored in the goal of Muslim mission (Arabic, *da'wah*; calling to the truth through preaching and propagation) to create a similar oneness of society in submission to God. This perspective contrasts sharply with a Christian view that affirms the social trinitarian nature of the Godhead (that God is one in three related persons). The Christian perspective of God enables, and actually encourages, immense diversity within society, while at the same time affirming that this variety finds its unity under the one God. Plurality is an inherently Christian notion.

Furthermore, Islam has no notion of *imago Dei* (image of God), the Christian and Jewish perspective that human beings are created in God's image and, therefore, possess value in themselves apart from their actions. That is, the *imago Dei* carries the idea that God is in some way present in human beings— there is some likeness between God and humankind. The Bible notes that Jesus Christ is the visible image of God (2 Cor. 4:4–7; Col. 1:13–15; Heb. 1:3).

> Say: "God is Unique! God, the Source [of everything]. He has not fathered anyone nor was He fathered, and there is nothing comparable to Him!"
>
> Qur'an 112:1–4

> Such was Jesus, the son of Mary; it is a statement of truth, about which they vainly dispute. It is not befitting to the majesty of God, that He should beget a son. Glory be to Him! When He determines a matter, He only says to it, "Be" and it is.
>
> Qur'an 19:34–35

Many Muslims interpret these passages in the Qur'an to mean that Jesus was not actually crucified.

> They did not kill him, nor did they crucify him, but they thought they did.
>
> Qur'an 4:156

> God lifted him up to His presence. God is Almighty, All-Wise.
>
> Qur'an 4:157

Although Jesus is nevertheless so significant that he is mentioned as second in importance only to Prophet Muhammad himself, Jesus is not considered God.

Prophet Muhammad and the Hadith

For those used to reading the Bible, reading the Qur'an can be a challenging experience, in part because the Qur'an is not a narrative but consists of a compilation of recitations divinely communicated to Prophet Muhammad in both Mecca and Medina. The only major narrative in the Qur'an is found in chapter 12. Muslims find guidance in the Qur'an, but the hadith provide much more practical advice and illustrations about living, despite their being a secondary source of knowledge in the Muslim community.

For living faithfully, Muslims appeal to the words and actions of Prophet Muhammad, as recorded in the hadith, a single item of prophetic tradition considered a report of words uttered by Prophet Muhammad or actions performed by him. Quoting a selection from the hadith helps adjudicate conflicts and guide behaviors, for Prophet Muhammad's life serves as the prime example of a whole host of issues facing Muslims.

> You have indeed in the Messenger of Allah an excellent exemplar for him who hopes in Allah and the Final Day, who remembers Allah much.
>
> Qur'an 33:21

Laws that govern Muslim custom (**sunnah**) are based on both the Qur'an and the hadith.

Text and Chain of Authorities

The hadith consist of two parts: *matn* (text) and *isnad* (chain of authorities). The strength of the *isnad* depends on the persons linked in the chain of transmission of its content. For example, the *isnad* usually take the form of something like, "I heard from A who was told by B who heard from C that the Prophet said . . . ," with the strongest hadith being rooted in one of the early Companions or in Prophet Muhammad himself. A detailed science of hadith criticism emerged, mainly to decipher the authenticity of any given hadith, classifying each as *sahih* (sound, authentic), *hasan* (good, acceptable), *da'eef* (weak), or *mawdoo'* (fabricated), with fabricated "hadith" actually not counting as hadith at all. Islamic law primarily utilizes *authentic* and *acceptable* hadith. Hadith range from presenting abstract ideas to quite practical help. (See sidebar 9.2 for some hadith selections.)

Figure 9.10. Muhammad at the Qa'abah, Istanbul, Turkey (1595)

Masjids usually have several hadith collections from which sermons are researched and preached. The path that Prophet Muhammad followed, and which all Muslims are enjoined to travel, is referred to as the "straight path." It is the straight path (Qur'an 3:51) that leads to a just and abundant life individually and corporately, the way revealed in the Qur'an and exemplified by the Prophet.

SHARIA

Another major source of knowledge and daily guidance for Muslims is sharia, the straight path, one of the most crucial concepts within Islam. Typically, sharia is translated as "Islamic law," but the term carries much more than a Western understanding of law, in a strict juridical sense. In Arabic, sharia literally means "way to the water hole," illustrated by the path worn by camels, the straight path—the implication being that the right way leads to water, the source of life.

Considered by Muslims to be God's immutable and eternal will for human beings, sharia is expressed in Prophet Muhammad's example (*sunnah*) and the Qur'an, as the first source of Islamic law, even though the Qur'an contains only about ninety verses directly concerned with law. The diversity of Muslim

Hadith Selections

Narrated by 'Umar bin Al-Khattab: I heard Allah's Apostle saying, "The reward of deeds depends upon the intentions and every person will get the reward according to what he has intended. So whoever emigrated for worldly benefits or for a woman to marry, his emigration was for what he emigrated for."

Sahih Bukhari, vol. 1, bk. 1, no. 1[a]

Narrated Anas bin Malik: The Prophet saw some sputum in the direction of the Qibla (on the wall of the mosque) and he disliked that and the sign of disgust was apparent from his face. So he got up and scraped it off with his hand and said, "Whenever anyone of you stand for the prayer, he is speaking in private to his Lord or his Lord is between him and his Qibla. So, none of you should spit in the direction of the Qibla but one can spit to the left or under his foot." The Prophet then took the corner of his sheet and spat in it and folded it and said, "Or you can do like this."

Sahih Bukhari, vol. 1, bk. 8, no. 399[b]

Anas reported that Allah's Apostle (may peace be upon him) forbade that a person should drink while standing. Qatada reported: We said to him: What about eating? Thereupon he (Anas) said: That is even worse and more detestable (abominable).

Sahih Muslim, bk. 23, no. 5018[c]

Abdullah (b. Mas'ud) (Allah be pleased with him) reported that Allah's Messenger (may peace be upon him) said to us: "O young men, those among you who can support a wife should marry, for it restrains eyes (from casting evil glances) and preserves one from immorality; but he who cannot afford it should observe a fast for it is a means of controlling sexual desire."

Sahih Muslim, bk. 8, no. 3233[d]

Hammam b. Munabbih who is the brother of Wahb b. Munabbih, said: This is what has been transmitted to us by Abu Huraira from Prophet Muhammad, the Messenger of Allah (may peace be upon him) and then narrated a hadith out of them and observed that the Messenger of Allah (peace be upon him) said: The prayer of none amongst you would be accepted in a state of impurity till he performs ablution.

Sahih Muslim, bk. 2, no. 435[e]

Narrated Abu Huraira: The Prophet said: "Every Prophet was given miracles because of which people believed, but what I have been given, is Divine Inspiration which Allah has revealed to me. So I hope that my followers will outnumber the followers of the other Prophets on the Day of Resurrection."

Sahih Bukhari, vol. 6, bk. 61, no. 504[f]

a. Available at http://www.iium.edu.my/deed/hadith/bukhari/001_sbt.html.
b. Available at http://www.iium.edu.my/deed/hadith/bukhari/008_sbt.html.
c. Available at http://www.iium.edu.my/deed/hadith/muslim/004a_smt.html.
d. Available at http://www.iium.edu.my/deed/hadith/muslim/008_smt.html.
e. Available at http://www.iium.edu.my/deed/hadith/muslim/002_smt.html.
f. Available at http://www.iium.edu.my/deed/hadith/bukhari/061_sbt.html.

opinions about any topic derives in part from the various ways that sharia is interpreted, with modern scholars distinguishing between the Qur'an and jurisprudence (*fiqh*).

Islamic Jurisprudence

The Islamic study and theory of law (jurisprudence) is called *fiqh*, a word that means "deep understanding." The person who possesses knowledge and deep understanding is called ***faqih***—that is, a jurist who has knowledge of

Christian Reflections

How do **Christians make** major decisions? Do all decisions, even what shirt to wear, require Christian reflection? Or just the big decisions? What are the sources of Christian decision making? What sources would you employ to make an important decision? The Bible? A priest or pastor's counsel? Church liturgy or creed? History? Personal experience? The Holy Spirit? Reason? Muslims encounter challenges in their daily lives similar to those confronting all people.

The major decisions Muslims make require the same sort of deep grappling with the sacred text, reason, and wise counsel as Christians typically make use of during such times. Something that distinguishes a Christian from a Muslim is the Christian affirmation that the Holy Spirit, referred to in the New Testament as the Advocate (John 14:15–17), enters the life of the follower of Jesus to guide and reassure her. Although Christian churches have different experiences of the Holy Spirit, as demonstrated most illustratively in styles of worship and theology, there is nevertheless general recognition that the Holy Spirit is the part of the Trinity whose purpose is to provide practical guidance and equip Christians, as God present to creation and believers.

Although Christians rely on Scripture, reason, personal experience, and tradition, they also recognize the power of the Holy Spirit to guide and console, in effect putting something of God into the heart of each believer. Since Muslims do not have a concept of an indwelling spirit of God, they rely on the insights of Islamic scholars, imams, and jurisprudence (*fiqh*), to decipher ethical decisions. Even Muslims within the Sufi traditions, who emphasize the closeness of God, as one nearer to a person than his jugular vein (Qur'an 50:16), focus more on the intimacy with God rather than direction, guidance, and comfort provided by the Spirit.

Some Muslims argue that Prophet Muhammad is none other than the Holy Spirit foretold in the Bible. Note that "Ahmad" means Prophet Muhammad in this following passage. "And when Jesus son of Mary said, 'Children of Israel, I am indeed the Messenger of God to you, confirming the Torah that is before me, and giving good tidings of a Messenger who shall come after me, whose name shall be Ahmad'" (Qur'an 61:6).

Islamic legislative rulings. *Fiqh*, then, is the human attempt to understand divine law (*shariah*). "Whereas shariah is immutable and infallible, fiqh is fallible and changeable."[7] Understanding Islamic law is a dynamic process that involves several methods of legal interpretation and analysis, depending on the law school that a jurist follows. While interpretations of Islamic law can be diverse throughout the Muslim community worldwide (*ummah*), the hadith clearly testify to the practical benefits of such knowledge.

> *Narrated Muawiya: I heard Allah's Apostle saying, "If Allah wants to do good to a person, He makes him comprehend [fiqh] the religion."*
>
> *Sahih Bukhari*, vol. 1, bk. 3, no. 71 (available at http://www .iium.edu.my/deed/hadith /bukhari/003_sbt.html)

We have to remember that Islam is considered as a way of life, and the religion seeks to address all areas of a Muslim community's existence and activity. Muslim historian Ibn Khaldun described *fiqh* as the "knowledge of the rule of God which concern the actions of persons who own themselves bound to obey the law respecting what is required (***wajib***), sinful (***haraam***), recommended (***mandub***), disapproved (***makruh***), or neutral (***mubah***)."[8] These five legal terms, here in Arabic, are consistent with the description of *fiqh* categories affirmed by Islamic jurists today.

Prophet Muhammad was a model Muslim by his own example, his behaviors and words, both during his life and after his death. He remains the best human example of being Muslim today. After the death of the Prophet, however, Muslims relied on additional sources as authoritative guides for their lives, with the recognition that jurists would play a major role in interpreting and adjudicating those sources to explicate Islamic law.

"If you do not know, ask people who know the Scripture."

Qur'an 21:7

Since Islamic law is applied to every area of life, from abstract philosophical methodologies of analysis to mundane issues of daily life, interpretations can be diverse. The most important foundational sources for *fiqh* are the Qur'an and the sunnah (i.e., hadith), which were discussed above.

In addition to the Qur'an and sunnah, the principles and investigative procedures through which practical laws are developed stem from what is collectively referred to as ***usul al-fiqh*** (principles of jurisprudence or sources of Islamic law). There are countless decisions made by Muslims that depend upon religious law. For instance, can a female Muslim college student date a male Christian student? Even after performing a ceremonial washing (ablution), should a Muslim perform another ablution if, on the way to the mosque, he steps into a puddle of mud? If involved in banking, how should one understand and incorporate Islamic economic jurisprudence in a global economy—for instance, the prohibition against usury (**riba**), that is, charging interest?

The first source of *fiqh* is **ijma** (consensus), which refers to the necessary agreement of all Muslim jurists on a particular issue not addressed in the Qur'an or sunnah. According to Islamic tradition, Prophet Muhammad declared, "My People will never agree together on an error."[9] For this reason, *ijma* is considered by most Muslims to be the strongest and most authoritative of the four sources of law. It is important to note that *ijma* is not a consensus of all jurists worldwide, but it does require agreement by jurists understood to have knowledge of the Qu'ran, sunnah, and other sources of jurisprudence. Naturally, it is not the consensus of ordinary Muslims that is authoritative, but rather the accord of those trained and accepted as interpreters of Islamic law. There is some difference between Sunni and Shia communities on the use of *ijma*, however, since most Sunni jurists consider consensus to be authoritative, whereas Shia jurists argue that *ijma* is impossible to achieve.

The second source is **qiyas** (analogical reasoning). When a difficulty in interpretation arises that neither the Qur'an nor hadith can resolve, an attempt can be made to find an analogous situation upon which a law has already been established. Also referred to as analogical deduction, jurists refer to the following hadith, where Prophet Muhammad questioned Mu'adh b. Jabal as the Prophet sent him to be judge in Yemen, as justification for using analogies to interpret Islamic law:

> "How will you decide when a question arises?"
> He replied, "According to the Book of Allah."
> "And if you do not find the answer in the Book of Allah?"
> "Then according to the *sunna* of the Messenger of Allah."
> "And if you do not find the answer either in the Sunna or in the Book?"
> "Then I shall come to a decision according to my own opinion without hestitation."
> Then the Messenger [Prophet Muhammad] of Allah slapped Mu'adh on the chest with his hand saying: "Praise be to Allah who has led the messenger of the Messenger of Allah to an answer that pleased him."[10]

The third principle for the interpretation of legal matters is **ijtihad**, independent legal reasoning or an independent decision not necessarily based on a traditional school of Islamic jurisprudence. *Fiqh* using *ijtihad* inherently assumes a degree of openness, freedom of thought, and rational thinking in pursuit of truth. *Ijtihad* carries with it the idea of struggle, since *ijtihad* comes from the same Arabic root as *jihad* (struggle, exertion). In addition, using *ijtihad* often requires exertion and diligence, which includes

Narrated Abu Musa: The Prophet said, "The example of guidance and knowledge with which Allah has sent me is like abundant rain falling on the earth, some of which was fertile soil that absorbed rain water and brought forth vegetation and grass in abundance."

Sahih Bukhari, vol. 1, bk. 3, no. 79 (available at http://www .quranwebsite.com/hadith /bukhari_volume_1.html)

personal opinion (*ra'y*). The idea of *ijtihad* is that it takes effort and struggle to achieve knowledge of Islamic law. Someone recognized as an Islamic jurist who is competent in interpreting *shariah* by *ijtihad* is a **mujtahid** (an authoritative interpreter of the religious law of Islam).[11]

In the early centuries of Islam, these kinds of interpretive strategies (i.e., *ijma, qiyas, ijtihad*) were common. Yet as time went on, legal rulings and procedures gradually solidified, and "Muslims tended more and more to imitate and accept on authority what their predecessors had to struggle to achieve."[12] This tendency to follow the past decisions and interpretations of Islamic jurisprudence is called **taqlid** ("to imitate," "to follow someone"). *Taqlid* means that one follows or imitates the decisions of a *mujtahid* in religious laws without engaging in original *ijtihad*. As such, *taqlid* is contrasted with independent reasoning (*ijtihad*). There is some debate as to what aspects of the tradition should be followed without going through *ijtihad* and those subsidiary elements that require ongoing interpretation.

And when it is said to them, "Come to what Allah has revealed and to the Messenger," they say, "Sufficient for us is that upon which we found our fathers." Even though their fathers knew nothing, nor were they guided?

Qur'an 5:104

And do not pursue that of which you have no knowledge. Indeed, the hearing, the sight, and the heart—about all those one will be questioned.

Qur'an 17:36

Rather, they say, "Indeed, we found our fathers upon a religion, and we are in their footsteps rightly guided." And similarly, We did not send before you any warner into a city except that its affluent said, "Indeed, we found our fathers upon a religion, and we are, in their footsteps, following."

Qur'an 43:22–23

There is a wide range of opinion about *taqlid* among various legal schools within Islam, since *taqlid* requires the unquestioning acceptance of the legal decisions of others without necessarily knowing the basis of those decisions.

Interpretation of Islamic jurisprudence remains a dynamic process today, and one that provides an indispensible guide to all aspects of Muslim life.

According to *Sahih Bukhari*, learning *fiqh* is one of the most honorable and best deeds for Muslims, since it promises abundance to those who have knowledge of Allah's laws.

Worship and Practice

The Five Pillars of Worship

Many people mistakenly condense Islam into what has become known as the "Five Pillars of Islam," when in fact the five pillars ought to be understood as part of Islamic worship rather than encapsulating Islam in its entirety. For instance, neither Islamic jurisprudence (*fiqh*), theology (**kalam**), nor Qur'anic interpretation (**tafsir**) are addressed directly in the five pillars. Yet all of Islam is permeated with the message of the Five Pillars. Muslims are enjoined to organize their lives on the basis of these ritual actions of worship that are based on the Qur'an, with the desire to accept one's dependence on God and the sovereignty of God. Each pillar contains social and ethical implications that impact the *ummah* (Muslim community worldwide).

THE FIRST PILLAR: SHAHADA

The first, and most significant, pillar is the confession of faith (**shahada**), which states, "There is no god but God, and Muhammad is his prophet." Said in Arabic, the *shahada* is the initial act of faith, giving testimony to one's belief about divine unity (i.e., *tawhid*) and the relationship between God and the Prophet Muhammad, as messenger and channel of God's word. Conversion to Islam requires that one say the *shahada* in front of two Muslim witnesses. Simply put, affirmation of the *shahada* communicates one's commitment to recognize no other gods than God and to follow the recitation received by Prophet Muhammad. Doing so begins the journey of submission.

THE SECOND PILLAR: SALAT

The second pillar of worship is prayer (**salat**), or ritual devotion, which is said in Arabic five times daily. Offering prayer reminds the faithful that "remembrance of God is indeed the greatest virtue." Formal prayer involves formulaic physical prostrations (*rakaah*), facing the Qa'abah in Mecca, toward which all daily prayers of the *ummah* are addressed. Another kind of prayer is **du'a** (Arabic, "supplication," "petitionary prayer"), which is usually said for forgiveness or intercession. The Qur'an contains examples of *du'a* that people can follow, or people can pray from their heart as a way to seek Allah's forgiveness. (See sidebar 9.3 for some examples of *du'a* from the Qur'an.)

Stephan Babuljak

Figure 9.11. Muslims in prayer, one of the Five Pillars of Islam

There is a story in the Qur'an (17:1) that says that Prophet Muhammad took a night journey (*Isra* and *Miraj*) when he traveled, either in a dream or physically, first to the Temple Mount in Jerusalem (which later contained the Al Aqsa Masjid), and then to the heavens, where he eventually spoke to God. According to hadith, Prophet Muhammad was told by God that the people should pray fifty times a day. After some discussion, God told Prophet Muhammad that praying five times daily would be as efficacious as praying fifty times daily, a message that Prophet Muhammad delivered to the people. That the entire *ummah* is called upon to pray toward the direction (*qibla*) of the Qa'abah daily draws Muslims from around the world together, finding unity in part through common geographic orientation.

THE THIRD PILLAR: *SAWM*

The third pillar of worship, fasting (***sawm***), occurs voluntarily throughout the year but is obligatory during the month of **Ramadan**, the ninth month of the calendar, when ritual fasting is practiced during the daylight hours. Fasting encourages Muslims to consider those who involuntarily fast because of physical poverty, reminding the faithful to be thankful to and reliant on God for his goodness and provision. Since Muslims follow a lunar calendar,

---

SIDEBAR 9.3

Examples of *Du'a* in the Qur'an

Our Lord! Take us not to task if we forget or fall into error. Our Lord! Impose not on us that which we have not the strength to bear, grant us forgiveness and have mercy on us. You are our Protector. Help us against those who deny the truth.

Qur'an 2:286

Our Lord! And grant us that which you have promised to us by Your messengers and save us from shame on the Day of Judgment. Verily You never fail to fulfill Your promise.

Qur'an 3:194

Our Lord! Bestow on us mercy from Your presence and dispose of our affairs for us in the right way.

Qur'an 18:10

the date of Ramadan changes each year. Ramadan is a time of heightened spiritual devotion and social cohesion as Muslims around the world forgo food, drink, sexual intercourse, and smoking during the daylight hours. The daily breaking of the fast is a festive occasion, usually celebrated each evening by Muslims at a masjid or other gathering place, where food is shared communally.

The arduousness of fasting for a month is broken finally at the end of twenty-nine or thirty days, depending on the calendar, with one of the great Islamic festivals, **Eid-ul-Fitr**, the "Feast of the Breaking of the Fast," which is accompanied by great celebrations, much like Christmastime, when gifts are distributed, special foods are eaten, and particular prayers are uttered. Eid-ul-Fitr takes on local flair depending on the region of the world where it is celebrated, and depending on how integrated and public Islam has become in the wider society. Hence, celebrations of Eid-ul-Fitr in the United States will be quite different from those in Muslim countries like Pakistan, Turkey, or Indonesia.

THE FOURTH PILLAR: *ZAKAT*

The fourth pillar of worship, almsgiving (*zakat*), should be understood as "purification of wealth," the annual giving of a fixed amount of excess personal assets or revenue for the benefit of the poor. The Qur'an insists on one purifying one's wealth by giving a portion of it away (Qur'an 9:60; 30:39). Charitable giving is based on one's ability to give, and while the Qur'an does not provide an exact percentage of giving, the hadith state that 2.5 percent of one's wealth should be donated and that one will receive a reward for doing so.

It should be noted that different schools of Islamic law have slightly different interpretations and policies surrounding *zakat*, its collection, and distribution. Like the other pillars, there is a social significance to *zakat*: the giver relies on God, is reconciled to his or her fellow human beings in need, and is reminded that all beneficence comes from the bounty of God.

THE FIFTH PILLAR: HAJJ

The fifth pillar, pilgrimage (**hajj**), when Muslims gather at Mecca for five days of prescribed ritual activities, is enjoined on all Muslims, unless personal circumstances such as financial limitations prevent them. The hajj occurs from the seventh to tenth day of Dhu al-Hijah, the twelfth month of the Islamic calendar. Nowadays numbering close to three million persons, the hajj is a gathering of diverse Muslims from around the world into a single community. Social statuses are relativized as pilgrims enter a sacred state of mind, and men don simple clothing consisting of long white robes.

Both the state of mind and the simple robes are referred to as the state of entering ***ihram***. While entering into a state of *ihram*, pilgrims often pray this invocation in Arabic:

> Here I am, O God, at Your command!
> Here I am at Your command!
> You are without associate!
> Here I am at Your command!
> To You are all praise, grace, and dominion!
> You are without associate![13]

Pilgrims perform prescribed acts of worship at the Grand Masjid in Mecca patterned on the story of Abraham (Ibrahim), Hagar (**Hajar**), and Ishmael (Isma'il), symbolizing the unity of the *ummah* and its historical continuity with the history of Abraham. Here is a breakdown of the ritual elements of the hajj:

Day 1: All pilgrims circumambulate (***tawaf***)—that is, walk around—the Qa'abah seven times, with many attempting to kiss, touch, or get near the Black Stone (Hajr Al Aswad), the stone that Muslims believe fell from heaven during the time of Adam and Eve, which is now framed in silver and attached to the side of the Qa'abah. Tradition says that originally the **Black Stone** was white, but its power to absorb sin has turned it black after years of being touched by pilgrims. Muslims believe that the Qa'abah was constructed originally by the Prophet Adam, then rebuilt by Abraham and **Isma'il**.

Figure 9.12. Sufi Muslims celebrating Eid al-Adha in Abiqui, New Mexico, USA

446

After the *tawaf*, the pilgrims, following the example of Hajar looking frantically for water for her son, Isma'il, walk or run seven times between the hills of Safa and Marwah, in a ritual called **sai**. According to Islamic tradition, as Hajar searched for water, the springs of the Zamzam Well burst and water gushed from the dry ground. Today's pilgrims are encouraged to drink from the well.

Day 2: After daybreak, pilgrims walk through Mina in order to reach **Mount Arafat**, where pilgrims pray fervently, employing the phrase, "*Labbayka Allahumma Labbayka*" ("At your service, O God, at your service"). The importance of spending time at Arafat is exemplified by the fact that if pilgrims do not spend the afternoon on Arafat, their pilgrimage is unacceptable.

For many Muslims, this "Day of Arafat" is the highlight of their pilgrimage, in part because on this day they seek forgiveness from God in the place where they believe Prophet Muhammad delivered his final sermon, so the location has spiritual potency for the faithful. At sunset, pilgrims leave Arafat and travel to a plain called Muzdalifah, where they spend the night praying and gathering small stones for the next day's rituals.

Day 3: Before sunrise, pilgrims travel to Mina, also known as the tent city, and approach the large pillars representing the temptations of Satan, who, according to Muslim tradition, tried to prevent Abraham from following God's command to sacrifice his son, Isma'il. By stoning the pillars of Satan, pilgrims reject Satan's temptation in their own lives. By the third day, pilgrims have traveled, mingled, prayed, and sought God together. Many are tired, but they have achieved what will be one of the highlights of their religious lives.

On this day, the last day of the formal hajj, pilgrims, joined by Muslims around the world, will celebrate **Eid al-Adha**, "the Festival of Sacrifice," the second of the two major Muslim festivals, commemorating the trials and victory of Abraham as well as the goodness of God that provided a ram for Abraham to sacrifice rather than his own son, demonstrating that a Muslim is committed to sacrificing anything to God.

Surely Abraham was an example, obedient to Allah,
by nature upright, and he was not of the polytheists.
He was grateful for Our [Allah] bounties. We [Allah] chose him and guided
him unto a right path. We gave him good in this world,
and in the next he will most surely be among the righteous.

Qur'an 16:120–21

Eid al-Adha entails sacrificing animals (i.e., camels, cows, sheep, goats), dividing the meat into three parts, with one third kept for one's family, one third given to friends and relatives, and one third gifted to the poor and needy around Saudi Arabia as well as to less fortunate Muslims throughout the world, keeping in mind that righteousness lies within one's heart rather than in the action itself: "Not their flesh, not their blood, reaches God, but what reaches him is your righteousness and doing of duty" (Qur'an 22:37). The hajj presents an immense logistical challenge for the Saudi Arabian government, which oversees the annual hajj through a permanent governmental office. Pilgrims who complete the hajj are given the honorific title **hajji** (male pilgrim; also *haji* or *hadji*) or **hajjah** (female pilgrim).

Jihad

Since the end of the twentieth century, particularly after the shocking events of September 11, 2001, when terrorists flew planes into the World Trade Center in New York City and the Pentagon in Washington, DC, scholars, students, media pundits, and religious people from around the world have grappled with the meaning of the Arabic term "**jihad**." Jihad comes from the Arabic root meaning "to strive," "to fight," "to exert," "to struggle"—struggling in the path of God—depending on the context.

Throughout the history of Islam there have been two types of jihad, sometimes called the "greater jihad" and the "lesser jihad." According to Islamic tradition, Prophet Muhammad claimed that the greater jihad entailed the inner struggle of the believer to submit everything to God and to improve himself and society, which requires great effort directed against temptations, Satan's influence, or oneself. Prophet Muhammad spoke of the lesser jihad as being the physical or external struggle, often interpreted as the use of physical force. According to a hadith, Prophet Muhammad exclaimed, "We have returned from the lesser jihad (battle) to the greater jihad (jihad of the soul)."

Striving is such a major theme within Islam that Muslims such as **Sayyid Qutb** have argued that jihad should be seen as the sixth pillar of Islam. So-called extremist Muslims, a term used to describe Muslims advocating and employing physical violence to implement their religious, social, and political agendas, justify their bloody struggle against unbelievers for failing to uphold a particular interpretation of Islam. Such groups—for example, Egyptian Islamic Jihad, al-Qaeda, and Jema'at Islamiyyah—terrorize Muslims and non-Muslims alike for their failure to adhere to a political interpretation of Islam.

Members of these extremist groups are referred to generally as jihadists, and the combination of their transnational reach and extremist ideology makes for a potent cocktail wreaking havoc around the world. It is important to note that the vast majority of Muslims advocate using violence only as a defensive strategy. However, if the beginning of the century is any indication of future events, the twenty-first century promises to witness ongoing contests within Islam as well as between Muslims and non-Muslims over the use of physical force.

Purification

Underlying the Muslim desire to worship is the profound need not only to submit to God but to purify oneself. Purification occurs prior to worship, but it also involves the entire life of a Muslim. The fundamental nature of purity is reflected in the Islamic concept of **fitrah** (human nature), which refers to the original state in which humans were created. It is said that God creates children according to *fitrah*, a kind of innate submission to God—Muslim—that gets corrupted by parents and society. Consequently, every child is born Muslim but later becomes impure.

Although the purity that characterizes birth is irretrievable, ritual purification is a precondition for worship, as every act of worship is an encounter with God. Sharia states that the two major rituals of purification are the major ablution (**ghusl**) and the minor ablution (*wudu*). Both kinds of purification

> *Cleanliness is half of faith.*
>
> *Sahih Muslim*, The Book of Purification [Kitab Al-Taharah] (available at http://www.salahtimes.com/hadiths/sahihmuslim/purification)

Charles E. Farhadian

Figure 9.13. *Wudu* before Friday worship

rituals utilize water that is clean, colorless, and odorless, and that has not already been used ritually.

The *ghusl* bath follows certain events, such as after having sexual relations or converting to Islam. *Ghusl*, a major bath that includes rinsing the mouth and nostrils, and bathing the entire body in a prescribed manner, is recommended before Friday congregational worship and on the days of the two major Muslim festivals.

Ghusl begins with stating the *Bismallah* ("In the Name of God, the Merciful, the Compassionate"), then declaring one's intention, "I intend to make *ghusl*." Failing to perform *ghusl* prevents one from engaging in ritual prayer, touching or reading the Qur'an, or entering the masjid for prayers.

The minor ablution (*wudu*) is a cleansing ritual consisting of washing hands, rinsing the mouth, brushing the teeth, rinsing the nostrils, then washing the arms, ears, neck, between the fingers, ending with the feet up to the ankles. *Wudu* is performed prior to prayer, and after sleep, sex, menstruation, and using the bathroom.

> For Allah loves those who turn to Him constantly and He loves those who keep themselves pure and clean.
>
> Qur'an 2:222

Prior to worship, then, rituals of purification need to be performed.

Modern Movements

The Popular Specter of Islam[14]

A religion that Westerners knew so little about a generation ago is now among the hottest topics in universities and the media. North American universities are on a hiring frenzy to recruit scholars of Islam. These, then, are good days. The world seems to be entering a new era of mutual encounter. Everybody seems to have an opinion about Islam, whether from countless media pundits pontificating on the meaning of Islamic resurgence throughout the non-Western world, from retired military generals providing insight on the "War on Terror," or from the local pastor. Some of us may think of Islam just in terms of events that have transpired in the recent decades. In the midst of paying so much attention to current events, it is too easy to overlook the fact that there are well over a billion Muslims worldwide who follow a religious tradition that began over thirteen hundred years ago.

In the postcolonial period, Muslims of all stripes are seeking representation and authenticity, and the ways of achieving these goals are immense and complicated. Attempts are uneven and vary according to a wide array of factors, including historical experience; economic, political, and social realities; and the relationship to European colonialism, exemplified by rampant sexual promiscuity. On the one hand, there are strong anti-American declarations and actions from extremist Islamist groups, even though they make up only a tiny fraction of the Muslim world (*ummah*). This kind of extremism represents only a small minority of world Muslim opinion, yet all too often in the West it is presumed to be the legitimate voice of the entire Muslim community. (See sidebar 9.4 for an example of an extremist Islamist statement.)

On the other hand, there are vigorous Muslim condemnations against such violent statements and actions. For instance, the **Organization of the Islamic Cooperation** (OIC), which consists of representatives of fifty-seven Muslim countries, and functions as a Muslim counterpart to the United

Wikimedia Commons

Figure 9.14. Islamic school in Touba, Senegal

Fatwa Declaration of Osama bin Laden

In February 1998 Osama bin Laden (1957–2011) issued this well-known anti-American **fatwa** (Arabic, "religious opinion"):

> To kill the Americans and their allies—civilians and military—is an individual duty for every Muslim who can do it in any country in which it is possible to do it, in order to liberate the al-Aqsa Mosque and the holy mosque [Mecca] from their grip, and in order for their armies to move out of all the lands of Islam, defeated and unable to threaten any Muslim. . . . We—with Allah's help—call on every Muslim who believes in Allah and wishes to be rewarded to comply with Allah's order to kill the Americans and plunder their money wherever and whenever they find it. We also call on Muslim ulama, leaders, youth, and soldiers to launch the raid on Satan's United States troops and the devil's supporters allying with them, and to displace those who are behind them so that they may learn a lesson.

> Available at http://www.pbs.org/newshour/updates /military/jan-june98/fatwa_1998.html

Nations, issued a formal seventeen-point declaration on international terrorism. (See sidebar 9.5 for examples from this declaration.)

How do we make sense of such diverse statements from the contemporary Muslim community? It is fair to say that with well over one billion people in the tradition, it is not surprising that not all Muslims would affirm resolutions passed by international representatives. But these resolutions do communicate the perspective and commitment of representative Muslims throughout the world.

Islam and the West

Let us begin by briefly considering the history of the encounter between Islam and the West. Within one hundred years after the death of Prophet Muhammad, Islam had established an empire greater than the Roman Empire. Muslims, whose origins were in the Arabian Peninsula, had conquered the empires of the Byzantines (to the west) and the Persians (Sassanids, to the east), creating an Islamic empire from North Africa to India. The first five hundred years of Islam, corresponding to the Dark Ages and the medieval period of Western history, were the golden age of Islam, marked by a robust development of Islamic sciences, literature, arts, crafts, and philosophy. This was a Muslim world where Muslims could traverse long distances between North Africa, the Middle East, western Asia, and central Asia, where Islam provided the ideological framework for state, society, and political leadership.

SIDEBAR 9.5

Some Points from the Declaration on International Terrorism

4. We affirm our commitment to the principles and true teaching of Islam which abhor aggression, value peace, tolerance and respect as well as prohibiting the killing of innocent people;

5. We reject any attempt to link Islam and Muslims to terrorism as terrorism has no association with any religion, civilization or nationality; . . .

14. We reaffirm our commitment to international action in combating international terrorism undertaken in conformity with the principles of the Charter of United Nations, including the principles of non-intervention in internal affairs and respect for sovereignty and territorial integrity, as well as international law and relevant international conventions and instruments.

Organization of Islamic Cooperation, "Kuala Lumpur Declaration on International Terrorism," adopted April 3, 2002, available at http://www.oic-oci.org

House of Submission versus House of Unbelief

For many Muslims, the world is divided between **Dar al-Islam** (House of Submission/Islam/belief) and **Dar al-Harb** (House of War/unbelief), and periods of violence marked Islamic expansion into non-Muslim regions, where the conquered were given three options: (1) convert to Islam; (2) become a member of the *dhimmi* class (protected scriptural class), requiring the payment of a poll tax in exchange for being protected by Islamic law; or (3) be killed. Citizenship, taxation, inheritance, and marriage were determined by sharia (Islamic law), and Jews and Christians were designated part of dhimmitude (protected scriptural minorities), protected people who possessed sacred scriptures.

During the Crusades (eleventh to thirteenth centuries) the West, having emerged from the Dark Ages, sought to drive Muslims from Spain, Italy, and the Mediterranean. When the Byzantine Empire sought assistance against the Muslim advance on its eastern borders, adjacent to the Arabian Peninsula, the church was deeply involved, and Pope Urban II called on Christians to fight against Muslims as crusaders. Muslim forces reconquered Jerusalem in 1187. Eventually, the Byzantine capital, Constantinople, fell in 1453, was renamed Istanbul, and became the seat of the Ottoman Empire.

Ongoing Influence of the Memory of the Crusades

For many Muslims, the memory of the Crusades lives on as an example of militant Christianity, and some Muslims continue to speak of the West's crusader mentality as a framework through which to understand the West's attitudes and motivations, particularly in the United States' military occupation in Afghanistan and Iraq. The great, sustained encounters between Islam and the West occurred during the era of Islamic empires (thirteenth to twentieth centuries): (1) the Ottomans (1281–1923) ruled over Turkey, southern Europe, Greece, and the Balkans, along with western Arabia (including Mecca and Medina), Egypt, and North Africa; (2) the Safavids (1501–1722) controlled Persia, establishing Shia Islam as the dominant religion in Persia; and (3) the Mughals (1526–1857) ruled most of the Indian subcontinent until the Indian mutiny in 1857, after which the Mughal Empire was formally abolished.

During the era of Islamic empires, Muslims were conscious of regional, linguistic, and ethnic differences, but they were united politically under the empires, marked by shifting borders and boundaries that did not coincide neatly with a nation-state but rather were marked by Islamic rule. That is, during the era of Islamic empires, there was no idea of a Muslim territorial state comparable to Western nationalism.

Legacy of European Colonialism

The West cannot gloss over the impact of European colonialism (fifteenth to twentieth centuries) on the history of Muslim states. There is a common legacy that Muslim states share as a result of their experiences with Western colonialism. And differing patterns of colonization account for different patterns of responses, from outright hatred to peaceful coexistence. European colonialism left indelible marks on the economies, social relations, geography, and political orders in areas that it dominated.

European colonization of Muslim territories began with the rise of European empires (e.g., Spanish, Portuguese, Dutch, English) that colonized much of the non-Western world (e.g., the Portuguese, the English, and the Dutch colonized the Malaysian-Indonesian archipelago; the Danes, the Portuguese, and the British Raj ruled South Asia). European colonialism challenged an Islamic way of life and identity in the Middle East, Africa, and Asia. Except for some regions, such as Macau and Hong Kong, the era of European colonialism ended after the Second World War, when Britain and France withdrew from the majority of their colonial territories, giving way to the emergence of Muslim states beginning around 1947 (i.e., West Pakistan and East Pakistan).

By the mid-1970s, most Muslim territories, from sub-Saharan Africa to Southeast Asia, had gained independence from colonial forces and become Muslim states. European colonialism precipitated a major identity crisis within the Muslim world. Said one scholar, "The fundamental spiritual crisis in Islam in the twentieth century stems from an awareness that something is awry between the religion which God has appointed [i.e., Islam] and the historical development of the world which He controls."[15]

Muslims interpreted the West as an imperial force that displaced Muslim institutions, local languages, and history and introduced Western curricula in schools, Western morals in major domains of life, and secular constitutions as the bedrock of jurisprudence. Today it would be absurd to suggest that all Muslims and all Muslim countries oppose the West. Yet tensions still exist today. How did Muslims respond in the colonial and postcolonial periods? How do Muslims understand themselves in a world increasingly dominated by Western nation-states?

A Spectrum of Muslim Voices

Muslim political discourse on the West is diverse, though based significantly on an experience of the West as powerfully transforming local lives. A major concern of many Muslims today is how to respond to Western ideas and economies, cultural influences, and religious and ethnic pluralities, given a Muslim history marked by significant periods of social, economic, religious, and political strength that later were undermined by colonizing forces.

Part of the critique runs like this: The notion of the secular state originated in the West. Western colonialism was imperialistic, imposing itself on the economic, political, religious, and cultural life of the Muslim world. The West continues to frequently support Israel and its policies; it enforces an economic open market that is devastating for many developing countries. However, the West supports the freedom of consciousness and religion, and many Muslims admire the developments of technology and science that also originated in the West. So the discourse is uneven and involves views of the secular order, politics, spirituality, and nation making. Generally, the typology of Muslim responses to the West consists of **traditionalists**, **modernists**, radicals or **Islamists**, and **moderates**/liberals. The following voices represent crucial perspectives that continue to animate the thinking of many Muslims today. Familiarity with these significant perspectives can help nuance one's understanding of contemporary Islam.

TRADITIONALISTS

The traditionalists are among the earliest voices that responded to colonizing forces, even to Islamic forces that colonized other Islamic regions. Common to these voices is a *nativistic return* to the original sources of Islam—that is, to the Qur'an and the hadith. *Nativistic return* refers to the strengthening of indigenous (i.e., "native") culture and religion, rather than allowing outside influences. Traditionalists can be highly legalistic and respond differently according to the context.

Ahmad Ibn Taymiyya

Among the most important traditionalist voices is that of **Ahmad Ibn Taymiyya**. Ibn Taymiyya (1263–1328) was born in Turkey and was known as a medieval scholar of Islamic law and theology, as well as a political activist. He lived during the fall of Baghdad, which was the center of learning and the headquarters of the Abbasid Caliphate (749–1258) until the conquest of the Mongol invaders. Ibn Taymiyya and his family were forced to flee to Damascus, where he developed his ideas on Islam, emphasizing the primacy and literal interpretation of the original Islamic sacred text, the Qur'an, and the hadith. It is worthwhile to note that the Mongols were fairly tolerant of most religions, including Christianity and Islam. In fact, the Mongols who conquered Baghdad were Muslim, yet they advocated the law codes of Genghis Khan instead of sharia.

Ibn Taymiyya established the precedent that even if rulers are Muslim, their failure to implement sharia rendered them apostates, so Muslims should wage physical jihad against them. Ibn Taymiyya was driven by a search for Muslim unity and an unceasing commitment to confronting foreign influences on Islamic culture, which in his context meant Greek philosophy, Sufism (Islamic mysticism), and Muslim prayers at saints' tombs. His work was foundational for Muhammad ibn Abd al Wahhab, whose ideology is known today as Wahhabism.

Muhammad ibn Abd al Wahhab

Another important traditionalist voice is that of **Muhammad ibn Abd al Wahhab** (1703–1792). Al-Wahhab was born in the Arabian Peninsula and followed Ibn Taymiyya's teachings, especially his legalistic leanings that sought to purify Islam of the cultural, religious, and social accoutrements it had accumulated through engagement with non-Islamic peoples and traditions. Al-Wahhab, for instance, convinced leaders to destroy the tombs of Muslim saints, and he also opposed the celebration of annual feasts for dead Muslim saints; condemned wearing charms and amulets and also believing in their healing powers; and banned all photographs, the use of tobacco, and even celebrating Prophet Muhammad's birthday. It is important to note that al-Wahhab made a pact with an emir (tribal chief) in Arabia, **Ibn Saud**, whose heirs eventually seized control of Arabia in 1932, after which they established Saudi Arabia and instituted the Wahhabi movement as its ideology. With the discovery of oil in Saudi Arabia in 1938, petrodollars fueled the spread of Wahhabism through religious schools, newspapers, and Wahhabi missionaries outside Saudi Arabia. Petrodollars continue to fund major *da'wah* (Muslim mission) activities that promote Islam around the world today.

MODERNISTS

Another group of Muslim intellectuals has influenced Islamic thought by shaping Muslim responses to modernism beginning in the late nineteenth century. Known generally as the modernists, they seek to interpret Islam to meet the changing conditions of modern life, and therefore they are distinct from the traditionalists because they permit some flexibility in the interpretation of Islam itself. Although Islamic modernism is not a systematic movement, a common element among modernists is their argument that Islam is compatible with reason, science, and technology.

The crucial interpretive question for Islamic modernists, as well as for traditionalists, hinges on a question of Qur'anic exegesis. How does one properly interpret the Qur'an? A critical debate among Qur'anic exegetes is between those who emphasize *ijtihad* (independent reasoning and independent decision that are not necessarily based on a traditional school of Islamic jurisprudence) and those who adhere to strict *taqlid* ("imitation"; following past decisions and interpretations by Islamic jurisprudence). That is, *ijtihad* inherently assumes a degree of openness, freedom of thought, and rational thinking in the pursuit of truth, whereas Qur'anic exegetes who advocate *taqlid* tend toward a closed exegetical approach, affirming that many interpretive decisions have already been made by earlier exegetes. Thus, *ijtihad* is more open, whereas *taqlid* tends to be more closed to interpretive innovation.

Examples of Muslim modernists include Sayyid Ahmad Khan, Muhammad Abduh, and Muhammad Iqbal. Briefly, **Sayyid Ahmad Khan** (1817–89) was born in India and was known for selectively adopting the best of the West while remaining true to Islamic principles. Khan had a lasting impact on India by pioneering modern education for the Muslim community in India and founding the well-known university Aligarh Muslim University. Khan encouraged the use of *ijtihad* (innovation) when interpreting the Qur'an to bring Islam in line with modern thinking and institutions. Khan was embraced by the West and was knighted by Queen Victoria as Sir Sayyid Ahmad Khan.

> *I say, let's have a debate. I'm not afraid of offending God by using my mind. . . . I think, therefore, I am a Muslim.*
>
> Muqtedar Khan, quoted in *News Journal*, April 2, 2006 (available at http://www.ijtihad.org/Soft%20Voice%20Strong%20Message.htm)

Muhammad Abduh (1849–1905) was an Egyptian religious reformer who strove to modernize Islam to show that it was rational; he rejected blind adherence to tradition (*taqlid*) and called for Islam to be the basis for modernization in Egypt. Muhammad Abduh studied logic at one of the most famous Muslim universities in the world, Al-Azar University in Cairo, Egypt. Abduh sought to show that properly used reason did not conflict with the religious revelation recorded in the Qur'an.

Finally, **Muhammad Iqbal** (1875–1938), who was born in India and studied philosophy and law in England and Germany, argued that Islam itself had to be reevaluated and reinterpreted to make sense to moderns. Iqbal was a committed Muslim and argued vigorously that Islam should be the source of government and society. Iqbal wanted the Qur'an to be the basis of society, although he also endorsed equal opportunity. Iqbal was knighted by the British government and showed great openness to the contributions of European thought. In Iqbal's own words, "With the reawakening of Islam, . . . it is necessary to examine, in an independent spirit, what Europe has taught and how far the conclusions reached by her can help us in the revision, and if necessary, reconstruction of theological thought in Islam."[16] Indeed, these words reflect a strikingly different social and religious orientation than that advocated by Islamic traditionalists.

Islamists

A third Muslim group have been variously called radicals, Islamists (*Islamiyya*), fundamentalists, or advocates of political Islam. This is a subset of the modernist strand. Whatever the nomenclature, the Islamists have not sought to interpret Islam in terms of dominant Western values. Here they differ from modernists, who maintain that some good things—indeed, many beneficial elements—can be adopted selectively by faithful Muslims. Rather, Islamists seek to assert the control of Islam by interpreting modernity according to Islamic values. For Islamists, the tension between Islam and the West is essentially a conflict between Islam and the secular order, which emerged out of the West.

Islamists support the state's control of Islam and seek to Islamize all aspects of life, including the political and jurisprudential domains. Many Islamists struggle to replace Western values with Islamic ones, repudiating the *"Baywatch* culture"—the promulgation of overly sexualized images and relationships through media outlets in the United States—of a morally degenerate West. The values associated with the *Baywatch* culture are perceived as universally endorsed by Americans and thus are part and parcel of American life. Islamists reject these values as failing to affirm human flourishing.

Sayyid Abu'l-A'la Mawdudi

Sayyid Abu'l-A'la Mawdudi (1903–79) was born in India and lived to witness the political independence of India from the British Raj. Mawdudi argued that British and French colonialism, and particularly its introduction of modern secular nationalism, was to blame for the decline of Muslim power in India. He mourned the dissolution of the Ottoman Empire and the power of Islam to control all ways of life. Mawdudi argued for the purging of all alien elements from Islam in India, including the severance of ties with Hindus and Christians because all non-Muslims were a threat to Islam.

The Jama'at al-Islamic Party was founded by Mawdudi in the northern part of South Asia (1941). He argued unapologetically that Islam was a revolutionary force and that physical force (militant jihad) was permissible to defend Islam and Islamic ideals, in order to bring the entire world under the rule of Islam.

> Islam is a revolutionary doctrine and system that overturns governments. It seeks to overturn the whole universal social order . . . and establish its structure anew. . . . Islam seeks the world. It is not satisfied by a piece of land but demands the whole

universe. . . . Islamic Jihad is at the same time offensive and defensive. . . . The Islamic party does not hesitate to utilize the means of war to implement its goal.[17]

Mawdudi's vision was all-encompassing:

Islam wants the whole earth and does not content itself with only a part thereof. . . . No, Islam wants and requires the earth in order that the human race altogether can enjoy the concept and practical program of human happiness, by which God has honored Islam and put it above the other religions and laws.[18]

Mawdudi was a radical revolutionary who believed that sharia was the blueprint for modern Muslim society, and therefore there was no need for any kind of dependence on the West. Jihad (both spiritual and physical struggle) must be continual to fully Islamize society.

Sayyid Qutb

Perhaps one of the most famous Islamists was Sayyid Qutb (1906–66), who was born in Egypt and was profoundly influenced by Mawdudi. Qutb was a member of the **Muslim Brotherhood** of Egypt, which was founded by **Hasan al-Banna**. The brotherhood, which began in Egypt and is now found in several Middle Eastern and Western countries, advocated a literalist interpretation of the Qur'an and sought the restoration of the caliphate (abolished by Ataturk in 1924), a pan-Islamic empire that unites Muslims worldwide. Today there are many different forms of the brotherhood. In June 2012, the Muslim Brotherhood–backed candidate, Mohammed Morsi, was declared the winner in Egypt's first free presidential election in history.

The brotherhood's creed is simple: "God [Allah] is our objective, the Qur'an is our constitution, the Prophet is our leader, struggle is our way, and death for the sake of God is the highest of our aspirations." Sayyid Qutb's ideas were fomented by his visit to the United States (1948–50), where, among other things, he visited a church dance and became convinced that the culture of the United States sexualized its women. He also experienced great prejudice and was shocked by the racial bigotry he witnessed and experienced in the United States. Qutb separated the world into two battling forces—things Islamic and things un-Islamic.

Ignorance versus Islam

More precisely, in the view of Qutb, the world is a battlefield between *jahiliyya* (era of darkness and ignorance) and Islam. It is the duty of all Muslims to fight whatever is characterized by *jahiliyya*, and thus is un-Islamic, even if that includes political leaders who called themselves Muslim but

Look at capitalism with its monopolies, its usury . . . at this individual freedom, devoid of human sympathy and responsibility for relatives except under force of law; at this materialistic attitude which deadens the spirit; at this behavior, like animals, which you call "Free mixing of the sexes"; at this vulgarity which you call "emancipation of women"; at these unfair and cumbersome laws of marriage and divorce, which are contrary to the demands of practical life; and at Islam, with its logic, beauty, humanity and happiness, which reaches the horizons to which man strives but does not reach. It is a practical way of life.

Qutb, *Milestones* (2007), 95

advocate, say, a secular constitution. Today, Qutb is seen as the godfather of modern Islamic terrorism. His book *Milestones* (or *Signposts*) lays out his vision of Islam as a total way of life and the need to eliminate non-Islamic influences, arguing forcefully that only Islam can fill the moral vacuum of the West.

Qutb was imprisoned for ten years in Egypt for his support of the attempted assassination of Gamal Abdel Nasser (1954), president of Egypt, then rearrested for trying to overthrow the Egyptian state. In 1966 Qutb was hanged for treason against Egypt. He was influenced by Islamic traditionalist Ibn Taymiyya and Islamist Mawdudi. Qutb himself discipled Osama bin Laden's second-in-command, Dr. Ayman al-Zawahiri.

Moderate or "Liberal" Islam

Finally, there are several voices that can be described as moderate or liberal. Prominent among them is **Abdurrahman Wahid** (1940–2009), who was born in Indonesia and served as the president of Indonesia from 1999 to 2001. Nearly blind, Wahid, known affectionately as "Gus Dur" (derived from a combination of an honorific title and shortened form of his first name), was the leader of the Nahdatul Ulama (Revival of Religious Scholars), the largest Islamic organization in Indonesia, with thirty-five million members. Wahid is neither modernist nor traditionalist and exhibits a surprisingly open honesty about his own struggle with important Qur'anic injunctions. For instance, according to the Qur'an, when living in a Muslim society Jews and Christians are to become members of the *dhimmi* (protected scriptural minority) class and thus pay the *jizya* (poll) tax for protection by Muslim rulers.

Abdurrahman Wahid has subjected the concept of *dhimmi* (protected scriptural minorities) to a radical critique, ultimately rejecting it. As the president of the largest Muslim country in the world, with significant religious minorities, Wahid has struggled with how to interpret the command to advance the notion of dhimmism among his citizens. Asked about the *jizya*, Wahid once replied:

It is very problematic for me until now, because it concerns the concept of *dhimmi*. To be frank I do not know what to do with it. It is there. But my belief and the very core of my own existence, you see, [is] to reject dhimmism because, as an Indonesian and because of our national priorities, my main thinking is that I have to reject it. All citizens are equal, you see. That is the problem. That is why I do not know what to do with it. It is there, but I reject it.[19]

Wahid suggests that Islam should not be the state religion, at least of Indonesia, and that Islam should be inclusive, democratic, and a pluralistic force rather than a state ideology. In Wahid's view, "there is no need for a nation-state with Islamic law." Wahid, then, advocates a dynamic, open, creative society where all religions can participate.

Conclusion

It is worthwhile to remember that Islam is not a monolithic tradition; it exhibits significant tension and variety within itself and among its interpreters. Nobel Prize–winner Amartya Sen reminds us of the mistake of a reductionistic view that equates individual identity exclusively with religious self-ascription. "For example, a Bangladeshi Muslim is not only a Muslim but also a Bengali and a Bangladeshi, typically quite proud of the Bengali language, literature, and music, not to mention the other identities he or she may have connected with class, gender, occupation, politics, aesthetic taste, and so on."[20] Religious people are embedded in social, cultural, and political systems that complicate attempts to construct an overly simplistic view of the "other" religious tradition as a single entity.

Commenting on the religious path of Islam, an imam in the United States declared that Muslims live "between hope and fear," with the hope that God, who is compassionate and merciful, will be gracious to them, yet fearful of a God who is so great and distinct from God's creation that no human being can know with assurance how God will judge each creature. Christians, we can say, live "between promise and fulfillment," with an assurance of salvation promised

Mankind today is on the brink of a precipice, not because of the danger of complete annihilation which is hanging over its head—this being just a symptom and not the real disease—but because humanity is devoid of those vital values which are necessary not only for its healthy development but also for its real progress. Even the Western world realizes that Western civilization is unable to present any healthy values for the guidance of mankind. It knows that it does not possess anything which will satisfy its own conscience and justify its existence.

Qutb, *Milestones* (2007), 1

All that the West sees in Islam is radicalism and its incompatibility with modern, open, democratic politics. Indonesia, however, has the opportunity to show that politics based on confession—as it is in Algeria and Iran—is not the only way. Not only can modernity and open politics exist in a Muslim-majority society, as it can here in Indonesia, but it can be nurtured so that democracy can flourish well in Islam.

Esposito and Voll, *Makers of Contemporary Islam*, 209

by a God who has extended salvation to all who would receive it, regardless of human imperfections and sin.

The declaration of Christianity is that God stooped to conquer sin and death and paid the price through Jesus Christ so that all could be saved. Even with these differences there is much that Christians can understand and be challenged by in Islam, such as the great honor given to God and the

Having suggested the existence of variety within Islam itself, I want to raise two questions that thoughtful Christians may want to keep in mind. First, what is the relationship between Islam and territory? Mecca is off-limits to non-Muslims because it is considered sacred territory. The pattern of the historical development of Islam began in Mecca and was, some say, linked with a desire for world empire. Islam is a missionary religion that calls its followers to prayer toward Mecca (i.e., the Qa'abah) five times daily.

The pilgrimage to Mecca (hajj) is an obligation for all faithful Muslims with the financial resources to make the trip, raising Mecca above all other domains. Islamic expansion moved out from its origin, Mecca, spreading in wider and wider circles, pointing the faithful back to Mecca, its epicenter, for spiritual sustenance and corporate identity. The history of Christianity, by contrast, is marked generally by accession and recession at the place of its origins, as it relativized geographic locations, making none more holy than any other.

The territoriality principle is so embedded within the tradition of Islam that Olivier Roy, research director at the French National Center for Scientific Research and a scholar of Islam, argues for deterritorialism as a root cause for current tensions between some Muslims and the West. Roy contends that Muslim immigrants to the West struggle in part because of the disjuncture they experience between their religion and the space (nation-state) they inhabit, where the territoriality principle has broken down. That is, the connection between Islam and the land (territory) has dissolved—no longer is Muslim identity tied to living in a Muslim land. Do Muslims have endless rights on claimed territory? How painful is the deterritorialization of Islam in the West for today's Muslims? As Islam continues to grow in the United States, how will Muslims continue to interpret and engage civil society and local neighborhoods and participate in national politics?

Second, what are the implications of the belief that Arabic is the language of God and the sacred text (Qur'an)? Because of the inseparable connection between language and culture, coupled with the untranslatability of the Arabic Qur'an, Arabic language and culture are given priority as a medium of religious faith and knowledge. Although diversity exists within Islam, Arabic language and culture are given special worth because it was through the Prophet Muhammad that the message was revealed.

struggle to submit everything to God's will—these can be seeds for fruitful conversation between Muslims and Christians and serve as the basis of civility and cooperation in mutually beneficial endeavors.

Timeline

570 CE	Birth of Muhammad
610	Muhammad receives first vision in a cave near Mecca
610–22	Muhammad preaches in Mecca
622	Muhammad and his followers flee Mecca to Medina; beginning of Islamic calendar (AH, Anno Hegirae)
624	Muslims successfully attack Meccan caravans at Badr
625	Muslims are defeated by Meccans at Uhud
630	Medinan Muslims capture Mecca; Qa'abah is purified; pilgrimage rites are Islamicized; most Arabian tribes are in alliance with Muhammad
632	Death of Muhammad; Abu Bakr chosen as first Rightly Guided Caliph
633	Muslim conquests (*Futuhat*) begin
634–44	Umar becomes caliph; Islam controls Egypt, Syria, Palestine, Mesopotamia, North African coast, parts of Persian and Byzantine Empires
650	Caliph Uthman, the third caliph, has the Qur'an written down
656	Caliph Uthman is murdered; 'Ali becomes fourth caliph
661	'Ali is murdered; Mu'awiya becomes caliph; beginning of Umayyad Caliphate (661–750)
680	Martyrdom of Husayn ('Ali's son) begins the Shia (partisans of 'Ali) sect
Late 600s	Ruling classes in East and West Africa convert to Islam
732	Muslim empires reach furthest extent; Battle of Tours prevents further advance northward
754	Baghdad (Madinat al-Salam, "City of Peace") becomes the new capital of the Abbasid Empire (754–1519)
765	Division within Shia Islam, majority being Imamiyya (Twelvers) and minority being Isma'iliyya (Seveners)
980–1037	Life of Avicenna, Iranian physician and Aristotelian philosopher
Late 900s	West Africa begins to convert to Islam
1030	Umayyad Caliphate in Cordoba, Spain, defeated by Christian Reconquista
1099	Christian crusaders control Jerusalem

1126–98	Life of Averroës, Muslim philosopher from Cordoba who sought to integrate Islam with Greek thinking
1221	Genghis Khan and the Mongols enter Persia
1241	Mongols control the Punjab
1258	Mongols capture Baghdad; end of Abbasid Caliphate
1281–1324	Reign of Uthman, who founds the Ottoman Empire (1299)
1400s	Islam enters the Philippines
1453	Mehmet Fatish (r. 1451–81) conquers Constantinople; the two parts of the Ottoman Empire unite and the sultan becomes Byzantine emperor
1501	Twelver Shia becomes official religion of Persia
1526	Babur, a Mongolian, seizes the Delhi sultanate and controls northern India
1556	Akbar founds the Mughal Dynasty in northern India
1700s	Muhammad Abd al-Wahhab rejects Sufism and founds what becomes the Saudi Arabian kingdom
1858	Last Mughal in India is deposed and India comes under British rule
1918	Fall of the Ottoman Empire; League of Nations grants Britain mandatory status over Palestine and Iraq, and France over Lebanon and Syria
1947	Pakistan founded as an Islamic nation
1979	Iranian Islamic revolution, when shah of Iran is overthrown by Ayatollah Ruhollah Khomeini, who established strict *sharia* principles
1990s	Taliban comes to power in Afghanistan
2001	Members of Al Qaeda, an Islamic terrorist organization, attack the United States
2006	Muhammad Yunus wins Nobel Peace Prize for successful application of microcredit programs to poor entrepreneurs in Bangladesh

Key Terms

Abduh, Muhammad

Abu Bakr

Abu Talib

al-Banna, Hasan

'Ali

Allah

Allahu Akbar

al-Mahdi

al-Masih

al-Qur'an

al-Rahim

al-Rahman

al-Wahhab, Muhammad ibn Abd

Asr

Bismallah al-Rahman al-Rahim

Black Stone

caliphate

Companions

da'eef

Dar al-Harb
Dar al-Islam
dhimmi
du'a
Eid al-Adha
Eid-ul-Fitr
Fajr
faqih
Fatimah
fatwa
fiqh
fitrah
ghusl
hadith
Hajar
hajj
hajjah
hajji
Hanafi
Hanbal
haraam
hasan
Ibn Saud
Ibn Taymiyya, Ahmad
Ibrahim (Abraham)
ihram
ijma
ijtihad
imam
Imams
Iqbal, Muhammad
Isa (Jesus)
Isha
Islamists
Isma'il
isnad

jahiliyya
jihad
jizya
jumu'ah
kalam
Khadijah
Khan, Sayyid Ahmad
Maghrib
makruh
Malik
mandub
masjid
matn
mawdoo'
Mawdudi, Sayyid
   Abu'l-A'la
Mecca
Medina
minaret
moderates
modernists
mosque
Mount Arafat
mubah
muezzin
mujtahid
Musa (Moses)
Muslim
Muslim Brotherhood
Nuh (Noah)
Organization of the Is-
   lamic Cooperation
Prophet Muhammad
Qa'abah
qibla
qiyas
Qur'an

Quraysh
Qutb, Sayyid
Ramadan
ra'y
riba
Rightly Guided Caliphs
sahih
sai
salat
sawm
Sevener Shiism
Shafi'i
shahada
sharia
Shia
sunnah
Sunni
surah
tafsir
Takbir
tanzil
taqlid
tawaf
tawhid
traditionalists
Twelver Shiism
ummah
usul al-fiqh
Uthman
Wahid, Abdurrahman
wajib
wilaya
wudu
Yathrib
zakat
Zuhr

Further Reading

Ali, Maulana Muhammad. *The Religion of Islam*. Columbus, OH: Ahmadiyya Anjuman Isha'at Islam, 1994.

Cragg, Kenneth. *The Call of the Minaret*. Oxford: Oneworld Publications, 2000.

———. *Jesus and the Muslim*. Oxford: Oneworld Publications, 1999.

———. *Muhammad and the Christian: A Question of Response*. Oxford: Oneworld Publications, 1999.

Esposito, John L. *Islam: The Straight Path*. New York: Oxford University Press, 2010.

Esposito, John L., and John O. Voll. *Makers of Contemporary Islam*. Oxford: Oxford University Press, 2001.

Peters, F. E. *Muhammad and the Origins of Islam*. Albany: SUNY Press, 1994.

Riddell, Peter G., and Peter Cotterell. *Islam in Context: Past, Present, and Future*. Grand Rapids: Baker Academic, 2003.

Smith, Wilfred Cantwell. *Islam in Modern History*. Princeton: Princeton University Press, 1957.

Volf, Miroslav, HRH Prince Ghazi Bin Muhammad Bin Talal, and Melissa Yarrington. *A Common Word: Muslims and Christians on Loving God and Neighbor*. Grand Rapids: Eerdmans, 2000.

ten

New Religious Movements

Contemporary Snapshot

On Saturday, November 29, 1997, the Reverend **Sun Myung Moon**, the self-proclaimed Messiah, stood before a large crowd at RFK Stadium in Washington, DC. Reverend Moon, then a seventy-seven-year-old Korean billionaire and convicted felon who had served thirteen years in a federal prison for income tax evasion in the mid-1980s, officiated over a mass wedding of 30,000 couples at the stadium while presiding simultaneously over the wedding ceremony of 3.6 million couples worldwide via video link. He officiated at the ceremony that day for many who had never met each other prior to the date of their wedding but were assigned spouses by Reverend Moon himself. Some of these arranged couples consisted of husbands and wives who could not speak each other's languages.

Reverend Moon, who was raised a Presbyterian, believed that Jesus did not fulfill his entire mission and so offered only partial salvation because of Jesus's failure to marry and have children. Consequently, Jesus appeared to Moon in a vision, asking Moon to complete Jesus's task of redeeming the world through marriage. Reverend Moon and his wife were called the "True

Parents" of humanity, who were fulfilling the mission that the original True Parents (Adam and Eve) and Jesus had failed to accomplish.

One way that Christians sometimes distinguish between religions claiming to be Christian is to categorize them as either a form of "Christianity" or a kind of "**cult**." In this context, the word "cult" is used negatively, with the assumption that Christianity is not a cult, and that a cult is sub-Christian or pagan. Another term that is used is "**new religious movements**" (NRM). Negatively, "cult" previously referred to strange and bizarre practices and beliefs—for Christians that would mean practices and beliefs outside the parameters of Christian orthodoxy—thus carrying with it the idea of deviancy and exoticism. Sociologically speaking, the term "cult" refers to beliefs and practices of a small group of people that are syncretistic—that is, they borrow elements from many different religious and philosophical traditions—individualistic, and esoteric. For our purposes, the most helpful definition of "cult," which also happens to be closest to the original and the broadest, is that "cult" refers to a system of worship—that is, reverential homage rendered to a divine being.

Christianity, then, can be seen as a cult, in the best sense of that term, as a structure through which people worship God. Sociologist **Max Weber** (1864–1920) and philosopher-theologian **Ernst Troeltsch** (1865–1923) argued that "church" referred to a large bureaucratic organization with a priesthood (or pastorate), marked by a formal statement of orthodoxy, efforts to recruit members through socialization, and ritualistic patterns of worship. Nowadays the expression "new religious movements" refers to those religious traditions that do not fit neatly into mainstream religious traditions. Many display a remarkable degree of organization, with the presence of religious leadership, such as priests, pastors, and spiritual guides. The older sociological term "cult," referring to a nontraditional small religious movement, has now been replaced by the generic term "new religious movements." The beliefs and practices of these movements are immensely diverse; however, most are highly syncretistic, with rituals and practices that have been influenced by the world religions, especially Hinduism, Buddhism, Judaism, Christianity, and Islam. Scholars Ron Enroth and J. Gordon Melton have written several worthwhile books regarding the phenomenon of the rise and appeal of new religious movements. Additionally, a plethora of recent releases of NRM handbooks and encyclopedias attest to the increasing interest in the field of emerging, "nontraditional" religions.[1]

Origins and Concepts

Although debate continues about the scope of the term "new religious movement"—for instance, when does an NRM become an accepted religion—most sociologists of religion and scholars of religious studies employ the term as an alternative to the word "cult."

World-Denying and World-Affirming Movements

NRMs are vastly different, with no overall structure into which they all fit comfortably. In a helpful way, sociologists have divided NRMs into "world-denying" and "world-affirming" movements. World-denying groups tend to be much more countercultural, are disillusioned with traditional religions and institutions, and thus shun the world, often by emphasizing spiritual experiences rather than reason and rationality. Some world-denying movements perceive the world as an evil force that must be overcome, and personal or communal renunciation plays a crucial role in the beliefs and practices of their adherents. World-affirming groups tend to focus more on illuminating deep truths and insights that help practitioners understand their hidden potential to live better on earth. Such movements seek to transform the individual by providing self-realization teaching and techniques. The authority structure of NRMs is just as broad, ranging from highly authoritarian to egalitarian. It is not unusual for NRMs to be led by a charismatic leader, but this is not always the case, as some NRMs exhibit a more loosely affiliated group of adherents not necessarily centered on an individual leader.

Given that there are thousands of NRMs worldwide, and the fact that it is impossible to illuminate more than a small number of them in this chapter, I present a few of the most popular NRMs that are found in the United States, categorizing them as either Western-oriented, that is, stemming historically from one of the monotheistic religions ("Movements of Judeo-Christian Orientation"), Asian-oriented, that is, rooted primarily in Asian religious traditions ("Movements of Hindu-Buddhist Orientation") or not directly related to Asian or Judeo-Christian orientations ("Movements of Distinctive Orientation"). While these NRMs exist primarily in the West, and particularly in the United States, they are increasingly found outside the West as well.

Movements of Judeo-Christian Orientation

MORMONISM

The largest new religious movement that originated in the United States is the **Church of Jesus Christ of Latter-Day Saints** (LDS), otherwise known as **Mormonism**. Boasting close to fourteen million members worldwide, Mormonism has expanded throughout segments of the world thanks to its assertive missionary outreach. Mormonism is the fifth largest religious body in the United States, listed just above the Evangelical Lutheran Church in America in numbers of adherents.[2] Its financial holdings are significant. Were it to be listed on the Fortune 500 list, the Mormon church would be located about midpoint on the list, just above Nike and the Gap.

Beginnings of Mormonism

Mormonism considers itself a **restoration movement** that continued the church from its demise after the death of Jesus's disciples. Known also as **primitivist movements**, restoration groups seek to reestablish the original form of Christianity, which they believe will retrieve the purer essence of Christianity. Mormonism began with **Joseph Smith Jr.** (1805–44), the founder, seer, and prophet of the religion. Smith was raised in Palmyra, New York, where as a teenager he was unsure about which Christian church to join. Following what he claimed were revelations from the heavenly personages Heavenly Father and Heavenly Son, who told Smith that he was set apart to do a special work on earth, Smith believed that he was called to restore the Christian church that had been corrupted in the postapostolic period. Through another revelation, the teenager Smith was told that no church in his day was correct, since they were abominable.

Figure 10.1. Joseph Smith Jr.

Charles William Carter/Wikimedia Commons

The following words are recorded in the **Book of Mormon**:

> And the angel said unto me, Behold the foundation of a church, which is most abominable above all churches, which slayeth the Saints of God, yea, and tortureth them and bindeth them down, and yoketh them with a yoke of iron, and bringeth them down into captivity. And it came to pass that I beheld this great and abominable church; and I saw the devil, that he was the founder of it.
>
> I Nephi 13:5–6

The angel told young Smith that the ancient prophet **Moroni** had buried golden tablets, along with seer stones (i.e., Urim and Thummim) to decipher the script, on which were recorded the story of the early inhabitants of the Americas—some of which are said to have originated near Jerusalem from the Prophet Lehi—and Jesus's postresurrection appearance to them. The story recorded on the golden tablets was translated by Smith and published as the Book of Mormon in 1830. The Book of Mormon began a series of revelations received by Joseph Smith Jr. until he died and, even if infrequently, throughout the history of the LDS presidency. Those revelations would not be without conflict.

Prophet Smith received revelations until his death in 1844. Two of the more controversial revelations were about men of black African descent and about plural wives. In 1978 the president of the LDS Church, Spencer W. Kimball, received the "Revelation on Priesthood," which permitted black men to hold the LDS priesthood. Prior to this revelation, President Kimball announced the construction of new LDS temples in the United States and Brazil. The eligibility of entrance into the priesthood was an obstacle, but during prayer the revelation came and all twelve men of the Quorum of the Twelve Apostles

Christian Reflections

The lack of historically verifiable archaeological and biological data mentioned in the Book of Mormon has raised serious doubts about the historicity of the stories. According to a statement by Smithsonian Institution archeologists, "The Smithsonian Institution has never used the Book of Mormon in any way as a scientific guide. Smithsonian archeologists see no direct connection between the archaeology of the New World and the subject matter of this book."[a] Likewise, in a letter written to Luke Wilson of the Institute for Religious Research, National Geographic researchers noted the Book of Mormon's lack of historicity regarding America's earlier inhabitants:

The *Book of Mormon* is clearly a work of great spiritual power; millions have read and revered its words, first published by Joseph Smith in 1830. Yet Smith's narration is not generally taken as a scientific source for the history of the Americas. Archeologists and other scholars have long probed the hemisphere's past, and the Society does not know of anything found so far that has substantiated the *Book of Mormon*.

In fact, students of prehistoric America by and large conclude that the New World's earliest inhabitants arrived from Asia via the Bering "land bridge."[b]

Because of the immense number of grammatical errors, the direct quotations from the King James Version (1611) of the Bible, and its resemblance to an unpublished novel, the authenticity of the Book of Mormon has come into question.

a. Available at http://www.mrm.org/smithsonian.
b. Available at http://mit.irr.org/national-geographic-society-statement-on-book-of-mormon.

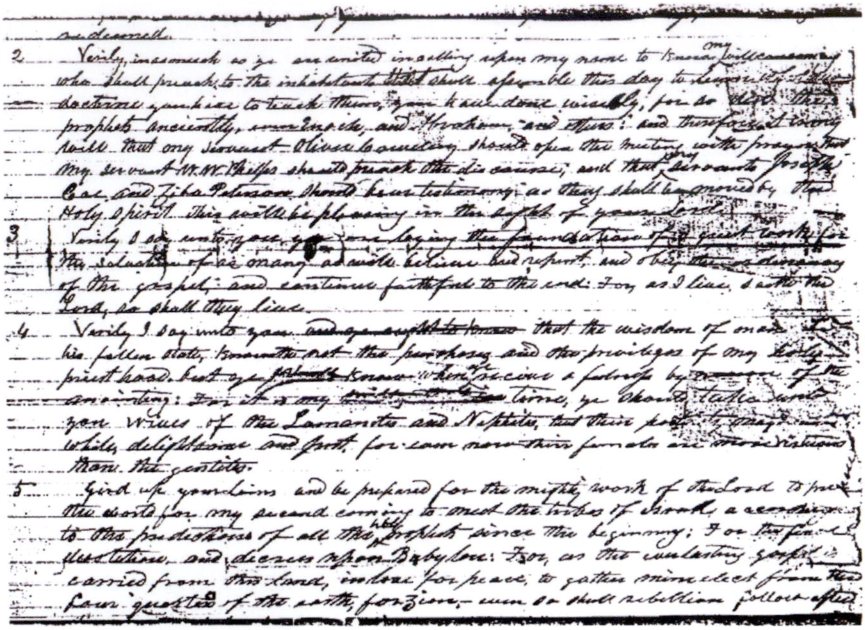

… as desired.
2 Verily, inasmuch as ye are united in calling upon my name to know my will concerning who shall preach to the inhabitants that shall assemble this day to learn the doctrine you have to teach them, you have done wisely, for so did the prophets anciently, even Enoch, and Abraham, and others: and therefore it is my will that my servant Oliver Cowdery should open the meeting with prayer; that my servant W. W. Phelps should preach the discourse; and that my servants Joseph Coe and Ziba Peterson should bear testimony, as they shall be moved by the Holy Spirit. This will be pleasing in the sight of your Lord.
3 Verily I say unto you, ye are laying the foundation of a great work for the salvation of as many as will believe and repent, and obey the ordinances of the gospel, and continue faithful to the end: For as I live, saith the Lord, so shall they live.
4 Verily I say unto you, ~~and ye ought to know~~ that the wisdom of man in his fallen state, knoweth not the purposes and the privileges of my holy priesthood, but ye shall know when ye receive a fulness by reason of the anointing: For it is my will, that in time, ye should take unto you wives of the Lamanites and Nephites, that their posterity may become white, delightsome and just, for even now their females are more virtuous than the gentiles.
5 Gird up your loins and be prepared for the mighty work of the Lord to prepare the world for my second coming to meet the tribes of Israel, according to the predictions of all the holy prophets since the beginning; For the final desolation and decrees upon Babylon: For, as the everlasting gospel is carried from this land, in love for peace, to gather mine elect from the four quarters of the earth, for Zion, — even so shall rebellion follow after

William W. Phelps/Wikimedia Commons

Figure 10.2. Polygamy revelation to Joseph Smith

(the most important governing body of the LDS Church) recognized that the Lord wanted the LDS Church to reverse its ban on allowing black men into the priesthood. Likewise, a new revelation changed the LDS perspective on plural marriage. In 1890 church president Wilford Woodruff issued a manifesto that officially ended the practice of polygamy. It would not be until 1904, when LDS Church president Joseph F. Smith entirely disavowed plural marriages in a second manifesto, that the LDS Church formally split from other Mormons who supported the practice of polygamy, such as the fundamentalist LDS groups. These groups will be introduced later in this chapter.

Smith received numerous revelations through heavenly personages until 1844 when he was murdered at the hands of the Illinois militia in Carthage, Illinois, while en route to find a headquarters for his new religious community.

Three Branches of Mormonism

Church of Jesus Christ of Latter-Day Saints

Three branches of Mormonism emerged following Prophet Smith's death. The first group, known today as the Church of Jesus Christ of Latter-Day Saints, finds its roots in the group that followed **Brigham Young** (1801–77) to the Salt Lake area of Utah, where Zion in the Wilderness was constructed as the worldwide headquarters of the LDS Church. Based in Salt Lake City, Utah, the LDS

Church is the largest of the three movements, and the branch of Mormonism that most people refer to when they speak of "Mormonism" or "Mormons."

FUNDAMENTALIST LATTER-DAY SAINTS (FLDS)

A second branch of Mormonism, known broadly as the **Fundamentalist Latter-Day Saints** (FLDS), consists of several disparate, mostly rural communities that adhere solely to the revelations of Prophet Joseph Smith Jr. The division between the LDS and the FLDS occurred primarily over the issue of plural marriage (**polygamy**), in which faithful men of the FLDS Church were instructed to marry several wives. With approximately ten thousand members spread throughout communities primarily in rural Arizona, Utah, South Dakota, and Texas, and holding to separation from its wider, non-FLDS surroundings, the FLDS Church is a relatively small movement.

Figure 10.3. Mormon temple headquarters in Salt Lake City, Utah, USA

The FLDS's promotion of plural marriage has led to arrests of some of the group's main leaders. The illegality of the FLDS is based not only on its infraction of antipolygamy laws in the United States but also on financial grounds, for it is common for a prophet of an FLDS community to register one marriage and receive state financial aid for all his other wives, who register with the state to receive state aid as single mothers.

REORGANIZED CHURCH OF THE LATTER-DAY SAINTS (RLDS)

The third branch of Mormonism is the **Reorganized Church of the Latter-Day Saints** (RLDS), also known as the **Community of Christ**, with headquarters in Independence, Missouri. Following the death of Prophet Joseph Smith Jr., a group supported Smith's son, Joseph Smith III (1832–1914), as leader of the Latter-Day Saints movement. Joseph Smith III fiercely opposed polygamy and the idea of evolving gods—that is, that God was once a man. Additionally, he rejected the notion that all LDS members had to gather in one location. Instead, he argued that they could worship wherever they lived. A large group of RLDS adherents eventually settled in Independence, Missouri. Most RLDS followers also reject the LDS Church practices of "baptism of the dead" and making covenants.

Reporting about 250,000 members, the RLDS Church is theologically closest to historic Protestantism and emphasizes spirituality, peace, and justice.

It retains belief in ongoing revelation, yet it has its own collection of Doctrine and Covenants (D&C) that includes revelations different from those compiled in the LDS Church D&C. For instance, in 1865 the RLDS Church ordained men of color into the priesthood. In 1984 the RLDS Church began ordaining women into the priesthood. The church also allows members of other churches to partake of Holy Communion (Lord's Supper), and the church is open to the public, unlike the LDS Church. In 2001 the RLDS Church renamed itself the Community of Christ. It maintains a commitment to the triune nature of God, which is distinct from the LDS perspective that God consists of three physical personages. However, the Community of Christ continues to uphold the Book of Mormon as scripture, while striking a balance between refusing to mandate Mormon belief in its historicity and affirming that Christ speaks through it. Today the Community of Christ has a cordial relationship with the larger LDS Church, which is based on a mutual acknowledgment of a common heritage.

Mormon Beliefs

Mormons perceive themselves as Christians who have restored the fallen church, which they believe had been apostate (i.e., had denied the faith) after the death of the disciples. They affirm Jesus Christ, the Holy Ghost, and Heavenly Father, but understand the Trinity as consisting of three separate, unrelated persons, with each individual member being a separate God. Thus, Mormon theology recognizes three Gods and rejects the orthodox Christian

Figure 10.4. Fundamentalist Latter-Day Saints Church in Eldorado, Texas, USA

understanding of the triune nature of God as three persons in one Godhead. Furthermore, while there is no formal doctrine, many LDS members believe that Heavenly Father is married to an exalted woman known as Heavenly Mother, who was a spirit daughter of heavenly parents. In the words of Mormon theologian Bruce McConkie, "Three separate personages—Father, Son, and Holy Ghost—comprise the Godhead. As each of these persons is a God, it is evident, from this standpoint alone, that a plurality of Gods exists. To us, speaking in the proper finite sense, these three are the only Gods we worship."[3]

Jesus, according to Mormon theology, is an offspring of Heavenly Father. Salvation is by repentance and baptism by immersion. The "baptism of the dead" gives those souls residing in the "spirit world" after death another chance to repent. Heaven itself consists of three levels, or degrees of glory, known as the Telestial Kingdom, the Terrestrial Kingdom, and the Celestial Kingdom; only the most committed Mormons who have accepted the teachings of Jesus Christ and followed what are known as the Laws and Ordinances of the Gospel are promised entrance into the Celestial Kingdom.

Mormon Sacred Texts

The sacred texts of Mormonism include four books. First, Mormons accept the Bible, which is the King James Version with several passages retranslated by Prophet Joseph Smith Jr., referred to as the Joseph Smith Jr. Translation (JST). A second sacred text is the **Pearl of Great Price**, which contains the history of Prophet Joseph Smith Jr., a translation of the Gospel of Matthew, the Mormon Thirteen Articles of Faith, and two lost books of the Bible, the *Book of Moses* and the *Book of Abraham*. A third sacred text is the Book of Mormon: Another Testament of Jesus Christ, which is considered a history of the early inhabitants of the Americas and a record of Jesus Christ's appearance among them. The fourth sacred text is the **Doctrine and Covenants**, a collection of revelations from God received primarily by Prophet Joseph Smith Jr. Contained within the Doctrine and Covenants are additional revelations from God to Mormon leaders John Taylor, Brigham Young, and Joseph F. Smith.

The presidents of the Church of Jesus Christ of Latter-Day Saints, who each are called "the prophet, seer, and revelator," can also receive direct revelations from God, such as when the President Wilford Woodruff received a revelation in 1890, later known as the "1890 Manifesto," prohibiting plural marriage in the LDS Church, thus upholding the antipolygamy laws of the United States at the time. Also, in 1978 President Spencer W. Kimball received a revelation that any man, regardless of skin color, can be ordained into the LDS Church, thereby reversing the racial policies of the LDS Church. President Kimball stated,

[God] has heard our prayers, and *by revelation* has confirmed that the long-promised day has come when every faithful, worthy man in the Church may receive the holy priesthood, with power to exercise its divine authority, and enjoy with his loved ones every blessing that flows there from. . . . Accordingly, all worthy male members of the Church may be ordained to the priesthood without regard for race or color.[4]

New revelations received by presidents of the LDS Church are published in new editions of the Doctrine and Covenants and are thus canonized for guidance of the faithful worldwide.

Mormon Church and Christian Orthodoxy

Since the LDS Church contends that it is the restoration of the Christian church, it understands itself as a Christian movement; yet many Christians throughout mainline, Roman Catholic, and Orthodox Christian traditions argue that Mormonism falls outside the parameters of orthodox Christianity and its theological affirmations. For instance, Mormons believe that Jesus was God evolved, since God was once a man.

> *God himself was once as we are now, and is an exalted man and sits enthroned in yonder heavens! This is the great secret.*
>
> J. Smith, *Teachings of the Prophet Joseph Smith*, 345

Later, President Brigham Young noted, "I tell you, when you see the Father in the Heavens, you will see Adam: when you see your Mother that bears your spirit, you will see Mother Eve."[5] Another particularly troublesome area of LDS belief for historic Christians is the Mormon understanding of Jesus Christ, who is believed to have married both Mary and Martha and needed saving, since Jesus is considered "a saved being."[6] Consequently, LDS theology holds perspectives on the identity and life of Jesus Christ different from those of historic, orthodox Christianity. The central role of Jesus Christ is that of a prototype of perfection:

He who said, "Come follow me" is our sure guide who marks the path all must follow to obtain salvation (see Ps. 48:14). "If we can find a saved being," Joseph Smith, Jr. asserted, "we may ascertain without much difficulty what all others must be in order to be saved. We think that it will not be a matter of dispute, that two beings who are unlike each other cannot both be saved; for whatever constitutes the salvation of one will constitute the salvation of every creature which will be saved; and if we find one saved being in all existence, we may see what all others must be, or else not be saved. We ask, then, where is the prototype? Or where is the saved being? We conclude . . . that it is Christ.[7]

476

Thirteen Articles of Faith

1. We believe in God, the Eternal Father, and in His Son, Jesus Christ, and in the Holy Ghost.

2. We believe that men will be punished for their own sins, and not for Adam's transgression.

3. We believe that through the Atonement of Christ, all mankind may be saved, by obedience to the laws and ordinances of the Gospel.

4. We believe that the first principles and ordinances of the Gospel are: first, Faith in the Lord Jesus Christ; second, Repentance; third, Baptism by immersion for the remission of sins; fourth, Laying on of hands for the gift of the Holy Ghost.

5. We believe that a man must be called of God, by prophecy, and by the laying on of hands by those who are in authority, to preach the Gospel and administer in the ordinances thereof.

6. We believe in the same organization that existed in the Primitive Church—namely, apostles, prophets, pastors, teachers, evangelists, and so forth.

7. We believe in the gift of tongues, prophecy, revelation, visions, healing, interpretation of tongues, and so forth.

8. We believe the Bible to be the word of God as far as it is translated correctly; we also believe the Book of Mormon to be the word of God.

9. We believe all that God has revealed, all that He does now reveal, and we believe that He will yet reveal many great and important things pertaining to the Kingdom of God.

10. We believe in the literal gathering of Israel and in the restoration of the Ten Tribes; that Zion (the New Jerusalem) will be built upon the American continent; that Christ will reign personally upon the earth; and, that the earth will be renewed and receive its paradisiacal glory.

11. We claim the privilege of worshiping Almighty God according to the dictates of our own conscience, and allow all men the same privilege, let them worship how, where, or what they may.

12. We believe in being subject to kings, presidents, rulers, and magistrates, in obeying, honoring, and sustaining the law.

13. We believe in being honest, true, chaste, benevolent, virtuous, and in doing good to all men; indeed, we may say that we follow the admonition of Paul—We believe all things, we hope all things, we have endured many things, and hope to be able to endure all things. If there is anything virtuous, lovely, or of good report or praiseworthy, we seek after these things.

Jessee and Esplin, *Joseph Smith Papers*, 1:427–37

This selection from Smith's *Lectures on Faith* reflects LDS theology on Jesus Christ—that is, that Jesus Christ was a model to emulate since Jesus himself was saved.

When asked to summarize the beliefs of the Church of Jesus Christ of Latter-Day Saints, Prophet Joseph Smith Jr. outlined the **Thirteen Articles of Faith**, which have been accepted as the foundational statement of LDS theology (see sidebar 10.1).

Salvation in Mormonism

On the question of salvation—that is, how is one saved—LDS theology affirms that both faith in Christ and performance of good works are necessary. Salvation entails affirming the beliefs of the LDS Church and doing the works described in the laws and ordinances of the gospel, which, according

---

Christian Reflections

What do **Christians think** of revelation—is it open and ongoing or closed and complete? All religious traditions that affirm the existence of a divine being who communicates with human beings also suggest that somehow the divine being communicates through a form of revelation. All mainstream, orthodox Christian denominations believe that revelation is closed, the scriptural canon is closed, and there will be no more new knowledge worthy of being canonized and inserted into the sacred text. For instance, the Roman Catholic catechism states, "Christian faith cannot accept 'revelations' that claim to surpass or correct the revelation of which Christ is the fulfillment, as is the case in certain non-Christian religions and also in certain recent sects which base themselves on such 'revelations.'"[a]

The Lutheran Church, Missouri Synod, notes, "We furthermore teach regarding the Holy Scriptures that they are given by God to the Christian Church for the foundation of faith, Eph. 2:20. Hence the Holy Scriptures are the sole source from which all doctrines proclaimed in the Christian Church must be taken and therefore, too, the sole rule and norm by which all teachers and doctrines must be examined and judged."[b] Thus, Lutherans reject any claim of revelation that seeks to add to the Word of God. Furthermore, a large group of evangelical scholars have written, "No new revelation (as distinct from Spirit-given understanding of existing revelation) will be given until Christ comes again."[c]

a. http://www.vatican.va/archive/ccc_css/archive/catechism/p1s1c2a1.htm.
b. http://www.lcms.org/doctrine/doctrinalposition#holyscriptures.
c. http://www.spurgeon.org/~phil/creeds/chicago.htm.

to LDS theology, include baptism for the dead and refraining from caffein-ated drinks. According to a basic belief outlined by Prophet Joseph Smith Jr. himself, "[Mormons] believe that through the Atonement of Christ, all mankind may be saved, by obedience to the laws and ordinances of the Gospel. . . . [The] ordinances of the Gospel are: first, Faith in the Lord Jesus Christ; second, Repentance; third, Baptism by immersion for the remission of sins; fourth, laying on of hands for the gift of the Holy Ghost."[8] According to the LDS Church, faith plus performing good works, being moral, getting baptized, and following Mormon laws and ordinances will lead to salvation. The current living prophet and president of the LDS Church is Thomas S. Monson (b. 1927), who was installed in 2008.

JEHOVAH'S WITNESSES

Beginnings of Jehovah's Witnesses

Another Christian-oriented new religious movement, the **Jehovah's Witnesses**, reports over one million adherents in the United States and over seven million worldwide. The Jehovah's Witnesses emerged from what was known as the Bible student movement started by **Charles Taze Russell** (1852–1916), a prominent Christian restorationist pastor from Pittsburgh, Pennsylvania. In 1909 Pastor Russell moved the printing offices to Brooklyn, New York, where he published a monthly religious journal called *Zion's Watch Tower*, which is now called the *Watchtower*.

Figure 10.5. Charles Taze Russell

Pastor Russell was a prolific writer and produced many books, articles, sermons, and pamphlets promoting biblical literalism, restorationist theology, and millenarianism—that is, the im-minent coming of the kingdom of God, arguing that the world was in "the last days." Russell also predicted that the end of the world would occur in 1873. When that year came to pass, and the world remained, Russell continued to postulate the end of the world, offering 1874 and then 1878. He argued that Christ had already arrived but was invisible to all except faithful Jehovah's Witnesses. Later Jehovah's Witness presidents would announce the world's end to be 1914, 1925, and 1975.

Joseph Rutherford (1869–1942), who had the reputation of being a strong orator, succeeded Russell as the leader of the Jehovah's Witness movement. Rutherford's immense influence on the tradition endures today; for instance, Rutherford required that Jehovah's Witnesses distribute their literature door-to-door, which became a unique characteristic practice of the Witnesses world-wide. Rutherford also predicted that **Armageddon**, the last battle between good and evil (Rev. 16:16), would occur in 1914, stating, "Millions now living will never die." Believing that in 1914 the kingdom of God was established on earth, Jehovah's Witnesses are enjoined to engage in door-to-door canvassing of neighborhoods to evangelize, sell their publication, the *Watchtower*, and attest to the fact that the world will soon end.

Theological Motifs of Jehovah's Witnesses

There is a strong emphasis on peace in the Jehovah's Witness movement, accompanied by the belief that in the future all races will live in peace, after the majority of the world's population is destroyed for not adhering to the Bible. After the events of Armageddon, 144,000 faithful will live with God in heaven, based on the Jehovah's Witness interpretation of biblical passages in Revelation (7:1, 4; 14:1, 3).

The theological beliefs of the Jehovah's Witnesses were articulated by the movement's founder, Charles Taze Russell, and they continue to be foundational to the identity of followers of the religion today. As the leader of a restorationist movement of Christianity, Russell believed in the Bible as a source of knowledge but argued that other Christians had misinterpreted major portions. While there are some significant similarities between the Jehovah's Witnesses and historic, orthodox Christianity, such as the affirmation that justification between God and humanity is by faith alone, there are several other Jehovah's Witnesses beliefs that lie outside the historic Christian faith.

Among the theological beliefs outside the bounds of Christian orthodoxy are the Jehovah's Witness understanding of the Trinity, Christ's second coming, and heaven and hell. Regarding the identity of the Trinity, Russell argued that Jesus Christ lived on earth as a human being and received his divinity as a gift from God the Father, whom he called Jehovah, after dying on the cross. Affirming a monotheism, an indivisible Supreme Being, without the three persons of Father, Son, and Holy Spirit, the Jehovah's Witnesses assert that Jesus was the first being created by Jehovah (God) and thus is a separate being from God. Jesus, it is affirmed, lived a sinless life, was crucified on a single stake (rather than on a cross), and was resurrected by Jehovah to live with God.

Jesus as King in 1914

Jehovah's Witnesses teach that Jesus was enthroned as king in 1914 and remains a heavenly king, an invisible, nonmaterial spirit accessible only to Jehovah's Witnesses. Jesus serves less as a savior than as an exemplar of God's truth, being a model of how to live a perfect life on earth. Furthermore, the Holy Spirit, rather than being a separate person as affirmed by historic Christianity, is "God's active force" or power through which Jehovah engages the world. Regarding Christ's second coming, which historic Christianity recognizes as a future event, Jehovah's Witnesses believe that it has already happened, not as a physical appearance but as an invisible event in 1914.

Heaven and Hell

Finally, the Jehovah's Witnesses' view of heaven and hell is directly related to their view of the end of the world. They advocate that after Armageddon, when the "Lamb of God" (Christ) will defeat the "Beast" (Satan's representative), 144,000 faithful will live with God in heaven, based on the Jehovah's Witness interpretation of biblical passages in Revelation (7:1, 4; 14:1, 3): "Then I looked, and there before me was the Lamb, standing on Mount Zion! And with him one hundred forty-four thousand who had his name and his Father's name written on their foreheads" (Rev. 14:1). The Jehovah's Witnesses believe that the Antichrist is not an individual, unlike the perspective held by many in historic Christianity. In terms of the timing of these catastrophic events, the **Watchtower** magazine notes that the United Nations will attack all religions as a prelude to Armageddon.

The Jehovah's Witnesses reject the notion of hell, instead arguing that the souls of wicked people will be annihilated. Until Armageddon, when all people will be given a chance to choose eternal life in heaven, "the dead are conscious of nothing." Salvation, according to the Jehovah's Witnesses, entails accepting and promoting the beliefs and practices of the Jehovah's Witnesses and Christ's death as a remission for Adam's sin. Worship for Jehovah's Witnesses is held in Kingdom Halls; adherents to the faith are assigned, according to their residence, which hall to attend. Such "meetings," as they are called, are devoted to studying the Watch Tower Society publications and the Bible, with prayers and congregational singing to open and close each gathering. Russell adopted several of his doctrines from the **Seventh-Day Adventists**, another nineteenth-century movement that also predicted the imminent end of the world.

Seventh-Day Adventists

Beginnings of Seventh-Day Adventists

William Miller

The Seventh-Day Adventist movement began with **William Miller** (1781–1849), who predicted that the world would end in 1843–44. Adventists believe that the second coming (advent) of Christ is literal and imminent. Miller, who was born in Pittsfield, Massachusetts, was an American Baptist pastor. After serving in the Vermont militia and becoming an affluent gentleman, he left the Baptist movement and became a deist—that is, he affirmed that

God created the world and initiated its laws but then allowed the world to follow its own course, as though God were a watchmaker allowing the watch to wind down through time, pursuing its own path.

Eventually, Miller left deism and, in a moment of great emotion, was convinced that Christ would return, predicting that the second coming would occur around the year 1843: "My principles in brief, are, that Jesus Christ will come again to this earth, cleanse, purify, and take possession of the same, with all the saints, sometime between March 21, 1843, and March 21, 1844."[9] Miller's estimates were based on his interpretation of Daniel 8:14–17.

> He said to me, "It will take 2,300 evenings and mornings; then the sanctuary will be reconsecrated." While I, Daniel, was watching the vision and trying to understand it, there before me stood one who looked like a man. And I heard a man's voice from the Ulai calling, "Gabriel, tell this man the meaning of the vision." As he came near the place where I was standing, I was terrified and fell prostrate. "Son of man," he said to me, "understand that the vision concerns the time of the end."
>
> Daniel 8:14–17 NIV

Miller's followers were known as **Millerites**, and their number began growing significantly beginning in the 1840s. When the predicted year of Christ's second coming passed without Christ's return, known by Adventists as the "Great Disappointment," most of the Millerites left the movement. Yet a small group remained faithful to Miller's vision and reinterpreted the passage in Daniel, contending that Christ's second coming was imminent even if the community could no longer predict the date.

Ellen G. White

Another significant pioneer of Seventh-Day Adventism was **Ellen G. White** (1827–1915), who was born and raised in Gorham, Maine. Although her family worshiped with the Methodists, they eventually left the Methodists because of their involvement with the Millerite movement. Known by Adventists as the "Spirit of Prophecy," White's writings remain authoritative for Adventist faith. According to Adventists, White was a prophet, and her restorationist writings focus on the "Great Controversy"—that is, the conflict between Christ and Satan.

White's emergence in a period when the Millerite movement was on the decline helped reenergize the movement. One of her major contributions to the Adventist movement was her writings, which in part were based on visions White received over a period of years. White is credited with writing more than five thousand articles and forty books, which are seen as inspired by God for

Adventist faith. She died in Saint Helena, California, in her home called Elmshaven, from which she dispensed her prophetic ministry. Today Elmshaven is the location of the Adventist Historical Site, a National Historic Landmark.

Twenty-Eight Fundamental Beliefs of Adventism

Seventh-Day Adventists affirm **Twenty-Eight Fundamental Beliefs** that serve as their only creed. These fundamental beliefs, which share many tenets with historic Christianity, cover a broad range of topics illuminated on the official Adventist website.[10] The topics included in the Twenty-Eight Fundamental Beliefs of the Seventh-Day Adventists include the following:

1. Holy Scriptures
2. Trinity
3. Father
4. Son
5. Holy Spirit
6. Creation
7. Nature of Man
8. Great Controversy between Christ and Satan
9. Life, Death, and Resurrection of Christ
10. Experience of Salvation
11. Growing in Christ
12. Church
13. Remnant and Its Mission
14. Unity in the Body of Christ
15. Baptism
16. Lord's Supper
17. Spiritual Gifts and Ministries
18. Gift of Prophecy
19. Law of God
20. Sabbath
21. Stewardship
22. Christian Behavior
23. Marriage and the Family
24. Christ's Ministry in the Heavenly Sanctuary
25. Second Coming of Christ
26. Death and Resurrection
27. Millennium and the End of Sin
28. New Earth

Adventist Sabbath

It is worthwhile to highlight some of the unique features of Adventism rather than rehearse the common elements shared with historic Christian faith. One of the unique aspects of Adventism is its understanding of the Sabbath, the day of rest. The fundamental Adventist belief about the Sabbath is that it should be observed on the seventh day—thus the religion's name, Seventh-Day Adventist—which Adventists believe is from Friday sunset to Saturday sunset. Adventists abstain from doing secular work on Saturdays, and some also refrain from watching television on that day. That is to say, Adventists worship on Saturday rather than on Sunday. The centrality of Saturday Sabbath is related to other fundamental beliefs, particularly numbers 25–28, which state that observance of the Sabbath will be a universal marker of faith in Christ when Jesus Christ visibly returns to earth.

Additionally, fundamental belief 24, also known as "investigative judgment," affirms who will receive salvation, contending that a divine judgment of Christians was initiated in 1844, the year that William Miller and the Millerite

---

SIDEBAR 10.2

The Heavenly Sanctuary

There is a sanctuary in heaven, the true tabernacle which the Lord set up and not man. In it Christ ministers on our behalf, making available the benefits of His atoning sacrifice offered once for all on the cross. He was inaugurated as our great High Priest and began His intercessory ministry at the time of His ascension. In 1844, at the end of the prophet period of 2300 days, He entered the second and last phase of His atoning ministry. It is a work of investigative judgment which is part of the ultimate disposition of all sin, typified by the cleansing of the ancient Hebrew sanctuary on the Day of Atonement. In that typical service the sanctuary was cleansed with the blood of animal sacrifices, but the heavenly things are purified with the perfect sacrifice of the blood of Jesus. The investigative judgment reveals to heavenly intelligences who among the dead are asleep in Christ and therefore, in Him, are deemed worthy to have part in the first resurrection. It also makes manifest who among the living are abiding in Christ, keeping the commandments of God and the faith of Jesus, and in Him, therefore are ready for translation into His everlasting kingdom. This judgment vindicates the justice of God in saving those who believe in Jesus. It declares that those who have remained loyal to God shall receive the kingdom. The completion of this ministry will mark the close of human probation before the Second Advent.

Seventh-Day Adventist Church, "Christ's Ministry in the Heavenly Sanctuary," *Fundamental Beliefs* 24, available at http://www.adventist.org/en/beliefs/apocalypse /christs-ministry-in-the-heavenly-sanctuary/

Mormonism, the Millerites, Jehovah's Witnesses, and Seventh-Day Adventists are examples of Christian restorationist movements that seek to restore Christianity, turning away from historic churches in order to reestablish "original" or "primitive" Christianity. The presence of restorationist or primitivist religious movements raises important questions about history, ecclesiology (the nature of the church), and the content of Christian faith. A useful benchmark with which to analyze restorationist movements is to consider the question of the content of the gospel, for most restorationist churches reinterpret the gospel to fit their particular set of doctrinal emphases. Has the gospel been compromised in the postapostolic church, as argued by most restorationist churches? Is there a "pure" gospel from which the universal church has strayed? Restorationists believe that the pure gospel has been compromised. If so, is that "pure form" recoverable? Or is there no such thing as a "pure, naked" gospel, an essential core that is corrupted through time and consequently needs restoration? Mission scholar **Lesslie Newbigin** (1909–98), bishop of the Church of South India, argues that there is no such thing as a pure gospel.

> Neither at the beginning, nor at any subsequent time, is there or can there be a gospel that is not embodied in a culturally conditioned form of words. The idea that one can or could at any time separate out by some process of distillation a pure gospel unadulterated by any cultural accretions is an illusion. It is, in fact, an abandonment of the gospel, for the gospel is about the word made flesh. Every statement of the gospel in words is conditioned by the culture of which those words are a part, and every style of life that claims to embody the truth of the gospel is a culturally conditioned style of life. There can never be a culture-free gospel.[a]

By reinterpreting the gospel—for instance, claiming that spirit is good and matter evil—restorationist movements insert their own understanding as gospel truth, often communicating that their interpretation carries deeper insight into Christian faith. But should Christians who follow the historic Christian faith see restorationist movements as just another way that the gospel is contextualized, in this case on American soil? Or should Christians recognize that these restorationist movements are outside the purview of historic faith and, therefore, offer a truncated or altered gospel? These questions force us to ask ourselves serious questions about the nature of the church, Christian faith, and the gospel. The answers to these questions will directly impact the way that we encounter other faith traditions.

a. Newbigin, *Foolishness to the Greeks*, 4.

Adventists expected Jesus Christ to return to earth. Investigative judgment relates to what Adventists call the Heavenly Sanctuary (see sidebar 10.2).

Adventism and Health

Adventist theology, then, affirms the pre-advent (second coming) judgment of believers since 1844, a doctrine that reflects their distinct identity as Seventh-Day Adventists. Finally, another Adventist emphasis is on health consciousness and healthful living, with an expectation that Adventists will follow Jewish dietary laws (kosher) outlined in the biblical book of Leviticus. That means Adventists abstain from "unclean foods and liquids" such as pork, shellfish, tobacco, and alcohol, as well as drinks containing caffeine (e.g., coffee, tea). Therefore, many Adventists follow a vegetarian diet and refrain from smoking and drinking alcohol, which seems to have contributed to their longer lifespan compared to other people within the same region.[11]

CHRISTIAN SCIENCE

Beginnings of Christian Science

Another nineteenth-century Christian-oriented movement was the **Church of Christ, Scientist**, also known as Christian Science. The Christian Science movement was founded by **Mary Baker Eddy** (1821–1910), who was born into a Congregationalist family in Bow, New Hampshire, and suffered chronic illness throughout her childhood. Her autobiography notes that beginning at the age of eight, Eddy heard voices calling her name. Much of Eddy's early life focused on her own need for physical healing. In 1862 Eddy began to learn from Phineas Parkhurst Quimby (1802–66), a New England healer and mesmerist, about the possibility of curing people without the intervention of medicine. Eddy herself claimed that Quimby had through his hypnotism relieved her from her persistent suffering.

In 1866 Eddy claimed to be cured of a severe spinal injury without the use of medicine. She based her convictions in part on Matthew 9:2, "And just then some people were carrying a paralyzed man lying on

Wikimedia Commons

Figure 10.6. Mary Baker Eddy

a bed. When Jesus saw their faith, he said to the paralytic, 'Take heart, son; your sins are forgiven.'" That healing marked a significant turning point for Eddy, who then spent the next three years studying the Bible in near seclusion while contemplating what God's mission was for her life. During those years Eddy attempted to recover the emphasis of healing that was present in the early church.

Christian Science Publications

In 1875 Eddy wrote *Science and Health with Key to the Scriptures* (*S&H*), which she called the textbook of Christian Science and which serves as the primary textual authority for the Christian Science movement today. The Church of Christ, Scientist was incorporated in 1879 with the explicit purpose, in Eddy's own words, "to commemorate the word and works of our Master, which should reinstate primitive Christianity and its lost element of healing."[12] Eddy became the head pastor of the "Mother Church" and wrote *The Manual of the Mother Church* as a guide to govern the movement. Her role as leader and author, however, was highly controversial.

Alongside the guidance provided in the *Science and Health with Key to the Scriptures*, *The Manual of the Mother Church*, and the Bible, the Christian Science movement publishes the newspaper the *Christian Science Monitor*, which Eddy herself founded in 1908, and has established Christian Science reading rooms worldwide, where people are encouraged to read Christian Science publications. Toward the end of her life, Eddy taught her followers and authorized them to promote her teachings throughout the country. She died in Newton, Massachusetts, on December 3, 1910, leaving behind the Mother Church in Boston and a new religious movement that today boasts of over 150,000 members worldwide. Many nonmembers also receive literature and frequent Christian Science reading rooms.

Mary Baker Eddy's experience of suffering chronic illness and seeking guidance from the Bible gave rise to the theological affirmations of the Christian Science movement. The Christian Science Church is similar to the broad movement of restorationists in that it sought to retrieve early Christian practices, particularly regarding healing, that it believed had been eliminated over time. As such, several themes within the Christian Science Church are shared by historic Christian faith, such as the belief in an omnipotent Creator God, the authority of the Bible, and the crucifixion and resurrection of Jesus Christ.

Christian Science Philosophy

Many beliefs of Christian Science, however, are outside the scope of Christian orthodoxy. First, Christian Science is distinct regarding the topic of creation and matter—that is, material reality—for it asserts that creation is entirely spiritual and matter (material reality) does not exist. This assertion is a philosophical claim about metaphysics, the nature of reality, and so has profound implications for the entire religious tradition. Given that matter does not exist as such, then sin, sickness, and death do not exist either but are a result of false belief. Belief, then, becomes the arbiter of what is real—of reality itself. In Eddy's words, "The only reality of sin, sickness, or death is the awful fact that unrealities seem real to human, erring belief, until God strips off their disguise" (*S&H* 472:27–29). This sentiment is reflected in the Christian Science "Scientific Statement of Being," which is read at weekly church services:

> There is no life, truth, intelligence, nor substance in matter.
> All is infinite Mind and its infinite manifestation, for God is All-in-All.
> Spirit is immortal Truth; matter is mortal error.
> Spirit is the real and eternal; matter is the unreal and temporal.
> Spirit is God, and man is His image and likeness.
> Therefore man is not material; he is spiritual.
>
> *S&H* 468

Second, God is understood as an incorporeal Spirit, referred to as "Father-Mother," as infinite Mind, Spirit, Life—"All-in-All." Third, Christian Science contends that Jesus is divine but not God: "Jesus is the name of the man who, more than all other men, has presented Christ, the true idea of God, healing the sick . . . and destroying the power of death" (*S&H* 473:10–17). Jesus was a healer who exemplified "scientific Christianity," which contains the laws of God. Jesus, then, was the divine Exemplar, the "way-shower" to demonstrate to human beings how to find life and mind (i.e., God). Jesus's death and resurrection illustrated that death itself is an illusion, and his blood atonement was useless as a means of securing salvation.

> The spiritual essence of blood is sacrifice. The efficacy of Jesus' spiritual offering is infinitely greater than can be expressed by our sense of human blood. The material blood of Jesus was not more efficacious to cleanse from sin when it was shed upon "the accursed tree," than when it was flowing in his veins as he went daily about his Father's business. His true flesh and blood were his Life; and they truly eat his flesh and drink his blood, who partake of that divine Life. . . . Jesus taught the way of Life by demonstration, that we may understand how this divine Principle heals the sick, casts out error, and triumphs over death. Jesus presented the ideal of God better than could any man whose origin was less spiritual.
>
> *S&H* 25:3–17

Fourth, the Holy Spirit is called the "divine Science," foreshadowed, Christian Scientists say, by Jesus's words:

> And I will pray the Father, and he will give you another Counselor [Comforter], to be with you for ever, even the Spirit of truth, whom the world cannot receive, because it neither sees him nor knows him; you know him, for he dwells with you, and will be in you.
>
> John 14:16–17 RSV

Being filled with the Holy Spirit means having knowledge of the "divine Science" and the ability to be healed of physical ailments through faith alone. Eddy wrote, "Spirit is immortal Truth; matter is mortal error. Spirit is the real and eternal; matter is the unreal and temporal. Spirit is God, and man is His image and likeness. Therefore man is not material; he is spiritual" (*S&H* 468:10–15).

Fifth, Eddy argued that the Trinity was tripartite, consisting of Life, Truth, and Love.

> God the Father-Mother, Christ the spiritual idea of sonship, and divine Science or the Holy Comforter.
>
> *S&H* 331:30

Figure 10.7. First Church of Christ, Scientist, in Boston, Massachusetts, USA

Wikimedia Commons

Sixth, heaven is portrayed not as a location but as a divine state of mind, where the Spirit reigns. Writing about heaven, Eddy noted that it is "not a locality, but a divine state of Mind in which all the manifestations of Mind are harmonious and immortal, because sin is not there and man is found having no righteousness of his own, but in possession of the 'mind of the Lord,' as the Scripture says" (*S&H* 291:12–17). Likewise, hell is a place of the mind—the result of believing in evil, pain, death, and sin creates its own evil (i.e., hell).

Mary Baker Eddy outlined the six basic beliefs of Christian Science in *Science and Health with Key to the Scriptures.*

The Six Basic Beliefs of Christian Science:

1. As adherents of Truth, we take the inspired Word of the Bible as our sufficient guide to eternal Life.

2. We acknowledge and adore one supreme and infinite God. We acknowledge His Son, one Christ; the Holy Ghost or divine Comforter; and man in God's image and likeness.

3. We acknowledge God's forgiveness of sin in the destruction of sin and the spiritual understanding that casts out evil as unreal. But the belief in sin is punished so long as the belief lasts.

4. We acknowledge Jesus' atonement as the evidence of divine, efficacious Love, unfolding man's unity with God through Christ Jesus the Way-shower; and we acknowledge that man is saved through Christ, through Truth, Life, and Love as demonstrated by the Galilean Prophet in healing the sick and overcoming sin and death.

5. We acknowledge that the crucifixion of Jesus and his resurrection served to uplift faith to understand eternal Life, even the allness of Soul, Spirit, and the nothingness of matter.

6. And we solemnly promise to watch, and pray for that Mind to be in us which was also in Christ Jesus; to do unto others as we would have them do unto us; and to be merciful, just, and pure.

S&H 497:1–27

Centrality of Healing by Faith

Healing is central to the Christian Science movement. Faith in God rather than in modern medicine is the cure for any ailment.

It is plain that God does not employ drugs or hygiene, nor provide them for human use; else Jesus would have recommended and employed them in his healing. The sick are more deplorably lost than the sinning, if the sick cannot rely on God for help and the sinning can. The divine Mind never called matter medicine, and matter required a material and human belief before it could be considered as medicine.

S&H 143:5

Belief in matter (material reality) is tantamount to sin, that which counteracts faith in the power of the Spirit alone to heal.

> The theology of Christian Science includes healing the sick. Our Master's first article of faith propounded to his students was healing, and he proved his faith by his works. The ancient Christians were healers. Why has this element of Christianity been lost? Because our systems of religion are governed more or less by our systems of medicine. The first idolatry was faith in matter. The schools have rendered faith in drugs the fashion, rather than faith in Deity. By trusting matter to destroy its own discord, health and harmony have been sacrificed. Such systems are barren of vital spiritual power, by which material sense is made the servant of Science and religion becomes Christlike.
>
> *S&H* 145:31

Christian Scientists hold Sunday worship services, where "Readers," who are leaders elected by the church, read and meditate on selections from the Bible and *Science and Health with Key to the Scriptures*. Christian Scientists reject the interpretation of the sacraments of historic Christianity and instead reinterpret them by emphasizing the purely spiritual meaning of the sacraments.

> Our baptism is a purification from all error. Our church is built on the divine Principle, Love. We can unite with this church only as we are new—born of Spirit, as we reach the Life which is Truth and the Truth which is Life by bringing forth the fruits of Love,—casting out error and healing the sick. Our Eucharist is spiritual communion with the one God. Our bread, "which cometh down from heaven," is Truth. Our cup is the cross. Our wine the inspiration of Love, the draught our Master drank and commended to his followers.
>
> *S&H* 35:19–29

Perhaps what the general public knows best about the Christian Science Church is its newspaper, the *Christian Science Monitor,* which was started in 1908 by Mary Baker Eddy and features reporting of both current national and international events. Christian Science is also known by the general public for its rejection of reliance on modern medicine. Christian Science followers reject modern medicine because they believe disease, suffering, and pain to have originated in the mind rather than in the body. Therefore, a spiritual remedy, rather than one based on conventional medicine, is necessary.

> In the Bible the word spirit is so commonly applied to Deity, that Spirit and God are often regarded as synonymous terms; and it is thus they are uniformly used and understood in Christian Science. As it is evident that

likeness of Spirit cannot be material, does it not follow that God cannot be in His unlikeness and work through drugs to heal the sick? When the omnipotence of God is preached and His absoluteness is set forth, Christian sermons will heal the sick.

S&H 344:32

Christian Reflections

All believers have to make sense of the relationship between matter and spirit. Is matter good, evil, or mixed? Likewise, is spirit good, evil, or a blend of good and evil? Biblical writers and Christian leaders of the Patristic Period (c. 100–500 CE) contended frequently against a perspective called **docetism** (Greek, *dokeo*, "to seem or appear"), which asserted a philosophical doctrine that viewed matter (material reality) as evil. The docetists, then, concluded that God could not be associated with matter.

Jesus's physical body was an illusion; he only *appeared* to have a physical body, but in reality he was pure spirit. In the late first century and early second century, docetism was the philosophical foundation of a movement called gnosticism, which was based on the quest to obtain "secret knowledge" (Greek, *gnosis*) that spirit was imprisoned in corrupt matter. Salvation required that spirit be freed from matter. The historic Christian faith clearly affirms the reality of both matter and spirit. The biblical narrative notes that there is no secret knowledge and that, in fact, the mystery of God has already been disclosed in Christ (e.g., Eph. 1:9; 3; 6:19; Col. 1:26–27; 2:1–3; 1 Tim. 3:16).

Gnostic gospels were written from the second to fourth centuries CE and were rejected by orthodox Christians in part on the grounds that they taught that salvation involved liberating oneself from the material world through secret knowledge within.[a] Given this context, the Christian claim that Jesus is fully human, fully divine—the "Word became flesh" (John 1:14)—is a striking affirmation that rejects an overly spiritualized view of Jesus and reality itself. Who but the God-man Jesus is able to absolve sin? Christian hymnody reflects the recognition that only the blood sacrifice of Jesus Christ can atone for sin, "For it is not possible that the blood of bulls and of goats should take away sins" (Heb. 10:4 KJV). The eighteenth-century hymnodist William Cowper (1731–1800) penned the hymn "There Is a Fountain Filled with Blood," which states, "There is a fountain filled with blood drawn from Emmanuel's veins/And sinners plunged beneath that flood lose all their guilty stains." Christians celebrate the Lord's Supper (Eucharist, Mass) with Jesus's own words, "This is my blood of the new covenant, which is poured out for many for the forgiveness of sins" (Matt. 26:28 NIV).

a. Some well-known gnostic gospels are the *Gospel of Mary*, *Gospel of Thomas*, *Gospel of Truth*, *Gospel of Philip*, and *Gospel of Judas*.

The Religious Path for Christian Science

The religious path for a Christian Science follower involves disciplining one's mind to overcome the false illusions that sin, death, and evil are real, while recognizing that human beings consist of divine spirits and minds: "Both sin and sickness are error, and Truth is their remedy" (*S&H* 461:16). Salvation is a progressive spiritual understanding that the material world is not real. Salvation is based on overcoming suffering and temptation by following Jesus as the divine ideal of Christ consciousness, leaving humanity with the paramount example of a perfected mind.

Movements of Hindu-Buddhist Orientation

By movements of Hindu-Buddhist orientation, I am referring to new religious movements heavily influenced by concepts that originate in the Asian religions, particularly from Hinduism and Buddhism. By creating a syncretistic movement, which blends together several Hindu-Buddhist notions (e.g., nature of the soul, reincarnation), packaging them for a Western audience, including congregational worship, these NRMs promise to provide "secret wisdom" about the nature of reality beyond the senses, psychological and physical techniques to enhance awareness of the mysteries of the universe, and a sense of tranquility and peace in the midst of unhappy life conditions. Frequently, the NRMs authenticate themselves through "scientific" investigation. The leaders of these NRMs often occupy the center of the religion, with their words forming the sacred text of the tradition.

THEOSOPHICAL SOCIETY

Madame Helena Blavatsky and Colonel Henry Steel Olcott

Another new religious movement that emerged in nineteenth-century America was the **Theosophical Society**. The Theosophical Society was cofounded by **Madame Helena Blavatsky** (1831–91) and **Colonel Henry Steel Olcott** (1832–1907) to promote what they believed was ancient spiritual wisdom and the idea that there is truth in every religion. Madame Blavatsky, who was born in Ukraine, left her first husband after four weeks of marriage and spent a decade traveling around the world (1848–58). She ended up in New York, where she claimed to possess strong psychic abilities, including clairvoyance (ability to see objects that cannot be perceived through senses), levitation (ability to raise her body as if floating on air), telepathy (mind-to-mind communication), and astro-projection (out-of-body projection).

In 1874 Madame Blavatsky was introduced to Colonel Olcott, a lawyer, and they soon worked together on their ideas about spiritualism—the belief that the dead communicate with the world through a spirit medium (a spiritualist). Colonel Olcott, an American journalist and lawyer who was born in New Jersey to a Presbyterian family, gained notoriety for being the first well-known American to convert to Buddhism. During the American Civil War, Olcott served in the United States Army and was promoted to the rank of colonel. After the war, he assisted in the investigation of the assassination of President Abraham Lincoln (1865) and later became a lawyer. While writing a series of articles about the spiritualists in 1874, Olcott met Blavatsky.

Promotion of Universal Brotherhood

The Theosophical Society was founded in 1875 in New York by Blavatsky, Olcott, and **William Quan Judge** (1851–96), a mystic born in Ireland and raised in the United States. In 1878 they moved the society headquarters from New York to Adyar (Chennai), India. The central aim of the Theosophical Society is the promotion of "Universal Brotherhood based on the realization that life, and all its diverse forms, human and non-human, is indivisibly One."[13] Based on the philosophy of theosophy, which affirms the presence of deep wisdom underlying all religions, the Theosophical Society does not affirm a sacred book but rather advocates that new insights through revelation come from individual beings seeking perfected spirituality.

What we desire to prove is, that underlying every once popular religion was the same ancient wisdom-doctrine, one and identical, professed and practiced by the initiates of every country who alone were aware of its existence and importance. To ascertain its origin and the precise way in which it was matured is now beyond human possibility.

Sinnett, *Purpose of Theosophy*, 10

Theosophy ("wisdom of God" or "knowledge of the divine") sought to demonstrate that the wisdom of God could be found in all religions. A. P. Sinnett (1840–1921), who was a friend of Blavatsky, a Theosophist, and president of the London Lodge of the Theosophical Society, contended that the goal of the Theosophists was to unearth and employ the ancient wisdom in all religions.

The Theosophical Society relies heavily on Hindu and Buddhist resources. In their "Three Fundamental Propositions," which are accepted as the three changeless doctrines of Theosophy, it is possible to discern some important Hindu and Buddhist themes that serve as crucial elements of Theosophical thinking (see sidebar 10.3). The Three Fundamental Propositions reflect an eclectic movement whose informal motto, "No religion higher than Truth," draws on Hindu and Buddhist resources. For instance, Theosophists affirm the essential unity of the individual soul and the divine, that the soul is the same as the preexistent Principle (e.g., the Absolute), a nontheistic entity. Theosophy posits that through time one's soul can be unified with the universe, which is similar to notions within the Hindu tradition.

The Soul Is the Absolute

The Theosophical Society believes that the soul is the same as the Absolute, which in Theosophical literature goes by the names "the Boundless," "the Self-Existing," "the First Cause," "the One Reality," "Divine Thought," "the Unknown," and "the Infinite Unity." Much like the Hindu notion of Brahman, the Absolute cannot be described and is without attributes. According to Blavatsky's *Secret Doctrine*, the Absolute is "An Omnipresent, Eternal, Boundless, and Immutable PRINCIPLE on which all speculation is impossible, since it transcends the power of human conception and could only be dwarfed by any human expression or similitude."[14]

Second, much like forms of Buddhism, Theosophy teaches that the individual soul passes through stages of human reincarnation, culminating in becoming a ***dhyani-chohan***, which in Sanskrit and Tibetan means "Lord of meditation," the highest spiritual beings. Blavatsky insisted on the presence of seven *dhyani-chohan*, which she described as "the collective hosts of spiritual beings—the Angelic Hosts of Christianity, the ***Elohim*** and 'Messengers' of the Jews—who are the vehicle for the manifestation of the divine or universal thought and will."[15] As such, *dhyani-chohan* are like archangels, and individuals have the potential to become them. Reincarnation is determined

---

Three Fundamental Propositions

The Secret Doctrine establishes three fundamental propositions: (a) An Omnipresent, Eternal, Boundless, and Immutable PRINCIPLE on which all speculation is impossible, since it transcends the power of human conception and could only be dwarfed by any human expression or similitude. It is beyond the range and reach of thought, "unthinkable and unspeakable." . . .

Further, *The Secret Doctrine* affirms: (b) The Eternity of the Universe *in toto* as a boundless plane; periodically "the playground of numberless Universes incessantly manifesting and disappearing." . . . "The appearance and disappearance of Worlds is like a regular tidal ebb, flux, and reflux. . . ."

Moreover, *The Secret Doctrine* teaches: (c) The fundamental identity of all Souls with the Universal Over-Soul, the latter being itself an aspect of the Unknown Root; and the obligatory pilgrimage for every Soul—a spark of the former—through the Cycle of Incarnation (or "Necessity") in accordance with Cyclic and Karmic law, during the whole term.

Blavatsky, *Secret Doctrine*, 1:14

Wikimedia Commons

Figure 10.8. Madam Helena Petrovna Blavatsky, Vera Petrovna de Zhelihovsky, Vera Vladimirovna de Zhelihovsky, Charles Johnston, and Colonel Henry Steel Olcott in London, 1888

by one's karma. Third, the goal of Theosophical thinking is the achievement of **universal brotherhood**. The methods to accomplish the objective of universal brotherhood are the study of religions and the elimination of any form of prejudice. Put succinctly, the goals of the Theosophical Society are threefold: (1) to form a nucleus of the universal brotherhood, without distinction of race, creed, sex, caste, or color; (2) to encourage the study of comparative religion, philosophy, and science; and (3) to investigate unexplained laws of nature and the powers latent in human beings.

Two Branches of the Theosophical Society

Following the death of Madam Blavatsky, the Theosophical Society split into two main branches. One branch of the society was guided by William Quan Judge, who led a movement out of the Theosophical Society in Adyar (Chennai, India) to form the Theosophical Society Pasadena (California). A group from this branch eventually split off to form a rival society headquartered in Point Loma, California. The second major branch that emerged after Blavatsky's death was guided by **Annie Besant**, who led the Theosophical Society Adyar. Annie Besant (1847–1933), a London-born Irish convert to the society, prominent women's rights activist, and powerful orator, joined the

496

Indian National Congress and fought for the independence of India from British colonial rule. Besant died in Adyar, India; one of Chennai's most elite neighborhoods, Besant Nagar, the location of the Theosophical Society Adyar headquarters, was named in her memory.

TRANSCENDENTAL MEDITATION

Maharishi Mahesh Yogi

Transcendental Meditation (TM) is a new religious movement started by **Maharishi Mahesh Yogi** (1918–2008). It stresses specific, systematic physical and mental techniques that guide the practitioner to "enlightenment" and "bliss." Maharishi Mahesh Yogi was born into the Kayath caste, a caste between the Brahmin and the Kshatriya classes, in Raipur, India. Maharishi studied physics at Allahabad University (Uttar Pradesh, India). In 1941 he became secretary for Swami Brahmananda Saraswati (1870–1953), the head (Sanskrit, *Shankaracharya*) of a Hindu monastery (Sanskrit, *matha*) and served him until the swami died in 1953.

Figure 10.9. *A Christian Martyr on the Cross (Saint Julia)*, by Gabriel Cornelius Ritter von Max, 1866. A Prague-born Austrian painter, von Max was a member of the Theosophical Society. Von Max studied various mystical movements and developed an allegorical-mystical pictoral language.

In 1955 Maharishi began teaching meditation techniques that he had learned from Swami Brahmananda, calling it Transcendental Meditation. From 1958 to 1964, Maharishi made five world tours to promote his ideas about TM. He visited countries throughout Africa, Asia, Europe, and North America, claiming that his method of meditation would relieve the world of discontentment. While on tour, Maharishi appeared on television, wrote books, trained practitioners, was interviewed for newsprint, and addressed world leaders, including U Thant, the secretary general of the United Nations. His popularity with Western celebrities, such as Clint Eastwood, the Beatles, the Beach Boys, the Rolling Stones, Jane Fonda, Stevie Wonder, and Deepak Chopra,

Figure 10.10. Maharishi Mahesh Yogi

was a testimony to the appeal of TM. Maharishi died on February 5, 2008, in Vlodrop, the Netherlands.

Transcendental Meditation Beliefs and Practices

The beliefs and practices of Transcendental Meditation focus on a seven-step method of mantra meditation, which consists of two introductory lectures, a personal interview, and four two-hour instruction sessions given daily for four days. Transcendental Meditation technique involves the employment of a **mantra** (sound, chant) for a twenty-minute period twice daily, while sitting in a comfortable position. Part of the appeal of TM is its immediate accessibility; its practice does not require long periods of training or expertise but rather involves a natural sense of meditation with the aim of quieting the mind, seeking a state of natural, restful alertness. Employing one's mantra helps TM practitioners pay full, undivided attention to one's conscious state, with the aim of experiencing love, creativity, bliss, and even humor.

Described as distinct from concentration or contemplation, TM claims to allow the mind to effortlessly experience "transcendental consciousness"—what TM devotees call "restful alertness." Maharishi argued that TM practices were based on ancient Vedas, the oldest recorded scriptures of the Hindu tradition. By paying full attention to the mantra, one can experience the source of all vibration (sound), the essence of the universe. TM-certified teachers assign mantras to individual students, based on the practitioner's nervous system.

Maharishi Mahesh Yogi and his Transcendental Meditation movement were not free from controversy. TM training can be costly, and students of TM may be asked to pay thousands of dollars to receive special mantras (chants). Although it was claimed that mantras were private and unique to each student, it was discovered in a 1977 court case that the mantras were meaningless sounds. Some TM advocates responded that while the mantra itself carried no meaning, the sound was sacred. Additionally, the TM movement offers a number of health and beauty products for those who want to improve their physical appearance. The organization has assets of over $3 billion, including large holdings in real estate (e.g., schools, health clinics) and the Maharishi University of Management, in Fairfield, Iowa. The Maharishi University of Management claims to offer "consciousness-based education" that enables students to discover the "field of pure consciousness within themselves as the source of all knowledge."[16] Several independent scientific studies conducted to investigate the impact of TM on individual health have resulted in irregular outcomes with regard to physical health measures, cognitive functioning, and psychological effects.

Movements of Distinctive Orientation

Church of Scientology

L. RON HUBBARD

L. Ron Hubbard (1911–86) created the **Church of Scientology** in New Jersey in 1953, after a successful stint as an American science-fiction author and self-help guru whose system, **Dianetics**, became the foundation for his new religious movement. L. Ron Hubbard was born in Tiden, Nebraska, and was distinguished as a young man by being the youngest Eagle Scout, the highest rank in the Boy Scouts of America, in the United States. His early success contrasts with his later years; he received poor grades as a civil engineering student at George Washington University and later failed other courses in physics at the Naval Training School in Princeton, New Jersey.

Figure 10.11. L. Ron Hubbard

Hubbard purported to be a nuclear physicist, then began his writing career and tried his hand as an expedition leader for various exploration clubs and organizations. Of his diverse experiences, Hubbard is best known for his published science-fiction and adventure stories. By 1938 he had written 138 novels. Hubbard frequently used the revenue from his fiction writing to fund his more serious research. Hubbard is also credited with cowriting a movie series, *The Secret of Treasure Island* (1938).

DIANETICS: THE MODERN SCIENCE OF MENTAL HEALTH

Of all of Hubbard's early work, the book and ideas that had lasting influence and gave rise to the Church of Scientology was ***Dianetics: The Modern Science of Mental Health*** (1950), which sold 150,000 copies in its first year. In *Dianetics* Hubbard presents his theory of the human mind and the relief of psychosomatic illness based on the concept of the engram. **Dianetics** (Greek, "through soul") means *what the soul is doing to the body through the mind*, and by using the term Hubbard sought to promote a spiritual technology by which he claimed unwanted ills, such as irrational fears and undesirable stress, could be eliminated. *Dianetics* became the foundational textbook for the Church of Scientology. Hubbard died in 1986 on his ranch near San Luis Obispo, California. After his body was cremated, followers said that Hubbard's spirit was living "on a planet a galaxy away."[17]

COMPOSITION OF A HUMAN BEING

Hubbard's work argues that the goal of Scientology is to improve life conditions and therefore is oriented toward pragmatic ends, rather than cognitive assent to a set of doctrines. Nevertheless, Scientology presents a unique set of beliefs and practices that are central to its identity as a new religious movement. First, Scientology pictures the human being as consisting of three parts, the **thetan** (spirit), the mind, and the body. The *thetan*, a term related to the Greek letter *theta*, is the basic life force that is good, but whose intrinsic, spiritual purity has been forgotten by people and therefore needs to be rehabilitated. The *thetan*, as an element of the cosmic force, is born into a physical body and is an individual's true identity.

As such, *thetan* is similar to the Hindu notion of **atman** (soul, self), the enduring identity of individuals. Scientology teaches that in order to regain knowledge of one's *thetan*, one needs "auditing," a kind of spiritual and mental counseling aimed at remembering one's true nature as a spiritual being.

Engrams

Second, Scientology asserts that painful memories, which serve as obstacles to our remembrance of our inherently pure *thetan*, are carried on **engrams**. According to Scientology, an engram is related to a person's unconscious mind.

> [An engram is] a recording made by the reactive mind when a person is "unconscious." An engram is not a memory—it is a particular type of mental image picture which is a complete recording, down to the last accurate detail, of every perception present in a moment of partial or full "unconsciousness." As a mental image, the engram is a recording of an experience containing pain, real or imaginary, which threatens survival.[18]

Engrams are debilitating, carried over from a past to one's present life, much like the Hindu notion of the reincarnation of soul or spirit (e.g., atman). There is a strong emphasis on counseling ("auditing") in Scientology as the means to improve one's condition, to free oneself of engrams. An E-meter, which Scientologists purport measures minute changes in electrical resistance in the body, is employed to detect engrams. Once an engram has been identified, the auditor (counselor) helps the counselee to eliminate

Abhijitsathe/Wikimedia Commons

Figure 10.12. Church of Scientology in Boston, Massachusetts, USA

the engram. A common way that Scientologists attempt to interest people in their movement is by offering a "free stress test," which utilizes the E-meter to demonstrate to the potential counselee the "scientific" validity of Scientology.

Counselees are classified according to "the emotional tone scale," which rates chronic emotions on a scale that Scientology argues indicates one's level of spiritual vitality. The emotional tone scale is employed to help guide auditing (counseling) procedures, with the assumption that the closer one approaches pain, the less happy one feels. Scientology claims to help people move up the emotional tone scale and liberate themselves to be pure, free beings. Additionally, Scientology proposes scales for other areas of life, including physical health, truth, and sexual activities.

CONTROVERSIES ABOUT THE CHURCH OF SCIENTOLOGY

Hubbard's work was considered unscientific by medical doctors. However, in the ensuing decades the Church has forged better relations with medical doctors who have come to understand that Scientology provides a spiritual practice, not a medical one. Debate about the motivation behind Hubbard's writing—with some claiming he set out as early as the 1940s to concoct a blend of psychology, science fiction, and religion to establish a new religion with the goal of making him wealthy—has beleaguered the movement since its founding. Scientology has been accused of aggressive and manipulative methods of recruiting converts. Regardless of the lasting controversies surrounding Scientology, many of which have been determined judicially to be false accusations, L. Ron Hubbard is credited by the Guinness World Records with being the world's most published author, with 1,084 fiction and non-fiction works attributed to him. Today the Church is recognized as a religion by the Australian High Court, United States Supreme Court, UK Supreme Court, and by the European Court of Human Rights.

Unification Church

REVEREND SUN MYUNG MOON

The **Holy Spirit Association for the Unification of World Christianity** (HSA-UWC), otherwise known as the **Unification Church**, was started by the Reverend Sun Myung Moon (1920–2012), considered by members to be the Messiah. Followers of the Unification movement are sometimes pejoratively called "Moonies." Sun Myung Moon was born on January 6, 1920, in what is today North Korea, which was then under Japanese rule. When Reverend Moon was about ten years old, his family converted from the Confucian tradition to become Christian, joining the Presbyterian Church. When he was sixteen years old, during a time of deep prayer, Reverend Moon purportedly received a revelation from Jesus inviting him to help establish God's kingdom on earth and bring world peace. Later Moon reported to have visited through "the spirit world" other great religious figures, such as Abraham, Moses, the Lord Buddha, and the Prophet Muhammad. Reverend Moon later declared, "The founders of five great religions and many other leaders in the spirit world, including even Communist leaders such as Marx and Lenin . . . and dictators such as Hitler and Stalin, have found strength in my teachings, mended their ways and been reborn as new persons."[19]

After developing his own interpretation of the Bible and preaching that message, Reverend Moon was arrested by North Korean officials on allegations of spying for South Korea; he then served a five-year sentence at a notorious labor camp. In 1954, following his liberation from the camp by American and United Nations forces, Reverend Moon established the Holy Spirit Association for the Unification of World Christianity in Seoul, South Korea. Reverend Moon's beliefs are summarized in his book *Divine Principle* (1966), which serves as the foundation of the theology of the Unification Church, as well as the church's sacred scripture.

Although Reverend Moon was married three times, he and his last wife, Hak Ja Han, were referred to as True Parents by devotees of the tradition, their family the True Family, and their children, the True Children. In 1971 Reverend Moon and his family moved to the United States, where he quickly circulated in powerful political circles, even receiving recognition by President Richard Nixon for Moon's support of the president during the Watergate scandal. Reverend Moon supported the election of Republican presidents Ronald Reagan and George H. W. Bush, for instance, contributing millions of dollars to the Bush election campaign. Moon also used his amassed wealth in part to found the *Washington Times*, spending nearly $2 billion to promote his ideas throughout the world. In 2004, during a United States congressional reception honoring Reverend Moon, he "declared himself the Messiah and said his teachings have helped Hitler and Stalin be 'reborn as new persons.'"[20]

> [Reverend Moon claimed he was] "sent to Earth . . . to save the world's six billion people. . . . Emperors, Kings, and Presidents . . . have declared to all Heaven and Earth that Reverend Sun Myung Moon is none other than humanity's Savior, Messiah, Returning Lord, and True Parent."
>
> Babington and Cooperman, "Rev. Moon Honored," *Washington Post*, June 23, 2004

Reverend Moon's Divine Principle

The Unification Church is based on the teachings found in Moon's *Divine Principle*, first published in Korean in 1966 and in English in 1973. *Divine*

Principle was cowritten by Reverend Moon and his early disciple Hyo Won Eu. Influenced by systematic Christian theology, *Divine Principle* includes reflection on God's purpose in creating human beings, the fall of human beings, and redemption. The book also reflects Moon's Confucian context, for it employs common polarities of Confucianism (e.g., divine-human, male-female) to argue that there is an inherent, God-ordained social hierarchy to the world, with God at the highest level, male and female below God, and children below male and female.

Unification Church Beliefs

Reverend Moon's goal was to build world peace through loving families and by unifying all religions. Reverend Moon himself fathered fourteen children. In terms of specific beliefs, the Unification Church recognizes a universal God, the universal salvation of all peoples regardless of their religious identification, the establishment of the real kingdom of God on earth, and that Sun Myung Moon is the Messiah. *Divine Principle*, a 536-page sacred scripture of the Unification Church, claims to provide the basis for seeking unity among all religions, but in actuality the scripture presents a religion that attempts to surpass Christianity. Affirming spiritualism—that is, the possibility of communicating with the spirits of the dead—*Divine Principle* notes that Moon himself had endured great suffering in the spirit world in order to shed light on the secrets of heaven. Sun Myung Moon was considered to be the third Adam; the first Adam was described in Genesis, and the second Adam was Jesus.

Unification Church Scandals

A series of scandals have followed Moon and his Unification Church. The United States government convicted him in 1982 of filing fraudulent income tax forms, costing him time in federal prison. There have been allegations that the church engages in mind control and numerous criticisms of Moon's lavish personal lifestyle as well as the performance of a mass marriage ceremony of approximately thirty thousand couples, some of whom had never previously met each other.

> *With the fullness of time, God has sent one person to this earth to resolve the fundamental problems of human life and the universe. His name is Sun Myung Moon. For several decades [Moon] wandered through the spirit world so vast as to be beyond imagining. He trod a bloody path of suffering in search of the truth, passing through tribulations that God alone remembers. Since he understands that no one can find the ultimate truth to save humanity without first passing through the bitterest of trials, he fought alone against millions of devils, both in the spiritual and physical worlds, and triumphed over them all. Through intimate spiritual communion with God and by meeting Jesus and many saints in Paradise, he brought to light all the secrets of Heaven.*
>
> Moon and Eu, introduction to *Exposition of the Divine Principle* (available at http://www.unification.net/dp96/dp96-1-0.html#Introduction)

Today this new religious movement is known by the alternate names of Family Federation for World Peace and Unification, Unification Church, Holy Spirit Association, the Holy Spirit Association for the Unification of World Christianity, Women's Federation for World Peace, and Collegiate Associate for the Research of Principles. The Unification Church now has a membership perhaps as high as three million, and it is led by Moon's son, Rev. **Hyung Jin Moon**.

Conclusion

A New Pluralism

Since the mid-twentieth century, the United States has been marked by the presence of a greater multiplicity of ethnicities and religions. Economic and political pressures, along with a desire for greater opportunities, have forced many to leave their countries to seek another home. Although there were many non-European immigrants in North America prior to the Second

Christian Reflections

The **popularity of** Hindu-Buddhist-oriented new religious movements among Westerners has demonstrated the attractiveness of "spirituality," that broad realm in religions that places heavy emphasis on the nature of the spirit world, incorporeality, and the supernatural. The appeal of spiritualistic NRMs may in part reflect the need of human beings to be connected to forces and powers greater than themselves. What the spiritualistic NRMs offer—namely, techniques of introspection, meditation, prayer, and a quest for wisdom and personal well-being—can also be found in historic Christianity. Part of the pull of these sorts of NRMs for Western Christians, however, may be due to the perception of some that the historic Christian church has become overly rational at the expense of engaging in the life of the spirit.

Indeed, it is not unusual to find that many participants in the spiritualistic NRMs have a Christian background. What they have discovered in their new religion is greater emphasis on holism—that is, for instance, the connection between mind and body, and tranquility through meditation. The burgeoning of the spiritualistic NRMs in the North Atlantic world attests to the failure of the secularization theory that conjectured that the rise of modernization and a scientific worldview would necessarily lead to the demise of spirituality and religion. Modernization, globalization, and science, while robust forces in modern societies, have not displaced the inherent need for people to find meaning in their lives through spirituality and religion.

World War, the diversity of immigrants to the United States increased significantly in the postwar period. People from the Global South have arrived in the United States in large numbers from the end of the Second World War until today. With immigration comes a changed religious landscape, where "new" religions, particularly from Asia, have contributed to the religious character of the United States. Immigration has led to a new religious situation, giving rise to a "new pluralism" that has forced Americans to question the nature of their identity as citizens and, for many, as religious people.

Our contemporary situation of new pluralism gives us as religious people an opportunity to encounter one another in fruitful ways that do not require discarding religious commitments. Encountering one another as religious people can be an excellent way to gain insights into the nature of the self, the natural world, and human problems. Interreligious encounter is important in helping reduce tensions through mutual understanding of truth—can religious people affirm that the "other" has something to teach us? By learning from others, we have the opportunity to learn about different ways of seeing the world. And these ways of thinking can help Christians too, without compelling Christians to give up the affirmations of their faith.

Reminding Christians

Religions can help remind us of practices and values that might even be a part of historic Christianity but have either been forgotten or simply are no longer a part of a given Christian tradition. To watch Muslims praying at a masjid can remind Christians of the seriousness with which we are to approach God—that God is transcendent and that the worship space is a place of prayer and submission. The Hindu tradition can teach Christians about the impossibility of narrowly defining God; God will always surprise us.

Regarding the East Asian notion of the Tao, can the God of the Bible be compared to the Tao as an unknowable force that can only be known as it unfolds itself in creation? Traditions of the Tao can remind Christians that God dwells in the light and the dark (e.g., "Even though I walk through the darkest valley, I will fear no evil, for you are with me," Ps. 23:4). Buddhism reminds Christians to consider the role of suffering in our world and in our vision of reality. It forces us to ask some important questions: What really matters? What am I holding on to that really is a distraction to what is ultimately important? Can Christians learn about the quietness of God—the silence—when they see Buddhists practice sitting or walking meditation ("Be still, and know that I am God!" Ps. 46:10)? Buddhists can teach Christians—and Americans in general—much about being fully present in the moment rather than being inattentive because of external or internal distractions. The new religious movements can remind Christians that an overly rationalistic approach to Christian faith can leave people wanting something more spiritual.

Yet encountering one another as religious people can also create immense challenges. A challenge is presented by Islam. If Muslims see their faith as incomplete unless it is integrated into every aspect of culture and society, what might be the best approach to Christian-Muslim dialogue? There is the challenge of Hinduism, which has no problem absorbing other deities, including Jesus Christ, into their immense pantheon of Gods, without changing the overall message or orientation. Is Jesus one of many Gods or the only God incarnate? Furthermore, it is increasingly common for people to create their own religions by combining appealing features of beliefs and practices of a variety of religions to create a smorgasbord of palatable tastes. Seeing the religious life as a smorgasbord, where we can pick and choose which elements we want to incorporate into our religious life, is undoubtedly one reflection of our post-Enlightenment condition that legitimizes us as autonomous individuals entitled to construct our own realities. This leaves us wanting to make our own decisions about what is best for us.

What Has New York to Do with Mecca?

In the second century, the church historian Tertullian asked, "What has Athens to do with Jerusalem?" Tertullian's provocative question aimed at exposing what in his mind was the incompatibility of Greek philosophy (i.e., "Athens") with Christian faith (i.e., "Jerusalem"). According to Tertullian, Christianity was a matter of faith, not philosophy. After two thousand years of Christian history, there are new questions that require new approaches to thinking about Christianity's relationship to cultures and religions.

Today the appropriate questions are more like, "What has New York to do with Mecca?" or "What has Jerusalem to do with Varanasi?" In the first case, New York represents secularism and the elimination of religion from the public square, while Mecca refers to the joining of religion, law, territory, and the nation-state. In the second case, Jerusalem represents "faith" of the monotheistic religious traditions, and Varanasi represents Asian religious traditions that recognize vast pantheons of Gods or no God at all (e.g., Theravada Buddhism). These sorts of questions point to realities in our contemporary world that are often challenging to navigate.

Theology of Religions

Since its emergence, Christianity has encountered every major world religion. Beginning with the ancient Near Eastern religions, to the religions

506

throughout the Roman Empire, Europe, Asia, Africa, and the Pacific, the history of Christianity conveys a story of those engagements. That history is replete with stories of both successes and failures. In general, Christians have thought about the relationship between Christianity and other religions in three ways. When we speak of Christianity's relationship with other religions, we are talking about a field of inquiry called the "theology of religions." The theology of religions considers the relationship between religions. Are all religions essentially the same, just with different names? Are religions mutually exclusive, with no similarities between them? It is one thing to learn about different religions, but it is another task to ask how those religions might relate to one another.

One general typology of the theology of religions consists of perspectives called (1) **exclusivist**, (2) **inclusivist**, and (3) **pluralist**. These should be seen not as mutually exclusive categories but rather as models that seek to organize our thinking about Christianity's relationship to other religions. One should keep two important points in mind when considering these perspectives. First, each category is broad and has many variations within it. That is, there are many types of exclusivists, and some adherents of exclusivism may not even use that term to define their theology of religions. Second, each theology of religions discussed below finds substantial support within the Christian community. So each particular perspective is considered to be within the scope of Christianity—at least according to the advocates themselves. Naturally, each Christian needs to decide which perspective best describes the relationship between Christianity and other religions. There are many examples of Christians who advocate for each perspective.

EXCLUSIVISTS

Exclusivists insist on the finality and uniqueness of the biblical revelation. They deny the possibility of salvation and salvific revelation outside Christianity—that is, as Peter Berger has noted, "outside the biblical orbit." This position typically holds that there is no significant overlap between Christianity and other religions, so exclusivists resist mixing elements of Christianity with other religions. Salvation is only through Jesus Christ. There is no revelation apart from Christ. While there are many examples of an exclusivist position within the theology of religion, perhaps the most influential twentieth-century theologian advocating this perspective was **Karl Barth** (1886–1968).

Barth contrasted *religion* with *revelation*. He asserted that human beings are naturally idol factories, and the idol they manufacture is religion. For Barth, *religion* is a human fabrication. Any attempt by human beings to initiate

Religion possesses no solution of the problem of life; rather it makes of the problem a wholly insoluble enigma. Religion neither discovers the problem nor solves it: what it does is to disclose the truth that it cannot be solved. Religion is neither a thing to be enjoyed nor a thing to be celebrated: it must be borne as a yoke which cannot be removed. Religion is not a thing to be desired or extolled: it is a misfortune which takes fatal hold upon some men, and is by them passed on to others; it is the misfortune which assailed John the Baptist in the desert, and drove him out to preach repentance and judgement; . . . Religion is the misfortune which every human being was to endure, though it is, in the majority of cases, a hidden suffering.

K. Barth, *Epistle to the Romans*, 258–59

The Gospel is not a truth among other truths. Rather, it is a question-mark against all truths. The Gospel is not the door but the hinge.

K. Barth, *Epistle to the Romans*, 35

a relationship with God can be a form of religion, and is ultimately an invalid way to know God. Religion is understood as the human attempt to know God.

In contrast, *revelation* is something totally new, coming directly from God. God reveals, pulls back the veil, to disclose himself. Whereas *religion* begins with human beings, *revelation* begins with God. What is revealed, according to Barth, is God's self-disclosure, Jesus Christ. In laying out his ideas, Barth was quite critical of a kind of Christianity that emphasizes the human initiative to know God.

Barth argued that Christianity could be false if it is seen as the human attempt to know God. However, Christianity should be recognized as the "true religion," since it is a creature of grace rather than of works. Barth argued strongly that the revelation of Jesus Christ was so dramatically different from anything humans had ever known that Christianity could not be compared to other kinds of knowledge, such as philosophy, psychology, or anthropology. The only truth is revealed by God, not by human nature, culture, or fabricated religion.

Inclusivists

Whereas exclusivists believe that truth comes only from the biblical witness, inclusivists are more willing to admit revelatory truth outside the Christian story. Inclusivists stress the centrality of biblical revelation, but they are more open to accept that God may be working outside the biblical witness—that is, outside Christianity. Some use the term "fulfillment" to describe an inclusivistic perspective. By using the term "fulfillment," inclusivists suggest that Christianity fulfills other religions; for instance, Christianity fulfills the yearnings reflected in religious rituals. There are good and valuable features of other religions; there is "truth" in the major religions. Other religions are seen as a ***praeparatio evangelica*** (preparation of the gospel). And Christianity is seen as the crown of other religions, fulfilling the longings and answering the ultimate questions provided by the other religions.

Inclusivists often employ Justin Martyr's notion of **Logos spermatikos** (i.e., seed-bearing word) to illustrate their perspective. *Logos spermatikos* was used by Justin Martyr to explain that God (as Father, Son, and Holy Spirit) left something of the Logos (word, truth) in all of creation, as a testimony of God. That is to say, the notion of *Logos spermatikos* asserts that God has not left human beings—nor their thought systems (e.g., philosophy)—without a witness of God. There are aspects of each culture, and philosophical and religious system, that are good and can be the foundation out of which the gospel can be communicated. There are numerous examples of this dynamic in both the Bible and the history of Christianity. For instance, the term "*Kyrios*" (Greek, "Lord," "Master") appears over seven hundred times in the New Testament. The term was adopted by the New Testament writers to refer to Jesus as Lord Jesus Christ. But *Kyrios* originally appeared in the context of worshiping the Greco-Egyptian God Kyrios Serapis (Lord Serapis). Biblical writers applied that term effectively to Jesus as "Lord Jesus Christ." Jesus was the fulfillment of the notion of "Lord"—as Lord of lords, King of kings (see 1 Tim. 6:14–16; Rev. 17:14; 19:16).

For the Christian apologists, symbols were pregnant with messages; they showed the sacred through the cosmic rhythms. The revelation brought by the faith did not destroy the pre-Christian meanings of symbols; it simply added a new value to them. True enough, for the believer this new meaning eclipsed all the others; it alone valorized the symbol, transfigured it into revelation. It was the resurrection of Christ that counted, not the signs that could be read in cosmic life. Yet it remains true that the new valorization was in some sort conditioned by the very structure of the symbolism; it could even be said that [a symbol] awaited the fulfillment of its deepest meaning through the new value contributed by Christianity.

Eliade, *Sacred and the Profane,* 137

Some **important questions** come to mind when thinking about the Christian exclusivist position. What are the sources of knowledge of God? Is the revelation of Christ the only way that we can know God? Or are there other ways that we can know God? What is the relationship between the revelation of Christ and different cultures? Is there a difference between knowing *something* about God and *fully* knowing God, or is this a false distinction? How helpful can different disciplinary perspectives be in knowing God, or are they mutually incompatible with the revelation of Jesus Christ? In other words, can the social sciences or hard sciences aid us in knowing God, or can the knowledge of God only come from God's revelation through Christ?

Christian Reflections

Anonymous Christianity means that a person lives in the grace of God and attains salvation outside of explicitly constituted Christianity—Let us say, a Buddhist monk—who, because he follows his conscience, attains salvation and lives in the grace of God; of him I must say that he is an anonymous Christian; if not, I would have to presuppose that there is a genuine path to salvation that really attains that goal, but that simply has nothing to do with Jesus Christ. But I cannot do that. And so, if I hold that everyone depends upon Jesus Christ for salvation, and if at the same time I hold that many live in the world who have not expressly recognized Jesus Christ, then there remains in my opinion nothing else but to take up this postulate of an anonymous Christianity.

Rahner, *Karl Rahner in Dialogue*, 135

An example of an inclusivist is **Karl Rahner** (1904–84), a preeminent Roman Catholic theologian of the twentieth century. Rahner suggested that at the creation, a portion of God's grace was part of the creative act, and that, therefore, God's grace is in creation and in all the major religions. Rahner argued that God's grace was so much a part of creation that faithful adherents to their respective religions can receive salvation through that religion. A Hindu could be saved through Hinduism, a Muslim through Islam, and a Buddhist through Buddhism. However, after religious people hear the gospel of Jesus Christ in what Rahner called "an existentially real way," then their religion cannot provide salvation. This is because the gospel of Jesus Christ completed the expectations and longings of their earlier religion. Christ fulfills the older religious traditions in much the same way as Jesus in the New Testament fulfilled the anticipation for a savior in the Old Testament. Rahner also introduced the notion of "**anonymous Christianity**" to describe his idea that even though people may never have heard of Christ, they might still attain salvation.

Rahner's insights sought to uphold the uniqueness of Christ with an inclusive understanding that God is already present and working in religions even before the gospel is communicated. Some contested Rahner's ideas because of his proposal of an overly generous view of salvation; for some, Rahner's generous soteriology was too inclusive. On the other hand, many have found Rahner's vision of respect for other religious traditions and recognition that God is working through them to be worthy of affirmation.

Pluralists

Pluralists give up the centrality of biblical revelation and argue that all truth is truth, whether it be conveyed in the Bible, another text, or a religious tradition. The reality to which religions refer is the same for all traditions. They just use different names for that reality. The truth of each religious tradition functions as a pointer to a more fundamental truth shared by all religions. All religious paths guide the religious person to the identical goal, since each religion is valid for its own cultural context but not for the entire world. A common analogy used by religious pluralists to describe their perspective is taken from the old Indian parable about six blind men touching an elephant. In the fable, the six blind men each touch a part of the elephant and report back what they have felt. The blind man touching a leg exclaims, "An elephant is like a pillar." Another feels the tail and exclaims, "An elephant is like a rope." Another touches the trunk and says, "An elephant is like a tree branch." Another feels the ear and notes, "An elephant is like a hand fan." And another, touching the belly, says, "An elephant is like a wall." Hindus, Jains, Buddhists, and Sufis have variations of this same story, but the point remains the same: it is impossible to fully express truth; we can perceive truth only partially. We are bound by our cultural and religious contexts.

Some would argue that by definition it is impossible for Christians to be pluralists—that is, it is inconsistent with the message of Christianity to suggest that Christianity conveys only a relativistic truth and that Christianity is just one road, along with others, moving toward the same spiritual summit. Yet Christian pluralists would disagree.

Paul Knitter (b. 1939) and **John Hick** (1922–2012) have led much of Christian pluralist discussion in the Global North. Knitter is a Catholic, and Hick was a Protestant. Both are theologians and have published several books promoting their theology of religion—for instance, *No Other Name? A Critical Survey of Christian Attitudes toward the World Religions* (Paul Knitter), *The Myth of Religious Superiority* (Paul Knitter), *God Has Many Names* (John Hick), and *The Metaphor of God Incarnate* (John Hick).

Knitter and Hick coedited *The Myth of Christian Uniqueness: Toward a Pluralistic Theology of Religions* (1987), in which twelve contributors lay out their visions of moving past the perspectives of exclusivism and inclusivism to embrace one that sees truth beyond the narrow confines of Christianity. The Christian pluralist position contends that the center of a theology of

The Christian is not to become a Hindu or a Buddhist, nor a Hindu or a Buddhist to become a Christian. But each must assimilate the spirit of the others and yet preserve its individuality and grow according to its own law of growth. If the [World Parliament of Religions] has shown anything to the world, it is this: It has proved to the world that holiness, purity, and charity are not the exclusive possessions of any church in the world, and that every system has produced men and women of the most exalted character. . . . if anybody dreams of the exclusive survival of his own religion and the destruction of the others, I pity him from the bottom of my heart.

Vivekananda, World Parliament of Religions, Address at the Final Session, September 27, 1893, quoted in Adiswarananda, *World Teacher*, 11

I do not deny for a moment that the truth of God has reached others through other channels—indeed, I hope and pray that it has. So while I have a special attachment to one mediator, I have respect for them all.

Macquarrie, *Mediators between Human and Divine*, 12

religions needs to be God rather than Jesus Christ. That is, Christian plural-ists suggest that it is more productive to be ***theocentric*** (God centered) than ***Christocentric*** (Christ centered). Thus, John Hick has called for a Coperni-can revolution that accepts that Christianity does not occupy the center of the universe. Instead, Hick suggests that Christianity is just one "planet" of several circling the "sun" of ultimate reality. Religions are different human responses to divinity, formed in different historical and cultural situations.

Hybrid Religions and Spiritualities

It is critically important to recognize that religious people do not follow their traditions perfectly. Part of our human condition is that we are incon-sistent; religious people often do the very things that their religions prohibit. Buddhists crave, Muslims do not pray five times daily, and Christians fail

Christian Reflections

The **Christian pluralist perspective** is an attractive option for modern Christians who seek an empathetic approach to the positive contributions of religions. Many feel uneasy claiming that they have knowledge of truth that may appear to judge other perspectives or that is considered worthy of providing peace with God unlike other religious traditions. Others feel constrained by moments in the history of Christianity when the church has been judgmental, unwilling to accept positive features of other religions.

Furthermore, many modern people highly value a spirit of tolerance. Religion is often seen as an opinion or value. The enlightened person is one who accepts the place of religion in modern society as one's opinion, without trying to win over other people to one's own religion. The adages "live and let live" or "don't judge me and I won't judge you" seem to be prevailing themes today. By claiming that all religions are equally valid ways to know God, Christian pluralists imply that they are in a position to know all religions. Other Christians would challenge this assumption.

Others would challenge this perspective that marginalizes Christ and seeks to understand the world, history, and truth apart from him. For example, Lesslie Newbigin states, "Once again, therefore, to speak of the finality of Christ is to speak of him as the clue to our interpretation of history as a whole. It implies that our conviction about Christ, and our commitment to serve him in the present hour, gives us the standpoint from which we can truly understand human history as a whole."[a]

a. Newbigin, *Finality of Christ*, 72.

to love others. To some extent, these failings are the battlegrounds for living faithfully in the world as persons of religious faith. We know what to do but fail to do it: "I do not understand what I do. For what I want to do I do not do, but what I hate I do" (Rom. 7:15 NIV).

In our post-Enlightenment and late-modern condition, the challenge lies not just in our failure to follow our religious traditions faithfully. A second challenge is that people have constructed their own religions. Many in the modern Global North no longer follow either one of the world religions or even a new religious movement. Rather, people gather features of religious life that appeal to them, creating a "religion" or "spirituality" consisting of an amalgamation of choice elements from any number of religious resources.

Today many feel free to choose religious options to satisfy their tastes for spirituality. Features of Jewish kabbalah, Buddhist meditation, Hindu notions of divine essence, and Christian morality can be combined to create a personalized religion that meets one's needs. These ad hoc hybridizations demonstrate that religions are not bounded, hermetically sealed systems, but that they exhibit a fluidity that is prone to mixing elements that might appear to be contradictory.

> *The apostolic testimony of Jesus as Lord is a claim for his finality in respect of matters of which the apostles themselves were necessarily ignorant. They knew nothing of Buddhism or Hinduism, yet claimed that Jesus was the only name given under heaven whereby we must be saved. They knew nothing of the sort of future for the human race which we are glimpsing in the second half of the twentieth century, yet they confessed him as the alpha and omega, the beginning and end of all things.*
>
> Newbigin, *Finality of Christ*, 78–79

Religion on the Rise

The world religions seem to have a bright future, since there is no indication of their waning. People worldwide continue to find meaning through the religious beliefs and practices that provide insight into and wisdom about the universal questions of life. Religions and spirituality are resurging worldwide, and with greater proliferation of diversity and hybridity. For some, the burgeoning of religions may be interpreted as a mixed bag, since changes in the religious landscape present challenges to one's self-understanding and raise the potential for conflict with one's own faith tradition.

Harvard professor Diana Eck, in her book *A New Religious America: How a "Christian Country" Has Become the World's Most Religiously Diverse Nation*, argues persuasively that the United States is the most religiously diverse nation in the world. However, by emphasizing the religious diversity in the United States, which actually accounts for only a tiny fraction of the overall population of the United States, one can easily overlook the clear numerical predominance of Christianity. Demographic surveys estimate that more than 75 percent of the people in the United States self-identify as Christian, with Jews, Muslims, and Buddhists combined making up only about 3 percent of the population. Such figures do not need to be cause for overconfidence among Christians. Rather, the numbers serve to remind Christians of the great opportunity and burden to exhibit the Christlike qualities that can benefit all human beings. It is worthwhile to note that although the overall percentage of American Muslims is fairly small (roughly 0.5 percent of the American population), there is no reason to believe that Islam will decline in the United States in the near future. Rather, current growth patterns point to the real possibility that Islam will one day be the second largest religion in the country, outnumbering the adherents of Judaism.

Christians have much to gain when encountering followers of other religious traditions. First, Christians can learn to appreciate the ways that God may already be working in other religious and cultural contexts. Some Christians may be surprised to learn that followers of other religious traditions exhibit virtues compatible with Christianity, such as charity, compassion, and environmental stewardship. Second, by listening empathetically to other believers, Christians may be reminded of important ideas and practices that some Christian traditions have forgotten or underplayed, such as the value of silent meditation and the recognition of mutual interdependence within the human community and between human beings and the environment. Recall that the Bible admonishes, "Be still, and know that I am God!" (Ps. 46:10). Third, by understanding other religions, Christians might gain confidence to engage others as world citizens, recognizing the "other" first as a fellow human being rather than as a religious adversary. Jesus himself never denigrated other religions, except for some of the Pharisees who Jesus said were hypocritical, proud, and pretentious. (Jesus continued to love the Pharisees—remember Nicodemus in John 3?) As David Bosch puts it, Christians are called to be witnesses to the truth they know in a spirit of "bold humility,"[21] relying on being empowered by the Holy Spirit to make meaningful the good news of the gospel.

Key Terms

anonymous Christianity	Besant, Annie	Christocentric
Armageddon	Blavatsky, Madame Helena	Church of Christ, Scientist (Christian Science)
atman	Book of Mormon	
Barth, Karl		

Church of Jesus Christ of Latter-Day Saints
Church of Scientology
Community of Christ
cult
dhyani-chohan
Dianetics
Dianetics: The Modern Science of Mental Health
Divine Principle
docetism
Doctrine and Covenants
Eddy, Mary Baker
Elohim
engrams
exclusivists
Fundamentalist Latter-Day Saints
gnostic gospels
Hick, John
Holy Spirit Association for the Unification of World Christianity
Hubbard, L. Ron

inclusivists
Jehovah's Witnesses
Judge, William Quan
Knitter, Paul
Logos spermatikos
mantra
Miller, William
Millerites
Moon, Hyung Jin
Moon, Sun Myung
Mormonism
Moroni
Newbigin, Lesslie
new religious movements
Olcott, Colonel Henry Steel
Pearl of Great Price
pluralists
polygamy
praeparatio evangelica
primitivist movements
Rahner, Karl
Reorganized Church of the Latter-Day Saints

restoration movement
Russell, Charles Taze
Rutherford, Joseph
Science and Health with Key to the Scriptures
Seventh-Day Adventist
Smith, Joseph, Jr.
theocentric
Theosophical Society
Theosophy
thetan
Thirteen Articles of Faith
Transcendental Meditation
Troeltsch, Ernst
Twenty-Eight Fundamental Beliefs
Unification Church
universal brotherhood
Watchtower
Weber, Max
White, Ellen G.
Yogi, Maharishi Mahesh
Young, Brigham

Further Reading

Blavatsky, H. P. *The Secret Doctrine*. Wheaton, IL: The Theosophical Publishing House, 1993.

Bromley, David G., and J. Gordon Melton. *Cults, Religion, and Violence*. New York: Cambridge University Press, 2002.

Daschke, Dereck, and Michael Ashcraft. *New Religious Movements: A Documentary Reader*. New York: New York University Press, 2005.

Dawson, Lorne L., ed. *Cults and New Religious Movements: A Reader*. Blackwell Readings in Religion. Malden, MA: Blackwell Publishing, 2003.

Eck, Diana L. *A New Religious America: How a "Christian Country" Has Become the World's Most Religiously Diverse Nation*. San Francisco: HarperOne, 2002.

Enroth, Ronald. *A Guide to New Religious Movements*. Downers Grove, IL: InterVarsity Press, 2005.

Glock, Charles Y., and Robert N. Bellah, eds. *The New Religious Consciousness*. Berkeley: University of California Press, 1976.

Lewis, James R., and J. Gordon Melton, eds. *Perspectives on the New Age*. Albany: SUNY Press, 1992.

Partridge, Christopher, and J. Gordon Melton, eds. *New Religions: A Guide; New Religious Movements, Sects, and Alternative Spiritualities*. New York: Oxford University Press, 2004.

Sinnett, A. P. *The Purpose of Theosophy*. Whitefish, MT: Kessinger Publishing, 2005.

Smith, Joseph, Jr. *Teachings of the Prophet Joseph Smith*. Salt Lake City: Deseret News Press, 1938.

Notes

Chapter 1: The Persistence of Religion

1. Key terms have been identified throughout the text by the use of boldface type. This will alert readers to important words or phrases. These appear in the key terms section at the end of each chapter and also in the glossary at the end of the book.

2. All citations of the Qur'an are taken from *Modern English Translation of the Holy Qur'an* (Kansas City, MO: Manar International, 1998).

3. Pals, *Seven Theories of Religion*, 4.

4. Quoted in Sharpe, *Comparative Religion*, 36.

5. Max Müller, "Westminster Lecture on Missions," (March 12 [1872]), in *Chips from a German Workshop*, 4:354.

6. Ibid., 4:251–80. See Sharpe, *Comparative Religion*, 35–45, for more details on Müller's ideas and influence.

7. In Lefebure and Feldmeier, *Path of Wisdom*, 57.

8. In Bhikkhu, *Access to Insight*.

9. Newbigin, *Foolishness to the Greeks*, 3.

10. For example, see Beckford, *Social Theory and Religion*; Evans-Pritchard, *Theories of Primitive Religion*; Kunin and Miles-Watson, *Theories of Religion*; Pals, *Eight Theories of Religion*; Preus, *Explaining Religion*; Segal, *Blackwell Companion*; and Stark and Bainbridge, *Theory of Religion*.

11. See Freud, *Civilization and Its Discontents*.

12. Ibid., 30.

13. Sigmund Freud, "Obsessive Actions and Religious Actions," in *Standard Edition*, 9:429.

14. Durkheim, *Elementary Forms of the Religious Life*, 10.

15. See Pals, *Seven Theories of Religion*, 124–57.

16. Marx and Engels, *Communist Manifesto*, 219.

17. Pals, *Seven Theories of Religion*, 142. Pals's chapter on Marx is particularly lucid.

18. Clifford Geertz, "Thick Description: Toward an Interpretive Theory of Culture," in his *Interpretation of Cultures*, 7.

19. Geertz, *Interpretation of Cultures*, 90. Geertz's complete presentation of religion can be found in "Religion as a Cultural System," in *Interpretation of Cultures*, 87–125.

20. Geertz, *Interpretation of Cultures*, 95.

21. Ibid., 112.

22. Mircea Eliade, quoted in Pals, *Seven Theories of Religion*, 160.

23. Eliade, *Patterns of Comparative Religion*, xvii.

24. Cf. Lewis, *Great Divorce*, where Lewis presents the themes of sacred and profane through an imaginary encounter between the citizens of hell (the phantoms) and those of heaven (those full of substance).

25. See Pals, *Seven Theories of Religion*, 161–63.

26. Eliade, *Sacred and the Profane*, 11.

27. For a focused discussion of Eliade's notion of sacred time, see Eliade, *Myth of the Eternal Return*.

28. Redfield, "Folk Society," 293.

29. Necromancy refers to practices of communicating with the spirits of the dead to reveal future events. As a broad category with a history dating to antiquity, necromancy can refer to practices of shamanism, witchcraft, black magic, spiritualism, channeling, voodoo, séances, and Santeria. A biblical example is the witch of Endor (1 Sam. 28:4–25), who called on the spirit of the recently deceased prophet Samuel.

30. Hiebert, Shaw, and Tiénou, *Understanding Folk Religion*, 175–95.

31. Ibid., 77.

32. Ibid., 73.

33. See Lu, *Japan*, 467.

34. Demographic and statistical data come from the Pew Forum on Religion and Public Life, analysis in December 2012, available at http://www.pewforum.org/global-religious-land scape-exec.aspx#geographic.

35. See Kahn, "Sunday Christians, Monday Sorcerers."

Chapter 2: Hinduism

1. Miller, trans., *The Bhagavad-Gita*, 107. All quotations from the Bhagavad Gita are from Miller's translation.

2. In Embree, *Hindu Tradition*, 25–26.

3. These are sometimes written as Rigveda, Yajurveda, Samaveda, and Atharvaveda.

4. Doniger, trans., *The Rig Veda*, 213–14.

5. Ibid., 149, 150.

6. Ibid., 99.

7. Ibid., 134–35.

8. F. Max Müller, ed. *Hymns of the Atharva-Veda*, 8.

9. Nikhilananda, *The Principal Upanishads*, 327–28.

10. Coward, Neufeldt, and Neumaier, eds., *Readings in Eastern Religions*, 28.

11. The expression is found in Chandogya Upanishad 6.8.7.

12. Jacobs, *The Principal Upanishads*, 267.

13. Ibid., 34.

14. The three categories of the Puranas are as follows: Those that honor (1) Vishnu (Vishnu Purana, Bhagavata Purana, Padma Purana, Naradiya Purana, Garuda Purana, Varaha Purana), (2) Brahma (Brahma Purana, Brahma-vaivarta Purana, Bhavisya Purana, Brahmanda Purana, Vamana Purana, Markandeya Purana), and (3) Shiva (Vayu Purana, Matsya Purana, Linga Purana, Skanda Purana, Agni Purana, Kurma Purana).

15. See "Deva," in Bowker, *Oxford Dictionary of World Religions*, 271.

16. A helpful outline of some of the Hindu responses to colonialism is presented in Embree, *Hindu Tradition*, chaps. 14–15. This classic introduction to Hinduism divides the Hindu responses into the two categories of acceptance and reform, and rejection and revival.

17. The quotation is from Rammohan Roy, *Translations of the Isa Upanishad*, pp. ii–iii, and is quoted in Embree, *Hindu Tradition*, 284.

Chapter 3: Buddhism

1. "Shakyamuni" refers to his tribe, "Gautama" is his clan, and "Siddhartha" is his personal name.

2. Cowell, *Buddhist Mahayana Texts*, 27–28.

3. Ibid., 30–31.

4. Ibid., 32.

5. Ibid., 34.

6. Ibid., 35.

7. Ibid., 51–52.

8. Ibid., 53.

9. Or "Middle Way."

10. "*Dhammacakkappavattana Sutta*" (Setting the Wheel of *Dhamma* in Motion), trans. Thanissaro Bhikkhu, *Access to Insight*, August 25, 2010. *Tathagata* means "one who has thus gone"—that is, one who has gone beyond the beyond—and refers to the Buddha. The historical Buddha preferred to use the term "tathagata" to refer to himself to communicate the absence of self—"The one who has arrived at the absolute."

11. Quoted in Strong, *Experience of Buddhism*, 35.

12. Grimes, *Concise Dictionary of Indian Philosophy*, 112–13.

13. *Dukkha* comes from *dur* = "bad" + *kha* = "state" and thus means literally "a bad state" because of impermanency.

14. Generally the prefix "a" or "an" functions as negation or indicates nonexistence of the thing. Technically, then, for instance, *anatta* (Pali) and *anātman* (Sanskrit) mean "nonabiding self" rather than "no-self."

15. R. King, *Indian Philosophy*, 79.

16. To make sense of human experience, the Buddha spoke of the existence of *skandhas*, which consist of five mutually conditioned bundles that do not exist in isolation from one another. Technically, *rupa* (material form) refers to the material givenness of experience, *vedana* (sensation) to the initial sensory apprehension of forms, *sanna* (cognition) to the classification of experience, *samskara* (disposition) to the volitional response that impacts the experience, and *vijnana* (consciousness) to the awareness of the six sensory images. Together these five work together to give an impression (appearance) of constancy and continuity. See R. King, *Indian Philosophy*, 79–81.

17. Ibid., 82.

18. Bowker, *Oxford Dictionary of World Religions*, 63.

19. The twelve links of dependent origination are as follows: (1) ignorance, (2) karmic actions, (3) consciousness, (4) body and mind, (5) senses, (6) sense impressions, (7) feelings, (8) craving, (9) clinging, (10) becoming, (11) rebirth, (12) old age and death. This process is followed by samsara, death, and rebirth, until liberation is achieved.

20. Grimes, *Concise Dictionary of Indian Philosophy*, 208.

21. Carter and Palihawadana, *The Dhammapada*, 20.

22. *Trikaya* (Sanskrit, *trikāya*; "three sheaths" of the Buddha) consist of (1) *Dharmakaya*— the sheath of the law, which is unmanifest, the reality, the void, the Absolute, which is the universal and transcendent Buddha; (2) *Sambhogakaya*—the sheath of enjoyment, manifest only to those with faith, in which Buddha dwells on earth or beyond; and (3) *Niranakaya*—the sheath of transformation, which is manifest empirically, and refers to the historical Buddha. Grimes, *Concise Dictionary of Indian Philosophy*, 322.

23. The countries and the Buddhist missionaries, in parentheses, that were sent include (1) Kasmira-Gandhara [Kashmir] (Majjhantikathera), (2) Mahisamandala [Mysore, India] (Mahadevathera), (3) Vanavasi [Tamil Nadu, India] (Rakkhitathera), (4) Aparantaka [Gujarat, India] (Yona-Dhammarakkhitathera), (5) Maharattha [Kālavāpi, Sri Lanka] (Mahadhammarakkhitathera), (6) Yona (Maharakkhitathera), (7) Himavanta (Majjhimathera), (8) Suvannabhumi [scholars debate location as being in either Southeast Asia or southern India] (Sonathera and Uttarathera), (9) Lankadipa [Sri Lanka] (Mahamahindathera). Furthermore, Asoka established embassies to the northwest (i.e., Syria, Egypt, Macedonia), to the east (i.e., lower Burma [Myanmar] and central Thailand), and to the south (i.e., southern India, Ceylon [Sri Lanka]). Buddhist monks most likely accompanied the embassies.

24. Harvey, *Introduction to Buddhism*, 101.

25. Buddhists worldwide do not use the same Pali term, "Theravada," to refer to the tradition. Other terms for the Theravada tradition include Shang-tso-pu (China), Jōzabu (Japan), and Sangjwabu (Korean).

26. Quotations from the Itivuttaka are from Bhikkhu, *Itivuttaka: The Group of Ones*.

27. A part of the Sutra Pitaka of the Pali Canon. This translation is quoted in Van Voorst, *Anthology of World Scriptures*, 4th ed., 99–100.

28. For instance, see Bowker, *Oxford Dictionary of World Religions*, 929.

29. In Van Voorst, *Anthology of World Scriptures*, 6th ed., 84.

30. Khyentse, *Heart of Compassion*, 27–28. These words were originally composed by the Tibetan Buddhist Ngulchu Thogme Zangpo (1295–1369) and are available at http://gnostictea chings.org/scriptures/buddhist/790-thirty-seven-verses-on-the-practices-of-bodhisattvas.html.

31. Dumoulin, *Zen Buddhism*, 1:9.

32. There are several good summaries of Tibetan Buddhism. See, for instance, Dalai Lama, *World of Tibetan Buddhism*; Powers, *Introduction to Tibetan Buddhism*; Wangyal, *Door of Liberation*; Richardson and Snellgrove, *Cultural History of Tibet*; Tucci, *Religions of Tibet*.

33. Harvey, *Introduction to Buddhism*, 145–47.

34. Bowker, *Oxford Dictionary of World Religions*, 713–14.

35. Harvey, *Introduction to Buddhism*, 260–61.

36. From Seng-Ts'an, *Hsin-hsin Ming*, "Verses on the Faith-Mind," available at http://www .csulb.edu/~wweinste/HsinHsinMing-print.html.

37. Suzuki, *Introduction to Zen Buddhism*, 58.

38. Suzuki, *Essays in Zen Buddhism*, 272; also quoted in Suzuki, *Introduction to Zen Buddhism*, 58.

39. Erye, *The Long Search* (DVD).

Chapter 4: Jainism

1. Loar, "In the Web of Life," *Los Angeles Times*, July 23, 1996.

2. Others suggest a date of 540–468 BCE or 549–477 BCE.

3. Quoted in Jacobi, *Jaina Sūtras*, 194–95.

4. Jacobi, *Gaina Sutras*, 194.

5. Jacobi, *Jaina Sūtras*, 80–81.

6. Ibid., 85.

7. *Acaranga Sutra* 2.15.20. Quoted in Müller, *Sacred Books of the East*, 195.

8. *Tattvas* (Sanskrit, "real," "truth," "the essence of things," "reality," "principle," "that-ness") is a term used in Indian philosophy that highlights the essence of anything, with each school of Indian philosophy advocating a different number of fundamental realities. Jainism recognizes nine fundamentals.

9. Varghese, *India*, 277–78.

10. The five categories of *ajiva* include (1) *pudgala*, matter that consists of uncreated and indestructible atoms; (2) *dharma-dravya*, the principle of motion; (3) *adharma-dravya*, the principle of rest; (4) *akasha*, space; and (5) *kala*, time. According to Jainism, the *jiva* has been in contact with *ajiva* from the beginning of time, and together they comprise reality. See Bowker, *Oxford Dictionary of World Religions*, 36.

11. Radhakrishnan and Moore, *Sourcebook in Indian Philosophy*, 254.

12. Nyayavijayaji, *Jaina Darśana*, 19.

13. Ibid., 25.

14. Dundas, *Jains*, 15.

15. Ibid., 15–16.

16. Bowker, *Oxford Dictionary of World Religions*, 953.

17. Ibid., 239.

18. Quoted in Embree, *Sources of Indian Tradition*, 1:80–82.

19. Nyayavijayaji, *Jaina Darśana*, 94.

20. Karan Singh, *A Treasury of Indian Wisdom*, 52–53.

21. Van Voorst, *Anthology of World Scriptures*, 6th ed., 117.

22. Jacobi, *Jaina Sūtras*, 79–80.

23. Ibid., 87.

24. Karan Singh, *A Treasury of Indian Wisdom*, 51–52.

25. *Acaranga Sutra* 1.8.6.1. Quoted in Dundas, *Jains*, 42.

26. You may recall that Triratna (Three Jewels) is a Sanskrit term employed by Buddhists as well to describe the fundamental refuges (Jewels) of Buddha, dharma, and *sangha*.

27. Quoted in Jacobi, *Jaina Sūtras*, 52.

28. Radhakrishnan and Moore, *Sourcebook in Indian Philosophy*, 257–58.

29. Available at http://www.jainnetwork.com/Prayers-and-Rituals-Ajainism_4/.

30. Jaini, *The Jaina Path of Purification*, 226–27.

31. Bowker, *Oxford Dictionary of World Religions*, 282.

Chapter 5: Sikhism

1. For instance, see Gohil and Sidhu, "Sikh Turban."

2. For a helpful general overview of the Sikh diaspora, as well as other south Indian communities, in Great Britain, see Brown, *Global South Asians*.

3. McLeod, "Influence of Islam," 302.

4. Noted in McLeod, *Exploring Sikhism*, 24.

5. For instance, see Lai, *Legacy of Muslim Rule in India*; Richards, *Mughal Empire*. Goel's *Hindu Temples* critiques Mughal rule and documents, among other things, forms of cultural and religious destruction.

6. See McLeod, *Exploring Sikhism*, 6.

7. Kitagawa, *Religious Traditions of Asia*, 112.

8. Ibid.

9. In Embree, *Sources of Indian Tradition*, 1:505.

10. Ibid., 1:501.

11. Ibid., 1:503.

12. Hinnells, *Handbook of Living Religions*, 318.

13. Available at http://www.srigurugranth.org/0044.html.

14. G. Singh, *History of the Sikh People*, 237.

15. Hinnells, *Handbook of Living Religions*, 315.

16. Dusenbery, "A Sikh Diaspora?," 24.

17. Mansukhani, *Introduction to Sikhism*, 48.

18. Baldev Singh, "Is Guru Nanak Hindu or Muslim?"

Chapter 6: Taoism and Confucianism

1. For more information, visit http://www.taoist.org/content/standard.asp?name=Home.

2. Unless otherwise indicated, quotations from the Tao Te Ching are from Lao Tsu, *Tao Te Ching*, trans. Gia-Fu Feng and Jane English (New York: Vintage Books, 1972).

3. Barrett, Kurian, and Johnson, *World Christian Encyclopedia*, 4.

4. See Sommer, *Chinese Religion*, vii.

5. Jaspers, *Origin and Goal of History*.

6. Many people confuse Qin Shi Huang with the Yellow Emperor of China (Huang Di). The Yellow Emperor was an ancient legendary figure, a cultural hero, born around 2704 BCE, who introduced the familiar Chinese cultural elements of carts, boats, wooden houses, and writing.

7. Thompson, *Chinese Way in Religion*, 57.

8. Since each chapter is fairly short and lacks specific verse notations, the references provided for the Tao Te Ching quotations in this chapter include just the chapter number.

9. Bowker, *Oxford Dictionary of World Religions*, 1047.

10. Sōhō, *Zen Teachings*, 59.

11. Zhiming, *Tao Te Ching*, 27.

12. Ibid., 118.

13. It is interesting to note that some translations of the Tao Te Ching use the word "God" instead of "emperors," which gives the passage a more pungent meaning.

14. Walker, trans., *Tao Te Ching of Lao Tzu*, 4.

15. Lao Tsu, *Tao Te Ching*, chap. 6.

16. Bowker, *Oxford Dictionary of World Religions*, 1047.

17. Mitchell, trans., *Tao Te Ching*, n.p.

18. See Zhuangzi, *Book of Chuang-tzu*, xxii.

19. Zhuangzi, *Teachings and Sayings of Chuang Tzu*, 26.

20. Creel, *What Is Taoism?*, 42.

21. Chan, *Source Book in Chinese Philosophy*, 189.

22. Sommer, *Chinese Religion*, 149.

23. See Bowker, *Oxford Dictionary of World Religions*, 554.

24. Sommer, *Chinese Religion*, 149.

25. Ibid., 150.

26. The Chinese believed that all things were composed of breaths; in the beginning the Nine Breaths mingled in Chaos. When the world emerged, the breaths separated, with purer breaths rising to create the sky and the grosser breaths descending to create the earth. Human bodies consist of gross breaths, so human beings need the Original Breath, the pure breath that enables the union with eternal Essence. See Thompson, *Chinese Way in Religion*, 61.

27. Company, *To Live as Long as Heaven and Earth*, 20.

28. Ibid., 30.

29. Legge, *Li Ki*, 239.

30. For instance, see Neville, *Boston Confucianism*.

31. Ibid., 17.

Chapter 7: Judaism

1. The Former Prophets contains the books of Joshua, Judges, Samuel, and Kings, and the Latter Prophets contains the books of Isaiah, Jeremiah, Ezekiel, and the Minor Prophets (i.e., Hosea, Joel, Amos, Obadiah, Jonah, Micah, Nahum, Habakkuk, Zephaniah, Haggai, Zechariah, and Malachi).

2. See http://www.jewishencyclopedia.com/articles/7698-hillel.

3. Bloxham, *The Final Solution*, 272.

4. De Lange, *Introduction to Judaism*, 44.

5. Ibid., 72.

6. Cohn-Sherbok, *Judaism*, 267.

7. Dorff, *Conservative Judaism*, 145.

Chapter 8: Christianity

1. See Dana Robert, "Shifting Southward: Global Christianity since 1945," *International Bulletin of Missionary Research*, 24, no. 2 (April 2000): 50–58.

2. Lupieri, *The Mandaeans*, 207.

3. The New Testament is divided into four Gospels, the book of Acts, thirteen Pauline epistles (letters attributed to Paul), seven general epistles (letters addressed to the church at large), and the book of Revelation (the final book of the New Testament).

4. Marius, *Martin Luther*, 355.

5. Roberts and Donaldson, *Ante-Nicene Fathers*, 3:246.

6. Parts of this section are gleaned from Andrew Walls, "The Gospel as Prisoner and Liberator of Culture," in his *Missionary Movement in Christian History*, 3–15. I recommend the entire book for its clear and engaging presentation of Christianity's engagement with culture.

7. For an introduction to some of the challenges and opportunities afforded Christians in the Global South, see Sanneh, *Disciples of All Nations*; Sanneh, *Whose Religion Is Christianity?*; Jenkins, *Next Christendom*; Jenkins, *New Faces of Christianity*; and Jenkins, *God's Continent*.

8. Walls, *Missionary Movement in Christian History*, 7.

9. Farhadian, *Christian Worship Worldwide*, discusses issues at the intersection of Christian worship and cultures and presents case studies of Christian worship in several locations in the Global South.

10. See Robert, "Shifting Southward."

11. Barrett, Johnson, and Crossing, "Missiometrics 2008."

12. M. L. King, *Testament of Hope*, 286.

13. Cox, *Cox's Book of Modern Saints and Martyrs*, 144.

14. See the online *Dictionary of African Christian Biography* for biographies, photos, and histories of African leaders, available at http://www.dacb.org/index.html.

15. Sanneh, *Whose Religion Is Christianity?*, 15.

16. Data on denominational affiliation and theological orientation comes from research provided by the Hartford Institute for Religion Research, available at http://hirr.hartsem.edu/megachurch/definition.html. According to the Hartford study, "the majority of megachurches (over sixty percent) are located in the southern Sunbelt of the United States—with California, Texas, Georgia, and Florida having the highest concentrations."

17. See McKnight, "Five Streams of the Emerging Church."

Chapter 9: Islam

1. Yusuf Ali's commentary on these verses notes, "*Iqra* may mean 'read,' or 'recite or rehearse,' or 'proclaim aloud,' the object understood being Allah's Message. In worldly letters [Muhammad] was unversed, but with spiritual knowledge his mind and soul were filled, and now had come the time when he must stand forth to the world and declare his mission" (*Modern English Translation*, trans. Ali, 1434).

2. Al-Bukhari 1:1; also in Ali, *Religion of Islam*, 20.

3. Their formal names are Abu Bakr As-Siddiq (Abdallah ibn Abi Quhafa) (c. 573–634), Umar ibn al-Khattab (c. 586–644), Usman ibn Affan (Uthman ibn Affan) (c. 579–656), and 'Ali ibn Abi Talib (c. 598–661).

4. Sunni hadith include *al-Bukhari* (d. 870), *Muslim* (d. 875), *al-Tirmidhi* (d. 892), *al-Nasai* (d. 915), *Ibn Maja* (d. 886), and *Abu Dawud* (d. 888), while the Shia hadith include *al-Kulayni* (d. 940), *al-Qummi* (d. 991), and *al-Tusi* (d. 1068).

5. Sanneh, *Translating the Message*, 253.

6. Khaldun, *Muqaddimah*, 2:156.

7. Esposito, *Oxford Dictionary of Islam*, 87.

8. Levy, *Social Structure of Islam*, 150.

9. Denny, *Introduction to Islam*, 190.

10. Ibid., 190.

11. One who exercises *ijtihad* is a *mujtahid*, meaning that the jurist has the ability to deduct religious rulings from the Qur'an and sunnah. In order to engage in *fiqh*, a *mujtahid* needs to know the following: (1) Arabic grammar, in order to understand the Qur'an; (2) *tafsir*, or qur'anic exegesis; (3) logic, in order to know how to define and deduce knowledge; (4) science of traditions, so that the *mujtahid* knows traditions and sources of knowledge of Islamic law; (5) science of *rijal*, the knowledge of the individuals in the chains of narrations in the hadith to verify the strength of the tradition; and (6) principles of Islamic jurisprudence, the rules that are applied to all the different sections of Islamic jurisprudence.

12. Denny, *Introduction to Islam*, 190.

13. Nimah Nawwab, "The Day of Arafah and Its Preparation," from *Understanding Islam*, available at http://www.onislam.net.

14. Portions of this section first appeared in Charles E. Farhadian, "Redeeming Islam," *Westmont Magazine* (Winter 2007): 12–16.

15. W. C. Smith, *Islam in Modern History*, 41.

16. Esposito, *Islam*, 137.

17. Roelle, *Islam's Mandate*, 99.

18. Rafiabadi, *Challenges to Religions and Islam*, 117–18.

19. Tahi-Farouki and Nafi, *Islamic Thought in the Twentieth Century*, 307.

20. See Sen, *Identity and Violence*, 15.

Chapter 10: New Religious Movements

1. For instance, see Enroth, *Guide to New Religious Movements*; Enroth, *Churches That Abuse*; Bromley and Melton, *Cults, Religion, and Violence*; Lewis and Melton, *Perspectives on the New Age*; Daschke and Ashcraft, *New Religious Movements*; Partridge and Melton, *New Religions*; Dawson, *Cults and New Religious Movements*; Glock and Bellah, *New Religious Consciousness*.

2. According to the National Council of Churches' *Yearbook of American & Canadian Churches* (2012), the largest religious bodies in the United States are as follows: Roman Catholic Church, 68,202,492 members; Southern Baptist Convention, 16,136,044; United Methodist Church, 7,679,850; Church of Jesus Christ of Latter-Day Saints, 6,157,238; Church of God in Christ, 5,499,875; National Baptist Convention, USA, 5,197,512; and Evangelical Lutheran Church in America, 4,274,855. It is noteworthy that four of the twenty-five largest churches are Pentecostal in belief and practice. Data also available at http://www.ncccusa.org/news/120209yearbook2012.html.

3. McConkie, *Mormon Doctrine*, 576.

4. Spencer W. Kimball, *Official Declaration—2*, Church of the Latter-Day Saints, June 8, 1978. Available at https://www.lds.org/scriptures/dc-testament/od/2?lang=eng.

5. Young, *Essential Brigham Young*, 99.

6. The notion that Jesus needed to be saved, and thus was saved, is attributed to Sidney Rigdon (1793–1876), an influential early leader of the LDS whose theology is recorded in J. Smith, *Lectures on Faith*.

7. Available at http://www.mormonbeliefs.com/lectures_on_faith.htm.

8. See https://www.lds.org/scriptures/pgp/a-of-f?lang=eng.

9. Dick, *William Miller and the Advent Crisis*, 96–97.

10. The "Twenty-Eight Fundamental Beliefs" of the Seventh-Day Adventists presented here are a summary of the beliefs as they appear on the Seventh-Day Adventist website, available at http://www.adventist.org/beliefs/fundamental/index.html.

11. One study showed that Adventists in California lived four to ten years longer than the average person in California. See Buettner, "Secrets of Long Life."

12. Eddy, *Church Manual of The First Church of Christ, Scientist*, 17–18.

13. See the Theosophical Society website at http://www.ts-adyar.org/.

14. Blavatsky, *Secret Doctrine*, 1:14.

15. Ibid., 1:38.

16. See the Maharishi University of Management website at http://www.mum.edu/.

17. Sappel and Welkos, "The Mind behind the Religion," A1.

18. "Engram," *The Official Scientology and Dianetics Glossary*, Church of Scientology International, available at http://www.scientology.org/gloss.htm.

19. Babington and Cooperman, "The Rev. Moon Honored at Hill Reception," A1.

20. Ibid.

21. Saayman and Kritzinger, eds., *Mission in Bold Humility*, 56.

Glossary

Abduh, Muhammad (1849–1905) Egyptian Islamic jurist, religious scholar, and liberal reformer; regarded as a key founding figure of Islamic modernism, breaking with the rigidity of Muslim ritual.

Abhidharma Ancient Theravada Buddhist texts that contain detailed philosophical and scientific analyses of doctrinal material appearing in the Buddhist Sutras; elaborations of the teachings of the Buddha.

Abu Bakr (573–634) Senior Companion (Sahabi) and father-in-law of Prophet Muhammad; ruled over Rashidun Caliphate (632–34) as first Rightly Guided Caliph after the death of Prophet Muhammad; referred to as al-Siddiq (The Truthful) among later generations of Muslims.

Abu Talib (549–619) Leader of the Banu Hashim clan of the Quraysh tribe of Mecca in Arabia; married to Fatimah bint Asad and was an uncle of Prophet Muhammad; protected the young Prophet until Abu Talib's death.

Acharya Nagarjuna (c. 150–c. 250) One of the most important Buddhist philosophers after Gautama Buddha; the founder of the Madhyamika school of Mahayana Buddhism.

Adi Granth Sikh scriptures compiled by Guru Arjan Dev; also referred to as the Final Guru or Sri Guru Granth Sahib.

Aggadic midrashim Homiletic and nonlegalistic exegetical texts from the classical rabbinic literature of Judaism; compendium of rabbinic homilies that incorporate moral exhortations and moral advice.

Agni Hindu Vedic deity, God of fire and ancestor of sacrifices; a messenger from and to other Gods; the mouthpiece of the Gods.

ahimsa In Hinduism, Buddhism, and Jainism, nonviolence to all living things; avoiding violence; doing no harm; the central concept in Jainism.

ajiva Jain concept of anything that does not have a soul or life; nonliving substance opposed to *jiva* (soul, life), e.g., pencil, plastic, chair.

Akali Dal Khara Sauda Bar Twentieth-century Sikh reform movement that worked to liberate Sikh shrines (*gurdwaras*) from control by the dominating Udasi and Nirmala priests, who considered shrines and lands associated with them as their personal property.

Akbar (the Great) (1542–1605) Third Mughal emperor, son of Emperor Humayun and grandson of Emperor Babur; known for religious tolerance and appreciation for the arts.

Al-Aqsa Mosque Third holiest site in Islam; site on which the Dome Mosque sits, along with the Dome of the Rock in the Old City of Jerusalem;

the location in Judaism where the temple is generally believed to have stood.

al-Banna, Hasan (1906–49) Egyptian schoolteacher and imam in Islam; founder of the Muslim Brotherhood, one of the largest and most influential twentieth-century Muslim revivalist movements.

alchemy Art of transmuting common metals, often into gold, for use in the attempt to achieve perfection, longevity or immortality; practice of the attempt to create an elixir of immorality.

'Ali (600–661) Cousin and son-in-law of Prophet Muhammad; the fourth and last of the Rightly Guided Caliphs, according to Sunni tradition; the first Imam, according to Shia tradition; son of Abu Talib and the first male convert to Islam.

Allah Arabic word for God; from the Arabic *al-ilah* (the God); used mainly by Muslims to refer to God, but also by Arab Christians and by Indonesian, Malaysian, and Maltese Christians.

Allahu Akbar Arabic term for "God is greater" or "God is [the] Greatest"; used in Islamic prayers, as an expression of Islamic faith, in times of distress, to celebrate a victory; also known as the *Tabir*.

Allen, Horace (1858–1932) Protestant medical missionary and diplomat from the United States to Korea at the end of the Joseon Dynasty (1392–1897).

al-Mahdi Divinely guided one; an eschatological figure who Muslims believe will usher in an era of justice and true belief just prior to the end of time; an honorific title applied to Prophet Muhammad and the first four caliphs by the earliest Muslims; a messianic deliverer who would return to champion Islam.

al-Masih In Arabic, "Messiah," "anointed one," "savior"; Muslim view of Jesus as Messiah (al-Masih), understood as prophet or messenger; Islamic messianism combines the belief that Jesus is the Messiah and will return at the end of time with the belief that a divinely appointed Mahdi (guide) will appear around the same time to deliver people from tyranny and oppression. *See also* al-Mahdi.

al-Qur'an The Recitation; the central sacred text of Islam, which Muslims believe to be the verbatim word of God given directly through angel Gabriel to Prophet Muhammad from 610 to 632 CE; only in Arabic; considered the finest piece of literature in the Arabic language. *See also* Qur'an.

al-Rahim One of the ninety-nine names for Allah in Islam; "the Exceedingly Merciful."

al-Rahman One of the ninety-nine names for Allah in Islam; "the Exceedingly Compassionate."

al-Wahhab, Muhammad ibn Abd (1703–92) Arabian Islamic Salafi theologian and founder of the Wahhabi movement; his pact with Muhammad bin Saud helped to establish the first Saudi state (1744), beginning a dynastic alliance between their families that continues to present-day Saudi Arabia; sought to purify Islam by returning Muslims to the original principles of Islam and eliminating corruptions that had crept into Islam; Wahhabism often refers to a puritanical form of Islam.

Amaladoss, Michael (b. 1936) Jesuit Indian theologian and writer born in Tamil Nadu, India; strong proponent of interreligious dialogue.

amrit Sanctified solution of sugar and water (nectar) used in a Sikh ceremony; "immortality"; related etymologically to the Greek "ambrosia."

Amritsar City in the state of Punjab, northwestern India; the spiritual center for the Sikh religion and home to the Harmandir Sahib, known as the Golden Temple; Sikh Guru Ram Das began the construction of the Golden Temple.

526

Anabaptist Christians of the Radical Reformation of sixteenth-century Europe, including the Amish, the Hutterites, and the Mennonites, who practice rebaptizing converts who have already been baptized as infants, arguing for "believer's baptism."

Analects (Lunyu) Collection of the words and actions of Confucius and his disciples as well as the discussions they held; most important text in Confucianism.

anatta Buddhist idea of "no-self" or the illusion of "self"; notion that all things perceived by the senses have no independent existence or substance.

anicca Buddhist notion of impermanence, one of the essential doctrines or three marks of Buddhism; all conditioned existence is in a constant state of flux; nothing is permanent.

anonymous Christianity Concept introduced by Jesuit theologian Karl Rahner (1904–84) declaring that people who have never heard the gospel might be saved through Christ as they faithfully respond to their own religious traditions.

anti-Semitism Discrimination, prejudice, or hatred against Jews based on their Jewish heritage.

aparigraha Jain concept of nonpossessiveness; limits possessions to what is necessary or important; one of the five principles of Jainism (also including nonviolence, not stealing, celibacy, and multiplicity of perspectives).

Apocrypha "To hide away"; term applied to the books in the Roman Catholic Bible and the Eastern Orthodox Bible that are not in the Protestant Bible; in biblical literature, works outside an accepted canon of Scripture.

Apollinarius (d. 390) Bishop of Laodicea in Syria, best known in church history as the chief opponent of Arianism.

apologists Any of the Christian writers, primarily in the second century, who attempted to provide a defense of Christianity; many of their writings were addressed to Roman emperors; generally refers to one who speaks or writes in defense of someone or something.

apostle One who is sent away; a messenger and ambassador; one sent away to convey a message; messenger; in Latin, "apostle" is translated into "mission," from which comes the English word "missionary."

apostolic authority Relating to a succession of spiritual authority from the twelve apostles of Christ; relating to or derived from the teaching or practice of the twelve apostles.

apotheosis Deification; elevation to divine rank; glorification of a subject to a divine level; idea that an individual has been raised to a godlike stature.

Appenzeller, Henry G. (1858–1902) Methodist missionary who, with four other missionaries (Horace Allen, Horace Underwood, William Scranton, and Mary Scranton), introduced Protestant Christianity into Korea.

Aranyakas "Forest books"; ancient Hindu Vedic texts that record philosophical speculation on the power of the Vedic sacrificial system; contains secret explanations of the allegorical meanings of Vedic rituals.

arhat In Theravada Buddhism, "one who is worthy"; a perfected person who has attained nirvana (liberation) or those who are far advanced along the path of Enlightenment but who may not have attained full Buddhahood.

Arianism Doctrines of Arius, denying that Jesus was of the same substance as God and holding instead that he was the highest of created beings; viewed as heretical by the Christian church.

Arius (256–336) Ascetic Christian priest in Alexandria, Egypt; opposed trinitarian Christology, making his ideas a primary topic of the First Ecumenical Council of Nicaea.

Armageddon According to the book of Revelation, Armageddon will be

527

the site of a battle during the "end of the world," interpreted either literally or symbolically; also used in a generic sense to refer to any "end of the world" scenario; in the New Testament, the place where the kings of the earth under demonic leadership will wage war on the forces of God at the end of history.

artha   Purpose, meaning, cause, motive, wealth; material prosperity; one of the four goals of life in Hinduism.

Aryan   "Noble people"; Indo-Iranian, Indo-European people influential in early Hindu Vedic tradition.

asatya   In Indian religions, untruthful words; a false statement; lying.

Ashimolowo, Matthew (b. 1952)   Nigerian-born senior pastor of Kingsway International Christian Centre (KICC) in London, who promotes prosperity theology (that financial blessing is the will of God for Christians and that faith always increases one's material wealth).

Ashkenazic Jews   Ethnoreligious group of Jews who trace their origins to the indigenous Israelite tribes of Canaan in the Middle East and eventually settled along the Rhine in Germany; today, descriptive for descendants of these settlers and those Jews who established communities in central Europe centuries later.

ashrama   Stages of life in Hinduism (student, householder, retirement, renunciant).

Asr   Afternoon daily prayer of Muslims; the third of five daily prayers of Islam; also referred to as *salat al-asr*.

asrava   Part of Jain karmic theory referring to the influence of the body and mind causing the soul to generate karma; influx of karma; ways in which the soul is exposed. *See also* Nav Tattvas.

asteya   Jain and Hindu notion of "avoidance of stealing" or "nonstealing."

astrology   Belief system that sees a relationship between astronomical phenomena and events in the human world; sometimes uses horoscopes and human personality to predict future events.

Athanasius (328–73)   Bishop of Alexandria; renowned Christian theologian, church father, and chief defender of trinitarianism (against Arianism); noted Egyptian Christian leader of the fourth century.

Atharva Veda   Collection of Hindu sacred texts consisting of spells and incantations, speculative hymns, and charms to repel evil influences.

atman   Self, soul; in Hinduism, the true self of an individual beyond identification with phenomena, the essence of an individual; in Buddhism, refers to self, ego, stressing the nonself teachings of the Lord Buddha (*anatma*); in Jainism, the soul, the principle of sentience and one of the *tattvas* (fundamental substances forming part of the universe).

atonement   In theology, a doctrine that describes how human beings can be reconciled with God; in Christian theology, refers to forgiving and pardoning of sin through the death and resurrection of Jesus Christ.

Augustine (354–430)   Church father and bishop in the Roman province of Africa whose writings are considered critically important in the development of Western Christianity and philosophy.

Aurangzeb   Sixth Mughal emperor, who ruled over most of the Indian subcontinent; a pious Muslim, he rejected the religious tolerance of his predecessors.

avatar   Descent of a Hindu deity to Earth; also incarnation; usually associated with Vishnu.

avidyā   Hindu and Buddhist concept of "ignorance" or "delusion"; when one is blind to reality; ignorance of reality as it really is.

avirati   Jain notion of nonrestraint that is the second cause of bondage; inability to refrain voluntarily from evil actions that harm oneself or others.

Axial Age Term coined by German philosopher Karl Jaspers to describe a period in which revolutionary thinking emerged in Persia, India, China, and the West (c. 800–200 BCE).

Ayodhya Ancient city of India, considered the birthplace of the Lord Vishnu avatar Rama and the setting of the Hindu epic Ramayana; located at the south end of the Indian state of Uttar Pradesh.

Babur (1483–1530) Conqueror from central Asia who laid the foundation of the Mughal Dynasty in the Indian subcontinent; he was a descendant of Genghis Khan through his mother.

Babylonian Talmud Important text of rabbinic Judaism compiled in late antiquity (third to fifth centuries) recording opinions of rabbis of Israel and Babylonia.

Balthasar, Hans Urs von (1905–88) Swiss theologian, Roman Catholic priest, prolific writer, considered one of the most important theologians of the twentieth century; along with Karl Rahner and Bernard Lonergan, he sought to offer an intellectual, faithful response to Western modernism's dismissal of Christianity; among his writing, he is well known for his sixteen-volume systematics, referred to as Trilogy.

bandha Part of Jain karmic theory referring to the bondage of karma to the soul.

bar mitzvah "Son of commandment"; ceremony when Jewish boys become accountable for their actions and become a bar mitzvah, a full-fledged member of the Jewish community with all its moral responsibilities.

Barth, Karl (1886–1968) Swiss Reformed theologian, regarded as the greatest Protestant theologian and most prolific theologian of the twentieth century; writings include *Church Dogmatics*, a thirteen-volume work, and *The Epistle to the Romans*; emphasized the paradoxical nature of divine truth.

bat mitzvah "Daughter of commandment"; ceremony when Jewish girls become accountable for their actions and become a bat mitzvah, a full-fledged member of the Jewish community with all its moral responsibilities.

beitzah In Judaism, the roasted egg used on the seder plate, said to be a reminder of the other festival sacrifice offered in the temple in Jerusalem; symbolizing sorrow at the destruction of the temple along with the hope that it will be rebuilt.

Besant, Annie (1847–1933) Prominent British socialist, theosophist, writer, women's rights activist, supporter of Irish and Indian self-determination; member of the Theosophical Society; helped established the Central Hindu College in India (1898); elected president of the Indian National Congress (1917); promoter of theosophy until she died.

Bhagavad Gita Hindu scripture, part of the massive Hindu epic the Mahabharata; tells the story of dialogues between Prince Arjuna and Lord Krishna about liberation.

bhakti Hindu and Buddhist religious devotion; in worship, warm devotion to the divine.

Bhattal, Rajinder Kaur (b. 1931) First woman Sikh chief minister of the Punjab, with a reputation for being a strong leader.

bimah In Judaism, the pedestal on which the Torah scrolls are placed when they are being read in the synagogue; the pulpit.

Bismallah al-Rahman al-Rahim "In the name of God, the Most Gracious, the Most Merciful"; Arabic phrase recited before each *surah* (chapter) of the Qur'an, except the ninth *surah*; usually the first phrase in the preamble of the constitutions of Islamic countries; known as *Basmala*.

Black Stone On the eastern cornerstone of the Qa'abah (cube, House of Allah) in the center courtyard of the Great

Mosque at Mecca; Muslim object of veneration, probably dating from the pre-Islamic religion of Mecca.

Blavatsky, Madame Helena (1831–91) Russian-German occultist who, with Henry Steel Olcott, established a research and publishing institute called the Theosophical Society, promoting the universal brotherhood of humanity without regard to race, creed, or color; sought to discover universal spiritual teachings throughout the world; wrote *The Secret Doctrine*. *See also* Theosophical Society.

bodhisattva In Buddhism, a "Buddha-to-be": anyone who is motivated by compassion, has achieved Enlightenment, and then takes the bodhisattva vow to help all sentient beings to be liberated; also refers to the Buddha in his former lives.

Book of Mormon Sacred text of the Church of Jesus Christ of Latter-Day Saints; Mormons believe the book contains writings of ancient prophets who lived on the American continent (c. 2200 BCE–421 CE); a record written on golden plates discovered and translated by Prophet Joseph Smith Jr.

Boston Confucianism Group of "New Confucians" from Boston, of whom the best known are Tu Wei-ming, of Harvard University, and Robert Neville, of Boston University; the perspective attempts to adapt Confucianism to Western culture.

Brahma Hindu God of creation; one of the Trimurti, as father of Manu; also known as "Lord of Speech and Sound."

Brahman In Hinduism, the "unchanging reality" that cannot be exactly defined; conceived as both personal and impersonal, the essence of all living things; universal cosmic energy; "the thread of the thread"; the power operative in the sacrifice; the True Self.

Brahmanas Commentaries on the Vedas; analyses of the mythology, philosophy, and rituals of the Vedas.

Brahmins Scholarly, priestly class in traditional Hindu society.

Braide, Garrick Sokari Pioneer of revival in Africa (1882–1918); born in Niger Delta, Braide adopted a practical approach to teaching and contextualized the gospel among the delta people.

Bright, Bill (1921–2003) American evangelist, founder of Campus Crusade for Christ; wrote *The Four Spiritual Laws* (1952) and produced the *Jesus Film* (1979).

British Raj British rule in the Indian subcontinent (1858–1947); also period of dominion of Indian subcontinent under British control.

Buddha "Awakened one"; the first awakened being in our era, with Siddhartha Gautama being regarded as the supreme Buddha; one who is enlightened to reality.

caliphate Politico-religious state comprising the Muslim community and the lands and people under its dominion in the centuries following the death of Prophet Muhammad in 632 CE.

Calvin, John (1509–64) Influential French theologian and pastor during the Protestant Reformation; principal figure in the development of the system of Christian theology called Calvinism.

canon Standard or criterion; a group of literary works that are generally accepted as representing a field; a basis for judgment; Scripture.

canonicity Conforming to orthodox or well-established rules or patterns; the quality or state of being canonical.

Cappadocian fathers Basil the Great (330–79), Gregory of Nyssa (c. 332–95), and Gregory of Nazianzus (329–89), who advanced early Christian theology, particularly the doctrine of the Trinity.

Caro, Rabbi Joseph (1488–1575) Author of the *Shulkhan Arukh*, the last of the great medieval codes of Jewish law, one of the most respected compilations of Jewish law ever written.

Catholic   Generally, the "universal" church; specifically, the Roman Catholic Church.

Catholics   Members of the Roman Catholic Church, the world's largest Christian church with over 1.2 billion members; led by the pope; offices include cardinals, patriarchs, and diocesan bishops.

Chalcedon Definition   Defines the nature of Christ as two natures that "come together into one person and hypostasis"; arose during the Fourth Ecumenical Church Council (451); union of Christ's humanity and divinity, in one hypostasis (shared existence).

charoset   Mixture of fruit, wine, and nuts eaten at Jewish Passover seder to symbolize mortar used by the Jewish slaves in Egypt.

chi   In traditional Chinese culture, an active principle forming part of any living thing; life energy; life force; energy flow; central energy underlying traditional Chinese medicine; "breath."

Christ   "Anointed"; translation of the Hebrew, the Messiah, used as title for Jesus in the New Testament.

Christian Zionism   Belief among some Christians that the return of the Jews to the Holy Land and the establishment of the State of Israel (1948) is in accordance with biblical prophecy; that the ingathering of Jews in the State of Israel is the prerequisite for the second coming of Jesus Christ.

Christocentric   Theological position describing Jesus Christ as the central point of focus or theme around which all other theological positions are oriented.

Christology   Field of study within Christian theology concerned primarily with the nature and person of Jesus Christ.

Ch'un-ch'iu   Chinese classic text; Confucianism's "Spring and Autumn Annals," which chronicles the history of the State of Lu (772–481 BCE).

church fathers   Influential theologians, eminent Christian teachers, and bishops from the first to sixth centuries, whose scholarly works were used as a precedent for centuries; also referred to as apostolic fathers, patristic fathers.

Church of Christ, Scientist (Christian Science)   Founded in 1879 in Boston by Mary Baker Eddy (1821–1910), a church that seeks to "reinstate primitive Christianity and its lost element of healing"; nineteenth-century restorationist movement, along with Jehovah's Witnesses, Seventh-Day Adventists and Latter-Day Saints, that sought to restore the church; focus on physical healings and faith brought through Christian Science prayer; emphasizes absolute goodness and perfection of God, and that sin, disease, and death cannot be real; Eddy's *Science and Health with Key to the Scriptures*, along with the Bible, are their scriptures. *See also* Eddy, Mary Baker.

Church of Jesus Christ of Latter-Day Saints   Nineteenth-century Christian restorationist movement, similar to Jehovah's Witnesses, Seventh-Day Adventists, and Christian Science, that sought to restore the Christian church along the lines of the apostolic early church; headquartered in Salt Lake City, Utah, the Latter-Day Saints church believes in an open canon and continuing revelation; sacred texts include the Bible, as corrected by Prophet Joseph Smith Jr., *Pearl of Great Price*, Book of Mormon, and *Doctrine and Covenants*; also known as Mormons.

Church of Scientology   Founded in 1953 in Camden, New Jersey, by popular author L. Ron Hubbard (1911–86), an organization devoted to the practice and promotion of the Scientology belief system, emphasizing self-knowledge as a means of realizing full spiritual potential; seeks to analyze mental aberrations and to offer means for overcoming them.

Clement of Alexandria (c. 150–c. 215) Christian theologian who taught at the Catechetical School of Alexandria, educated in classical Greek philosophy and literature; united Greek philosophical traditions with Christian doctrine; teacher of Origen; also known as Titus Flavius Clemens.

cleromancy Form of divination, usually by casting lots, bones, stones, or dice, to illuminate the will of God or other supernatural power.

collective experience Experience characteristic of individuals acting in cooperation; concept used in social sciences.

Communist Manifesto, The One of the world's most influential publications; an 1848 work written by Karl Marx and Friedrich Engels that proposes a history of class struggle and the problems of capitalism.

Community of Christ American-based international church, established in 1930, that is part of the Latter-Day Saints movement, a restorationist movement; formerly known as the Reorganized Church of Jesus Christ of Latter-Day Saints; closest of the three branches of the Latter-Day Saints movement to mainline Protestantism, except for their belief in continuing prophetic revelation; headquarters in Independence, Missouri.

Companions Disciples, scribes, family of the Prophet Muhammad; those believed to have lived, interacted with, heard, or seen the Prophet Muhammad. In Sunni Islam, considered to be the most authoritative sources of information about the conduct of Prophet Muhammad; Shia consider many Companions guilty of preventing their first Imam (Ali ibn Abi Talib) from succeeding to the caliphate.

Confucius (551–479 BCE) Chinese teacher and philosopher who emphasized personal and governmental morality, correctness in human relationships, and justice; Confucius's thoughts were adopted during the Han Dynasty (206 BCE–220 CE) as state ideology in China.

Conservative Judaism Modern movement originating within Ashkenazic Judaism as a reaction against liberal religious positions taken by Reform Judaism; seeks to conserve Jewish traditions rather than reform or abandon them.

consubstantiation Theological doctrine describing the nature of the Christian Eucharist (Lord's Supper), holding that during the sacrament the fundamental substance of the body and blood of Christ are present alongside the substance of the bread and wine, which remain present.

Council of Chalcedon Fourth Ecumenical Church Council (451); repudiated the idea that Jesus had only one nature (Monophysitism), adopted the Chalcedonian Creed (hypostatic union).

Council of Constantinople Second Ecumenical Church Council (381); repudiated Arianism (that Christ was created by and subordinate to God the Father); declared that Christ is "born of the Father before all time."

Council of Ephesus Third Ecumenical Church Council (431); repudiated Nestorianism (emphasized disunion between the human and divine natures of Christ); proclaimed the Virgin Mary as the *Theotokos* (God-bearer); repudiated Pelagianism (that original sin did not taint human nature, thus rejecting the notion of inherited, generational sin).

Council of Jerusalem Early church council (c. 50) held in Jerusalem; affirmed that gentile converts to Christianity were not obligated to keep most of the Mosaic law, particularly male circumcision.

Council of Nicaea First Ecumenical Church Council (325); repudiated Arianism, declaring that Christ is homoousios (of the same substance) with the Father; recognized the primacy of the See of Rome, Alexandria, and Antioch.

covenant   Formal alliance, contract, or agreement made by God with a particular religious community or with humanity in general.

covenantal   Theological concept of the covenant (contract, promise) as an organizing principle for Christian theology.

Crowther, Samuel Ajayi (c. 1809–91)   Linguist and the first African Anglican bishop in Nigeria: a member of the Niger expedition of 1841.

cult   Ritual practice, from Latin, *cultus* (worship); a particular system of religious worship, especially with reference to its rituals and ceremonies; sociologically, a group having a sacred ideology and a set of rites centering around their sacred symbols; currently, a pejorative term for a new religious movement or group whose beliefs or practices are considered abnormal.

da'eef   Part of Islamic hadith classification, notably "weak" authenticity of the hadith.

Dalit   "Crushed"; traditionally, untouchables, outcastes, classless people; refers to those outside the Hindu class system.

Dar al-Harb   Territory of War; denotes place or territory bordering on Dar al-Islam (territory of Islam), whose leaders are called upon to convert to Islam; jurists trace the concept to Prophet Muhammad, who demanded that people choose between conversion and war; when leaders of Dar al-Harb accept Islam, the territory becomes part of Dar al-Islam.

Dar al-Islam   Territory of Islam; region of Muslim sovereignty where Islamic law prevails; abode, home, place of peace and submission; an area under the rule of Islam; compare to Dar al-Harb.

darshana   Hindu notion of seeing the divine; means "sight" and "to see"; refers to seeing the divine with reverence and devotion; also refers to Hindu philosophy.

Darwin, Charles (1809–82)   English naturalist who established the notion that all species of life have descended from common ancestors; advocated belief in natural selection as a form of evolution; author of *On the Origin of Species* (1859).

dasa   Ancient term for enemies of the Indo-Aryan tribes in the Rig Veda; also means "servant of God" and "devotee."

Das Kapital   Karl Marx's critique of the political economy of capitalism and the capitalist mode of production; the first volume was published in 1867.

dastar   Sikh head covering (Persian, "turban") mandatory for all Amritdhari (baptized) Sikh men; required for all members of the Khalsa; the *dastar* in central and South Asia connotes royalty and dignity.

Data   Sikh characteristic of God as the Great Giver.

Da Xue   The Great Learning, one of the four books in the Confucian Canon.

Deva   Deity; any benevolent supernatural being in Hinduism; devi is the feminine term, Goddess.

Devanandan, P. D. (1901–62)   Indian Protestant theologian, ecumenist, and notable pioneer in interreligious dialogues in India.

devapuja   In Jainism, worship of *tirthankaras* (spiritual role models, leaders).

dhamma   "That without which nothing can stand"; duty, teaching, truth; same as dharma.

dharma   In Hinduism, natural law governing conduct of an individual and a group; duty, custom, degree, vocation, and moral rectitude.

dharmasala   In Sikhism, a place of worship; village hospice that functions as a religious asylum, a place set apart so that believers could meet for worship;

predecessor to the Sikh *gurdwara* (place of worship).

dhimmi   In Islam, a protected scriptural minority; a non-Muslim citizen of an Islamic state; allowed rights of residence in return for taxes (*jizya*), accompanied by several other restrictions on dress, occupation, and residence; a covenant of protection with conquered "Peoples of the Books."

dhyani-chohan   In Theosophy, the Lord of meditation, the highest spiritual being; a general term for celestial beings beyond human evolution.

Dianetics   Set of metaphysical ideas and practices about the relationship between the mind and the body, created by Scientologist L. Ron Hubbard and practiced by followers of Scientology; a pseudoscience of dividing the mind into three parts (conscious, subconscious, and somatic), with the goal of removing the "reactive mind" that prevents happiness; use of "auditing," with a series of questions, to attempt to rid one of painful past experiences that cause the "reactive mind."

Dianetics: The Modern Science of Mental Health   Book by L. Ron Hubbard that set out self-improvement techniques (1950) based on Hubbard's description of the human mind; describes counseling ("auditing") techniques designed to rid one of engrams, mental images of past experience that produce negative emotional effects; the book was a major commercial success, yet met with major controversy because of its scientific invalidity.

diasporic people   People who have migrated or moved away from an established homeland; people settled far from their ancestral homelands; mass dispersions of people with common ethnic roots.

Digambara   One of two main sects of Jainism; "sky-clad"; a male-only ascetic tradition in which members shun all property and wear no clothes, being clothed by the sky, following the practice of Mahavira.

divination   Attempt to foresee; to gain insight into a situation or question; to divine by way of occultic ritual.

Divine Principle   Main theological textbook (1966) of the Unification Church; written by church founder Rev. Sun Myung Moon (1920–2012) and Moon's early disciple Hyo Won Eu (1914–70).

diwan   Main hall where Sikh congregational worship occurs in a *gurdwara* (worship center).

docetism   From the Greek, "to seem"; Christian heresy and one of the earliest sectarian doctrines that affirmed that Jesus Christ did not have a real or natural body during his life on earth but only an apparent or phantom one; became more fully developed as an important doctrinal position of gnosticism, a religious dualist system of belief arising in the second century that held that matter was evil and the spirit good.

Doctrine and Covenants   One of the four scriptures of the Church of Jesus Christ of Latter-Day Saints (Mormonism); contains the ongoing revelations from Prophet Joseph Smith Jr. to contemporary presidents of the Mormon church; new revelations received by the current Mormon president (prophet) are added to the Doctrine and Covenants.

dreidel   A four-sided spinning top played with during the Jewish holiday of Hanukkah; each side bears a letter of the Hebrew alphabet of an acronym (N-G-H-S) meaning "a great miracle happened there."

du'a   Appeal or innovation; usually refers to supplicatory prayers in Islam, regarded as a profound act of worship within Islam, when Muslims ask Allah for forgiveness and favors.

dualism   Denotes a state of two parts; a binary opposition, usually between good and evil.

dukkha   Suffering, stress, anxiety, dissatisfaction, dis-ease; the first truth of Buddhism.

dukkha-dukkha   Buddhist notion of obvious physical or emotional suffering, anxiety, dissatisfaction.

dukkha nirodha   Buddhist truth of the cessation of suffering (*dukkha*).

dukkha nirodha gamini patipada magga   Buddhist path leading to the cessation of suffering *(dukkha)*.

dukkha nirodha marga   Buddhist notion of the path toward the liberation of suffering (*dukkha*); also known as the Noble Eightfold Path.

dukkha samudaya   Buddhist term meaning "origin of suffering"; also known as the Second Noble Truth of Buddhism.

Durga   Hindu Goddess, depicted with multiple arms, carrying weapons, and riding a lion; she slays demons, such as Mahishasura, the buffalo demon.

Durkheim, Émile (1858–1917)   French sociologist, often considered the father of sociology; wrote about religious life, suicide, the division of labor in society.

ccumenical   Whole household of God; usually refers to Christian unity and cooperation across denominational lines.

Eddy, Mary Baker (1821–1910)   Founder of Christian Science, a restorationist movement; author of the movement's *Science and Health with Key to the Scriptures*, which focused on physical healing and miracles performed by Jesus.

Eid al-Adha   In Islam, Feast of the Sacrifice celebrated at the end of the annual pilgrimage to Mecca (hajj); unblemished animals are sacrificed in commemoration of the ram substituted by Allah when Abraham was commanded to sacrifice his son, Isma'il, as a test of faith; also known as Id al-Adha and Greater Bayram.

Eid-ul-Fitr   In Islam, Feast of the Breaking of the Fast celebrated at the end of Ramadan, the month of fasting; begins upon sighting of the crescent moon and lasts for three days; also known as Id al-Fitr and Lesser Bayram.

Eliade, Mircea (1907–86)   Romanian historian of religion; founder of the "history of religions" approach to studying religion; advocated the study of hierophanies (appearances of the sacred) as the basis of religion.

Elohim   God of Israel in the Old Testament; the Hebrew word "God"; a plural form of majesty, employed in the Old Testament for the one and only God of Israel whose personal name was revealed to Moses as YHWH (Yahweh).

emerging church   Christian movement of the late twentieth and early twenty-first centuries that crosses several theological boundaries—for example, as Protestant, post-Protestant, Catholic, evangelical, postevangelical, liberal, postliberal, conservative, post-conservative, Anabaptist, reformed, charismatic; attempt for Christians to live their faith in a late-modern or postmodern society.

emic   Insider perspective; an approach to investigation that illuminates how local people think; analysis of cultural phenomena from the perspective of one who participates in the culture being studied.

Emperor Constantine (c. 272–337)   Roman emperor known for being the first Roman emperor to convert to Christianity, proclaiming tolerance of all religions throughout the Roman Empire; summoned the Council of Nicaea (325), the First Ecumenical Church Council.

Emperor Hirohito (1901–89)   124th emperor of Japan, grandson of Emperor Meiji; reigned during Japan's imperial expansion, militarization, and involvement in World War II; today he is referred to as Emperor Showa (abundant benevolence).

emptiness   Buddhist doctrine of openness, thusness, absence of inherent existence in all phenomena.

engrams In Dianetics and Scientology, defined as mental images of a past experience that produce a negative emotional affect in an individual's life; a stimulus impression, mental trace.

Enlightenment European intellectual movement of the seventeenth and eighteenth centuries whose revolutionary ideas changed intellectual, scientific, cultural, and religious life; posited that reason was the primary source for legitimacy and authority.

etic Outsider perspective; analysis of cultural phenomena from the perspective of one who does not participate in the culture being studied.

Eucharist Christian sacrament, ritual commemoration of Jesus's Last Supper with his disciples, at which he gave them bread with the words, "This is my body," and wine with the words, "This is my blood"; a central focus of the Roman Catholic Mass; also referred to as Holy Communion, Sacrament of the Altar, the Lord's Supper.

evangelicalism Worldwide Protestant Christian movement that began in the 1730s, with the emergence of the Methodists in England, and became significant in the United States during the Great Awakenings of the eighteenth and nineteenth centuries; Christian movement that emphasizes conversion (being "born again"), high regard for biblical authority, proclamation of the saving death and resurrection of Jesus Christ offering forgiveness, and activities to share the gospel in word and action.

exclusivists In Christian theology of religions, those who insist on the finality and uniqueness of the biblical revelation; deny the possibility of salvation and salvific revelation outside Christianity; assert that there is no overlap, in any way, between Christianity and other religions.

Fajr First of five daily prayers in Islam; begins at dawn.

fall In Christianity, the transition of the first human beings from a state of innocent obedience to God to a state of guilty disobedience to God and the resulting corruption of the entire natural world, including human nature, causing people to be born into original sin.

Falun Gong "Dharma Wheel Practice"; a spiritual practice first introduced in China in 1992, combining meditation, slow-moving *qigong* (balancing intrinsic life energy), and moral philosophy.

Falwell, Jerry (1933–2007) Influential American fundamentalist Southern Baptist pastor, televangelist, and political commentator; founded Thomas Road Baptist Church, Lynchburg, Virginia, and Liberty University; cofounded the Moral Majority (1979); promoted Christian fundamentalism.

faqih An expert in *fiqh*, or Islamic jurisprudence; a jurist, someone who has deep understanding of Islamic legislative rulings, pertaining to the actions of human beings, based primarily on the Qur'an, Sunnah, *ijma* (consensus), and *qiyas*.

Fatimah Daughter of Muhammad and Khadijah; wife of the fourth caliph, 'Ali, and mother of Hasan and Husayn; known as "Mother of the Imams."

fatwa Authoritative legal opinion given by a mufti (Islamic legal scholar) in response to a question posed by an individual or a court of law; typically requested in cases not covered by the *fiqh* (Islamic jurisprudence) literature and is neither binding nor enforceable; its authority is based on the mufti's education and status within the Muslim community.

feng shui Chinese system of geomancy, method of divination that interprets markings on the ground or patterns on the earth, to improve life; "wind-water"; used to orient the human environment on spots with good *chi* (*qi*), life force.

filial piety Confucian virtue of respect for one's parents and ancestors; to be good to one's parents, engage in good conduct inside and outside the home in order to reflect favorably on one's parents and ancestors.

fiqh   Human attempt to understand Islamic divine law (sharia); whereas sharia is infallible, *fiqh* is fallible and changeable; the science of jurisprudence.

fitrah   According to the Qur'an, the original state in which human beings are created by Allah as naturally good and with innate inclination toward *tawhid* (Oneness of God); Allah creates children according to *fitrah*, and their parents make them Jews or Christians; human nature.

Five Aggregates   Buddhist phenomenology of five aspects that constitute the world of appearances, which essentially do not exist; the aggregates that must be extinguished, attachments to be relinquished for liberation; also known as *skandhas*. See also *rupa, vedana, sanna, samskara, vijnana.*

folk religion   Synthesis of popular beliefs and practices that are developed within a local culture, aimed at handling everyday problems; also referred to as "local religions" or "popular religions."

fordfinders   Jain concept of a human being who helps achieve liberation and enlightenment by being a role model and leader for spiritual insight; someone who has crossed over life's stream of rebirths and made a path for others to follow. See also *tirthankara.*

Four Noble Truths   Buddhist truth regarding the nature of *dukkha* (suffering), its causes, its cessation, and the path leading to liberation from suffering.

Frazer, James (1854–1941)   Scottish social anthropologist; an early founder of modern anthropology; wrote *The Golden Bough* (1890), documenting similarities among magical and religious beliefs worldwide.

free association   Technique created by Sigmund Freud whereby patients speak for themselves freely as a method of unearthing unconscious thinking.

Freud, Sigmund (1856–1939)   Austrian neurologist who became known as the founder of psychoanalysis, a way of treating psychopathologies; major influence on Western thinking, with concepts of Oedipus complex, libido, dreams, ego, superego, and id.

fundamentalism   Strict adherence to specific theological doctrines and sacred texts; in Christianity, usually understood as a reaction against modernist theology, a movement within the Protestant community in the United States beginning in the late nineteenth century with strong stance against aspects of culture and knowledge; most religions have some form of fundamentalism that advocates a return to fundamental principles by rigid adherence to those principles and opposition to others.

Fundamentalist Latter-Day Saints   One of the largest fundamentalist organizations in the United States; practices polygamy; consists of roughly ten thousand members residing in small towns primarily in the United States and Canada; the disparate movement consists of various small communities led by a succession of men regarded as prophets who continue to receive revelations and advocate plural marriage.

Gandhi, Mahatma (Mohandas Karamchand) (1869–1948)   Preeminent leader of Indian nationalism during the British Raj; employed nonviolent civil disobedience that led to Indian independence; argued for *swaraj* (self-rule) of Indians.

Ganesha   Elephant-headed Hindu deity who removes obstacles; also known as the Remover of Obstacles.

Geertz, Clifford (1926–2006)   American anthropologist who advocated the approach of symbolic anthropology, investigating patterns of symbols and "thick description"; wrote *The Interpretation of Cultures* (1973).

Geiger, Abraham (1810–74) German rabbi and scholar who led the founding of Reform Judaism; sought to remove all nationalistic elements (e.g., "chosen people" doctrine) from Judaism.

Gemara Commentaries on the Mishnah; the Mishnah and the Gemara together form the Judaic Talmud.

gentile Person who is not Jewish; a pagan or heathen; relating to a gentile; non-Israelite populations.

gentile breakthrough First-century communication of the Christian gospel to gentiles in Antioch based on gentile cultural forms; gentile entrance and inclusion into the redemptive history, which became the basis for Christian mission and understanding the relationship between gospel and culture.

ghusl Major purification ritual in Islam; consists of washing hands and sexual organs, performing *wudu* (minor purification), rubbing water into roots of hair, and pouring water over entire body, beginning with the right side; the water used must be clean, colorless, and odorless and cannot have been used for a previous ritual. See also *wudu*.

glossolalia Sacred language marked by fluid vocalizing of speech-like syllables that lack any readily comprehended meaning; "speaking in tongues"; in Christianity, a gift of the Holy Spirit for prayer and edification of the church; many religions have some form of *theopneustic glossolalia* (God-inspired speaking in tongues).

gnosis Spiritual knowledge in the sense of mystical experience or insight; intuitive apprehension of spiritual truths, an esoteric form of knowledge sought by the gnostics.

gnostic gospels Collection of about fifty-two ancient texts based on the teachings of several spiritual leaders written from the second to fourth centuries but not included in the Christian canon (Bible); the writings emphasize secret knowledge and enlightenment, with the belief that salvation lies not in worshiping Jesus Christ, but in psychic or pneumatic souls learning to free themselves from the material world via a revelation; part of the New Testament Apocrypha, e.g., *Gospel of Thomas, Gospel of the Lord, Gospel of Truth, Gospel of Judas*.

gnostics Followers of diverse, syncretistic religious movements in antiquity consisting of various belief systems united in the teaching that the material cosmos was created by an imperfect God (the Demiurge); salvation is understood as a reawakening (*gnosis*); belief that the material world created by the Demiurge should be shunned and the spiritual world should be embraced.

Golden Temple In Sikhism, a holy temple of God (the Harmandir Sahib) located in Amritsar, Punjab, with four doors representing the openness of the Sikhs toward all religions.

gospel Good news; in Christianity, the account that describes the life of Jesus Christ, communicated through the four canonical Gospels of Matthew, Mark, Luke, and John; the good news of the redemption through the propitiatory offering of Jesus Christ, the Son of God, for sin; in Islam, the Arabic term (*Injil*) that has undergone many changes as the original words of *Isa* (Jesus); *Injil* was given by Allah to the Prophet Isa (Jesus).

Graham, Billy (b. 1918) Influential American Christian evangelist who has preached in person to more people around the world than any other preacher in history; spiritual advisor to twelve United States presidents.

Granth Sahib Sacred text of Sikhism. *See also* Adi Granth.

Great Commission In Christian tradition, the instruction of the resurrected Jesus Christ to his disciples that they spread his teachings to all the nations of the world; emphasizing mission work, evangelism, and baptism; the primary basis for Christian mission and the nature of the church in the world; for example, see Matthew 28:16–20; Mark 16:14–20; Luke 24:44–47; John 20:19–23.

Great Schism Division of Roman Catholic Church and Eastern Orthodox Church in the year 1054.

gurdwara Place of worship for Sikhs; "Gateway to the Guru."

Gurmukh In Sikh tradition, a "person oriented toward the Guru"; a term describing one who has obtained the status of *mukhti* (Sanskrit, "release," "liberation").

guru Teacher or master who transmits religious knowledge or wisdom.

Guru In Sikhism, one of the Ten Gurus (Teachers) of Sikh tradition, enshrined in the Adi Granth.

Guru Amar Das (1479–1574) In Sikh tradition, the third Guru.

Guru Angad Dev (1504–54) In Sikh tradition, the second Guru.

Guru Arjan Dev (1563–1606) In Sikh tradition, the fifth Guru; the first Guru to be born in a Sikh family, made one of the most important contributions to Sikhism, the final compilation of the Adi Granth in 1604.

Guru Gobind Singh (1666–1708) In Sikh tradition, the tenth and final human Guru.

Guru Hargobind (1595–1644) In Sikh tradition, the sixth Guru, noted for building the chief Sikh shrine located in the Golden Temple.

Guru Har Krishan (1656–64) In Sikh tradition, the eighth Guru; installed as Guru at the age of five, he died only three years later.

Guru Har Rai (1630–61) In Sikh tradition, the seventh Guru.

Guru Nanak (1469–1539) In Sikh tradition, the first Guru, who traveled far and wide teaching people the message of one God who dwells in every one of God's creations; his teachings are found in the Guru Granth Sahib.

Guru Ram Das (1534–81) In Sikh tradition, the fourth Guru.

Guru Tegh Bahadur (1621–75) In Sikh tradition, the ninth Guru.

hadith Report of the words and actions of Prophet Muhammad and other early Muslims; considered an authoritative source of revelation, second only to the Qur'an. Sunni and Shia traditions have different collections of hadith.

Hajar (Hagar) Mother of Ibrahim's (Abraham's) son Isma'il (Ishmael); servant of Ibrahim and Sarah.

hajj In Islam, the annual pilgrimage to Mecca during the month of Dhu al-Hijaah; performance of the hajj is one of the Five Pillars of Islam, required by all adult Muslims at least once in their lifetime if they are physically and financially able.

hajjah In Islam, an honorific term for a female pilgrim who has made the pilgrimage to Mecca (hajj); in some Muslim communities, a term of honor and respect.

hajji In Islam, an honorific term for a male pilgrim who has made the pilgrimage to Mecca (hajj); in some Muslim communities, a term of honor and respect.

halakhah Path that one walks; Jewish law; the complete body of rules and practices that Jews are bound to follow, including biblical commandments, commandments instituted by the rabbis, and authoritative customs.

halakhic midrashim Ancient Judaic rabbinic method of Torah study that expounded on laws by identifying their sources in the Hebrew Bible (Tanakh) and interpreting these passages as proof of the authenticity of the laws; investigation of the Torah.

Hanafi Islamic school of legal thought (*madhhab*) whose origins are attributed to Abu Hanifah in Kufa, Iraq, in the eighth century; most widespread Islamic school of legal thought, followed by roughly one-third of the world's Muslims; uses reason, logic, opinion (*ray*), analogy (*qiyas*), and preference (*istihsan*) in the formulation of Islamic laws.

Hanbal   Islamic school of legal thought (*madhhab*) whose origins are attributed to Ahmad ibn Hanbal in ninth-century Baghdad, Iraq; the official school of Islamic law in Saudi Arabia, with adherents in Palestine, Syria, and Iraq; uses the Qur'an, hadith, fatwas of Muhammad's Companions, sayings of a single Companion, traditions with weaker chains of transmission or those lacking the name of a transmitter in the chain, and reasoning by analogy (*qiyas*) when necessary.

Hanukkah   Festival of Lights in Judaism; a Jewish holiday commemorating the rededication of the second temple in Jerusalem.

haraam   In Islamic law, one of the five categories that define the morality of human action; "sinful"; in Islamic jurisprudence, an act that is forbidden by Allah. See also *wajib, mandub, makruh,* and *mubah.*

Harappa   Early Indus Valley Civilization city that emerged c. 2600 BCE along the Indus River Valley.

Harijans   Terms used by Mahatma Gandhi for Dalits; "children of God."

Harmandir Sahib   In Sikh tradition, "the Abode of God"; the sacred Sikh *gurdwara* located in the city of Amritsar; also known as the Golden Temple; the four entry doors to the Harmandir Sahib symbolize the openness of the Sikhs toward all people and religions.

Harris, William Wade (c. 1860–1929)   Liberian evangelist who preached in Liberia, Ivory Coast, and Ghana against indigenous fetishes and occult practices, and approved of polygamy; baptized over one hundred thousand new converts in Africa.

hasan   In Islam, means "good" and is used to describe hadith whose authenticity is not as well established as that of *sahih* hadith (sound hadith) but is stronger than *daif* hadith (weak hadith); *hasan* hadith is sufficient for use as religious evidence.

heathens   Unconverted member of a people or nation that does not acknowledge the God of the Bible; an irreligious person.

Hegel, Georg Wilhelm Friedrich (1770–1831)   German idealist philosopher; argued that the human mind is the highest expression of the Absolute; developed the concept of the dialectic, in which contradiction between a thesis and its antithesis is resolved at a higher level of truth (synthesis).

Hellenism   Influence of ancient Greek culture and philosophy outside Greece; a body of humanistic and classical ideals associated with ancient Greece, including reason, pursuit of knowledge and the arts, moderation, civic responsibility, and bodily development.

heresy   Any belief or theory that strongly varies from established beliefs or customs; violation of religious or traditional laws or legal codes.

Herzl, Theodor (1860–1904)   Founder of the Zionist political movement in the late 1800s whose ideas influenced the foundation of the State of Israel.

Hick, John (1922–2012)   Philosopher of religion and theologian; strong advocate of religious pluralism; reinterpreted Christology metaphorically, arguing that Jesus Christ did not teach or believe that he was God incarnate; that Jesus was not literally God in the flesh, but was metaphorically the presence of God; stressed a theocentric, rather than Christocentric, view of religion.

Hiebert, Paul (1932–2007)   Mennonite professor of mission and anthropology; born in India, taught at Trinity Evangelical Divinity School.

hierophany   Appearance of the sacred; used by Mircea Eliade for his analyses of religion.

Hillel   One of the greatest rabbis recorded in the Talmud and one of the most important figures in Jewish history; he is associated with the development of the Mishnah and the Talmud.

Hinayana   "Lesser Vehicle" applied to some schools of early Buddhism that contrasted with Mahayana ("Greater Vehicle") Buddhism; used as a synonym for Theravada Buddhism.

Hirsch, Samson Raphael (1808–88)   German rabbi known as the intellectual founder of a school of contemporary Orthodox Judaism; major influence on the development of Orthodox Judaism.

history of religions   Written record of human religious experiences and ideas; this approach considers common patterns of religion throughout history.

Hitler, Adolf (1889–1945)   Austrian-born German politician and leader of the Nazi Party; chancellor of Germany from 1933 to 1945; promoted Pan-Germanism, anti-Semitism, and anti-Communism; instrumental in the Holocaust (mass extermination) of roughly twelve million Jews and other minorities.

Hoffman, Melchoir (c. 1495–1543)   Anabaptist prophet and visionary leader in northern Germany and the Netherlands; influenced the development of the Mennonites.

Holdheim, Samuel (1806–60)   German rabbi and author; one of the most extreme leaders of the Reform Movement in Judaism; pioneer of modern Jewish homiletics.

Holocaust   Genocide of about six million Jews, in addition to millions of Roma, Slavs, communists, homosexuals, disabled individuals, and other "undesirables," by Nazi German forces during World War II; systematic state-sponsored murder of Jews led by Adolf Hitler.

Holy Spirit Association for the Unification of World Christianity   New religious movement founded in South Korea (1954) by Rev. Sun Myung Moon; also known as Family Federation for World Peace and Unification, Unification Church, or Unificationism. *See also* Moon, Sun Myung.

homoiousios   Of similar being, substance, essence; used in the context of Christian discussions about the nature of the Godhead; concept promoted by Arianism that Jesus was "of similar substance" as the Father.

homoousios   Of the same being, substance, essence; used in the context of Christian discussions about the nature of the Godhead; Christian concept of the relationship between Jesus and the Father, that Jesus is "of the same substance as" the Father.

Hubbard, L. Ron (1911–86)   American pulp-fiction author and founder of the Church of Scientology; wrote science fiction and fantasy stories and developed a self-help system called Dianetics that became the foundation of the Church of Scientology. *See also* Church of Scientology; Dianetics.

Humayun (1508–56)   Second Mughal emperor, who ruled a large territory consisting of what is now Afghanistan, Pakistan, and parts of northern Indian.

huppah   Canopy under which a Jewish couple stands during their wedding ceremony; a sheet stretched over four poles, symbolizing that the couple will build a home together.

hypostasis   Technical term predating Christianity, but employed during the Christian Ecumenical Church Councils as "substance"; subsistence; actual, concrete existence; essence; person.

Ibn Saud (d. 1953)   Founder and first ruler of present kingdom of Saudi Arabia; his religious and political ideas formed the foundation of the kingdom; promoted and protected Wahhabi doctrines. *See also* al-Wahhabi, Muhammad ibn Abd.

Ibn Taymiyya, Ahmad (d. 1328)   Prominent and controversial Syrian thinker, theologian, Hanbali jurist within Islam; promoted supremacy of the

Qur'an and the *sunnah* of Prophet Muhammad and early Muslim community, literal interpretation of the Qur'an, and condemned popular practices of saint worship and pilgrimages to saints' tombs; influenced radical Islamic perspectives of Muhammad ibn Abd al-Wahhab, Hasan al-Banna, and Sayyid Qutb, forming the basis for aspects of modern Islamic physical jihad.

Ibrahim (Abraham) In Islam, the original monotheist, purifier of God's house, builder of the Qa'abah, and first Muslim; rewarded by Allah for his faithful preparation to obey Allah's command to sacrifice his son, Isma'il; father of both Ishmael and Isaac, he is the common ancestor of Jews, Christians, and Muslims.

I Ching "Classic of Changes"; contains a divination system; a book of the Six Classics of Confucianism.

ihram State of purity necessary to perform pilgrimage (hajj and *umrah*), achieved through ritual cleansing and symbolized by wearing a seamless two-piece white garment covering the upper and lower parts of the body for males; women in a state of *ihram* are allowed to wear any clothing they wish as long as it fulfills Islamic conditions of public dress.

ijma In Islamic jurisprudence, an Arabic term referring to agreement or consensus of the Muslim community on religious matters; use of consensus to interpret Islamic law.

ijtihad In Islam, "independent reasoning"; one of four sources of Sunni law and hermeneutics; opposed to *taqlid* (imitation).

imam One who stands in front; a role model for the Muslim community in all its spiritual and secular undertakings; leader of the congregational prayers in the mosque.

Imams In Shia Islam, the divinely appointed successors to Prophet Muhammad, who are regarded as infallible, with the ability to make binding decisions in all areas of human activity; the two traditions of Shia Islam affirm the existence of seven and twelve Imans—thus, Sevener Shiism and Twelver Shiism, respectively.

inclusivists In Christian theology of religions, those more willing to admit revelatory truth outside Christianity, while stressing the centrality of biblical revelation; usually inclusivists recognize that truth may appear outside Christianity, but salvation remains only through Jesus Christ.

Indra Hindu Vedic nature deity; the God of rain and thunderstorms who wields a lightning thunderbolt; warrior deity of the Kshatriya class.

Indus River Valley Valley of major river that flows through Pakistan, western Tibet, and northern India; site of some of the largest human habitations of the ancient world and early forms of Hinduism.

intifada Shaking off, uprising, rebellion; the Palestinian resistance to the Israeli occupation of the West Bank of the Jordan River and the Gaza Strip; also used generally as resistance or revolt against oppression—for example, in 2011, against Assad's rule in Syria.

Iqbal, Muhammad Muslim South Asian political and religious writer, lawyer, professor, poet, ideologue (d. 1938) who supported the foundation of Pakistan as a homeland for the Muslims of India; delivered presidential address to the All India Muslim League (1930) that became a landmark in the Muslim nationalist movement for the creation of Pakistan, emphasizing Muslim nationalism and self-determination.

Isa (Jesus) In Islam, Jesus; a righteous prophet, messenger to Israel, spirit from God, messiah; human, conceived miraculously, but not God; a great spiritual leader and teacher; also known as Isa ibn Maryam (Jesus son of Mary).

Isha The fifth of five daily prayers in Islam; night prayer.

Islamists Muslim individuals or movements that attempt to implement Islamic values and Islamic law in all spheres of life; sometimes those who emphasize implementation of Sharia (Islamic law), pan-Islamic political unity, and selective removal of non-Muslim influences.

Isma'ili Major Shia Muslim community named after Isma'il, the eldest son of Imam Jafar al-Sadiq (d. 765); today, the movement consists of several branches and groupings.

isnad In Islam, chain of authority; refers to the line of transmitters of a particular saying or doctrine, particularly with regard to hadith; indicates authority of given hadith.

Israel-Palestine conflict Ongoing struggle between Israelis and Palestinians that began in the early twentieth century involving in part issues of mutual recognition, security, borders, water rights, and control of Jerusalem.

Isserles, Rabbi Moses Influential Ashkenazic Jewish rabbi known for his work on halakhah (Jewish law).

Jahangir Fourth Mughal emperor (1569–1627), the eldest son of Emperor Akbar.

jahiliyya Pre-Islamic period; "ignorance" of monotheism; secular modernity; some Muslim leaders argue for physical jihad against *jahiliyya*.

Janamsakhi In Sikh tradition, "birth testimony," "life stories"; a collection of uncritical biographies of Guru Nanak.

Japji In Sikh tradition, a set of verses recited every morning by faithful Sikhs.

Jataka Tales Edifying narratives of the previous lives of Lord Buddha in both human and animal forms, consisting of 547 poems; important within Theravada Buddhism.

jati Hindu caste; denotes thousands of clans, tribes, and communities in India; a subset of class in the ancient Hindu class system.

Jehovah's Witnesses Millenarian restorationist Christian denomination with nontrinitarian beliefs distinct from orthodox Christianity; founded by Charles Taze Russell in the late 1870s, with the formation of Zion's Watch Tower Tract Society; Jehovah's Witnesses reject the Trinity and do not observe holidays such as Christmas, Easter, and birthdays; leaders have predicted the end of the world several times.

jen Confucian virtue of "fellow feeling," the good feeling a virtuous person experiences when being altruistic; as an expression of Confucian ideals, an inner virtue from which all other Confucian virtues emanate.

Jerusalem Talmud Collection of rabbinic notes on second-century Mishnah.

Jew Member of the Jewish people, an ethnoreligious group; a member of the religion of Judaism, who may be a convert to Judaism without being ethnically Jewish.

jihad In Islam, to strive, to exert, to fight; applied in instances such as against one's evil inclinations, to convert unbelievers, for ethical betterment of the Islamic community; applied against Muslims perceived as unbelievers and non-Muslims; two types: Greater Jihad (spiritual) and Lesser Jihad (physical).

jina Jain concept of a spiritual conqueror; one venerated as a *tirthankara*.

jiva Hindu and Jain concept of a living being; the immortal essence of a living organism that survives death; this is an individual "living being" rather than atman, which refers to "the cosmic self."

jivanmukta Hindu concept of someone who has gained knowledge of the self and is liberated while living in a human body.

jizya Islamic law of poll tax, per capita tax, levied on non-Muslim citizens (*dhimmi*) who meet certain criteria; a material proof of the non-Muslims' acceptance of subjugation to a Muslim state and its laws.

John of Leiden (c. 1509–36) Anabaptist leader from Leiden, Netherlands, who established a polygamous theocracy.

Judge, William Quan (1851–96) Mystic, esotericist, occultist, and one of the founders of the original Theosophical Society.

jumu'ah In Islam, Friday congregational prayers; also known as *salat al-jumu'ah*.

junzi Confucian notion of ideal human being; "superior person" or "exemplary person"; a ruler animated by superior ethics and morality who serves as a role model by acting virtuously.

Justin Martyr (100–c. 165) Early Christian apologist regarded as the foremost interpreter of the theory of Logos (word, speech, reason, principle of order and knowledge); also known as Saint Justin.

kabbalah Esoteric discipline and school within Judaism; set of esoteric teachings that seek to explain the relationship between the eternal, mysterious, and the finite, moral; Jewish mystical tradition.

Kabir (1440–1518) mystic poet and saint of India, whose writings influenced the bhakti movement within Sikhism.

kaccha In Sikh tradition, short trousers, undershorts, used practically during the period of the human Gurus to enable quick action in war, especially if surprised by an enemy; worn as an undergarment to symbolize self-restraint and self-control of sexual desires like lust.

kaddish Prayer in Aramaic praising God, usually associated with mourning practices.

Kagawa, Toyohiko (1888–1960) Japanese Christian pacifist and labor activist who employed Christian principles in his vocation to advance a rightly ordered society and in his cooperatives to help the poor by living

among them and establishing schools, hospitals, and churches.

kalam In Islam, philosophical or mystical discussions about revealed truth; theology; focuses on seven major issues: concept of Allah; ontological and cosmological proofs for Allah's existence; cosmology and the relationship between Allah and creation; free will of human beings and theodicy; role of imagination; relationship between reason and revelation; application of divine law to community and society.

Kali Hindu goddess associated with empowerment (Shakti); goddess of time, change, and death who annihilates evil forces.

kama In Hinduism and Buddhism, sexual desire, sexual pleasure, sensual gratification; also desire, wish, passion, pleasure of the senses, and enjoyment of life and love without sexual connotations.

kami Shinto notion of spiritual being, for example, natural forces, spirits.

kangha In Sikh tradition, a small comb usually made of wood or ivory; its purpose is to keep the hair neat and tangle free at all times.

Kant, Immanuel (1724–1804) German philosopher who argued that reason was the source of morality; sought to unite reason with experience in his book *Critique of Pure Reason* (1781).

Kapany, Narinder Singh (b. 1926) Considered the father of fiber optics, he has fundamentally shaped the world of technology and communications through his research in fiber optics communications, biomedical instrumentation, and solar energy; also known for his work as a philanthropist, art collector, artist, and farmer.

Kaplan, Rabbi Mordecai M. (1881–1983) Jewish rabbi and educator who cofounded Reconstructionist Judaism.

kara In Sikh tradition, a steel bangle bracelet worn on the right wrist; reminds the wearer of his or her unity with God and other Sikhs in bondage to the Guru, restraining the wearer from evil action.

karma   Ancient Indian notion of action, both mental and physical, that causes the cycle of life and death (samsara); that which binds one to existence.

karpas   Traditional ritual in the Jewish Passover seder; refers to the vegetable, usually parsley or celery, that is dipped in salty water and eaten; symbolizes the salty tears that the Jews shed in their slavery in Egypt.

kasaya   Jain concept of negative emotions or passions of which there are four (anger, greed, ego, deceit), which continue to cause the soul to be in bondage to existence.

Kaur   In Sikh tradition, "Princess" or "Lioness"; a mandatory name for female Sikhs, often used as a last or middle name.

kesh   In Sikh tradition, long, uncut hair and unshorn beard; no hair may be removed from the body since doing so interferes with God's will.

Ketuvim   Third and final section of the Hebrew Bible (Tanakh) consisting in part of the Wisdom literature.

kevala   Jainist concept of the highest form of knowledge that a soul can attain; also known as Supreme Knowledge; one who has attained *kevala* is a "spiritual victor" (*jina*).

kevala jnana   Jain notion of Supreme Knowledge. See also *kevala*.

kevalin   Jain name for one who has achieved Supreme Knowledge (*kevala jnana*).

Khadijah (d. 619)   First wife of Prophet Muhammad and his only wife until she died; mother of Fatimah; first person to believe in Prophet Muhammad's prophethood.

Khalsa   Collective body of all initiated Sikhs.

Khan, Sayyid Ahmad (1817–98)   Indian Muslim philosopher and social activist born in India; jurist for the British East India Company, remained loyal to the British during the Indian mutiny (1857), later blamed British policies for the revolt; promoted Western-style scientific education; founded Muhammadan Anglo-Oriental College (1875).

khanda   Sikh symbol consisting of a double-edged sword.

Khasam   In Sikh tradition, the characteristic of God, the Master.

Kim, Heup Young, (b. 1949)   Korean Christian theologian and scholar of East Asian religions, particularly Confucianism and Taoism; specialist in constructive theology, interfaith dialogue, and religion and science.

Kimbangu, Simon (1887–1951)   Congolese religious leader whose followers considered him the special envoy of Jesus Christ; founder of Kimbanguism and the Kimbanguist Church.

King, Martin Luther, Jr. (1929–68)   American Christian clergyman, activist, and leader in the African American civil rights movement; known for his role in advancement of civil rights using nonviolent civil disobedience to protest racism against blacks.

kirpan   In Sikh tradition, a sword; this ceremonial sword can be five to ninety centimeters long and can be worn at the waist, the neck, or in the *kangha* (comb), representing quick defense of truth and the prevention of violence.

Kivengere, Festo (1919–88)   A Ugandan Anglican leader who played a significant role in a Christian revival in southwestern Uganda; often referred to as "the Billy Graham of Africa."

Knitter, Paul (b. 1939)   Paul Tillich Professor of Theology, World Religions, and Culture at Union Theological Seminary in New York City; a Roman Catholic who, with former colleague John Hick, promotes religious pluralism.

Konkokyo   New religion of Japan; type of Shinto sect that worships God under the name of Tenchi Kane No Kami; God is seen as present within this world and the universe as the body of the Parent God (No Kami).

Kotel Western Wall, Wailing Wall located in the Old City of Jerusalem at the foot of the western side of the Temple Mount; a remnant of the ancient wall that surrounded the Jewish temple's courtyard.

Koyama, Kosuke (1929–2009) Japanese Protestant Christian theologian considered one of the leading Japanese Christian theologians of the twentieth century; wrote *Water Buffalo Theology, No Handle on the Cross,* and *Three Mile an Hour God.*

Krishna Avatar of the Hindu God Vishnu; various depictions include an infant, a young boy, and a charioteer in the Bhagavad Gita.

Kshatriyas One of the four classes (*varnas*) within ancient Hinduism, constituting the class of kings, princes, and the ruling and military elite of the Vedic-Hindu system.

Kurozumikyo "Teachings of Kurozumi," a Japanese Shinto sect; believes that Amaterasu is the source of light and life, and human beings can gain access to her divine power to perform miracles.

langar In Sikh tradition, free kitchens; common kitchen where food is served in a *gurdwara* to all the visitors, Sikh or non-Sikh; only vegetarian food is served in a *langar.*

Laozi (c. sixth century BCE) Chinese philosopher credited as founder of philosophical Taoism and author of Tao Te Ching; revered as a deity in most religious forms of Taoist philosophy.

Legalists One of the major traditional Chinese schools of philosophy; upholds the rule of law as a means to restore harmony in society; notion that a ruler should govern his subjects by the law, method, and charisma.

li Confucian concept of ritual and behavioral protocol; customs, etiquette, morals; rules of proper behavior.

liberalism Within Christianity, an umbrella term covering diverse philosophically and biblically informed religious movements and ideas from the late eighteenth century onward; stemming from F. E. D. Schleiermacher (1768–1834), who sought to reformulate Christian doctrine in contemporary terms, emphasizing the use of reason, science, freedom, and experience while focusing on human goodness.

liberation Freedom from an unwelcomed condition (e.g., as experienced in salvation, nirvana, *moksha*).

Li Qi "Book of Ritual"; one of the Six Classics of Confucianism; set of codes of behavior for the privileged classes, with emphasis on morality, geared toward regulating human conduct.

Livingstone, David (1813–73) Scottish Congregationalist pioneer medical Christian missionary with the London Missionary Society and explorer in Africa; one of the most popular national heroes of the late nineteenth century in Victorian Britain; proponent of Christian missions and trade, with motto, "Christianity, Commerce, and Civilization."

Logos Important term in religion, philosophy, rhetoric, and psychology that means "word," "speech," "reason"; a principle of order and knowledge. In Christianity, the Gospel of John identifies the Logos through which all things are made as the incarnation of Jesus.

Logos spermatikos Seed-bearing Word; used by Justin Martyr to assert that God had prepared a way to his final revelation in Jesus Christ through hints of truth found in classical philosophy.

Lunyu (Analects) Collection of the words and actions of Confucius and his disciples as well as the discussions they held; most important text in Confucianism. See also *Analects.*

Luther, Martin (1483–1546) German monk, former Catholic priest, and seminal figure in the sixteenth-century Protestant Reformation, who strongly disputed efficacy of Roman Catholic indulgences; posted Ninety-Five Theses (1517), which was the catalyst for the Protestant Reformation; argued that salvation was by grace alone through faith; translated the Bible into vernacular German; founder of Lutheran movement.

Maghrib   One of the five daily prayers in Islam; the sunset prayer; also means "the West," referring mainly to northwest Africa, including Morocco, Algeria, Tunisia, and sometimes Libya.

Mahabharata   Major, massive epic poem in ancient India, narrating the Kurukshetra War and the conflicts between the Kaurava and Pandava princes; contains significant devotional and philosophical material.

Mahasanghikas   "The Great Assembly"; one of the two earliest schools of Buddhism.

Mahavira   Propagator of Jain tradition, regarded as the twenty-fourth, and last, *tirthankara*, Jain name for a human being who helps others achieve liberation by being a role model and leader; also known as "fordfinder" and *jina*.

Mahayana   "Greater Vehicle" in Buddhism; largest major branch of Buddhism; promotes bodhisattvas as vehicles of liberation.

mahzor   Prayer book used by Jews on the High Holidays of Rosh Hashanah and Yom Kippur.

Maimonides, Moses (1135–1204)   Pre-eminent medieval Sephardic Jewish philosopher and prolific and influential scholar of the Torah in the Middle Ages.

Majjhima Patipada   The Middle Way or Middle Path, discovered by Lord Buddha, that leads to liberation.

makruh   In Islamic law, one of the five categories that define the morality of human action; an offensive act; detestable or disapproved actions to be avoided by Muslims, though not

forbidden (*haraam*). See also *wajib*, *haraam*, *mandub*, and *mubah*.

Malik (d. 795)   Founder of the Maliki school of Islamic law; compiled a collection of hadith (*Al-muwatta*), used widely by Sunnis; emphasized hadith as basis for legal principles; used personal opinion (*ray*) and analogy (*qiyas*) in legal matters.

mandala   Hindu and Buddhist ritual symbol used for meditation, usually a depiction of the cosmos metaphysically or symbolically; representation of a principal deity for purposes of meditation.

mandub   In Islamic law, one of the five categories that define the morality of human action; actions that are approved in Islamic law; recommended duties, but not essential.

manji   In Sikh tradition, a territorial division or district, as well as a missionary order for the purpose of preaching.

Manmukh   In Sikh tradition, "person guided by inclination," an ego-centered, perverse, self-willed individual who is controlled by human impulses rather than the truth of the Gurus.

mantra   Sound, syllable, word, or group of words considered capable of creating spiritual transformation; these can be ritual prayers or sounds that imitate, reflect, or respond to the divine; a sacred utterance considered to possess mystical or spiritual efficacy.

maror   Bitter herbs eaten at the Jewish Passover seder, symbolizing the bitterness of slavery in Egypt.

Marx, Karl (1818–83)   German philosopher and revolutionary socialist; had a profound influence on understanding labor in relation to capital; wrote *The Communist Manifesto* (1848) and *Das Kapital* (1867–94).

masand   In Sikh tradition, a territorial deputy or vicar charged with the care of Sikh congregations and who seeks to establish new and restore older *gurdwaras* (Sikh worship spaces).

masjid House of prayer in Islam; "a place of prostration" to Allah; Muslim place of worship.

matn In Islam, the content or text of a hadith report; with its chain of transmission (*isnad*), one of the two main parts of a hadith report.

matzo Unleavened bread traditionally eaten by Jews during the Jewish Passover holiday, reflecting the haste with which the Jews fled Egypt, thus having no time for yeast to rise.

mawdoo' Part of Islamic hadith classification; fabricated hadith.

Mawdudi, Sayyid Abu'l-A'la (d. 1979) South Asian Muslim revivalist thinker, prolific writer, politician, founder of Jamaat-I Islami; advocated an Islamic anti-imperialist perspective, for restitution and purification of Islamic institutions and practices, and for a separate cultural homeland for Indian Muslims but not the creation of an independent Muslim state.

maya Indian term meaning "illusion" or cause of illusion; unwholesome mental factor obscuring enlightenment and thus inhibiting liberation.

McPherson, Aimee Semple (1890–1944) Canadian-American Los Angeles–based Christian Pentecostal evangelist in the 1920s and 1930s; founded Foursquare Church and pioneered the use of modern media, especially radio, in her evangelistic efforts.

Mecca Holiest city of Islam; birthplace of Prophet Muhammad, site of the Qa'abah and the annual pilgrimage (hajj); the city Muslims face during prayer.

Medina Second holiest city of Islam, to which Prophet Muhammad and early followers emigrated (*hijra*) in 622 CE; means "City of the Prophet"; place of Prophet Muhammad's burial site.

megachurches Christian church having two thousand or more in average weekly attendance.

Meiji Restoration Transition of Japan under Emperor Meiji from a feudal system to a constitutional monarchy (1868–1912); led to enormous changes in Japan's political and social structures.

men "Door"; Confucian concept referring to the door that leads to long life, enlightenment, and immortality.

Mengzi (372–289 BCE) Chinese philosopher who was the most famous Confucian after Confucius himself; one of the principal interpreters of Confucianism.

menorah Nine-branched candelabrum lit during the eight-day holiday of Hanukkah; a symbol of Judaism.

Messiah Savior or liberator, usually "anointed one," commonly used as a title in the Abrahamic religions. In the Hebrew Bible, an "anointed" individual or object, such as a Jewish king or high priest, an expected deliverer of the Jews; in the Christian tradition, Jesus Christ is considered the Messiah, the Savior of the world; in Islam, Jesus is considered the Messiah (*Masih*) and Prophet who will wage war against the false messiah at the end of time, but he is not considered Lord and Savior.

Messianic Jews Blending of Christian theology with elements of Jewish ideas and practices; Jewish belief that Jesus is the Messiah, the Son of God, and that salvation is only through him.

metaphysical dualism Notion that reality is composed of two types of underlying substances in the world.

metaphysical monism Notion that reality is composed of only one ultimate substance.

Middle Way Buddhist insight into emptiness that transcends opposites; Buddhist idea that the path to liberation is between the extremes of hedonism and asceticism.

midrash Homiletic stories told by Jewish rabbis to explain passages of the Hebrew Bible (Tanakh).

Miller, William (1782–1849) American Baptist preacher from upstate New York who founded the restorationist movement of Adventism, which emphasizes the belief that the personal, visible return of Jesus Christ (e.g., second coming; "advent") is imminent; Miller was a farmer, deputy sheriff, justice of the peace, and chaplain in the infantry during the War of 1812; prophesied that the second advent of Jesus Christ would occur roughly in the year 1843.

Millerites   Followers of the teachings of William Miller who first shared his belief in the coming second advent of Jesus Christ (Adventism) in roughly the year 1843, based on Miller's study of the symbolic meaning of the prophecies of the biblical book of Daniel.

minaret   Islamic beacon; tower on a mosque from which the call to prayer is issued five times daily.

minjung   Korean word meaning "the mass of the people," referring to those who are oppressed politically, exploited economically, marginalized sociologically, despised culturally, and condemned religiously; as a worldview, it came to inform the struggle for democracy in Korea.

minjung sinhak   Korean "theology of the people"; a form of Korean Christian liberation theology.

minyan   Refers to the quorum of ten Jewish adults required for certain religious obligations, such as performing public prayers; sometimes means prayer service.

Mishnah   First major written work of rabbinic Judaism; early written compilation of Jewish oral tradition that forms the basis of the Talmud.

mission   Organized effort for the purpose of propagating an idea, faith, or organization. In Christianity, the sending of the church into the world for the purpose of sharing the gospel in word and deed; proclamation of the gospel and humanitarian work based on the Bible. In Islam (*dawah*), inviting people to understand and embrace Islam.

missionaries   Member of a religious group sent into an area as a witness to their faith, doing ministries of service, education, literacy, social justice, health care, and economic development; one who is sent to preach in Christ's name; apostle.

mithyatva   Jain concept of wrong or false belief; ignoble activity; not having interest in faith in the path of liberation.

moderates   Individuals or groups that selectively interpret religion to maintain crucial elements of the tradition while being open to change and interpretation of the religious tradition; this immensely broad category is relative to context and other perspectives.

modernists   Individuals or groups that interpret religion to meet changing conditions of modern life; most religions have some kind of modernist perspective that permits flexibility in interpretation of the religion to be compatible with reason, science, and technology.

Mohenjodaro   One of the largest human settlements of the ancient Indus Valley Civilization; built around 2600 BCE.

moksha   Eternal freedom; to let loose; liberation from the cycle of rebirth (samsara).

moksha-marga   In Indian religions, way to liberation; entails perfect knowledge, perfect action, and perfect surrender.

monism   Philosophical position that argues that the variety of existing things can be explained in terms of a single substance or reality; that all things can be traced to a common source; unity of all essences. *See also* metaphysical monism.

Monophysite   Christological view, regarded by the early church as heretical, which taught that Jesus Christ had only one nature rather than both a divine and a human nature that were united in one person.

monotheism Belief in the existence of one God; sometimes, belief in one personal and transcendent God (e.g., as in Judaism, Christianity, Islam).

monotheistic Pertaining to belief in one God. *See also* monotheism.

Moon, Hyung Jin (b. 1979) International president of the Unification Church; he is the youngest son of Rev. Sun Myung Moon, who appointed Hyung Jin Moon to be the new leader of the Family Federation for World Peace and Unification.

Moon, Sun Myung (1920–2012) Korean religious leader best known for founding the Unification Church and for his claim that he was a messiah; a media mogul and anti-Communist activist; Moon and his wife, Hak Ja Han, presided over mass wedding ceremonies uniting thousands of participants; he and his wife were referred to as the True Parents by members of the Unification Church, his family as the True Family, and his children as the True Children.

Mormonism Predominant religious tradition of the Church of Jesus Christ of Latter-Day Saints, founded by Prophet Joseph Smith Jr. in the 1820s in upstate New York; the term "Mormon" refers to the author of the Book of Mormon, considered by Mormons to be a Nephite, a member of one of the four main groups of settlers of the ancient Americas.

Moroni According to Mormons, an angel or resurrected being who appeared to Prophet Joseph Smith Jr. in 1823 to inform Smith that he had been chosen to restore God's church on earth; Moroni was the son of Mormon, the Nephite prophet for whom the Book of Mormon is named.

mosque Muslim place of prayer and worship; place of ritual prostration. *See also* masjid.

Mother Teresa (1910–97) Albanian Roman Catholic nun who founded the Missionaries of Charity, a Roman Catholic religious congregation of women dedicated to the poor, particularly the destitute of India; dedicated her life of service to the poorest of Kolkata; recipient of the Nobel Peace Prize; beatified by the Roman Catholic Church in 2003.

Mount Arafat Mountain located outside Mecca, on whose plain pilgrims gather on the ninth day of Dhu al-Hijjah, where they pray continuously from just after noon until shortly after sunset; many believe that Allah's spirit descends closest to earth at this spot at this time.

Mozi Chinese philosopher during early Warring States Period; founded school of Mohism, strongly arguing against Confucianism and Taoism by emphasizing self-reflection and authenticity rather than obedience to ritual; advocated "universal love."

mubah In Islamic law, one of the five categories that define the morality of human action; an action that is neither forbidden nor recommended; a religiously neutral action; often synonymous with "halal." See also *wajib*, *haraam*, *mandub*, and *makruh*.

muezzin Male Muslim who issues *adhan* (call to prayer) in Arabic for Muslims from atop the minaret five times daily; today a CD or tape recording is amplified through loudspeakers mounted on the minaret to announce the time for Islamic prayer.

Mughal Imperial power in the Indian subcontinent (c. 1526–1757) of Turkic-Mongol origin.

mujtahid In Islamic jurisprudence, an authoritative interpreter of the religious law of Islam.

mukhti "Release," "liberation"; liberation from successive rebirths and therefore the achievement of peace through the ultimate union with God.

Müller, Friedrich Max (1823–1900) German philologist; a founder of the Western academic discipline of Indian studies and comparative religion.

Münster, Thomas (1489–1525) Early German theologian who became a rebel leader during the Peasants' War, turning against Martin Luther through his writings and supporting the Anabaptists.

Musa (Moses) In Islam, the prophet who led the Israelites out of slavery in Egypt; he set down the tablets containing Allah's commandments, rather than breaking them, after discovering the Israelites worshiping the golden calf.

Muslim One who submits to the will of Allah.

Muslim Brotherhood Founded in 1928 in Egypt by Hasan al-Banna; one of the largest Islamic movements in the world; a pan-Islamic, religious, political, and social movement that has become a model of political activism combined with Islamic charity work.

mystery religions Religious cults of the Greco-Roman world that restricted participation to initiates; main characteristic was secrecy associated with the particularities of the initiation and ritual practices.

myth Sacred narrative that usually explains the origins of the world, humankind, or the first creation; refers to any traditional story that can be allegorical but has an explanatory function.

Nam In Sikh tradition, "name," which encompasses the whole of creation; name of God; the word repeated daily by all Sikhs to refer to the All-Pervading Supreme Reality.

Namaskar Mantra Most important prayer in Jainism; exemplifies deep respect toward beings that Jains believe are more spiritually advanced within the Jain tradition.

naraka Hindu, Jain, Buddhist, and Sikh notion of hell; place of torment; in Islam in Indonesia and Malaysia, the term refers to the Islamic concept of hell.

Nav Tattvas Nine Fundamentals of Jain karmic theory and the nature of the soul (*jiva*).

Neo-Confucianism Moral, ethical, and metaphysical Chinese philosophy based on Confucianism, originating in the Tang Dynasty (618–907), that emphasized rationalism over against superstitious and mystical elements of Taoism and Buddhism that had influenced Confucianism during the Han Dynasty.

Nestorian Church Christian church originating in Asia Minor and Syria following the condemnation of Nestorius and his teachings by the ecumenical church councils of Ephesus (431) and Chalcedon (451); in modern times, known as the Church of the East, the Persian Church, or the Assyrian Church.

Nestorius (c. 386–450) Early bishop of Constantinople whose views on the nature and person of Jesus Christ led to the calling of the Ecumenical Church Council of Ephesus (431) and to Nestorianism being declared a heresy. *See also* Council of Ephesus.

Nevi'im Second main division of the Hebrew Bible (Tanakh) consisting of the Former and Latter Prophets.

Newbigin, Lesslie (1909–98) British theologian, missiologist, missionary, author who spent much of his life serving as a missionary in India; bishop of the Church of South India (CSI) and influential in ecumenism and mission studies; wrote several books, including *The Gospel in a Pluralistic Society*.

new covenant Christian belief that Jesus Christ is the mediator of a new relationship between God and human beings that includes all people who recognize Jesus Christ as Lord and Savior; Christians believe that the new covenant was celebrated at the Last Supper and that Jesus is the mediator of the new covenant through the shedding of his blood.

new religious movements Religious communities or ethical, spiritual, or philosophical groups of modern origin that occupy a peripheral place in a dominant religious culture; while they may share some elements of belief and practice with preexisting religions or denominations, they are separate from mainstream society; some use this expression rather than the pejorative term "cult."

nirjara One of the Nine Fundamentals of Jain karmic theory; refers to the shedding of accumulated karma from the atman (soul).

nirvana Liberation; freedom from samsara; freedom from suffering; union with Brahman; literally means "blown out," as with a candle.

Nishan Sahib Sikh holy triangular flag, used outside most *gurdwaras* (Sikh churches).

Nitobe, Inazo (1862–1933) Japanese Christian, agricultural economist, author, educator, politician; founding president of Tokyo Woman's Christian University.

Noble Eightfold Path One of the principal teachings of Lord Buddha; the way leading to the cessation of suffering (*dukkha*).

nonanthropomorphic Not comparable in form to a person or human being.

nonbeing Emptiness; forms of reality that do not have substance, particularly important in Buddhism and Taoism.

Nonchurch Christianity Indigenous Japanese Christian movement (Mukyokai) founded by Uchimura Kanzo in 1901 that rejected liturgy, sacraments, and ordained clergy; monthly meetings nurture Christian faith and morals.

Nuh (Noah) In Islam, a prophet who was saved from the Great Flood in an ark while the rest of the world was destroyed due to its unrighteousness.

Okami Amaterasu Major deity in Shinto religion; the sun goddess; Amaterasu ("shining in heaven") is worshiped at Ise Shrine, Honshu, Japan.

Olcott, Colonel Henry Steel (1832–1907) American military officer, journalist, lawyer, and cofounder and first president of the Theosophical Society; first well-known American to make a formal conversion to Buddhism; interpreted Buddhism through a Western perspective; wrote *Buddhist Catechism* (1881).

Organization of the Islamic Cooperation International organization consisting of fifty-seven member states that represents the collective voice of the Muslim world and works to safeguard the interests of Muslims in the spirit of promoting peace; the OIC has a permanent delegation to the United Nations and is the largest international organization outside the United Nations.

Orientalism Depiction of aspects of Middle Eastern and other Asian cultures by Westerners as static and underdeveloped, including other deprecatory views of the "East" that shaped Western imperialism.

Origen (c. 185–c. 254) Early Christian theologian and church father of the Greek church; prolific writer in theology, covering topics of textual criticism, biblical exegesis, preaching, hermeneutics, and spirituality.

Orthodox Christian tradition of Eastern Orthodox churches.

Orthodox Judaism Judaism that adheres to the interpretation and application of the laws and ethics of the Torah as legislated in the Talmud; also referred to as Torah Judaism or traditional Judaism.

orthodoxy That which is considered correct or proper belief as defined by official ecclesiastical bodies; "right belief"; in general, refers to basic Christian beliefs that are accepted by all Christian churches, often seen as expressed in the traditional Apostles' and Nicene Creeds.

Otto, Rudolph (1869–1937) German theologian and scholar of comparative religion; famous for his book *The Idea of the Holy* (1917), which defines the concept of holy as that which is numinous ("non-rational, non-sensory experience or feeling whose primary and immediate object is outside the self").

pagan Broad term pertaining to indigenous polytheistic and nontheistic religious traditions, primarily those in the classical world; also used as a label for any non-Abrahamic ethnic religion; "heretic"; polytheism, shamanism, animism; in the twentieth century, paganism and neopaganism referred to new religious movements attempting to revive historical pre-Abrahamic religions.

Pali Language of the earliest Buddhist scriptures (e.g., Pali Canon, Tripitaka).

Panjabi Pracharni Sabha Society for the promotion of Punjabi language.

panth Sikh term meaning pathway, sect, denomination, or religious society; Sikh Panth refers to the entire community, fellowship, or religious body of Sikhs.

pap One of the Nine Fundamentals of Jain karmic theory; refers to the results of bad deeds (bad karma); demeritorious karma.

paramatman In Hindu philosophy, refers to Absolute Atman or Supreme Soul in Vedanta and yoga practices; the Oversoul or Soul Beyond, which is nearly identical with the Absolute, where individuality/personality vanishes.

parinirvana Complete liberation in Buddhism, occurring upon the death of the body of someone who has attained complete enlightenment (*bodhi*).

Parshva Twenty-third *tirthankara* in Jainism.

Parvati Hindu Goddess (Shakti), wife of Shiva and mother of Ganesha; has wrathful incarnations, such as Durga, Kali, Tara, and Chandi.

Passover Major Jewish festival commemorating Jewish liberation by God from slavery in ancient Egypt as recounted in the story of the exodus in the Hebrew Bible (Tanakh).

Passover seder Jewish gathering on the first night of Passover for a special dinner where the story of the exodus is retold using text and food.

Pax Romana Roman Peace; the period of relative peace and minimal expansion by military force experienced by the Roman Empire (27 BCE–180 CE).

Pearl of Great Price One of the four scriptures of the Church of Jesus Christ of Latter-Day Saints (Mormons); contains selections from the Book of Mormon; portions of the Joseph Smith Translation of the Bible (JST); the *Book of Abraham*, which tells of the plurality of Gods; autobiographical statement of Prophet Joseph Smith Jr.; and Thirteen Articles of Faith, a concise listing of the fundamental doctrines of Mormonism.

Pentecostalism Christian renewal movement that places special emphasis on direct personal experience of God through baptism with the Holy Spirit; adherence to the inerrancy of Scripture and the necessity of accepting Christ as personal Lord and Savior; emphasis on experiencing a Holy Spirit–led and empowered Christian life, represented by the spiritual gifts of speaking in tongues and divine healing; can be interpreted as an institutional body (church) or a characteristic of Christian living.

phenomenology The study of that which appears; study of the structures of subjective experience and consciousness; study of appearances (e.g., of the sacred).

Pita In Sikh tradition, a characteristic of God as Father; a "personal" God as Father.

pluralists In Christian theology of religions, those who give up the centrality of the biblical revelation and argue that all truth is truth, whether conveyed in the Bible or other religious traditions; religions possess different names, but the ultimate reference is the same; Christianity is just one way of attaining salvation, since there is a wide variety of salvific religious paths.

polygamy Marriage that includes more than two partners; when a man is married to more than one wife at a time, the relationship is called polygyny; when a woman is married to more than one husband at a time, it is called polyandry.

polytheism Belief in many deities.

popular religion *See* folk religion.

praeparatio evangelica Preparation for the gospel; in Christian theology of religions, the view that religions are preparations for the gospel; that religions and systems of symbols can be fulfilled, completed only by the revelation of Jesus Christ.

Prakrit The name of any of several Middle Indo-Aryan vernacular languages derived from dialects of Old Indo-Aryan languages; Prakrit languages are related to Sanskrit.

pramada Jain notion of being careless or negligent.

prasad Material substance of food used as a religious offering in Hinduism and Sikhism and consumed by worshipers; a gracious gift that is first offered to a deity and assumed to receive the deity's blessing.

primitivist movements Movements based on the belief that Christianity should be restored along the lines of what is known about the apostolic early church, which primitivists see as the search for a purer and more ancient form of Christianity; appealing to the primitive church as a normative model; also referred to as restorationist or restorationism.

Pritam In Sikh tradition, the characteristic of God, the Lover.

profane In the phenomenology of religion, means mundane, ordinary, repeatable and can be applied to anything (e.g., space, time, language, cosmos, bodies, nature).

Prophet Muhammad (570–632) In Islam, the final prophet in a long line of prophets; referred to as the "Seal of the Prophets"; Allah's messenger sent to proclaim in Arabic the same revelation that had been proclaimed by earlier Jewish and Christian prophets; founder of the religion of Islam.

Protestant One of the major branches of Christianity; emerged with Martin Luther in the sixteenth century as a reaction against medieval Roman Catholic doctrines and traditions; emphasized salvation by grace alone (*sola gratia*), faith alone (*sola fide*), and Scripture alone (*sola scriptura*).

Protestants Members of one of the major branches of Christianity; members of any of several church denominations affirming the principles of the sixteenth-century Protestant Reformation as justification by faith alone, priesthood of all believers, and the primacy of the Bible.

puja In Hindu, Buddhist, and Jain religious traditions, devotional acts that express honor, worship, and devotional attention; worship. In Hindu tradition, a prayer ritual to honor one or more deities; in Jain tradition, worship of the *tirthankaras*; in Buddhist tradition, a devotional act that usually involves bowing before a sacred object or person of honor.

punya Hindu, Jain, and Buddhist concept of merit; that which accumulates as a result of good deeds, acts, or thoughts; results of meritorious actions.

Puranas Ancient Hindu texts eulogizing various deities, especially Brahma, Vishnu, and Shiva.

Purim Jewish holiday that commemorates the deliverance of the Jewish people from the ancient Persian Empire, as recounted in the biblical book of Esther.

Purim *gragger* Noisemaker used during Purim, symbolizing the disapproval whenever the name of Haman, the main antagonist of the story, is mentioned.

Purusha Cosmic man or self; a primeval giant who was sacrificed by the Gods and from whose body came the classes (*varna*) of Hindu tradition.

Qa'abah Cube-shaped "House of God" located in Mecca, Saudi Arabia; the focal point of the hajj pilgrimage and the spiritual center that all Muslims face during daily prayers; Muslims believe it was built by Adam, and then rebuilt by Ibrahim (Abraham) and Isma'il; also known as *ka'bah*.

qibla "Direction"; direction that Muslims face during prayer, which is toward the Qa'abah in Mecca; a prayer wall in the mosque into which the *mihrab* (niche) is set, indicating the direction of prayer, which is always toward the Qa'abah in Mecca.

qiyas In Islamic jurisprudence, an Arabic term referring to the process of deductive analogy in which the teachings of the Hadith are compared and contrasted with those of the Qur'an; use of analogy to interpret Islamic law.

Qur'an The Recitation; central religious text of Islam revealed through the angel Gabriel to Prophet Muhammad; guides Muslims in all areas of life and testifies to the one God (Allah). *See also* al-Qur'an.

Quraysh Influential Meccan tribe during the life of Prophet Muhammad, of which Muhammad was a member; prosperous merchants who controlled Mecca and trade in the region; custodians of the Qa'abah.

Qutb, Sayyid (1906–66) Muslim Egyptian novelist, literary critic, poet, activist, and leader of Islamist perspectives that advocated strict adherence to Islamic law; promoted idea that even Muslim leaders should be replaced (even assassinated) if they lived in a state of ignorance (*jahiliyyah*); executed in 1966 for trying to overthrow Egypt's President Gamal Nasser (1952); influential ideologue on contemporary Islamists advocating physical jihad; strongly criticized the society and culture of the United States.

rabbi In Judaism, a teacher of the Torah; "master," "great one," "teacher."

Rahner, Karl (1904–84) German Jesuit theologian; one of the most influential Roman Catholic theologians of the twentieth century; known for his work in Christology and for his integration of an existential philosophy of personalism with Thomistic realism.

Ramadan Ninth month of the Islamic calendar when Muslims worldwide observe a month of fasting, one of the Five Pillars of Islam; an obligatory fast for all adult Muslims, except those who are sick, traveling, pregnant, have menstrual bleeding, or have health concerns; during Ramadan, Muslims fast from dawn until sunset and also refrain from consuming food and liquids, smoking, and sexual relations during that time.

Ramakrishna, Sri (1836–86) Hindu mystic, Brahmin Vaishnava priest of the Dakshineswar Kali Temple (near Kolkata); promoted God-consciousness and the idea that all religions lead to the same goal, communion with God.

Ramananda Vaishnava who lived in Varanasi in the fifteenth century; a pioneer of the bhakti movement and a social reformer in northern India who promoted devotion to Rama and Sita.

Ramayana One of the great epic poems of India; depicts duties of relationships between husband and wife, devotee and divine; tells the story of Rama, an avatar of Vishnu, who saves his wife, Sita, from the king of Sri Lanka, Ravana.

Rammohan Roy (1772–1833) Modern Hindu reformer; sought several social and religious reforms, such as the abolishment of sati (widow immolation) and child marriage.

Rashi Medieval French rabbi who made a major contribution to Torah study; the author of a comprehensive commentary on the Talmud and the Hebrew Bible (Tanakh).

ra'y In Islamic jurisprudence, personal opinion used to interpret Islamic law.

Reconstructionist Judaism Modern, American-based Jewish movement based on the ideas of Mordecai Kaplan (1881–1983); considers Jewish law (halakhah) not binding but to be treated as a valuable cultural remnant.

Redfield, Robert (1897–1958) American anthropologist and ethnolinguist; wrote on archeology, linguistics, cultural anthropology, and ethnology; author of *The Primitive World and Its Transformation* (1953) and *Peasant Society and Culture* (1956).

Reform Judaism Movement that maintains that Judaism and Jewish traditions should be modernized in order to be compatible with modern culture; Jewish law (halakhah) is considered a guideline rather than a restrictive list.

release In Hinduism, Buddhism, and Jainism, the concept of *moksha*; emancipation, liberation, or release from the cycle of death and rebirth; in epistemological and psychological terms, release connotes freedom, self-realization, and self-knowledge.

Reorganized Church of the Latter-Day Saints American-based international church that is part of the Latter-Day Saints movement; also known as Community of Christ. *See also* Community of Christ.

restoration movement Nineteenth-century movement consisting of several churches that sought to restore the Christian church to a purer form, like the apostolic early church; to reestablish Christianity in its original form. *See also* primitivist movements.

riba In Islamic economic jurisprudence, "usury"; unjust gains in trade or business, considered a major sin in Islam; often defined as "interest" charged in an economic system.

Ricci, Matteo (1552–1610) Italian Jesuit priest who helped found the Jesuit China Mission; Christian missionary to China who adopted Chinese customs and language to communicate Christian faith; the first to translate the Confucian classics into a Western language, Latin, with assistance from the scholar Xu Guangqi.

right conduct In Buddhism and Jainism, the devotee's commitment to be morally upright; not acting in ways that would be corrupt or bring harm to oneself or to others.

right knowledge One of the triple gems of Jainism (right vision, right knowledge, right conduct).

Rightly Guided Caliphs For Sunni Muslims, the first four successors of Prophet Muhammad: Abu Bakr, Umar, Uthman, and 'Ali; all were the Prophet's Companions and from the tribe of Quraysh; their rule is considered a golden age of Islam, but is contested by Shia Muslims.

right vision One of the triple gems of Jainism (right vision, right knowledge, right conduct); determination to discern the meaning of the essence of reality; having the right view of the Nine Fundamentals (Nav Tattvas) in Jainism.

Rig Veda Ancient Hindu sacred texts containing hymns to be recited by Brahmin priests; organized by family books.

rita Hindu Vedic notion of order, rule, truth; the principle of natural order that regulates and coordinates the operation of the universe and everything within it, including the natural world, human, moral and sacrificial orders; cosmic unity.

rituals Formulized actions and behaviors, prescribed by the tradition of a community; includes, for example, various worship practices, rites of passages, purification rites, oaths of allegiance, marriages and funerals, and sports events.

Roberts, Oral (1918–2009) American Methodist-Pentecostal televangelist; one of the best-known and most controversial American religious leaders of the twentieth century; influenced the development of prosperity gospel and abundant life teachings; founded

Oral Roberts University in Tulsa, Oklahoma.

Romero, Oscar (1917–80) Archbishop of San Salvador, El Salvador; strong advocate for the rights of the poor; critic of the United States for giving military aid that led to increased injustice and political repression in El Salvador; denounced persecution of members of the Roman Catholic Church who had worked on behalf of the poor; assassinated by a right-wing death squad while celebrating Mass in March 1980.

Rosh Hashanah Jewish New Year; a two-day celebration that includes the sounding of the ram's horn (shofar) and eating foods such as apples dipped in honey.

rupa Buddhist notion of external or internal matter; form; the physical world; one of the Five Aggregates. See also *skandhas*.

Russell, Charles Taze (1852–1916) Prominent Christian restorationist minister from Pittsburgh, Pennsylvania, whose ideas led to the founding of the Jehovah's Witnesses; began publishing a monthly religious journal, *Zion's Watch Tower and Herald of Christ's Presence*; among his beliefs, Russell agreed with the imminent second coming of Christ and maintained that there was a heavenly resurrection of 144,000 righteous, and that Christ had already returned invisibly in 1874.

Rutherford, Joseph (1869–1942) Succeeded Charles Taze Russell as the second president of the Watch Tower Bible and Tract Society and principle organizer of the Jehovah's Witnesses; born in Missouri, Rutherford emphasized that the Witnesses were the true chosen followers of God.

Sabbath Weekly day of rest or time of worship observed in the Abrahamic religions, but on different days and with different practices.

sacraments Outward signs instituted by God to convey an inward or spiritual grace; liturgical practices of churches; Roman Catholicism recognizes seven sacraments; Protestants recognize two sacraments.

sacred State of being holy, separated; worthy of spiritual respect and devotion; inspires awe among believers.

sacred actions (rituals) Prescribed actions performed in a sacred context; communicative event between the human and the divine.

Sacred and the Profane, The Book by Mircea Eliade (1961) arguing that understanding religion begins with the distinction between the sacred and the profane; religion concerns hierophany (manifestation of the sacred).

sacred community Assembly of religious believers for religious purposes.

sacred corpus Body of holy scripture.

sacred experience Actual experiences of religious believers, distinct according to religious tradition.

sacred objects Material objects set apart for religious purposes.

sacred places Places set apart from ordinary space for religious purposes.

sacred writings Writings that communicate religious truth or insight that shapes the religious community.

sacrifices Offerings of food, objects, animals, or the self as an act of worship or propitiation.

sadhu In Hinduism, a "good man," "a holy man"; a religious ascetic or holy person; one solely dedicated to achieving *moksha* (liberation); in Buddhism, a Pali word that means good, excellent, or auspicious, chanted three times to show appreciation and happiness of something related to the *dhamma*.

sages Spiritual guides, holy teachers, learned persons, pious persons.

sahih In Islam, a term used to classify hadith; "genuine," "authentic," conveyed by a trustworthy and completely competent person; contains neither a serious concealed flaw nor irregularity.

sai Ritual of the hajj pilgrimage in Islam when pilgrims, imitating

Hajar's quest for water for her son, Isma'il, walk or run seven times between the hills of Safa and Marwah.

salat   The second of the Five Pillars of Islam; prayer or worship required five times daily: daybreak (salat al-fajr), noon (salat al-duhr); midafternoon (salat al-asr), sunset (salat al-maghreb), and evening (salat al-isha); times of prayer are determined by the sun's position and announced by the muezzin (prayer announcer) from the minaret (tower) of a mosque.

sallekhana   Jain religious ritual of self-starvation; vow of suicide by fasting taken when one feels that one's life has served its purpose.

salvation   Being saved or delivered from a dire situation, the human condition, sin. See also liberation.

Sama Veda   Ancient Hindu sacred texts containing hymns to various nature deities; organized by instrumental accompaniment.

samkara-dukkha   In Buddhism, ignorance of thinking that anything will permanently satisfy; a form of suffering.

samsara   Hindu, Buddhist, and Jain cycle of death and rebirth; "continuous flow"; existence; reincarnation.

samskara   Buddhist notion of mental habits; predispositions from past impressions; impulses, volition; mental formations triggered by an object; one of the Five Aggregates. See also skandhas.

samvar   Part of Jain karmic theory meaning blockage or stoppage of the inflow of karmas to the soul (jiva).

Sangat   In Sikh tradition, the body of men and women who meet in the presence of the Guru Granth Sahib; the congregation of the Sikh community.

sangha   In Hindu, Jain, and Buddhist traditions "association," "assembly," "community"; usually refers to monastic community of ordained monks and, depending on the tradition, nuns; also may refer to lay believers.

sanna   Buddhist notion of perceptions; capacity to conceptualize and recognize things by associating them with other things; one of the Five Aggregates. See also skandhas.

Sanneh, Lamin (b. 1942)   D. Willis James Professor of Missions and World Christianity and Professor of History at Yale Divinity School; his works include Translating the Message (1989) and Whose Religion Is Christianity? (2003).

sannyasi   Renouncer; final life stage in Hindu tradition in which a devotee renounces worldly and material pursuits and dedicates his or her life to the attainment of spiritual insight.

Sanskrit   Liturgical language in Hinduism; scholarly and literary language in Buddhism and Jainism; an Indo-European language.

Sant   To be good; to be real; refers to those who sing the name of God and worship him, particularly the Hindu bhakti poets.

Sarasvati   Hindu Goddess of wisdom (knowledge), music, arts, and science; companion of Brahma; revered as Brahma's power (Shakti).

Sarasvati, Dayananda   Modern Hindu reformer who argued for supremacy of the Vedic tradition; exhorted India to go back to the Vedas for its identity; called for "India for Indians."

Sat Guru   Guru who dispels the darkness from all three elements of human existence (physical, psychic, and spiritual spheres); someone who enables one to overcome the ego.

Sat Nam   In Sikhism, "everlasting name," referring to the All-Pervading Supreme Reality that sustains the universe; "True Name" that refers to God.

satori   Japanese term for Buddhist notion of "awakening," "comprehension," "understanding"; in Zen Buddhism, seeing one's true nature or essence.

Sattler, Michael (c. 1490–1527)   Monk who left the Roman Catholic Church during the Protestant Reformation to become one of the early leaders of the Anabaptist movement; influential for his role in developing the Schleitheim Confession, the most representative statement of Anabaptist principles.

satya In Hinduism, Jainism, and Buddhism, reality; absolute truth; "unchangeable"; "that which pervades the universe in all its constancy."

sawm In Islam, one of the Five Pillars; fasting; required during Ramadan, when Muslims seek to gain heightened awareness of the presence of Allah; spiritually, to remind Muslims of those who fast involuntarily, because of poverty; time to acknowledge gratitude to Allah.

Schechter, Solomon (1847–1915) An English rabbi and scholar who was founder and president of the United Synagogue of America, the Jewish Theological Seminary of America (New York), and the American Conservative Jewish movement.

Schindler, Oskar (1908–74) German industrialist, spy, and member of the Nazi party credited with saving the lives of more than 1,200 Jews during the Holocaust by employing them in his factories.

Schleiermacher, Friedrich (1768–1834) German theologian, philosopher, and biblical scholar known for his attempt to reconcile criticisms of the Enlightenment with traditional Protestant Christianity; influential in the evolution of higher criticism used in biblical studies; referred to as the "Father of Modern Liberal Theology."

School of Principle Neo-Confucian school, started by Zhu Xi, that saw knowledge as a preparation for action.

School of the Heart/Mind Neo-Confucian school, started by Wang Yangming, that emphasized that one should look to one's own heart or mind to understand morality; regarded as heterodox by some Confucians.

Science and Health with Key to the Scriptures Central text of the Christian Science (1875) religion; written by Mary Baker Eddy and inspired by her personal experience of healing; argues a view of Christianity in which sin, disease, and death are not of God and are therefore not real, contending that by striving for a spiritual understanding of the world as God's perfect creation one can eliminate false beliefs and be healed.

Scranton, Mary F. (1832–1909) Methodist Episcopal Church missionary; first Women's Foreign Missionary Society representative to Korea and the founder of the Ewha Girls School (today's Ewha Womans University).

Second Vatican Council Twenty-first council of the Roman Catholic Church (1962–65), convened by Pope John XXIII; the council enacted extensive church reforms and cast traditional Catholic doctrines such as revelation, salvation, and the church in new theological frameworks.

Sect Shinto Forms of Shinto that include worship or veneration of founders of Shinto sects, separate from government-owned shrines.

sefiroth In Jewish mysticism, the ten attributes or powers in kabbalah through which God created the world and manifests himself, and by which God can be discerned.

Sephardic Jews Members or descendants of the Jews who lived in Spain and Portugal (Iberian Peninsula) until their expulsion in the last decades of the fifteenth century, during the Spanish Inquisition.

Sevener Shiism Major Shia Muslim community; named after Isma'il, the eldest son of Imam Jafar al-Sadiq (d. 756). *See* Imams.

Seventh-Day Adventist Christian denomination distinguished by its observance of Saturday as the Sabbath day of worship and its emphasis on the imminent second coming (advent) of Jesus Christ; the denomination grew out of the Millerite movement as part of restorationism; emphasizes diet and health, holistic understanding of the person, promotion of religious liberty, and conservative principles; part of the larger Adventist movement. *See also* Millerites, restoration movement.

Seymour, William J. (1870–1922) African American minister and initiator of the American Pentecostal movement; son of former slaves, he believed in glossolalia (speaking in tongues) as a confirmation of the gifts of the Holy Spirit; preached against racial barriers in favor of unity in Christ; his preaching influenced the Azusa Street Revival, which launched Pentecostalism in the United States.

shabad Sound, speech; in Sikhism, refers to a hymn or paragraph of the Sikh Holy Scripture.

Shabbat Jewish day of rest and the seventh day of the week.

Shafi'i (d. 820) Muslim jurist, theologian, founder of the Shafi'i school of Islamic law; called the architect of Islamic law; first jurist to insist that hadith were critical sources of law over customary doctrines of the earlier schools of legal thought; rejected use of personal opinion (*ray*) in favor of analogy (*qiyas*).

shahada First of the Five Pillars of Islam; witness; recitation of the Islamic witness of faith: "There is no god but God and Muhammad is the messenger of God"; declaration of acceptation to convert to Islam.

Shahid Sikh Missionary College Located in Amritsar, this college trains Sikh preachers and teaches Sikh sacred texts, philosophy, history, and music.

Shah Jahan (1592–1666) Fifth Mughal emperor, grandson of Akbar the Great; reigned during the golden age of Mughal architectural achievements, such as the Taj Mahal, Moti Masjid, Red Fort, and Jama Masjid.

Shakti Feminine creative power in Hinduism; worshiped as Supreme Being.

sharia Islamic law; "path to the water hole," refers to the fact that water is the whole way of life and source of good; "the right path"; the straight path."

Shavuot Jewish holiday commemorating the anniversary of the day God gave the Torah to the nation of ancient Israel assembled at Mount Sinai.

Shaw, Daniel Professor of anthropology and translation, Fuller Theological Seminary, who grew up in India and the Philippines.

Shema Yisrael "Hear, O Israel: the LORD is our God, the LORD is one"; communicates monotheism of Judaism and Christianity; part of the Jewish morning and evening prayer services.

Shembe, Isaiah Mdliwamafa (1870–1935) Founder of Zulu Nazareth Baptist Church, an indigenous church for the Zulu people, and leading figure in the African Independent Church (AIC) movement in South Africa; itinerant evangelist who healed and prophesied.

shen In indigenous Chinese religion, "spirit," a beneficent spirit of the dead; a deified person; gods; refers also to supernatural or heavenly beings.

Shia Party of 'Ali; followers of 'Ali who believe that 'Ali has Prophet Muhammad's spiritual authority and that divine guidance was passed on to his descendants; the defining moment of Shiism was the martyrdom of Husayn (the son of 'Ali), his male family members, and many companions at Karbala, Iraq, in 681 by the Umayyads.

Shih Ching "Classic of Poetry"; one of the Six Classics of Confucianism, containing the oldest authenticated Chinese poems, dating from the Western Zhou period (1046–771 BCE).

Shi Huang Di, Emperor (260–210 BCE) King of the Chinese State of Qin during the Warring States Period; became the first emperor of a unified China in 221 BCE; first to call himself the emperor of China.

Shinto "Way of the Deities"; indigenous spirituality of Japan and the Japanese.

Shinto Taikyo One of thirteen Shinto sects, with approximately forty thousand members.

Shiromani Gurdwara Prabandhak Committee Parliamentary body responsible for preservation of Sikh places of worship (*gurdwaras*) in northern India by managing the religious, financial, and security facets of *gurdwaras*; also known as the Parliament of the Sikhs.

Shiva Hindu God; the supreme God within Shaivism.

shmriti "That which is remembered"; a classification of Hindu sacred text that is believed to have been passed down orally from one generation to another.

Shoah Destruction; catastrophe in Hebrew; usually refers to the Holocaust.

shofar Ram's horn blown during Rosh Hashanah. *See also* Rosh Hashanah.

shramana Ancient Indian religious movements usually of renunciate ascetics; wandering ascetics; "one who strives"; masculine is *shramana*, feminine is *shramani*.

shramani Female renunciate ascetics or wandering ascetics. See also *shramana*.

Shrine Shinto A form of Shinto religion of Japan that focuses on the worship of *kami* (spirit beings) in public and private shrines.

shruti Classification of Hindu sacred texts believed to be directly from the Gods; cosmic sound of truth; sacred texts of divine origin.

Shu Ching "Classic of History"; one of the Six Classics of Confucianism, among the earliest examples of Chinese prose recording speeches from the early Zhou Dynasty (eleventh century BCE); preserves sayings and recalls deeds of ideal leaders.

Shudras Fourth class in the ancient Hindu *varna* system; functions to serve the other three classes (*varnas*); traditionally, artisans, laborers, and servants; lowest class.

Shvetambara One of the two main denominations of Jains; "white-clad," describing its ascetics' practice of wearing white clothes; believe that women are unable to obtain liberation (*moksha*).

siddha Jain notion of liberated souls who have destroyed all karmic bonding; do not have any kind of body, since they are soul in its purest form.

Siddhartha Personal name of the historic Buddha (Gautama Buddha).

siddha-sila Jain cosmological concept referring to the apex of the universe, where people with infinite knowledge go after they attain liberation (*moksha*); people are called *siddhas* after they discard their mortal bodies.

siddur Jewish prayer book containing daily prayers; Jewish liturgy used on the ordinary Sabbath and on weekdays for domestic and synagogue ritual.

sikha In Sikh tradition, the Pali term for "learner" and "disciple," referring to disciples of the Sikh Gurus. In Hindu tradition, refers to the lock of hair left on top or on the back of the shaven head of a male Orthodox Hindu; today, mainly seen among celibate Hindu monks and temple priests.

Sikh Students Federation Sikh students' union and political organization in India; primarily political but also promotes Sikh heritage and values.

Simons, Menno (1496–1561) Anabaptist religious leader from Friesland, Netherlands, whose movement became known as the Mennonites, emphasizing a radical separation from the world, community discipline, pacifism, independent local congregations, believers' baptism, and the life of holiness.

sin In Christian theology, the human condition of separation from God that arises from opposition to God's purposes; missing the mark; breaking God's law, failing to do what God wills, or rebellion; most of the world religions have some notion of sin as the human problem or condition to be overcome through the insights and practices of the religion (e.g., ignorance, *adharma*, *shirk*).

Singh "Lion"; common name used in South Asia; used as a surname for male Sikhs.

Singh, Manmohan (b. 1932) Best known worldwide as the first Sikh prime minister of India; a renowned economist credited with instituting economic reforms as prime minister that dramatically reduced regulations, thus stimulating the Indian economy.

Singh, Sobha (1890–1978) Prominent Sikh builder and real-estate owner in Delhi; known as *adhi da malik* (the owner of half of Delhi).

Singh Sabha Movement Sikh movement aimed at the revival of the Sikh Guru's teaching, in response to Hindu and Christian mission activities.

Six-Day War War fought between Israel and Egypt (then called United Arab Republic), Jordan, and Syria (June 5–10, 1967), ending with Israel's victory with the capture of the Sinai Peninsula, Gaza Strip, West Bank, Old City of Jerusalem, and Golan Heights.

skandhas In Buddhism, the Five Aggregates; five aspects that constitute the human being. *See also* Five Aggregates.

slamatan Communal feast from Java, Indonesia, symbolizing the social unity of those participating in it; major ritual in Javanese religion.

Smith, Joseph, Jr. (1805–44) American religious leader and founder of the Church of Jesus Christ of Latter-Day Saints movement, a restorationist movement, the predominant branch being Mormonism; published the Book of Mormon, attracted thousands of followers; considered a prophet in a line of biblical prophets; led Latter-Day Saints until he was killed by an armed mob in Carthage, Illinois.

sociocentric Identity that is oriented toward or focused on one's own social group.

sola fide By faith alone; slogan of the Protestant Reformation used by Martin Luther (1483–1546) to indicate that justification of the sinner (salvation) comes only to those who have faith and is not achieved through any "good works" (Rom. 3:28).

sola gratia By grace alone; slogan of the Protestant Reformation indicating that the basis for Christian salvation is solely the grace of God and not any human achievement. It is God's initiative and action that is the agent of salvation.

sola scriptura Scripture alone; slogan of the Protestant Reformation indicating that the church's authority extends only to the Holy Scriptures and not ecclesiastical traditions or human opinions; this was called the "formal principle" or Scripture Principle of the Reformation.

soli Deo gloria For glory to God alone; slogan of the Protestant Reformation meaning that everything that is done is for God's glory to the exclusion of humankind's pride; Christians are to be motivated by God's glory rather than their own.

solus Christus Christ alone; slogan of the Protestant Reformation indicating that Christian salvation is through Christ alone and that Christ is the only mediator between God and human beings.

Soma Hindu Vedic nature deity, depicted as a plant and drink used by Kshatriya class.

Son of Man Hebrew or Aramaic expression that may be a synonym for humankind; mortal; or refer to an apocalyptic figure who will judge the righteous and unrighteous at the end time; used as a title for Jesus.

State Shinto State religion of the Empire of Japan (1868–1945); used as state ideology in Japan.

Sthanakavasi   One of the major Jain denominations; a subsect of Svetambara Jains; reform movement that rejects the use of all images.

Sthaviravadins   "Teaching of the Elders"; one of two of the earliest Buddhist schools.

Stott, John (1921–2011)   English Christian leader, author, and Anglican cleric who was a noted leader of the worldwide evangelical movement; one of the principle authors of the Lausanne Covenant; a rector at All Souls Church, Langham Place; leader of Anglican evangelicalism.

stupa   Buddhist relic house; a mound-like or semihemispherical structure containing Buddhist relics; used as a place of meditation and pilgrimage.

Suffering Servant   Image from the Servant Songs of Isaiah (e.g., 52:13–53:12) indicating that the servant of the Lord is one who suffers on behalf of the people; Judaism sees this as prophetic of Israel, Christians as a prophecy of the sufferings of Jesus Christ for the sin of the world.

Sukkoth   Festival of Booths; Jewish autumn festival of double thanksgiving when a temporary hut is constructed for the weeklong festival commemorating the time when God provided for the ancient Israelites in the wilderness as they were freed from slavery in Egypt.

sunnah   In Islam, custom, normative precedent, conduct, tradition; usually based on Prophet Muhammad's example; Prophet Muhammad's words and actions are believed to complement the divinely revealed message of the Qur'an.

Sunni   Largest branch of the Muslim community, represented by nearly 90 percent of the Muslim world; name derived from the sunnah, the exemplary behavior of Prophet Muhammad. *See also* sunnah.

sunyata   In Buddhism, "emptiness," "voidness," "vacuity"; emptiness as a quality of dharmas and anything pertaining to one's self; a meditative state when one enters and remains in internal emptiness.

surah   In Arabic, "chapter"; usually refers to chapters in holy scripture, especially the Qu'ran; also used to refer to chapters in the Bible in regions influenced by the Arabic language, such as Indonesia and Malaysia.

Sutras   Literally, "thread"; in South Asian religions, a collection of precepts summarizing teaching; one of the discourses or collections of discourses of the Buddha that constitute the basic text of the Buddhist scripture; in Jainism, refers to canonical sermons of the Venerable Mahavira.

Swami Vivekananda (1863–1902)   Modern Hindu reformer, follower of Ramakrishna; key figure introducing Vedanta to the West.

symbol   Object, word, or action that represents or suggests an idea or belief; takes the form of words, gestures, and sounds that serve as pointers or signs.

synagogue   Assembly; Jewish house of prayer considered to be consecrated space used for prayer.

syncretism   Union of two parties against a third; a blending together of views from different philosophical or religious perspectives to the extent that the identity of each part is lost.

tafsir   Qur'anic exegesis; elucidation, interpretation, commentary on the Qur'an; Prophet Muhammad is considered the most authoritative interpreter of the Qur'an.

tai chi   Chinese martial art practiced for defense and health benefits; use of leverage through the joints based on coordination and relaxation in order to balance chi; seeks a healthy balance of yin and yang forces, thereby aiding the flow of chi; also known as tai chi chuan.

tai chi chuan   *See* tai chi.

Taj Mahal   Built by Mughal emperor Shah Jahan in memory of his wife, Mumtaz Mahal; this white marble mausoleum, a UNESCO World

Heritage Site located in Agra, India, is considered the finest example of Mughal architecture.

Takbir God is Great. See *Allahu Akbar.*

tallit Jewish prayer shawl worn over the outer clothes during morning prayers and during all prayers on Yom Kippur; contains special twined and knotted fringes.

Talmud Central text of rabbinic Judaism considered second to the Torah; consists of two parts, Mishnah and Gemara.

Tanakh In Judaism, the canon of the Hebrew Bible, containing the Torah, Nevi'im, and Ketuvim.

tanha Buddhist notion of thirst, craving, desire that drives human beings back into existence (samsara); desire to hold on to pleasurable experiences, identified by Lord Buddha as the principle cause in the arising of suffering (*dukkha*).

tanzil In Islam, to send down; descent; the transmission of divine guidance for human beings through prophets, beginning with Adam and culminating in the mission of Prophet Muhammad.

Tao Chinese concept signifying "path," "way," or "principle": metaphysical concept originating with Laozi that became the basis for religious and philosophical Taoism as well as Confucianism and Zen Buddhism.

Taoshi Taoist priests; the scholars and ritual functionaries of religious Taoism.

Tao Te Ching "Classic of the Way and Its Virtue"; Chinese classic text, ascribed to Laozi; fundamental text for both philosophical and religious Taoism.

tapas A Hindu Vedic and Jain notion denoting spiritual suffering, austerity; the fire that burns within that is needed for the ascetic to foster self-control and attain enlightenment; striving for liberation by undertaking ascetic practices.

taqlid In Islam, imitation; conformity to legal precedent and doctrines; juxtaposed with *ijtihad* (independent reasoning); modern reformers criticize *taqlid* for advocating cultural and intellectual stagnation.

tathagata "One who has thus gone"; term Lord Buddha applied to himself to mean that he had attained a superior state of being and that he was beyond suffering.

tawaf In Islam, the circumambulating of the Qa'abah, House of God, seven times by pilgrims on the pilgrimage (hajj) to Mecca; imitation of angels and all created beings circumambulating the throne of God; the first major ritual performed at the hajj.

tawhid "Divine Unity"; doctrine of God in Islam that communicates the concept of monotheism; that God is One and Unique.

Temple Mount One of the most important religious sites in the Old City of Jerusalem, used by Jews, Christians, and Muslims.

ten Boom, Corrie (1892–1983) Dutch Christian who helped many Jews escape the Holocaust during World War II; later imprisoned by the Nazis for helping Jews; wrote *The Hiding Place.*

Tenrikyo Nineteenth-century Japanese religion that originated in revelations to Nakayama Miki, known as Oya-sama by devotees.

terefah In Judaism, any animal whose death is due to mortal injuries or physical defects; food unfit to eat.

Tertullian (c. 160–c. 255) Early Christian church father, author, theologian from Carthage in the Roman Province of Africa; notable Christian apologist against heresy; referred to as the "Father of Latin Christianity" and the "Founder of Western theology"; oldest Latin writer to use the term "Trinity."

theocentric Belief that God is the central aspect of human existence; in Christian theology of religions, recognizing God, by several names, as the center of the theological universe, rather than Christ

(Christocentrism) or the Holy Spirit (Pneumocentricism).

Theosophical Society   Formed in New York City (1875) by Helena Blavatsky, Henry Steel Olcott, William Quan Judge, and others, the society promoted occultism and the universal brotherhood of humanity through incorporation of Brahmanic and Buddhist teachings.

Theosophy   Divine wisdom; refers to systems of esoteric philosophy concerning direct knowledge of mysteries of being, nature, and God; the attempt to understand the mysteries of the universe and the bonds that unite the universe, human beings, and the divine.

Theravada   Oldest form of Buddhism, derived from term meaning "Teaching of the Elders"; predominant form of Buddhism in mainland Southeast Asia and Sri Lanka.

thetan   In Scientology, a concept similar to soul or spirit; a term derived from the Greek letter *theta*, which in Scientology represents the source of life itself; Scientology asserts that it is the *thetan* that commands the body; Scientology describes *thetan* as a person—not a thing, but creator of things—the immortal spiritual being.

Thirteen Articles of Faith   Creed composed by Prophet Joseph Smith Jr. as a concise listing of fundamental doctrines of Mormonism; Latter-Day Saint denominations consider these articles an authoritative statement of basic theology.

Thomas, M. M. (1916–96)   Renowned Indian Christian theologian, social thinker, activist, and former governor of Nagaland, India; chairperson of the Central Committee of the World Council of Churches; born into a Mar Thoma family and advocate of the ecumenical movement.

Thomas, Robert Jermain (1839–66)   Protestant Christian missionary who served with the London Missionary Society in China and Korea; the second known Protestant missionary to Korea.

Three-Self Patriotic Movement   Only state-sanctioned (registered) Protestant church in mainland China; three guiding principles include self-governance, self-support, and self-propagation, ideas first articulated by Henry Venn (1796–1873) and Rufus Anderson (1796–1880); the attempt in China to remove foreign influences from the Chinese churches and to assure the Chinese communist government that the churches would be patriotic to the People's Republic of China.

t'ien   One of the oldest Chinese terms for the cosmos; a key concept in Chinese mythology, philosophy, and religion; in Taoism and Confucianism, *t'ien* means "Heaven."

T'ien ming   Mandate of Heaven; in Confucian thought, notion that Heaven (*t'ien*) conferred the right to rule directly upon an emperor; continuation of the Mandate of Heaven is conditioned by the personal behavior of the ruler, who is expected to possess righteousness and benevolence.

Tiénou, Tite   Dean and professor of theology of missions at Trinity Evangelical Divinity School.

T'ien Shih   In religious Taosim, "Celestial Master" or "Heavenly Lord"; applied to Chang Lu, who introduced the role of Taoist priests, the scholars and ritual functionaries of religious Taoism who organize Taoist communities and are sometimes marked by a monastic lifestyle.

Tipitaka   Pali word for Three Baskets; the classical Theravada scripture consisting of the Vinaya Pitaka, Sutta Pitaka, and the Abhidhamma Pitaka; same as Tripitaka.

tirthankara   Jain concept of a human being who helps others achieve liberation after succeeding in crossing over life's stream of rebirths and becoming a role model for others; also known as *jina*.

Torah Central concept in Judaism referring to the first five books of the Hebrew Bible (Tanakh), the rabbinic commentaries on it, and the totality of Jewish teaching and practice.

torii Traditional Japanese gate most commonly found at the entrance of a Shinto shrine.

traditionalism Refers to past traditions as the basis for current belief and practice.

traditionalists Social, cultural, and religious perspective that advocates a return to the original sources of a religion to strengthen indigenous, native culture and religion, rather than allowing for outside influence; embraces nativism.

Transcendental Meditation Specific form of mantra meditation (TM), introduced in India in the mid-1950s by Maharishi Mahesh Yogi (1918–2008); TM technique uses a sound or mantra, practiced for fifteen to twenty minutes twice daily with the aim of achieving relaxation and stress reduction.

transubstantiation In Roman Catholic theology, the doctrine that in the Eucharist the substance of the bread and wine used in the sacrament is literally, in actual reality, changed into the substance of the body and blood of Jesus Christ.

triloka Hindu and Buddhist concept of "three worlds," "three realms" of desire, form, and formlessness. Among Jains, refers to three levels of Jain cosmology: (1) the heavens, populated by disembodied souls; (2) the middle, the world inhabited by human beings; and (3) the lower world, inhabited by hell-beings.

Trimurti "Three forms"; Hindu concept in which the cosmic functions of creation, maintenance, and destruction are personified by the Gods Brahma (creator), Vishnu (sustainer), and Shiva (destroyer); the Hindu triad.

Tripitaka Sanskrit word for Three Baskets; the classical Theravada canon consisting of Sutra Pitaka, Vinaya Pitaka, and Abhidharma Pitaka; same as Tipitaka.

Triratna Buddhist creed; "I take refuge in Lord Buddha, I take refuge in the dharma, I take refuge in the *sangha*"; also known as the Three Jewels, Three Refuges of Buddhism, Triple Gem. In Jain tradition, the Three Jewels refer to "correct perception," "correct knowledge," and "correct conduct."

tritheists Those who believe in three separate and individual Gods; some early formulations by Christian theologians were considered to move in this direction, and Christian apologists sought to defend their faith against these charges.

Troeltsch, Ernst (1865–1923) German Protestant theologian, philosopher of religion and history who wrote *The Social Teachings of the Christian Churches* (1912); sought to understand the varied relationship between Christianity and culture, especially modernity; distinguished between church, sect, and mysticism as primary types of religious life, arguing that the church is more inclusive and achieves greater accommodation to other institutions.

tsumi Japanese word that indicates violation of morality; a divine punishment resulting from the violation of a divine command or taboo; sin.

Twelver Shiism In Shia Islam, those who recognize twelve Imams; the largest subdivision within Shia Islam; also known as Ithna Asharis.

Twenty-Eight Fundamental Beliefs Core set of theological beliefs held by the Seventh-Day Adventist Church, understood as descriptors rather than prescriptors; they describe the official theological position of the church, but adherence to them is not a criterion for church membership; the Fundamental Beliefs cover doctrines of God, humankind, salvation, Christian life, the church, and end times.

Tylor, Edward Burnett (1832–1917) English anthropologist; advocated cultural evolutionism; wrote *Primitive Culture* (1871) and *Anthropology* (1881), in which he argues that animism is the first stage of religious development.

Tzom Gedaliah Jewish fast day from dawn until dusk to lament the assassination of the righteous governor of Judah by that name (Gedalia), which ended Jewish rule following the destruction of the first temple (587 BCE).

Uchimura, Kanzo (1861–1930) Japanese Christian author, evangelist, and founder of the Nonchurch Christianity (Mukyokai) in the Meiji and Taisho period in Japan. *See also* Nonchurch Christianity.

ummah Muslim community worldwide; expresses essential unity and equality of all Muslims from diverse cultural and geographical settings.

Underwood, Horace G. (1859–1916) English-born American Presbyterian missionary, educator, and Bible translator who dedicated his life to developing Korean society and Christianity in Korea; worked with the first Protestant missionaries in Korea, established the Seoul YMCA, helped translate the Bible into Korean, and became president of the Joseon Christian College, the predecessor of Yonsei University.

Unification Church New religious movement founded in South Korea in 1954 by Rev. Sun Myung Moon; also known as Holy Spirit Association for the Unification of World Christianity, Family Federation for World Peace and Unification, and Unificationism. *See also* Moon, Sun Myung.

universal brotherhood One of the goals of the Theosophical Society, to form a nucleus of the universal brotherhood of humanity, without regard for race, creed, sex, caste, or color; to oppose bigotry in every form and to promote a feeling of brotherhood among all people and nations.

Upanishads Collection of ancient Hindu philosophical texts that are considered the "end of the Vedas" (Vedanta); develops major concepts of Brahman, atman, karma, and samsara.

usul al-fiqh Roots of Islamic jurisprudence; for Sunni, includes four foundamental sources of knowledge: Qur'an, sunnah, *ijma* (consensus), *qiyas* (analogy); for Shia there is less emphasis on *ijma*.

Uthman (d. 656) Companion of Prophet Muhammad; third Rightly Guided Caliph, from the powerful Umayyad clan; under his leadership, the Qur'an was compiled and standardized.

Vaishnava Ramanandi An egalitarian Hindu sect started by Ramananda, who called for radical equality, even between genders; the group stresses the need to worship the one God, Rama, through bhakti (warm devotion) commitment.

Vaishyas Third class of the ancient Hindu class system; perform tasks of cattle raising, pastoral work, agricultural labor, trade, and business.

Vajrayana Diamond Vehicle; includes Tantric Buddhism and Tibetan Buddhism; emphasis on tantric literature, with goal to become a bodhisattva or enlightened without returning.

Varanasi Most important Hindu place of pilgrimage; one of the oldest continuously inhabited places in the world; according to Hinduism, Varanasi was founded by Shiva; located on the Ganges River, it is also known as Benares.

varna Class division within ancient Hinduism consisting of four groups (Brahmin, Kshatriya, Vaishya, Shudra).

Varnashrama-dharma Hindu notion of acting according to one's class (*varna*), stage of life (*ashrama*), and duty (dharma).

Varuna Hindu Vedic nature deity of the sky who maintains cosmic order.

vedana Buddhist notion of feeling; sensation; sensing an object as either pleasant, unpleasant, or neutral; one of the Five Aggregates. See also *skandhas*.

Vedanta "End of the Vedic hymns"; the summary and goal of the Vedas; philosophical traditions concerned with self-realization and the understanding of the ultimate nature of reality; also known as Upanishad.

Vedas Ancient Hindu sacred texts; the oldest Hindu scriptures (*shruti*) used for the performance of Vedic sacrifices.

vijnana Buddhist notion of consciousness; discernment; that which discerns; one of the Five Aggregates. See also *skandhas*.

Vinaya Literally, "leading out," "education," and "discipline"; a Pali and Sanskrit word that is the regulatory framework for the Buddhist monastic community (sangha); Vinaya Pitaka is one of the three parts that make up the Tripitaka.

virparinama-dukkha Suffering caused by loss of something valuable; a type of the Buddhist notion of suffering (*dukkha*).

Vishnu Hindu supreme God who has ten *avatara*; recognized as the All-Pervading One who sustains the universe. See also avatar.

Wahid, Abdurrahman (1940–2009) Indonesian Islamic thinker, writer, politician; president of Indonesia (1998–2001); chair of the Nahdatul Ulama; moderate Muslim who promoted Islamic boarding schools, religious pluralism and tolerance, social justice, democracy.

Wailing Wall Western Wall located in the Old City of Jerusalem at the foot of the western side of the Temple Mount; a remnant of the ancient wall that surrounded the Jewish temple's courtyard. *See also* Kotel.

wajib In Islamic law, one of the five categories that define the morality of human action; denotes a religious duty commanded by Allah; obligatory or required actions for Muslims. See

also *haraam, mandub, makruh*, and *mubah*.

Walls, Andrew (b. 1928) British historian and missiologist; major thinker and promoter of the study of Christian missions; pioneer in the studies of African church history; wrote *The Missionary Movement in Christian History* (1996), among other works.

Wang Yangming (1472–1529) Regarded as the most important Chinese Neo-Confucian philosopher, he denied the rationalist dualism of the orthodox philosophy of Zhu Xi.

Warren, Rick (b. 1954) An American evangelical Christian pastor and author; founder and senior pastor of Saddleback Church and author of the popular book *The Purpose Driven Life*.

Warring States Period Period in ancient China that culminated in the unification of China (475–221 BCE) under the Qin Dynasty; a period of violent civil disorders when smaller states disappeared and seven larger states remained to fight ruthlessly for supremacy until 221 BCE.

Watchtower Illustrated religious magazine of the Jehovah's Witnesses printed monthly in 209 languages; the magazine was started by Charles Taze Russell to draw attention to what he believed were the last days and to draw attention to the kingdom of God, which he believed would replace earthly governments.

Weber, Max (1864–1920) German sociologist, philosopher, and political economist, who is considered one of the founders of the discipline of sociology; influenced social theory and social research and introduced the "rationalization thesis" and the "Protestant Ethic thesis"; Weber was a massive intellectual figure who had far-reaching impact across a vast array of academic disciplines.

Western Wall Wailing Wall located in the Old City of Jerusalem at the foot of the western side of the Temple Mount; a remnant of the ancient wall that surrounded the Jewish temple's courtyard. *See also* Kotel.

White, Ellen G, (1827–1915) Born and raised in Gorham, Maine, White was one of the founders of the Seventh-Day Adventist Church; she was considered a prophet and her restorationist writings and prophecies were central to that denomination's early growth; among Adventists, her writings hold a secondary role to the Bible; she wrote *Steps to Christ*, *The Ministry of Healing*, and several books concerning the Great Controversy theme held centrally by Adventists, the cosmic battle between Jesus Christ and Satan.

wilaya In Islam, concept of guardianship, important within Twelver Shiism, where it signifies the legitimacy of 'Ali's claim to lead the Islamic community; in Islamic law, the term refers to guardianship of minors or to authority to contract marriage on behalf of a previously unmarried Muslim woman.

World Council of Churches Interchurch, ecumenical organization founded in 1948, describing itself as "a worldwide fellowship of 349 global, regional, and sub-regional, national and local churches seeking unity, a common witness, and Christian service"; consists of mostly mainline Protestant churches from 150 countries, representing 520,000 local congregations.

worldview Comprehensive orientation of an individual or society and its knowledge; includes natural philosophy, existential and normative affirmations; also, a fundamental orientation of the heart expressed in story or a set of presuppositions.

wudu In Islam, minor ablution; obligatory cleansing rituals performed in order to render the believer ritually pure; required prior to prayer for both men and women; consists of washing the hands, mouth, face, arms up to the elbows, and feet; defilements such as sleep, sex, menstruation, and going to the toilet require minor ablution.

wu-wei Taoist concept of nonaction, nondoing; notion that beings that are wholly in harmony with the Tao behave in a completely natural way; action without action.

xiao Confucian concept of filial piety. *See also* filial piety.

xin Chinese Confucian concept of mind; refers to one's disposition or feeling, since ancient Chinese people believed the heart was the center of human cognition.

Yahweh God of the ancient kingdoms of Israel and Judah, whose name was revealed to Moses as four Hebrew consonants (YHWH), called the Tetragrammaton.

Yajur Veda One of the Hindu Veda collections; organized by sacrifice.

yanban Korean concept of ruling class or nobles during Joseon Dynasty.

yang In Chinese religion, one of two fundamental cosmic forces of the universe; considered the positive principle of light, warmth, dryness, maleness, and activity.

Yathrib Second holiest city of Islam, to which Prophet Muhammad and early followers emigrated (*hijra*) in 622 CE; following the successful negotiation of a truce by Prophet Muhammad, the city was renamed Medina. *See also* Medina.

Yeshua Hebrew name, common alternative form of the name Joshua; name corresponding to the Greek (*Iesous*), from which comes the English spelling, Jesus.

YHWH Tetragrammaton representing the God of the ancient kingdoms of Israel and Judah, whose name was revealed to Moses as four Hebrew consonants (YHWH); Yahweh. *See* Yahweh.

yi The Confucian virtue of righteousness and justice; the moral disposition to do good.

Yi, Gwang-jeong Korean diplomat who in 1603 returned from Beijing carrying several theological books written by Matteo Ricci, a Jesuit missionary to China; he disseminated the information in the books, planting the first seeds of Christianity in Korea.

Yiddish High Germanic language of Ashkenazic Jewish origin, spoken in many parts of the world; developed as a fusion of different German dialects with Hebrew, Aramaic, and Slavic vocabulary; the international language of the Ashkenazic Jews.

yin In Chinese religion, one of two fundamental cosmic forces of the universe; considered the negative principle of dark, wetness, cold, passivity, and femaleness.

Yin-Yang Cosmologists One of the six major Chinese schools of philosophy that emerged during the Warring States Period (403–221 BCE), it promoted the investigation of the art of yin and yang; based rituals, actions, and divination on natural rhythms of the universe, particularly the patterns of the four seasons.

yoga Physical, mental, and spiritual discipline originating in ancient India, with a goal of attaining peace and liberation.

Yogasutras Hindu teachings that present eight stages ("limbs") or steps that guide the practitioner to union with Brahman; these steps form the basis for nearly all future yogic practices.

Yogi, Maharishi Mahesh (1918–2008) Born in Madya Pradesh, India, and developed the Transcendental Meditation (TM) technique; organized a movement to spread the teaching of TM throughout the world.

yogic breathing Originally a Hindu discipline of seeking to control breath as part of the overall practice of yoga; means "extension of the life force," used by many South Asian religions and New Religious Movements.

Yom Kippur Day of Atonement, when Jews seek to expiate their sins and achieve reconciliation with God; holiest day of the year for Jews, with the central themes of atonement and repentance.

Young, Brigham (1801–77) American religious leader, second president of the Church of Jesus Christ of Latter-Day Saints, who led his followers, the Mormon pioneers, in an exodus through a desert to Zion in the Wilderness, Salt Lake Valley, Utah, the headquarters of the Church of Jesus Christ of Latter-Day Saints.

Yueh Ching One of the Six Classics of Confucianism, "Classic of Music" lost by the time of the Han Dynasty; argued that the scholarly gentleman should be adept at music.

Yun, Sung-Bum (1916–80) Korean Christian theologian who studied with Karl Barth; wrote in support of Korean Confucianism as a lens through which to understand Christian ethics; controversial figure who sought to create an indigenous Korean Christian theology—for example, interpreting the Christian notion of the Godhead through the ancient Korean mythologies of divine figures.

zakat One of the Five Pillars of Islam; required almsgiving; purification of wealth; Muslims are required to give 2.5 percent of their net worth annually; connotes path to purity and spirituality; collection is used for the poor.

Zen A Mahayana school of Japanese Buddhism that developed first in China (known as Ch'an), emphasizing attainment of enlightenment by direct insight into Buddhist teaching; seeks direct understanding through sitting meditation (*zazen*) and use of a brief paradoxical statement or question (*koan*) to exhaust the analytic intellect and will in order to be awakened.

zeroah Roasted lamb shanks used for the Jewish Passover seder to represent the lamb that was sacrificed during the ancient Jews' exodus from Egypt.

Zhuangzi In Chinese religion, known as "Master Zhuang," a defining historical figure in Chinese Taoism and writer of the book *Zhuangzi*.

Zhung Yung One of the four books of Confucian philosophy, "Doctrine of the Mean"; philosophical treatment of Confucian metaphysics, politics, and ethics.

Zhu Xi A Song Dynasty Confucian scholar who led the School of Principle; the most influential Neo-Confucian in China.

Zionism Jewish nationalist movement whose goal has been the creation and support of a Jewish national state in Palestine, the ancient homeland of the Jews; the nationalist attachment of the Jews and of Judaism to the historical region of Palestine, where one of the hills of ancient Jerusalem was called Zion.

Zohar Book of Radiance; in the Jewish mystical tradition of kabbalah, a collection of several commentaries on the Torah attributed to Simeon ben Yohai (second century CE).

Zuhr Second of five daily prayers in Islam; midday prayer; Dhuhr prayer or Salat-ul-Zuhr.

Zwingli, Ulrich (1484–1531) Leader of the Reformation in Switzerland; Roman Catholic priest in Zurich who opposed the sale of indulgences, clerical celibacy; along with Martin Luther, Zwingli represented early leadership of the Protestant Reformation; his ideas were taken up by John Calvin to create Reformed theology.

Bibliography

Adiswarananda (Swami). *Vivekananda, World Teacher: His Teachings on the Spiritual Unity of Humankind*. Woodstock: SkyLight Paths, 2006.

Ahlstrom, Sydney E., ed. *Theology in America: The Major Protestant Voices from Puritanism to Neo-orthodoxy*. Indianapolis: Bobbs-Merrill, 1967.

Ali, Maulana Muhammad. *The Religion of Islam*. Columbus, OH: Ahmadiyya Anjuman Isha'at Islam, 1994.

Amaladoss, Michael. *The Asian Jesus*. Maryknoll, NY: Orbis Books, 2006.

Aritonang, Jan Sihar, and Karel Steenbrink, eds. *A History of Christianity in Indonesia*. Leiden: Brill Academic, 2008.

Augustine. *The Confessions*. Translated by R. S. Pine-Coffin. New York: Penguin Classics, 1961.

Babb, Lawrence. *Absent Lord: Ascetics and Kings in a Jain Ritual Culture*. Berkeley: University of California Press, 1996.

———. *Redemptive Encounters: Three Modern Styles in the Hindu Tradition*. Berkeley: University of California Press, 1986.

Babington, Charles, and Alan Cooperman. "The Rev. Moon Honored at Hill Reception: Lawmakers Say They Were Misled." *Washington Post,* June 23, 2004.

Baron, Joseph L., ed. *A Treasury of Jewish Quotations*. Northvale, NJ: Jason Aronson, 1996.

Barrett, David B., Todd M. Johnson, and Peter F. Crossing. "Missiometrics 2008: Reality Checks for Christian World Communions." *International Bulletin of Missionary Research* 32, no. 1 (January 2008): 27–31.

Barrett, David B., George T. Kurian, and Todd M. Johnson, eds. *World Christian Encyclopedia: A Comparative Survey of Churches and Religions in the Modern World*. New York: Oxford University Press, 2001.

Barth, Frederik. *Ethnic Groups and Boundaries*. Boston: Little, Brown, 1969.

Barth, Karl. *Church Dogmatics*. Edited by G. W. Bromiley and T. F. Torrence. Vol. I/2. Translated by G. T. Thomson and Harold Knight. Edinburgh: T&T Clark, 1956.

———. *Church Dogmatics*. Edited by G. W. Bromiley and T. F. Torrence. Vol. II/1. Translated by T. H. L. Parker et al. Edinburgh: T&T Clark, 1957.

———. *The Epistle to the Romans*. London: Oxford University Press, 1968.

Bays, Daniel. *Christianity in China: From the Eighteenth Century to the Present*. Stanford, CA: Stanford University Press, 1996.

Bear, Laura. *Lines of the Nation: Indian Railway Workers, Bureaucracy, and the Intimate Historical Self*. New York: Columbia University Press, 2007.

Beckert, Heinz, and Richard Gombrich, eds. *The World of Buddhism*. New York: Thames-Hudson, 1987.

Beckford, James A. *Social Theory and Religion*. Cambridge: Cambridge University Press, 2003.

Bellah, Robert N. "Religious Evolution." *American Sociological Review* 29 (1964): 358–74.

Bellah, Robert N., and Steven M. Tipton. *The Robert Bellah Reader*. Durham, NC: Duke University Press, 2006.

Benedict, Ruth. *Patterns of Culture*. Boston: Houghton-Mifflin, 1934.

Berg, Herbert. *The Development of Exegesis in Early Islam: The Authenticity of Muslim Literature from the Formative Period*. Richmond, Surrey: Curzon Press, 2000.

Berger, Peter L. *The Heretical Imperative*. New Delhi: Doubleday, 1979.

Berger, Peter L., and Thomas Luckmann. *The Social Construction of Reality*. London: Penguin Books, 1967.

Bevans, Stephen B. *Models of Contextual Theology*. Maryknoll, NY: Orbis Books, 2004.

Bhikkhu, Thanissaro, trans. *Itivuttaka: The Group of Ones, Access to Insight (Legacy Edition)*. http://www.accesstoinsight.org/tipitaka/kn/iti/iti.1.001-027.than.html.

———, trans. *Therigatha: Access to Insight (Legacy Edition)*. http://www.accesstoinsight.org/tipitaka/kn/thag/thag.01.00x.than.html#top.

Blavatsky, H. P. *The Secret Doctrine*. Wheaton: Theosophical Publishing House, 1993.

Bloxham, Donald. *The Final Solution: A Genocide*. New York: Oxford University Press, 2009.

Bowker, John. *The Oxford Dictionary of World Religions*. New York: Oxford University Press, 1997.

Bromley, David G., and J. Gordon Melton. *Cults, Religion, and Violence*. New York: Cambridge University Press, 2002.

Brown, Judith M. *Global South Asians: Introducing the Modern Diaspora*. New York: Cambridge University Press, 2006.

Brown, Judith M., and Robert Eric Frykenberg, eds. *Christians, Cultural Interactions, and India's Religious Traditions*. Grand Rapids: Eerdmans, 2002.

Buettner, Dan. "The Secrets of Long Life." *National Geographic*, November 16, 2005, 2–27.

Burridge, Kenelm. *In the Way: A Study of Christian Missionary Endeavors*. Vancouver: University of British Columbia Press, 1991.

———. *Someone, No One: An Essay on Individuality*. Princeton: Princeton University Press, 1979.

Buswell, Robert E., and Timothy S. Lee, eds. *Christianity in Korea*. Honolulu: University of Hawaii Press, 2007.

Calvin, John. *Institutes of the Christian Religion*. 1559. Translated by Ford Lewis Battles. Vol. 1. Philadelphia: Westminster Press, 1967.

Carter, John Ross, and Mahinda Palihawadana, trans. *The Dhammapada: The Sayings of the Buddha*. New York: Oxford University Press, 2008.

Casanova, José. *Public Religions in the Modern World*. Chicago: University of Chicago Press, 1994.

Chan, Wing-tsit. *China*. Berkeley: University of California Press, 1946.

———. *A Source Book in Chinese Philosophy*. Princeton: Princeton University Press, 1969.

Ching, Julia. *The Religious Thought of Chu Hsi*. New York: Oxford University Press, 2000.

Cohn-Sherbok, Dan. *Judaism: History, Belief and Practice*. Philadelphia: Psychology Press, 2003.

Cole, W. Owen. "Sikhism." In *The New Penguin Handbook of Living Religions*, edited by John R. Hinnells, 331–32. New York: Penguin Books, 2003.

Cole, W. Owen, and Piara Singh Sambhi. *The Sikhs: Their Religious Beliefs and Practices*. New York: St. Martin's Press, 1993.

Company, Robert Ford. *To Live as Long as Heaven and Earth: A Translation and Study of Ge Hong's Traditions of Divine Transcendents*. Berkeley: University of California Press, 2002.

Confucius. *The Analects*. Translated by D. C. Lau. New York: Penguin Books. 1979.

Conze, Edward. *Buddhist Meditation*. New York: Allen & Unwin, 1956.

Coward, Harold, Ronald Neufeldt, and Eva K. Neumaier, eds. *Readings in Eastern Religions*. Waterloo, Ontario: Wilfrid Laurier University Press, 2007.

Cowell, E. B., trans. *Buddhist Mahayana Texts*. Sacred Books of the East 49. London: RoutledgeCurzon, 2001.

Cox, Caroline. *Cox's Book of Modern Saints and Martyrs*. New York: Continuum International, 2006.

Cragg, Kenneth. *Call of the Minaret*. Oxford: Oneworld, 2000.

Cragg, Kenneth, and Marston Speight. *Islam from Within*. Belmont, CA: Wadsworth, 1950.

Creel, Herrlee Glessner. *What Is Taoism? and Other Studies in Chinese Cultural History*. Chicago: University of Chicago Press, 1982.

Dalai Lama. *The World of Tibetan Buddhism: An Overview of Its Philosophy and Practice*. Somerville, MA: Wisdom, 1995.

Daschke, Dereck, and Michael Ashcraft. *New Religious Movements: A Documentary Reader*. New York: New York University Press, 2005.

Dass, Nirmal. "Raga Basant." In *Songs of the Saints from the Ādi Granth*, 162–63. Albany: State University of New York Press, 2000.

Davis, Winston. *Japanese Religion and Society: Paradigms of Structure and Change*. Albany: State University of New York Press, 1992.

Dawson, Lorne L., ed. *Cults and New Religious Movements: A Reader*. Blackwell Readings in Religion. Malden, MA: Blackwell, 2003.

De Lange, Nicholas. *An Introduction to Judaism*. New York: Cambridge University Press, 2000.

De Michelis, Elizabeth. *A History of Modern Yoga*: *Patañjali and Western Esotericism*. New York: Continuum, 2004.

Denny, Frederick Mathewson. *An Introduction to Islam*. New York: Macmillan, 1993.

Devanandan, P. D. *Preparation for Dialogue*. Bangalore: CISRS, 1964.

Dick, Everett N. *William Miller and the Advent Crisis*. Berrien Springs: Andrews University Press, 1994.

Dictionary of African Christian Biography. http://www.dacb.org/index.html.

Doniger, Wendy. *The Hindus: An Alternative History*. New York: Penguin Books, 2009.

———. trans. *The Rig Veda*. New York: Penguin Books, 1981.

Doniger, Wendy, and Brian K. Smith. *The Laws of Manu*. London: Penguin Books, 1991.

Doran, Robert. *Birth of a Worldview: Early Christianity in Its Jewish and Pagan Context*. New York: Westview Press, 1995.

Dorff, Elliot N. *Conservative Judaism: Our Ancestors to Our Descendants*. New York: United Synagogue of Conservative Judaism, 1977.

Douglas, Mary. *Purity and Danger*. London: Routledge & Kegan Paul, 1966.

Dumont, Louis. *Homo Hierarchicus*. Chicago: University of Chicago, 1970.

Dumoulin, Heinrich. *Zen Buddhism: A History*. Vol. 1, *India and China*. Translated by James W. Heisig and Paul Knitter. Bloomington, IN: World Wisdom, 2005.

Dundas, Paul. *The Jains*. New York: Routledge, 2002.

Durkheim, Emile. "The Dualism of Human Nature and Its Social Conditions." In *Emile Durkheim on Morality and Society*, edited by Robert Bellah, 149–66. Chicago: University of Chicago Press, 1973.

———. *The Elementary Forms of the Religious Life*. Translated by Joseph Ward Swain. New York: Free Press, 1965.

Dusenbery, Verne A. "A Sikh Diaspora? Contested Identities and Constructed Realities." In *Nation and Migration: The Politics of Space in the South Asian Diaspora*, edited by Peter van der Veer, 17–42. Philadelphia: University of Pennsylvania Press, 1995.

Earhart, H. Byron. *Japanese Religion: Unity and Diversity*. Belmont, CA: Wadsworth, 1983.

Eck, Diana. *A New Religious America: How a "Christian Country" Has Become the World's Most Religiously Diverse Nation*. San Francisco: HarperOne, 2002.

Eddy, Mary Baker. *Church Manual of The First Church of Christ, Scientist*. Boston: The First Church of Christ Scientist, 1910.

———. *Science and Health with Key to the Scriptures*. Boston: The First Church of Christ, Scientist, 1875. Available online at http://mbeinstitute.org/ScienceAnd Health/SandH.pdf

Eliade, Mircea. *Myth and Reality*. New York: Harper & Row, 1963.

———. *The Myth of the Eternal Return: Or, Cosmos and History*. Translated by Willard R. Trask. Princeton: Princeton University Press, 1954.

———. *Patterns of Comparative Religion*. Translated by Rosemary Sheed. Lincoln: University of Nebraska Press, 1958.

———. *The Sacred and the Profane*. Translated by Willard R. Trask. New York: Harcourt Brace Jovanovich, 1959.

Ellwood, Robert, and Richard Pilgrim. *Japanese Religion: A Cultural Perspective*. Englewood Cliffs, NJ: Prentice Hall, 1985.

Embree, Ainslee T. *The Hindu Tradition: Readings in Oriental Thought*. New York: Vintage Books, 1972.

———. *Sources of Indian Tradition*. Vol. 1, *From the Beginnings to 1800*. New York: Columbia University Press, 1988.

Enroth, Ronald. *Churches That Abuse*. Grand Rapids: Zondervan, 1993.

———. *A Guide to New Religious Movements*. Downers Grove, IL: InterVarsity, 2005.

Erye, Ronald. *The Long Search: Land of the Disappearing Buddha*. DVD. Directed by Jonathan Stedall. UK: British Broadcasting Corporation, 1977.

Esposito, John L. *Islam: The Straight Path*. New York: Oxford University Press, 1988.

———, ed. *The Oxford Dictionary of Islam*. New York: Oxford University Press, 2003.

———. *Unholy War: Terror in the Name of Islam*. New York: Oxford University Press, 2003.

Esposito, John L., and John O. Voll. *Makers of Contemporary Islam*. Oxford: Oxford University Press, 2001.

Evans-Pritchard, E. E. *Nuer Religion*. New York: Oxford University Press, 1971.

———. *Theories of Primitive Religion*. Oxford: Clarendon Press, 1965.

Farhadian, Charles E., ed. *Christian Worship Worldwide*. Grand Rapids: Eerdmans, 2007.

Fischer, Louis. *Quotes from Gandhi: His Life and Message for the World*. New York: Mentor, 1982.

Fishbane, Michael. *Judaism*. Hagerstown, MD: Torch, 1987.

Fox, Richard G. *Lions of the Punjab*. Berkeley: University of California Press, 1985.

Freud, Sigmund. *Civilization and Its Discontents*. New York: W. W. Norton, 2005.

———. *Future of an Illusion*. Translated by James Strachey. New York: W. W. Norton, 1989.

———. *The Standard Edition of the Complete Psychological Works of Sigmund Freud*. Edited by James Strachey with Anna Freud. London: Hogarth Press, 1961.

Frykenberg, Robert Eric, ed. *Christians and Missionaries in India: Cross-Cultural Communication since 1500*. Grand Rapids: Eerdmans, 2003.

———. "Constructions of Hinduism at the Nexus of History and Religion." *Journal of Interdisciplinary History* 23, no. 3 (Winter 1993): 523–50.

———. "The Emergence of Modern 'Hinduism' as a Concept and as an Institution: A Reappraisal with Special Reference to South India." In *Hinduism Reconsidered*, edited by Gunther Sontheimer and Hermann Kulke, 82–107. New Delhi: Manohar Books, 1997.

———. "India." In *A World History of Christianity*, edited by Adrian Hastings, 147–89. London: Cassell, 1999.

———. *Pandita Ramabai's America: Conditions of Life in the United States*. Grand Rapids: Eerdmans, 2003.

Geertz, Clifford. *The Interpretation of Cultures*. New York: Basic Books, 1973.

———. *Negara: The Theatre State in Nineteenth-Century Bali*. Princeton: Princeton University Press, 1981.

———. *The Religion of Java*. Chicago: University of Chicago Press, 1976.

Gellner, Ernst. *Nations and Nationalism*. Ithaca, NY: Cornell University Press, 2009.

Gibbs, Eddie, and Ryan K. Bolger. *Emerging Churches: Creating Christian Community in Postmodern Cultures*. Grand Rapids: Baker Academic, 2005.

Glock, Charles Y., and Robert N. Bellah, eds. *The New Religious Consciousness*. Berkeley: University of California Press, 1976.

Goel, Sita Ram. *Hindu Temples: What Happened to Them*. New Delhi: Voice of India, 2000.

Gohil, Neha Singh, and Dawinder S. Sidhu. "The Sikh Turban: Post-9/11 Challenges to This Article of Faith." *Rutgers Journal of Law and Religion* 9, no. 2 (Spring 2008): i–60.

Gombrich, Richard. *Buddhism Transformed: Religious Change in Sri Lanka*. Princeton: Princeton University Press, 1990.

González, Justo L. *A History of Christian Thought*. Vol. 3, *From the Protestant Reformation to the Twentieth Century*. Nashville: Abingdon, 1987.

Grimes, John. *A Concise Dictionary of Indian Philosophy: Sanskrit Terms Defined in English*. Albany: State University of New York, Albany, 1996.

Gutiérrez, Gustavo. *A Theology of Liberation*. Maryknoll, NY: Orbis Books, 1988.

Hannerz, Ulf. *Cultural Complexity: Studies in the Social Organization of Meaning*. New York: Columbia University Press, 1992.

Harvey, Peter. *An Introduction to Buddhism: Teachings, History, and Practices*. Cambridge: Cambridge University Press, 2012.

———. *The Selfless Mind*. New York: Routledge, 1995.

Hauerwas, Stanley, and William H. Willimon. *Resident Aliens: Life in the Christian Colony*. Nashville: Abingdon, 1989.

Hefner, Robert W. *Conversion to Christianity: Historical and Anthropological Perspectives on a Great Transformation*. Berkeley: University of California Press, 1993.

Hefner, Robert W., and Patricia Horvatich. *Islam in an Era of Nation-States*. Honolulu: University of Hawaii Press, 1997.

Hiebert, Paul R., Daniel Shaw, and Tite Tiénou. *Understanding Folk Religion*. Grand Rapids: Baker Books, 1999.

Hinnells, John R. *Handbook of Living Religions*. London: Penguin Books, 1997.

Holdheim, Samuel. *Das Ceremonialgesetz in Messiasreich*. Schwerin, Germany: C. Kürschner, 1845.

Hucker, Charles O. *China's Imperial Past: An Introduction to Chinese History and Culture*. Stanford, CA: Stanford University Press, 1975.

Jacobi, Hermann, trans. *Gaina Sutras*. Sacred Books of the East 22. 1884. Reprint, Oxford: Clarendon Press, 2001.

———. *Jaina Sūtras*. Richmond, Surrey: Curzon Press, 2001.

Jacobs, Alan. *The Principal Upanishads*. New York: O Books, 2003.

Jacobsen, Knut A., Helene Basu, Angelika Malinar, and Vasudha Narayanan, eds. "Ramanandi." In *Brill's Encyclopedia of Hinduism*. Vol. 3, *Society, Religious Specialists, Religious Traditions, Philosophy*, 478–89. Leiden: Brill, 2011.

Jaini, Padmanabh S. *The Jaina Path of Purification*. Berkeley: University of California Press, 1979.

Jaspers, Karl. *The Origin and Goal of History*. Translated by Michael Bullock. London: Routledge & Keegan Paul, 1953.

Jenkins, Philip. *God's Continent: Christianity, Islam, and Europe's Religious Crisis*. New York: Oxford University Press, 2009.

———. *The New Faces of Christianity: Believing the Bible in the Global South*. New York: Oxford University Press, 2008.

———. *The Next Christendom: The Coming of Global Christianity*. New York: Oxford University Press, 2007.

Jessee, Dean C., and Ronald K. Esplin, eds. *The Joseph Smith Papers*. Vol. 1, *Journals*. Salt Lake City: Church Historian's Press, 2008.

Kahn, Miriam. "Sunday Christians, Monday Sorcerers: Selective Adaptation to Missionization in Wamira." *Journal of Pacific History* 18 (1983): 96–112.

Keay, Frank Ernest. *Kabir and His Followers*. New Delhi: Aravali Books International, 1997.

Kee, Howard Clark, Jerry W. Frost, Emily Aibu, and Carter Lindberg. *Christianity: A Social and Cultural History*. New York: Macmillan, 1991.

Khaldun, Ibn. *The Muqaddimah: An Introduction to History*. Vol. 2. Translated by Franz Rosenthal. Princeton: Princeton University Press, 1967.

Khyentse, Dilgo. *The Heart of Compassion: The Thirty-Seven Verses on the Practice of a Bodhisattva*. Translated by Padmakara Translation Group. Boston: Shambhala, 2007.

Kim, Heup Young. *Christ and the Tao*. Eugene, OR: Wipf and Stock Publishers, 2010.

King, Martin Luther, Jr. *A Testament of Hope: The Essential Writings and Speeches of Martin Luther King, Jr.* New York: HarperCollins, 1990.

King, Richard. *Indian Philosophy: An Introduction to Hindu and Buddhist Thought*. Washington, DC: Georgetown University Press, 1999.

———. *Orientalism and Religion: Post-Colonial Theory, India and "The Mystic East."* London: Routledge, 1999.

King, Winston L. "Religion." In *The Encyclopedia of Religion*. Vol. 12, edited by Mircea Eliade, 282–93. New York: Simon and Schuster Macmillan, 1995.

Kitagawa, Joseph M. *On Understanding Japanese Religions*. Princeton: Princeton University Press, 1987.

———. *Religious Traditions of Asia: Religion, History, and Culture*. London: Routledge, 2002.

Klostermaier, Klaus K. *A Survey of Hinduism*. Albany: State University of New York Press, 1989.

Kohn, Livia. *Daoist Body Cultivation: Traditional Models and Contemporary Practices.* Cambridge, MA: Three Pines Press, 2006.

———. *Daoist Mystical Philosophy.* Cambridge, MA: Three Pines Press, 2007.

Kohn, Livia, and Robin R. Wang, eds. *Internal Alchemy.* Cambridge, MA: Three Pines Press, 2009.

Kosambi, Meera. *Pandita Ramabai through Her Own Words.* New York: Oxford University Press, 2000.

Koyama, Kosuke. *Water Buffalo Theology.* Maryknoll, NY: Orbis Books, 1999.

Kulke, Hermann, and Dietmar Rothermund. *A History of India.* 3rd ed. New York: Routledge, 2003.

Küng, Hans. *Christianity and World Religions: Paths to Dialogue.* Maryknoll, NY: Orbis Books, 1993.

Kunin, Seth Daniel, and Jonathan Miles-Watson, eds. *Theories of Religion.* Piscataway, NJ: Rutgers University Press, 2006.

Lai, Kishori Saran. *Legacy of Muslim Rule in India.* New Delhi: Aditya Prakashan, 1992.

Lao Tsu. *Tao Te Ching.* Translated by Gai-Fu Feng and Jane English. New York: Vintage Books, 1972.

Latourette, Kenneth Scott. *A History of Christianity: Beginnings to 1500.* Peabody, MA: Prince Press, 1997.

———. *A History of Christianity: Reformation to the Present.* Peabody, MA: Prince Press, 1997.

Layton, Bentley. *The Gnostic Scriptures: A New Translation with Annotations and Introductions.* Garden City, NY: Doubleday, 1987.

Lee, Timothy S. *Born Again: Evangelicalism in Korea.* Honolulu: University of Hawaii Press, 2010.

Lefebure, Leo D., and Peter Feldmeier. *The Path of Wisdom: A Christian Commentary on the* Dhammapada. Grand Rapids: Eerdmans, 2011.

Legge, James, trans. *The Li Ki or the Collection of Treatises on the Rules of Propriety or Ceremonial Usages.* Sacred Books of the East 28. Oxford: Clarendon, 1885. Reprint, Delhi: Motilal Banarsidass, 1968.

Levy, Reuben. *The Social Structure of Islam.* Cambridge, UK: Cambridge University Press, 1957.

Lewis, C. S. *The Great Divorce.* New York: HarperOne, 2001.

Lewis, James R., and J. Gordon Melton, eds. *Perspectives on the New Age.* Albany: State University of New York Press, 1992.

Lings, Martin. *What Is Sufism?* London: I. B. Taurus, 1999.

Loar, Russ. "In the Web of Life, Jain Religion Reveres Even the Tiniest Forms." *Los Angeles Times*, July 23, 1996.

Lojong Texts: An Anthology. Translated by Adam Pearcey. 2013. http://www.lotsawa house.org/Downloads/LojongTexts-AnAnthology.pdf.

Lu, David John. *Japan: A Documentary History.* Armonk, NY: M. E. Sharpe, 1997.

Lupieri, Edmondo. *The Mandaeans: The Last Gnostics.* Grand Rapids: Eerdmans, 2002.

Luther, Martin. *Luther's Works*. Translated by Roger Hornsby. 55 vols. Muhlenberg Press, 1958.

Macquarrie, John. *Mediators between Human and Divine: From Moses to Muhammad*. New York: Continuum, 1996.

Mahabharata. Translated by William Buck. Berkeley: University of California Press, 2000.

Mann, Gurinder Singh. *The Making of Sikh Scriptures*. New York: Oxford University Press, 2001.

———. *Sikhism*. Upper Saddle River, NJ: Prentice Hall, 2004.

Mansukhani, G. S. *Introduction to Sikhism*. New Delhi: Hemkunt Press, 2007.

Marius, Richard. *Martin Luther: The Christian between God and Death*. Cambridge, MA: Harvard University Press, 1999.

Marx, Karl. "Contribution to the Critique of Hegel's Philosophy of Right." In *Karl Marx: Early Writings*. Translated and edited by T. B. Bottomore, 43–59. New York: McGraw-Hill, 1963.

Marx, Karl, and Friedrich Engels. *The Communist Manifesto*. 1888. Introduced and annotated by Gareth Stedman Jones. Translated by Samuel Moore. New York: Penguin Classics, 2002.

Mbiti, John S. *African Religions and Philosophy*. Portsmouth, NH: Heinemann, 1992.

McConkie, Bruce. *Mormon Doctrine*. Salt Lake City: Bookcraft, 1991.

McConkie, Joseph Fielding, and Donald W. Parry. *A Guide to Scriptural Symbols*. Salt Lake City: Bookcraft, 1990.

McFague, Sallie. *Metaphorical Theology: Models of God in Religious Language*. Minneapolis: Augsburg Fortress, 1982.

McKnight, Scot. "Five Streams of the Emerging Church." *Christianity Today* 52, no. 2 (February 2007): 34.

McLeod, W. H. *Exploring Sikhism: Aspects of Sikh Identity, Culture, and Thought*. New Delhi: Oxford University Press, 2000.

———. "The Influence of Islam upon the Thought of Guru Nanak." *History of Religions* 7, no. 4 (May 1968): 302–16.

Mencius. Translated by Irene Bloom. New York: Columbia University Press, 2009.

Meyer, Marvin W. *The Gnostic Gospels of Jesus: The Definitive Collection of Mystical Gospels and Secret Books about Jesus of Nazareth*. San Francisco: HarperCollins, 2005.

Migne, J.-P., ed. *Patrologia Graeca*. Vol. 46. Paris: Garnier Fratres, 1863.

Miller, Barbara Stoler, trans. *The Bhagavad-Gita: Krishna's Counsel in Time of War*. New York: Bantam Books, 1986.

Mitchell, Stephen, trans. *Tao Te Ching: An Illustrated Journey*. London: Frances Lincoln Limited, 1988.

Modern English Translation of the Holy Qur'an. Translated by A. Yusuf Ali. Kansas City, MO: Manar International, 1998.

Moon, Sun Myung, and Hyo Won Eu. Introduction to *Exposition of the Divine Principle*. New York: Holy Spirit Association for the Unification of World Christianity, 1996.

Müller, F. Max. *Chips from a German Workshop*. Vol. 4. New York: Charles Scribner's Sons, 1891.

———, ed. *Hymns of the Atharva-Veda*. New Delhi: Atlantic Publishers & Distributors, 1990.

———. *The Sacred Books of the East: Gaina Sutras, pt. 1*. Translated by Hermann Jacobi. Oxford: Clarendon, 1884.

Nasr, Seyyed Hossein. *Ideals and Realities of Islam*. 2nd ed. Chicago: Kazi, 2001.

Nawwab, Nimah. "The Day of Arafah and Its Preparation." *Understanding Islam*. http://www.onislam.net.

Neusner, Jacob. *The Death and Birth of Judaism*. New York: Basic Books, 1987.

———. *Judaism's Theological Voice: The Melody of the Talmud*. Chicago: University of Chicago Press, 1997.

———. *Self-Fulfilling Prophecy: Exile and Return in the History of Judaism*. Boston: Beacon Press, 1987.

Neville, Robert Cummings. *Boston Confucianism: Portable Tradition in the Late-Modern World*. Albany: State University of New York Press, 2000.

Newbigin, Lesslie. *The Finality of Christ*. Richmond: John Knox Press, 1969.

———. *Foolishness to the Greeks: The Gospel and Western Culture*. Grand Rapids: Eerdmans, 1986.

———. *The Gospel in a Pluralistic Society*. Grand Rapids: Eerdmans, 1989.

Nida, Eugene A. *Message and Meaning: The Communication of the Christian Faith*. Pasadena, CA: William Carey Library, 1990.

———. *Signs, Sense, and Translation*. Cape Town: Bible Society of South Africa, 1991.

Nikhilananda (Swami), trans. and ed. *The Principle Upanishads*. Mineola, NY: Dover Publications, Inc., 1963.

Nyayavijayaji, Muni Shri. *Jaina Darśana*. Translated by Nagin J. Shah. Delhi: Bhogilal Lehar Chand Institute of Indology, 2000.

Oduyoye, Mercy Amba. *Hearing and Knowing: Theological Reflections on Christianity in Africa*. Maryknoll, NY: Orbis Books, 1986.

Oliver, Roland. *The African Experience*. Boulder, CO: Westview Press, 2000.

Orobator, Agbonkhianmeghe E. *Theology Brewed in an African Pot*. Maryknoll, NY: Orbis Books, 2008.

Pagels, Elaine. *The Gnostic Gospels*. New York: Random House, 2004.

Pals, Daniel L. *Eight Theories of Religion*. Oxford: Oxford University Press, 2005.

———. *Seven Theories of Religion*. New York: Oxford University Press, 1996.

Partridge, Christopher, and J. Gordon Melton, eds. *New Religions: A Guide; New Religious Movements, Sects, and Alternative Spiritualities*. New York: Oxford University Press, 2004.

Pascal, Blaise. *Pensées*. Mineola, NY: Dover Publications, 2003.

Pelikan, Jaroslav. *The Christian Tradition: A History of the Development of Doctrine*. Vol. 1, *The Emergence of the Catholic Tradition (100–600)*. Chicago: University of Chicago Press, 1971.

Peters, F. F. *Muhammad and the Origins of Islam*. Albany: State University of New York Press, 1994.

Placher, William C. *A History of Christian Theology: An Introduction*. Philadelphia: Westminster Press, 1983.

———. *Readings in the History of Christian Theology*. Vol. 1. Philadelphia: Westminster Press, 1988.

Pohl, Christine D. *Making Room: Recovering Hospitality as a Christian Tradition*. Grand Rapids: Eerdmans, 1999.

Powers, John. *Introduction to Tibetan Buddhism*. Ithaca, NY: Snow Lion, 1995.

Preus, J. Samuel. *Explaining Religion: Criticism and Theory from Bodin to Freud*. American Academy of Religion Texts and Translation Series. Oxford: Oxford University Press, 2000.

Qutb, Sayyid. *Milestones*. Beirut: Dar El-Ilm, 2007.

Radhakrishnan, Sarvepalli, and Charles A. Moore, eds. *A Sourcebook in Indian Philosophy*. Princeton: Princeton University Press, 1967.

Rafiabadi, Hamid N. *Challenges to Religions and Islam: A Study of Muslim Movements, Personalities, Issues and Trends*. Pt. 1. New Delhi: Sarup & Sons, 2007.

Rahman, Fazlur. *Islam*. Chicago: University of Chicago Press, 1979.

Rahner, Karl. *Karl Rahner in Dialogue: Conversations and Interviews, 1965–1982*. Edited by Paul Imhof and Hubert Biallowons. Danvers, MA: Crossroad, 1986.

———. *Theological Investigations*. Vol. 2, *Man in the Church*. London: Darton, Longman & Todd, 1963.

Ramabai, Pandita. *A Testimony*. 9th ed. Clinton, NJ: Pandita Ramabai Mukti Mission, 1968.

Rambo, Lewis R. *Understanding Religious Conversion*. New Haven: Yale University Press, 1995.

Rambo, Lewis R., and Charles E. Farhadian, eds. *The Oxford Handbook of Religious Conversion*. New York: Oxford University Press, 2014.

Reader, Ian. *Religion in Contemporary Japan*. Honolulu: University of Hawaii Press, 1998.

Redfield, Robert. "The Folk Society." *Journal of Sociology* 52, no. 4 (January 1947): 293–308.

Reynolds, Frank E., and Jason A. Carbine, eds. *The Life of Buddhism*. Berkeley: University of California Press, 2000.

Richards, John. *The Mughal Empire*. The New Cambridge History of India, pt. 1, vol. 5. New York: Cambridge University Press, 1995.

Richardson, Don. *Eternity in Their Hearts*. Ventura, CA: Regal Books, 1981.

Richardson, Hugh, and David Snellgrove. *A Cultural History of Tibet*. Boston: Shambhala, 1995.

Robert, Dana. "Shifting Southward: Global Christianity since 1945." *International Bulletin of Missionary Research* 24, no. 2 (April 2000): 50–58.

Roberts, Alexander, and James Donaldson, eds. *The Ante-Nicene Fathers*. Translated by Peter Holmes. Vol. 3. Buffalo: Christian Literature, 1884–86.

Roelle, Patrick J. *Islam's Mandate: A Tribute to Jihad*. Bloomington, IN: Author-House, 2010.

Saayman, Willem, and Klippies Kritzinger, eds. *Mission in Bold Humility: David Bosch's Work Considered*. Maryknoll: Orbis Books, 1997.

Sahlins, Marshall. *Islands of History*. Chicago: University of Chicago Press, 1987.

Said, Edward W. *Orientalism*. New York: Vintage Books, 1978.

Sanneh, Lamin. *Disciples of All Nations: Pillars of World Christianity*. New York: Oxford University Press, 2007.

———. *Translating the Message: The Missionary Impact on Culture*. 1989. Revised and expanded ed. Maryknoll, NY: Orbis Books, 2009.

———. *Whose Religion Is Christianity? The Gospel beyond the West*. Grand Rapids: Eerdmans, 2003.

Sappel, Joel, and Robert W. Welkos. "The Mind behind the Religion." *Los Angeles Times*, June 24, 1990.

Schmidt, William. *Becoming a Storyteller: Wisdom, Trauma and the Dalai Lama*. Bloomington, IN: AuthorHouse, 2009.

Schweitzer, Albert. *The Quest of the Historical Jesus*. Baltimore: Johns Hopkins University Press, 1998.

Seager, Richard Hughes. *Buddhism in America*. New York: Columbia University Press, 2000.

Segal, Robert A., ed. *The Blackwell Companion to the Study of Religion*. Oxford: Blackwell, 2006.

Sen, Amartya. *Identity and Violence: The Illusion of Destiny*. New York: W. W. Norton, 2007.

Seng-Ts'an, Chien-chih. *Hsin-hsin Ming, Verses on the Faith-Mind*. Translated from the Chinese by Richard B. Clarke. Buffalo: White Pine Press, 2001. http://www.csulb.edu/~wweinste/HsinHsinMing-print.html.

Sharma, Arvind. *A Guide to Hindu Spirituality*. Bloomington, IN: World Wisdom, 2006.

———. *Modern Hindu Thought*: *The Essential Texts*. New York: Oxford University Press, 2002.

Sharpe, Eric J. *Comparative Religion: A History*. La Salle, IL: Open Court, 1986.

Sri Guru Granth Sahib 1. New Delhi: Allied Publishers Private Limited, 2005.

Singh, Baldev. "Is Guru Nanak Hindu or Muslim?" *Sikh Spectrum* 30 (November, 2007). http://www.sikhspectrum.com/2007/11/was-guru-nanak-a-hindu-or-a-muslim/#/0.

Singh, Bhagat. *Japji: The Sikh Morning Prayer*. New Delhi: Hemkunt Press, 2007.

Singh, Gopal. *A History of the Sikh People, 1469–1988*. Mumbai: World Book Centre, 1988.

Singh, Karan, ed. *A Treasury of Indian Wisdom*. New York: Penguin Group, 2010.

Singh, Khushwant, trans. *Hymns of Guru Nanak*. Andhra Pradesh, India: Orient Blackswan, 1991.

Sinnett, A. P. *The Purpose of Theosophy*. Whitefish, MT: Kessinger, 2005.

Smelser, Niel J., ed. *Karl Marx on Society and Social Change*. Chicago: University of Chicago Press, 1973.

Smith, Joseph. *Lectures on Faith*. Salt Lake City: Deseret, 1985.

———. *Teachings of the Prophet Joseph Smith*. Salt Lake City: Deseret, 1938.

Smith, Wilfred Cantwell. *Islam in Modern History*. Princeton: Princeton University Press, 1957.

Sōhō, Takuan. *Tao Te Ching: Zen Teachings on the Taoist Classic*. Translated by Thomas Cleary. Boston: Shambhala, 2010.

Sommer, Deborah. *Chinese Religion: An Anthology of Sources*. New York: Oxford University Press, 1995.

Stark, Rodney, and William Sims Bainbridge. *A Theory of Religion*. Piscataway, NJ: Rutgers University Press, 1996.

Strong, John S. *The Experience of Buddhism: Sources and Interpretations*. 2nd ed. Belmont, CA: Wadsworth/Thompson Learning, 2002.

Sugirtharajah, R. S. *The Bible and Empire: Postcolonial Explorations*. New York: Cambridge University Press, 2005.

Sutton, Matthew Avery. *Aimee Semple McPherson and the Resurrection of Christian America*. Cambridge, MA: Harvard University Press, 2007.

Suzuki, Daisetz Teitaro. *Essays in Zen Buddhism*. New York: Grove Press, 1949.

———. *An Introduction to Zen Buddhism*. New York: Grove Press, 1964.

Swearer, Donald. *The Buddhist World of Southeast Asia*. Albany: State University of New York Press, 1996.

Tacitus, Publius Cornelius. *Annals of Imperial Rome*. Translated by Michael Grant. New York: Penguin Books, 1989.

Tahi-Farouki, Suha, and Basheer N. Nafi, eds. *Islamic Thought in the Twentieth Century*. New York: I. B. Taurus, 2004.

Taylor, Charles. *Sources of the Self: The Making of the Modern Identity*. Cambridge, MA: Harvard University Press, 1989.

ten Boom, Corrie. *The Hiding Place*. Old Tappan, NJ: Chosen Books, 1971.

Tennent, Timothy. *Christianity at the Religious Roundtable*. Grand Rapids: Baker Academic, 2002.

Teresa, Mother. *Mother Teresa: Come Be My Light; The Private Writings of the Saint of Calcutta*. Edited and with a commentary by Brian Kolodiejchuk. New York: Doubleday Religion, 2007.

Thompson, Laurence G. *The Chinese Way in Religion*. Belmont, CA: Wadsworth, 1973.

Tsunoda, Ryusaku, Theodore deBary, and Donald Keene, eds. *Sources of Japanese Tradition*. Vol. 1. New York: Columbia University Press, 1958.

Tu, Wei-ming. *Neo-Confucian Thought in Action: Wang Yang-ming's Youth (1472–1509)*. Berkeley: University of California Press, 1976.

Tucci, Giuseppe. *The Religions of Tibet*. Berkeley: University of California Press, 1988.

Tudor, Parfitt. *The Jews of Ethiopia: The Birth of an Elite*. London: Routledge Press, 2005.

Turner, Harold W. *From Temple to Meeting House: The Phenomenology and Theology of Sacred Space*. New York: Walter de Gruyter, 1979.

———. *Religious Innovation in Africa: Collected Essays on New Religious Movements*. Boston: Hall, 1979.

Turner, Victor. *The Forest of Symbols*. Ithaca, NY: Cornell University Press, 1967.

Tweed, Thomas A. *Crossing and Dwelling: A Theory of Religion*. Cambridge, MA: Harvard University Press, 2006.

Van Voorst, Robert E., ed. *Anthology of World Scriptures*. 4th ed. Belmont, CA: Wadsworth Thomson Learning, 2003.

————, ed. *Anthology of World Scriptures*. 6th ed. Belmont, CA: Wadsworth Thomson Learning, 2008.

Varghese, Alexander P. *India: History, Religion, Vision and Contribution to the World*. Vol. 1. New Delhi: Atlantic, 2008.

Vaudeville, Charlotte Kabir. *Kabir*. Vol. 1. Oxford: Clarendon Press, 1974.

Voll, John O. *Islam: Continuity and Change in the Modern World*. Syracuse: Syracuse University Press, 1994.

Walker, Brian Browne, trans. *The Tao Te Ching of Lao Tzu*. New York: St. Martin's Press, 1995.

Walls, Andrew. *The Missionary Movement in Christian History: Studies in the Transmission of Faith*. Maryknoll, NY: Orbis Books, 1996.

Walters, Donald J. (Swami Kriyananda). *The Essence of Self-Realization: The Wisdom of Paramahansa Yogananda*. Nevada City: Crystal Clarity, 1990.

Walters, Kerry, and Robin Jarrell. *Blessed Peacemakers: 365 Extraordinary People Who Changed the World*. Eugene, OR: Cascade Books, 2013.

Wangyal, Geshe. *The Door of Liberation: Essential Teachings of the Tibetan Buddhist Tradition*. Boston: Wisdom, 1995.

Watt, Montgomery. *Muhammad: Prophet and Statesman*. New York: Oxford University Press, 1974.

Webber, Robert E. *Worship Old and New*. Grand Rapids: Zondervan, 1994.

Weber, Max. *The Protestant Ethic and the Spirit of Capitalism*. Translated by Talcott Parsons. New York: Charles Scribner's Sons, 1958.

Whiteman, Darrell L. "Contextualization: The Theory, the Gap, the Challenge." *International Bulletin of Missionary Research* (January 1997): 2–7.

Wiesel, Elie. *Night*. Translated by Marion Wiesel. New York: Hill & Wang, 2006.

Wilken, Robert Louis. *The First Thousand Years: A Global History of Christianity*. New Haven: Yale University Press, 2012.

————. *The Spirit of Early Christian Thought: Seeking the Face of God*. New Haven: Yale University Press, 2005.

Yao, Xinzhong. *An Introduction to Confucianism*. New York: Cambridge University Press, 2005.

Young, Brigham. *The Essential Brigham Young*. Salt Lake City: Signature Books, 1992.

Zhiming, Yuan. *Tao Te Ching*. Translated by Daniel Baida Su and Chen Shangyu. Bloomington, IN: AuthorHouse, 2010.

Zhuangzi. *The Book of Chuang-tzu*. Translated by Martin Palmer with Elizabeth Breuilly. New York: Penguin Books, 1996.

————. *Teachings and Sayings of Chuang Tzu*. Translated by Herbert A. Giles. Mineola, NY: Courier Dover, 2001.

Index